PSYCHOLOGY

A NEW INTRODUCTION

STUDY GUIDE

**Nick Shackleton-Jones
Richard Gross and Rob McIlveen**

Hodder & Stoughton

A MEMBER OF THE HODDER HEADLINE GROUP

British Library Cataloguing in Publication Data
A catalogue record for this title is available from the British Library

ISBN 0 340 74264 X

First published 1999

Impression number 10 9 8 7 6 5 4 3 2 1
Year   2003 2002 2001 2000 1999

Typeset by GreenGate Publishing Services, Tonbridge, Kent.

Printed and bound in Great Britain for Hodder and Stoughton Educational,
a division of Hodder Headline plc, 338 Euston Road, London NW1 3BH,
by Redwood Books Limited, Trowbridge, Wiltshire.

CONTENTS

Unit 4 Developmental Psychology

Unit 5 Social Psychology

Unit 6 *Abnormal Psychology and Atypical Development*

Unit 7 *Perspectives*

Appendices

An A level in psychology is quite an achievement. The syllabus itself is large and wide-ranging, whilst the assessment measures used require students to demonstrate both depth and breadth of knowledge, together with a critical awareness of the issues relating to that knowledge. In addition, psychology may be a subject which is new to many students, which in turn makes the unfamiliar jargon and sheer volume of material all the more daunting.

In this Study Guide we have attempted to meet the needs of the A level Psychology student by answering the questions 'What do I need to know?', 'How can I remember it?' and 'How can I do well in an exam?' as directly as possible. The Guide is a companion to the textbook *Psychology – A New Introduction* and follows its structure closely, with a study chapter for each chapter in the textbook. By ensuring a high degree of consistency with this text, the Study Guide is able to consolidate and deepen students' understanding of the main text. The Guide also contains additional materials to assist students in their preparation for exams, essay-writing and completion of coursework, although there is no separate references section (since these can all be found in the main textbook).

For each chapter of the main text there is a corresponding *schema* (or map of a topic) and a set of *self-test questions and answers* in the Study Guide. There are also six additional 'super-schemas', which provide an overview of entire syllabus areas (e.g. developmental psychology) at a single glance. The principal aim of the *schemas* is to make the material as memorable and accessible as possible, allowing students simultaneously to review the whole of a topic, the key facts, and the way in which the material is structured. The schematic form is based on the findings of several psychologists interested in learning and memory processes, and has been developed with the help of a great many A level Psychology students.

The *schemas* summarise central information contained in the corresponding textbook chapter and organise information into an overall structure by the use of links and headings. They possess the following properties:

- Central information contained in corresponding textbook chapters is condensed, summarised and broken into discrete 'chunks', which are presented in a visual arrangement. Where helpful, diagrams are also included.
- Items of information are contained in boxes whose borders and style indicate the type of information contained in them.

- Black boxes indicate the main topic area.

Attribution Theories & Bias

- The main areas into which the topic can be divided are indicated by shaded, rounded boxes, connected to the main topic by heavy lines.

Attribution Biases

- Sub-headings are contained in non-shaded rounded boxes.

Pursuit of common goals

- Theory, applications and evaluation are mostly contained in boxes with a normal border.

Conflict approaches
Hostility arises from competition.
Solutions:
- remove competition and replace it with goals requiring co-operation

- Important research studies are contained in boxes with a heavy dotted border.

Conflicting Research:
- Gilligan (1982): Kohlberg's stages are based on male morality and female morality is oriented more towards compassion.

- A light dotted border above and below a piece of text indicates the introduction of a key term or definition.

Attribution: an explanation of why an individual behaved in a certain way

The boxes are connected in such a way as to suggest the structure of the material. Where boxes are connected to the main topic box by a narrow line, this suggests material which might be used by way of introduction of a topic. In many cases, the schemas can provide the basis for an essay structure.

The *self-test questions* are aimed at developing students' critical abilities, as well as providing a way for students to monitor and vary their own learning. Each section contains questions which range in type and difficulty, so that most students should find it difficult to answer all questions correctly. Moreover, the questions tend to focus on information which is central to a topic and would therefore be useful in answering an exam question.

From an evolutionary perspective, our memory systems were not really 'designed' to acquire large amounts of information presented in symbolic form. In fact, we are better at remembering the plot of a good movie, how to get to our favourite places, how our teachers talked and acted or unusual things that happened to us. However, the 'information age' means that we are increasingly required to assimilate information rapidly, and it seems we will need to develop new strategies for doing so by adapting the form of information to suit our specialised processing capabilities. We hope that you will find this Guide to be a useful step in that direction.

Please note that the Appendices on Exam Preparation, Essay Writing and Coursework apply specifically to the AEB syllabus. However, these also contain a great deal of advice and guidance that are relevant to other A level syllabuses.

ACKNOWLEDGEMENTS

Nick would like to thank his wife Rose and daughter Nadia for their love and support. Rob would like to thank Gill for her usual patience. Richard sends his love as usual to Jan, Tanya and Jo. Many thanks to Tim and Greig at Hodder & Stoughton, Dave and his team at GreenGate Publishing and Ian at De Morgan Communications. Our best wishes go to all the unforgettable students who shared the adventure.

UNIT 1

Introduction

AN INTRODUCTION TO PSYCHOLOGY AND ITS APPROACHES

KEY QUESTIONS
- What is psychology?
- What do psychologists do?
- What are the major theoretical approaches in psychology?

Section 1: What is psychology?

1 What do the two Greek words *psyche* and *logos* mean?
2 What does *introspection* mean?
3 What name was given to Wundt's (1879) approach, in which he attempted to analyse the structure of conscious thought?
4 What criticism did Watson (1913) make of introspectionism?
5 Complete the sentence: 'Watson proposed that psychologists should confine themselves to studying —————, since this is measurable and observable'.
6 What is the difference between Freud's *psychodynamic approach* and *psychoanalysis*?
7 What were Gestalt psychologists mainly interested in?
8 What are *cognitive processes*?
9 What is the *computer analogy*?

Section 2: Classifying psychologists' work

10 What is the difference between pure research and applied research?
11 How does the *process approach* to psychology differ from the *person approach*?
12 Identify two areas of study in which a biopsychologist might be interested.
13 What is the *nature–nurture issue* concerned with?
14 Identify four cognitive processes which are of interest to cognitive psychologists.
15 What do developmental psychologists study?
16 Why might some psychologists claim that all psychology is social psychology?
17 What is the study of interpersonal perception concerned with?
18 What types of investigatory methods are most likely to be employed by the process and person approaches to psychology, respectively?
19 According to Hartley & Branthwaite (1997), in what way can the psychologist be seen as a 'toolmaker'?
20 What might be the role of a clinical psychologist in working with the elderly?

21 What do criminological (or forensic) psychologists attempt to do?
22 Which type of psychologist is most likely to be involved in planning educational programmes for people with learning difficulties?
23 What are the main responsibilities of occupational psychologists?

Section 3: Major theoretical approaches

24 What does a *methodological behaviourist* believe?
25 How does this view differ from that of a *radical behaviourist*?
26 What are the two types of conditioning (or learning) which are central to the behaviourist approach?
27 What do the letters 'S' and 'R' stand for, in the term *S–R psychology*?
28 Identify one practical contribution of behaviourist principles to the field of abnormal psychology.
29 How can the behaviourist approach be criticised for the way in which it defines the *response*?
30 Identify one further criticism of the behaviourist approach.
31 Identify one technique which Freud believed could be used to access the unconscious mind.
32 What is *repression*?
33 What claim is made by the *theory of infantile sexuality*?
34 What was the principal difference between Adler's psychodynamic approach and Freud's?
35 What is the link between rational emotive therapy (RET) and psychoanalysis?
36 What does it mean to say that Freudian theories are *unfalsifiable*?
37 Complete the sentence: 'Humanistic psychologists believe in ———— ———— and people's ability to choose how they act'.
38 What is an *actualising tendency*?
39 What is a *phenomenal field*?
40 What is 'lay therapy', to which Rogers contributed?
41 Why is the humanistic approach subject to the 'nominal fallacy'?

Q

Section 1: What is psychology?

1 *Psyche* means mind, soul or spirit, whilst *logos* means discourse or study.

2 Introspection describes the attempt of an individual to observe and analyse his/her own mental processes.

3 Wundt's (1879) approach was called *structuralism*.

4 Watson (1913) pointed out that the results of introspection could never be proved or disproved, and were therefore subjective and unscientific.

5 'Watson proposed that psychologists should confine themselves to studying *behaviour*, since this is measurable and observable.'

6 Freud's psychodynamic approach is based on his *psychoanalytic theory*, whilst *psychoanalysis* describes the therapeutic techniques which he developed.

7 Gestalt psychologists were mainly interested in perception.

8 Cognitive processes are mental processes, such as perception, attention, memory and thinking in general.

9 The *computer analogy* is the notion that human cognitive processes can be compared with the operation of computer programs.

Section 2: Classifying psychologists' work

10 Pure research is research done for its own sake, and intended to increase our knowledge, whilst applied research is aimed at solving a particular problem.

11 The *process approach* investigates the mechanisms underlying behaviour, whilst the *person approach* focuses more directly on the individual.

12 A biopsychologist might be interested in the functions of the nervous system, the endocrine (hormonal) system, brain activity, and genetics.

13 The *nature–nurture issue* is concerned with the degree to which characteristics are inherited (nature) or a product of learning and the environment (nurture).

14 Attention, memory, perception, language, thinking, problem-solving, reasoning and concept-formation are all of interest to cognitive psychologists.

15 Developmental psychologists study the biological, cognitive, social and emotional changes that occur in people over time.

16 Because all behaviour takes place within a social context and our behaviour may be influenced by others even when we are alone.

17 The study of interpersonal perception is concerned with how we form impressions of others and judge the causes of their behaviour.

18 The process approach is typically confined to the laboratory, where experiments are undertaken, whilst the person approach makes greater use of field studies and non-experimental methods.

19 Hartley & Branthwaite (1997) see psychologists as 'tool-makers' in their use and development of measures and techniques to help in the analysis and assessment of problems.

20 The clinical psychologist may be involved in assessing the elderly for their fitness to live independently.

21 Criminological psychologists attempt to apply psychological principles to the criminal justice system.

22 An educational psychologist.

23 Occupational psychologists are involved in the selection and training of individuals for jobs, and in vocational guidance, including the administration of aptitude tests and tests of interest.

Section 3: Major theoretical approaches

24 A *methodological behaviourist* believes that the subject matter of psychology should be behaviour.

25 The *radical behaviourist* believes not only that we should not study mental activities, but that these can be explained by (reduced to) an analysis of behaviour.

26 *Respondent* conditioning and *operant* conditioning.

27 *Stimulus* and *response*.

28 The behaviourist approach has led to the development of behaviour therapy and behaviour modification, used in the treatment of psychological disorders.

29 The behaviourist approach tends only to consider the frequency of a behaviour (the *response*) and not its intensity, duration or quality.

30 The behaviourist approach fails to account for the influence of people's *thoughts* on their behaviour.

31 *Free association*, *dream interpretation* and *transference* are all psychoanalytic techniques used to access the unconscious mind.

32 *Repression* refers to the process whereby threatening or unpleasant experiences are 'forgotten' by being removed to the unconscious.

33 The *theory of infantile sexuality* claims that the sexual instinct is active from birth and develops through a series of psychosexual stages.

34 Adler rejected Freud's emphasis on sexuality, stressing instead the *will to power* (striving for superiority and the rejection of inferiority).

35 The founder of rational emotive therapy, Ellis, was originally trained in Freudian techniques.

36 *Unfalsifiable* means 'incapable of being disproved'. For example, the claim that some unacceptable impulses are concealed in the unconscious mind is impossible to falsify.

37 'Humanistic psychologists believe in *free will* and people's ability to choose how they act.'

38 An *actualising tendency* is an intrinsic desire to grow, develop and enhance our capacities.

39 A *phenomenal field* refers to the way in which we each create our own world, shaped by our perceptions.

40 'Lay therapy' is therapy which is provided by non-medically qualified therapists.

41 The humanistic approach describes but does not explain personality. This is the *nominal fallacy*.

What is psychology?

- The word *psychology* derives from the Greek *psyche* (mind, soul or spirit) and *logos* (discourse or study).
- Wilhelm Wundt (1879) opened the first psychological laboratory at the University of Leipzig, attempting to record and measure conscious mental processes, using *introspection* under controlled conditions (*structuralism*).
- Watson (1913) proposed that psychologists should confine themselves to studying behaviour, since this can be measured and studied objectively (*behaviourism*).
- Freud (1900) published his *psychoanalytic theory* of personality, in which the *unconscious mind* plays a central role.
- Cognitive psychology emerged in the late 1950s, as psychologists became able to model cognitive processes on *computers*.

Process approach — **Classifying psychologists' work** — **Person approach**

Biopsychology
(Ch 3–20)
- Interested in the biological basis of behaviour (e.g. nervous system, endocrine system)
- Genetics and the role of the environment (nature vs nurture) are central issues.

Cognitive psychology
(Ch 21–37)
- Studies processes such as attention, memory, perception, language and thought
- Links to social psychology (social cognition) and developmental (Piaget's theory of cognitive development).

Developmental psychology
(Ch 38–50)
- Studies the biological, social, cognitive and emotional changes which take place over time.

Social psychology
(Ch 51–64)
- Studies the way in which our behaviour is influenced by others (e.g. interpersonal perception, attraction, prejudice).

Abnormal psychology
(Ch 65–80)
- Studies the underlying causes of deviant behaviour and psychological abnormality.

Introducing Psychology

Clinical psychologists – major functions
- Assessing people with learning difficulties/brain damage/the elderly
- Planning/carrying out programmes of therapy
- Carrying out research into abnormal psychology (e.g. therapeutic effectiveness)
- Involvement in community care
- Teaching other groups of professionals (e.g. nurses, social workers).

Educational psychologists – responsibilities
- Administering psychometric tests
- Planning and supervising remedial teaching
- Research into teaching, interview and counselling methods
- Planning educational programmes for people with impairments/special educational needs
- Advising parents and teachers on how to deal with children with impairments/behaviour problems
- Teacher training.

Applied psychology

Seven major skills/roles
- **Counsellor:** helping people to overcome problems
- **Colleague:** focusing on human issues, as part of a team
- **Expert:** drawing on specialised knowledge in advising on issues
- **Toolmaker:** using and developing psychometric measures
- **Detached investigator:** assessing the evidence for a point of view
- **Theoretician:** attempting to explain observed phenomena
- **Agent for change:** helping people and institutions to change for the better.

Criminological psychologists – research areas
- Jury selection and presentation of evidence
- Eyewitness testimony
- Improving the recall of child witnesses
- False memory syndrome
- Offender profiling and crime prevention
- Treatment programmes (e.g. anger management).

Occupational psychologists – responsibilities
- The selection and training of people for jobs
- Helping people who need to re-train for a new career (industrial rehabilitation)
- Designing training schemes as part of 'fitting the person to the job'
- Helping design equipment as part of 'fitting the job to the person'
- Maximising productivity
- Helping with communication and industrial relations (organisational psychology)
- Helping to sell products (advertising).

Major theoretical approaches

The behaviourist approach — **The psychodynamic approach** — **The humanistic approach**

	The behaviourist approach	The psychodynamic approach	The humanistic approach
Assumptions	• Advocates the study of observable behaviour (methodological behaviourism) and rejects introspectionism • Emphasises the role of learning (either respondent or operant conditioning) and environmental factors in influencing behaviour • Stresses the use of operational definitions (where concepts are defined in measurable terms) • Holds that a science of behaviour should aim to predict and control behaviour.	• Sees much of our behaviour as determined by unconscious thoughts, desires and memories • Experiences or thoughts which are threatening or unpleasant may be repressed (a major form of ego defence) • The mind is composed of three interacting (often conflicting) forces: the id, ego and superego • Infants are sexually active from birth and pass through a series of psychosexual stages which influence adult personality.	• Believes that people are free to choose how they act • Argues that behaviour must be understood in terms of the individual's subjective interpretation of it (phenomenological approach) • Individuals aim to grow, develop and enhance their capacities ('self-actualisation'), unless blocked by external factors • Stresses the importance of understanding the whole person (not 'bits' of behaviour).
Contributions	• Used to explain learning, language development, moral development, gender development, memory (e.g. interference theory of forgetting) and abnormal behaviour • Used in behaviour therapy and behaviour modification. Also used in biofeedback and programmed learning (e.g. computer assisted learning).	• Used to explain motivation, dreams, forgetting, attachment, moral and gender development and abnormality. Influenced Erikson ('psychosocial stages'), Jung ('analytical psychology') and Adler ('individual psychology') • Psychoanalysis is used in the treatment of disorders such as depression and anxiety.	• Rogers' client-centred therapy is used widely, and Rogers helped develop lay therapy (administered by psychoanalysts and others who are not medically qualified) • Rogers helped develop ways of measuring self-concept and ideal self, in order to explore the importance of therapist qualities.
Evaluation	• Behaviourists have tended to measure frequency of responses (e.g. of a rat in a Skinner box) and ignore intensity, duration and quality of responses • What people think is often very important in determining their behaviour (Garrett, 1996) and this is not recognised by the behaviourist.	• Freudian theories are unfalsifiable (incapable of being disproved) • Freudian ideas about repression, early sexuality and the unconscious have become a part of Western culture • 'Hermeneutic strength': the theory allows us to interpret meaning in a way appropriate to our complex human experience.	• The theory has wide appeal as an alternative to more mechanistic theories, but its concepts are difficult to test empirically and it only succeeds in describing, not explaining personality. • The approach counterbalanced behaviourist and psychodynamic approaches, recognising the importance of the self.

2

PSYCHOLOGY AND ITS METHODS

KEY QUESTIONS
- What is an experiment?
- What is an observation?
- What is a survey?
- What is a case study?
- What is a correlation?

Q

Section 1: Experiments in psychology

1 What is a *variable*?
2 Complete the sentence: 'Only the experimental method permits psychologists to talk in terms of ___ ___ ___'.
3 Define the term *hypothesis*.
4 What is the difference between an *independent variable* and a *dependent variable*?
5 What is the point of providing *operational definitions* of those things which will be investigated?
6 What is the difference between a control group and an experimental group?
7 What does it mean to say that a participant is *randomly allocated* to the various conditions in an experiment?
8 In what way does a *repeated measures design* differ from an *independent measures (groups) design*?
9 Identify one disadvantage of the independent measures design.
10 What is the objective of using standardised experimental procedures and instructions?
11 What is a *confounding (or extraneous) variable*?
12 What is predicted by the *null hypothesis*?
13 Why are most psychological experiments conducted in psychological laboratories?
14 What is the principal weakness of the laboratory as a setting for experiments?
15 Why might the findings of many psychology experiments fail to generalise to many groups of people?
16 What does Orne (1962) mean by the term *demand characteristics*?
17 In what way does the field experiment differ from the laboratory experiment?
18 What advantage does the field experiment have over the laboratory experiment?
19 Complete the sentence: 'Field experiments commonly involve a loss of ___ over the IV, DV and extraneous variables'.

Section 2: Observations

20 What name is given to the type of observation in which a researcher observes behaviour in its natural environment and does not attempt to interfere with what is being observed?
21 What is *observer bias*?
22 What is *intra-observer reliability*?
23 What ethical issue is often raised by participant observation?

Section 3: Case studies and surveys

24 What is a *case study*?
25 What name is given to the daily recording of descriptions and observations of the behaviour of a specific person (as used by Piaget)?
26 Identify two major limitations which are likely to apply to case studies.
27 Why is it important to researchers using the survey method that their sample is representative of the population they are studying?
28 What advantage do questionnaires have over the interview method of conducting surveys?
29 What is the principal advantage of the survey as a method of collecting data over the laboratory experiment?
30 What element of the survey is most likely to introduce unreliability?

Section 4: Correlations

31 What is the purpose of the correlation, as an investigative tool?
32 What does it mean to say that two variables are correlated?
33 What value would the correlation coefficient have for a perfect negative correlation?
34 Under what conditions would a correlational study be most useful?
35 What is the major weakness of correlational studies compared with experimental studies?

Section 1: Experiments in psychology

1 A *variable* is any element that can change or vary over time, between individuals or across situations.

2 'Only the experimental method permits psychologists to talk in terms of *cause and effect*.'

3 A *hypothesis* is an unambiguously phrased prediction that can be tested empirically.

4 The *independent variable* (*IV*) is independently under the experimenter's control, whilst the *dependent variable* (*DV*) is not manipulated but is the outcome of manipulating the IV.

5 *Operational definitions* narrow down what will be investigated and provide unambiguous (and measurable) descriptions of what a term means.

6 A control group comprises the individuals who are not exposed to the IV and it is frequently used as a comparison with the experimental group (which is exposed to the IV and variations of it).

7 The participant has an equal chance of being allocated to any one of the conditions.

8 In the *repeated measures design*, each participant is tested in all of the conditions, whilst in the *independent measures (groups) design* different participants are allocated to different conditions.

9 Results may be affected by individual differences between the groups of participants in each condition.

10 Standardised experimental procedures and instructions ensure the uniformity of experience, thereby controlling for extraneous variables.

11 *Confounding (or extraneous) variables* are factors other than the IV which may affect the outcome.

12 The *null hypothesis* predicts that the IV will *not* affect the DV and that any differences between groups will be due to chance factors alone.

13 A psychological laboratory facilitates control and reduces the possibility of confounding variables.

14 The laboratory is an artificial setting, and this may lead to participants displaying artificial behaviours.

15 Many psychology experiments involve participants who are undergraduates and are not, therefore, representative of other groups of people.

16 The term *demand characteristics* refers to perceptions and expectations which participants may have regarding how they are expected to behave, and what will happen to them.

17 The field experiment takes place in the real world.

18 The field experiment is likely to have greater *ecological validity* than the laboratory experiment.

19 'Field experiments commonly involve a loss of *control* over the IV, DV and extraneous variables.'

Section 2: Observations

20 A *naturalistic* observation.

21 *Observer bias* refers to the tendency of observers to distort what they see so that it conforms to what they expect to see.

22 *Intra-observer reliability* refers to the consistency of observation by the *same* observer on different occasions.

23 Participant observation commonly raises the issue of disclosure, which concerns whether or not participants should be deceived by those observing them.

Section 3: Case studies and surveys

24 A *case study* is an in-depth investigation of a single 'unit' (e.g. a person or event).

25 The diary method.

26 Case studies lack control over important variables. The 'unit' studied may not be representative, so the findings cannot be generalised. There is the potential for observer and participant bias, and the case study is an unconvincing basis for establishing the relationship between two variables.

27 If the sample is not representative of the population, then the results cannot be generalised to that population.

28 Questionnaires are anonymous and may result in more truthful answers; they are also cheaper and quicker than interviews.

29 The survey allows more data to be collected than can practically be studied in the laboratory. In addition, it requires less investment in terms of time and money.

30 The self-reports of participants may be unreliable.

Section 4: Correlations

31 A correlation summarises the *relationship* between two variables.

32 Two variables are correlated when changes in the value of one are associated with changes in the value of the other.

33 The correlation coefficient for a perfectly negative correlation is -1.

34 A correlational study is likely to be most useful when an experiment is impractical or unethical.

35 Correlational studies do not allow causality to be inferred.

A

Psychology & its Methods

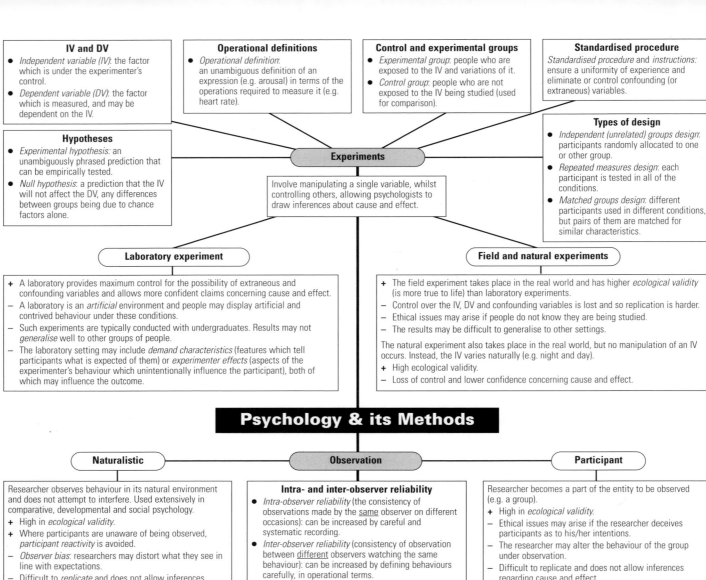

Experiments

Involve manipulating a single variable, whilst controlling others, allowing psychologists to draw inferences about cause and effect.

IV and DV
- *Independent variable (IV)*: the factor which is under the experimenter's control.
- *Dependent variable (DV)*: the factor which is measured, and may be dependent on the IV.

Operational definitions
- *Operational definition*: an unambiguous definition of an expression (e.g. arousal) in terms of the operations required to measure it (e.g. heart rate).

Control and experimental groups
- *Experimental group*: people who are exposed to the IV and variations of it.
- *Control group*: people who are not exposed to the IV being studied (used for comparison).

Standardised procedure
Standardised procedure and *instructions*: ensure a uniformity of experience and eliminate or control confounding (or extraneous) variables.

Hypotheses
- *Experimental hypothesis*: an unambiguously phrased prediction that can be empirically tested.
- *Null hypothesis*: a prediction that the IV will not affect the DV, any differences between groups being due to chance factors alone.

Types of design
- *Independent (unrelated) groups design*: participants randomly allocated to one or other group.
- *Repeated measures design*: each participant is tested in all of the conditions.
- *Matched groups design*: different participants used in different conditions, but pairs of them are matched for similar characteristics.

Laboratory experiment
- + A laboratory provides maximum control for the possibility of extraneous and confounding variables and allows more confident claims concerning cause and effect.
- – A laboratory is an *artificial* environment and people may display artificial and contrived behaviour under these conditions.
- – Such experiments are typically conducted with undergraduates. Results may not *generalise* well to other groups of people.
- – The laboratory setting may include *demand characteristics* (features which tell participants what is expected of them) or *experimenter effects* (aspects of the experimenter's behaviour which unintentionally influence the participant), both of which may influence the outcome.

Field and natural experiments
- + The field experiment takes place in the real world and has higher *ecological validity* (is more true to life) than laboratory experiments.
- – Control over the IV, DV and confounding variables is lost and so replication is harder.
- – Ethical issues may arise if people do not know they are being studied.
- – The results may be difficult to generalise to other settings.

The natural experiment also takes place in the real world, but no manipulation of an IV occurs. Instead, the IV varies naturally (e.g. night and day).
- + High ecological validity.
- – Loss of control and lower confidence concerning cause and effect.

Observation

Naturalistic

Researcher observes behaviour in its natural environment and does not attempt to interfere. Used extensively in comparative, developmental and social psychology.
- + High in *ecological validity*.
- + Where participants are unaware of being observed, *participant reactivity* is avoided.
- – *Observer bias*: researchers may distort what they see in line with expectations.
- – Difficult to *replicate* and does not allow inferences regarding cause and effect.

Intra- and inter-observer reliability
- *Intra-observer reliability* (the consistency of observations made by the <u>same</u> observer on different occasions): can be increased by careful and systematic recording.
- *Inter-observer reliability* (consistency of observation between <u>different</u> observers watching the same behaviour): can be increased by defining behaviours carefully, in operational terms.

Participant

Researcher becomes a part of the entity to be observed (e.g. a group).
- + High in *ecological validity*.
- – Ethical issues may arise if the researcher deceives participants as to his/her intentions.
- – The researcher may alter the behaviour of the group under observation.
- – Difficult to replicate and does not allow inferences regarding cause and effect.

Case studies

In-depth investigations of a single 'unit' (e.g. person or event). Data is derived from observation, psychometric testing, self- and other-report. A *diary method* may also be used.

- Used to understand and help people with mental disorders (e.g. Freud's work).
- Used to illustrate psychological principles.
- Used as a research tool to suggest theories or hypotheses.
- + May shed light on things which are unethical or impractical to study in other ways.
- – A single 'unit' may not be representative, so results cannot be generalised.
- – Little control over variables, so does not allow inferences regarding cause and effect.
- – Potential for observer and participant bias.

Surveys

Provide information about groups of people. Data is collected by interview or questionnaire. Researchers begin by identifying the population (those to which the findings will apply) of people they wish to study. A random, *representative* sample is selected. Sampling can also be carried out on a *quota* basis or an *opportunity* basis (although the latter is less representative).
- + Surveys allow more data to be collected than can be obtained in the laboratory and may require less investment (of time and money).
- – Survey results can only be generalised to the population from which the sample was drawn.
- – Responses may be unreliable, or influenced by the researcher.
- + People are more likely to be truthful in questionnaires (which are often anonymous) and these are cheaper and quicker than interviews.
- + Interviewers can clarify questions.

Correlations

Positive correlation (> +1)

e.g. shoe size vs height

A statistical analysis which allows us to determine whether or not a relationship exists between two (or more) variables (i.e. whether a change in one is associated with a change in another). Correlation coefficients range from +1 (*perfect positive correlation*) through 0 (*no correlation*) to –1 (*perfect negative correlation*).
- + Correlations are useful when experimentation is impractical.
- – Correlations do not allow *causality* to be inferred.
- – Correlations usually only detect *linear* relationships between two variables, e.g. shoe size and height.

Negative correlation (> –1)

e.g. test time vs. I.Q. score

UNIT 2

Biopsychology

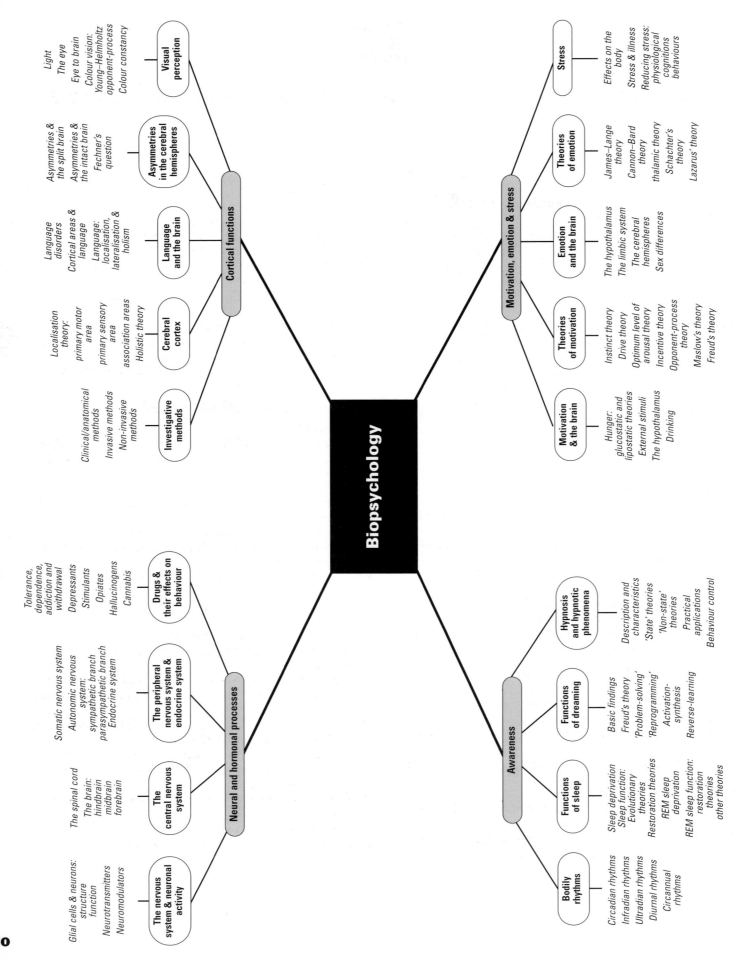

10

THE NERVOUS SYSTEM AND NEURONAL ACTIVITY

KEY QUESTIONS
- What is the nervous system?
- What are glial cells and neurons?
- What is the structure of a neuron?
- How do neurons function?
- What are the principal neurotransmitters and neuromodulators?

Section 1: Introducing the nervous system
1 What do the abbreviations *PNS* and *CNS* stand for?
2 Which of these two is the point of origin for complex commands, decisions and evaluations?
3 What are the two functions of the PNS?
4 Complete the sentence: 'The NS is a complicated network of ___ and ___ events'.

Section 2: Glial cells and neurons
5 What is a *neuron*?
6 Where are most neurons to be found?
7 Identify four functions of glial cells.
8 Name the three types of neuron.
9 What, in evolutionary terms, is the value of *reflex arcs*, which bypass the brain?
10 What name is given to the part of a neuron which houses the nucleus?
11 What is the principal difference between *dendrites* and *axons*?
12 What name is given to a group of axons bundled together in the peripheral nervous system?
13 What is the principal function of the *myelin sheath* which wraps around some axons?

Section 3: The function of neurons
14 What are the three major functions of neurons?
15 What function does the *sodium–potassium pump* perform when a neuron is in a resting state?
16 What is meant by saying that in its resting state a neuron is *polarised*?
17 What happens to a neuron when it is activated by a stimulus?
18 What is an *action potential*?
19 How is the *resting state* of a neuron restored, following activation?
20 What term is used to describe the 'leaping' of the action potential from one Node of Ranvier to another along the axon?

21 How does the '*all-or-none rule*' apply to neurons?
22 What is the difference between a neuron's *absolute refractory period* and its *relative refractory period*?
23 In the case of most neurons, where does the journey of an action potential end?

Section 4: Neurotransmitters and neuromodulators
24 How does *communication* take place *across a synaptic cleft*?
25 What is the name of the membrane which contains *receptor sites*?
26 What is *cotransmission*?
27 In what sense are some neurotransmitters '*excitatory*' and some '*inhibitory*'?
28 To what process does the term *summation* refer?
29 Identify the two ways in which the effect of a neurotransmitter can be ended.
30 How do *psychoactive drugs* affect the functioning of the nervous system?
31 What effect does *acetylcholine* (ACh) have when released to muscle cells?
32 How does *curare* exert its effects?
33 Identify one disorder which is thought to be related to the function of ACh.
34 Identify three functions in which dopamine is involved.
35 Which disorder is thought to be linked to over-utilisation of *dopamine*?
36 Identify three psychological states which have been linked to deficiencies in *serotonin* levels.
37 *Amphetamines* function by increasing the amount of a neurotransmitter responsible for general arousal. Name this neurotransmitter.
38 What is the major role played by *gamma-amino butyric acid*?
39 What is a *neuromodulator*?
40 Identify the principal functions of *endorphins*.

Section 1: Introducing the nervous system

1 The abbreviations *PNS* and *CNS* stand for *peripheral nervous system* and *central nervous system*, respectively.

2 The *central nervous system* is the point of origin for complex commands, decisions and evaluations.

3 The PNS is responsible for sending information to the CNS from the external world, muscles and organs, and for sending messages from the CNS to the muscles and glands.

4 'The NS is a complicated network of *electrical* and *chemical* events.'

Section 2: Glial cells and neurons

5 A *neuron* is a cell that processes and transmits information.

6 Most neurons (80 per cent) are to be found in the brain.

7 *Glial cells* supply nutrients and provide structural support to neurons, insulate neurons by forming myelin sheaths, remove debris following a cell's death and provide the brain with a barrier to certain harmful substances carried in the blood.

8 *Sensory* (or *afferent*), *motor* (or *efferent*), and *association* (or *connector*) neurons.

9 *Reflex arcs* are useful since they allow actions to be taken very quickly, before much damage has been done by a harmful stimulus.

10 The *cell body* (or *soma*).

11 *Dendrites* carry action potentials *towards* the cell body (i.e. inputs) whereas *axons* carry action potentials *away* from the cell body (i.e. outputs).

12 A *nerve*.

13 The *myelin sheath* serves to insulate the axon from other axons, and from ions found in the surrounding fluids, helping to prevent neurons from 'scrambling' messages.

Section 3: The function of neurons

14 *Neurons* are responsible for receiving, responding to, and sending messages.

15 The *sodium–potassium pump* keeps negative sodium ions out of the cell.

16 This means that the inside of the cell is negatively charged relative to its surroundings.

17 When a neuron is activated by a stimulus, the sodium channels open, allowing sodium ions to flood into it, and it becomes *depolarised*.

18 An *action potential* is the momentary change in electrical charge of the cell from –70 millivolts to around +40 millivolts.

19 Following activation, the *resting state* of a neuron is restored by the closing of sodium channels and the opening of potassium channels, which allow positively charged potassium ions out of the cell.

20 *Saltatory conduction.*

21 Neurons either 'fire' or do not 'fire' in response to a stimulus. There are no intermediate states of activity.

22 During the *absolute refractory period*, immediately after firing, the neuron cannot 'fire' again, irrespective of the strength of the stimulus. During the *relative refractory period*, the neuron *can* 'fire', providing the stimulus is considerably stronger than its threshold of response.

23 For most neurons, the journey of an action potential ends with its arrival at a *terminal button*.

Section 4: Neurotransmitters and neuromodulators

24 *Communication* takes place across a synaptic cleft by the action of *neurotransmitters* which travel across this gap.

25 The *post-synaptic membrane* contains *receptor sites*.

26 *Cotransmission* refers to the ability of terminal buttons to release more than one neurotransmitter, depending on the pattern of the action potential which reaches them.

27 Some neurotransmitters increase the likelihood that a receiving neuron will fire (*excitatory*), whilst others decrease the likelihood that a receiving neuron will fire (*inhibitory*).

28 *Summation* refers to the process whereby the effects of excitatory and inhibitory synapses are combined.

29 The effect of a neurotransmitter can be ended by *de-activation* (usually by destruction by enzymes) or *re-uptake* of the neurotransmitter.

30 Psychoactive drugs *inhibit* the process of re-uptake of certain neurotransmitters, thereby increasing their effect.

31 Acetylcholine *contracts* muscle cells.

32 Curare is a poison which causes paralysis by preventing *ACh* from lodging in receptor sites.

33 *Alzheimer's disease* is thought to be related to the functions of *ACh*.

34 *Dopamine* is involved in *voluntary movements*, *learning* and *arousal*.

35 *Schizophrenia* is thought to be linked to over-utilisation of *dopamine*.

36 Deficiencies in serotonin levels have been linked to *anxiety*, *mood disorders* and *insomnia*.

37 *Noradrenaline.*

38 The major role of *gamma-amino butyric acid* is in *motor behaviour*.

39 A *neuromodulator* is any chemical substance which 'primes' neurons, so that they increase or decrease their response to certain neurotransmitters.

40 *Endorphins*, like morphine, *relieve pain*.

Nervous System & Neuronal Activity

Central nervous system (CNS)
Is the point of origin of all complex commands and evaluations. Consists of:
- The brain
- The spinal cord

Peripheral nervous system (PNS)
Has two functions; Sending:
- information to the CNS from the outside world, muscles and glands
- messages from the CNS to the body's muscles and glands.

Glial cells and neurons

Glial cells – functions
- Supply nutrients and provide structural support to neurons.
- Insulate neurons by providing *myelin sheaths*.
- Remove debris following a cell's death and provide the brain with a barrier to certain harmful substances carried in the blood.

Neurons – functions
- A neuron is a cell that processes and transmits information.
- *Sensory* (or *afferent*) neurons respond directly to external stimuli and transmit information to the CNS.
- *Motor* (or *efferent*) neurons carry messages from the CNS to the muscles and glands.
- *Association* (or *connector*) neurons integrate the activities of the other two kinds of neuron.

The structure of neurons

Myelin sheaths and Nodes of Ranvier
- Myelin sheaths are part protein, part fat, and consist of the membrane of a type of glial cell called a *Swann cell*.
- The myelin sheath surrounding an axon is segmented rather than continuous, with the axon exposed at points called *nodes of Ranvier*.
- The action potential transmitted down a myelinated neuron 'leaps' from one node to another (*saltatory conduction*) allowing information to be conducted more quickly.

- The *cell body* (or *soma*) houses the nucleus of the cell and controls the cell's metabolism and maintenance.
- *Dendrites* branch out from the cell body and receive information from other neurons.
- The *axon* transmits messages away from the neuron to other neurons, muscles or glands.
- *Myelin sheaths* coat some nerves (a nerve is a bundle of axons in the PNS), which acts to insulate axons from one another and speed up the transmission of information.

The function of neurons

The transmission of information *within* a neuron

Resting state
- Inactive neurons contain positively charged potassium ions and large, negatively charged protein molecules.
- The fluid surrounding a neuron has a high concentration of positively charged sodium ions and negatively charged chloride ions.
- A *sodium–potassium pump* in the cell membrane keeps sodium ions out, so that in its inactive state the inside of the cell is negatively charged relative to the outside (by about −70 millivolts). The neuron is 'polarised'.

Active state
- When a neuron is activated by a stimulus, the sodium channels open for about one millisecond, resulting in depolarisation of the cell as it becomes positively charged (to about +40 millivolts). This is called an *action potential*.
- A chain reaction is then set off, causing sodium channels to open at adjacent sites down the axon, causing the action potential to 'travel' down the axon. With myelinated axons, the action potential 'leaps' from one node (where myelin is segmented) to another (*saltatory conduction*).
- Neurons respond according to an 'all-or-none' rule: they will only respond with an action potential if a stimulus exceeds a certain *threshold of excitation*.

Recovery
- Following excitation, potassium channels open, allowing positively charged potassium ions to move out of the cell, restoring the resting state potential of −70 millivolts.
- A cell which has just fired cannot fire again for a short period (the *absolute refractory period*) of one or two milliseconds.
- Following this, there is another short period (the *relative refractory period*) during which the cell will only fire if the stimulus is very strong.

The transmission of information *between* neurons

The synapse
- For most neurons, an action potential's journey ends where the axon ends in a *terminal* button.
- Terminal buttons house tiny sacs called *synaptic vesicles*, which contain chemical messengers called *neurotransmitters*.
- Terminal buttons do not touch other cells. Instead, they discharge neurotransmitters across a microscopic gap (called a *synaptic cleft*) which are then picked up by receptor sites on the receiving neuron.
- The releasing end of the terminal button is called the *pre-synaptic membrane*, and the receptor site the *post-synaptic membrane*.

Excitation, inhibition and summation
- Terminal buttons may release more than one neurotransmitter and these neurotransmitters may have *excitatory* or *inhibitory* effects on receiving neurons, causing them to become more (or less) likely to fire.
- A neuron may have connections to many other neurons, some of which are excitatory and some inhibitory, so that the decision to fire depends on the combined effects of these neurons (a process called 'summation').

Deactivation and re-uptake
- The effects of a neurotransmitter are ended either by *deactivation* (where it is destroyed by certain enzymes) or *re-uptake* (taken back by the terminal button that released it).
- *Psychoactive drugs* can affect the nervous system by altering the rate of neurotransmitter re-uptake, causing the neurotransmitter to stimulate the post-synaptic membrane for a longer period of time.

Neurotransmitters and neuromodulators

Gamma-amino butyric acid (*inhibitory*)
- Plays a role in motor behaviour and may also be involved in the modulation of anxiety.

Serotonin (*primarily inhibitory*)
- Deficiencies have been linked to anxiety, mood disorders, and insomnia.
- Elevated levels have been linked to autism.

Dopamine (*primarily inhibitory*)
- Involved in voluntary movements, learning, memory, and arousal.
- Reduced uptake has been linked to Parkinson's disease.
- Over-utilisation is linked to schizophrenia.

Neuromodulators
- Any chemical substance which 'primes' neurons so that they increase or decrease neurotransmitter production.
- *Endorphins* are inhibitory and, like morphine, relieve pain.
- Endorphin levels have been shown to increase during pregnancy and labour.
- May also play a role in hunger, sexual behaviour, mood regulation, and body temperature.

Noradrenaline (*also a hormone*)
- Increases heart rate and processes involved in arousal.
- Implicated in learning, memory and eating.
- Excesses and deficiencies are linked to mood disorders.
- Amphetamines increase the amount of available noradrenaline and act as stimulants.

Acetylcholine (**ACh**: *primarily excitatory*)
- Causes muscle cells to contract when released to them.
- Curare prevents ACh from lodging in receptor sites and causes paralysis.
- Concentrated in the hippocampus (which plays a role in memory), and implicated in Alzheimer's disease.

4

THE CENTRAL NERVOUS SYSTEM

SYLLABUS
3.1 Basic neural and hormonal processes and their influences on behaviour
● the organisation, structure and functioning of the central nervous system

KEY QUESTIONS
● What is the role of the spinal cord?
● How does the brain develop?
● What roles are played by the hindbrain, midbrain and forebrain respectively?

Q

Section 1: The spinal cord
1 What is the *spinal cord*?
2 What is the role of the *spinal vertebrae*?
3 Of what two types of neuron are spinal nerves principally composed?
4 What is the difference between the *dorsal root* and the *ventral root*?

Section 2: The development of the brain
5 According to MacLean's (1973, 1982) *triune model* of the brain, which is the oldest part of the brain?
6 What name does MacLean give to the *limbic system*?
7 What name is given to the *three sets of membranes* which encase the brain?
8 What is the role of *cerebrospinal fluid*?
9 What are the three main functions of the brain?

Section 3: The hindbrain
10 Where is the *medulla* located?
11 What does the term *contralateral connection*, used to apply to the nerve fibres crossing the medulla, mean?
12 Identify four vital functions regulated by the medulla.
13 What vital integrative role does the *pons* play?
14 Identify one other role played by the pons.
15 What are the two principal functions of the *cerebellum*?
16 What type of memories are stored in the *cerebellum*?
17 Complete the sentence: 'For Eccles (1973), the cerebellum is a computer controlling complex motor behaviour, leaving the rest of the brain free for ___ activity'.

Section 4: The midbrain
18 What two parts of the brain are connected by the *reticular formation*?
19 What is the *orienting reflex* (controlled by the *reticular formation*)?
20 Identify one *eye reflex* controlled by the reticular formation.

21 Why is the reticular formation sometimes also called the *reticular activating system* or *consciousness system*?
22 Identify one likely consequence of damage to the *reticular formation*.
23 What term is used to describe the process by which the reticular formation learns to screen out constant sources of uninformative stimuli?

Section 5: The forebrain
24 What name is given to the structures which act as a '*sensory relay station*' for all sensory information except olfaction?
25 What is the *lateral geniculate nucleus* involved in?
26 In what way is the *hypothalamus* able to affect the *endocrine (hormonal) system*?
27 What is *homeostasis*?
28 Identify three behavioural impairments likely to be caused by damage to the hypothalamus.
29 What is the likely consequence of damage to the *basal ganglia*?
30 Which important neurotransmitter is produced by the *basal ganglia*?
31 Which disease has been linked to degeneration of neurons in the basal ganglia?
32 Identify the structures included in the *limbic system*.
33 Name the largest structure in the limbic system, which is involved in the formation of new memories.
34 Complete the sentence: 'The limbic system is particularly involved in behaviours satisfying ___ and ___ needs'.
35 What percentage of neurons are located in the *cerebrum*?
36 What is the *corpus callosum*?
37 What name is given to the surface layer of the cerebrum?
38 What name is given to the 'valleys' which divide the brain into lobes?
39 Name the four lobes into which the brain is divided.

Section 1: The spinal cord

1 The *spinal cord* is a thick column of nerve fibres that emerges from the bottom of the brain and runs down the back.
2 The *spinal vertebrae* are bony structures which encase and protect the spine.
3 *Spinal nerves* are principally composed of *sensory* and *motor neurons*.
4 The *dorsal root* contains *sensory neurons*, whilst the *ventral root* contains *motor neurons*.

Section 2: The development of the brain

5 MacLean's (1973, 1982) *triune model* identifies the '*reptilian brain*' (or *central core*) as the oldest brain structure.
6 MacLean calls the limbic system the '*old mammalian brain*'.
7 *Meninges*.
8 *Cerebrospinal fluid* acts as a 'liquid cushion' and protects the brain against injuries caused by movements of the head.
9 The brain functions to *take in information, interpret this information*, and *act on it*.

Section 3: The hindbrain

10 The *medulla* is located on the spinal cord, as it widens on entering the skull.
11 '*Contralateral connection*' describes the manner in which nerve fibres cross the medulla so that one side of the body is connected to the other side of the brain.
12 The medulla regulates *heart rate, blood pressure, body temperature* and *respiration*.
13 The *pons* integrates movements of the two halves of the body.
14 The *pons* also plays a role in functions related to *attention, respiration, alertness* and *sleep*.
15 The *cerebellum* is principally responsible for *maintaining balance* and '*smoothing*' (or co-ordinating) *movements*.
16 *Motor memories* are stored in the *cerebellum*.
17 'For Eccles (1973), the cerebellum is a computer controlling complex motor behaviour, leaving the rest of the brain free for *conscious* activity.'

Section 4: The midbrain

18 The *spinal cord* and *forebrain* are connected by the *reticular formation*.
19 The *orienting reflex* is a general response to a novel stimulus.
20 The *pupillary reflex* is controlled by the reticular formation.
21 The reticular formation is sometimes also called the *reticular activating system* or *consciousness system*, as it is involved in maintaining general arousal levels, sleep and waking.
22 Damage to the reticular formation may produce a *comatose state*.
23 *Habituation*.

Section 5: The forebrain

24 The *thalami*.
25 The *lateral geniculate nucleus* is involved in processing visual information.
26 The *hypothalamus* helps to regulate the *pituitary gland*, which in turn controls the body's endocrine glands.
27 *Homeostasis* is the maintenance of a proper balance of physiological variables.
28 Damage to the hypothalamus may cause *changes to food intake, sterility* and the *stunting of growth*.
29 Damage to the *basal ganglia* may cause *changes in posture, muscle tone, jerks, tremors* and *twitches*.
30 *Dopamine* is produced by the *basal ganglia*.
31 *Parkinson's disease* has been linked to degeneration of neurons in the basal ganglia.
32 *Limbic system* structures include the *olfactory bulbs, hippocampus, amygdala, septum pellucidum, cingulate gyrus, mamillary body, fornix* and *anterior commissure*.
33 The *hippocampus* is involved in the formation of new memories.
34 'The limbic system is particularly involved in behaviours satisfying *motivational* and *emotional* needs.'
35 *Seventy-five per cent* of neurons are located in the *cerebrum*.
36 The *corpus callosum* is a dense mass of joining fibres which convey information back and forth between the brain's two hemispheres.
37 The surface layer of the cerebrum is called the *cerebral cortex*.
38 The 'valleys' which divide the brain into lobes are called *fissures*.
39 The brain is divided into *frontal, parietal, occipital* and *temporal* lobes.

A

The Central Nervous System

The spinal cord
- A thick column of nerve fibres that emerges from the bottom of the brain and runs down the back.
- The main 'communication cable' between the CNS and the PNS.

The Brain

Triune model
(MacLean, 1973, 1982)
Identifies three main parts of the brain:
- *The reptilian brain* (central core) is the oldest of the 3 parts and virtually identical to the brains of reptiles.
- *The old mammalian brain* (limbic system) developed in early mammals about 100 million years ago.
- *The new mammalian brain* (cerebral cortex) developed in the last 2 million years in some mammals.

The development of the brain
The brain has three main functions:
- Taking in information from the senses,
- Interpreting this information,
- Acting upon this information.

It is not the size of the brain, but the complexity of the interconnections between the neurons which gives it its processing power.

Foetal development model
Identifies brain sections based on foetal development:
- The nervous system develops from a single tube of neural tissue, the lower part becoming the spinal cord.
- The top of the tube swells and the *hindbrain* (lowest section), *midbrain* and *forebrain* can be clearly identified.
- As these develop, the forebrain 'folds back' over the midbrain.

The hindbrain

The medulla oblongata
- The first structure that emerges as the spinal cord enters the skull and widens.
- Although only 1½ inches long, it regulates heart rate, blood pressure, respiration and body temperature.
- The medulla also plays a role in vomiting, coughing and sneezing.
- Contains all the nerve fibres connecting the spinal cord to the brain, most of which cross so that one side of the brain controls the other side of the body (*contralateral connection*).

The pons
- A bulge of white matter lying forward of the medulla.
- It is an important connection between the midbrain and the medulla, and is vital in integrating the movements of the two halves of the body.
- The pons plays a role in functions related to attention, respiration, alertness and sleep.

The cerebellum
- Lies behind the pons, and consists of two convoluted hemispheres which extend outward towards the back of the skull.
- The cerebellum is involved in maintaining reflex actions such as breathing and balance and 'smoothing' muscular movements.
- The cerebellum is important in learning and storing muscular memories.
- Eccles (1973): it is a computer, controlling complex motor behaviour, leaving the rest of the brain free for conscious activity.

The midbrain

The reticular formation
- Consists of a tangle of nerve cells and fibres which ascend from the spinal cord to the forebrain carrying mainly motor information. Important in maintaining muscle tone and controlling various reflexes.
- Also called the *reticular activating system*, it is vital in maintaining general arousal levels. Stimulation of this area causes messages to be sent to the cerebral cortex, increasing alertness.
- In humans the reticular formation includes an area controlling eye reflexes (e.g. pupil dilation and eye movements) as well as being one of several locations where pain is registered.

The reticular formation and attention
- The reticular formation is also involved in screening incoming information, filtering out irrelevant information.
- It allows us to *habituate* to uninformative information (such as the ticking of a clock), but alerts us to other information (such as the crying of a baby) even if we are asleep.

The forebrain

The thalamus
- We possess two *thalami* (joined egg-shaped structures near the centre of the brain).
- Each acts as a *sensory relay station* for all sensory information except olfaction.
- Nerves from sensory systems enter the thalami from below and information is transmitted to the *cerebral cortex* by nerve fibres exiting from above.
- The thalami also receive information *from* the cortex, mainly dealing with complex limb movements.

Sub-structures
- The *medial geniculate body* is responsible for auditory sensory information.
- The *ventrobasal complex* transmits information about body position and the sense of touch.
- The *lateral geniculate nucleus* is involved in vision.

The hypothalamus
- A tiny collection of *nuclei* located beneath the *thalami*.
- Functions include helping to regulate the *sympathetic branch* of the *ANS*, controlling the *pituitary gland* which in turn controls other *endocrine glands*.
- Damage can cause changes in food intake, sterility and stunting of growth.
- Also plays a major role in *species-typical behaviour* (the four Fs: feeding, fighting, fleeing and 'reproduction') and *homeostasis* (maintaining a proper balance of physiological variables)

Major areas
- *anterior, supraoptic* (both involved in water balance)
- *presupraoptic* (heat control)
- *ventromedial* (hunger)
- *posterior* (sex drive)
- *dorsal* ('pleasure')

The basal ganglia
- Should really be called the basal nuclei, since 'ganglia' is usually used to describe collections of cell bodies outside the nervous system.
- Embedded in the mass of white matter and lie in front of the thalami.
- Involved in the coordination of muscular movement, controlling slower movements.
- Damage leads to changes in posture and muscle tone leading to jerks, tremors and twitches.
- Produces much of the brain's dopamine and degeneration is linked to Parkinson's disease.

The limbic system
- A series of structures located near the border between the cerebellum and parts of the hindbrain.
- The limbic system is involved in behaviours satisfying motivational and emotional needs.
- Destruction of the amygdala causes monkeys to become docile, whilst electrical stimulation can cause rage.
- Only fully evolved in mammals.
- The limbic system includes the *olfactory bulbs, hippocampus, amygdala, septum pellucidum, cingulate gyrus, mamillary body, fornix* and *anterior commissure*.

The hippocampus
- The largest structure in the limbic system and involved in memory.
- Damage results in the inability to form new memories.

The cerebrum
- Accounts for 80% of the brain's weight.
- Increases information-processing capacity.
- Lower vertebrates have no cerebrum.
- Divided into two *cerebral hemispheres*, connected by the *corpus callosum*, which conveys information back and forth.
- The surface layer is called the *cerebral cortex* and is the most recently evolved part.
- The cortex is folded into convolutions which increase the total area.

The brain's lobes
- The cortex is divided by *gyri* and *fissures*. The *lateral* and *central* fissures demarcate the *frontal, parietal, occipital* and *temporal* lobes.
- Different areas of the cortex are specialised for motor, sensory and associative functions.

5

THE PERIPHERAL NERVOUS SYSTEM AND THE ENDOCRINE SYSTEM

SYLLABUS

3.1 Basic neural and hormonal processes and their influences on behaviour
- the organisation, structure and functioning of the autonomic system and endocrine systems, and interactions between them
- the influence of these systems on physiological and behavioural functions including homeostasis

KEY QUESTIONS
- What are the somatic nervous system (SNS) and the autonomic nervous system (ANS)?
- What are the functions of the sympathetic and parasympathetic branches of the ANS?
- What glands comprise the endocrine system?

Section 1: The peripheral nervous system

1 What are the two essential functions of the *peripheral nervous system* (PNS)?
2 Complete the sentence: 'The somatic nervous system is concerned with the ___ world, whilst the autonomic nervous system is concerned with the ___ world'.
3 What two types of neurons allow the somatic nervous system to connect the central nervous system to sensory receptors and the skeletal muscles?

Section 2: ANS: the two branches

4 To what do the nerves of the autonomic nervous system (ANS) connect the central nervous system (CNS)?
5 What is the primary function of the ANS?
6 How are the neurons of the *sympathetic branch* of the ANS arranged, relative to the spinal cord?
7 What feature of the *sympathetic branch* results from the large number of interconnections between neurons?
8 According to Cannon (1927), what is the major function of the sympathetic branch of the ANS?
9 Identify the two *hormones* which are secreted in response to ANS activation.
10 Identify three bodily effects which are increased as a result of heightened ANS activity.
11 How does the distribution of nerve fibres in the *parasympathetic branch* of the ANS differ from that in the *sympathetic branch*, and what effect does this have?
12 What are the major functions of the *parasympathetic branch* of the ANS?
13 When does parasympathetic activity dominate?
14 Identify two bodily processes that are stimulated by the *parasympathetic branch* of the ANS.
15 What is involved in *biofeedback*?

Section 3: The endocrine system

16 What is the difference between an *exocrine gland* and an *endocrine gland*?
17 What are *hormones*?
18 In what way are *hormones* similar to *neurotransmitters*?

19 What is the role of a *negative feedback loop* in hormonal regulation?
20 Which CNS structure is responsible for regulating the *pituitary gland*?
21 What is the *infundibulum*?
22 What is the role of *somatotrophin*?
23 Name one other hormone produced by the *anterior pituitary*.
24 Identify one way in which the anterior pituitary is able to influence the hypothalamus, via the endocrine system.
25 Identify one role of *oxytocin*, a hormone produced by the *posterior pituitary*.
26 What is the function of *anti-diuretic hormone*?
27 What names are given to the outer layer and inner core of the *adrenal glands*?
28 What collective name is given to the hormones secreted by the outer layer of the adrenal glands?
29 Identify three functions of these hormones.
30 What branch of the ANS is activated by *adrenaline*?
31 Identify another hormone also produced by the inner core of the adrenal glands.
32 Name the primary hormone produced by the *thyroid gland*.
33 What condition occurs as a result of *over-production* of this hormone?
34 The *parathyroid glands* secrete *parathormone*. Identify the two mineral levels this affects.
35 What condition occurs as a result of the pancreas over-secreting *insulin*?
36 What names are given to the *gonads* in women and men, respectively?
37 What two aspects of development do hormones secreted by the gonads control?
38 What is the role of *testosterone*?
39 Name the two hormones responsible for regulating the *menstrual cycle*.
40 According to Cantin & Genest (1986), which endocrine gland is responsible for secreting *atrial natriuretic factor*?

Q

Section 1: The peripheral nervous system

1 The *peripheral nervous system* sends information to the CNS from the outside world, and transmits information from the CNS to the muscles.

2 'The somatic nervous system is concerned with the *external* world, whilst the autonomic nervous system is concerned with the *internal* world.'

Section 2: ANS: the two branches

3 *Sensory (afferent)* and *motor (efferent) neurons.*

4 The nerves of the autonomic nervous system (ANS) connect the central nervous system (CNS) to the *skeletal muscles.*

5 The primary function of the ANS is to *regulate internal bodily processes.*

6 The neurons of the *sympathetic branch* of the ANS are arranged so that they form a long vertical chain on either side of the spinal cord.

7 Because of the interconnections between neurons, the sympathetic branch is able to act as a unit.

8 Cannon (1927) claims that the major function of the sympathetic branch of the ANS is to mobilise the body for an emergency ('*fight-or-flight*').

9 *Adrenaline* and *noradrenaline* are secreted in response to the activation of the ANS.

10 *Heart rate, respiration rate* and *pupil size* are three bodily effects increased by heightened ANS activity.

11 Nerve fibres in the *parasympathetic branch* of the ANS are *more widely distributed*, and tend to *act less as a unit* and more on individual organs.

12 The *parasympathetic branch* of the ANS stimulates processes that serve to *restore or conserve energy*, and those which carry out the *body's 'maintenance needs'.*

13 *Parasympathetic* activity dominates when we are *relaxed* or *inactive.*

14 *Salivation* and *digestion* are both stimulated by the *parasympathetic branch* of the ANS.

15 *Biofeedback* involves *learning to control ANS activity* by the use of equipment which records (and provides 'feedback' on) a bodily process not normally under conscious control.

Section 3: The endocrine system

16 *Exocrine glands* have *ducts*, whilst *endocrine glands* secrete their products *directly into the bloodstream.*

17 *Hormones* are powerful *chemical messengers* secreted by endocrine glands.

18 Hormones, like neurotransmitters, act *only* on receptors at particular locations in the body (i.e. they are specific).

19 A *negative feedback loop* enables a steady state to be maintained by feeding information back to the glands, instructing them to stop when sufficient hormone has been released.

20 The *hypothalamus* is responsible for regulating the pituitary gland.

21 The *infundibulum* is a network of blood vessels connecting the *pituitary gland* to the *hypothalamus.*

22 *Somatotrophin* is a *growth hormone*, secreted by the *anterior pituitary.*

23 The *anterior pituitary* also produces *prolactin (lactogenic hormone).*

24 The anterior pituitary is able to influence the *gonads* to produce *hormones* which, in turn, influence the hypothalamus.

25 *Oxytocin* instructs the uterus to *contract during childbirth* and shortly after birth *stimulates the breasts to produce milk.*

26 *Anti-diuretic hormone* acts on the kidneys, regulating the amount of water which is drawn from the tissues and passed to the bladder.

27 The *outer layer* and *inner core* of the adrenal glands are called the *cortex* and *medulla*, respectively.

28 *Corticosteroids.*

29 Corticosteroids *promote muscle development, increase resistance to stress* and *stimulate the liver to release sugar.*

30 The *sympathetic branch* of the ANS is activated by adrenaline.

31 *Noradrenaline.*

32 *Thyroxin.*

33 Over-production of this hormone leads to *hyperthyroidism*, characterised by excitability, insomnia and weight loss.

34 *Parathormone* affects *calcium* and *phosphate* levels in the blood and tissue fluids.

35 Oversecretion of insulin results in *hypoglycaemia*, characterised by fatigue, shakiness and dizziness.

36 The *gonads* are called *ovaries* in women and *testes* in men.

37 Hormones secreted by the gonads control the *development of primary and secondary sexual characteristics.*

38 *Testosterone* is a masculinising hormone, and acts prenatally in order to *differentiate the male sex organs.*

39 *Estrogen* and *progesterone* are responsible for regulating the menstrual cycle.

40 Cantin & Genest (1986) claim that the *heart* is responsible for secreting *atrial natriuretic factor.*

The peripheral nervous system

The somatic nervous system (external world)

- The *somatic nervous system* (SNS) connects the *central nervous system* (CNS) to *sensory receptors and skeletal muscles.*
- This allows voluntary movement.
- *Sensory neurons* carry messages to the CNS, whilst *motor neurons* carry instructions from the CNS to the muscles.
- Damage to these neurons can cause loss of sensation and paralysis.

The autonomic nervous system (internal world)

- The autonomic nervous system (ANS) connects the CNS to the internal organs (viscera), glands and smooth muscles (e.g. those involved in digestion).
- The ANS functions to regulate internal bodily processes, by sending information to and from the CNS.
- The ANS appears to operate autonomously (independently), controlling functions such as urination and defecation in the absence of conscious control.
- The ANS is divided into two branches:

The sympathetic branch

Effects of activation
- Dilates pupils
- Inhibits salivation
- Accelerates breathing
- Increases heartbeat
- Increases blood pressure
- Inhibits digestion
- Inhibits bladder contraction
- Stimulates secretion of adrenaline and noradrenaline
- Contracts bladder
- Increases blood flow to muscles
- Releases sugar from the liver.

- Comprises bundles of neurons which form a long vertical chain on either side of the spinal cord.
- The interconnections between the neurons allow the sympathetic branch to act as a unit.
- The sympathetic branch prepares the body to expend energy.
- Cannon (1927) suggested that the major function of the sympathetic branch was to prepare the body for *fight-or-flight.*

The parasympathetic branch

- Comprises bundles of neurons originating at either end of the spinal cord.
- Nerve fibres are widely distributed and as a result act less as a unit and more on individual organs.
- The parasympathetic branch stimulates processes that restore or conserve energy.
- Also carries out the body's maintenance needs (e.g. digestion, waste elimination, tissue repair) and is most active when we are inactive.

Effects of activation
- Constricts pupils
- Stimulates salivation
- Slows breathing
- Slows heartbeat
- Stimulates digestion
- Contracts bladder.

Biofeedback
- Miller pioneered the application of ANS control with *biofeedback,* in which equipment is used to provide feedback on bodily processes not normally under conscious control (Walker, 1984).

The Peripheral Nervous System

The thyroid gland
- Produces thyroxin in response to anterior pituitary secretions.
- Thyroxin raises metabolism by increasing oxygen use.
- Over-production leads to *hyperthyroidism* (characterised by excitability, insomnia and weight loss)

The parathyroid gland
- Embedded in the thyroid gland.
- Secretes *parathormone* which controls calcium and phosphate levels in the blood and tissues.
- The amount of calcium in the blood directly affects the nervous system's excitability.

The pituitary gland
- Located deep within the brain, slightly below the *hypothalamus* to which it is connected.
- The anterior pituitary functions separately from the posterior pituitary.

The adrenal glands
- They have an *outer layer* (*cortex*) and an *inner core* (*medulla*).
- Regulated by the anterior pituitary.
- The cortex secretes corticosteroids which promote muscle development and increase resistance to stress.

The endocrine system

- Endocrine glands are glands without ducts which release their products directly into the bloodstream.
- Such glands secrete *hormones* (powerful chemical messengers) which act on certain receptors at locations around the body.
- Information is fed back to these glands (via a *negative feedback loop*), enabling the hormones to maintain a steady state.
- The endocrine system plays a major role in regulating development and co-ordinating complex psychological reactions.
- The system is regulated by the *hypothalamus*, which exerts its influence via the *pituitary gland.*

The anterior pituitary
Produces at least 8 hormones including:
- *Somatotrophin* (growth hormone)
- *Prolactin* (stimulates milk production during pregnancy).

The posterior pituitary
Produces:
- *Oxytocin* causes uterus to contract during childbirth.
- *Antidiuretic hormone* acts on the kidneys, causing water to be conserved.

Adrenaline and noradrenaline
The adrenal medulla produces these two hormones:
- *Adrenaline* activates the sympathetic branch of the ANS (fight-or-flight response)
- *Noradrenaline* triggers the release of *adrenocorticotrophic hormone*, which regulates the activity of the adrenal cortex, increasing resistance to stress.

Pancreas
- Plays a major role in controlling blood and urine sugar levels by secreting *insulin* and *glucagon.*
- *Hypoglycaemia* occurs when insulin is oversecreted, leaving too little sugar.
- *Hyperglycaemia* occurs when insulin is undersecreted, leaving too much sugar in the blood. The kidneys then secrete too much water, causing poisonous wastes to accumulate.

The gonads
These are the sexual glands – *ovaries* in women and *testes* in men.
Three main types of hormone are secreted by the gonads, controlling *primary sex characteristics* (e.g. penis growth and sperm production) and *secondary sex characteristics* (e.g. body hair and deepening of the voice).
- *Testosterone* (a masculinising hormone) stimulates the prenatal differentiation of the male sex organs.
- *Estrogen* (female sex hormone) leads to the development of the female reproductive capacity and secondary sexual characteristics (e.g. breasts).
- *Progesterone* (female sex hormone) stimulates the growth of the female reproductive organs and maintains pregnancy.
- Both estrogen and progesterone regulate the menstrual cycle.

The heart
- Cantin & Genest (1986) discovered that the heart secretes a powerful hormone called *atrial natriuretic factor* (ANF).
- This plays an important role in regulating blood pressure and blood volume, and in excreting water, sodium, and potassium.
- The blood vessels, kidneys, adrenal glands and other regulatory glands may all, in turn, be affected.

SOME METHODS AND TECHNIQUES USED TO INVESTIGATE CORTICAL FUNCTIONS

<table>
<tr><td>

SYLLABUS
3.2 **Cortical functions**
• methods and techniques used to investigate cortical functioning.

</td><td>

KEY QUESTIONS
• How do clinical/anatomical methods investigate cortical functioning?
• What invasive methods have been developed to investigate cortical functioning?
• What non-invasive methods have been developed to investigate cortical functioning?

</td></tr>
</table>

Section 1: Clinical/anatomical methods

1 In what way do *clinical/anatomical methods* study the brain?
2 What type of patients were studied in Broca and Wernické's investigations into language?
3 Identify three difficulties with such studies.

Section 2: Invasive methods of investigation

4 What is involved in *ablation*?
5 What discovery was made by Flourens, using this technique with rabbits, birds and dogs?
6 Apart from the difficulty of generalising the results of ablation studies to humans, what is another problem with these studies?
7 What is involved in *lesion production*?
8 Complete the sentence: 'Lesions in one area of the hypothalamus cause extreme ___ in rats'.
9 Identify one therapeutic use of lesions in humans.
10 What do the letters ESB stand for?
11 How were Olds & Milner (1954) able to discover a '*pleasure centre*' in the brains of rats?
12 What classic research was carried out by Penfield during the 1940s and 1950s?
13 How has ESB been used therapeutically?
14 Identify three criticisms of ESB made by Valenstein (1977).
15 What does *micro-electrode recording* aim to measure?
16 Which sensory system has been investigated by Hubel and Wiesel using micro-electrode recording?
17 Identify two drawbacks associated with this method.

Section 3: Non-invasive methods of investigation

18 In what way can radioactive forms of sugar be used to study anatomic pathways?
19 What does an *EEG* (*electroencephalogram*) measure?
20 In what form are the results of an EEG machine produced?
21 When are *alpha waves* most likely to be be recorded by an EEG?

22 Identify three conditions in which the EEG can assist diagnosis.
23 Identify one further area in which the EEG has proved an indispensible tool for researchers.
24 What is the principal criticism of the EEG as a method of investigating cortical functioning?
25 In what way is *computerised electroencephalography* able to partially overcome limitations of the EEG?
26 In what way does a *magnetoencephalograph* (MEG) differ from an EEG?
27 How does EEG imaging allow brain functioning to be measured 'on a millisecond by millisecond basis' (Fischman, 1985)?
28 How does *computerised axial tomography* (CAT) allow researchers to investigate cortical functioning?
29 What type of information is yielded by a CAT scan?
30 What do the letters MRI stand for, when referring to scanning devices?
31 What is the role of radio waves in MRI scanning?
32 What limitation do CAT and MRI scans share, when providing us with information about the brain?
33 What is the first step in investigating the brain functioning of an individual when using *positron emission tomography* (PET)?
34 What is the biggest advantage of PET over MRI and CAT?
35 In what way is PET useful in the study of mental disorders?
36 What conclusion was reached by Gur *et al.* (1994) in studying the brain metabolism of men and women using this method?
37 What is the advantage of newer techniques (such as *SPET* and *SQUID*) over other scanning techniques?
38 How does SPET measure brain activity?
39 Complete the sentence: 'SPET is also useful in detecting the brain areas affected in people with ___ difficulties (Matthews, 1996a)'.

Section 1: Clinical/anatomical methods

1 *Clinical/anatomical methods* look at the behavioural consequences of *accidental brain damage*.

2 Broca and Wernické studied patients who had suffered a *stroke*, and had difficulty producing or understanding speech.

3 Such studies are not very helpful in studying subtle changes, since accurate records of behaviour prior to the damage often do not exist. It is also difficult to determine the location and amount of damage, and researchers have to wait for the 'right kind' of injury to occur in order to study a given area.

Section 2: Invasive methods of investigation

4 *Ablation* involves surgically *removing* or *destroying brain tissue* and observing the behavioural consequences.

5 Flourens discovered that the cerebellum plays a vital role in co-ordination and balance.

6 Ablation methods cannot tell us if a removed part of the brain controlled a particular behaviour or was simply involved in it.

7 *Lesion production* involves deliberately injuring part of the brain, then observing the behavioural consequences.

8 'Lesions in one area of the hypothalamus cause extreme *overeating* (or *undereating*) in rats.'

9 Lesions are used to reduce the severity of epileptic seizures.

10 *Electrical stimulation of the brain*.

11 Olds & Milner (1954) fitted implanted electrodes to a control mechanism which the rat could operate. Since the rat would self-stimulate this region at over 100 times per minute, and in preference to food or water, it was assumed that this was a *pleasure centre*.

12 Penfield stimulated the cortex of conscious patients being treated for epilepsy, to map cortical functions.

13 *ESB* has been used to treat pain by 'blocking' pain messages in the spine before they reach the brain.

14 Valenstein (1977) points out that no single brain area is likely to be the sole source of a given behaviour, that ESB-provoked behaviour is not normal but compulsive and stereotypical, and that identical stimulation produces different effects at different times on the same individual.

15 *Micro-electrode recording* aims to measure the electrical activity in a single neuron.

16 Hubel and Wiesel used this technique to investigate the visual system in monkeys.

17 The method is slow (since only one neuron can be studied at a time), and is confined to non-humans since the electrodes can destroy brain tissue.

Section 3: Non-invasive methods of investigation

18 Radioactive forms of sugar can be injected into non-humans, the animal made to perform a task, and slices of the sacrificed animal's brain pressed against a radioactivity-sensitive film in order to determine which areas were most active.

19 An EEG measures changes in the electrical activity of the brain.

20 An EEG machine produces results by tracing the impulses in pen on paper attached to a revolving drum.

21 *Alpha waves* are most likely to be be recorded in adults who are awake, relaxed, with their eyes closed.

22 Tumours, damaged brain tissue, and epilepsy.

23 The EEG has also proved helpful in investigating *sleep and dreaming*.

24 The EEG only reflects the gross activity of neurons and tells us only that something is happening, not what is happening.

25 In *computerised electroencephalography*, a stimulus is repeatedly presented and a computer screens out activity unrelated to the stimulus.

26 A *magnetoencephalograph* (MEG) detects weak magnetic fields, whereas an EEG detects electrical activity.

27 During EEG imaging, the activity recorded by 32 electrodes is sent to a computer, which translates this information into coloured, moving images.

28 The *CAT scan* examines the brain by taking a large number of X-rays of the brain, using a rotating X-ray tube and detector.

29 A CAT scan yields structural information about the brain.

30 *Magnetic resonance imaging*.

31 Radio waves are used to excite hydrogen atoms in the brain which in turn disturb a magnetic field. This disturbance is measured.

32 Both CAT and MRI scans can only provide a still image of a cross-section of the brain.

33 The first step in *PET* is to inject the person with a small amount of radioactive material, bonded to a substance which is metabolised.

34 PET is able to examine the relationship between brain activity and mental processes.

35 PET can reveal differences in the pattern of neural activity between those with and without mental disorders.

36 Gur *et al.* (1994) concluded that men have a more active metabolism in the primitive brain centres controlling sex and violence.

37 Newer techniques (such as *SPET* and *SQUID*) are able to focus on very small areas of the brain.

38 SPET measures brain activity by monitoring blood flow to different brain areas.

39 'SPET is also useful in detecting the brain areas affected in people with *learning* difficulties (Matthews, 1996a).'

A

Investigating Cortical Functioning

Invasive methods

Ablation and lesion production

Ablation involves surgically removing or destroying brain tissue and observing the behavioural consequences.

- Flourens pioneered the technique in the 1820s, showing that the removal of thin slices from the cerebellum of rabbits, birds and dogs resulted in poor co-ordination and balance.
- However, where behaviour does change, we cannot be sure if the brain region *controls* or is merely *involved* in a behaviour.

Lesion production involves deliberately injuring part of the brain and observing the behavioural consequences.

- Animals are placed under anaesthetic, an electrode inserted into a specific brain site, and used to 'burn' out a small area.
- Lesions to the hypothalamus of rats produce over- or under-eating.
- However, we cannot be sure that such findings can be generalised to humans.

Electrical stimulation of the brain (ESB)

ESB involves inserting one or more electrodes into a living animal's brain and applying an electric current which does not cause any damage.

- Olds & Milner (1954) electrical stimulation of the *hypothalamus* in rats caused them to increase the frequency of whatever they were engaged in.

Also used in studying the *cortex* of humans (Penfield, 1940s and 1950s) and can be used to '*map*' brain regions, as well as *therapeutically* (e.g. by 'blocking' pain messages in the spine before they reach the brain).

Problems

Valenstein (1977) points out that (i) no single brain area is likely to be the sole source of a behaviour, (ii) ESB produces compulsive, not natural behaviours, and (iii) the effects of ESB on the *same area* vary over time.

Micro-electrode recording

The insertion of tiny electrodes to record a single neuron's activity in a living animal's brain. The electrode is attached to an electrical connector cemented to the brain, which leads to an apparatus which measures electrical activity.

- Hubel & Wiesel (1965) used this technique to investigate the ways in which a monkey's brain processes visual information.

Problems

- Since the brain contains billions of neurons, building up a picture of how the brain works using this method is very slow.
- Micro-electrodes can destroy brain tissue, so their use has been confined to non-humans, making it difficult to generalise findings to humans.

Clinical/anatomical methods

- Involve looking at the behavioural consequences of accidental brain damage.
- Unfortunately it may be difficult to determine the precise *location* and *amount of* damage, and just how *much* behaviour change has resulted from the damage.

Chemical stimulation

Involves introducing a chemical into the brains of non-humans to determine its behavioural and physiological effects.

- The chemical is delivered using a small tube (*micro-pipette*).
- The most commonly used chemicals are those believed to affect synaptic transmission.

- Has been used to trace anatomic pathways in the brain, using a radioactive form of sugar. Cells involved in a task use more sugar, so radioactivity builds up in them.
- The animal is then 'sacrificed' and slices of brain tissue exposed to a photographic film sensitive to radioactivity.

Problems

- The data are often difficult to interpret, with different non-humans responding differently to the same chemical.
- As with all invasive methods, there are practical and ethical issues.

Non-invasive methods

Recording the brain's electrical activity

- Adrian & Matthews (1934) developed the *electroencephalogram* (or EEG) which measures changes in brain activity in different brain parts.
- The EEG allows researchers to measure brain activity in response to specific experiences, using an amplifier which passes information to pens which trace impulses onto paper.
- The EEG is used in *clinical diagnosis* since EEG patterns from tumours and damaged tissue are distinctive.
- The EEG is also used to investigate *sleep and dreaming*.
- Recordings can only represent the gross and simultaneous activity, revealing that *something* is happening but not *what*.

4 main types of 'brain waves'

- **Delta** (1–3 Hz): mainly found in infants, adults in 'deep' sleep, or adults with brain tumours.
- **Theta** (4–7 Hz): common in infants aged 2–5 years, observed in adults with antisocial personality disorder.
- **Alpha** (8–13 Hz): seen in adults who are awake, relaxed and whose eyes are closed.
- **Beta** (13Hz +): seen in adults who are awake, alert, have their eyes open, and are concentrating on a task.

Modern techniques

- *Computerised electro-encephalography* involves repeatedly presenting a stimulus and having a computer filter out activity unrelated to it.
- *Magnetoencephalograms* (*MEGs*) detect the weak magnetic fields caused by the brain's electrical activity.
- *EEG imaging* allows researchers to measure brain functioning on a millisecond by millisecond basis, by feeding information from 32 electrodes placed on the scalp into a computer which produces moving images.

Scanning and imaging devices

Computerised axial tomography (CAT)

- The brain is examined by taking a large number of X-ray photographs of it.
- A person's head is placed in a tube with an X-ray source and X-ray detector opposite each other. These two then rotate, and the amount of penetration of X-rays is recorded.
- Information is then fed into a computer which displays a 3-D representation of the brain's structures.

Magnetic resonance imaging (MRI)

- MRI uses a strong magnetic field, rather than X-rays, to form an image of the brain.
- A person is placed in a powerful magnetic field, then harmless radio waves, which excite hydrogen atoms in the brain, are emitted.
- The changes in the magnetic field are recorded by computer, producing a more sensitive and clearer picture than the CAT scan.

Positron emission tomography (PET)

- PET measures metabolic activity in the brain.
- A person is injected with a harmless radioactive substance 'bonded' to glucose.
- As the brain metabolises this glucose, the most active areas can be detected.
- PET can provide information about brain functioning *during* behaviour and *differences* of functioning in abnormality.

SPET and SQUID

- *Superconducting quantum imaging devices* (SQUIDs) and *single positron emission devices* (SPETs) are able to focus on the activity of very small areas of the brain.
- SPET measures blood flows into different brain areas, having first injected a person with a small amount of radioactive iodine.
- Useful in detecting areas of brain involved in learning difficulties.

22

THE CEREBRAL CORTEX

KEY QUESTIONS
• What is localisation theory?
• What are the primary motor areas?
• What are the sensory motor areas?
• What are the primary association areas?
• What is holistic theory?

Section 1: Localisation theory
1 What is the central claim of *localisation theory*?
2 How did *phrenologists* claim to be able to detect the unusual development of the 'organs' which make up the brain?
3 Which *invasive method* is commonly used to assist in understanding localised brain function?

Section 2: The primary motor area
4 What did Delgado (1969) discover when he stimulated part of the *primary motor area* in a patient's left hemisphere?
5 What is a *contralateral connection*?
6 What did Penfield discover when he stimulated the top of the primary motor area?
7 What did Penfield discover regarding those body areas (such as fingers) which require more precise control?
8 What aspect of movement is the primary motor area *not* responsible for?

Section 3: The primary sensory areas
9 What is the principal role of the *primary somatosensory area*?
10 In what two ways is this area similar to the primary motor area?
11 According to Robertson (1995), what difference exists between the somatosensory areas of Braille readers and non-Braille readers?
12 What is a likely consequence of damage to the primary somatosensory area?
13 In which lobe is the *primary auditory area* located?
14 What did Penfield discover when stimulating this area in his patients?
15 What is meant by saying that hearing involves *ipsilateral connections* as well as *contralateral connections*?
16 What is a likely consequence of slight damage to the auditory area?
17 In which lobe is the *primary visual area* located?
18 What did Penfield discover was the consequence of stimulating this area?

19 What is a likely consequence of damage to part of the visual area?
20 What is the *optic chiasma*?
21 Why doesn't damage to one eye result in one hemisphere 'missing out' on visual input?

Section 4: Association areas
22 Complete the sentence: 'The motor association areas are involved in the ___ and ___ of movements'.
23 What do the *motor association areas* in the left parietal lobe keep track of?
24 What is *cross-modal matching*?
25 What is a likely consequence of damage to the *auditory association area* in the left hemisphere?
26 What is *visual agnosia*, and from what type of damage does it result?
27 What example of this phenomenon is given by Sacks (1985)?
28 Identify three other cognitive functions which are performed by association areas involved in neither motor nor sensory functions.
29 Complete the sentence: 'Frontal lobe damage does not cause significant impairments in ___ functioning'.
30 What example does Luria (1980) give of *perseveration*?
31 Identify three ways in which frontal lobe damage may affect intentions.
32 What is *behavioural inertia*, caused by excessive frontal lobe damage?
33 What name is given to the procedures in which brain damage is deliberately inflicted with the intention of treating mental disorders?
34 Identify three roles played by association areas in the *temporal lobes*.

Section 5: Holistic theory
35 What is the central claim made by *holistic theory*?
36 What did Lashley (1926) discover when studying the effects of destroying parts of rats' brains on their ability to remember their way through a maze?
37 What is the *law of mass action*?

Q

Section 1: Localisation theory

1 According to *localisation theory*, different areas of the brain are specialised for different psychological functions.
2 *Phrenologists* claimed to be able to detect unusual developments of people's brains by the pattern of bumps on their skulls.
3 *Electrical stimulation of the brain* (ESB).

Section 2: The primary motor area

4 Delgado (1969) discovered that this caused the patient to form a clenched fist with his right hand.
5 A *contralateral connection* is one in which nerve fibres cross over, connecting one side of the body to the opposite hemisphere.
6 Penfield discovered that stimulating the top of the *primary motor area* resulted in twitching in the *lower* part of the body.
7 Those body areas which require more precise control have more cortical area devoted to them than areas requiring less precise control.
8 The primary motor area is *not* responsible for 'commanding' or planning movements.

Section 3: The primary sensory areas

9 The *primary somatosensory area* is responsible for receiving information from the skin senses (and the sense of taste).
10 This area also represents the body in an approximately 'upside-down' fashion, and more sensitive body parts have more cortex devoted to them.
11 Robertson (1995) found that Braille readers have more cortical area devoted to the tip of the right forefinger than do non-Braille readers.
12 Damage to the primary somatosensory area is likely to cause deficits or disturbances in the sense of touch.
13 The *primary auditory area* is located in the *temporal lobe*.
14 Penfield discovered that stimulation of this area caused patients to report hearing sounds.
15 Whilst much of the information from each ear crosses to the opposite hemisphere (*contralateral connection*), some information is processed by the hemisphere on the same side as the ear (*ipsilateral connection*).
16 Slight damage to this area is likely to produce partial hearing loss.
17 The *primary visual area* is located in the *occipital lobe*.
18 Penfield discovered that stimulation of this area caused patients to report 'seeing' different kinds of visual displays.
19 Damage to part of this area is likely to cause blindness in part of the visual field.

20 The *optic chiasma* is the location in the brain where nerve fibres from each eye meet and then divide.
21 Damage to one eye doesn't result in one hemisphere 'missing out' on visual input, since both hemispheres receive half of the visual input from each eye.

Section 4: Association areas

22 'The motor association areas are involved in the *planning* and *execution* of movements.'
23 The motor association areas in the left parietal lobe keep track of the location of the body's moving parts.
24 *Cross-modal matching* is a complex sensory function in which information from one sense modality (such as touch) may be translated into another (such as sight). This allows us to identify by sight something which we have previously only touched.
25 Damage to the *auditory association area* in the left hemisphere is likely to result in difficulties in producing or comprehending language.
26 *Visual agnosia* is an inability to recognise objects by sight, and results from damage to the visual association area.
27 Sacks (1985) gives an example of a man who, suffering from visual agnosia, mistook his wife for his hat.
28 Other association areas are involved in *learning*, *thinking* and *memory*.
29 'Frontal lobe damage does not cause significant impairments in *intellectual* functioning.'
30 Luria (1980) gives the example of a man who continued to try to light a match after it had been lit.
31 Frontal lobe damage may affect the *ability to set goals*, *plan actions*, and *make decisions*.
32 *Behavioural inertia* is a condition in which a person *lacks spontaneity*, *remains motionless*, and *stares vacantly into space*.
33 *Psychosurgery*.
34 Association areas in the *temporal lobes* play a role in *memory*, *social behaviour*, and certain *emotional responses*.

Section 5: Holistic theory

35 *Holistic theory* claims that psychological functions are controlled by neurons throughout the brain.
36 Lashley (1926) found that destruction of one particular area did not lead to greater difficulties than destruction of any other area.
37 The *law of mass action* says that the greater the amount of cortex destroyed, the greater are the behavioural effects.

The Cerebral Cortex

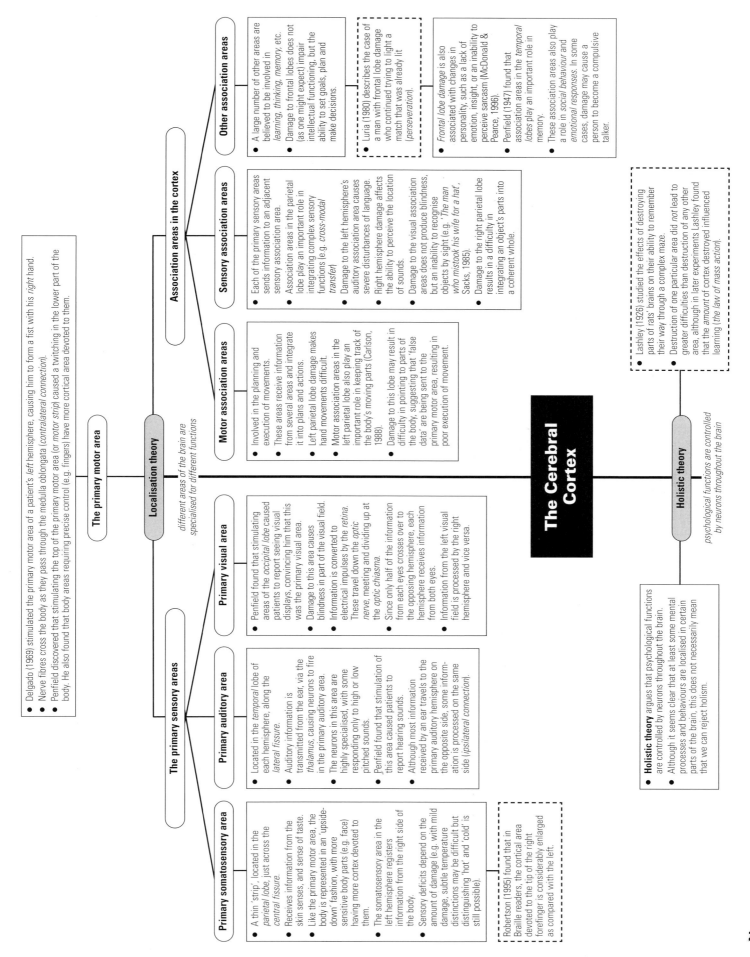

- Delgado (1969) stimulated the primary motor area of a patient's *left* hemisphere, causing him to form a fist with his *right* hand.
- Nerve fibres cross the body as they pass through the medulla oblongata (*contralateral connection*).
- Penfield discovered that stimulating the top of the primary motor area (or *motor strip*) caused a twitching in the lower part of the body. He also found that body areas requiring precise control (e.g. fingers) have more cortical area devoted to them.

Localisation theory

different areas of the brain are specialised for different functions

The primary motor area

Association areas in the cortex

Motor association areas

- Involved in the planning and execution of movements.
- These areas receive information from several areas and integrate it into plans and actions.
- Left parietal lobe damage makes hand movements difficult.
- Motor association areas in the left parietal lobe also play an important role in keeping track of the body's moving parts (Carlson, 1988).
- Damage to this lobe may result in difficulty in pointing to parts of the body, suggesting that 'false data' are being sent to the primary motor area, resulting in poor execution of movement.

Sensory association areas

- Each of the primary sensory areas sends information to an adjacent sensory association area.
- Association areas in the parietal lobe play an important role in integrating complex sensory functions (e.g. *cross-modal transfer*)
- Damage to the left hemisphere's auditory association area causes severe disturbances of language.
- Right hemisphere damage affects the ability to perceive the location of sounds.
- Damage to the visual association areas does not produce blindness, but an inability to recognise objects by sight (e.g. '*The man who mistook his wife for a hat*', Sacks, 1985).
- Damage to the right parietal lobe results in a difficulty in integrating an object's parts into a coherent whole.

Other association areas

- A large number of other areas are believed to be involved in *learning, thinking, memory,* etc.
- Damage to frontal lobes does not (as one might expect) impair intellectual functioning, but the ability to set goals, plan and make decisions.
- Luria (1980) describes the case of a man with frontal lobe damage who continued trying to light a match that was already lit (*perseveration*).
- *Frontal lobe damage* is also associated with changes in personality, such as a lack of emotion, insight, or an inability to perceive sarcasm (McDonald & Pearce, 1996).
- Penfield (1947) found that association areas in the *temporal lobes* play an important role in memory.
- These association areas also play a role in *social behaviour* and *emotional responses*. In some cases, damage may cause a person to become a compulsive talker.

The primary sensory areas

Primary somatosensory area

- A thin 'strip', located in the *parietal lobe*, just across the *central fissure*.
- Receives information from the skin senses, and sense of taste.
- Like the primary motor area, the body is represented in an 'upside-down' fashion, with more sensitive body parts (e.g. face) having more cortex devoted to them.
- The somatosensory area in the left hemisphere registers information from the right side of the body.
- Sensory deficits depend on the amount of damage (e.g. with mild damage, subtle temperature distinctions may be difficult but distinguishing 'hot' and 'cold' is still possible).
- Robertson (1995) found that in Braille readers, the cortical area devoted to the tip of the right forefinger is considerably enlarged as compared with the left.

Primary auditory area

- Located in the *temporal* lobe of each hemisphere, along the *lateral fissure*.
- Auditory information is transmitted from the ear, via the *thalamus*, causing neurons to fire in the primary auditory area.
- The neurons in this area are highly specialised, with some responding only to high or low pitched sounds.
- Penfield found that stimulation of this area caused patients to report hearing sounds.
- Although most information received by an ear travels to the primary auditory hemisphere on the opposite side, some information is processed on the same side (*ipsilateral connection*).

Primary visual area

- Penfield found that stimulating areas of the *occipital lobe* caused patients to report seeing visual displays, convincing him that this was the primary visual area.
- Damage to this area causes blindness in part of the visual field.
- Information is converted to electrical impulses by the *retina*. These travel down the *optic nerve*, meeting and dividing up at the *optic chiasma*.
- Since only half of the information from each eyes crosses over to the opposing hemisphere, each hemisphere receives information from both eyes.
- Information from the left visual field is processed by the right hemisphere and vice versa.

Holistic theory

psychological functions are controlled by neurons throughout the brain

- Lashley (1926) studied the effects of destroying parts of rats' brains on their ability to remember their way through a complex maze.
- Destruction of one particular area did *not* lead to greater difficulties than destruction of any other area, although in later experiments Lashley found that the *amount* of cortex destroyed influenced learning (*the law of mass action*).

- **Holistic theory** argues that psychological functions are controlled by neurons throughout the brain.
- Although it seems clear that at least some mental processes and behaviours are localised in certain parts of the brain, this does not necessarily mean that we can reject holism.

25

LANGUAGE AND THE BRAIN

Section 1: Language disorders

1 What did Broca discover when he carried out a post-mortem on his patient 'Tan'?
2 What was the central difference between the patients studied by Broca and those studied by Wernické?
3 What is an *aphasia*?
4 Why does Milner (1971) argue that the term *dysphasia* is more appropriate than *aphasia*?
5 Upon what basis does the *Boston classification* (Kertesz, 1979) distinguish different forms of aphasia?
6 Complete the sentence: 'Usually a person with Broca's aphasia can ___ spoken or written language either normally or near normally, but has great difficulty in ___ speech'.
7 What is meant by saying that the speech of *Broca's aphasics* often has a '*telegraphic*' quality to it?
8 What are *phonemic paraphrasias*?
9 What does *Broca's area* store?
10 What is the major characteristic of *Wernické's aphasia*?
11 Williams (1981) identifies an important difference between the disturbed communication of some aphasics and similar disturbances in people suffering from a mental disorder. What is this difference?
12 What are *semantic paraphrasias*?
13 Complete the sentence: 'Wernické's aphasics are capable of using some language. However, there are few ___ words, and the words that are produced often do not make sense'.
14 What is the probable function of *Wernické's area*?
15 What is the major characteristic of *anomic aphasia*?
16 How is anomic aphasia different from similar speech difficulties experienced occasionally by non-aphasics?
17 What is the likely role of the *angular gyrus*?
18 What is the typical symptom of *conduction aphasia*?
19 Conduction aphasia probably occurs as a consequence of lesions interrupting the *arcuate fasciculus*. What role does this structure play?

20 What are the symptoms of *transcortical aphasia*?
21 What is the essential difference between transcortical aphasia and Wernické's or Broca's aphasia?
22 Geschwind *et al.* (1968) studied a female patient suffering from *isolation aphasia*. How was she still able to use language?

Section 2: Cortical areas and language

23 According to the *Wernické–Geschwind model*, what are the first two areas of the cortex to process information when an individual is asked to repeat a word just heard?
24 When asked to repeat a word we have just read, information is first processed by the visual cortex. What is the *next* structure involved in processing the information?
25 In both cases, which area is responsible for the movements which produce speech?

Section 3: Language: localisation and lateralisation

26 What is the difference between *localisation* and *lateralisation*?
27 In what percentage of right-handers is language lateralised in the left hemisphere?
28 What is *bilateral representation*?
29 What difference did Kimura (1993) discover between the ways in which speech production is organised in men and women?
30 According to Kimura, why are men more likely to suffer aphasia than women?
31 According to Lashley (1926), what is the *law of equipotentiality*?
32 Connor (1997) cites the case of a ten-year-old boy who had his left hemisphere surgically removed in an effort to treat *Sturge–Weber syndrome*. What was the consequence of this operation?

Section 1: Language disorders

1 Broca discovered that 'Tan' had suffered stokes which had caused multiple lesions in a cortical area of the frontal lobe of the left hemisphere.

2 Broca's patients had difficulty in *producing* speech, whilst Wernické's patients had difficulty in *understanding* language but were able to produce it (even though what was produced was typically meaningless).

3 An *aphasia* is a language disorder arising from brain damage.

4 Milner (1971) points out that the word *aphasia* comes from the Greek word meaning '*speechless*' and that *dysphasia* is a more appropriate term to describe *partial loss of language*.

5 The *Boston classification* distinguishes different forms of aphasia based on the particular skill that has been lost.

6 'Usually a person with Broca's aphasia can *understand* spoken or written language either normally or near normally, but has great difficulty in *producing* speech.'

7 The speech of Broca's aphasics contains few 'function words' and consists almost entirely of 'content words' (i.e. is 'telegraphic').

8 *Phonemic paraphrasias* are mispronunciations of certain words (e.g. saying 'likstip' instead of 'lipstick').

9 *Broca's area* stores the 'motor plans' for the formulation of words.

10 The major characteristic of *Wernické's aphasia* is a difficulty in understanding spoken or written language.

11 People suffering from a mental disorder (e.g. schizophrenia) may produce language similar to that produced by some aphasics. However, in the former case language seems to be irrelevant, whilst in the latter case the individual tries hard to communicate.

12 In *semantic paraphrasias*, the word that is produced does not have the intended meaning, though it may be related to the intended word.

13 'Wernické's aphasics are capable of using some language. However, there are few *content* words, and the words that are produced often do not make sense.'

14 Wernické's area probably stores memories of the sequence of sounds contained in words.

15 *Anomic aphasics* have few problems in producing or understanding language, but are unable to find correct nouns to name objects.

16 Non-aphasics may occasionally have difficulties in finding a correct word, but for anomic aphasics this difficulty is extended to everyday objects such as a 'pen'.

17 The *angular gyrus* is probably involved in retrieving the appropriate word for a given meaning from a memory store.

18 The typical symptom of *conduction aphasia* is difficulty in repeating a sentence that has just been heard.

19 The *arcuate fasciculus* contains fibres which connect Broca's area with Wernické's area.

20 *Transcortical aphasics* have few comprehension skills and/or cannot produce normal speech. They are, however, able to repeat back what somebody has just said.

21 In transcortical aphasia the damage has occurred beyond Wernické's and Broca's areas.

22 Geschwind *et al.*'s (1968) female patient was able to *finish familiar poems* and *repeat words* which were spoken to her, *correcting grammatical errors*.

Section 2: Cortical areas and language

23 According to the *Wernické–Geschwind model*, the first two areas of the cortex involved in processing the word are the *primary auditory area* and *Wernické's area*.

24 Once the word has been processed by the visual cortex, it is then passed to the *angular gyrus*.

25 In both cases the *primary motor area* is responsible for the movements of the tongue, mouth and larynx which produce speech.

Section 3: Language: localisation and lateralisation

26 *Localisation* is the view that specific functions and processes have relatively precise and circumscribed locations, whereas *lateralisation* is the view that certain functions occur only in one or other of the cerebral hemispheres.

27 Language is lateralised in the left hemisphere in *95 per cent* of right-handers.

28 *Bilateral representation* is when the language structures are more or less *equally represented* in both hemispheres.

29 Kimura (1993) discovered that speech is more *bilaterally organised* in women than in men.

30 Kimura has found that men are more likely to incur aphasia as a result of damage to the *back* of the brain than are women (who are more likely to incur aphasia as a result of *frontal* damage), and damage to the *back* of the brain is more likely.

31 The *law of equipotentiality* (Lashley, 1926) refers to the ability of other areas of the brain to reorganise themselves and take over a damaged part's functions.

32 The operation resulted in the boy learning to speak at the age of ten, having previously been mute.

Cortical areas and language disorders

- Broca studied patients (such as 'Tan') who had difficulty in producing speech.
- Wernické described patients who could produce speech but had difficulty understanding it.
- Post-mortems suggested that such language deficits arose from brain damage to the left frontal lobe.
- Such deficits are called *aphasias*. Milner (1971) argues that unless speech loss is complete, deficits should be called *dysphasias*.
- The *Boston classification* (Kertesz, 1979) classifies aphasias based on the linguistic skill that has been lost.

Wernické's aphasia

Damage to Wernické's area causes Wernické's aphasia:

- The major characteristic is difficulty in *understanding* written or spoken language.
- Wernické's aphasics produce language which is virtually unintelligible and lacking in coherence.
- Sufferers may produce *jargon* (nonsense words) or *neologisms* (invented words).
- The lack of content words, and the fact that some sufferers may be unaware that they have a speech deficit, suggests that they are *unable to monitor* their own language.
- Wernické's area may store memories of the sequences of sounds contained in words.
- To assist comprehension, non-verbal responses must be elicited (e.g. pointing) to discover whether of not a question has been *understood*.

Semantic paraphrasias

- Wernické's aphasics characteristically produce words which are related to the word they *intended* to produce (e.g. 'chair' instead of 'table').

Broca's aphasia

Damage to Broca's area causes 'Broca's aphasia':

- The major characteristic is great difficulty in *producing* speech. Usually, a Broca's aphasic can *comprehend* written or spoken language. However, speech is typically slow, non-fluent and difficult to understand, with grammatical words omitted.
- Broca's area stores the 'motor plans' for the formulation of words. Damage to this area causes *faulty data* to be sent to the primary motor area.

Conduction aphasia

Conduction aphasics can understand and produce speech relatively well.

- The major characteristic is difficulty in repeating a sentence that has just been heard.
- Conduction apahsia probably occurs as a result of lesions interrupting the nerve fibres (*arcuate fasciculus*) which connects Broca's area with Wernické's area.

Transcortical aphasia

Transcortical aphasics *can* repeat back what somebody has just said to them.

- The major characteristic of transcortical aphasia is poor comprehension skills and/or an inability to produce normal speech.
- Different forms of transcortical aphasia resemble Broca's aphasia and Wernické's aphasia, although the damage has occurred *beyond* these areas.

Isolation aphasia

The brain's speech mechanisms receive auditory input and can control the muscles used for speech, but receive no information from other senses, or from neural circuits containing memories of the meaning of words.

Geschwind *et al.* (1968) studied a female patient who suffered severe brain damage as a result of carbon monoxide inhalation. She made few voluntary movements, never said anything meaningful on her own, nor gave any sign of understanding speech, but was able to repeat phrases (correcting grammatical errors) and finish familiar poems.

Anomic aphasia

Anomic aphasics have few problems in understanding and producing language.

- The major characteristic is an inability to find the correct nouns to name objects.
- This happens to most of us at times, but the anomic aphasic has difficulty in naming common objects (e.g. a pen), causing them to circumlocute (speak in a roundabout way).
- Anomic aphasia seems to result from damage to the *angular gyrus*, which retrieves the word corresponding to a particular meaning.

Language and the Brain

The relationship between cortical areas and language

The Wernické–Geschwind model (1979)

Repeating a word we have heard:

1. The word is passed (via the thalamus and auditory area) to Wernické's area,
2. Activity there allows word recognition and comprehension to take place,
3. The formulation of the word is then passed to Broca's area where memories and the sequence of movements needed to produce it are stored,
4. Broca's area then passes this information to the primary motor area, which programs muscles of the face, tongue, and larynx to produce the word.

Repeating a word we have read:

1. Words are registered in the visual area of the cortex,
2. Words are sent to the angular gyrus,
3. This area transforms a word's visual representation into a form which is recognised by Wernické's area,
4. Wernické's area receives the code and understands the meaning, then initiates the sequence of events for producing the word, via Broca's area.

Language: localisation, lateralisation and holism

Not only are certain language functions localised, but in most people they are found in one or other of the cerebral hemispheres (lateralised).

- Geschwind & Behan (1984): for most of us, language is lateralised in the left hemisphere.

Left- and right-handedness and language

Satz (1979): in 95% of right-handed individuals, language is localised in the left hemisphere (in the remaining 5% is is localised in the right hemisphere). 75% of left-handers have language localised in the left hemisphere, with *bilateral representation* in the remaining 25% (language processed in both hemispheres).

Gender and language

Kimura (1993): speech is more bilaterally organised in women. In addition, women are less likely to incur aphasia than men since women are more likely to suffer aphasia when the front of the brain is damaged, and damage to the back of the brain (which affects men more) is more common.

Holism

The brain appears to have remarkable *plasticity*, so that when an area is damaged other areas are able to reorganise themselves and take over that area's functions.

- Connor (1997) reports on the case of a 10-year-old boy with 'Sturge–Weber syndrome', which caused the left side of the brain to become shrunken. Removal of the left side of his brain resulted in him learning to speak, having previously been mute.

9

ASYMMETRIES IN THE CEREBRAL HEMISPHERES
AND THE 'SPLIT-BRAIN'

KEY QUESTIONS
- What research has been done into cerebral asymmetries, using 'split-brain' patients?
- Can cerebral asymmetries be demonstrated in the intact brain?
- Does each half of the brain have a different conscious experience?

Section 1: 'Split-brain' studies
1 What does it mean to say that the brain is *bilaterally symmetrical*?
2 What was Fechner's (1860) answer to the question, 'What would happen if a living brain were split in half?'?
3 What is a *commisurotomy*?
4 What was the *medical* aim of the commisurotomy?
5 What did Sperry *et al.* (1964) discover after conducting commissurotomies followed by surgery on the optic nerves of cats?
6 What were researchers able to conclude, on the basis of such experiments, concerning the role of the *corpus callosum*?
7 In what way does the *visual information* reaching each hemisphere differ in normal humans?
8 What was Sperry's method for delivering visual information to only one cerebral hemisphere?
9 Using Sperry's method, under what conditions is a split-brain patient able to report *verbally* on what has been presented?
10 How can the above finding be explained?
11 Under which conditions is a split-brain patient able to identify correctly a stimulus which has been presented in the left visual field?
12 What is suggested by the finding that the right hemisphere *is* able to follow an instruction to identify items closely related to a given stimulus?
13 How does the *divided field technique* differ from Sperry's technique?
14 If the words 'case' and 'key' are presented in the right and left visual fields respectively, which of the two words would the left hand write in response to the question 'What did you see?'?
15 Complete the sentence: 'Gazzaniga (1983) claimed that 20 years of empirical research showed that the cognitive skills of the disconnected right hemisphere are vastly ___ to the cognitive skills of a chimpanzee'.

16 What did Zaidel (1983) conclude about the *right* hemisphere's linguistic abilities?
17 What was discovered by studies which looked at the ability of split-brain patients to reproduce *drawings*?
18 What are *chimerics*?
19 In what sense is the left hemisphere an '*analyser*'?
20 What happens when different decision tasks are presented to both hemispheres of split-brain patients simultaneously?
21 Identify one reason why the results of split-brain studies should be treated with caution.
22 What is involved in the *Wada test*?
23 When would the Wada test be used?

Section 2: Asymmetries in the intact brain
24 Identify additional ways in which it is possible to study cerebral asymmetries in the intact brain.
25 What is involved in a *dichotic listening task*?
26 Complete the sentence: 'Ornstein (1986) concluded that the left hemisphere processes information ___ (one item at a time), and its mode of operation is ___'.
27 Identify four activities in which the right hemisphere demonstrates superior synthetic ability.

Section 3: Answering Fechner's question
28 Why is the idea of people being 'logically left-brained' or 'intuitively right-brained' incorrect.
29 Complete the sentence: 'Sperry sees the bisected brain as a divided organism in which two mental units ___ for control over the organism'.
30 What is Pucetti's (1977) argument concerning the nature of mind?
31 How does '*bundle theory*' explain the unity of consciousness?

Q

Section 1: 'Split-brain' studies

1 The brain is *bilaterally symmetrical* in that it consists of two hemispheres which are apparently mirror images of each other.

2 Fechner (1860) believed that if a living brain were split in half, each half would have a *different conscious experience.*

3 A *commisurotomy* is a surgical operation which involves severing the *corpus callosum*, which connects the two cerebral hemispheres.

4 The aim of the commisurotomy was originally to reduce the severity of *epileptic seizures* by preventing the corresponding brain activity from 'bouncing' back and forth between the two hemispheres.

5 Sperry *et al.* (1964) discovered that when each of the cat's hemispheres received information from one of its eyes, a cat which had learned a task with a patch over one eye behaved as if it had never learned the task when the patch was placed over the other eye.

6 On the basis of such experiments, researchers were able to conclude that the *corpus callosum* functions as a means by which information can be transmitted back and forth between the two hemispheres.

7 Normally, the right hemisphere receives information about the left visual field, and the left hemisphere information about the right visual field.

8 Sperry's method involved presenting a visual stimulus for a tenth of a second in either the right or left visual field, causing it to be perceived in only the left or right hemisphere of split-brain patients.

9 When split-brain patients are shown objects in the *right* visual field, they are able to report *verbally* on what has been shown.

10 The visual information is processed by the *left hemisphere*, which usually contains the *language structures*. These enable split-brain patents to report on what they have seen.

11 When a stimulus which has been presented in the *left visual field* of a split-brain patient, it will be processed by the *right hemisphere*, allowing the patient to use the *left hand* to select the stimulus seen.

12 The finding suggests that although the right hemisphere is incapable of speech production, it nevertheless can *comprehend language* to some extent.

13 In the *divided field technique,* a stimulus is presented to the left and right visual fields of patients simultaneously, whereas in Sperry's technique a stimulus is presented to either the right or left visual field.

14 The left hand is controlled by the primary motor area of the right hemisphere, which receives information from the left visual field, so the left hand should write the word 'key'.

15 'Gazzaniga (1983) claimed that 20 years of empirical research showed that the cognitive skills of the disconnected right hemisphere are vastly *inferior* to the cognitive skills of a chimpanzee'.

16 Zaidel (1983) concluded that the comprehension abilities of the right hemisphere are roughly equivalent to those of a *ten-year-old child*.

17 Such studies found that the *right hemisphere is superior* to the left at copying drawings. The left hemisphere seems to be incapable of duplicating 3-D forms.

18 *Chimerics* are composite pictures of two faces.

19 The *left hemisphere* is skilled at handling discrete information which can be stated verbally in the form of mathematical propositions. Hence it is an '*analyser*'.

20 Split-brain patients are able to perform two tasks simultaneously better than are people with an intact corpus callosum (Ellenberg & Sperry, 1980).

21 Split-brain patients have all had a history of epileptic seizures and so may not be *representative* of people in general.

22 The *Wada test* involves injecting an anaesthetic (sodium amytal) into the left or right carotid artery, then observing what happens.

23 The Wada test is used *prior to brain surgery* in order to determine whether language structures might be affected.

Section 2: Asymmetries in the intact brain

24 *Cerebral asymmetries* can be studied in the intact brain using an *EEG, measurements of blood flow and glucose consumption*, and through studying *people who have suffered strokes*.

25 A *dichotic listening task* involves presenting different auditory information to a person's right and left ears simultaneously.

26 'Ornstein (1986) concluded that the left hemisphere processes information *serially* (one item at a time), and its mode of operation is *linear*.'

27 The *right hemisphere* demonstrates superior synthetic ability in *spatial tasks*, *artistic activities*, *body image* and *facial recognition*.

Section 3: Answering Fechner's question

28 The idea of people being 'logically left-brained' or 'intuitively right-brained' is incorrect because it *exaggerates and oversimplifies* the differences. Normally the two hemispheres co-operate and can perform at least some of the tasks normally performed by the other.

29 'Sperry sees the bisected brain as a divided organism in which two mental units *compete* for control over the organism.'

30 Pucetti (1977) argues that even in normal people, in whom the two hemispheres are connected, the individual *is two minds*.

31 *Bundle theory* explains the unity of consciousness by claiming that a sense of self is no more than a collection ('*bundle*') of experiences (e.g. the sensations accompanying respiration, of the tongue and eyes, and so on).

Asymmetries in the Cerebral Hemispheres

Fechner's question. In 1860 Fechner asked what would happen if a living person's brain were split in half along the two hemispheres. His own answer was that each half would have a separate conscious experience (i.e. that there are two 'minds' within one brain).

Asymmetries & the 'split brain'

The split-brain procedure

The commissurotomy

- In the early 1960s, Vogel & Bogen suggested that epileptic seizures were caused by an amplification of brain activity which 'bounced' back and forth between the two hemispheres.
- They suggested that severing the *corpus callosum* (which contains 250 million axons connecting the two hemispheres) could be used as a therapy of last resort (a *commissurotomy*).

- Research with cats and monkeys revealed that the commissurotomy did not seem to cause any ill-effects.
- In humans, the operation was successful in reducing the severity of epileptic seizures, and did not cause any obvious ill-effects (Sperry, 1964).
- Sperry also severed some of the nerve fibres connecting a cat's eyes to its brain, so that each of the disconnected hemispheres received information from only one eye. Cats who learned tasks with an eye patch over one eye behaved as if no learning had occurred when the patch was placed over the other eye!

Such findings suggested that the *corpus callosum* is a means of transferring information between the two hemispheres, and that if this is severed, each hemisphere is unaware of the sensations and processes occurring in the other.

Procedures for studying split-brain patients

Sperry's technique

Because of the way our eyes are connected to our brain, both hemispheres receive information from both eyes. However, the *left* hemisphere processes information from the *right* side of the visual field and the *right* hemisphere from the *left* side of our visual field. Normally, as our eyes move, both hemispheres are able to receive the same visual information.

- Sperry's method involved presenting a stimulus for one tenth of a second on the right or left side of a projector screen, with the participant looking straight ahead.
- Because the eyes do not have sufficient time to move, the information is only received by one or other hemisphere.

The divided field technique

A word or picture is presented to the left visual field (right hemisphere) and a different word or picture presented simultaneously to the right visual field (left hemisphere). Words and pictures are flashed up briefly onto a projector screen as in Sperry's technique.

Zaidel's contact lens technique

Zaidel (1983) developed a technique of presenting information to the left or right visual field using a contact lens which moves with the eye. This allows a stimulus to be presented for long periods.

Basic findings of split-brain studies

- When a picture is shown to the *right* visual field and a patient asked to report verbally what was shown, the task is done easily.
- When a picture is shown to the *left* visual field the patient *cannot* do the task (since the right hemisphere usually lacks language structures).
- However, in the above situation a patient is able to use the *left* hand (which is out of sight, beneath the screen) to *correctly* select the object seen by the *right* hemisphere (since the left hand is controlled by the right hemisphere).

- In one study the word 'case' was presented to the right visual field and the word 'key' to the left visual field. The patient reported that the word 'case' had been seen, but the left hand wrote the word 'key'.
- Other studies showed that when asked to find an object that corresponded to a word seen, right and left hands ignored objects that had been seen by the hemisphere controlling the other hand.

- The right hemisphere was given vocabulary questions requiring it to choose a picture that corresponded to a word. Although the right hemisphere cannot produce language, language *comprehension* was shown to be roughly equivalent to that of a ten-year-old-child.

Differences between the hemispheres

- The right hemisphere is superior to the left at copying drawings (even though it controls the less co-ordinated left hand). The left hemisphere seems incapable of duplicating 3-D forms.
- Levy *et al.* (1972) showed patients *chimerics* (composite pictures of two different faces). When asked to describe the picture, the left hemisphere dominated, but the right hemisphere was better able to select a picture that had been seen.

Analytic and synthetic hemispheres

Analyser: the *left hemisphere* is better at using discrete information that can be handled verbally in the form of mathematical propositions.

Synthesiser: the *right hemisphere* is superior when information cannot be described adequately in words or symbols, but is able to synthesise it and recognise it as a whole.

Other findings

- A female split-brain patient may occasionally pick out different dresses with the left and right hands.
- Ellenberg & Sperry (1980) found that split-brain patients were able to perform two simple decision tasks simultaneously, and better than people with an *intact* corpus callosum.

Asymmetries in the intact brain

The Wada test

- Involves anaesthetising one hemisphere by injecting sodium amytal into the left or right carotid artery.
- The person then raises both arms and counts backwards. The arm on the opposite side will fall limp and counting will continue if the verbal hemisphere is unaffected.

Divided field technique

The divided field technique can also be used with people with intact brains. If one type of stimulus is best identified in the right/left visual field, this implies that the relevant hemisphere is best at processing that type of information.

Ornstein (1986) concluded that:

- The *left hemisphere* is specialised for analytical and logical thinking, and processes information sequentially (one item at a time).
- The *right hemisphere* is specialised for synthetic thinking, processes information more diffusely.

Answering Fechner's question

- Ornstein (1986) suggests that a commissurotomy does not produce a 'splitting' of the mind, but helps to manifest a duality that is there all the time.
- According to Sperry, a 'split' brain is essentially a divided organism with two mental units competing for control, each possessing its own private sensations, thoughts, feelings and memories.
- Pucetti (1977) argues that even when the hemispheres are connected we are two minds, which appear to be unified because the existence of two selves is undetectable.
- Parfit (1987) argues that we should not consider split-brain patients as constituting two 'persons', since there is no such thing as a person – only a succession of conscious states.

THE NEUROPHYSIOLOGICAL BASIS OF VISUAL PERCEPTION

SYLLABUS

3.2 Cortical functions
- the structure and processes involved in visual perception, including the relevance of neurophysiological explanations of perceptual phenomena.

KEY QUESTIONS
- What are light and colour?
- How do the eye and visual pathways function?
- How can colour vision and colour constancy be explained?

Q

Section 1: Light and the eye

1 What name is given to the *energy particles* of which light consists?
2 Which two forms of electromagnetic radiation lie either side of the visible spectrum?
3 What determines the *intensity* of a light wave?
4 What is *hue*?
5 What determines our experience of *saturation*?
6 What did Sir Isaac Newton discover when light was passed through a prism?
7 What name is given to the tough outer coat which encloses the eyeball?
8 How is the amount of light which enters the eye controlled?
9 What is the next structure which light reaches when it has passed through the aqueous humour?
10 What is the role of the *ciliary muscles*?
11 What do *cones*, *rods*, *bipolar cells* and *ganglion cells* all have in common?
12 What type of cell are *rods* and *cones*, and what is their role?
13 Complete the sentence: 'Rods help us to see ___ colour, whilst cones respond to different wavelengths allowing us to see ___ colour'.
14 How does the distribution of rods and cones around the retina differ?
15 What is the *optic disc*?
16 Place the following in order according to which is most and least numerous in the retina: bipolar cells, rods and cones, ganglion cells.
17 According to Hubel & Wiesel (1962), what is a *receptive field*?

Section 2: From the eye to the brain

18 Describe what occurs at the *lateral geniculate nucleus* (LGN).
19 What is the *geniculostriate path*?
20 What is '*blindsight*'?

21 Name the three types of cortical cell Hubel & Wiesel (1965) propose decode light information.
22 What are *hypercolumns*?
23 What is *ocular dominance*?
24 What did Zeki (cited in Highfield, 1997b) discover when studying GY, a man blinded in an accident when he was seven?

Section 3: Understanding colour vision

25 What was the principle behind Newton's *colour circle*?
26 What term is used to describe the type of colour mixing which occurs when we mix different coloured paints? Why is this term used?
27 What type of colour mixing takes place in the visual system?
28 How does the *Young–Helmholtz theory* explain colour vision?
29 What did Ohtsuka (1985) discover about the way in which light of a certain wavelength stimulates receptor cells?
30 Identify two perceptual phenomena which cannot be explained by the Young–Helmholtz theory.
31 Name the three types of receptor proposed by the *opponent-process theory* of colour vision.
32 Why is the *opponent-process theory* of colour vision so called?
33 Which two types of individuals suffer from *dichromatic vision*?
34 How can the opponent-process theory explain why we see a green after-image having stared for some time at a red patch?
35 Complete the sentence: 'Opponent-process theory does not seem to operate at the level of the ___, but along the ___ ___ from the cones to the visual area'.
36 What is *colour constancy*?
37 What was Land (1977) able to demonstrate, using a *colour Mondrian*?
38 What theory did Land advance to explain his findings?

Section 1: Light and the eye

1 Light consists of energy particles called *photons*.

2 *Ultraviolet rays* and *infrared rays* lie either side of the visible spectrum.

3 The *number of photons* in a stream of light determines the wave's intensity.

4 *Hue* refers to the colour we perceive something to be.

5 Our experience of *saturation* is determined by the proportion of coloured light to non-coloured light in a light stream.

6 Sir Isaac Newton discovered that white light is a mixture of wavelengths corresponding to all colours in the visible spectrum.

7 The tough outer coat which encloses the eyeball is called the *sclera*.

8 The amount of light which enters the eye is controlled by the *iris*, which contracts or expands, altering the size of the *pupil*.

9 Having passed through the aqueous humour, light reaches the *lens*.

10 The *ciliary muscles* expand or contract so as to change the shape of the lens, allowing light to be focused on the retina.

11 *Cones*, *rods*, *bipolar cells* and *ganglion cells* are all *neurons* (and are all present in the retina).

12 Rods and cones are *photosensitive cells* (or *photoreceptors*), which convert light energy into electrical nerve impulses.

13 'Rods help us to see *achromatic* colour whilst cones respond to different wavelengths allowing us to see *chromatic* colour.'

14 Rods are fairly evenly distributed around the retina whilst cones are much more numerous towards its centre (especially at the *fovea*).

15 The *optic disc* is the part of the retina where the optic nerve leaves the eye.

16 Rods and cones are the most numerous, followed by bipolar cells and ganglion cells.

17 Hubel & Wiesel define a *receptive field* as the area of the retina to which a single ganglion cell is sensitive.

Section 2: From the eye to the brain

18 At the *lateral geniculate nucleus* (LGN), the optic nerve fibres terminate at synapses with cells belonging to the thalamus, which combine the information from both eyes before sending it to the cortex.

19 The *geniculostriate path* is the neural pathway which carries visual information from the thalami to the cortex.

20 *Blindsight* is a term used to describe the ability to identify objects without being consciously aware of them.

21 Hubel & Wiesel (1965) suggested the existence of *simple cells*, *complex cells* and *hypercomplex cells*, each involved in decoding information.

22 *Hypercolumns* are 1 mm square blocks of tissue which extend from the surface of the cortex down to the white matter below.

23 *Ocular dominance* refers to the manner in which cells in the visual cortex always respond more strongly to a stimulus in one eye or the other.

24 Zeki discovered that GY could detect fast moving cars and the direction in which they were travelling, and that such detection did not involve the primary visual processing area.

Section 3: Understanding colour vision

25 Newton's *colour circle* was designed so that colours which produced either white or neutral grey were placed at opposite ends of the circle's diameter.

26 When we mix different coloured paints, *subtractive* colour mixing occurs. This term is used since each colour absorbs all those wavelengths which it does not reflect. Mixing the paints causes both sets of absorbed wavelengths to be 'subtracted' from the light reflected.

27 *Additive* colour mixing takes place in the visual system.

28 The *Young–Helmholtz theory* proposes that the eye contains three types of receptor, responding to red, green and blue light respectively, and that the perception of colour is created by combining information from them.

29 Ohtsuka (1985) discovered that light of a particular wavelength may stimulate more than one type of receptor.

30 Neither *colour blindness* nor *negative after-images* can be explained by the Young–Helmholtz theory.

31 The *opponent-process theory* of colour vision proposes the existence of *red-green*, *yellow-blue* and *black-white* receptors.

32 The theory is so called since each member of a pair is *opposed* to the other, so that when one is excited the other is inhibited.

33 People who are red–green, or yellow–blue colourblind suffer from *dichromatic vision*.

34 According to the opponent-process theory, staring at a red patch causes the red component to tire, so that only the green component is 'fresh' enough to fire when we stare at a neutral surface.

35 'Opponent-process theory does not seem to operate at the level of the *cones*, but along the *neural path* from the cones to the visual area.'

36 *Colour constancy* refers to the manner in which the colours we perceive are not determined solely by the wavelength of light reflected from an object, but by other factors such as knowledge and experience.

37 Land (1977) was able to demonstrate that participants would judge a colour to be the same, despite alterations in the wavelength of the light actually reflected from it.

38 Land's *retinex theory* attempts to explain his findings.

A

About 90% of the information about the external world reaches us through the eye, which has a complex structure:
- **The sclera:** a tough outer coat, which is opaque except for the front, where it bulges out to form a transparent membrane (cornea).
- **The lens:** a crystalline structure which focuses light waves, and whose shape is controlled by a ring of **ciliary muscles**.
- **The vitreous humour:** a jelly-like substance through which light passes, which helps the eye to maintain its shape.
- **The retina:** a delicate membrane lining the back of the eye, containing photosensitive cells.

The **iris** controls the amount of light entering the eye by expanding or contracting to vary the size of the **pupil**. Abnormalities in the shape of the eye make it impossible for the lens to focus light (*accommodation*) correctly, causing short- or long-sightedness.

The retina

Contains two types of *photoreceptor* cells, which convert light into electrical nerve impulses:
- **Rods:** (120 million, evenly distributed around the retina) help us to see *achromatic* colour (black, white and greys) and are specialised for vision in dim light (*scotopic vision*).
- **Cones:** (7 million, packed densely around the centre of the retina, especially the *fovea*) help us to see *chromatic* colour (red, green, blue, etc.) and are specialised for bright light vision (*photopic vision*).

These cells convert light to neural signals which are passed to smaller numbers of **bipolar cells** which in turn pass signals to **ganglion cells**. These travel across the retina's inner surface and converge to form the **optic nerve**. A single ganglion cell is connected to all/most of the rods in its *receptive* field.

Types of ganglion cells
- *On-centre and off-surround:* most active when light falls on the centre of its receptive field.
- *Off-centre and on-surround:* most active when light falls on the edge of the receptive field.
- *Transient cells:* respond to movements in the receptive field.

Visual sensory information travels to the **thalamus** and on to the **primary visual area** of the cortex:
- Optic nerve fibres terminate at synapses at the **lateral geniculate nucleus** (LGN), a part of the thalamus.
- The LGN in each thalamus combines the information from both eyes before sending it to the cortex, via the **geniculostriate path**.

Types of cortical cells
Hubel & Wiesel (1965) suggested the existence of 3 types of cortical cells, which play a role in decoding light information:

Simple cells: respond *only* to particular features of a stimulus in a particular orientation and location in the visual field.

Complex cells: respond to particular features of a stimulus in a particular orientation *no matter where they occur* in the visual field.

Hypercomplex cells: respond to corners, angles, bars of a particular length moving in a certain direction.

- Hubel & Wiesel (1977) showed that the visual area is divided into roughly 1 mm square blocks of tissue extending down through the cortex to the white matter below. These *hypercolumns* contain cells with the same 'orientation preference'. In addition, cells always respond more strongly to a stimulus in one eye rather than the other (*ocular dominance*).
- Maunsell & Newsome (1987) have identified as many as 19 areas, besides the primary visual area, which are involved in vision and which transmit and receive information from each other.

Visual Perception

Light is a form of electromagnetic radiation, consisting of energy particles called *photons*, which travel in waves.

2 important characteristics:
- The number of photons in a stream of light determines its *intensi*ty.
- The distance between peaks of a light wave determines its *wavelength*.

3 important properties:
- *Brightness:* determined by the intensity of a wave.
- *Hue:* the colour we perceive is partly determined by a light's wavelength.
- *Saturation:* how colourful light is (determined by the proportion of coloured light to non-coloured light).

Sir Isaac Newton discovered that white light is a mixture of all the colours of the spectrum. He Íalso discovered that mixing two colours far apart in the spectrum produced white, and produced a 'colour circle' to record which these were.

Subtractive and additive colour mixing
- *Subtractive colour mixing:* blue and yellow paint appears blue and yellow because they absorb all other wavelengths. Mixing them causes all wavelengths except green to be absorbed.
- *Additive colour mixing:* when lights with different wavelengths strike the retina, these are combined by the visual system.

Familiarity with, and knowledge of, an object, can both affect the perception of an object's colour (*colour constancy*)

- Land (1977): Asked participants to select two colours from a *colour Mondrian* (a patchwork of different colours). Land adjusted the red, green and blue light being reflected from the second colour, so that it matched the first – nevertheless, participants still saw the colour as remaining the same!

Land proposed the '*retinex theory of colour constancy*' to explain this phenomenon.

- Proposes that the eye contains *3 types of receptor cells* corresponding to red, green and blue.
- The perception of colour is created by *combining* the information from these receptors, the ratio of blue:green:red receptors activated determining the colour perceived.
- Over 100 years later, research confirmed the existence of three such receptors, each containing a *photopigment* sensitive to different wavelengths of light.
- The wavelengths to which the cone types are sensitive *overlap*, so that light of a particular wavelength may stimulate more than one type of cone (Ohtsuka, 1985).
- However, *colour blindness* and the perception of *negative after-images* cannot easily be explained by this theory.

The theory is also called *trichromatic theory* and derives from the work of Young (who in 1802 demonstrated that combinations of red, green and blue light could produce all the colours of the spectrum) and von Helmholtz (who, 50 years later, suggested that the eye contains 3 types of receptor corresponding to these wavelengths).

- Hering (1870) also proposed the existence of *3 types of receptor cells*, with two responsive to pairs of colours (red–green receptors and yellow–blue receptors) and one sensitive to black-white (contributing to the perception of brightness and saturation).
- A response to one of the colours for which a receptor is sensitive means that the other colour of the pair is '*inhibited*' (so that a colour can be reddish-yellow, but never 'reddish-green').
- Hering's theory *can* explain *colour blindness* (e.g. where red and green cannot be seen but blue and yellow can) and *negative after images* (where receptors become 'overstimulated' by a colour causing the opposite of the pair to fire more readily).

Opponent-process theory does *not* seem to operate at the level of the cones, but along the neural pathways connecting them to the visual area:
- Studies of the bipolar, ganglion and LGN cells suggest that messages from the cones may be relayed to the brain in an opponent-process fashion (DeVallois & Jacobs, 1984), e.g. some neurons are excited by red light but inhibited by green.

BODILY RHYTHMS

KEY QUESTIONS

What is the nature of the following bodily rhythms:
- circadian rhythms
- infradian rhythms
- ultradian rhythms
- diurnal rhythms
- circannual rhythms?

What has research revealed about these bodily rhythms?

Section 1: Circadian rhythms

1 What is a *bodily rhythm*?
2 Over what period of time do *circadian rhythms* vary?
3 Which physiological variables vary in a circadian way.
4 What are *Zeitgebers*?
5 What is an *oscillator*?
6 The SN are the location of one of the oscillators. What do the letters SN stand for?
7 What research, conducted by Morgan (1995), supports the view that the cycle length of such rhythms is dependent on genetic factors?
8 According to Loros *et al.* (cited in Highfield, 1996b), what are the evolutionary origins of the *internal clock*?
9 What does it mean to say that circadian rhythms are primarily an *endogenous property*?
10 What did Luce & Segal (1966) discover when investigating the sleep patterns of people living in the Arctic Circle?

Section 2: Infradian rhythms

11 How long do *infradian rhythms* last?
12 Complete the sentence: 'The menstrual period is the ___ of a four-week cycle of activity'.
13 What is the role of the menstrual cycle?
14 Identify two psychological symptoms associated with pre-menstrual syndrome (PMS).
15 Identify the behavioural changes which Dalton (1964) claimed are clustered around the pre-menstrual interval.
16 Identify two reasons for thinking that PMS is not simply a 'denial of femininity'.
17 Which *gland* is responsible for governing the phases of the menstrual cycle?
18 What was shown in Reinberg's (1967) study of a young woman who spent three months in a cave?

Section 3: Ultradian rhythms

19 What are *ultradian rhythms*?

20 Which two discoveries were made in Loomis *et al.*'s (1937) pioneering studies of sleep using the EEG?
21 What do the letters '*REM*' stand for in the term '*REM sleep*'?
22 What did Dement & Kleitman (1957) discover about REM sleep?
23 When are *beta waves* replaced by *alpha waves*?
24 What type of waves mark the onset of *Stage 1 sleep*?
25 What is a *hypnogogic state* and when does it occur?
26 What are *sleep spindles* and during which stage of sleep are they most likely to occur?
27 What do *Stage 3 sleep* and *Stage 4 sleep* have in common?
28 After falling asleep, when do we enter REM sleep for the first time?
29 Why has REM sleep also been termed '*paradoxical sleep*'?
30 During which cycles of sleep do *Stages 3 and 4* of sleep occur?
31 How do sleep patterns change with age.

Section 4: Diurnal rhythms

32 What are *diurnal rhythms*?
33 What did Gunter *et al.* (cited in Marks & Folkhard, 1985) discover when testing participants' immediate recall of news information?
34 According to Adam (1983), what were students better at in the afternoon?
35 What are the two '*diurnal types*' identified by Horne & Osterberg (1976)?

Section 5: Circannual rhythms

36 What are *circannual rhythms*?
37 Why are circannual rhythms commonly found amongst species from temperate latitudes?
38 What do the letters *SAD* stand for?
39 Which *hormone* is normally only produced when it is dark?
40 What is the name of the therapy used to treat SAD?

Section 1: Circadian rhythms

1 A *bodily rhythm* is a cyclical variation over some period of time in a physiological or psychological process.
2 *Circadian rhythms* vary over periods of about 24 hours.
3 *Heart rate, metabolic rate, breathing rate, body temperature* and *hormones* all vary in a circadian way.
4 *Zeitgebers* are external cues about the time of day.
5 An *oscillator* is an *internal* (or *body*) *clock*.
6 The letters SN stand for *suprachiasmatic nuclei*.
7 Morgan (1995) gave hamsters brain transplants of SN cells from a mutant strain whose cycles were shorter than those of the recipients. The recipients adopted the same cycles as the mutant strain.
8 Loros *et al.* argue that internal clocks were developed by primitive bacteria so that they could adjust their metabolism in anticipation of the sun's rays.
9 Circadian rhythms are primarily an *internal* (*endogenous*) *property* and do not depend on external cues.
10 Luce & Segal (1966) discovered that people living in the Arctic Circle slept for normal periods, despite the fact that the sun does not set during the summer months.

Section 2: Infradian rhythms

11 *Infradian rhythms* last for longer than one day.
12 'The menstrual period is the *end* of a four-week cycle of activity.'
13 The menstrual cycle prepares the womb to house and nourish a fertilised egg (a *zygote*).
14 *Irritability, depression, headaches,* a *decline in alertness and visual acuity,* and *changes in appetite* are all associated with *pre-menstrual syndrome.*
15 Dalton (1964) claimed that *crimes, suicides, accidents* and a *decline in the quality of schoolwork and intelligence test scores* are all clustered around the pre-menstrual interval.
16 PMS occurs in all cultures, and similar effects occur in primates.
17 The *pituitary gland* is responsible for governing the phases of the menstrual cycle.
18 Reinberg's (1967) study found that the woman's day lengthened and her menstrual cycle shortened.

Section 3: Ultradian rhythms

19 *Ultradian rhythms* are rhythms which are shorter than one day.
20 Loomis *et al.*'s (1937) studies found that the brain is active during sleep and that certain types of activity seem to be related to changes in the type of sleep.

21 *Rapid eye movement.*
22 Dement & Kleitman (1957) found that people woken during REM sleep usually reported that they were *dreaming*.
23 *Beta waves* are replaced by *alpha waves* when people change from being awake and alert to relaxed with eyes closed.
24 *Theta waves* mark the onset of *Stage 1 sleep*.
25 A *hypnogogic state* is one in which we experience hallucinatory and dream-like images, and occurs at the transition from relaxation to *Stage 1 sleep.*
26 *Sleep spindles* are brief bursts of mental activity which usually occur during *Stage 2 sleep.*
27 *Stage 3 sleep* and *Stage 4 sleep* are both characterised by *delta waves, unresponsiveness to the environment,* a *lack of eye movement* and *complete relaxation of the muscles.*
28 We enter REM sleep for the first time having first 'descended' to Stage 4 sleep, then 'climbed' to Stage 2 sleep.
29 REM sleep is '*paradoxical sleep*' in that the eyes and brain are very active, whilst the body is virtually paralysed.
30 Stages 3 and 4 of sleep occur only during the first *two cycles of sleep.*
31 As we get older, we sleep for *less time*, and spend *less time in REM sleep.*

Section 4: Diurnal rhythms

32 *Diurnal rhythms* are rhythms which occur during the waking day.
33 Gunter *et al.* found that participants' immediate recall of news information seemed to decline over the course of the day.
34 Adam (1983) found that students were better at extracting the main theme of lectures in the afternoon.
35 Horne & Osterberg (1976) identified *morning types* and *evening types.*

Section 5: Circannual rhythms

36 *Circannual rhythms* are those which have a period of about a year.
37 Circannual rhythms promote species' survival when the climate fluctuates predictably.
38 The letters *SAD* stand for *seasonal affective disorder.*
39 *Melatonin* is normally only produced when it is dark.
40 *Phototherapy.*

Bodily Rhythms

Circadian rhythms

These are consistent cyclical variations *over a period of about 24 hours*. Heart rate, metabolic rate, breathing rate, temperature and hormones all vary during the day, and such variations persist for a time if we reverse our activity patterns.

Internal clocks

- *External cues* (*Zeitgebers*) are used by the body to synchronise internal (or body) clocks called *oscillators*, in a process called *entrainment*.
- Folkhard *et al.* had students spend a month isolated from external cues. Recordings of mood, activity and temperature levels confirmed the existence of several internal clocks.
- **Location:** One of these clocks lies in the *suprachiasmatic nuclei* (SN), which receives information directly from the retina.
- **Evolution:** Loros *et al.* (cited in Highfield, 1996b): internal clocks were developed by primitive bacteria in order to adjust their metabolism in anticipation of the sun.

Research

- Hamsters given brain transplants of SN cells from a mutant strain adopt the same activity cycles as the mutants (suggesting a genetic basis).
- Luce & Segal (1966) found that people living near the Arctic Circle sleep normally even during the light summer months, suggesting that the sleep-waking cycle is an *endogenous* (internal) property.
- Some people take longer than others to adjust to changes (e.g. *'jet lag'*) and not all functions reverse at the same time.

Infradian rhythms

These are rhythms which *last for longer than one day*. The most commonly studied infradian rhythm is *menstruation* (an endocrine cycle).

Menstruation

The end of a 4-week cycle of activity in which the womb has prepared for the job of housing and nourishing a fertilised egg.

- Onset is irregular at first, but becomes well-established in a few months.
- Sabbagh & Barnard (1984): the menstrual periods of women who spend a lot of time together often become synchronised (possibly due to some chemical scent).

Pre-menstrual syndrome

- A variety of effects typically occurring 4/5 days before the onset of menstruation. Includes mild irritation, depression, headaches, a decline in alertness and sometimes changes in appetite.
- Dalton (1964) reported that crimes, suicides, accidents and a decline in the quality of schoolwork are all clustered around the pre-menstrual interval.
- Traditionally, PMS was attributed to a denial of femininity, although the finding that the effects of PMS occur in all cultures (and also in primates) challenges this.

Research

The *pituitary gland* governs menstruation by influencing changes in the walls of the uterus (the endometrium):

- Timonen *et al.* (1964) found that conceptions increased during the lighter (summer) months.
- Reinberg (1967) found that the menstrual cycle of a woman who spent 3 months in a cave shortened. Reinberg speculated that this was due to low light levels.

Ultradian rhythms

These are rhythms which are *shorter than a day* (e.g. heart rate and renal excretion). The most well-researched are those occurring during sleep.

- Loomis *et al.* (1937) used the EEG to discover that the brain is active during sleep and that types of activity seemed to relate to types of sleep.
- Dement & Kleitman (1957) found that people woken during REM (rapid eye movement) sleep usually reported dreaming.
- During REM sleep, the body's muscles are in a state of *virtual paralysis* although heart rate and blood pressure fluctuate.
- Rechtschaffen & Kales (1968) divided NREM (non-REM) sleep into four stages:

Stage and EEG	Characteristics
Stage 1 *theta waves*	Onset sometimes accompanied by a *hypnagogic* (hallucinatory) state. We are easily awoken.
Stage 2 *sleep spindles*	Characterised by brief bursts of activity. Brain responds to some external stimuli (*K-complexes*).
Stage 3 *delta waves*	In Stages 3 and 4, we are unresponsive and difficult to wake. Muscles are relaxed.
Stage 4 *delta waves*	Delta waves make up more than 50% of the EEG. Heart rate, temperature and blood pressure low.

- After we have 'descended' to Stage 4 sleep we 'climb' the sleep *staircase*, entering REM sleep instead of Stage 1.
- Typically, we have 5 or so such cycles of sleep, each lasting on average 90 mins.
- Stages 3 and 4 occur only in the first two cycles of sleep, whilst episodes of REM sleep increase in length.
- As we age we spend less time asleep, and the percentage of REM sleep decreases.

Diurnal rhythms

These are rhythms which *occur during the waking day*. Research has centred on how the time of day affects task performance.

Memory and time of day

- Gunter *et al.* (cited in Marks & Folkhard, 1985) found that participants' immediate recall of television news information declined over the course of the day.
- Adam (1983): the information remembered by students did not depend on the time of day of the lecture, though the main theme was more easily extracted in the afternoon.

Diurnal types

- Horne & Osterberg (1976) used a '*morningness–eveningness*' questionnaire to establish the existence of two *diurnal types*: morning types are tired in the evening and awake alert, whilst *evening types* perform best in the evening and are tired in the morning. However such differences may be associated with introversion/extroversion.

Problems

It is generally believed that differences in task performance during the day cannot solely be explained in terms of circadian variations, but are likely to be the result of many different rhythms reflecting cognitive functions.

Circannual rhythms

These are rhythms which have *a period of about one year* (e.g hibernation, migration, pair-bonding) and are adaptive in fluctuating climates.

The gold-mantled ground squirrel

- Pengelley & Fisher (1957) found that even when the squirrel was kept at a constant temperature and under regular periods of illumination, it hibernated in October, becoming active in April.

Seasonal affective disorder (SAD)

- Some mood disorders are under seasonal control and related to secretions of *melatonin* by the *pineal gland*, which in turn lowers *serotonin* levels.
- Melatonin production is suppressed when it is dark, and may be 'de-synchronised' in winter.

Phototherapy

- In phototherapy, sufferers of SAD are seated in front of an extremely bright light for just one hour each evening.
- Symptoms reverse within 3–4 days, presumably by lowering the levels of melatonin and rephasing its production.

THE FUNCTIONS OF SLEEP

KEY QUESTIONS

- What have studies of total sleep deprivation shown?
- What theories of sleep function have been proposed?
- What have studies of REM sleep deprivation shown?
- What theories of REM sleep function have been proposed?

Q

Section 1: Studies of total sleep deprivation

1 What was the nature of Patrick & Gilbert's (1898) pioneering study of *sleep deprivation*?
2 Why was it impossible for researchers to assess the psychological functioning of Peter Tripp towards the end of his 'wakeathon'?
3 What pattern of sleeping is common in participants following sleep deprivation?
4 What are periods of *micro-sleep*?
5 According to Hüber-Weidman (1976), after how many nights without sleep may *delusions* be experienced?
6 What is the principal symptom of *sleep deprivation psychosis*?
7 How did Rechtschaffen *et al.* (1983) investigate the effects of sleep deprivation in rats?
8 What was the likely cause of death in Rechtschaffen *et al.*'s rats?

Section 2: Evolutionary and restoration theories

9 According to Meddis (1975), what that two factors may affect the amount of time which an animal spends sleeping?
10 Complete the sentence: 'Webb (1982) argues that sleep is an ___ response which does not satisfy a ___ need in the way that food does'.
11 What is the principal claim made by the *hibernation theory* of sleep function?
12 Why are explanations which relate sleep function to risk of predation *non-falsifiable*?
13 According to Oswald's (1966) *restoration theory* of sleep function, what are the functions of sleep?
14 How does Shapiro *et al.*'s (1981) study of people who had completed an 'ultra-marathon' support Oswald's theory?
15 How does Ryback & Lewis's (1971) study of healthy individuals who spent six weeks in bed contradict Oswald's theory?
16 What did Kales *et al.* (1974) discover when studying insomniacs?

Section 3: Studies of REM sleep deprivation

17 How was Dement (1960) able to investigate the effects of *REM sleep deprivation* in volunteers?
18 What finding of Dement's suggests that his volunteers began to experience *REM starvation*?
19 What is the *REM rebound effect*?
20 What did Greenberg *et al.* (1972) discover after showing REM-deprived volunteers a film of a circumcision rite performed without anaesthetic?
21 Complete the sentence: 'Alcohol suppresses ___ sleep without affecting ___ sleep'.

Section 4: Restoration and other theories

22 What is synthesised more rapidly during REM sleep than during NREM sleep?
23 What percentage of a newborn baby's sleep is REM sleep?
24 What caused an increase in REM sleep in non-humans in Bloch's (1976) study?
25 Which aspect of REM sleep is difficult for restoration theorists to explain?
26 How did Empson & Clarke (1970) support the *memory consolidation theory* of sleep function?
27 Identify one other finding relating to humans which supports memory consolidation theory.
28 What does the *sentinel theory* propose is the function of REM sleep?
29 What is the main weakness of this theory?
30 What is the role of REM sleep according to the *oculomotor system maintenance theory*?

Section 5: The physiology of sleep

31 Complete the sentence: 'When night falls the ___ gland secretes the hormone ___ which influences neurons that produce serotonin'.
32 What did Jouvet (1967) demonstrate was the effect of substances which inhibit serotonin synthesis?
33 According to Jouvet, which two neurotransmitters, produced by the *locus coeruleus*, are responsible for the onset of REM sleep?

Section 1: Studies of total sleep deprivation

1 Patrick & Gilbert's (1898) study deprived three 'healthy young men' of sleep for a period of ninety hours.

2 Towards the end of Peter Tripp's 'wakeathon', he experienced *intense delusions*, which made tests of psychological functioning impossible.

3 Following sleep deprivation, participants typically sleep for longer than normal, then return to their usual pattern of sleeping on subsequent nights.

4 *Micro-sleep* occurs when we stop what we are doing and stare into space for a few seconds.

5 Hüber-Weidman (1976) claims that *delusions* may be experienced after five nights without sleep.

6 The principal symptom of *sleep deprivation psychosis* is *depersonalisation* (the loss of a clear sense of identity).

7 Rechtschaffen *et al.* (1983) placed a rat on a disc above a bucket of water, with an EEG monitoring its brain activity. When the rat attempted to sleep, the disc rotated, forcing the rat to walk to avoid falling into the water.

8 The rats were probably unable to *regulate their own body heat*.

Section 2: Evolutionary and restoration theories

9 Meddis (1975) suggests that the animal's *method of obtaining food* and its *exposure to predators* affect the amount of time it spends sleeping.

10 'Webb (1982) argues that sleep is an *innate* response which does not satisfy a *physiological* need in the way that food does.'

11 The *hibernation theory* of sleep function claims that sleep is an adaptive instinctual behaviour which keeps us quiet and out of harm's way.

12 Such explanations can explain *both* sleeping very little *and* sleeping a lot by reference to a decreased risk of predation. Hence they are impossible to falsify.

13 Oswald's (1966) *restoration theory* claims that the functions of sleep are to restore depleted energy reserves, eliminate waste products from the muscles, repair cells, and recover physical abilities lost during the day.

14 Shapiro *et al.*'s (1981) study found that people who had completed an 'ultra-marathon' slept for longer than normal for two nights following the race.

15 Ryback & Lewis (1971) found that healthy individuals who spent six weeks in bed did *not* sleep for less time than normal.

16 Kales *et al.* (1974) found that insomniacs suffer from far more psychological problems than healthy people.

Section 3: Studies of REM sleep deprivation

17 Dement (1960) deprived volunteers of REM sleep by waking them up every time they entered REM sleep, and compared them with volunteers who were woken during NREM sleep.

18 *REM starvation* was shown by volunteers because they made more and more attempts to enter REM sleep as the amount of REM deprivation increased.

19 The *REM rebound effect* refers to the increase in REM sleep following a period of deprivation.

20 Greenberg *et al.* (1972) discovered that the anxiety experienced when repeatedly viewing the film did not diminish in volunteers deprived of REM sleep, as would normally be the case in healthy individuals.

21 'Alcohol suppresses *REM* sleep without affecting *NREM* sleep.'

Section 4: Restoration and other theories

22 *Proteins* are synthesised more rapidly during REM sleep than during NREM sleep.

23 Around *50 per cent* of a newborn baby's sleep is REM sleep.

24 Bloch's (1976) study found that REM sleep increases when non-humans are given training on a new task.

25 The fact that REM sleep uses a substantial amount of energy, which would *prevent* protein synthesis.

26 Empson & Clarke (1970) found that participants were less able to recall unusual phrases which they heard before bedtime if they were deprived of REM sleep.

27 The proportion of time spent in REM sleep *decreases* with age.

28 The *sentinel theory* proposes that awakening after REM sleep allows animals to check their surroundings for signs of danger.

29 The sentinel theory sees only the *end* of REM sleep as serving any function, not the time during REM sleep.

30 The *oculomotor system maintenance theory* proposes that the function of REM sleep is to keep the eye muscles 'toned up'.

Section 5: The physiology of sleep

31 'When night falls the *pineal* gland secretes the hormone *melatonin* which influences neurons that produce serotonin.'

32 Jouvet (1967) demonstrated that substances which inhibit serotonin synthesis *prevent* sleep.

33 The *locus coeruleus* produces *noradrenaline* and *acetylcholine*.

A

Total sleep deprivation in humans
- Patrick & Gilbert (1998) deprived three 'healthy young men' of sleep for 90 hours. Desire to sleep increased gradually. Two of them experienced perceptual disorders after the second night. When allowed to sleep, all three slept for longer than usual, then returned to normal.
- In 1959, Peter Tripp staged a charity 'wakeathon', staying awake for eight days. Towards the end he experienced hallucinations and delusions.

The effects of sleep deprivation
(after Hüber-Weidman, 1976)
Night 1: experience is uncomfortable, but tolerable.
Night 2: urge to sleep is greatest between 3 and 5 a.m.
Night 3: complex information-processing is impaired.
Night 4: confusion, irritability, and micro-sleep occur.
Night 5: delusions may be experienced.
Night 6: *depersonalisation* and symptoms of *sleep deprivation psychosis*.

Total sleep deprivation in rats
- Rechtschaffen *et al.* (1983) placed a rat on a rotating disc above a bucket of water. An EEG monitored its brain activity, causing the disc to rotate whenever it showed signs of sleep. This forced the rat to walk to avoid falling into the water.
- **Result:** all sleep-deprived rats had died after 33 days. The rats had suffered progressive physical deterioration until they were unable to regulate their own body temperature.

Restoration theories of sleep
- Oswald (1966): the purpose of sleep is to restore depleted reserves of energy, eliminate waste products, repair cells and recover physical abilities.
- The pituitary gland releases a hormone during Stage 4 sleep which is important for tissue growth, formation of red blood cells and protein and RNA synthesis.

- Shapiro *et al.* (1981): people completing an ultramarathon slept for $1\frac{1}{2}$ hours longer than normal following the race.
- Ryback & Lewis (1971): healthy individuals who spent 6 weeks in bed did not sleep for less time (*contradicting* the theory).
- Kales *et al.* (1974): insomniacs suffer from more *psychological* problems, suggesting a psychologically restorative function.

Evolutionary theories of sleep

Predators and prey
- Meddis (1975): points out that animals that cannot find a safe place to sleep have high metabolic rates (which require a lot of food-gathering) or are at risk from predators (e.g. sheep) sleep very little, whilst predators sleep more.

The hibernation theory of sleep function
The enforced inactivity of sleeping aids survival by:
1) reducing the risk of predation or accidents by night
2) preventing us from wasting energy foraging or hunting
However, Evans (1984) points out that we are potentially *vulnerable* during sleep, and that such accounts are 'non-falsifiable' since they can explain either more or less sleep by reference to reduced vulnerability.

The Functions of Sleep

Dement (1960): volunteers were allowed to sleep normally but woken every time they entered REM sleep. A control group was woken the same number of times during NREM sleep.
- Compared with the control group, the REM-deprived group were more irritable, aggressive and less able to concentrate on tasks.
- After several nights they began to show *REM-starvation*: they attempted to go into REM sleep as soon as they slept and were increasingly hard to wake. The number of attempts to enter REM sleep also increased greatly.

REM sleep deprivation

REM rebound
When people are allowed to sleep normally after REM-deprivation, they show a REM rebound effect (they spend longer in REM sleep than is normal), suggesting that they are trying to make up for 'lost' REM sleep time.

REM, anxiety and alcohol
- Greenberg *et al.* (1972): participants watched an anxiety-provoking film of a circumcision rite (performed without anaesthetic). Repeated viewing usually causes the anxiety to subside, but this did not occur in REM-deprived participants.
- Alcohol suppresses REM sleep without affecting NREM sleep. With severe alcohol abuse, a REM rebound effect may manifest itself as the disturbing hallucinations experienced during alcohol withdrawal (Greenberg & Pearlman, 1967).

Restoration theories
- Oswald (1966): REM sleep is related to brain restoration and growth.
- Studies have shown a greater rate of *protein synthesis* during REM sleep than in NREM sleep, and this may be an organic basis for changes in the personality (Rossi, 1973).
- Infants spend 50% of their sleep time in REM sleep (compared with 20% for adults) and REM sleep may promote the cell manufacture and growth necessary for the developing nervous system.

Bloch (1976): REM sleep increases when non-humans are given training on a new task, suggesting that protein synthesis during REM sleep may be involved in the formation of new memories.
Problem: REM sleep uses a substantial amount of energy which would actually *prevent* high levels of protein synthesis.

Other theories

Memory consolidation theory
REM sleep may stimulate neural tissue and consolidate memories:
- Empson & Clarke (1970) found that REM-deprived participants who heard unusual phrases before bedtime were less likely to remember them the next morning than those deprived of NREM sleep.

The sentinel theory
- Short periods of wakefulness sometimes occur at the end of REM sleep. Snyder (cited in Borbely, 1986) believes this allows animals to check for danger.
- However, this does not suggest a function for REM sleep itself.

The oculomotor system maintenance theory
- The function of REM sleep is to keep the eye muscles toned up.

The physiology of sleep

Night falls
↓
Eyes inform the *suprachiasmatic nuclei*
↓
Pineal gland informed
↓
Pineal gland secretes *melatonin*
↓
Melatonin influences *serotonin* production
↓
Serotonin acts on the *reticular activating system*

The monoamine hypothesis of sleep
- Jouvet (1967): destruction of the *raphe nuclei* produces sleeplessness. Serotonin (a *monoamine neurotransmitter*) is concentrated in this structure.
- Chemicals which *inhibit* serotonin production prevent sleep.
- Destruction of the *locus coerulus* (in the pons) causes REM sleep to disappear completely. This structure produces *noradrenaline* and *acetylcholine*, which Jouvet proposed were responsible for the onset of REM sleep.
- Jouvet (1983): interactions between the *raphe nuclei* and *locus coerulus* cause sleep cycles.

Problems
- The complete picture is probably more complicated: stimulation of the *thalamus* can induce sleep and stimulation of other areas can prevent waking.
- The *ventrolateral preoptic area* of the hypothalamus provides direct input to neurons which contain *histamine*, *noradrenaline* and *serotonin*, and may serve as an 'off-switch' allowing simultaneous deactivation of all arousal systems.

THE FUNCTIONS OF DREAMING

SYLLABUS
3.3 Awareness
- research into the physiological and psychological factors involved with states of awareness, including dream states

KEY QUESTIONS
What is the function of dreaming, according to:
- Freud's theory
- 'problem-solving' theory
- 'reprogramming' theories
- 'activation–synthesis' theory
- 'reverse-learning' theory?

Section 1: Dreams: some basic findings
1 Approximately how many episodes of REM sleep do we experience per night?
2 What percentage of the time do we report vivid dreams when woken from REM sleep?
3 Identify the major differences between dreams occurring in REM sleep and those occurring in NREM sleep.
4 How did Dement & Wolpert (1958) demonstrate that external events can be incorporated into a dream?
5 Identify two differences between men's dreams and women's dreams.
6 Why can't sleepwalking occur during REM sleep?

Section 2: Freudian and problem-solving theories
7 Complete the sentence: 'Freud argued that a dream was a sort of 'psychic ___ ___'.
8 According to Freud, why is a dream's content disguised in symbolic form?
9 What term describes the *real (deeper) meaning* of a dream?
10 Which of the following would Freud *not* consider to be symbols for the male genital organs: hoses, bottles, feet, trees, ships, umbrellas?
11 In what way have Foulkes & Cohen (1973) challenged Freud's claim that part of the function of dreaming is to 'protect sleep'?
12 What is probably the major problem for Freud's theory of dream function?
13 How does Webb & Cartwright's (1978) *problem-solving theory* view the function of dreams?
14 Complete the sentence: 'Like Freud, Cartwright makes much use of the role of ___ in dreaming'.
15 How does Hartmann's (1973) research support Webb & Cartwright's (1978) theory of dream function?

Section 3: Reprogramming and activation–synthesis theories
16 According to Evans' (1984) *reprogramming theory*, what are the two functions of REM sleep?

17 What did Herman & Roffwarg (1983) discover caused participants to spend longer than usual in REM sleep?
18 According to Foulkes (1985), how does 'spontaneous activity' in the nervous system relate to the content of dreams?
19 Identify the four functions which Foulkes attributes to dreams.
20 According to Koukkou & Lehman's (1980) theory, with what do we combine recently acquired information during dreams?
21 What was Hobson (1989) able to demonstrate regarding the activity of neurons in sleeping cats?
22 What do Hobson & McCarley (1977) mean by saying that the dream is the brain's effort 'to make the best out of a bad job'?
23 According to Hobson (1988), what is the effect of *acetylcholine* on *giant cells*?
24 Why, according to Hobson & McCarley's (1977) *activation–synthesis theory*, are we unable to remember dreams?
25 How does Foulkes criticise Hobson and McCarley's theory?

Section 4: Reverse-learning theory
26 According to Crick & Mitchison's (1983) *reverse-learning theory*, what is the function of dreams?
27 How does the finding that neither the dolphin nor the spiny anteater dream provide some support for this theory?
28 What does Crick and Mitchison's theory suggest regarding the significance of a dream's content?
29 Complete the sentence: 'All theories of dreaming have difficulty in accounting for the observation that something very like REM sleep occurs in the ___ ___'.
30 What is Jouvet's (1983) explanation for the above observation?
31 What did Maquet et al. (cited in Highfield, 1996d) find when using PET scans to investigate brain activity during dreaming?

Section 1: Dreams: some basic findings

1 We experience *four or five episodes* of REM sleep per night.
2 People woken from REM sleep report dreaming about *80 per cent* of the time.
3 Dreams occurring during *REM sleep* are *clearer, more detailed, more vivid,* and *more likely to have a plot* than those occurring during NREM sleep.
4 Dement & Wolpert (1958) lightly sprayed cold water onto dreamers' faces and found that they were more likely to dream about water.
5 *Men's dreams* are more likely to take place in *outdoor settings* and be more *aggressive and sexual in content* than women's dreams.
6 Sleepwalking can't occur during REM sleep since the body is in a state of '*virtual paralysis*'.

Section 2: Freudian and problem-solving theories

7 'Freud argued that a dream was a sort of 'psychic *safety valve*'.'
8 A dream's content is disguised in symbolic form since it consists of drives and wishes that would be threatening if expressed directly.
9 The real (deeper) meaning of a dream is its *latent content*.
10 Bottles and ships symbolise the *female* genital organs, according to Freud.
11 Foulkes & Cohen (1973) point out that disturbing events during the day tend to be followed by disturbing dreams, rather than 'protective imagery'.
12 The major problem is that the interpretation of a dream is not something which can be objectively achieved.
13 Webb & Cartwright's (1978) theory sees dreams as a way of dealing with problems (such as those relating to work, sex, health and relationships).
14 'Like Freud, Cartwright makes much use of the role of *metaphor* in dreaming.'
15 Hartmann (1973) found that people experiencing interpersonal or occupational problems spend longer in REM sleep than people without such problems.

Section 3: Reprogramming and activation–synthesis theories

16 Evans (1984) claims that during REM sleep the brain *assimilates/processes new information*, and *updates information already stored*.
17 Herman & Roffwarg (1983) discovered that spending a day *wearing distorting lenses* (that turned the world upside-down) caused participants to spend longer than usual in REM sleep.
18 Foulkes (1985) argues that spontaneous activity in the nervous system is interpreted by cognitive processes, presenting them as more structured dreams.
19 Foulkes believes that dreams may *relate newly acquired knowledge to our own self-consciousness, help integrate newly acquired specific knowledge with past general knowledge, prepare us to deal with new, unexpected events* and *reveal the nature of our cognitive processes*.
20 Koukkou & Lehman (1980) believe that during dreams we combine recently acquired information with ideas and strategies of thinking that originated in childhood.
21 Hobson (1989) demonstrated that neurons deep within the brain fire in a seemingly random way during sleep.
22 Hobson & McCarley (1977) argue that during dreams the brain receives signals which suggest that it is moving, and attempts to synthesise this random activity by imposing order on it.
23 Hobson (1988) argues that *giant cells* fire in an unrestrained way in the presence of *acetylcholine*.
24 We are unable to remember dreams since the neurons in the cortex that control the storage of new memories are turned 'off'.
25 Foulkes (1985) points out that the content of dreams is influenced by our waking experiences, so that they cannot be as random and meaningless as Hobson and McCarley suggest.

Section 4: Reverse-learning theory

26 According to Crick and Mitchison (1983), the function of dreams is to enable the brain to get rid of information it does not need.
27 Both the dolphin and the spiny anteater have an unusually large cortex for their size (possibly to accommodate all the useless information which cannot be disposed of).
28 A dream's content is an accidental result that does not lend itself to meaningful interpretation.
29 'All theories of dreaming have difficulty in accounting for the observation that something very like REM sleep occurs in the *developing foetus*.'
30 Jouvet's (1983) explanation is that REM sleep serves to program the brain for genetically determined functions (such as instincts).
31 Maquet *et al.* (cited in Highfield, 1996d) found that both the *left and right amygdalas are active* during sleep.

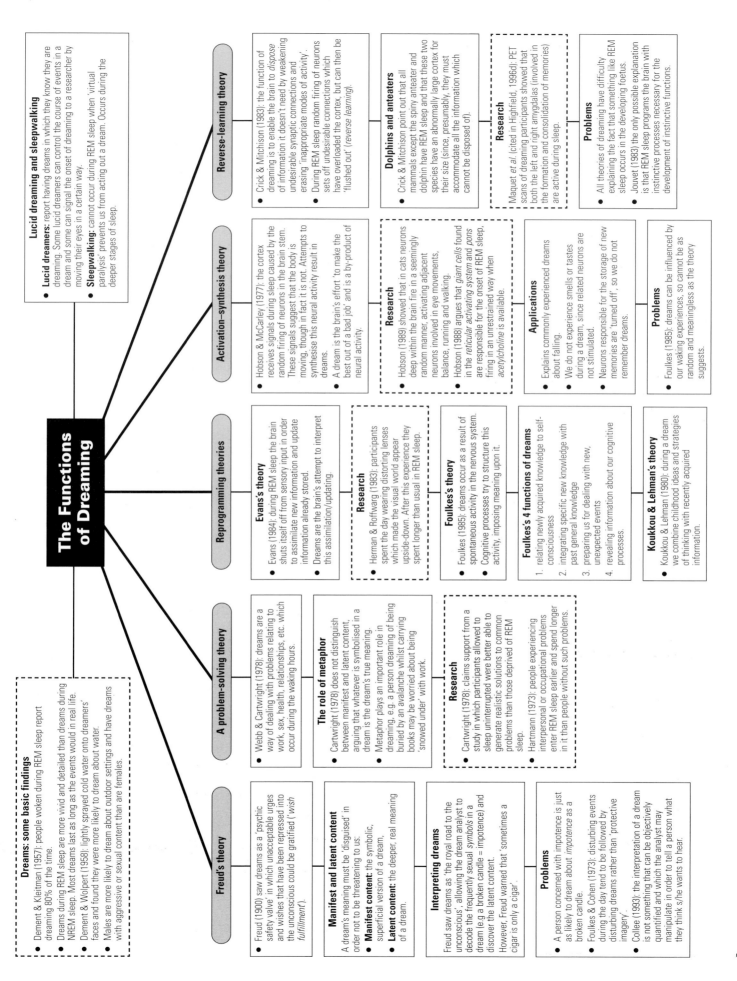

The Functions of Dreaming

Freud's theory

- Freud (1900) saw dreams as a 'psychic safety valve' in which unacceptable urges and wishes that have been repressed into the unconscious could be gratified ('*wish fulfilment*').

Manifest and latent content

A dream's meaning must be 'disguised' in order not to be threatening to us:

- **Manifest content:** the symbolic, superficial version of a dream,
- **Latent content:** the deeper, real meaning of a dream.

Interpreting dreams

Freud saw dreams as 'the royal road to the unconscious', allowing the dream analyst to decode the frequently sexual *symbols* in a dream (e.g a broken candle = impotence) and discover the latent content.

However, Freud warned that 'sometimes a cigar is only a cigar'.

Problems

- A person concerned with impotence is just as likely to dream about *impotence* as a broken candle.
- Foulkes & Cohen (1973): disturbing events during the day tend to be followed by disturbing dreams rather than 'protective imagery'.
- Collee (1993): the interpretation of a dream is not something that can be objectively quantified and which the analyst may manipulate in order to tell a person what they think s/he wants to hear.

A problem-solving theory

- Webb & Cartwright (1978): dreams are a way of dealing with problems relating to work, sex, health, relationships, etc. which occur during the waking hours.

The role of metaphor

- Cartwright (1978) does not distinguish between manifest and latent content, arguing that whatever is symbolised in a dream is the dream's true meaning.
- Metaphor plays an important role in dreaming, e.g. a person dreaming of being buried by an avalanche whilst carrying books may be worried about being 'snowed under' with work.

Research

- Cartwright (1978): claims support from a study in which participants allowed to sleep uninterrupted were better able to generate realistic solutions to common problems than those deprived of REM sleep.
- Hartmann (1973): people experiencing interpersonal or occupational problems enter REM sleep earlier and spend longer in it than people without such problems.

Reprogramming theories

Evans's theory

- Evans (1984): during REM sleep the brain shuts itself off from sensory input in order to assimilate new information and update information already stored.
- Dreams are the brain's attempt to interpret this assimilation/updating.

Research

- Herman & Roffwarg (1983): participants spent the day wearing distorting lenses which made the visual world appear upside-down. After this experience they spent longer than usual in REM sleep.

Foulkes's theory

- Foulkes (1985): dreams occur as a result of spontaneous activity in the nervous system.
- Cognitive processes try to structure this activity, imposing meaning upon it.

Foulkes's 4 functions of dreams

1. relating newly acquired knowledge to self-consciousness
2. integrating specific new knowledge with past general knowledge
3. preparing us for dealing with new, unexpected events
4. revealing information about our cognitive processes.

Koukkou & Lehman's theory

- Koukkou & Lehman (1980): during a dream we combine childhood ideas and strategies of thinking with recently acquired information.

Activation–synthesis theory

- Hobson & McCarley (1977): the cortex receives signals during sleep caused by the random firing of neurons in the brain stem. These signals suggest that the body is moving, though in fact it is not. Attempts to synthesise this neural activity result in dreams.
- A dream is the brain's effort 'to make the best out of a bad job' and is a by-product of neural activity.

Research

- Hobson (1989) showed that in cats neurons deep within the brain fire in a seemingly random manner, activating adjacent neurons involved in eye movements, balance, running and walking.
- Hobson (1988) argues that *giant cells* found in the *reticular activating system* and *pons* are responsible for the onset of REM sleep, firing in an unrestrained way when *acetylcholine* is available.

Applications

- Explains commonly experienced dreams about falling.
- We do not experience smells or tastes during a dream, since related neurons are not stimulated.
- Neurons responsible for the storage of new memories are 'turned off', so we do not remember dreams.

Problems

- Foulkes (1985): dreams can be influenced by our waking experiences, so cannot be as random and meaningless as the theory suggests.

Reverse-learning theory

- Crick & Mitchison (1983): the function of dreaming is to enable the brain to *dispose* of information it doesn't need by weakening undesirable synaptic connections and erasing 'inappropriate modes of activity'.
- During REM sleep random firing of neurons sets off undesirable connections which have overloaded the cortex, but can then be 'flushed out' (*reverse learning*).

Dolphins and anteaters

- Crick & Mitchison point out that all mammals except the spiny anteater and dolphin have REM sleep and that these two species have an abnormally large cortex for their size (since, presumably, they must accommodate all the information which cannot be disposed of).

Research

- Maquet *et al* (cited in Highfield, 1996d): PET scans of dreaming participants showed that both the left and right amygdalas (involved in the formation and consolidation of memories) are active during sleep.

Problems

- All theories of dreaming have difficulty explaining the fact that something like REM sleep occurs in the developing foetus.
- Jouvet (1983) the only possible explanation is that REM sleep programs the brain with instinctive processes necessary for the development of instinctive functions.

HYPNOSIS AND HYPNOTIC PHENOMENA

KEY QUESTIONS
• What is the nature of hypnosis?
• How do 'state' theories explain hypnosis?
• How do 'non-state' theories explain hypnosis?
• What are the practical applications and ethical implications of hypnosis and hypnotic phenomena?

Q

Section 1: The nature of hypnosis

1 What was the mysterious force which Franz Anton Mesmer believed filled the universe?
2 What was the conclusion reached by King Louis XVI's committee investigating Mesmer's cures?
3 For what purpose did Ward, a British physician, use hypnosis in 1842?
4 What is the requirement common to all ways of inducing a hypnotic state?
5 How do psychologists know that hypnotised people are not asleep?
6 What is usually the first step in inducing a hypnotic state?
7 What is an *ideosensory suggestion*?
8 What is meant by a *suspension of planning*, which is shown by hypnotised people?
9 What is the difference between a *positive hallucination* and a *negative hallucination*?
10 What is a *post-hypnotic suggestion*?
11 According to Hilgard (1977), approximately what percentage of people are highly susceptible to hypnosis?
12 How is the *Stanford hypnotic suggestibility scale* used?
13 Identify three personality traits which are highly correlated with *hypnotic susceptibility*.
14 What did Crawford (1994) discover concerning the pattern of *hemispheric activation* prior to and during hypnosis?
15 What do Spanos *et al.* (1983) propose is the essential difference between hypnotised and non-hypnotised (faking) individuals?
16 What did Coe & Yashinki (1985) discover by using a 'lie detector' test?
17 What is *trance logic*?
18 According to Bowers (1976), how do hypnotised and faking participants differ behaviourally, when told that they cannot see a chair?

Section 2: 'State' theory of hypnosis

19 What is the central claim made by Hilgard's (1977) *neodissociation theory*?
20 What is the *hidden observer*?

21 What is involved in the *cold pressor test* (CPT)?
22 How did Hilgard use the CPT to investigate the hidden observer phenomenon?
23 Identify three areas in which hypnosis has been used as an *analgesic*.
24 What does the term *strategic enactment* mean, as used by Spanos (1991) to explain analgesic effects?

Section 3: 'Non-state' theory of hypnosis

25 What is Barber's (1979) argument against the existence of a special 'state' of hypnosis?
26 Complete the sentence: 'Non-state theorists see hypnotised people as acting out a ___ ___ which is defined by their expectations and the situation'.
27 What term is used to describe the phenomenon in which, for example, we allow actors in a film to lead us through a fantasy?
28 In what way does the *'human plank' trick* lend support to non-state theory?
29 What is the origin of the hidden observer, according to non-state theorists?

Section 4: Practical applications and ethical implications

30 What is *hypermnesia*?
31 What is involved in the *television technique*?
32 Identify two reasons for doubting the reliability of information gained from a witness during hypnosis.
33 What occurs during *age regression*?
34 What finding led Charcot to conclude that the origins of *hysterical disorders* were psychological rather than physical?
35 In what way did Freud see hypnosis as useful?
36 Why did Freud eventually abandon hypnosis as a therapeutic technique?
37 What claim is made by the *Hollywood theory of hypnosis* (Hayes, 1994)?
38 Identify one source of *ethical concern* over the use of hypnosis.
39 Why is it difficult to resolve ethical concerns relating to behaviours performed during hypnosis?

Section 1: The nature of hypnosis

1 Mesmer believed that a mysterious form of '*magnetism*' filled the universe.

2 King Louis XVI's committee concluded that Mesmer's cures probably occurred through '*aroused imagination*' (the *placebo effect*).

3 Ward used hypnosis as an anaesthetic in an operation to *amputate* a man's leg.

4 All ways of inducing a hypnotic state require that the person understands that hypnosis will take place.

5 Hypnotised people do not show the EEG recording characteristic of people who are asleep.

6 The first step in inducing a hypnotic state is usually to focus the individual's attention on a target.

7 An *ideosensory suggestion* is a suggestion is made by the hypnotist regarding sensations (such as feeling warm).

8 A *suspension of planning* is a loss of ability to initiate actions, although the individual will respond to the hypnotist's suggestions.

9 *Positive hallucinations* involve responding to something that is not present, whilst *negative hallucinations* involve failing to respond to something that is present.

10 A *post-hypnotic suggestion* is an instruction given to people during a hypnotic session which subsequently influences their behaviour in some way.

11 According to Hilgard (1977), roughly *15 per cent* of people are highly susceptible to hypnosis.

12 The *Stanford hypnotic suggestibility scale* comprises a series of suggestions which are made after the induction of a hypnotic state in order to deduce susceptibility.

13 *Absorption*, *expectancy* and *fantasy-proneness* are highly correlated with hypnotic susceptibility.

14 Crawford (1994) discovered that *frontal* and possibly *left-biased* activity prior to hypnosis is followed by a more posterior and possibly *right-biased activation* during induction.

15 Spanos *et al.* (1983) propose that whilst hypnotised people believe their responses are involuntary, non-hypnotised (faking) individuals *know* that they are pretending.

16 Coe & Yashinki (1985) discovered that people with post-hypnotic amnesia experienced improved recall for the hypnotic episode when they believed they were to be tested using a 'lie detector'.

17 *Trance logic* is the difference in performance between the hypnotised and those pretending to be hypnotised.

18 According to Bowers (1976), hypnotised participants will walk around the chair (as if sleepwalking), whereas faking participants will bump into it.

Section 2: 'State' theory of hypnosis

19 Hilgard's (1977) *neo-dissociation theory* proposes that hypnosis is the division of consciousness into separate channels of mental activity.

20 The *hidden observer* is a dissociated part of consciousness which remains separate and monitors all that happens during hypnosis.

21 The *CPT* involves plunging one or both forearms into circulating icy water and keeping them immersed for as long as possible.

22 Hilgard asked the hidden observer to 'remain out of awareness', and write down ratings of pain on a ten point scale, whilst the hypnotised participant underwent the CPT.

23 Helping children with *bone-marrow transplants* for cancer, the *removal of teeth*, tonsils and *breast tumours*, and *amputations*.

24 *Strategic enactment* is used by Spanos (1991) to refer to strategies (such as mental distractions) to which hypnosis's analgesic effects can be attributed.

Section 3: 'Non-state' theory of hypnosis

25 Barber (1979) argues that it is difficult to see why the brain should have evolved in such a way that it can be hypnotised.

26 'Non-state theorists see hypnotised people as acting out a *social role* which is defined by their expectations and the situation.'

27 *Suspension of self-control.*

28 Behaviours which can be performed under hypnosis, such as the '*human plank*' *trick*, are also possible in a normal waking state.

29 Non-state theorists claim that the hidden observer is a product of a script which is supplied by the hypnotist.

Section 4: Practical applications and ethical implications

30 *Hypermnesia* is the apparent ability of a hypnotised person to recall details and entire memories of events.

31 The *television technique* involves instructing the hypnotised witness to 'zoom in' on details, or 'freeze the frame' to examine details.

32 Witnesses may *pick up on suggestions made by the hypnotist* and incorporate these into memory, or '*recall*' information *which is simply incorrect.*

33 *Age regression* involves asking people to play themselves as infants or children.

34 Charcot discovered that hysterical symptoms could be simulated under hypnosis.

35 Freud saw hypnosis as useful in gaining access to the unconscious and uncovering the causes of disorders.

36 Freud felt that hypnosis elicited childhood *fantasies*, rather than *experiences*.

37 The *Hollywood theory of hypnosis* suggests that hypnotists are able to induce people to act in ways which violate their own moral codes.

38 Reports of 'porno-hypnotist' shows in America, 'striptease' in a British show, and indecent assaults on patients by hypnotherapists, all give rise to ethical concerns.

39 It is difficult to determine whether a behaviour occurs because the hypnotist has control or because the person *wants* to behave in that way.

Characteristics

- **Suspension of planning:** a loss of ability to initiate actions, although the person will respond to the hypnotist's suggestions.
- **Distortion in information processing:** e.g. accepting inconsistencies which would normally be noticed.
- **Narrowing of attention:** lowered awareness of sensations.
- **Post-hypnotic amnesia:** a person may be instructed to forget all that has happened during the session.
- **Post-hypnotic suggestion:** instructions given during the session may influence subsequent behaviour.
- **Positive and negative hallucinations:** people may respond to something that is *not* present, or fail to respond to something that *is* present.

Individual differences

- Hilgard (1977) estimates that 5–10% of people are *highly susceptible* to hypnosis, 5–10% *highly resistant* and 75–80% between the two.
- The *Stanford hypnotic susceptibility scale* comprises a series of suggestions made to a hypnotised person to determine susceptibility (e.g. taste hallucinations, age regression, negative visual hallucinations).
- Oakley *et al.* (1996): susceptibility is not limited to personality types, although traits of *absorption, expectancy,* and *fantasy-proneness* are all correlated with susceptibility.

A brief history
- **1780's** – Mesmer used 'mesmerism' to treat patients, claiming to harness a mysterious magnetic force.
- **1842** – Ward amputated a man's leg using only hypnosis as an anaesthetic.
- **1845–1851** – Eskdale performed many operations in India, using only hypnosis. Patients showed no sign of suffering.

Hypnosis

Inducing a hypnotic state
- A person needs to understand that hypnosis will take place.
- The individual is required to focus attention whilst the hypnotist makes suggestions of tiredness/relaxation.
- Suggestions that the arms and legs feel heavy (*ideomotor* suggestions) or warm (*ideosensory* suggestion) may be made.

'State' theories

Hypnosis is a unique and altered state of consciousness.
- Hilgard's (1977) *neo-dissociation theory* proposes that hypnosis is the division of consciousness into separate channels of mental activity, allowing us to focus attention on the hypnotist and perceive other events 'subconsciously'.
- Hilgard maintained that a (dissociated) part of consciousness remains aware of everything that happens during hypnosis and monitors it (the *hidden observer*).

The hidden observer and the cold pressor test (CPT)
- In the CPT, a participant plunges one or other forearm into circulating icy water. Immersion causes pain which most people cannot tolerate for more than 25 seconds.
- Hypnotised participants told that they would feel no pain would remove their forearms after about 40 seconds.
- When Hilgard asked the 'hidden observer' to remain out of awareness and to write down rating of pain these were much higher than those reported verbally by the hypnotised participant.

The analgesic properties of hypnosis
Hypnosis has been used to help children undergoing bone-marrow transplants, in the removal of teeth, tonsils and breast tumours.
- Hilgard's findings suggest that hypnosis does not eliminate pain, but enables it to be better tolerated because there is no conscious awareness of it.
- Spanos (1991) argues that hypnosis incorporates *strategic enactments* (strategies such as mental distractions which can seem to cause analgesia).
- Relaxation may help the brain to produce *endorphins*, or people may not report pain for fear of giving offence (Barber, 1970).

'Non-state' theories

Hypnosis involves acting out a social role.
- Non-state theorists see hypnotised people as acting out a role defined by their own expectations and the situation. The hypnotist's instructions govern the rules of the situation.
- Hypnosis involves the suspension of *self-control* (such as that we might experience when actors in a film lead us through a fantasy).

The origins of hypnotic phenomena
- Barber (1979): argues that it is difficult to see why the brain should have evolved in such a way that people can be hypnotised (since hypnotic phenomena occur only under very specialised conditions).
- Barber believes that a *functional analysis* of hypnosis as a behavioural phenomenon points to a plausible reason for its occurrence (i.e. hypnosis serves a social function and is not an altered state of consciousness).

Research
- Spanos *et al.* (1983) used the CPT with hypnotised participants and gave instructions to the 'hidden observer' to be more or less aware of what was going on. The hidden observer reported more or less pain, depending on the instruction, suggesting that the 'hidden observer' is actually a product of a *script* supplied by the hypnotist.
- Non-state theory is also supported by the finding that behaviours possible under hypnosis (e.g. the 'human plank' trick) are also possible in non-hypnotic conditions.
- However, it is difficult for such theories to explain the apparent analgesic effects of hypnosis during painful surgical procedures.

Practical applications

Hypermnesia: the apparent ability of a hypnotised person to focus on details of an event or reconstruct an entire memory.
- Some police departments use the *television technique* in which the witness is told to 'zoom in' on details or 'freeze the frame'.
- However, hypnotised witnesses may pick up on the hypnotist's suggestions (and incorporate these into memory), or report *incorrect* information.

Age regression: people are asked to play themselves as infants or children.
- Age regression seems to give better access to childhood memories rather than literally returning people to an earlier stage.

Psychoanalytic theory: Freud believed that hypnotic states produced regression.
- Freud saw hypnosis as useful in gaining access to the unconscious, although he later rejected it.

Ethical concerns

- The '*Hollywood theory of hypnosis*' (Hayes, 1994) suggests that hypnotists are able to induce people to act in ways which violate their moral code.
- Reports of 'porno-hypnotist' shows in America, 'striptease' in the stage show of one British hypnotist and indecent assaults on patients by hypnotherapists all raise serious ethical questions (Rogers, 1994).
- However, it is difficult to determine the extent to which individuals perform behaviours because the hypnotist has control or because they want to behave in that way (e.g. keeping to the 'script').

Genuineness

Spanos *et al.* (1983): the essential difference between hypnotised and non-hypnotised people is that the former *believe* their responses are involuntary, whereas the latter *know* they are pretending.

Research
- Coe & Yashinki (1985) found that hypnotised people with post-hypnotic amnesia would show dramatically improved recall for the session if given a 'lie detector' test.
- Kinnunen *et al.* (1995) found different measures of skin conductance (a measure of deception) for hypnotised individuals as compared with 'simulators'.
- Bowers (1976) found that genuinely hypnotised participants will walk around a chair which they have been told they cannot see (as if sleepwalking), whereas people faking hypnosis will bump into it.

15

SOME DRUGS AND THEIR EFFECTS ON BEHAVIOUR

SYLLABUS
3.1 Basic neural and hormonal processes and their influences on behaviour
- research into the effects of drugs on behaviour

KEY QUESTIONS
What effects do the following types of drug have on behaviour?
- depressants
- stimulants
- opiates
- hallucinogens
- cannabis

Section 1: Introducing drugs
1 What does the term *psychoactive drug* usually refer to?
2 How do *recreational drugs* and *drugs of abuse* differ?
3 What phenomenon is described by the term *tolerance*?
4 What is *physiological dependence*?
5 Identify two effects of depressants.
6 Complete the sentence: 'Apart from differences in body weight and sex, the effects of drugs also depend on ___'.

Section 2: Depressants and stimulants
7 Why do small amounts of *alcohol* have a 'stimulating' effect?
8 Identify three cognitive functions which are affected by alcohol.
9 Which other functions are affected by alcohol?
10 Why are long-term alcohol users at risk from brain damage?
11 How does a large amount of alcohol affect the functioning of neurons?
12 What explanation does the *disease model of alcoholism* offer for alcoholism?
13 Identify two conditions for which *barbiturates* may be prescribed.
14 How do the effects of the *minor tranquillisers* differ from those of barbiturates?
15 Identify four effects of *stimulants*.
16 To which naturally occurring chemical are *amphetamines* similar?
17 Identify three clinical uses of amphetamines.
18 What happens to users when amphetamine wears off?
19 Which clinical condition does *amphetamine psychosis* resemble?
20 Identify four additional effects associated with long-term amphetamine use.
21 How do the effects of *cocaine* and amphetamines differ?
22 Identify four effects associated with chronic use of cocaine.
23 What type(s) of dependence does cocaine unquestionably produce?

24 The release of which two *neurotransmitters* is facilitated by cocaine?
25 What is the common name for *MDMA*?
26 How long do the effects of MDMA last?
27 Which two *neurotransmitters* does MDMA affect?
28 What two adverse physiological effects are associated with MDMA?

Section 3: Opiates and hallucinogens
29 What are the general effects of the *opiates*?
30 Why was *heroin* originally developed?
31 What are the immediate effects of heroin?
32 What effects of heroin have been observed in long-term users?
33 To what extent do *tolerance* to, and *dependence* on, heroin develop?
34 According to Snyder (1977), why does the regular use of opiates lead to such severe withdrawal symptoms?
35 For what purpose was *methadone* developed?
36 What are the general effects of the *hallucinogens*?
37 What are *synaesthesia* and *depersonalisation* (two of the effects of *LSD*)?
38 Does LSD lead to physiological dependence, withdrawal or tolerance?
39 What does Carlson (1988) suggest is a possible effect of the suppression of *serotonin* by hallucinogens?
40 What are the four 'Cs' identified by Smith *et al.* (1978) as being effects of long-term PCP use?

Section 4: Cannabis
41 What is the difference between *marijuana* and *hashish*?
42 Identify four features associated with the 'high' produced by *cannabis*.
43 How long does the active component of cannabis (*THC*) remain in the body?
44 What is *reverse tolerance*, which is sometimes reported with cannabis use?
45 Identify three *medical applications* of cannabis.

Q

Section 1: Introducing drugs

1 *Psychoactive drugs* are chemicals which alter perceptions and behaviour by changing conscious awareness.

2 *Recreational drugs* have no legal restrictions on their use, whilst *drugs of abuse* are taken outside of society's approval.

3 *Tolerance* is the lessening of the effects of a drug with continued use, leading the user to take more to achieve the same effect.

4 *Physiological dependence* means that the body cannot do without a drug because it has adjusted to, and becomes dependent on, that drug's presence.

5 Depressants *depress neural activity, slow down bodily functions*, inducing *calmness* and *sleep*.

6 'Apart from differences in body weight and sex, the effects of drugs also depend on *expectations*.'

Section 2: Depressants and stimulants

7 Small amounts of alcohol lower social inhibitions, and the ability to foresee negative consequences or recall acceptable standards of behaviour.

8 The *transfer of information to long-term memory, visual acuity*, and *depth perception* are all affected by alcohol.

9 Alcohol also affects *motor functions*.

10 Alcohol interferes with the absorption of vitamin B, causing a vitamin deficiency which affects the brain in long-term users.

11 In large amounts, alcohol reduces the ability of the cell membranes of neurons to conduct nerve impulses.

12 The *disease model of alcoholism* proposes that it is a weakness caused by a genetic predisposition.

13 *Barbiturates* may be prescribed for *insomnia* or *anxiety*.

14 The *minor tranquillisers* have much *milder effects* than the barbiturates and do not cause sleep.

15 *Stimulants* temporarily *excite neural activity, increasing physiological arousal, enhancing positive feelings*, and *heightening alertness*.

16 *Amphetamines* are similar to *adrenaline*.

17 Amphetamines have been used to treat *asthma, narcolepsy*, and children with *attention-deficit/hyperactivity disorder*.

18 Users experience a 'crash' when the drug wears off, characterised by extreme fatigue and depression.

19 *Amphetamine psychosis* resembles *paranoid schizophrenia*.

20 Long-term use has been associated with *severe depression, suicidal tendencies, disrupted thinking*, and *brain damage*.

21 The effects of cocaine are *briefer* in duration than those of amphetamines, lasting only for 15–30 minutes.

22 Chronic use of cocaine may lead to *convulsions, respiratory failure, bleeding into the brain*, and *formication* (a prickling sensation of the skin).

23 Cocaine certainly produces *psychological dependence* (it is debatable whether or not it causes physiological dependence).

24 The release of both *noradrenaline* and *dopamine* is facilitated by cocaine.

25 *MDMA* is commonly called '*ecstasy*'.

26 The effects of MDMA may last for *up to ten hours*.

27 MDMA affects *serotonin* and *dopamine* levels.

28 *Dehydration* and *heatstroke* are associated with *MDMA*.

Section 3: Opiates and hallucinogens

29 The opiates *depress activity in the central nervous system*, and *produce pain insensitivity* without a loss of consciousness.

30 *Heroin* was originally developed as a 'cure' for physiological dependence on morphine.

31 Heroin causes a pleasurable '*rush*' similar to an orgasm, but affecting the whole body.

32 Long-term use of heroin may lead to *increases in aggression, social isolation* and a *reduction in physical activity*. The *immune system may also be depressed*.

33 *Tolerance* develops very quickly, and heroin produces both *physiological* and *psychological* dependence.

34 Snyder (1977) argues that the regular use of opiates leads the brain to stop producing its own opiates (*endorphins*). When the user abstains, the internal mechanisms for regulating pain are severely disrupted.

35 *Methadone* was developed to treat the physiological dependence associated with opiate use.

36 The *hallucinogens* produce alterations in perception and evoke sensory images in the absence of any sensory input (hallucinations).

37 *Synaesthesia* refers to the blending of sensory modalities so that an experience in one leads to an experience in another (e.g. 'seeing' sounds). *Depersonalisation* is where the user perceives the body as being separate from the self.

38 *LSD* does not seem to lead to physiological dependence or withdrawal, although tolerance develops rapidly.

39 Carlson (1988) suggests that this may activate '*dream mechanisms*' while the user is still awake, causing hallucinations.

40 *Combativeness, catatonia, convulsions* and *coma* (Smith *et al.*, 1978).

Section 4: Cannabis

41 *Marijuana* is extracted from the branches and leaves of male and female cannabis plants, whilst *hashish* derives from the resin of the female plant.

42 A cannabis 'high' involves *relaxation*, a *loss of social inhibitions, intoxication* and a *humorous mood*.

43 THC remains in the body for as long as a month.

44 *Reverse tolerance* occurs when regular use of a drug leads to a *lowering* of the amount needed to achieve the initial effects.

45 Cannabis has been used with *glaucoma sufferers*, patients being treated for *cancer* with chemotherapy, and to reduce the symptoms of *multiple sclerosis*.

Some Drugs and their Effects

Tolerance is the lessening of the effects of drugs with continued use.
Physiological dependence is when the body adjusts to, and cannot do without, a drug.
Psychological dependence is feeling compelled to continue taking a drug even though the body is not dependent on its presence.
Withdrawal is the adverse symptoms (e.g. hallucinations) when a drug is stopped.
Drug addiction is the combination of physiological dependence and tolerance.

Depressants

Depress neural activity, slow down bodily functions and induce sleep.

Alcohol

Over 90% of British adults drink alcohol to some extent.

- **Short-term effects:** depend partly on *expectations*. Small amounts have a 'stimulating effect', by lowering social inhibitions and impairing our ability to recall standards of behaviour. Affects *cognitive functions* (such as transfer to long-term memory) and *motor functions* (80 mg slows reaction times by 10%). Larger amounts cause staggering and sedation; very large amounts may cause death.
- **Long-term effects:** may augment *depression*, cause *malnutrition* (by interfering with absorption of vitamin B), which may lead to *brain damage*. Other consequences include liver damage, heart disease, and a reduction in the efficiency of the immune system. Babies of women who drink during pregnancy may suffer from *foetal alcohol syndrome*.
- **Dependence:** physiological and psychological occur after prolonged and severe intoxication. Symptoms of withdrawal include restlessness, nausea, fever and hallucinations.
- **Action:** has a relaxing effect on the ANS. In large amounts, decreases neural activity by reducing the ability of neurons to conduct nerve impulses. Increases the inhibitory effects of the neurotransmitter GABA, reducing activity in areas associated with arousal.

Barbiturates

- **Effects:** similar to alcohol. Prescribed to induce sleep or reduce anxiety.
- **Action:** depress neural activity by reducing the release of excitatory neurotransmitters in several areas.
- **Dependence:** physiological, leading to withdrawal and tolerance.

Tranquillisers (e.g. valium)

- **Effects:** milder than barbiturates and do not induce sleep.

Aromatic solvents (e.g. some glues)

Abused by as many as 9% of secondary school children (Mihill, 1997) and associated with a number of deaths.

Stimulants

Temporarily excite neural activity, arouse bodily functions, enhance positive feelings and heighten alertness.

Amphetamines

- **Short-term effects:** increase *energy* and *confidence*, and suppress appetite. Small amounts cause increased *wakefulness* and *arousal*. Users experience a 'crash' (fatigue and depression) as the drug wears off. Large amounts cause *hallucinations* and *paranoid delusions*.
- **Long-term effects:** paranoid delusions (*amphetamine psychosis*) similar to *paranoid schizophrenia*. Associated with *severe depression, disrupted thinking* and *brain damage*.
- **Dependence:** tolerance and psychological dependence develop quickly. The amphetamine 'hang-over' suggests some physiological dependence.
- **Action:** chemically similar to adrenaline. Used to raise the attention span of children with attention-deficit/hyperactivity disorder.

Cocaine

A powerful CNS stimulant extracted from the coca shrub native to South America.

- **Short-term effects:** similar to amphetamines, but briefer in duration (minutes, not hours), since it is metabolised more quickly. Leads to *euphoria, deadening of pain, self-confidence and energy*, followed by a 'crash'. Can cause cardiac arrest.
- **Long-term effects:** *cocaine psychosis* (similar to amphetamine psychosis), *convulsions, respiratory failure* and *bleeding into the brain* may all occur.
- **Dependence:** psychological dependence, although it is not clear whether physiological dependence, tolerance or withdrawal are produced.
- **Action:** stimulates the *sympathetic nervous system*, facilitates release of *noradrenaline* and *dopamine*, increasing neuronal activity.

MDMA *'ecstasy'*

- **Short-term effects:** small amounts produce a mild euphoric 'rush' and elation (lasting up to 10 hours). Large amounts trigger hallucinations. Causes dehydration and hyperthermia which can lead to collapse and death.
- **Long-term effects:** associated with depression, panic attacks, kidney and liver failure.
- **Dependence:** tolerance occurs, but physiological dependence does not (Department of Health, 1994).

The opiates

Depress activity in the CNS but act as analgesics, producing pain insensitivity without loss of consciousness.

Morphine and heroin

Morphine was used to relieve pain during the Franco-Prussian war. Heroin was produced in an attempt to cure the physiological dependence which morphine causes, but it too causes dependence.

- **Short-term effects:** Heroin causes a 'rush' similar to sexual orgasm which affects the whole body. Rapidly decomposes into morphine, producing euphoria, relaxation and drowsiness.
- **Long-term effects:** associated with aggressiveness, social isolation and immune system damage.
- **Dependence:** both physiological and psychological. Tolerance develops quickly. Withdrawal symptoms include cramps, chills, insomnia and diarrhoea.
- **Action:** mimic the effects of the brain's naturally occurring opiates (*endorphins*), released when we engage in behaviours important to survival. Opiate abuse may cause natural production of opiates to cease (Snyder, 1977).

Methadone

A synthetic opioid used to treat the dependence associated with opiate use.

- **Short-term effects:** acts more slowly than heroin and does not produce the 'rush'.
- **Dependence:** users are less likely to take heroin, but in avoiding the withdrawal symptoms associated with heroin, they may become psychologically dependent on methadone.

Hallucinogens

Produce alterations in perception and sensory images in the absence of sensory input.

LSD

- **Short-term effects:** onset may be delayed for an hour or more. Produces heightened and distorted sensory experiences which may be pleasurable or terrifying. *Depersonalisation* and *synaesthesia* may occur.
- **Long-term effects:** may cause *flashbacks*.
- **Dependence:** does not seem to cause dependence or withdrawal, although tolerance develops rapidly.
- **Action:** chemically similar to *dopamine* and *serotonin*. May cause 'dream mechanisms' to become activated by suppressing natural serotonin.

PCP *'angel dust'*

- **Short-term effects:** distortions in body image, depersonalisation and euphoria. Large amounts may lead to violence, panic, psychotic behaviour.
- **Long-term effects:** Combativeness, catatonia, convulsions and coma (Smith *et al*, 1978).
- **Dependence:** psychological but not physiological.

Cannabis

Derives from the cannabis plant. Has been classed as a hallucinogen, but can have stimulant and depressant effects.

- **Short-term effects:** small amounts produce a mild pleasurable 'high' consisting of relaxation and loss of social inhibition. Short-term memory is impaired. Some users report fear and confusion. Large amounts cause hallucinogenic reactions.
- **Long-term effects:** may lead to *amotivational syndrome* (lack of motivation).
- **Dependence:** psychological dependence almost certainly occurs, although *reverse tolerance* has been reported (regular use increases sensitivity).

49

16

MOTIVATION AND THE BRAIN

SYLLABUS
3.4 Motivation, emotion and stress
- research into the relationship between brain systems and motivation
- physiological and non-physiological theories of motivation

KEY QUESTIONS
- What causes hunger?
- What is the role of the hypothalamus in eating?
- What causes drinking?

Q

Section 1: The causes of hunger
1 Define the term *motive*.
2 What is *homeostasis*?
3 Complete the sentence: 'An early theory proposed that the ___ sent information about hunger to the brain via the ___ ___.'
4 How did Cannon & Washburn (1912) study the relation between hunger pangs and stomach contractions?
5 Identify two reasons why hunger mechanisms are more complex than early theories suggest.
6 What finding suggests that the liver also plays a role in controlling hunger?
7 According to *glucostatic theory*, what is the primary stimulus for hunger?
8 In what way do *insulin injections* support glucostatic theory?
9 Where did Meyer & Marshall (1956) believe glucoreceptors to be, following their experiments with mice?
10 What does the finding that animals who eat diets high in fats, but maintain a relatively constant calorie intake, suggest?
11 What are *adipose tissues*?
12 According to Nisbett's (1972) version of *lipostatic theory*, what determines the *body-weight set-point*?
13 Identify one finding relating to humans which supports lipostatic theory.
14 What condition usually results in rats in whom the *lateral hypothalamus* (LH) has been damaged?
15 What is the likely role of the lateral hypothalamus?
16 Identify four *external factors* which may influence eating.
17 What is encouraged by *sensory-specific satiety*?

Section 2: The hypothalamus and eating
18 What did Hetherington & Ranson (1942) discover was the effect of producing lesions in the *ventromedial hypothalami* (VMH) of rats?
19 What is the difference between the *dynamic* and *static phases* of VMH *hyperphagia*?
20 What role does the *dual hypothalamic control theory* of eating give to the LH and the VMH?
21 Under which conditions do VMH-damaged rats *not* eat more food than normal?
22 Under which conditions can LH damaged rats be persuaded to eat normally?
23 Identify three other effects of LH damage in rats.
24 What overall conclusion concerning the importance of the LH and VMH can be reached, based on the research findings?
25 Which *neurotransmitter level* is increased by *carbohydrates*?
26 O'Rahilly *et al.* (cited in Radford, 1997) found low levels of *leptin* in the bodies of two obese cousins. What is the likely role of leptin?

Section 3: Drinking
27 What explanation for drinking does the *dry-mouth theory* of thirst propose?
28 Identify one problem with the dry-mouth theory.
29 To what are certain cells in the *lateral preoptic area* of the hypothalamus sensitive?
30 What is *osmosis*?
31 What is the role of *antidiuretic hormone*, which is produced by osmoreceptors in response to fluid depletion?
32 What causes *volumetric thirst*?
33 What is the role of the hormone *angiotensin*?
34 Which aspect of drinking behaviour is particularly difficult for researchers to explain?
35 What is the difference between *primary* and *secondary* drinking?

Section 1: The causes of hunger

1 *A motive* is an inner directing force which arouses an organism and directs its behaviour towards some goal.

2 *Homeostasis* refers to the body's tendency to maintain a steady state.

3 'An early theory proposed that the *stomach* sent information about hunger to the brain via the *vagus nerve*.'

4 Washburn swallowed a balloon attached to a tube so that his stomach contractions could be measured, whilst at the same time recording his hunger pangs.

5 People whose stomachs have been removed still report feeling hungry, and cutting the connections between the gastrointestinal tract and the brain has little effect on food intake (Pinel, 1993).

6 Injections of glucose into the liver cause a decrease in eating.

7 According to *glucostatic theory*, the primary stimulus for hunger is a decrease in the level of blood-glucose below a certain set-point.

8 *Insulin injections* lower blood glucose levels and stimulate eating.

9 Meyer & Marshall (1956) believed that glucoreceptors were located in the *ventromedial hypothalamus*.

10 The finding suggests that it cannot be glucose levels alone which regulate eating behaviour, since the animals' blood glucose levels are lowered slightly despite the constant calorie intake.

11 *Adipose tissues* are the fatty tissues of the body.

12 Nisbett's (1972) theory claims that fat levels in the adiposites (fat cells) determine the body-weight set-point.

13 Short-term dieting programmes do *not* produce long-term weight loss in humans.

14 *Hypophagia* (the cessation of eating to the point of starvation) usually results in rats in whom the *lateral hypothalamus* has been damaged.

15 The *lateral hypothalamus* affects feeding by altering the body-weight set-point.

16 *Habit, environment, culture*, and *palatability of foods* may all influence eating.

17 *Sensory-specific satiety* (we become tired of one food after a time) encourages the consumption of a *varied diet*.

Section 2: The hypothalamus and eating

18 Hetherington & Ranson (1942) discovered that lesions in the *ventromedial hypothalamus* of rats caused them to *overeat*, doubling or trebling their body weight.

19 In the *dynamic phase* of VMH *hyperphagia*, the animal eats rapidly for several weeks and gains weight. During the *static phase*, the animal attempts to defend a stable level of obesity.

20 The *dual hypothalamic control theory* of eating proposes that the LH 'turns' hunger on and the VMH 'turns' it off.

21 VMH-damaged rats do *not* eat more food than normal if they have to *work* for their food.

22 LH damaged rats can be persuaded to eat normally if they are fed for several weeks through a tube.

23 LH damage in rats also causes them to *cease grooming themselves*, have *difficulty with balance*, and *show little interest in any stimuli*.

24 The LH and VMH are likely to affect the body-weight *set-point*, but are *not* absolutely essential in regulating eating in the long-term.

25 *Carbohydrates* increase *serotonin* levels.

26 *Leptin's* role is apparently to keep the brain informed and regulate appetite and the rate at which calories are consumed.

Section 3: Drinking

27 The *dry-mouth theory* of thirst proposes that receptors in the mouth and throat play a major role in determining thirst.

28 When water is prevented from passing into the stomachs of animals who have swallowed it, they quickly resume drinking ('*sham drinking*' studies).

29 Certain cells in the *lateral preoptic area* of the hypothalamus are sensitive to *cellular dehydration* (an increase in salt levels in the blood).

30 *Osmosis* is the process whereby fluid levels in the cells are affected by salt levels in the blood.

31 *Antidiuretic hormone* causes the kidneys to reabsorb water which would otherwise be excreted as urine.

32 *Volumetric thirst* is caused by a lowering of the volume of blood in the body, which in turn lowers blood pressure.

33 *Angiotensin* is released by the kidneys and circulates to the hypothalamus, resulting in the initiation of drinking behaviour.

34 It is difficult to explain why we normally stop drinking well before the new supply of fluid reaches the blood.

35 *Primary* drinking occurs when there is a physiological need, whilst *secondary* drinking is drinking not caused by such a need.

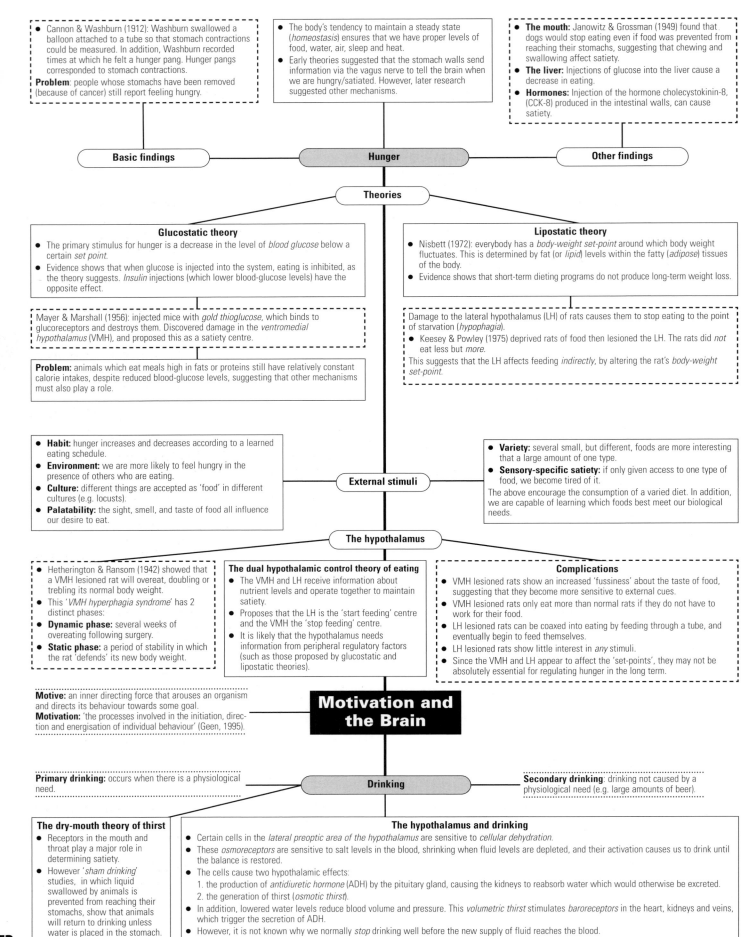

Hunger

Basic findings

- Cannon & Washburn (1912): Washburn swallowed a balloon attached to a tube so that stomach contractions could be measured. In addition, Washburn recorded times at which he felt a hunger pang. Hunger pangs corresponded to stomach contractions.
- **Problem**: people whose stomachs have been removed (because of cancer) still report feeling hungry.

- The body's tendency to maintain a steady state (*homeostasis*) ensures that we have proper levels of food, water, air, sleep and heat.
- Early theories suggested that the stomach walls send information via the vagus nerve to tell the brain when we are hungry/satiated. However, later research suggested other mechanisms.

Other findings

- **The mouth:** Janowitz & Grossman (1949) found that dogs would stop eating even if food was prevented from reaching their stomachs, suggesting that chewing and swallowing affect satiety.
- **The liver:** Injections of glucose into the liver cause a decrease in eating.
- **Hormones:** Injection of the hormone cholecystokinin-8, (CCK-8) produced in the intestinal walls, can cause satiety.

Theories

Glucostatic theory

- The primary stimulus for hunger is a decrease in the level of *blood glucose* below a certain *set point*.
- Evidence shows that when glucose is injected into the system, eating is inhibited, as the theory suggests. *Insulin* injections (which lower blood-glucose levels) have the opposite effect.

Mayer & Marshall (1956): injected mice with *gold thioglucose*, which binds to glucoreceptors and destroys them. Discovered damage in the *ventromedial hypothalamus* (VMH), and proposed this as a satiety centre.

Problem: animals which eat meals high in fats or proteins still have relatively constant calorie intakes, despite reduced blood-glucose levels, suggesting that other mechanisms must also play a role.

Lipostatic theory

- Nisbett (1972): everybody has a *body-weight set-point* around which body weight fluctuates. This is determined by fat (or *lipid*) levels within the fatty (*adipose*) tissues of the body.
- Evidence shows that short-term dieting programs do not produce long-term weight loss.

Damage to the lateral hypothalamus (LH) of rats causes them to stop eating to the point of starvation (*hypophagia*).
- Keesey & Powley (1975) deprived rats of food then lesioned the LH. The rats did *not* eat less but *more*.
This suggests that the LH affects feeding *indirectly*, by altering the rat's *body-weight set-point*.

External stimuli

- **Habit:** hunger increases and decreases according to a learned eating schedule.
- **Environment:** we are more likely to feel hungry in the presence of others who are eating.
- **Culture:** different things are accepted as 'food' in different cultures (e.g. locusts).
- **Palatability:** the sight, smell, and taste of food all influence our desire to eat.

- **Variety:** several small, but different, foods are more interesting that a large amount of one type.
- **Sensory-specific satiety:** if only given access to one type of food, we become tired of it.
The above encourage the consumption of a varied diet. In addition, we are capable of learning which foods best meet our biological needs.

The hypothalamus

- Hetherington & Ransom (1942) showed that a VMH lesioned rat will overeat, doubling or trebling its normal body weight.
- This 'VMH hyperphagia syndrome' has 2 distinct phases:
- **Dynamic phase:** several weeks of overeating following surgery.
- **Static phase:** a period of stability in which the rat 'defends' its new body weight.

The dual hypothalamic control theory of eating
- The VMH and LH receive information about nutrient levels and operate together to maintain satiety.
- Proposes that the LH is the 'start feeding' centre and the VMH the 'stop feeding' centre.
- It is likely that the hypothalamus needs information from peripheral regulatory factors (such as those proposed by glucostatic and lipostatic theories).

Complications
- VMH lesioned rats show an increased 'fussiness' about the taste of food, suggesting that they become more sensitive to external cues.
- VMH lesioned rats only eat more than normal rats if they do not have to work for their food.
- LH lesioned rats can be coaxed into eating by feeding through a tube, and eventually begin to feed themselves.
- LH lesioned rats show little interest in *any* stimuli.
- Since the VMH and LH appear to affect the 'set-points', they may not be absolutely essential for regulating hunger in the long term.

Motive: an inner directing force that arouses an organism and directs its behaviour towards some goal.
Motivation: 'the processes involved in the initiation, direction and energisation of individual behaviour' (Geen, 1995).

Motivation and the Brain

Drinking

Primary drinking: occurs when there is a physiological need.

Secondary drinking: drinking not caused by a physiological need (e.g. large amounts of beer).

The dry-mouth theory of thirst
- Receptors in the mouth and throat play a major role in determining satiety.
- However 'sham drinking' studies, in which liquid swallowed by animals is prevented from reaching their stomachs, show that animals will return to drinking unless water is placed in the stomach.

The hypothalamus and drinking
- Certain cells in the *lateral preoptic area* of the hypothalamus are sensitive to *cellular dehydration*.
- These *osmoreceptors* are sensitive to salt levels in the blood, shrinking when fluid levels are depleted, and their activation causes us to drink until the balance is restored.
- The cells cause two hypothalamic effects:
  1. the production of *antidiuretic hormone* (ADH) by the pituitary gland, causing the kidneys to reabsorb water which would otherwise be excreted.
  2. the generation of thirst (*osmotic thirst*).
- In addition, lowered water levels reduce blood volume and pressure. This *volumetric thirst* stimulates *baroreceptors* in the heart, kidneys and veins, which trigger the secretion of ADH.
- However, it is not known why we normally *stop* drinking well before the new supply of fluid reaches the blood.

17

THEORIES OF MOTIVATION

SYLLABUS
3.4 Motivation, emotion and stress
- research into the relationship between brain systems and motivation
- physiological and non-physiological theories of motivation

KEY QUESTIONS
- What different types of motive are there?
- How do instinct theories explain motivation?
- How do drive theories explain motivation?
- How do optimum level of arousal and incentive theories explain motivation?
- How do Maslow and opponent-process theorists explain motivation?

Section 1: Types of motive

1 What name is given to *motives* which are rooted primarily in body tissue needs?
2 What are *sensation-seeking motives*?
3 Identify two effects of sensory deprivation.
4 Identify two types of sensation-seeking motive which are often activated by the new or unknown.
5 What is the sensation-seeking motive known as *manipulation*?
6 What does Brehm (1966) mean by *psychological reactance*?
7 What do psychologists generally believe is the purpose of the motivation to *seek stimulation*?
8 In what important way do complex *psychosocial motives* differ from other classes of motive?
9 What psychosocial need does McClelland (1958) suggest can be measured using the *thematic apperception test*?
10 What is the *need for affiliation*?
11 Identify two other complex psychosocial needs.

Section 2: Instinct theories

12 What is the principal claim made by *instinct theories* of motivation?
13 Why were such theories particularly popular in the early twentieth century?
14 In what way was the reasoning of early instinct theorists 'circular'?
15 What does the term *fixed action pattern*, used by ethologists, mean?
16 What is the role of the self-vocalisations produced by ducklings whilst still within the egg?

Section 3: Drive theories

17 What do *sociobiologists* see as the primary motivation for all our behaviours?
18 To what did Woodworth (1918) liken human behaviour?
19 What is the major difference between *homeostatic drive theory* and *drive reduction theory*?
20 How did Cannon (1929) define *homeostasis*?
21 Complete the sentence: 'When we are thirsty a ___ need leads to an internal ___ which causes a ___ drive'.
22 According to drive reduction theory, what is a '*drive state*'?
23 In what way do such states activate behaviour?
24 In what way are *primary drives* different from *secondary drives*?
25 Why is it difficult for drive theories to explain behaviours such as 'stamp collecting'?
26 Why do people who refuse to eat snacks (despite being hungry) in order to enjoy their lunch more, apparently contradict drive reduction theory?

Section 4: Arousal and incentive theories

27 What did Olds & Milner (1954) discover when they allowed a rat to stimulate its own '*pleasure centre*' by means of an electrode placed in its hypothalamus?
28 What does *optimum level of arousal* (OLA) *theory* suggest is an important motivation?
29 According to Zuckerman (1979), what are '*sensation-seekers*'?
30 What is the major problem with OLA theory?
31 How does *incentive theory* differ from other theories of motivation mentioned above?
32 How do experiments with rats and saccharin (Sheffield & Roby, 1955) support incentive theory?
33 What is *work motivation*?
34 Under which three conditions is work motivation high?
35 How do *intrinsic* and *extrinsic rewards* differ?

Section 5: Opponent-process and Maslow's theories

36 According to *opponent-process theory*, what does every emotional experience elicit?
37 What has opponent-process theory been particularly useful in explaining?
38 According to Maslow (1954), how can our needs be organised?
39 How do *D-motives* and *B-motives* differ?
40 What is the principal difficulty with concepts such as *self-actualisation*?

Section 1: Types of motive

1 *Biologically-based motives*.

2 *Sensation-seeking motives* are apparently largely unlearned needs for certain levels of stimulation.

3 *Sensory deprivation* commonly produces *hallucinations, difficulty in thinking clearly, boredom, anger* and *frustration*.

4 *Curiosity* and *exploration* are often activated by the new or unknown.

5 *Manipulation* refers to our desire to touch, handle or play with a specific object before we are satisfied.

6 *Psychological reactance* is the term that describes our tendency to re-assert our freedom when it is threatened.

7 The motivation to *seek stimulation* probably evolved to increase an organism's chances of survival by motivating it to gather information about its surroundings.

8 *Complex psychosocial motives*, unlike other classes of motive, are acquired by learning, and aroused by psychological events.

9 McClelland (1958) suggests that *need for achievement* can be measured using the *thematic apperception test*.

10 The *need for affiliation* is the desire to maintain close, friendly relations with others.

11 The *need for power* and the *need for approval* are both psychosocial needs.

Section 2: Instinct theories

12 *Instinct theories* of motivation see us as possessing innate predispositions to act in a particular way in response to a certain stimulus.

13 Such theories were popular largely due to Darwin's emphasis on the similarity between humans and other animals.

14 Early instinct theorists argued for the existence of instincts on the basis of observed behaviours, and also explained behaviours by reference to these instincts.

15 A *fixed action pattern* is an unlearned behaviour (universal to all members of a species) which occurs in the presence of a naturally occurring stimulus.

16 The self-vocalisations enable the duckling to *discriminate maternal calls*.

Section 3: Drive theories

17 *Sociobiologists* see the desire to ensure the future survival of our genes as the primary motivation for all our behaviours.

18 Woodworth (1918) likened human behaviour to the *operation of a machine*.

19 *Homeostatic drive theory* is a *physiological* theory whilst *drive reduction theory* is primarily a *learning* theory.

20 Cannon (1929) defined *homeostasis* as an optimum level of physiological functioning that maintains an organism in a constant internal state.

21 'When we are thirsty a *tissue* need leads to an *internal* imbalance which causes a *homeostatic* drive.'

22 A drive state is an unpleasant state of bodily arousal.

23 *Drive states* activate behaviour by motivating us to reduce the tension associated with them.

24 *Primary drives* are biological needs, whilst *secondary drives* help reduce primary drives and are learned by association.

25 Stamp collecting is not a behaviour which can sensibly be explained by proposing a 'stamp collecting *drive*'.

26 Such behaviours seem to increase rather than reduce certain drives.

Section 4: Arousal and incentive theories

27 Olds & Milner (1954) discovered that rats would stimulate this area in preference to doing anything else, and that this behaviour *never satiated*.

28 *Optimum level of arousal theory* suggests that the *desire for a certain level of stimulation* is an important motivation.

29 Zuckerman (1979) identifies *sensation-seekers* as those people with high optimum levels of arousal.

30 *OLA theory* cannot be tested since we cannot measure an organism's level of arousal.

31 *Incentive theory* proposes that we are motivated by external stimuli (incentives) rather that internal states.

32 Sheffield & Roby (1955) found that rats will work hard for a sip of saccharin even though saccharin cannot reduce a tissue need (it has no nutritional value).

33 *Work motivation* is our tendency to expend effort and energy on a job.

34 Work motivation is high when hard work will improve performance, performance will *yield rewards* and these rewards are *valued*.

35 *Intrinsic rewards* are the pleasure and satisfaction which a task brings, whilst *extrinsic rewards* are those which are given beyond a task's intrinsic pleasures.

Section 5: Opponent-process and Maslow's theories

36 According to *opponent-process theory*, every emotional experience elicits a more intense opposite emotional experience.

37 Opponent-process theory been particularly useful in explaining *drug addiction*.

38 Maslow (1954) argues that our needs can be organised in a *hierarchy*, with basic physiological needs at the bottom, and more complex and psychological needs higher up.

39 *D-motives* are those relating to deficiencies which are associated with our survival, whilst *B-motives* give rise to behaviours which relate to 'self-actualisation' or 'being'.

40 Concepts such as *self-actualisation* are difficult to define operationally, and consequently difficult to study experimentally.

Sensation-seeking motives

Needs for certain levels of stimulation, largely learned:

- **Activity:** all animals need to be active; sensory deprivation studies show that inactivity is intolerable.
- **Curiosity and exploration:** humans and non-humans are motivated by the unknown and the desire to 'find out'.
- **Manipulation:** primates seem to have the need for tactile experiences which they direct towards a specific object.

In addition, many species demonstrate a need for *play* (which is often 'practice play'), *contact* (touching others), and *control* (the need to determine our own actions)

Types of motive

Biologically-based motives

- Rooted primarily in body tissue needs (e.g. need for food, air, water, sleep).
- Although these needs are in-built, their expression is often learned

Complex psychosocial motives

Needs aroused by psychological events and acquired by learning:

- **Need for achievement** (nAch): the need to meet or exceed some standard.
- **Need for affiliation** (nAff): the desire to maintain close, friendly relations with others.
- **Need for power** (nPower): a concern with being in charge, having status and prestige.
- **Need for approval** (nApp): the desire for some sign that others like us or think we are good.

Theories of Motivation

Instinct theories

Propose that we possess *innate* or *genetically pre-determined dispositions* to act in a certain way. Largely due to the Darwinian emphasis on the similarity of humans to animals.

- Early theories fell into disrepute due to disagreement over the number of instincts (up to 15,000 were identified), and a tendency of theorists to propose a new instinct to explain any observed behaviour (e.g. a 'cleanliness instinct').
- *Ethologists* revived and revised instinct theory, coining the term '*fixed action pattern*' to describe unlearned behaviours which are 'released' automatically in the presence of certain stimuli (e.g. aggressive behaviour in sticklebacks in response to a red patch (Tinbergen, 1951)).

Sociobiology

- Sociobiologists argue that innate tendencies play an important role in complex human behaviour, with the primary motive to ensure the survival of one's genes.
- However, such 'selfish gene' explanations of human behaviour may underestimate the role of situational and personal variables.

Drive theories

Homeostatic drive theory

- Cannon (1929) saw organisms as trying to achieve an optimum level of physiological functioning by maintaining a constant internal state (*homeostasis*).
- Tissue needs (e.g. dehydration) lead to imbalances which lead to homeostatic drives, causing the organism to behave in a way which restores the balance (e.g. eating when hungry).

Drive reduction theory

- States of need lead to unpleasant states of bodily arousal *(drive states)* which activate behaviours required to reduce them.
- *Primary drives* (such as hunger) are supplemented by *secondary drives* (e.g. the drive for money), which we acquire through association.
- However, not all behaviours are obviously motivated by drives – and some seem to *increase* rather than reduce certain drives (e.g. carefully preparing a meal). Finally, Olds & Milner (1954) discovered that a rat that could stimulate an electrode placed in the 'pleasure centre' of its hypothalamus, would do so *endlessly*.

Optimum level of arousal theory

- We have a preference for an optimum level of arousal (OLA) and that when arousal falls *below* this level, we are motivated to raise it by increasing stimulation; when arousal rises *above* this level, we decrease stimulation.
- People with a *low* OLA may prefer sedentary lifestyles, whereas those with a *high* OLA ('*sensation-seekers*') may prefer to engage in activities such as driving fast cars.
- Unfortunately, there is no way of measuring an organism's OLA independently of its behaviour.

Incentive (expectancy) theory

- *External* stimuli (instead of internal drives) motivate us in certain directions in the absence of physiological states.
- The expectation of achieving a desirable goal (incentive) motivates us to perform behaviours. Undesirable goals inhibit behaviours.
- *Work motivation* describes our tendency to expend effort and energy on a job and will be increased if a) hard work improves performance, b) good performance yields rewards, c) such rewards are valued (Mitchell & Larson, 1987).
- Rotter (1966) proposes that expectations and values affect whether a behaviour is performed or not.

Opponent-process theory

Solomon & Corbit (1974) point to the fact that some motives are clearly acquired.

- Argue that every emotional experience elicits a more intense *opposite* emotional experience which persists long after the primary emotion it developed from, and diminishes the intensity of the primary emotion.
- Repeated pleasurable experiences eventually lose their pleasantness (shifting the driving force from pleasure to pain).
- Repeated unpleasurable experiences eventually lose their unpleasantness (shifting the driving force from pain to pleasure).

Drug addiction

- The initial pleasure produced by the drug is followed by a gradual decline and then a minor craving for it.
- When addiction occurs the drug is taken to avoid the pain of withdrawal rather than the experiences of pleasure.

Maslow's theory

Maslow (1954): behaviour is motivated by the desire for personal growth (*self-actualisation*).

- Human needs can be organised into a hierarchy. Lower needs need to be satisfied before higher, more complex needs.
- Behaviours related to survival have '*deficiency*' (D-motive) causes. Behaviours related to self-actualisation have '*being*' (B-motive) causes.
- Critics point out that the 'self-actualisation' is difficult to define, and that the order in which needs are satisfied often differs from the order in the hierarchy.

Freud's theory

Behaviour is controlled by unconscious motives closely related to instincts.

- Originally Freud saw all human behaviour as rooted in '*Eros*' (the drive for 'bodily pleasure').
- Later he argued that '*Thanatos*' (a drive for self-destruction) also influences behaviour.
- Unfortunately, it is difficult to test such a theory since unconscious motives cannot be observed directly.

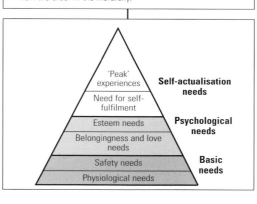

18

EMOTION AND THE BRAIN

SYLLABUS
3.4 Motivation, emotion and stress
- research into the relationship between brain systems and emotion
- physiological theories of motivation and emotion

KEY QUESTIONS
- What is the role of the hypothalamus in emotion?
- What is the role of the limbic system in emotion?
- What is the role of the cortex in emotion?
- What sex differences are there in emotion?

Q

Section 1: The hypothalamus
1 What did Bard (1928) discover was the effect of destroying parts of the cerebral cortex in cats and dogs?
2 Complete the sentence: 'Bard concluded that the cortex normally acts as an ___ of sub-cortical structures responsible for the production of emotional behaviour'.
3 What was the consequence of removing the *hypothalamus* following decortication?
4 What is the behavioural consequence of stimulating the *dorsal part* of the hypothalamus of non-humans?
5 What did Sem-Jocobsen (1968) discover when investigating *hypothalamic stimulation* in humans?

Section 2: The limbic system
6 What is *Klüver–Bucy syndrome*?
7 What is *hyperorality* (one of the symptoms of Klüver–Bucy syndrome)?
8 Identify four other symptoms of Klüver–Bucy syndrome.
9 According to Klüver & Bucy (1937), how does damage to the *limbic system* affect fearfulness and aggression in monkeys?
10 What is the effect of destroying the *amygdala* of wild monkeys?
11 What two effects associated with the stimulation of different parts of the amygdala have been observed in cats?
12 In the case study conducted by Mark & Ervin (1970), what procedure was carried out to reduce Julia's aggressive behaviour?
13 What effect did the destruction of areas of the amygdala have on DR (Calder *et al.*, cited in Spinney, 1997b)?
14 What did Brady & Nauta (1953) discover was the effect of lesions in the *septum* of rats?
15 Complete the following sequence of structures involved in the Papez circuit (1937): 'hippocampus, ___, anterior thalamus, ___ ___, entorhinal cortex, hippocampus'.
16 What evidence did Delgado (1969) produce for the existence of an *aggression centre*?

17 What was Valenstein's (1973) criticism of Delgado's claims?

Section 3: The cerebral hemispheres
18 What is the role of the *corpus callosum*?
19 What do studies in which the corpus callosum is surgically divided tell us about the two hemispheres?
20 Which side of the body is likely to be paralysed in a patient displaying an *indifference reaction* following brain damage?
21 What stimuli were used by Ley & Bryden (1979) in studying the processing of emotional states in people with normally functioning hemispheres?
22 Under what conditions were fewer recognition errors made by the right hemisphere in Ley and Bryden's study?
23 Complete the sentence: 'PET scans have shown that the left hemisphere is more active during ___ emotional experiences'.
24 What are the two difficulties which Ross (1981) identifies as being caused by damage to different areas of the *right hemisphere*?
25 According to Day & Wong (1996), how does the hemispheric functioning of *dissocial individuals* differ from that of normal people?

Section 4: Sex differences
26 What two explanations did Broca (cited in Kohn, 1995) give for the lower average weight of the female brain?
27 According to Kimura (1993), in what two abilities do male and female brains differ?
28 What are the hypothesised roles of the *temporal–limbic system* and the *cingulate gyrus*?
29 What did Gur *et al.* (cited in Highfield, 1995a) discover when using PET to investigate sex differences in the functioning of these two systems?

Section 1: The hypothalamus

1 Bard (1928) discovered that destroying parts of the cerebral cortex in cats and dogs caused a lower threshold of emotional excitation.

2 'Bard concluded that the cortex normally acts as an *inhibitor* of sub-cortical structures responsible for the production of emotional behaviour.'

3 The rage produced by decortication disappeared if the hypothalamus was also removed.

4 Stimulating the *dorsal part* of the hypothalamus causes non-humans to make frantic attempts to escape the cage in which they are housed.

5 Sem-Jocobsen (1968) discovered that *hypothalamic stimulation* in humans had little effect on emotional experiences.

Section 2: The limbic system

6 *Klüver–Bucy syndrome* is the name given to the five main consequences of damage to the temporal lobes of monkeys.

7 *Hyperorality* is the tendency of monkeys to eat any food given to them, and to put moveable objects into their mouths.

8 Klüver–Bucy syndrome also includes *visual agnosia, hypersexuality*, becoming *tame and easier to handle*, and displaying a *complete lack of fear*.

9 Klüver and Bucy (1937) found that damage to the *limbic system* decreases fearfulness and increases aggression in monkeys.

10 Destroying the *amygdala* causes the monkeys to become tame and placid.

11 Stimulation of different parts of a cat's amygdala causes either preparation to attack or cowering in terror.

12 Julia's aggressive behaviour was reduced by *psychosurgery* in the form of a small lesion to her amygdala.

13 DR was unable to differentiate whether people were angry, happy or sad from the tone of their voices, and could not detect facial expressions of emotion.

14 Brady & Nauta (1953) discovered that lesions in the *septum* of rats resulted in the lowering of the rat's 'rage threshold'.

15 'hippocampus, *hypothalamus*, anterior thalamus, *cingulate gyrus*, entorhinal cortex, hippocampus.'

16 Delgado (1969) showed that stimulating a charging bull's limbic system resulted in the bull stopping in its tracks.

17 Valenstein's (1973) argued that the bull was simply 'confused' and 'frustrated' and gave up (rather than ceasing to be aggressive).

Section 3: The cerebral hemispheres

18 The *corpus callosum* connects the two cerebral hemispheres and allows them to exchange information.

19 Such studies suggest that the two hemispheres are not functionally symmetrical, but specialised for the performance of different tasks.

20 An *indifference reaction* is most likely to be produced in people with *left-sided paralysis*.

21 Ley & Bryden (1979) showed participants drawings of faces displaying different emotional expressions.

22 Fewer recognition errors were made by the right hemisphere when the drawings displayed clear emotional states.

23 'PET scans have shown that the left hemisphere is more active during *positive* emotional experiences.'

24 Ross (1981) identifies difficulty in producing facial gestures and difficulty in recognising facial gestures as being caused by damage to different areas of the *right hemisphere*.

25 Day & Wong (1996) found that *dissocial* individuals do not show a right ('emotional') hemisphere advantage as do normal people when responding to negative emotional words.

Section 4: Sex differences

26 Broca believed that '*physical inferiority*' and '*intellectual inferiority*' were the causes of the lower average weight of the female brain.

27 Kimura (1993) claims that male and female brains differ with regard to *spatial ability* and *language ability*.

28 The *temporal–limbic system* has been associated with 'action-oriented' responses such as sexual arousal and violence, whilst the *cingulate gyrus* has been associated with 'symbolic' modes of expression.

29 Gur *et al.* (cited in Highfield, 1995a) discovered that brain metabolism was identical for the two sexes, except in the *temporal–limbic system*, where metabolism was higher in men than in women, and the *cingulate gyrus*, where metabolism was higher in women than in men.

The limbic system

The cerebral hemispheres

Klüver & Bucy's (1937) research

Klüver–Bucy syndrome

Describes the five main consequences of damage to the temporal lobes of monkeys:

1. *Hyperorality*: the monkeys ate any food given to them and tended to put anything movable into their mouths.
2. *Visual agnosia*: they were unable to recognise objects by sight.
3. *Hypersexuality*: increased and often inappropriate sexuality.
4. Tamer and safer to handle.
5. Displayed a complete lack of fear.

Klüver and Bucy – further research

- Showed that damage to the limbic system affected the emotional behaviour of monkeys (e.g. increased aggression and decreased fearfulness).
- Noted that the destruction of the amygdala made wild and ferocious monkeys tame and placid. Similar results were found in other species.
- Electrical stimulation of the amygdala in cats caused different responses depending on the part stimulated. Cats would either a) arch their backs, hiss and show signs of attack or b) cower in terror (e.g. in response to a small mouse).

Applications – psychosurgery

Klüver, Bucy and others' findings were instrumental in developing psychosurgery:

- Mark & Ervin (1970): cite the case of Julia, a young woman who committed unprovoked attacks on 12 people. Tests suggested that the amygdala was damaged, and a small lesion produced by surgeons in the amygdala greatly reduced her aggressive behaviour.
- However, some people have pointed out that there is an important (and ethical) distinction to be drawn between the removal of damaged tissue and the damaging of otherwise healthy tissue by psychosurgery.
- Calder *et al.* (cited in Spinney, 1997b), report the case of DR, whose operation to treat epilepsy resulted in the destruction of her left amygdala and partial destruction of her right. Her subsequent inability to tell if people are happy or detect emotion from facial expressions or tone of voice suggest that the amygdala interprets all emotional signals.

The Papez circuit

Papez (1937) proposed that a complex set of interconnected pathways and centres in the limbic system form a closed loop which underlie emotional experience:

- *hippocampus → hypothalamus → anterior thalamus → cingulate gyrus → entorhinal cortex → hippocampus.*

However, Maclean (1949) has suggested that the *amygdala* and hippocampus play a central role in the mediation of aggression whilst the cingulate gyrus does not.

The corpus callosum and hemispheric specialisation

The two cerebral hemispheres are connected by the corpus callosum. Split-brain studies suggests that this acts as a '*channel of communication*' between the two hemispheres which are specialised for different tasks (see Ch. 9).

- A study in 1908 reports of a mentally disturbed woman whose left hand tried to choke her whilst her right tried to pull it away. A post-mortem revealed that the corpus callosum was badly damaged.

Studies of brain-damaged patients

- People with *right* hemisphere damage suffer paralysis of the left side but seem unmoved by this (*indifference reaction*), whereas those with *left* hemisphere damage suffer anxiety and depression in response to their paralysis (*catastrophic reaction*).
- This suggests that the right hemisphere is specialised for recognising and responding to emotion-provoking stimuli (such as brain damage), whilst the left hemisphere is not.
- However, Davidson (1992) points out that the left hemisphere is not 'unemotional' and has been shown (using PET scans) to be more active during the experience of *positive* emotions.
- Ross (1981) found that damage to different areas of the right hemisphere caused difficulty in interpreting or producing facial expressions, depending on where the damage occurred, suggesting that different cortical areas play different roles.

Studies of people with normal hemispheric function

- Ley & Bryden (1979) showed participants drawings of faces depicting emotional expressions, in such a way that they were only perceived by one or other of the hemispheres.
- The right hemisphere made fewer recognition errors when the drawings depicted clear emotional states, suggesting that the right hemisphere has an advantage in recognising clear facial expressions of emotion.

Reciprocal activity

According to Sackheim (1982), the two hemispheres operate in a *reciprocal* manner, with activity in one producing reciprocal activity in the other:

- extremely excited reactions might be caused by a failure of the right hemisphere to reciprocate the activity of the left hemisphere,
- extremely sad or angry reactions might be caused by a failure of the left hemisphere to reciprocate the activity of the right hemisphere.

Studies of non-humans

- Bard (1928) found that destroying part of the cerebral cortex in cats or dogs resulted in a lowered threshold of emotional excitation.
- Bard concluded that the cortex normally acts to *inhibit* sub-cortical structures, which are responsible for producing emotional behaviour.
- Bard also discovered that the 'rage' produced by decortication largely disappeared if the hypothalamus was also removed. *Stimulation* of the hypothalamus can also produce the rage described above.

The hypothalamus

Studies of humans

- Sem-Jacobsen (1968) found that hypothalamic stimulation had little effect on the emotional experiences of humans.
- Studies of people with damage to the hypothalamus show little change in emotional experiences.

Studying the hypothalamus – techniques

The hypothalamus controls the endocrine system via connections to the pituitary gland. Large hypothalamic lesions kill an animal by disrupting the endocrine system.

- Ellison & Flynn (1968) developed a technique in which two knives rotated around the hypothalamus preserved the connection to the pituitary whilst severing all other connections. However, even under these circumstances, some aggressive behaviours could be elicited in cats.

Research

- Gur *et al.* (cited in Highfield, 1995a) used PET to study the brain activity in men and women who were relaxed.
- Brain metabolism was identical except in the *temporal–limbic system* (where metabolism was higher in men) and the *cingulate gyrus* (where metabolism was higher in women).

Gender differences

The average male brain weighs more than the average female brain, and seems to differ in some respects (such as spatial ability and language ability: Kimura, 1993).

Explanations

- It has been hypothesised that the temporal–limbic system is associated with 'action-oriented' emotional responses, and the cingulate gyrus with 'symbolic' modes of expression.
- Gur *et al.* propose that their findings suggest a biological basis for a male tendency to express themselves physically, whilst women are more inclined to 'talk things through'.

THEORIES OF EMOTION

SYLLABUS

3.4 Motivation, emotion and stress
- research into the relationship between brain systems and emotion
- physiological and non-physiological theories of emotion

KEY QUESTIONS
- How does the James–Lange theory explain emotion?
- How does the Cannon–Bard theory explain emotion?
- How does Schachter's theory explain emotion?
- How does Lazarus's theory explain emotion?

Section 1: The James–Lange theory

1 How does the *James–Lange theory* of emotion run counter to common sense?
2 Complete the sentence: 'For the James–Lange theory, emotions are a ___-___ of automatic behavioural or physiological responses'.
3 Which brain structure is responsible for interpreting bodily changes as an emotion?
4 What does the James–Lange theory imply about the pattern of physiological responses fed back to the brain with respect to different emotions?
5 What findings were reported by Wolf & Wolff (1947)?
6 What was demonstrated in Marañon's (1924) study, in which participants were injected with adrenaline?
7 What did Hohmann (1966) discover when investigating the emotional experiences of patients with spinal cord injuries?
8 What claim is made by *facial feedback theory*?
9 How did McCanne & Anderson (1987) provide experimental support for facial feedback theory?
10 What physiological processes would explain McCanne & Anderson's (1987) findings?

Section 2: The Cannon–Bard thalamic theory

11 What is the name of the physiological response which Cannon saw as underlying all emotional states?
12 According to the *thalamic theory*, to which two areas does the thalamus simultaneously send impulses?
13 Complete the sentence: 'The sensations of emotion produced in the cortex and the physiological and behavioural responses are seen as ___ from one another'.
14 Identify the two brain structures which are likely to play a more central role in emotion than the thalamus.

Section 3: Schachter's theory

15 According to *Schachter's theory*, what are the two factors upon which an emotion depends?
16 According to Schachter's theory, what determines the *intensity* of an emotion and the *particular emotion* that is experienced?
17 In what way does Schachter's theory view physiological states differently from the James–Lange theory?
18 What was the purpose of Schachter & Singer (1962) injecting participants with *epinephrine*?
19 Which two types of behaviour were exhibited by 'stooges' in Schachter & Singer's (1962) experiment?
20 Why should participants in the '*epinephrine-ignorant*' condition experience changes in their emotional states?
21 Why should participants in the '*epinephrine-informed*' condition *not* experience changes in their emotional states?
22 What were the two experimental conditions in Dutton & Aron's (1974) study?
23 What are people taught in *misattribution therapy*?
24 What three criticisms did Hilgard *et al.* (1979) make of Schachter and Singer's original experiment?

Section 4: Lazarus's theory

25 What does Lazarus (1982) regard as an *essential pre-requisite* for the experience of emotion?
26 Complete the sentence: 'According to Lazarus, emotion reflects a constantly changing ___-___ relationship'.
27 What argument has Zajonc (1984) raised against Lazarus's theory?
28 What does Lazarus use the term *primitive evaluative perception* to describe?
29 What argument concerning the emotional responses of different individuals has been raised by Ekman *et al.* (1985) in support of Lazarus's theory?

Section 1: The James–Lange theory

1 The *James–Lange theory* suggests that rather than emotional states (e.g. sadness) giving rise to behavioural changes (e.g. crying), behavioural changes give rise to emotional states (e.g. crying causes sadness).

2 'For the James–Lange theory, emotions are a *by-product* of automatic behavioural or physiological responses.'

3 The *cortex* is responsible for interpreting bodily changes as emotions.

4 The theory implies that the pattern of physiological responses would have to be *different for each emotion*, if the cortex were to be able to determine which emotion should be experienced.

5 Wolf & Wolff (1947) found that different people display different patterns of physiological activity whilst experiencing the same emotion.

6 Marañon (1924) found that participants did not report emotional overtones to the physiological changes caused by adrenaline.

7 Hohmann (1966) discovered that there was a diminishing of emotional experience for events after the injury, and that the further up the spinal cord the injury was, the less intense were the reported emotional experiences.

8 *Facial feedback theory* claims that facial expressions can produce changes in emotional state as well as mirror them.

9 McCanne & Anderson (1987) asked participants to suppress or exaggerate facial expressions when thinking of either pleasant or unpleasant events, and found that facial expressions can heighten reported emotional reactions.

10 It is possible that contraction of facial muscles affects blood flow to the brain, which in turn influences the release of *serotonin* and *noradrenaline* (believed to play a role in emotion).

Section 2: The Cannon–Bard thalamic theory

11 Cannon saw the *'fight-or-flight'* response as underlying all emotional states.

12 The *thalamus* simultaneously sends impulses to the *cortex* and the *hypothalamus*.

13 'The sensations of emotion produced in the cortex and the physiological and behavioural responses are seen as *independent* from one another.'

14 The *limbic system* and the *hypothalamus* are likely to play a more central role in emotion than the *thalamus*.

Section 3: Schachter's theory

15 According to Schachter's theory, an emotion depends on *physiological arousal in the ANS* and the *cognitive appraisal* (interpretation) of this arousal.

16 The *intensity* of an emotion is determined by the *degree of arousal*, whilst the *particular emotion* that is experienced is determined by the *interpretation* of the arousal.

17 Schachter's theory sees a single physiological state as being responsible for all emotions, whilst the James–Lange theory proposed different states for different emotions.

18 *Epinephrine* was injected in order to produce increased heart rate, respiration rate, blood pressure and muscle tremors.

19 Stooges in these experiments behaved either *'angrily'* or *'euphorically'*.

20 Participants in the *'epinephrine-ignorant'* condition should experience arousal and have no obvious explanation for it, so should attribute it to some change in emotional state.

21 Participants in the *'epinephrine-informed'* condition should experience arousal, but since they are expecting these effects they will attribute them to the drug and *not* to a change in emotional state.

22 Dutton & Aron (1974) had female researchers approach male participants on either a high, unstable, suspension bridge or a low, stable, wooden bridge.

23 During *misattribution therapy*, people are taught to attribute maladaptive arousal (e.g. a phobia) to some other source (e.g a pill they have just taken).

24 Hilgard *et al.* (1979) criticised the experiment for overlooking that epinephrine does not affect everyone in the same way, for failing to assess the mood of the participants before they were given the injection, and for ignoring the fact that some people are extremely afraid of injections.

Section 4: Lazarus's theory

25 Lazarus (1982) regards some *cognitive processing* as an essential pre-requisite for the experience of emotion.

26 'According to Lazarus, emotion reflects a constantly changing *person–environment* relationship.'

27 Zajonc (1984) argues that cognition and emotion operate as *independent* systems.

28 Lazarus uses the term *primitive evaluative perception* to describe the sorts of unconscious cognitive appraisal involved in primitive emotional responses (such as fear).

29 Ekman *et al.* (1985) have pointed out that there is no known stimulus which reliably produces the same emotion in everybody.

- According to this theory, an emotional experience is the *result* (not the cause of) bodily and/or behavioural changes (e.g. crying) to some emotion-provoking stimulus. James argued that 'we feel sorry *because* we cry'.
- When we experience a stimulus, physiological reactions and behavioural responses occur which trigger the emotional experience. Emotions are a by-product of such automatic responses. The brain receives sensory feedback from the body's internal organs and parts that respond to the emotion-provoking stimuli. The brain then labels this as an emotion.

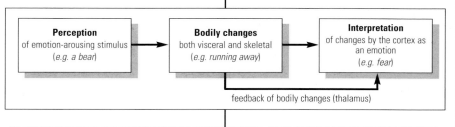

| **Perception** of emotion-arousing stimulus (*e.g. a bear*) | → | **Bodily changes** both visceral and skeletal (*e.g. running away*) | → | **Interpretation** of changes by the cortex as an emotion (*e.g. fear*) |

feedback of bodily changes (thalamus)

3 criticisms of the theory (Cannon, 1927)

| Each emotion would need a distinct pattern of physiological activity or the cortex would be unable to determine which is to be felt:
• Wolf & Wolff (1947): different people experience different patterns of physiological activity when experiencing the same emotion. | Physiological changes do not themselves produce changes in emotional state:
• Marañon (1924) injected participants with adrenaline which caused a physiological change but participants did *not* report an emotional change. | Total separation of the viscera from the CNS does not eliminate emotions:
• Cannon found that when visceral feedback was abolished in cats and dogs, emotional experience was unaffected (although this ignores feedback from the muscles). |

Facial feedback theory

Argues in support of the James–Lange theory that facial expressions can produce changes in emotional state as well as reflect them (e.g. we feel happier when we smile).
- McCanne & Anderson (1987): participants experienced emotions more strongly when they exaggerated facial expressions, and less strongly when they suppressed them.
- Contraction of facial muscles apparently heightens physiological arousal and may affect blood flow to the brain.

Human emotions have four elements: *subjective feelings, cognitive processes, physiological arousal* and *behavioural reactions*.

Theories of Emotion

- Cannon saw all emotions as producing the same pattern of responses (the *fight-or-flight* response).
- External stimuli activate the *thalamus* which sends information to the cortex for interpretation and messages to the viscera and skeletal muscles (via the PNS).

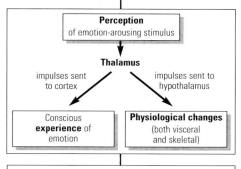

Perception of emotion-arousing stimulus

Thalamus

impulses sent to cortex ← → impulses sent to hypothalamus

| Conscious **experience** of emotion | **Physiological changes** (both visceral and skeletal) |

Because the information sent to the cortex is *independent* of the physiological and behavioural responses, the experience of emotion neither causes nor is a result of bodily changes.

Problems
- The claim that bodily activity is a 'side-effect' of emotion is not supported by the evidence.
- Other brain structures (such as the hypothalamus and the limbic system) seem to be more directly involved in emotion than the thalamus.

- Schachter's (1964) *'two-factor theory of emotion'* proposes that emotional experience depends on two factors: *physiological arousal* in the ANS, and *cognitive appraisal* (interpretation of this arousal).
- Unlike the James–Lange theory, Schachter argues that the same physiological changes underlie all emotional states, and that it is the *meaning* attributed to them that determines different emotions. The interpretation may be influenced by situational cues.

Perception of emotion-arousing stimulus

Physiological changes — *Thalamus sends impulses to cortex* → **Awareness of arousal**

Interpreting the arousal *as an* emotion in the light of the situation

Schachter & Singer (1962):
- Participants were given an injection of *epinephrine* (which causes physiological arousal) and either informed or misinformed as to its effects.
- Participants were exposed to 'stooges' who behaved in either an angry or euphoric way.
- Participants who were *not* informed of the drug's effects reported similar feelings to those of the stooge to whom they were exposed (apparently interpreting their arousal similarly).

Other research
- Dutton & Aron (1974) found that male participants approached by a female researcher whilst crossing an unstable suspension bridge were more likely to invent stories with a high amount of sexual imagery than those approached on a solid wooden bridge (the former interpreting their arousal as sexual attraction).
- Other researchers (e.g. Marshall & Zimbardo, 1979) have had difficulty replicating Schachter and Singer's findings: Maslach (1978) found that participants were more likely to attach negative emotional labels to their arousal, irrespective of the situation.
- Hilgard *et al.* (1979) have pointed out that epinephrine does not affect everyone in the same way, that Schachter and Singer failed to assess the mood of participants *prior* to the experiment, and that some people are extremely afraid of injections.

- Lazarus (1982) argues that some cognitive processing is an essential pre-requisite for the experience of emotion.
- Emotion occurs when 'central life agendas' (e.g. survival, personal values) become an issue in the changing person–environment relationship.

Problems
- Zajonc (1984) argues that cognition does not have primacy over emotion, and that they operate as independent systems.
- Zajonc argues that we have evolved the ability to detect affective qualities without cognitive mediation (e.g. when we meet a person for the first time and form a positive or negative impression despite having processed very little information about the person).

- Lazarus disagrees and argues that even primitive emotional responses (e.g. fear) require some unconscious appraisal ('primitive evaluative perception').
- Ekman *et al.* (1985) point out that there is no known stimulus which reliably produces the same response in all people, supporting Lazarus's theory.

20

STRESS

SYLLABUS
3.4 Motivation, emotion and stress
* theories and research findings concerning the effects of stress on the body, including the relationship between stress and illness
* methods used to reduce stress (e.g. biofeedback and anxiolytic drugs)

KEY QUESTIONS
* What is stress?
* How does stress affect the body?
* What is the relation between stress and illness?
* How can stress be reduced?

Q

Section 1: Introducing stress

1 What did Seyle (1936) discover when he exposed rats to conditions like extreme cold, fatigue, electric shock or the injection of toxic fluids?
2 What term is used to describe any stimulus which produces stress?
3 What is *eustress* (Selye, 1980)?
4 Complete Lazarus & Folkman's (1984) definition of stress: 'Stress is a pattern of ___ physiological states and ___ responses occurring in situations where people perceive ___ to their well-being which they may be unable to meet'.

Section 2: The effects of stress on the body

5 What name is given to the *non-specific response* discovered by Selye?
6 What name is given to the first of the three stages of this response?
7 What is the role of *corticosteroids*, released during the first stage?
8 Identify three physiological factors that are increased by the action of *adrenaline* and *noradrenaline*.
9 What general name is given to the response in which we prepare for physical action?
10 How is the *immune system* affected during the second stage (the *resistance stage*)?
11 During which stage are *stress-related illnesses* most likely to occur?
12 Identify two criticisms of Selye's account of the non-specific responses occurring in response to a stressor.
13 What is involved in the *primary appraisal* of a stressor?
14 Identify two negative emotional states associated with stress.

Section 3: Stress and illness

15 Identify two illnesses with which stress is apparently linked.
16 What is the relationship between *antibodies* and *antigens*?
17 How does the persistent secretion of *steroids* affect the immune system?

18 Identify three events which Esterling & Rabin (1987) found to cause immunological deficiencies in non-humans.
19 What was the stressor that caused wounds to heal more slowly in Sweeney's (1995) study?
20 What are the effects of *acute* and *chronic stressors* on the levels of defensive agents?
21 How were Visintainer *et al.* (1983) able to draw a link between stress and cancer?
22 According to Tache *et al.* (1979), among which groups of people does cancer occur more frequently?
23 What is the principal difficulty with studies of the relationship between stress and cancer in humans?
24 What explanation did Friedman and Rosenman propose for the finding that men are more susceptible to heart disease than women?
25 What are the major characteristics of *Type A personalities* (Friedman & Rosenman, 1974).

Section 4: Reducing stress

26 According to Dixon (1980), how can *humour* help in reducing stress?
27 Identify two disadvantages of using *psychotherapeutic drugs* to reduce stress.
28 What does a *biofeedback machine* do?
29 How is Jacobson's (1938) *progressive relaxation technique* carried out?
30 What did Morris (1953) discover in his study of London bus drivers and conductors?
31 Identify the three main ways in which *hardy* and *non-hardy individuals* differ.
32 What two terms do Lazarus & Folkman (1984) use to distinguish different *coping strategies*?
33 What is *super-person syndrome*?
34 What did Berkman's (1984) research reveal about the effects of *social support*?
35 Identify the three traits/tendencies which are altered in Friedman & Ulmer's (1984) advocated approaches to '*Type A management*'.

Section 1: Introducing stress

1 Seyle (1936) discovered that the *same (non-specific) pattern* of *physiological responses* occurred.

2 A *stressor*.

3 *Eustress* is stress which is healthy and necessary to keep us alert.

4 'Stress is a pattern of *negative* physiological states and *psychological* responses occurring in situations where people perceive *threats* to their well-being which they may be unable to meet.'

Section 2: The effects of stress on the body

5 Selye (1936) called the non-general response the *general adaptation syndrome* (GAS).

6 The first of the three stages is the *alarm reaction*.

7 *Corticosteroids* help to fight inflammation and allergic reactions.

8 *Adrenaline* and *noradrenaline increase heart rate and blood pressure*, the *release of glucose from the liver, respiration rate, blood coaguability*, and *sweating*.

9 The *'fight-or-flight' response* is the general name given to the response in which we prepare for physical action.

10 During the second stage (the *resistance stage*), the immune system's ability to deal with infection or physical damage is reduced.

11 *Stress-related illnesses* are most likely to occur during the *exhaustion stage* (the third stage) of the GAS.

12 Selye's account was largely based on the responses of non-humans to stressors, and fails to take into account psychological factors in the production of stress.

13 The *primary appraisal* of a stressor involves deciding whether it has *positive, negative* or *neutral implications*.

14 *Anger, hostility, embarrassment, depression, helplessness* and *anxiety* are all associated with stress.

Section 3: Stress and illness

15 A link apparently exists between stress and *headaches, asthma, cancer, cardiovascular disorders, hypertension* and the *malfunctioning of the immune system*.

16 *Antibodies* are produced by the immune system and bind to *antigens*, identifying them as targets for destruction.

17 The persistent secretion of *steroids* depresses the immune system by interfering with antibody production.

18 Esterling & Rabin (1987) found that s*eparation from the mother, electric shocks*, and *exposure to loud noise* all cause immunological deficiencies in non-humans.

19 Caring for an elderly relative with dementia caused participants' wounds to heal more slowly in Sweeney's (1995) study.

20 *Acute stressors* are associated with an *increase* in the levels of defensive agents, whilst *chronic stressors* are associated with a *decrease* in these levels.

21 Visintainer *et al.* (1983) injected cancerous cells into non-humans and found that exposure to an uncontrollable stressor dramatically weakened their abilities to resist the cells' effects.

22 Tache *et al.* (1979) found that cancer occurs more frequently among *widowed, divorced* or *separated adults* (compared to those who are married).

23 Studies of the relationship between stress and cancer in humans tend to be *retrospective*, and therefore likely to contain *inaccuracies*.

24 Friedman and Rosenman proposed that the finding that men are more susceptible to heart disease than women may be due to *job-related stress*.

25 *Type A personalities* are *ambitious, competitive, easily angered, time-conscious, hard-driving* and *demanding of perfection* (Friedman & Rosenman, 1974).

Section 4: Reducing stress

26 Dixon (1980) has suggested that *humour* can help by *stimulating endorphin production*.

27 *Psychotherapeutic drugs* lead to *physical dependence* in at least some people, and also have *unpleasant side-effects*.

28 A *biofeedback machine* produces precise information (or feedback) about bodily processes such as heart rate and/or blood pressure.

29 Jacobson's (1938) *progressive relaxation technique* involves tightening, then relaxing, groups of muscles until the whole body is relaxed.

30 Morris (1953) discovered that the conductors were far less likely to suffer from cardiovascular disorders than the sedentary drivers.

31 *Hardy people* are *highly committed* to/involved in whatever they do, *view change as a challenge*, and have a *stronger sense of control* over events in their lives, as compared with *non-hardy individuals* (Kobasa, 1979).

32 Lazarus & Folkman (1984) use the terms *problem-focused* and *emotion-focused* strategies to distinguish different *coping strategies*.

33 *Super-person syndrome* refers to the tendency to take on many tasks and find it difficult to complete any one of them.

34 Berkman (1984) found that people with fewer family, friendship and community ties were more likely to die at a given age than those who had strong ties.

35 Friedman & Ulmer's (1984) *'Type A management'* advocates altering *time-urgency, hostility* and *self-destructive tendencies*.

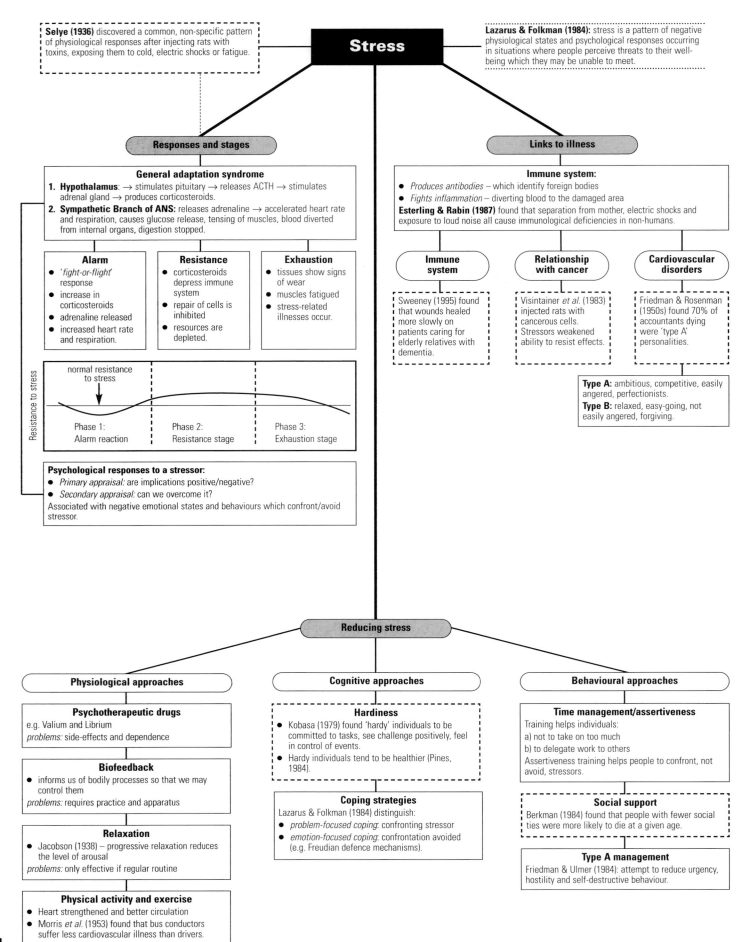

Stress

Selye (1936) discovered a common, non-specific pattern of physiological responses after injecting rats with toxins, exposing them to cold, electric shocks or fatigue.

Lazarus & Folkman (1984): stress is a pattern of negative physiological states and psychological responses occurring in situations where people perceive threats to their well-being which they may be unable to meet.

Responses and stages

General adaptation syndrome
1. **Hypothalamus**: → stimulates pituitary → releases ACTH → stimulates adrenal gland → produces corticosteroids.
2. **Sympathetic Branch of ANS**: releases adrenaline → accelerated heart rate and respiration, causes glucose release, tensing of muscles, blood diverted from internal organs, digestion stopped.

Alarm
- 'fight-or-flight' response
- increase in corticosteroids
- adrenaline released
- increased heart rate and respiration.

Resistance
- corticosteroids depress immune system
- repair of cells is inhibited
- resources are depleted.

Exhaustion
- tissues show signs of wear
- muscles fatigued
- stress-related illnesses occur.

Resistance to stress

normal resistance to stress

Phase 1: Alarm reaction

Phase 2: Resistance stage

Phase 3: Exhaustion stage

Psychological responses to a stressor:
- *Primary appraisal:* are implications positive/negative?
- *Secondary appraisal:* can we overcome it?
Associated with negative emotional states and behaviours which confront/avoid stressor.

Links to illness

Immune system:
- *Produces antibodies* – which identify foreign bodies
- *Fights inflammation* – diverting blood to the damaged area

Esterling & Rabin (1987) found that separation from mother, electric shocks and exposure to loud noise all cause immunological deficiencies in non-humans.

Immune system

Sweeney (1995) found that wounds healed more slowly on patients caring for elderly relatives with dementia.

Relationship with cancer

Visintainer *et al.* (1983) injected rats with cancerous cells. Stressors weakened ability to resist effects.

Cardiovascular disorders

Friedman & Rosenman (1950s) found 70% of accountants dying were 'type A' personalities.

Type A: ambitious, competitive, easily angered, perfectionists.
Type B: relaxed, easy-going, not easily angered, forgiving.

Reducing stress

Physiological approaches

Psychotherapeutic drugs
e.g. Valium and Librium
problems: side-effects and dependence

Biofeedback
- informs us of bodily processes so that we may control them
problems: requires practice and apparatus

Relaxation
- Jacobson (1938) – progressive relaxation reduces the level of arousal
problems: only effective if regular routine

Physical activity and exercise
- Heart strengthened and better circulation
- Morris *et al.* (1953) found that bus conductors suffer less cardiovascular illness than drivers.

Cognitive approaches

Hardiness
- Kobasa (1979) found 'hardy' individuals to be committed to tasks, see challenge positively, feel in control of events.
- Hardy individuals tend to be healthier (Pines, 1984).

Coping strategies
Lazarus & Folkman (1984) distinguish:
- *problem-focused coping:* confronting stressor
- *emotion-focused coping:* confrontation avoided (e.g. Freudian defence mechanisms).

Behavioural approaches

Time management/assertiveness
Training helps individuals:
a) not to take on too much
b) to delegate work to others
Assertiveness training helps people to confront, not avoid, stressors.

Social support
Berkman (1984) found that people with fewer social ties were more likely to die at a given age.

Type A management
Friedman & Ulmer (1984): attempt to reduce urgency, hostility and self-destructive behaviour.

UNIT 3
Cognitive Psychology

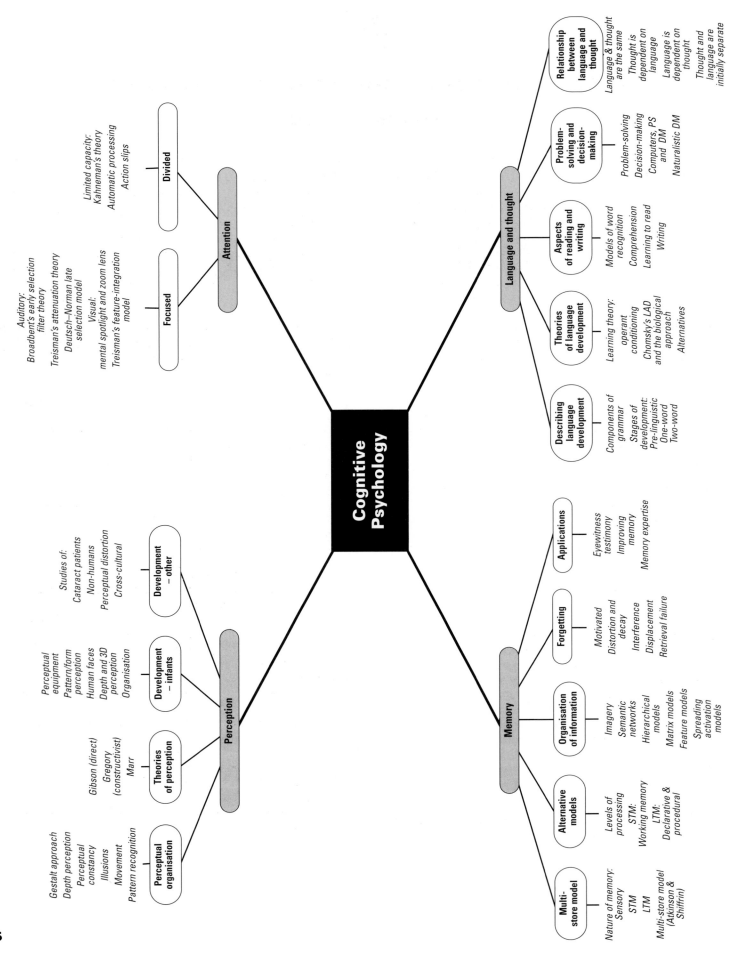

21

VISUAL PERCEPTION AND PERCEPTUAL ORGANISATION

KEY QUESTIONS
- What are sensation and perception?
- How, according to Gestalt psychologists, do we organise perception?
- What cues are used in depth perception?
- How do we perceive illusions, constancies and movement?
- How does pattern recognition occur?

Section 1: Introducing perception
1 How do psychologists define *sensation*?
2 How do psychologists define *perception*?

Section 2: Gestalt psychology
3 Ehrenfels (1890) claimed that many stimuli acquire a pattern quality which gave them 'emergent properties' (e.g. 'squareness') – what name did he give this characteristic?
4 According to Gestalt psychologists, where do the principles for organising sensory information originate?
5 What are 'figure' and 'ground'?
6 Name two factors which may determine whether something is perceived as figure or ground.
7 How does Rubin's vase (Rubin, 1915) demonstrate the figure–ground principle?
8 Gestalt psychologists believed that objects are perceived as *Gestalten*. What does this mean?
9 What is the *law of Prägnanz*?
10 Name three Gestalt laws of perception.
11 What criticisms did Greene (1990) make of the Gestalt approach?
12 What experiment did Navon (1977) perform to test the idea that the whole is perceived before the parts?
13 Why did some critics claim that Gestalt laws have low ecological validity?

Section 3: Depth perception
14 What is depth perception?
15 What is the difference between *monocular* and *binocular depth cues*?
16 What is *retinal disparity*?
17 What is *accommodation*?
18 Name any four monocular depth cues.

Section 4: Illusions, constancies and movement
19 What is *perceptual constancy*?
20 Define the term size constancy.

21 Why is shape constancy needed when perceiving objects?
22 How does the brain prevent us from perceiving the world as spinning around when the eyes and head move?
23 What is colour constancy?
24 Define an *illusion*.
25 Name two of the four types of illusion identified by Gregory.
26 What perceptual tendency is demonstrated by the *horizontal–vertical illusion*?
27 What do Rubin's vase and the Necker cube have in common?
28 Why, according to Hochberg (1970), does it take us a few seconds to see that impossible figures are impossible?
29 Why, according to Gregory (1973), does the *autokinetic effect* occur?
30 What is *induced movement*?

Section 5: Pattern recognition
31 What, according to Eysenck (1993), is one of the principal functions of visual perception?
32 According to the *template-matching hypothesis* (TMH), how do we identify objects in our visual field?
33 What is the principal problem with the template-matching hypothesis?
34 According to *prototype theories*, what is a 'prototype'?
35 What, according to Eysenck (1993), is the main weakness of this approach?
36 How, according to *feature detection theories*, do we see stimulus patterns?
37 What did Rabbit (1967) discover when participants searched lists of letters to find a target letter?
38 What did Hubel & Wiesel (1968) find when looking at cortical cells?
39 Name the different types of 'demon' in Selfridge's *Pandemonium model*.

Section 1: Introducing perception

1 *Sensations* are the physical experiences that physical stimuli elicit in the sense organs.

2 *Perception* is the organisation and interpretation of incoming sensory information to form internal representations of the external world.

Section 2: Gestalt psychology

3 Ehrenfels (1890) called 'emergent properties', such as 'squareness', *Gestalt qualität*.

4 Gestalt psychologists claimed that the principles for organising sensory information are innate.

5 '*Figure*' and '*ground*' are the object and surroundings respectively in any scene.

6 Such factors include familiarity, surroundedness, contour, size orientation and symmetry.

7 Rubin's vase demonstrates the figure–ground principle; either the 'vase' or two 'faces' can be perceived as the figure.

8 *Gestalten* are 'organised wholes', 'configurations' or 'patterns'. Gestalt psychologists believe that we perceive these rather than combinations of sensations.

9 'Psychological organisation will always be as good as the prevailing conditions allow' (Koffka, 1935). Often this means that we prefer simple, stable patterns to more complex ones.

10 The Gestalt laws of perception are: proximity, similarity, good continuation, closure, the part–whole relationship, simplicity, common fate.

11 Greene (1990) criticised the Gestalt approach for being at best descriptive and at worst imprecise and difficult to measure.

12 Navon (1977) constructed alphabetical letters made up of smaller letters. He found that participants perceived the larger letters more readily.

13 Gestalt laws may have low ecological validity because they tend to concentrate on perceptions of single objects, rather than scenes in which objects are parts.

Section 3: Depth perception

14 *Depth perception* is the ability to organise three-dimensional perceptions from the two-dimensional information which falls on our retinas.

15 *Monocular depth cues* can be perceived with one eye, whilst *binocular depth cues* require both eyes in order to be perceived.

16 *Retinal disparity* describes the difference between the images cast upon each retina.

17 *Accommodation* describes the thickening or flattening of the lenses of the eye in order to focus on an object.

18 The following are monocular depth cues: relative size, superimposition, relative height, texture gradient, linear perspective, shadowing, relative brightness, aerial haze, aerial perspective, motion parallax.

Section 4: Constancies, illusions and movement

19 *Perceptual constancy* is the ability to perceive objects as unchanging despite changes in the sensory information which reaches our eyes.

20 *Size constancy* refers to the perception of objects as remaining of fixed size, despite their casting smaller images on the retina as they get further away.

21 Shape constancy is needed in order to perceive an object as staying the same despite changes in the retinal image at different orientations.

22 The brain uses kinaesthetic feedback (information about movement) from the muscles and balance organs of the ear, filtering out movements of the head and eyes from our perception of the world.

23 The ability to see objects as having constant colour despite changes in the actual wavelength of light which they reflect.

24 An *illusion* is a perception of an object which does not match its true physical characteristics.

25 Gregory (1983) identifies distortions, ambiguous figures, paradoxical figures and fictions.

26 The *horizontal–vertical illusion* illustrates our tendency to overestimate the size of vertical objects.

27 They are both *ambiguous figures*; i.e. both can be perceived in more than one way.

28 Hochberg (1970) claims that it takes us time to organise the parts of an object into a meaningful whole.

29 Gregory (1973) claims that the autokinetic effect occurs due to small, uncontrollable eye movements which, in the absence of any surroundings, cannot be filtered out.

30 *Induced movement* is the apparent movement of an object which is stationary, when its surroundings are moving.

Section 5: Pattern recognition

31 Eysenck (1993) maintains that one of the principal functions of visual perception is to assign meaning to objects in the visual field by pattern recognition.

32 According to the *template-matching hypothesis*, we identify objects in our visual field by matching them against miniature copies of patterns stored in memory.

33 Too many templates would have to be stored, and it would take too long to search through them.

34 'Prototypes' are 'abstract forms representing the basic elements of a set of stimuli' (Eysenck, 1993). They are idealised models of a class of objects.

35 The approach cannot explain how perception of a stimulus is affected by context (Eysenck, 1993).

36 *Feature detection theories* claim that we see stimulus patterns as combinations of more elementary features.

37 Rabbit's (1967) participants found it more difficult to identify a target letter from a list of letters when the letters shared similar features.

38 Hubel & Wiesel (1968) found that cortical cells responded selectively to lines of differing orientation.

39 Selfridge's *Pandemonium model* involved image, feature, cognitive and decision demons.

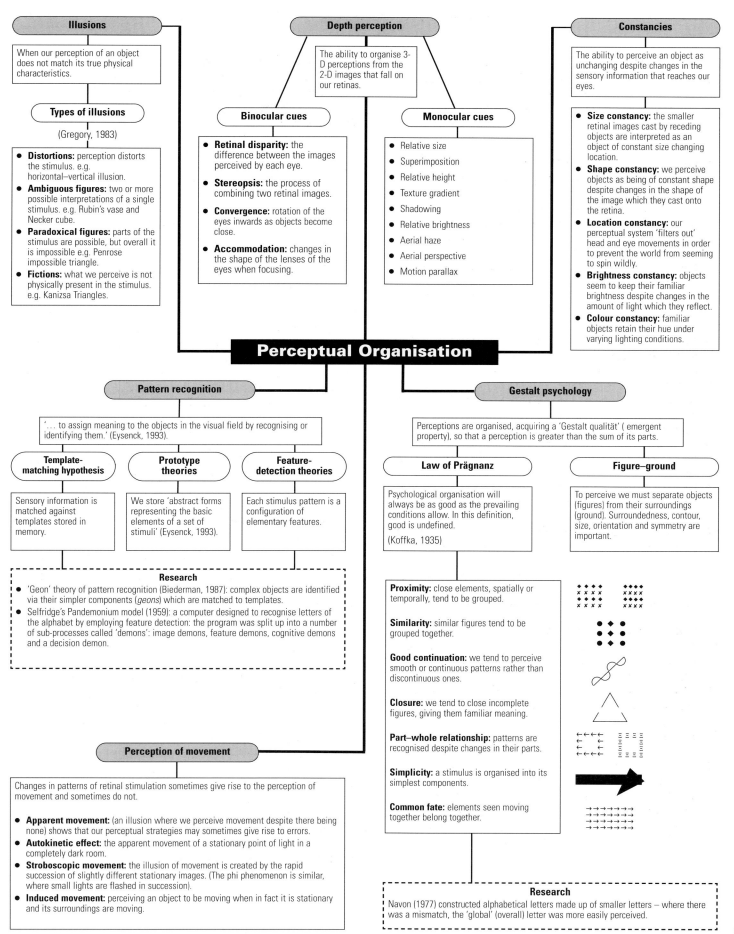

Illusions

When our perception of an object does not match its true physical characteristics.

Types of illusions

(Gregory, 1983)

- **Distortions:** perception distorts the stimulus. e.g. horizontal–vertical illusion.
- **Ambiguous figures:** two or more possible interpretations of a single stimulus. e.g. Rubin's vase and Necker cube.
- **Paradoxical figures:** parts of the stimulus are possible, but overall it is impossible e.g. Penrose impossible triangle.
- **Fictions:** what we perceive is not physically present in the stimulus. e.g. Kanizsa Triangles.

Depth perception

The ability to organise 3-D perceptions from the 2-D images that fall on our retinas.

Binocular cues

- **Retinal disparity:** the difference between the images perceived by each eye.
- **Stereopsis:** the process of combining two retinal images.
- **Convergence:** rotation of the eyes inwards as objects become close.
- **Accommodation:** changes in the shape of the lenses of the eyes when focusing.

Monocular cues

- Relative size
- Superimposition
- Relative height
- Texture gradient
- Shadowing
- Relative brightness
- Aerial haze
- Aerial perspective
- Motion parallax

Constancies

The ability to perceive an object as unchanging despite changes in the sensory information that reaches our eyes.

- **Size constancy:** the smaller retinal images cast by receding objects are interpreted as an object of constant size changing location.
- **Shape constancy:** we perceive objects as being of constant shape despite changes in the shape of the image which they cast onto the retina.
- **Location constancy:** our perceptual system 'filters out' head and eye movements in order to prevent the world from seeming to spin wildly.
- **Brightness constancy:** objects seem to keep their familiar brightness despite changes in the amount of light which they reflect.
- **Colour constancy:** familiar objects retain their hue under varying lighting conditions.

Perceptual Organisation

Pattern recognition

'… to assign meaning to the objects in the visual field by recognising or identifying them.' (Eysenck, 1993).

Template-matching hypothesis

Sensory information is matched against templates stored in memory.

Prototype theories

We store 'abstract forms representing the basic elements of a set of stimuli' (Eysenck, 1993).

Feature-detection theories

Each stimulus pattern is a configuration of elementary features.

Research

- 'Geon' theory of pattern recognition (Biederman, 1987): complex objects are identified via their simpler components (*geons*) which are matched to templates.
- Selfridge's Pandemonium model (1959): a computer designed to recognise letters of the alphabet by employing feature detection: the program was split up into a number of sub-processes called 'demons': image demons, feature demons, cognitive demons and a decision demon.

Gestalt psychology

Perceptions are organised, acquiring a 'Gestalt qualität' (emergent property), so that a perception is greater than the sum of its parts.

Law of Prägnanz

Psychological organisation will always be as good as the prevailing conditions allow. In this definition, good is undefined.

(Koffka, 1935)

Figure–ground

To perceive we must separate objects (figures) from their surroundings (ground). Surroundedness, contour, size, orientation and symmetry are important.

Proximity: close elements, spatially or temporally, tend to be grouped.

Similarity: similar figures tend to be grouped together.

Good continuation: we tend to perceive smooth or continuous patterns rather than discontinuous ones.

Closure: we tend to close incomplete figures, giving them familiar meaning.

Part–whole relationship: patterns are recognised despite changes in their parts.

Simplicity: a stimulus is organised into its simplest components.

Common fate: elements seen moving together belong together.

Perception of movement

Changes in patterns of retinal stimulation sometimes give rise to the perception of movement and sometimes do not.

- **Apparent movement:** (an illusion where we perceive movement despite there being none) shows that our perceptual strategies may sometimes give rise to errors.
- **Autokinetic effect:** the apparent movement of a stationary point of light in a completely dark room.
- **Stroboscopic movement:** the illusion of movement is created by the rapid succession of slightly different stationary images. (The phi phenomenon is similar, where small lights are flashed in succession).
- **Induced movement:** perceiving an object to be moving when in fact it is stationary and its surroundings are moving.

Research

Navon (1977) constructed alphabetical letters made up of smaller letters – where there was a mismatch, the 'global' (overall) letter was more easily perceived.

SOME THEORIES OF VISUAL PERCEPTION

KEY QUESTIONS
- What are top-down and bottom-up theories?
- How do Gregory, Gibson and Marr explain perceptual processes?
- What are the strengths and weaknesses of these three theories?
- Can top-down and bottom-up approaches be combined?

Section 1: Top-down and bottom-up approaches

1 What do *top-down theorists* of perception believe?
2 What is another name for top-down processing?
3 What do *bottom-up theorists* of perception believe?
4 What is another name for bottom-up processing?

Section 2: Gregory's theory

5 According to Gregory (1966), what does our perceptual system 'search for' when it detects a stimulus?
6 How do perceptual constancies show that perception is an indirect process?
7 What is an illusion?
8 Why do illusions support Gregory's top-down approach to perception?
9 Why, when viewing the Necker Cube, does the cube seem to reverse repeatedly?
10 How does Gregory's *misapplied size constancy theory* apply to the Müller–Lyer illusion?
11 How does Allport (1955) define *perceptual set*?
12 Name three factors which may influence perceptual set.
13 Gordon (1989) makes a number of criticisms of Gregory's theory – describe one of them.
14 Eysenck & Keane (1995) make a further criticism of Gregory's approach – what is it?

Section 3: Gibson's theory

15 What is meant by Gibson's claim that perception is 'direct'?
16 What term does Gibson (1966) use to describe the pattern of light extended over time and space?
17 What three main forms of information does this pattern contain?
18 What kinds of information are provided by the flow of the environment around a moving observer?
19 What are *affordances*?
20 According to Marr (1982), Gibson failed to recognise two things – what are they?

21 Why is it unlikely that Gibson's concept of affordances applies well to humans?
22 What, according to Fodor & Pylyshyn (1981), is the difference between 'seeing' and 'seeing as'?
23 What do *transactionalists* argue?
24 How does the 'Ames room' work?
25 How does Gibson defend his approach against the criticism that it cannot explain visual illusions?

Section 4: Comparing Gregory and Gibson

26 Name two things which Gibson's and Gregory's approaches have in common.
27 How do Gregory and Gibson differ in their views of perceptual learning?
28 When, according to Eysenck & Keane (1995), is top-down processing likely to be most important?
29 What is the name of Neisser's (1976) model which proposes that perception involves a perceptual cycle?
30 What are the two sources of information in this model?
31 What are the two processes which relate these sources of information to one another?

Section 5: Marr's theory

32 What, according to Marr (1982), is the central 'problem' of perception?
33 Marr (1982) claims that there are three levels at which any process must be understood – what are they?
34 How did Marr see visual representation as being organised?
35 According to Marr, how does his model's *raw primal sketch* differ from its *full primal sketch*?
36 What is the role of the *2½-D sketch*?
37 To what does the *3-D-model representation* correspond?
38 What was Marr & Nishihara's (1978) answer to how the visual system can identify objects from the 2½-D sketch?
39 Which is the least well-supported stage in Marr's theory?
40 According to Gardner (1985), to what types of forms does Marr's model apply best?

Section 1: Top-down and bottom-up approaches

1 *Top-down theorists* of perception believe that our perception is the end result of a process which involves making inferences about what things are like.

2 Top-down processing can also be called *conceptually-driven processing*.

3 *Bottom-up theorists* believe that our perception of the world is essentially determined by the information presented to the sensory systems.

4 Bottom-up processing can also be called *data-driven processing*.

Section 2: Gregory's theory

5 Gregory (1966) claims that our perceptual system searches for the best interpretation of a stimulus.

6 Perceptual constancies show that perceptions must 'go beyond' the often sketchy information provided in the retinal image, drawing on expectations and past experience.

7 An illusion is a perceptual hypothesis which is not confirmed by the data.

8 Illusions support Gregory's approach because they show that perception is an active process of suggesting and testing hypotheses.

9 The Necker Cube seems to reverse repeatedly as the perceptual system continually tests two equally plausible hypotheses about the nature of the object.

10 Gregory's *misapplied size constancy theory* suggests that we interpret the 'fins' of the Müller–Lyer illusion as perspective cues, and therefore overestimate the length of the apparently more distant line.

11 Allport (1955) defines *perceptual set* as: 'a perceptual bias or predisposition or readiness to perceive particular features of a stimulus'.

12 Perceptual set may be influenced by motivation, values, beliefs, cognitive style, cultural background, context and expectations.

13 Gordon (1989) criticises Gregory on three counts: he fails to explain how we begin 'constructing' our perceptions and why we end up sharing so many; it seems unlikely that sensations are really very ambiguous if perception is usually accurate; such theories underestimate the richness of the sensory data available in the real world.

14 Eysenck & Keane (1995) believe Gregory's theory to be better at explaining illusions than real-world perception.

15 Gibson's claim that perception is 'direct' means that perception involves 'picking up' information provided by the optical array in a way which involves little or no information processing.

16 Gibson (1966) uses the term '*optical array*' to describe the pattern of light extended over time and space.

Section 3: Gibson's theory

17 This pattern contains information such as optic flow patterns, texture gradients and affordances.

18 The flow of the environment provides information regarding direction, speed and altitude.

19 *Affordances* are directly perceivable, potential uses of objects.

20 Marr (1982) claimed that Gibson failed to recognise that detecting physical invariants involved considerable information processing, and the sheer difficulty of this task.

21 Gibson's concept of affordances does not take into account the fact that humans inhabit a cultural environment, from which they derive much information.

22 Fodor & Pylyshyn (1981) claim that 'seeing' depends on what a thing is and 'seeing as' depends on knowing what a thing is (e.g. a Martian might well 'see' a table but not see it *as* a table).

23 *Transactionalists* argue that past experience is used to select interpretations of ambiguous sensory data.

24 The 'Ames room' works by being constructed in such a way as to give the impression that the people standing at either corner are of unusual sizes.

25 Gibson claims that visual illusions do not occur in the natural environment.

Section 4: Comparing Gregory and Gibson

26 Gibson's and Gregory's approaches both see visual perception as mediated by reflected light, as requiring physiological systems, and as an active process influenced by learning.

27 For Gregory, perceptual learning involves using experience and memory to make sensations coherent; for Gibson, we learn to identify features given in the optical array.

28 Eysenck & Keane (1995) maintain that top-down processing is most important where stimuli are brief or ambiguous.

29 Neisser's (1976) model was called the *analysis-by-synthesis* model.

30 Within this model, the stimulus environment and schemas provide information.

31 *Feature analysis of sensory cues* and *perceptual exploration* are the two processes relating this information.

Section 5: Marr's theory

32 Marr (1982) claims that the central 'problem' of perception is identifying the mechanisms and computations used to extract information from a scene.

33 Marr's three levels are the *computational theory* level, the *algorithmic* level, and the *hardware/implementation* level.

34 Marr saw visual representation as four successive stages in processing information of progressive complexity.

35 The *raw primal sketch* identifies regions and boundaries, the *full primal sketch* fits these together as structures.

36 The *2½-D sketch* makes explicit the orientation and depth of visible structures.

37 The *3-D-model representation* corresponds to object recognition.

38 Marr & Nishihara (1978) suggested that objects could be recognised from a library of 'generalised cylinder representations'.

39 The 3-D-model stage of Marr's theory is the least well supported.

40 According to Gardner (1985), Marr's model applies best to mammalian bodies.

Perception: Top-down vs. Bottom-up

Top-down/ indirect/constructivist approach: perception is an active process involving knowledge and experience, and hypotheses or 'best guesses' about the world (*conceptually-driven processing*).

Bottom-up/direct approach: the perceptual environment is information-rich, containing many cues which allow us to perceive without interpretation (*data-driven processing*).

Gregory

Gregory (1966): 'Perception is not determined simply by stimulus patterns. Rather, it is a dynamic searching for the best interpretation of the available data … [which] involves going beyond the immediately given evidence of the senses. We draw inferences from sensory information, forming hypotheses/best guesses as to what we see.'

Illusions

A perceptual hypothesis which is not confirmed by the data (see Ch 21).

Key example: Müller–Lyer illusion where:
1. figure is interpreted in 3-D using fins as depth cues
2. size constancy is misapplied, the more 'distant' lines being scaled up to appear larger.

Constancies

Supplementing available sense data to give objects familiar meaning (see Ch 21).

Perceptual set

A perceptual bias or predisposition or readiness to perceive particular features of a stimulus (Allport, 1955).

Shows that perception can be influenced by perceiver and stimulus variables, e.g.
- Motivation
- Context/expectations
- Beliefs and values

Gibson

Optical array

The pattern of light striking the retina.
Perception involves 'picking up' the rich information provided by the optical array, in a way which requires little or no information processing. The optic array contains '*physical invariants*':

Optic flow

The flow of the visual environment around a moving observer.

Texture gradients

The greater roughness of textures when close up.

Affordances

Directly perceivable potential uses of objects – linked to the concept of 'ecological optics'

Research

- Lee & Lishman (1975) built a 'swaying room' which appeared to sway around a stationary participant standing in it. They found that adults adjust their balance and children fall over.
- Lee & Lishman (1975):also argue that 'time to contact' estimations are an important function of perception and that optic flow plays a key role in this calculation.

Marr

Marr (1982): the central problem of perception is identifying the computations which allow information to be extracted from a scene. There are three levels at which any process must be understood:
1. **Computational** theory level: an analysis of the goals and tasks of a system.
2. **Algorithmic** level: the actual operations (or program) by which tasks can be achieved.
3. **Hardware**/Implementation level: a description of the physical mechanisms underlying a system's operation.
Visual representation is organised as an information-processing system consisting of four successive stages (modules).

Image level

A description of the intensity of light at each point in the image (similar to retina). Allowing regions and boundaries to be identified.

Primal sketch

Raw primal sketch describes potentially significant regions. *Full primal sketch* describes how these regions go together.

$2\frac{1}{2}$D Sketch

Makes explicit the orientation and depth of visible structures. It describes only visible parts, so is not fully 3D.

3D Model

Matches shapes and orientations to 3D objects, possibly by using a library of models stored in memory (such as generalised cylinders).

Combining top-down and bottom-up processing

Transactionalists argue that whether top-down or bottom-up processing is used will depend on past experience.

Research: Ames' distorted room (cited in Ittelson, 1952) showed that whether the distortion resulted in a judgement that the person is very small or that the room is abnormal depended on familiarity/unfamiliarity with the person in the room.

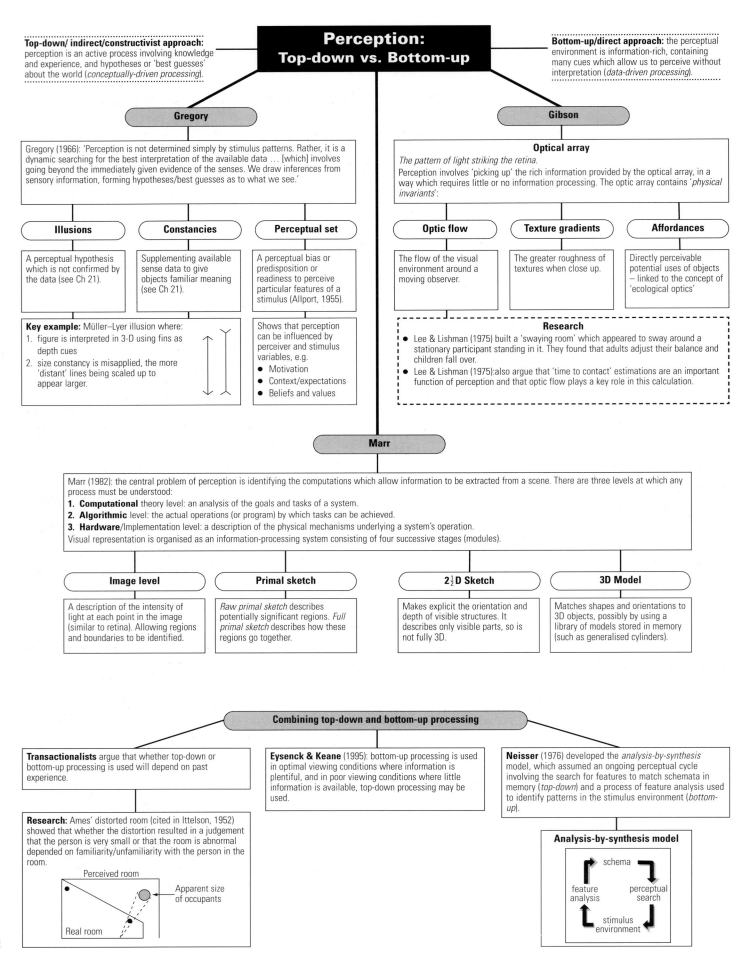

Eysenck & Keane (1995): bottom-up processing is used in optimal viewing conditions where information is plentiful, and in poor viewing conditions where little information is available, top-down processing may be used.

Neisser (1976) developed the *analysis-by-synthesis* model, which assumed an ongoing perceptual cycle involving the search for features to match schemata in memory (*top-down*) and a process of feature analysis used to identify patterns in the stimulus environment (*bottom-up*).

Analysis-by-synthesis model

23

STUDYING THE DEVELOPMENT OF VISUAL PERCEPTUAL ABILITIES 1: HUMAN NEONATE AND INFANT STUDIES

SYLLABUS
5.1 Perceptual processes
- perceptual development and the methods used in the study of this area

KEY QUESTIONS
- How does the nature–nurture debate apply to the study of perception?
- What methods are used in the study of infant perception?
- What perceptual equipment do infants have?
- Are perceptual abilities inborn or learned?

Section 1: Nature vs. nurture
1 Why are psychologists interested in studying the perceptual abilities of human infants?
2 What is the principal problem in studying infant perceptions?
3 What is the nature–nurture debate as it applies to perception?
4 What is a *nativist*?
5 What is an *empirist*?

Section 2: Studying infant perception
6 How does the *preferential looking technique* work?
7 What two things can this technique tell us?
8 What would you expect to happen to a baby's sucking rate when it detects a novel stimulus?
9 What is *habituation*?
10 What is the principle behind the technique of *conditioned head rotation*?
11 What are two physiological measures which you would expect to change when a baby detects a novel stimulus?
12 What is a *visually evoked potential* and how is it measured?

Section 3: Perceptual equipment
13 How good is an infant's colour perception when it is a few months old?
14 Which technique did Bornstein (1976) use to discover that infants could distinguish between yellow and green?
15 What is the *pupillary reflex*?
16 When is the *blink reflex* first present?
17 What is the *optokinetic reflex*?
18 When do babies first show *convergence* and *accommodation*?
19 What is *visual acuity*?
20 Which technique did Gwiazda *et al.* (1980) use to study visual acuity?
21 How far can neonates see before things start to become blurred?

Section 4: Perceptual abilities
22 Which technique did Fantz (1961) use to investigate the perceptions of 1–15-week-old infants?
23 What was Fantz's first finding, using this technique?
24 In a later experiment, Fantz used six discs, each with a different appearance. Which was the most popular stimulus?
25 When scanning a triangle, which areas do babies spend longest looking at?
26 What do these findings suggest regarding pattern or form perception?
27 Give two explanations for the finding that infants prefer looking at human faces.
28 What was Fantz's aim in presenting children with normal and 'scrambled' faces?
29 What did Hershenson *et al.* (1965) discover when presenting infants with a real face, a distorted picture and Fantz's 'scrambled' face?
30 How do babies respond to facial expressions, minutes after birth?
31 Is a preference for human faces innate?
32 What did Gibson & Walk (1960) call their apparatus, used to test depth perception in infants?
33 What was the reaction of 6–14-month-old infants placed on their apparatus?
34 What is the principal problem with their study?
35 How did Campos *et al.* (1970) overcome this problem?
36 What is an *integrated avoidance response*?
37 How did infants respond when unable to grasp the 'virtual object' created by Bower's (1979) apparatus?
38 What does this show?
39 What method did Bower (1966) use to investigate size constancy in his 'peek-a-boo' experiments?
40 What can we conclude from this?
41 How did Bower use triangles to investigate whether or not infants exhibited the Gestalt principle of *closure*?
42 What was Slater's (1994) conclusion regarding the perceptual abilities of the new-born infants?

Q

Section 1: Nature vs. nurture

1 Psychologists are interested in studying the perceptual abilities of human infants, since it is a direct way of assessing which abilities are present at birth.

2 The principal problem in studying infant perception is their inability to tell us what they perceive; we have to *infer* what it is that they can perceive.

3 The nature–nurture debate, in the area of perception, concerns whether or not perceptual abilities are inborn or the product of experience and learning.

4 A *nativist* is someone who argues that we are born with capacities to perceive the world in certain ways.

5 An *empirist* argues that our perceptual abilities develop through experience.

Section 2: Studying infant perception

6 The technique works by presenting the infant with two stimuli simultaneously, and observing which the infant spends most time looking at.

7 This technique tells us whether the infant can discriminate between two stimuli, and which it prefers.

8 A baby's *sucking rate* tends to increase or decrease when it detects a novel stimulus.

9 *Habituation* is the weakening of a response to a stimulus to which an organism has become accustomed.

10 The technique of *conditioned head rotation* works by operantly conditioning an infant to make a response to a stimulus, then varying the stimulus to discover whether the conditioned response is still made.

11 When a baby detects a novel stimulus it is usual for its heart rate and breathing rate to change.

12 A *visually evoked potential* is a measure of brain activity made by attaching electrodes to an infant's scalp.

Section 3: Perceptual equipment

13 An infant's colour perception is almost as good as an adult's by the time it is a few months old.

14 Bornstein (1976) used habituation to discover that infants could distinguish between yellow and green.

15 The *pupillary reflex* is the narrowing of the pupil as a result of the contraction of the muscles of the iris. It protects the retina from bright light.

16 The *blink reflex* is present at birth.

17 The *optokinetic reflex* is a reflex which allows the infant to follow moving objects with its eyes.

18 Babies do not show *convergence* and *accommodation* until a few months old.

19 *Visual acuity* refers to the ability to discriminate fine detail.

20 Gwiazda *et al.* (1980) used the *preferential looking technique* to study visual acuity.

21 Neonates can only see about twenty centimetres before things start to become blurred.

Section 4: Perceptual abilities

22 Fantz (1961) used the *preferential looking technique* to investigate the perceptions of 1–15-week-old infants.

23 Fantz found that infants demonstrated a distinct preference for *complexity*.

24 The most popular of the six discs which Fantz (1961) presented to infants was the picture of a face.

25 When scanning a triangle babies spend longest looking at the corners of the triangle, the areas of highest contrast.

26 These findings suggest that ability to discriminate some detail is present at birth and that a preference for complexity is probably innate.

27 Infants may prefer looking at human faces because this preference is innate, or simply because a face combines complexity, pattern and movement, all of which babies prefer.

28 Fantz presented children with normal and 'scrambled' faces in an attempt to discover whether they preferred faces, or just complexity and contrast.

29 Hershenson *et al.* (1965) claimed that infants did not show any preference when presented with a real face, a distorted picture and Fantz's 'scrambled' face.

30 Shortly after birth babies will tend to imitate facial expressions.

31 Fantz argues that a preference for human faces is innate, whilst other researchers disagree. Slater (1994) believes that a neonate's tendency to imitate faces shows that some knowledge of faces must be innate.

32 Gibson & Walk's (1960) apparatus was called the *visual cliff*.

33 Six- to 14-month-old infants placed on the visual cliff would not crawl onto the deep side, even when beckoned by their mothers.

34 The infants in Gibson & Walk's study were not neonates and may have learned to perceive depth by the time they were able to crawl.

35 Campos *et al.* (1970) got round this problem by placing younger babies on the deep side and monitoring their heart rates.

36 An *integrated avoidance response* occurs when an infant shields its face, throws back its head and even cries in response to an object moving towards its face.

37 Infants unable to grasp Bower's (1979) 'virtual object' appeared surprised and occasionally distressed.

38 Bower claims that infants have an innate expectation that they can touch what they see.

39 Bower's (1966) experiments used *conditioned head rotation* to discover whether an infant could recognise cubes of different sizes at different distances.

40 This experiment found that size constancy does appear to be innate.

41 Bower conditioned infants to respond to a triangle partially covered by a rectangle – and found they responded similarly to a complete triangle.

42 Slater (1994) concluded that the new-born infant 'comes into the world with a remarkable range of visual abilities'.

Perceptual Development: Infants (*Nature vs. Nurture*)

Empirists (not empiricists!) believe that our perceptual capacities and abilities develop through experience.

Nativists (innate theorists) argue that we are born with certain capacities and abilities to perceive the world in particular ways.

Methods of study

Preferential looking
Two stimuli are presented simultaneously. If the infant spends more time looking at one than the other then:
a) it perceives difference
b) that stimulus is preferred.

Sucking rate
Baby's sucking rate (of dummy) is measured, then a new stimulus introduced. If sucking rate increases or decreases, then the infant has detected the new stimulus.

Habituation
If a baby knows a stimulus it will tend to ignore it (*habituation*). New stimuli will then re-excite the baby and result in increased attention.

Conditioned head rotation
The infant is operantly conditioned to turn its head in response to a stimulus (e.g. a sound). The stimulus can then be varied and the infant's behaviour noted.

Physiological measures
Heart rate and breathing rate can be monitored. If these change when a new stimulus is presented, then the infant can *discriminate* new and old stimuli.

Brain activity
Electrodes attached to the infant's scalp measure VEPs (visually evoked potentials). Changes suggest that the infant can perceive a stimulus change.

Perceptual equipment

Colour perception
- Retina, rods and cones are well developed at birth.
- Bornstein (1976): used habituation and found 3-month-olds could distinguish yellow from green and blue-green from white.
- Bornstein (1988): at 2 months most infants have normal colour vision.

Brightness
- *Fovea* is well developed at birth.
- *Blink reflex* is present at birth.
- *Pupillary reflex* (protects retina from bright light) present in premature babies.
- Adams & Maurer (1984): ability to discriminate brightnesses reaches adult levels within one year.

Movement
- *Optokinetic reflex* (enables infant to follow a moving object) present within 2 days of birth. *Tracking* is initially 'jerky' but improves rapidly in first 3 months.
- *Convergence* is absent at birth.
- *Accommodation* approaches adult levels by 4 months.

Visual acuity
Gwiazda *et al.* (1980) used preferential looking to discover that the ability to discriminate fine detail is roughly 30 times poorer than an adult's – at birth everything beyond 30 cm is a blur.
- Between 6 and 12 months acuity approaches adult's.

Perceptual abilities

Pattern/form perception
Fantz (1961) used preferential looking technique with 2–4-month-old infants. Six discs presented (red, yellow, white, bullseye, text and face).
- Infants preferred more complex figures.
- Face preferred most of all.

Preference for complexity increases with age, possibly as the infant's ability to scan improves. Salapatek (1975): very young infants only scan one corner of a triangle; later on they explore internal features.

Perception of human faces
Human faces combine complexity, pattern and movement, all of which babies innately prefer. Some researchers believe that a special preference for faces is innate (Fantz, 1961) whilst others do not (Hershenson *et al.*, 1965)

Fantz (1961) used preferential looking technique with infants from 4 days to 6 months. Babies preferred to look at a normal diagram of a face than a 'scrambled' one (matched for pattern, complexity and contrast)

Depth perception
Gibson & Walk (1960) constructed a *visual cliff.*
- most 6–14-month-olds wouldn't crawl onto 'deep' side. (However, by this age babies might have learned to perceive depth.)

Campos *et al.* (1970): even 2-month-olds showed a decreased heart rate when placed on the deep side, suggesting that they perceived depth.

Bower *et al.* (1970): 20-day-olds show an *avoidance response* when approached by a large object.

Perception of 3D objects
Bower (1979) devised an apparatus which creates the illusion of 3D objects. The infant wears polarising goggles which makes a 3D virtual object appear to be suspended in front of it.
- Infants aged 16 to 24 weeks expressed surprise when they could not grasp the object, and some were distressed. Bower believes this shows infants perceive objects as solid and 3D.

Perceptual organisation
Bower (1966) conditioned 2-month-olds to turn their heads whenever they saw a 30 cm cube at 1 metre distance (by playing 'peek-a-boo'). He then presented a 30 cm cube at 3 metres and a 90 cm cube at 3 metres. Infants responded more to the former, suggesting that *size constancy is innate.*

Bower (1966): *closure is innate.* Infants made similar conditioned responses to a complete triangle as they did to one which was partially obscured by a bar.

24

STUDYING THE DEVELOPMENT OF VISUAL PERCEPTUAL ABILITIES 2: OTHER APPROACHES

SYLLABUS

5.1 Perceptual processes
- perceptual development and the methods used in the study of this area.
- individual, social and cultural variations in the nature of perceptual organisation

KEY QUESTIONS
- What does the study of cataract patients tell us about perception?
- What do studies using non-humans show?
- Is the human visual system adaptable?
- What conclusions can we draw from cross-cultural studies of perception?

Q

Section 1: An overview of approaches

1 What are the four alternatives to infant studies, used to study perceptual development?
2 What is the most common procedure for investigating perceptual development in non-humans?
3 What is the rationale behind studying humans' ability to adapt their visual systems?
4 If a difference in perception exists between two cultures which is not biological in origin, what does this suggest?

Section 2: Human cataract patients

5 Why are psychologists interested in the perceptual capabilities of cataract patients?
6 What is a cataract?
7 In terms of which two abilities did Hebb analyse Von Senden's case histories of cataract removal?
8 Which of these two abilities did Hebb conclude is most dependent on learning?
9 Name one ability which SB did not have, following cataract removal (Gregory & Wallace, 1963)?
10 Give two reasons why we must be cautious in our interpretations of the data from cataract patients.

Section 3: Sensory restriction with non-humans

11 Why are non-humans used to shed light on the issue of perceptual development, rather than humans?
12 Briefly describe the nature of Riesen's first (1947) experiment with chimpanzees.
13 What was the central criticism which Weiskrantz (1956) made of this study?
14 In his second study, Riesen (1965) fitted translucent goggles to one of the chimpanzees. Why?
15 Which two principal conclusions can be derived from Riesen's work?
16 What was the name of the apparatus in which Held & Hein (1963) raised an 'active' kitten and a 'passive' kitten?
17 Can we conclude from these experiments that depth perception does not develop if kittens cannot guide their own movements?

18 What were the effects of raising kittens in vertical-only environments (as in Blakemore & Cooper's, 1970, experiments)?
19 What is the principal problem in drawing conclusions from Blakemore & Cooper's (1970) experiment?

Section 4: Distortion and readjustment studies

20 What experiment did Stratton (1896, 1897) carry out on himself?
21 Briefly describe the effect which this had on Stratton's ability to accomplish simple tasks.
22 When Stratton removed the lenses, what important observation did he make about the world's appearance?
23 What does this suggest?

Section 5: Cross-cultural studies

24 What did Rivers (1901) discover when comparing the responses to the Müller–Lyer Illusion of English participants with those of Murray Islanders?
25 What is one possible explanation for the finding that in Segall *et al.*'s (1963) study, Africans living on the plains were more susceptible to the horizontal–vertical illusion?
26 What is the central claim made by Segall *et al.*'s *carpentered world hypothesis*?
27 Did the findings of Mundy-Castle & Nelson's (1962) study of Knysma forest-dwellers support this hypothesis?
28 Which perceptual ability was not displayed by the pygmy in Turnbull's (1961) study?
29 What was the aim of Hudson's (1960) study in which he showed African participants hunting scenes?
30 Why might one argue that non-Westerners were at a 'double disadvantage' in trying to interpret Hudson's drawings?
31 What does Serpell (1976) mean by saying that research may have mistaken 'stylistic preference' for perceptual differences?
32 What is the *transactional perspective*?

Section 1: An overview of approaches

1 The four alternatives to infant studies are: studies of cataract patients, studies of the effects of sensory deprivation on non-humans, perceptual readjustment studies, and cross-cultural studies.

2 The most common procedure with non-humans involves depriving them of early sensory experience in order to study what effect this has on their perceptual abilities.

3 We can assume that the more a visual system is capable of adaptation, the greater the role learning is likely to have played in the development of perceptual abilities.

4 If a difference in perception exists between two cultures (and we can rule out biological origins), this suggests that environmental factors have influenced perceptual abilities.

Section 2: Human cataract patients

5 Psychologists are interested in the capabilities of cataract patients, since any perceptual abilities which are discovered to have persisted in the absence of patterned light are presumably innate.

6 A cataract is a film over the eyes which allows only diffuse light to be perceived.

7 Hebb analysed Von Senden's case histories in terms of *figural unity* (the ability to detect a stimulus) and *figural identity* (the ability to say what it is).

8 Hebb concluded that figural identity is the most dependent on learning.

9 Following cataract removal, SB could not judge distances by sight alone, nor could he interpret facial expressions (Gregory & Wallace, 1963).

10 The data from cataract patients cannot easily be generalised to the abilities of neonates, since other perceptual abilities which have subsequently developed (such as hearing) may interfere with vision; also, some deterioration of the visual system may have occurred during blindness, and some of the patients did not have cataracts from birth.

Section 3: Sensory restriction with non-humans

11 Non-humans are used, rather than humans, because experimenters are able to manipulate environments in ways not ethically permissible with humans.

12 Riesen's first (1947) experiment involved rearing chimpanzees in total darkness for the first sixteen months of their lives.

13 Weiskrantz (1956) pointed out that in the absence of light the retina is likely to degenerate, making it difficult to determine which abilities are present at birth.

14 Riesen (1965) fitted translucent goggles to one of the chimpanzees (Kova) to study perceptual development in the absence of patterned light.

15 Riesen's work indicated that light is necessary for normal development of the visual system and that patterned light is necessary for the development of some complex abilities.

16 Held & Hein's (1963) apparatus was called the '*kitten carousel*'.

17 No. It may simply be that the kittens had not had the opportunity to develop normal motor responses.

18 Kittens raised in vertical-only environments (Blakemore & Cooper, 1970) did not respond to horizontal movements of a rod and did not possess cortical cells responsive to such movements.

19 Blakemore & Cooper's (1970) experiment may have caused cells receptive to certain stimuli to have deteriorated during the experiment.

Section 4: Distortion and readjustment studies

20 Stratton (1896, 1897) fitted himself with a lens which inverted and reversed his visual world.

21 Stratton was able to walk around and accomplish simple tasks after five days.

22 When Stratton removed the lenses, his world was definitely not upside down.

23 This suggests that he had learned to adapt his motor responses, not his perceptions.

Section 5: Cross-cultural studies

24 Rivers (1901) discovered that Murray Islanders were less susceptible than the English participants.

25 Africans living on the plains are perhaps more likely to perceive vertical objects as important focal points and, therefore, more likely to overestimate their length.

26 Segall *et al.*'s *carpentered world hypothesis* holds that Westerners are more likely to interpret angles in 3D terms, since we live in a world where most angles are realistically interpretable as right-angled corners.

27 No. Mundy-Castle & Nelson's (1962) study of Knysma forest-dwellers found that they were not susceptible to the Müller–Lyer illusion, despite living in carpentered buildings.

28 The pygmy in Turnbull's (1961) study did not appear to possess *size constancy*.

29 Hudson's (1960) 'hunting scenes' study aimed to classify participants as having 2D or 3D vision, depending on their interpretation of the scene.

30 Non-Westerners were at a 'double disadvantage' in trying to interpret Hudson's drawings because of the unfamiliarity of the task (e.g. the paper used) and because different cultures emphasise the importance of depth cues other than those used in Hudson's drawings.

31 Serpell (1976) points out that non-Westerners may 'reject' Western pictorial representations on aesthetic grounds ('stylistic preference'), because they do not conform to their notions of artistic representation.

32 The *transactional perspective* holds that we are born with certain capacities whose development is strongly influenced by environmental influences.

A

Human cataract patients

Hebb (1949): analysed 65 cases of cataract removal collected by Von Senden between 1700 and 1928. Analysed results in terms of:

Figural unity
The ability to detect the presence of a stimulus, scanning and tracking objects.
Conclusion: probably innate.

Figural identity
The ability to name/identify an already familiar stimulus through vision alone.
Conclusion: depends on learning.

Gregory & Wallace (1963) described the case of SB who received his sight at 52:
- was able to identify some objects by sight alone.
- could not judge distances by sight alone.
- could not interpret facial expressions.

Problem: many patients are confused by the visual world, and we cannot know how much deterioration of the visual system has occurred – this makes it difficult to generalise from adults to infant abilities.

Perceptual adaptation

The greater an organism's ability to adapt its perceptions, the greater the role of learning is likely to be.

Stratton (1896, 1897) wore a lens which inverted and reversed his visual world.
- began to adapt after 3 days.
- by the 5th day he could walk around and do simple things.
- by the 8th day everything seemed 'harmonious'.
However, he was often unsure as to which hand to use to grasp objects.

Problem: Stratton's world was not inverted when he removed the lens, suggesting that it was his *motor responses* not his perception which had adapted.

Snyder & Pronko (1952) reported on participants who adapted to inversion and reversal over a period of 30 days. When tested 2 years later, adaptation was swift, suggesting that motor adaptations are remembered.
Conclusion: probably learned.

Perceptual Development – Other Approaches

Studies of non-humans

Chimpanzees

Riesen (1947) reared chimps in total darkness for first 16 months of life.
Results
- Failed to show blink response.
- Only noticed objects if they accidentally bumped into them.

Weiskrantz (1956) argued that results were inconclusive since visual system degenerates in absence of light. Riesen only showed that light is necessary to *maintain* visual system.

Riesen (1965) raised three chimps:
- Debi – complete darkness
- Kova – 1½ hours per day in opaque goggles.
- Lad – normal lighting.
Results
- Kova did not suffer retinal damage but receptive fields failed to develop normally.

Conclusion
- Simple perceptual abilities (e.g. differentiating colour, size, brightness) are inborn.
- Complex abilities (e.g. following moving objects) are learned.

Kittens

Held & Hein (1963): placed kittens in a 'kitten carousel' for three hours per day. One kitten could move, and controlled the other, which could not.
Results
- 'passive kittens had poorer paw–eye coordination.
- 'passive kittens' showed little evidence of depth perception.
Problems
Kittens may simply have failed to learn correct motor responses.

Blakemore & Cooper (1970) raised kittens in chambers with only vertical or horizontal lines.
Results
- Kittens failed to respond to movements in a direction which they hadn't experienced.
- Micro-electrodes found cells of visual cortex to be insensitive to stimuli in unfamiliar orientations.
Problem
Cells may have been present at birth but degenerated.

Cross-cultural studies

Visual illusions

Rivers (1901) compared adults and children from England and the Murray Islands.
Results
- Murray Islanders less susceptible to Müller–Lyer, more susceptible to horizontal–vertical.

Segall *et al.* (1963) compared African and Filipinos with Americans and white South Africans on Müller–Lyer.
Results
- Africans and Filipinos less susceptible.
- However, Africans who live on plains were more susceptible than those living in jungle.

Carpentered world hypothesis (Segall *et al.*, 1963)

Westerners live in a culture where 90% of the angles around us belong to corners of objects/buildings. Therefore, we are more likely to interpret the Müller–Lyer in 3D terms.

Problem
Mundy-Castle & Nelson (1962) studied Knysma (isolated illiterate white S.Africans).
Results
- Did not interpret Müller–Lyer in 3D terms, despite rectangular environments – so perhaps culture *is* the key factor.

Other phenomena

Turnbull (1961) took a Bambuti pygmy from dense jungle. Pygmy identified distant buffalo as insects and seemed unable to use size constancy over long distances.

Hudson (1960) showed Africans pictures of a hunting scene. Participants needed to use relative size and overlap to interpret depth. Both children and adults found it difficult to perceive depth in the picture.

Deregowski (1972): Africans preferred the non-perspective drawing of an elephant (flattened out) to a drawing in perspective. (However, so did young Europeans.)

Problem
Serpell (1976) points out that it may not be a difference in perception but in artistic conventions which is being studied.

25

FOCUSED ATTENTION

SYLLABUS

5.2 Attention and performance limitations
- theories and evidence relating to focused auditory attention and focused visual attention

KEY QUESTIONS
- Why do psychologists study attention?
- What theories are there to explain focused auditory attention?
- What theories are there to explain focused visual attention?
- What are the strengths and weaknesses of these theories?

Section 1: Early studies of attention

1 Why did behaviourists argue that attention was not worthy of experimental study?
2 What important claim did Broadbent make in his 1958 book *Perception and Communication*?
3 What is the *cocktail-party phenomenon* (Cherry, 1953)?
4 What is a *binaural listening task*?
5 What is a *dichotic listening task*?
6 What is involved in *shadowing*?
7 How much of a shadowed message is remembered?
8 Broadbent (1954) used a *split-span procedure* to investigate attention. What did this involve?

Section 2: Focused auditory attention

9 What is the common feature of all *single-channel theories of attention*?
10 According to Broadbent's (1958) theory, at what stage does filtering occur in the processing of information?
11 What is the purpose of the *short-term store* in this model?
12 What features of the stimulus does the selective filter operate upon?
13 What does the *limited-capacity channel* correspond to?
14 How does this model suggest that we deal with two simultaneous stimuli?
15 Why is Moray's (1959) finding that we will sometimes switch our attention to a 'non-attended ear' if our name is presented in that ear a problem for Broadbent's model?
16 What did Treisman (1960) discover when she switched information, mid-sentence, to a non-attended ear?
17 What were Underwood's (1974) participants, trained in shadowing, able to do?
18 According to Treisman's *attenuation theory*, what types of analyses are carried out on incoming information?
19 What does it mean to say a message is 'attenuated'?
20 What types of information is attention likely to be switched to, according to this theory?
21 According to the Deutsch–Norman theory, when does filtering or selection occur?

22 Why is this theory sometimes called *pertinence theory*?
23 Why is the finding (Treisman & Riley, 1969) that target words are best identified in a shadowed message (vs. the non-shadowed message) a problem for this theory?
24 What is meant by saying that the major problem with these single-channel theories is that they are inflexible?

Section 3: Focused visual attention

25 Which area of the retina allows maximum visual processing?
26 What is *covert attention* (Posner, 1980)?
27 What did Posner liken covert attention to?
28 What conclusion can be drawn from LaBerge's (1983) experiment, in which participants identified numbers at varying distances from the centre of their attention?
29 What did LaBerge discover when he investigated the 'width' of the 'mental spotlight'?
30 What did Eriksen (1990) mean by the *zoom-lens model* of visual attention?
31 When Neisser & Becklen (1975) superimposed two films, what implications did their results have for the the *spotlight model*?
32 What is a *visual search procedure*?
33 According to Treisman's (1988) *feature–integration theory* of visual processing, what are the two stages of visual processing?
34 In Treisman & Gelade's (1980) experiments, which of the two letters 'Y' or 'Z' increased the time taken by participants to spot a letter 'T', and why?
35 When McLeod *et al.* (1991) asked participants to identify a moving 'X' from among moving 'O's and stationary 'X's, what did they find?
36 Does this support Treisman's feature integration theory – why/why not?
37 Overall, what do the above studies suggest regarding the fate of unattended information?

Section 1: Early studies of attention

1 Behaviourists argued that since attention was not directly observable, it was not worthy of study.

2 Broadbent's book *Perception and Communication* argues that humans cannot cope with all the information available to their senses, and must therefore selectively attend to some of it.

3 The *cocktail-party phenomenon* (Cherry, 1953) describes our ability to focus attention on one conversation, whilst ignoring other conversations.

4 A *binaural listening task* involves listening to pairs of messages spoken simultaneously, using both ears.

5 A *dichotic listening task* involves presenting different messages to participants' right and left ears, respectively.

6 *Shadowing* is a procedure which requires participants to repeat out loud one or other of the messages presented in a dichotic listening task.

7 Moray (1959) found that *very little* of the shadowed message is remembered.

8 Broadbent's (1954) *split-span procedure* involved presenting six numbers to participants, three in one ear and three in the other, and recording how many were recalled.

Section 2: Focused auditory attention

9 All single-channel theories of attention propose that at some stage in the processing of information there is a 'bottleneck' or filter, which limits the amount of information to be passed on for further processing.

10 Broadbent's (1958) *early selection filter theory* claims that filtering occurs *early* on in processing.

11 The *short-term store* is a temporary buffer which holds information until it can be processed further.

12 The selective filter operates upon purely *physical characteristics* of the stimulus (such as tone and volume).

13 The *limited-capacity channel* corresponds to our 'stream of consciousness', i.e. all that we are aware of, now.

14 According to this model, it is possible for us to process two simultaneous stimuli by returning to the stimuli still held in the short-term store (one at a time).

15 Moray's (1959) finding is a problem since, according to Broadbent's model, selective filtering does not involve analysis of *meaning*, so we should not notice that our name is presented in a non-attended ear.

16 Treisman (1960) found that participants would occasionally shift their attention to the non-attended ear.

17 Underwood's (1974) participants, trained in shadowing, were able to recall most of the material presented to the non-shadowed ear.

18 Treisman's *attenuation theory* claims that incoming information is analysed in terms of its grammar, meaning and sound patterns.

19 An attenuated message is not rejected completely but 'turned down', so that it is still processed to some extent.

20 According to this theory, attention is likely to be switched to biologically relevant or important information.

21 The Deutsch–Norman theory claims that filtering and selection of information occur late in processing, only after all inputs have been analysed at a high level.

22 This theory is sometimes called *pertinence theory*, since the pertinence (or relevance) of information plays a key role in determining whether or not it is selected for attention.

23 The finding (Treisman & Riley, 1969) that target words are best identified in a shadowed message (vs. the non-shadowed message) is a problem for this theory, since *both* sensory inputs should have been analysed in terms of their meaning before being attended to: target words should be equally easy to identify.

24 Single-channel theories are inflexible in that they claim that certain amounts of processing occur at certain stages, whereas this may vary depending on the task and the nature of the information.

Section 3: Focused visual attention

25 The *fovea* (an area of the retina with the densest concentration of receptor cells) allows maximum visual processing.

26 *Covert attention* (Posner, 1980) refers to our ability to shift our attention without shifting our gaze (i.e. making eye movements).

27 Posner likened covert attention to an *internal mental spotlight*.

28 LaBerge (1983) asked participants to identify numbers at varying distances from the centre of their attention, concluding that visual attention is most concentrated at the centre of the internal spotlight.

29 LaBerge discovered that the 'width' of the mental spotlight's 'beam' varied, depending on the task.

30 Eriksen's (1990) *zoom-lens model* of visual attention proposed that the beam of the internal mental spotlight may be very narrow or broad.

31 Neisser & Becklen (1975) found that when they superimposed two films, participants could attend to one or the other, but not both. This contradicts the spotlight model, since both films were at the centre of attention.

32 A *visual search procedure* involves presenting participants with an array of stimuli, from which they must identify a 'target' item.

33 Treisman's (1988) two stages of visual processing are processing the features of a stimulus, and combining those features to form objects.

34 Treisman & Gelade's (1980) experiments found that the letter 'Z' increased the time taken by participants to spot a letter 'T' (since it shares the horizontal bar).

35 McLeod *et al.* (1991) found that participants could quickly identify a moving 'X' from among stationary 'X's and moving 'O's.

36 No, since the surrounding stimuli shared features with the moving 'X'.

37 Overall, these studies support the idea that unattended information is processed to some extent, but to what extent and how this is done is still unclear.

Internal mental spotlight
Posner (1980) likened attention to an internal spotlight which illuminates the attended region, allowing it to be perceived in greater detail.

- Posner *et al.* (1978, 1980): participants could switch their attention to areas 7 degrees either side of their visual field without making eye movements (covert attention).
- LaBerge (1983): asked participants to identify the middle letter of a series, occasionally presenting numbers to identify at different distances from the centre. The further from the centre, the longer identification took.

Zoom-lens model
Eriksen (1990) accepts spotlight model but proposed that the beam can be very narrow or quite broad, depending on the task.

Neisser & Becklen (1975): showed adults and children two superimposed films. Participants had to identify key events in the films. Unable to attend to both films simultaneously (contradicts zoom-lens model).

Treisman's feature-integration theory:
Objects possess features (such as colour, curvature).
Features and objects are recognised in two distinct stages of visual processing:

Stage1: features of visual input processed rapidly (in parallel)

Stage2: features combined to form objects. Occurs slowly (serially)

Research
- Treisman's (1988) theory was developed using findings from a **visual search procedure** in which participants must identify a target item from an array of other items (such as letters).
- Treisman & Gelade (1980): participants could rapidly detect a 'T' from amongst 'I's and 'Y's, irrespective of the size of the array, but only slowly from amongst 'I's and 'Z's. This suggests that **feature-detection** was being used to identify the letters.

Visual attention

Focused Attention

Auditory attention

Binaural listening tasks: listening to two messages at once through both ears.
Voice intensity, sex, location affected ability to separate messages.

Cocktail party phenomenon (Cherry, 1953): the ability to focus attention on one conversation whilst ignoring others.

Dichotic listening tasks: listening to a different message in each ear.
Participants shadowed one of the messages but very little was remembered of the non-shadowed message.

Single-channel theories

Broadbent's early selection filter theory

- Incoming info. goes into short-term store.
- Info. is held until it can be processed.
- Selection operates on info.'s physical characteristics.
- Filtered info. passes into consciousness.
- Info. analysed and response made.
- Processing can return to info. still in short-term store.

Stimulus inputs → Senses → Short-term store → Selective filter → Limited capacity channel → Store of past events & outcomes / Output varying system → Effectors → Response

Inconsistent Research
- Treisman (1960): if shadowed material was switched mid-sentence to other ear, participants would sometimes switch attention.
- Moray (1959): if participant's name was presented in non-attended ear, attention would switch a third of the time.

Treisman's attenuation (or stimulus analysis system) theory

- Information enters filter via senses
- Non-shadowed message is attenuated (turned down)
- Info. is analysed in terms of syllables, grammar and meaning.
- Biologically relevant and emotionally important info is attended to.
- Attenuated info is still available if important.

Stimulus inputs → Senses → Selective filter (attenuator) → Semantic analysis (recognition processes) → Response processes

Research
Treisman & Riley (1969): participants stopped shadowing when a target word was heard in either the attended or non-attended ear. Performance was better for the shadowed message (76%) than the non-shadowed message (33%).

The Deutsch–Norman late selection filter theory

- Filtering or selection only occurs after all inputs have been analysed at a high level.
- Memory system is used for analysis.
- Pertinence is taken into account when analysing info.
- One representation is then chosen for response/further attention.

Stimulus inputs → Processing / Pertinence / Memory → Selection → Attention

Research
Norman (1969): participants could remember words presented to a non-attended ear if asked immediately following a shadowing task.

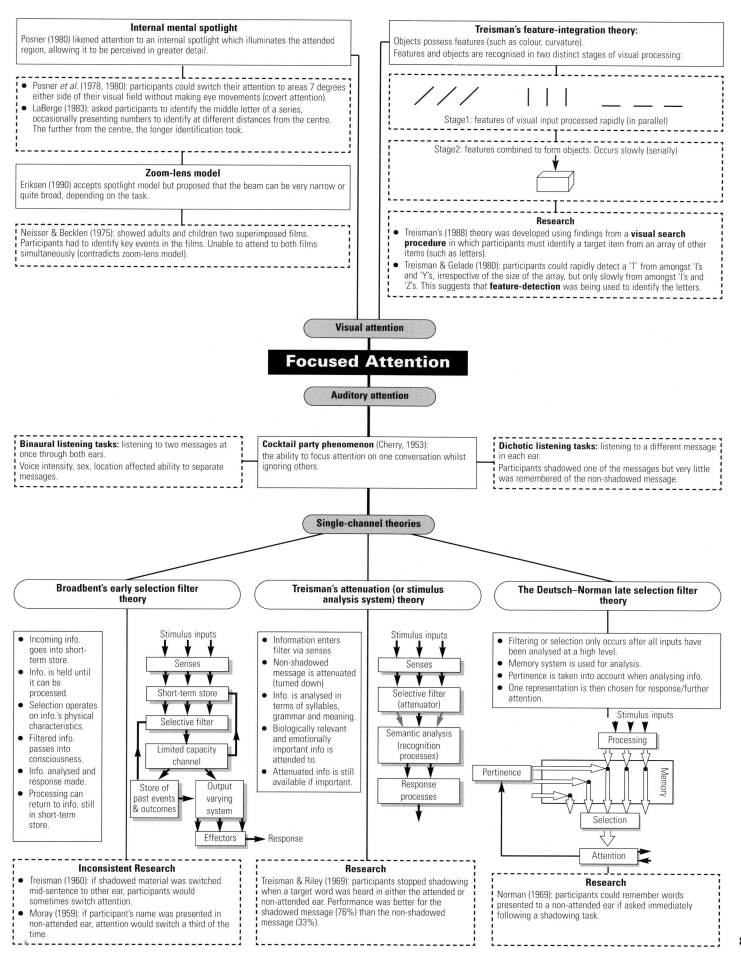

26

DIVIDED ATTENTION

SYLLABUS
5.2 Attention and performance limitations
- theories and evidence relating to divided attention
- the nature of automatic processing and research evidence in this area; theories and research into performance deficits, including action slips and dual task limitations

KEY QUESTIONS
- What is dual-task performance and which factors affect it?
- How do limited-capacity and multi-channel theories explain divided attention?
- How does automatic processing occur?
- What are 'action slips'?

Q

Section 1: Dual-task performance
1 What is the difference between studies of focused attention and studies of divided attention?
2 What did Spelke *et al.* (1976) discover about students' abilities to perform two tasks simultaneously?
3 According to Hampton (1989), why do factors which make one task easier tend to make the other easier too?
4 What three factors do Eysenck & Keane (1995) identify as affecting our ability to perform two tasks simultaneously?

Section 2: Theories of divided attention
5 Name two factors which (according to Kahneman's, 1973, model of attention) may affect how capacity is allocated.
6 What is the role of arousal in Kahneman's model?
7 What is meant by the *allocation policy* in Kahneman's (1973) model?
8 According to Norman & Bobrow's (1975) *central capacity interference theory*, in what two ways may performance be limited?
9 What does it mean to say that this theory is *unfalsifiable*?
10 What is meant by the term 'module' in Allport's *multi-channel approach*?
11 Why, according to this model, can dissimilar tasks be performed simultaneously?
12 Give one criticism of this approach.
13 How do *synthesis models* attempt to combine capacity and module accounts of attentional processing?

Section 3: Automatic processing
14 What does it mean to say that a task is processed automatically?
15 According to Schneider & Shiffrin (1977), what is the distinction between *controlled* and *automatic processing*?
16 Give an everyday example of a task which is initially controlled, but through practice becomes automatic.

17 What two suggestions have been made as to how we change from controlled to automatic processing?
18 What is the *Stroop Effect* (Stroop, 1935)?
19 According to Manstead & Semin (1980), what is the distinction between *open-loop control* and *closed-loop control*?
20 According to Abrams & Manstead (1981), why does our performance on simple tasks improve when we are being watched?
21 Why does our performance on complex tasks worsen when we are being watched?
22 What are the two separate control systems which Norman & Shallice (1986) proposed in their attentional model?
23 According to this model, when does partially automatic processing occur?

Section 4: Action slips
24 What is an '*action slip*'?
25 Name three of the five categories of action slip identified by Reason (1979, 1992).
26 What relationship does Reason (1992) suggest exists between action-slips and open-loop control?
27 Name two reasons why action slips occur, according to Sellen & Norman's (1992) *schema theory* of action slips.
28 What, according to this theory, is the difference between a parent schema and a child schema?
29 What, according to Eysenck (1994), would be one way of avoiding all action-slips?
30 What is one criticism of the *diary method* employed by Reason to record his participants' data concerning action-slips?
31 What overall conclusion can we draw regarding whether or not it is possible to divide attention between two tasks?

Section 1: Dual-task performance

1 Studies of focused attention require participants to process information from one of two inputs, whereas studies of divided attention require participants to process both stimulus inputs.

2 Spelke *et al.* (1976) discovered that students could learn to take notes and read short stories simultaneously, but only after six weeks of training.

3 Hampton (1989) claimed that factors which make one task easier will make the other easier, since such factors reduce the interference occurring between the two tasks.

4 Eysenck & Keane (1995) identify *difficulty* of task, *amount of practice* at task, and *similarity of tasks* as affecting dual-task performance.

Section 2: Theories of divided attention

5 Kahneman's (1973) model of attention claimed that *enduring dispositions*, *momentary intentions* and an *evaluation of attentional demands* all affect the way that processing capacity is allocated.

6 Arousal plays a key role in Kahneman's (1973) model, with more attentional resources being available when we are aroused.

7 The *allocation policy* was Kahneman's (1973) attempt to explain the system of rules used by an attentional system for deciding which possible activities should be allocated attention.

8 Norman & Bobrow's (1975) *central capacity interference theory* claims that performance may be *data-limited* (e.g. reading at a distance) or *resource-limited* (e.g. holding a conversation whilst negotiating a roundabout).

9 An *unfalsifiable* theory is one which cannot be disproved, i.e. which is consistent with any set of findings.

10 A 'module', according to Allport's *multi-channel approach*, is a specialised processing mechanism.

11 Dissimilar tasks can be performed simultaneously, because they use separate processing modules and so do not interfere with each other.

12 The approach is unfalsifiable, since we can propose any number of modules to explain observations. In addition, the number and function of the modules has yet to be specified, as has the manner in which they co-operate to produce behaviour.

13 *Synthesis models* propose the existence of a modality-free central processor which co-ordinates and controls the operation of more specific processing systems. Baddeley's (1986) working memory model is an example.

Section 3: Automatic processing

14 A task which has become automatic is one which makes no attentional demands.

15 Schneider & Shiffrin (1977) claim that *controlled processing* makes heavy demands on attentional resources, is slow, and involves conscious attention to a task. *Automatic processing* makes no demands on attentional resources, is fast,

unavoidable, unaffected by capacity limitations and difficult to modify.

16 Such tasks include learning to drive a car, tying one's shoelaces, and reading.

17 Psychologists are unsure as to how, precisely, controlled processing may become automatic, although it may involve a speeding up of the processing or a change in the nature of the processing.

18 The *Stroop Effect* (Stroop, 1935) refers to the difficulty of naming the colour of words which themselves refer to a different colour.

19 According to Manstead & Semin (1980), *open-loop control* is equivalent to automatic processing and *closed-loop control* to controlled processing.

20 Abrams & Manstead (1981) claim that our performance on simple tasks improves when we are being watched, because we normally leave them under open-loop control and pay little attention to what is going on. We focus our attention when we are being watched.

21 Manstead & Semin (1980) explain that when performing complex tasks which require all our attentional capacity, an audience acts as a distraction.

22 Norman & Shallice's (1986) attentional model proposes the existence of *contention scheduling* and the *supervisory attentional system*.

23 *Partially automatic processing* results from the monitoring of fully automatic processes by the contention scheduling system.

Section 4: Action slips

24 An *action slip* is the performance of an action which is unintended.

25 Reason (1979, 1992) identified *storage failures*, *test failures*, *sub-routine failures*, *discrimination failures* and *programme assembly failures* as the five categories of action slip.

26 Reason (1992) suggests that action-slips occur because we become over-reliant on open-loop control (automatic actions) when we should be paying more attention (closed-loop control).

27 Sellen & Norman's (1992) *schema theory* claims that action slips occur because of errors in the formation of intentions, activating incorrect schema, activation of the correct schema is lost, or faulty triggering of an active schema.

28 A *parent schema* corresponds to overall intentions, whilst a *child schema* corresponds to sets of actions involved in achieving the intention.

29 Eysenck (1994) claims that we could avoid all action slips by relying solely on closed-loop control.

30 Reason's *diary method* is flawed in that participants may not have detected all of their action slips.

31 It does sometimes seem possible to divide attention between two tasks, although how this is achieved has not yet been satisfactorily explained.

A

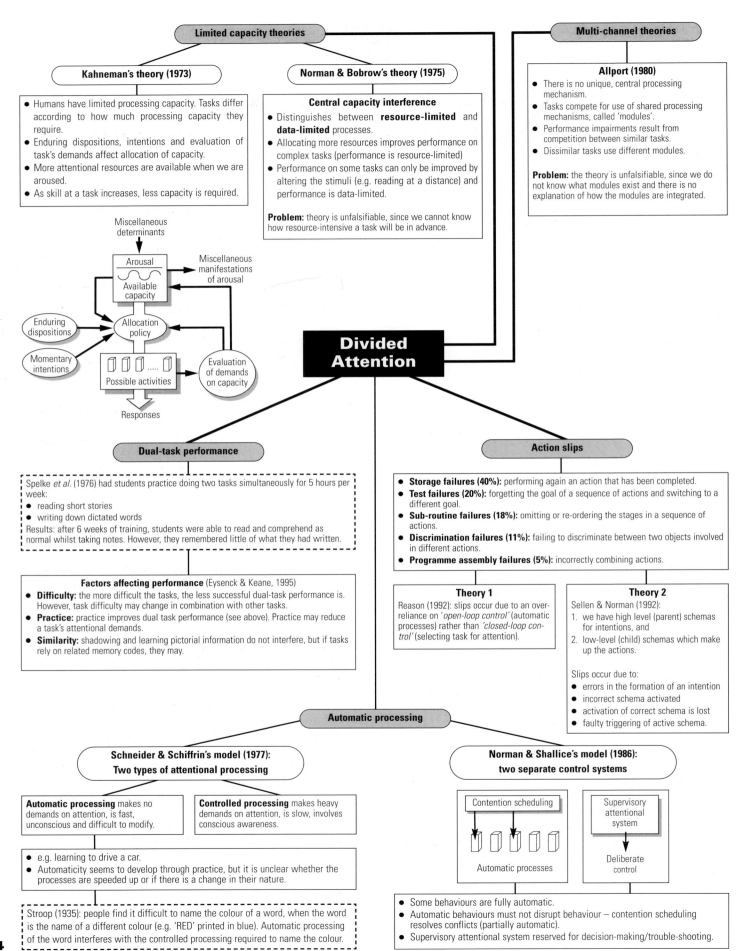

Limited capacity theories

Kahneman's theory (1973)

- Humans have limited processing capacity. Tasks differ according to how much processing capacity they require.
- Enduring dispositions, intentions and evaluation of task's demands affect allocation of capacity.
- More attentional resources are available when we are aroused.
- As skill at a task increases, less capacity is required.

Norman & Bobrow's theory (1975)

Central capacity interference

- Distinguishes between **resource-limited** and **data-limited** processes.
- Allocating more resources improves performance on complex tasks (performance is resource-limited)
- Performance on some tasks can only be improved by altering the stimuli (e.g. reading at a distance) and performance is data-limited.

Problem: theory is unfalsifiable, since we cannot know how resource-intensive a task will be in advance.

Multi-channel theories

Allport (1980)

- There is no unique, central processing mechanism.
- Tasks compete for use of shared processing mechanisms, called 'modules'.
- Performance impairments result from competition between similar tasks.
- Dissimilar tasks use different modules.

Problem: the theory is unfalsifiable, since we do not know what modules exist and there is no explanation of how the modules are integrated.

Miscellaneous determinants

Arousal

Available capacity

Miscellaneous manifestations of arousal

Enduring dispositions

Momentary intentions

Allocation policy

Possible activities

Evaluation of demands on capacity

Responses

Divided Attention

Dual-task performance

Spelke *et al.* (1976) had students practice doing two tasks simultaneously for 5 hours per week:
- reading short stories
- writing down dictated words
Results: after 6 weeks of training, students were able to read and comprehend as normal whilst taking notes. However, they remembered little of what they had written.

Factors affecting performance (Eysenck & Keane, 1995)
- **Difficulty:** the more difficult the tasks, the less successful dual-task performance is. However, task difficulty may change in combination with other tasks.
- **Practice:** practice improves dual task performance (see above). Practice may reduce a task's attentional demands.
- **Similarity:** shadowing and learning pictorial information do not interfere, but if tasks rely on related memory codes, they may.

Action slips

- **Storage failures (40%):** performing again an action that has been completed.
- **Test failures (20%):** forgetting the goal of a sequence of actions and switching to a different goal.
- **Sub-routine failures (18%):** omitting or re-ordering the stages in a sequence of actions.
- **Discrimination failures (11%):** failing to discriminate between two objects involved in different actions.
- **Programme assembly failures (5%):** incorrectly combining actions.

Theory 1
Reason (1992): slips occur due to an over-reliance on 'open-loop control' (automatic processes) rather than 'closed-loop control' (selecting task for attention).

Theory 2
Sellen & Norman (1992):
1. we have high level (parent) schemas for intentions, and
2. low-level (child) schemas which make up the actions.

Slips occur due to:
- errors in the formation of an intention
- incorrect schema activated
- activation of correct schema is lost
- faulty triggering of active schema.

Automatic processing

Schneider & Schiffrin's model (1977):
Two types of attentional processing

Automatic processing makes no demands on attention, is fast, unconscious and difficult to modify.

Controlled processing makes heavy demands on attention, is slow, involves conscious awareness.

- e.g. learning to drive a car.
- Automaticity seems to develop through practice, but it is unclear whether the processes are speeded up or if there is a change in their nature.

Stroop (1935): people find it difficult to name the colour of a word, when the word is the name of a different colour (e.g. 'RED' printed in blue). Automatic processing of the word interferes with the controlled processing required to name the colour.

Norman & Shallice's model (1986):
two separate control systems

Contention scheduling

Automatic processes

Supervisory attentional system

Deliberate control

- Some behaviours are fully automatic.
- Automatic behaviours must not disrupt behaviour – contention scheduling resolves conflicts (partially automatic).
- Supervisory attentional system reserved for decision-making/trouble-shooting.

27

THE NATURE OF MEMORY AND AN INTRODUCTION TO THE MULTI-STORE MODEL OF MEMORY

SYLLABUS
5.3 Memory
- theories and research findings relating to the nature of memory (i.e. structure, processes and types of memory)

KEY QUESTIONS
- How do psychologists measure memory?
- What basic processes are involved in memory?
- What is the nature of memory?
- How does the multi-store model of memory explain the flow of information in memory?

Section 1: Introducing memory
1 Reber (1985) identifies three meanings of the term 'memory'. What are they?
2 What is the relationship between learning and memory?
3 How did Ebbinghaus (1885) investigate the nature of memory?
4 What did he conclude, concerning the nature of forgetting over time?
5 What was Bartlett's (1932) principal criticism of Ebbinghaus's research?
6 What do psychologists record when measuring memory by *relearning*?
7 What is the difference between *recall* and *recognition* tests of learning?
8 What three basic *information-processing operations* are involved in memory?
9 Which of the following refers to the inability to retrieve stored information: unavailability, inaccessibility?

Section 2: The nature of memory
10 What is the principal function of *sensory memory*?
11 What did Sperling (1960) discover about the capacity of the *iconic store* (visual sensory memory)?
12 How long does it take for iconic memory to fade?
13 Why does *echoic memory* (auditory sensory memory) fade more slowly than visual sensory memory?
14 What does it mean to say that sensory memory is '*modality-specific*'?
15 What, according to Miller (1956), is the capacity of short-term memory?
16 What is '*chunking*'?
17 When Conrad (1964) presented participants with lists of six consonants for a brief period of time, what sort of errors did they make in recalling these consonants?
18 How is it possible to maintain information in short-term memory for long periods of time?
19 How did Peterson & Peterson (1959) discover the duration for which information is held in STM?
20 What is the capacity of long-term memory?

21 When Baddeley (1976) investigated the nature of long-term memory, what type of information did his participants have most difficulty recalling?

Section 3: The multi-store model of memory
22 What is another name for Atkinson & Shiffrin's (1969, 1971) *multi-store model of memory*?
23 What are the two *permanent structural components* referred to by this model?
24 What is the key process which accounts for the transfer of information from STM to LTM?
25 When Murdock (1962) tested participants by asking them to free-recall from a list of forty words presented to them, what did he discover?
26 How can the multi-store model account for the *primacy effect*?
27 How can the multi-store model account for the *recency effect*?
28 What would you expect to find if participants were asked to count backwards for thirty seconds at the end of presentation of the words to be recalled?
29 Which ability is commonly impaired in people suffering from *Korsakoff's syndrome*?
30 Which type of memory was impaired in the case of KF (Shallice & Warrington, 1970)?
31 In what way do such studies support the multi-store model?
32 What is the principal way in which Atkinson and Shiffrin's model has been challenged?
33 How did De Groot (1966) explain why expert chess players possess phenomenal memory for the position of chess pieces on a board provided they are placed according to the rules of the game?
34 What is the difference between *maintenance rehearsal* and *elaborative rehearsal*?
35 Is the multi-store model an adequate explanation of how different types of memory are linked?

Q

Section 1: Introducing memory

1 According to Reber (1985), 'memory' can refer to the function of retaining information, the storage system that holds information, or the stored information itself.

2 Learning is a relatively permanent change in behaviour as a result of experience. Without memory, we could not benefit from past experiences.

3 Ebbinghaus (1885) investigated the nature of memory by inventing nonsense syllables, learning these lists, then testing himself on his ability to recall them at different times.

4 He concluded that memory declines sharply at first, but then levels off after a couple of days.

5 Bartlett (1932) pointed out that Ebbinghaus's research bore very little relation to memory in everyday life.

6 When measuring memory by *relearning*, psychologists record the number of trials taken to learn information initially, then compare these with the number of trials taken to re-learn it at a later date.

7 *Recall tests* require participants to remember items without any cues being present, whilst *recognition tests* involve deciding whether or not a piece of information has been presented previously.

8 *Registration*, *storage* and *retrieval* are the three basic information-processing strategies involved in memory.

9 Inaccessibility refers to the inability to retrieve stored information.

Section 2: The nature of memory

10 The principal function of *sensory memory* is to retain information long enough for us to decide if it is worthy of further processing.

11 Sperling (1960) discovered that the *iconic store* (visual sensory memory) seemed to hold most of the visual information available to our senses for a short period.

12 Iconic memory fades in less than a second.

13 *Echoic memory* (auditory sensory memory) may fade more slowly than visual sensory memory because we are required to retain all of the sounds which make up a word before that word can be processed.

14 Sensory memory is '*modality-specific*' in that information is stored in the form in which it is received.

15 Miller (1956) claimed that, for most people, the capacity of short-term memory is seven items (plus or minus two items).

16 '*Chunking*' refers to the process of combining independent pieces of information into larger 'chunks' of information.

17 Conrad (1964) found that acoustic confusion errors occurred when participants attempted to recall consonants from their short-term memory.

18 Information can be maintained indefinitely in short-term memory by *rehearsing* (repeating over and over) the information.

19 Peterson & Peterson (1959) discovered the duration of STM by presenting participants with a list of trigrams (such as XPJ) and asking them to count backwards for varying time periods after presentation (which prevents rehearsal). They were then asked to recall the information.

20 The capacity of long-term memory is not known, but no limit has ever been discovered. However, we do not remember all that we experience or every aspect of a stimulus, so some 'cognitive economising' seems likely.

21 Baddeley (1976) found that his participants had most difficulty recalling semantically-similar words from LTM suggesting that information is coded semantically in LTM (i.e. converted into its meaning).

Section 3: The multi-store model of memory

22 Atkinson & Shiffrin's (1969, 1971) *multi-store model of memory* is also called the *dual-memory model*.

23 The two *permanent structural components* are *short-term memory* and *long-term memory*.

24 The key process which accounts for the transfer of information from STM to LTM is *rehearsal*.

25 Murdock (1962) discovered that participants were most likely to recall the words presented early on or towards the end of the list, but recalled few of those presented in the middle.

26 The multi-store model claims that the *primacy effect* results from the transfer of the first few words into LTM through rehearsal.

27 The multi-store model claims that the *recency effect* results from the last few words remaining in STM at the time of recall.

28 Counting backwards for thirty seconds at the end of presentation of a list of words would tend to *eliminate* the recency effect.

29 People suffering from *Korsakoff's syndrome* are commonly unable to transfer information from STM to LTM.

30 KF (Shallice & Warrington, 1970) had impaired STM but normal LTM.

31 Such studies suggest that STM and LTM are separate structural components, since they can be damaged independently.

32 The principal criticism of Atkinson and Shiffrin's model is that it is not necessary to distinguish various storage systems as it does.

33 De Groot's (1966) explanation of expert chess players' abilities was that they were able to draw on information from LTM in order to aid recall from STM.

34 According to Craik and Watkins, *maintenance rehearsal* is rehearsing material in the form in which it is presented, whilst *elaborative rehearsal* involves forming links with other material or making it meaningful in some way.

35 The multi-store model is not an adequate explanation of how different types of memory are linked, as it is overly simplistic.

Sensory memory

capacity

Sperling (1960) investigated visual sensory memory (iconic store) by flashing up a grid of letters and then testing recall immediately after.
Results: almost all information could be retrieved but memory faded very quickly with a delay.

duration

- Sperling found that iconic store faded within 1 second.
- Auditory sensory memory (echoic store) lasts longer – about 4 seconds.
- Echoic store needs to be longer so that all sounds in a word can be processed.

coding

Sensory memory holds info long enough for it to be processed by attentional systems – as such, coding is **modality specific** i.e. information is held in a relatively raw state close to the relevant sensory system (e.g. the retina), rather than centrally.

Short-term memory

capacity

- Miller (1956): 7 (±2) independent items or 'chunks'.
- Bower & Springston (1970): the letters FBIPHDTWAIBM could be remembered if 'chunked' so as to relate to items in long-term memory (FBI, etc.).

duration

Info can be held indefinitely by *rehearsal*.
- Peterson & Peterson (1959) prevented rehearsal by getting participants to count backwards before recalling nonsense 'trigrams' (e.g. XPJ).

Results: recall fell to 5% after 18 seconds.

coding

Conrad (1964) presented participants with 5 consonants (e.g. BKSJLR) for less than 1 second.
Results: mistakes were often similar in sound to the target, suggesting that coding is principally acoustic.

Long-term memory

capacity

There is no evidence of a limit to LTM's capacity. Nevertheless, we do not remember images or stories precisely, which suggests that some 'cognitive economising' occurs.

duration

Ebbinghaus (1885) memorised lists of nonsense syllables, then tested himself at intervals.
Results: memory declined sharply at first, then levelled off after a couple of days.

coding

Baddeley (1966): participants required to recall acoustically similar ('mad', 'mat') or semantically similar ('big', 'long') words.
Results: Semantically similar words were harder to recall in the long-term, suggesting LTM is largely coded semantically.

Nature of memory

The Nature of Memory

Measuring memory

Relearning: recording the number of repetitions needed to learn material vs. the number required to relearn it (e.g. revision speed).

Recognition: deciding whether or not a piece of information has been encountered before (e.g. multiple choice questions).

Recall: recalling items either in the order of presentation (*serial recall*) or any order (*free recall*) (e.g. essay questions).

Paired-associates: participants learn a list of paired items, are later presented with the one and must remember the other.

Information processing

Operations involved in memory:

- **Registration:** transformation of sensory input into a form which can be stored.
- **Storage:** holding or retaining information in memory.
- **Retrieval:** extracting stored info from memory.
- **Forgetting:** may occur because information is stored but irretrievable (inaccessible) or it may never have been stored (unavailable)

Multi-store model

Atkinson & Shiffrin (1968, 1971) attempted to explain flow of information from short-term to long-term memory:
- STM and LTM are permanent structural components.
- Control processes are transient and control flow of info.
- Rehearsal is a process which functions as a buffer between sensory memory and LTM and enables transfer of information to LTM.

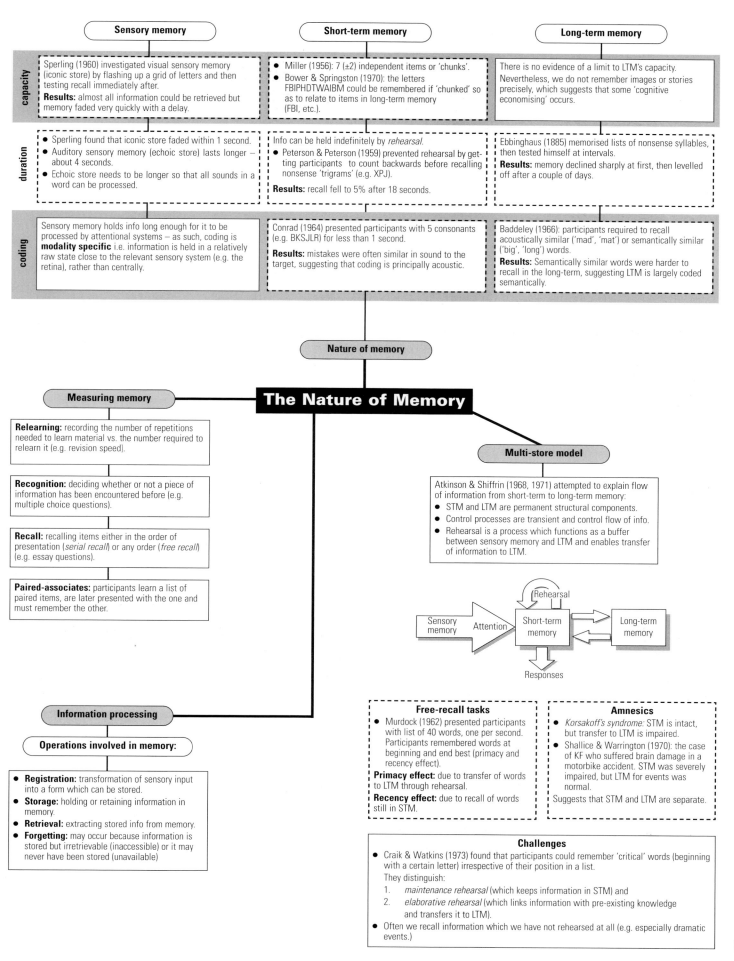

Free-recall tasks
- Murdock (1962) presented participants with list of 40 words, one per second. Participants remembered words at beginning and end best (primacy and recency effect).
Primacy effect: due to transfer of words to LTM through rehearsal.
Recency effect: due to recall of words still in STM.

Amnesics
- *Korsakoff's syndrome:* STM is intact, but transfer to LTM is impaired.
- Shallice & Warrington (1970): the case of KF who suffered brain damage in a motorbike accident. STM was severely impaired, but LTM for events was normal.

Suggests that STM and LTM are separate.

Challenges
- Craik & Watkins (1973) found that participants could remember 'critical' words (beginning with a certain letter) irrespective of their position in a list.
  They distinguish:
  1. *maintenance rehearsal* (which keeps information in STM) and
  2. *elaborative rehearsal* (which links information with pre-existing knowledge and transfers it to LTM).
- Often we recall information which we have not rehearsed at all (e.g. especially dramatic events.)

28

SOME ALTERNATIVES TO THE MULTI-STORE MODEL OF MEMORY

KEY QUESTIONS
- How does the levels-of-processing model explain memory?
- How does the working memory model view short-term memory?
- In what ways can long-term memory be reconceptualised?

Q

Section 1: The levels-of-processing model

1 Why is the distinction between *maintenance rehearsal* and *elaborative rehearsal* a key element in Craik & Lockhart's (1972) alternative to the multi-store model?

2 What are some of the features of Craik and Lockhart's *central processor*?

3 How is memory related to the activity of this central processor?

4 What features of a stimulus are analysed at a shallow level?

5 At which level is a word's meaning analysed?

6 How did Craik & Tulving's (1975) experiment make participants process tachistoscopically presented words at different levels?

7 What is *elaboration*?

8 Apart from elaboration and level of processing, which other factor is most likely to determine whether or not a word is remembered?

9 What did Eysenck & Eysenck (1980) discover about the memorability of information processed at shallow levels?

10 What is meant by the criticism that the model is descriptive rather than explanatory (Eysenck & Keane, 1995)?

11 Why is it a problem for the model that there is no way of measuring depth of processing independently of a person's actual retention score?

Section 2: The working memory model

12 What feature of the multi-store model did Baddeley & Hitch's (1974) working memory model elaborate?

13 What is meant by the claim that the *central executive* in this model is *modality free*?

14 What are the three *slave-systems* which make up working memory?

15 What is the name of the experimental method used by Baddeley to investigate the working memory model?

16 If two tasks can be performed as well together as separately, what does this tell us about the slave-systems which they use?

17 According to Baddeley (1990), which system within working memory may be responsible for specific problems in learning to read?

18 Give one criticism of Baddeley's central executive.

Section 3: Reconceptualising long-term memory

19 What does the finding that people suffering from certain types of amnesia are unable to learn new information but may be able to learn new skills suggest about LTM?

20 According to Squire (1987), what is the distinction between *procedural* and *declarative memory*?

21 According to Tulving (1972), declarative memory can be further subdivided. Which two further types does he propose?

22 In Baddeley's (1995) view, are these two types of memory entirely separate?

23 What is meant by Brown and Kulik's term *flashbulb memory*?

24 According to Brown & Kulik (1977), what kind of event most commonly produces flashbulb memories?

25 What further discovery did they make when investigating flashbulb memories for the death of Martin Luther King?

26 Why, according to evolutionary explanations, do flash-bulb memories occur?

27 When Neisser & Harsch (1992) investigated the accuracy of students' recollections of the space-shuttle explosion, three years after the event, what did they find?

28 What is a critical difference between procedural memory and *episodic* or *semantic memory*?

29 Name two of the cortical/subcortical areas thought to be involved in declarative memory (Baddeley, 1995).

30 Is either short-term memory or long-term memory a unitary store, as the multi-store model suggests?

Section 1: The levels-of-processing model

1 According to Craik & Lockhart (1972), *maintenance* (or *rote*) *rehearsal* serves only to maintain information in STM, whilst *elaborative rehearsal* (forming meaningful links) is more likely to transfer information to LTM. This suggests that simple rehearsal is not sufficient for information to be transferred to LTM.

2 Craik and Lockhart's *central processor* is capable of analysing data on a variety of levels and is of finite capacity.

3 According to Craik and Lockhart, memory is a *by-product* of the activity of this central processor.

4 The surface features of a stimulus (such as whether a word is in upper or lower case) are analysed at a shallow level.

5 The deepest level of analysis, *semantic analysis*, involves analysis of a word's meaning.

6 In Craik & Tulving's (1975) experiment, participants were presented with words tachistoscopically, then asked one of four questions (e.g. Is the word in capital letters? Does the word rhyme with 'wait'? Would the word fit the sentence …?). Different question types required different types of processing.

7 *Elaboration* refers to the amount of processing of a particular type at a particular level.

8 *Distinctiveness* has been shown to have a strong influence on whether or not a word is remembered.

9 Eysenck & Eysenck (1980) discovered that even when information was processed at a shallow level, it was likely to be remembered if it was distinctive.

10 The model is descriptive in that it accurately describes the findings that different types of processing lead to differential memories, but it does not explain how this works or why it should be so.

11 Because there is no way of measuring depth of processing independently of a person's actual retention score, the logic of the model is circular, since depth is supposed to explain better retention scores, and retention scores indicate depth of processing.

Section 2: The working memory model

12 Baddeley & Hitch's (1974) working memory model constitutes an elaboration of short-term memory (STM).

13 The *central executive* is *modality free* in the sense that it can process information in any sensory form (e.g. visual or acoustic information).

14 The three *slave-systems* which make up working memory are the articulatory loop, the primary acoustic store, and the visuo-spatial scratchpad.

15 Baddeley used the *concurrent-* (or *interference-*) *task method*, presenting participants with two tasks to perform simultaneously.

16 If two tasks can be performed as well together as separately, this suggests that they employ separate slave-systems.

17 According to Baddeley (1990), deficits in the articulatory loop may well be responsible for specific problems in learning to read.

18 Baddeley's central executive is suspiciously multi-purpose. We know very little about how it functions, despite its central role in working memory.

Section 3: Reconceptualising long-term memory

19 Amnesics, who are unable to learn new information but can learn new skills, suggest that LTM itself is composed of separate memory systems.

20 According to Squire (1987), *procedural memory* is 'skill' memory, storing knowledge of how to do things, whereas *declarative memory* is 'fact' memory, storing knowledge of specific information.

21 Tulving (1972) proposes that declarative memory can be further subdivided into *episodic memory* (EM), a record of events, and *semantic memory*, a record of general factual knowledge.

22 In Baddeley's (1995) view, semantic memory can be built up from episodic memories.

23 *Flashbulb memory* is the term used by Brown and Kulik to refer to a special kind of EM, in which we can supply a vivid and detailed recollection of where we were and what we were doing when we heard about or saw some important event.

24 Brown & Kulik (1977) found that personal shocking events were most likely to precipitate flashbulb memories (commonly, the sudden death of a relative).

25 Brown and Kulik also discovered that whilst 75 per cent of black participants had flashbulb memories for the assassination of Martin Luther King, only 33 per cent of whites did, suggesting that personal relevance is an important factor.

26 Evolutionary explanations suggest that flashbulb memories occur in response to events which threaten survival, so that the organism can remember and avoid recurrences of the event.

27 When Neisser & Harsch (1992) investigated the accuracy of students' recollections of the space-shuttle explosion three years after the event, none produced an entirely accurate report of what they were doing, and over one-third produced a completely inaccurate report.

28 The critical difference between procedural memory and episodic or semantic memory is that the former cannot be consciously inspected, whilst the latter are objective and can be examined consciously.

29 Cortical/subcortical areas thought to be involved in declarative memory are the hippocampus, the temporal lobes, the thalamus and mamillary bodies (Baddeley, 1995).

30 Contrary to the multi-store model, most research suggests that STM comprises a variety of processing systems (as in the working memory model), and that LTM stores different information in different ways and cannot, therefore, be considered unitary.

Alternative Memory Models

Levels of processing

Working memory

Craik & Lockhart (1972):
- It is not the *amount* but the *type* of rehearsal which is important.
- Instead of structures (STM and LTM) organised by processes, the model proposes a single attentional process which is structured in stages.
- Memory is seen as a by-product of perceptual analysis.
- Incoming information is subjected to a series of analyses of increasing depth – the greater the depth the more likely it is to be retained.
- The level used depends on the stimulus and the time available.

Baddeley & Hitch (1974):
- STM is more complex and versatile than the multi-store model proposed, and it is not unitary.
- Emphasised that it is an active store, combining a *central executive* (which allocates resources and can process any kind of information) and three *slave/sub-systems*:
  1. **Articulatory loop:** a verbal rehearsal loop, also used to hold words we are preparing to speak.
  2. **Visuo-spatial scratch-pad:** a visual rehearsal system, used to recall spatial layouts and images.
  3. **Primary acoustic store:** stores a variety of information in acoustic form.

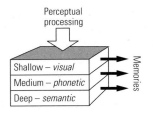

Perceptual processing

Shallow – *visual*
Medium – *phonetic*
Deep – *semantic*

Memories

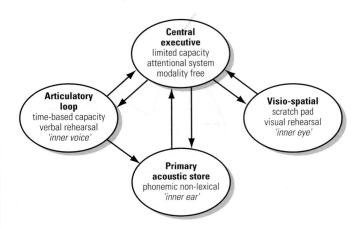

Central executive
limited capacity
attentional system
modality free

Articulatory loop
time-based capacity
verbal rehearsal
'inner voice'

Visio-spatial
scratch pad
visual rehearsal
'inner eye'

Primary acoustic store
phonemic non-lexical
'inner ear'

Research
- Craik & Tulving (1975) presented participants with words on a tachistoscope. Asked one of four questions after each word:
1. Is the word in capitals? (*visual processing*)
2. Does the word rhyme with 'wait'? (*phonetic processing*)
3. Is the word a type of food? (*semantic processing*)
4. Would the word fit the sentence 'He kicked the ... into the tree'? (*semantic processing*).

Results: an unexpected test of recognition showed that participants recognised more of the words processed at deeper levels.

Research
Baddeley *et al.* (1975) used the *concurrent/interference task* method to determine the number of systems. Participants must perform two tasks simultaneously: if the tasks interfere, then a single system is being used for both; if not, then it suggests the existence of separate systems.

Conflicting studies
- Bransford *et al.* (1979): the nature of elaboration was more important than the amount of elaboration. Distinctive material was more likely to be remembered.
- Eysenck & Eysenck (1980): even shallow processing could lead to good remembering if the stimulus was distinctive.
- Eysenck & Keane (1995): the model is more descriptive than explanatory – e.g. it does not explain why deeper processing leads to better recall.
- Morris (1977): rhyming recognition tests produced better recall when processed at the shallow, rather than deep level.

Practical application
- Gathercole & Baddeley (1990): children with specific problems learning to read often show impaired memory span and often do poorly on tasks such as judging if words rhyme. Baddely (1990) argues that this may be related to a deficit in the phonological loop, which might be detectable at an early stage.

Reconceptualising LTM

Squire (1987): distinguishes

Declarative
'fact' memory – *knowing that* something is the case

Procedural
'skill' memory – *knowing how* to do something

Tulving (1985): distinguishes EM from SM

Episodic memory (EM)
Autobiographical memory, recording events, people, objects we have encountered.

Semantic memory (SM)
A store of factual knowledge about the world, including concepts, rules and language. May also be built up from experience (EM).

- Cannot be inspected consciously.
- Initially we learn something *declaratively* (e.g. driving a car) and this eventually becomes *procedural* (this corresponds to the controlled/automatic processing distinction in attention (see Ch 26)

Flashbulb memories
Vivid and detailed memories of important events (e.g. the death of John F. Kennedy) , possibly triggered by a special neural mechanism (Brown & Kulik, 1982).

The case of HM: HM was unable to transfer information from STM to LTM following brain surgery. He was able to learn new skills, however (e.g. mirror-reading), although he had to be reminded that he had learned them.

- Brown & Kulik (1977) found that 73 out of 80 participants had flashbulb memories associated with personal shock.
- Personal relevance matters: more black participants had a flashbulb memory of Martin Luther King's assasination than did whites.

29

THE ORGANISATION OF INFORMATION IN MEMORY

SYLLABUS
5.3 Memory
- explanations of the organisation of information in memory

KEY QUESTIONS
- What is the role of imagery in organising memories?
- How do semantic-network models explain the organisation of information in memory?
- How can schemas help us to understand the organisation of memory?

Section 1: Introducing memory organisation

1 According to Baddeley (1995), what is the secret of a good memory?
2 What did Bousfield (1953) discover when participants recalled lists of 60 words drawn from four categories?
3 What are the two terms used by Tulving (1968) to describe whether or not participants or experimenters are responsible for the organisation of material?
4 What did Bower *et al.* (1969) discover when participants were asked to learn lists of words arranged either as a hierarchy or randomly?

Section 2: Imagery as organisation

5 What is the *method of loci*?
6 What did Bower (1972) discover when his participants learned words either by 'memorising' them or forming mental images of them?
7 According to Anderson (1995b), what type of mental images are most effective?
8 What is the name of Paivio's model which attempts to explain our superior memory for images?
9 Which type of noun would you expect to remember more easily – concrete or abstract? Why?

Section 3: Network models of memory

10 What is the assumption common to all network models about how information is stored in memory?
11 What does it mean to say that this type of model is concerned with *lexical memory*?
12 How does Collins & Quillian's (1969) *hierarchical network model* represent a *concept*?
13 What is the advantage of organising concepts in a hierarchy?
14 What did Collins and Quillian discover when participants performed *sentence verification tasks* on statements such as 'a canary can sing'?
15 Is Rips *et al.*'s (1973) finding that people typically take longer to verify 'a bear is a mammal' than 'a bear is an animal' consistent with this model? Explain your answer.

Section 4: Matrix and feature models

16 What did Broadbent discover when comparing the recall scores of groups presented with words arranged in a hierarchy vs. those for whom the words were arranged in a matrix?
17 When, according to Smith *et al.*'s (1974) *feature approach*, should it be easiest to verify a statement?
18 What is the difference between a *defining feature* and a *characteristic feature*?

Section 5: Spreading-activation models

19 What is *semantic distance*?
20 What does *spreading activation* mean?
21 In Jones & Anderson's (1987) *lexical-decision experiments*, participants were primed with certain words before being asked to identify target words flashed very briefly. What conclusions did they draw?
22 Give one criticism of spreading-activation models.

Section 5: Schemas

23 What is a *schema*?
24 Name two features of schemas.
25 How did Allport & Postman (1947) investigate the distorting effect of schemas?
26 How was Neisser (1981) able to explain inconsistencies in John Dean's account of his meeting with President Nixon?
27 What is meant by saying that schemas comprise *fixed compulsory values* and *variable values*?
28 What types of information can schemas represent?
29 How are schemas used, other than to store information?
30 Who was SAM (Schank & Abelson 1977)?
31 What is Cohen's (1993) view of the practical use of schemas?
32 How are MOPs arranged in Schank's (1982) *dynamic-memory theory*?
33 What overall conclusion can be drawn about the nature of the organisation of memory?

Section 1: Introducing memory organisation

1 According to Baddeley (1995), the secret of a good memory is 'systematic encoding of incoming material, integrating and relating it to what is already known'.

2 Bousfield (1953) found that participants tended to recall words in clusters of related items, suggesting that they had tried to organise them during learning.

3 Tulving (1968) used the term *subjective organisation* to refer to participants' own organisation of material and *experimenter organisation* to refer to an organisation imposed by the researcher.

4 Bower *et al.* (1969) discovered that 65 per cent of words were recalled correctly when they were presented hierarchically compared with only 19 per cent when presented randomly.

Section 2: Imagery as organisation

5 The *method of loci* is a mnemonic technique used to improve memory by imagining items to be recalled at familiar locations.

6 Bower (1972) discovered that 80 per cent of words were recalled by participants who had formed mental images of them vs. only 45 per cent by those who had not been instructed to do so.

7 According to Anderson (1995b), bizarre, interacting and vivid images are most effective at improving recall.

8 Paivio's model is called the *dual-code model* (or *dual-code hypothesis*).

9 According to Paivio, concrete nouns should be more easily remembered, since it is possible to form a mental image of them, thereby coding them in two forms.

Section 3: Network models of memory

10 Network models share the common assumption that information is stored in memory by being embedded in an organised, structured network.

11 *Lexical memory* refers to memory for particular words rather than grammar or sentences.

12 Collins & Quillian's (1969) model represents a *concept* as being *a node in a network* connected by pointers which give the concept its meaning.

13 The advantage of organising concepts in a hierarchy is that properties shared by concepts can be stored jointly at a higher level: this is cognitively economical (the same information is not stored twice).

14 Collins and Quillian discovered that when participants performed *sentence verification tasks*, they typically took longer to verify statements involving information further up the hierarchy (e.g. 'a bird has skin').

15 Rips *et al.*'s (1973) finding is *inconsistent* with this model, since 'mammal' is lower than 'animal' in the hierarchy, and therefore 'a bear is a mammal' should be verified quicker than 'a bear is an animal'.

Section 4: Matrix and feature models

16 Broadbent discovered that groups presented with words arranged in a matrix were just as likely to recall those words as when they were presented in a hierarchy.

17 According to Smith *et al.*'s (1974) *feature approach*, it should it be easiest to verify a statement when the concepts to be compared share few or many features.

18 A *defining feature* is a characteristic sufficient for a concept to belong to a category (e.g. having feathered wings = bird), whilst a *characteristic feature* is a feature which an object possesses independently of its belonging to a category (e.g. having yellow feathers).

Section 5: Spreading-activation models

19 *Semantic distance* is a way of identifying objects as being more or less closely related by representing them as closer or further apart.

20 *Spreading activation* refers to the 'activation' of concepts in order of closeness to a central concept.

21 In Jones & Anderson's (1987) *lexical-decision experiments*, participants identified target words more quickly if they were related to a 'prime' word. This supported the notion of 'spreading activation'.

22 The spreading-activation model may be guilty of the 'symbolic fallacy': it only tells us how different symbols are related to each other, but ultimately what they will *refer to* can vary according to the situation.

Section 5: Schemas

23 A *schema* is a 'mental map' or representation of a given area of knowledge.

24 Schemas provide us with preconceived expectations, help us to interpret information, and affect the way that memories are encoded.

25 Allport & Postman (1947) investigated the distorting effect of schemas by showing participants a picture of a white man threatening a black man with a razor. After several re-tellings of the story, the razor changed from the white man's hand to the black man's hand in participants' accounts.

26 Neisser (1981) explained inconsistencies in John Dean's account by claiming that he had recalled details from a schema for such meetings.

27 Schemas comprise *fixed compulsory values* (such as the fact that restaurants involve eating and sitting down) and *variable values* (such as what might be on the menu).

28 Schemas can represent any kind of information at any level of abstraction (from 'sucking' schemas to schemas for 'justice').

29 Schemas are also active recognition devices.

30 SAM (Schank & Abelson, 1977) was a computer program, programmed with a restaurant script.

31 Cohen (1993) believed that the concept of a schema is too vague to be of practical use.

32 MOPs (*memory organisation packets*) store specific details about specific events, and are at the bottom of a hierarchy in Schank's (1982) *dynamic-memory theory*.

33 The evidence does support the view that memory is highly organised, but precisely how it is organised is still unclear.

Organisation of Memory

Imagery

Paivio's (1986) dual-coding approach
proposed that information can be stored in two forms:
- *verbal codes* (as words) or
- *sensory codes* (as images or sounds).

Abstract nouns (such as 'economics') were harder to recall than concrete nouns (such as 'cat'). Paivio argued this was because concrete nouns can also be stored in image form.

Bower (1972) presented participants with 100 cards each with two unrelated words printed on it (e.g. cat and brick). One group was told simply to memorise the words, the other to form vivid mental images which linked the words.
Results: those using imagery scored 80% recall vs. only 43% for the non-imagers.

Anderson (1995b) found that bizarre, interacting and vivid images were the most effective.

Schemas

The nature of schemas

- A schema is a 'mental map' of events, objects or people, containing relevant information.
- Schemas provide us with preconceived expectations.
- Schemas help us to interpret the world, and to make it more predictable.
- Schemas affect the way memories are encoded and can have a distorting effect (see below).

Allport & Postman (1947) showed participants a drawing of two men in an argument (one white, one black). The white man held a cut-throat razor.
When participants described the scene to another, who in turn described it to another, the razor typically 'changed hands' in line with prevailing prejudice.

Schema theories

Common features of schema theories:
- Schemas are packets of information comprising fixed values and variable values.
- Schemas can be combined to form systems.
- Schemas can represent knowledge at abstract or practical levels (e.g. a schema for justice vs. a schema for faces).
- Schemas represent knowledge and experience of the world.
- Schemas are active recognition devices.

Schank & Abelson (1977) wrote a computer program (SAM) around a restaurant 'script'. SAM was able to answer questions about what to do in a restaurant.

Schank's (1982) *dynamic memory theory* sees schemas for specific events as 'memory organisation packets' (MOPS) stored at the bottom of a hierarchy.

Semantic network models

Hierarchical network model
(Collins & Quillian, 1969, 1972)

A concept is a node in a network connected by pointers. Pointers give the meaning of a word.
Two types of pointer:
1. property pointers
2. category pointers

Features:
- *Cognitive economy:* shared properties stored at higher level.

```
             has skin
   Animal
             breathes
   Fish   Bird
                can fly
                has wings
   Pigeon   Canary
                is yellow
                can sing
```

Matrix and feature models

Broadbent *et al.* (1978) gave participants a list of 16 words to remember. Words were presented:
1. randomly
2. in a hierarchical organisation
3. In a matrix (see below).

Results: recall was significantly better for groups 2 and 3 but neither was superior.

	Mammals	Birds
Farmyard	Cow	Chicken
	Sheep	Turkey
	Pig	Duck
	Goat	Goose
Pets	Dog	Budgerigar
	Cat	Canary
	Guinea-pig	Parrot
	Hamster	Macaw

Revised network model
Collins & Loftus (1975)

A concept is still a node in a network but the model has new features.

Features:
- The network is no longer hierarchically organised – more flexible.
- *Semantic distance* varies – represents how closely concepts are related.
- New links: 'is a', 'is not a', 'has', 'has not', 'can', 'cannot'.
- *Spreading activation:* more distant properties are recognised more slowly with activation spreading in *all* directions.

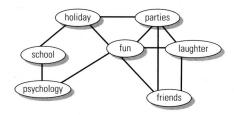

Research (Hierarchical network model)

- *Sentence verification tasks* found that participants took longer to say if 'a canary has skin' is true than if asked to say if 'a canary can sing' is true – supporting the model.
- Baddeley (1990): it took longer to verify 'an ostrich is a bird' than 'a canary is a bird' – but the model predicts they should take the same amount of time.
- Rips *et al.* (1973): it takes longer to verify 'a bear is a mammal' than 'a bear is an animal' when, according to the model, 'animal' is higher up the hierarchy than 'mammal' (and so should take longer to verify).

Smith *et al.*'s (1974) **feature** approach:
- Concepts are stored together with their features.
- Verification takes place by a comparison of features.
- Where shared features are many (e.g. 'a cat is an animal') or few (e.g. 'a cat is sand') verification is swift.
- Where only some features are shared, we look to see whether it is *defining features* or *characteristic features* which are shared.

Research (Revised network model)

Participants are shown a 'prime' (such as the word 'dog'), then target words are shown very briefly.
Where target words are closer to the prime (such as 'dalmation') they are identified more quickly (as the model suggests), because they are 'activated' by the prime.

30

THEORIES OF FORGETTING

Q

Section 1: Introducing forgetting

1 What is the distinction between the *availability* and *accessibility* of information?
2 Which of these two is most likely to account for failures of short-term memory?

Section 2: Motivated forgetting

3 According to Freud, what is *repression*?
4 What sort of information does Freud suggest we are likely to repress?
5 What is *psychogenic amnesia*?
6 Which aspect of psychogenic amnesia does the *motivated forgetting theory* have most difficulty accounting for?
7 According to Parkin (1993), in what circumstances may motivated forgetting have a beneficial role?
8 How, according to Loftus (1997), are *false memories* constructed?

Section 3: Distortion and decay theories

9 What is the central principle behind the *Gestalt* theory of forgetting?
10 Are there any studies which support this theory?
11 What is an *engram*?
12 According to decay theories, under what circumstances will the engram tend to decay?
13 What, according to Hebb (1949), are the two stages in the formation of an engram?
14 What types of memory are *not* lost through decay?
15 What did Jenkins & Dallenbach's (1924) study of recall in sleeping participants conclude about the role of decay in forgetting?

Section 4: Interference theory

16 What are the *two types of interference* which may occur between information which is learned?
17 How is *paired-associate learning* used to investigate these two types of interference?
18 What term describes the interference of later learning with material learned earlier?

19 What, based on Wickens' (1972) research, is the most likely cause of *proactive interference*?
20 Why have the results of interference experiments been criticised for possessing 'low ecological validity'?

Section 5: Displacement theory

21 In what sort of memory system would you expect displacement of material to occur?
22 What was involved in Waugh & Norman's (1965) *serial probe task*?
23 What were their findings?

Section 6: Retrieval-failure theory

24 According to retrieval-failure theory, why are we sometimes unable to recall memories?
25 What is the *tip-of-the-tongue phenomenon*?
26 What did Brown & McNeill (1966) discover when investigating the tip-of-the-tongue phenomenon?
27 When Tulving & Pearlstone (1966) asked participants to recall words which they had tried to memorise, why was the experimental group able to recall many more than the control group?
28 What is Tulving & Thomson's (1973) *encoding specificity principle*?
29 Tulving (1974) used the term *cue-dependent forgetting* to apply to which two types of forgetting?
30 Would you prefer to take your A level Psychology exam in the same room or a different room to the one in which your lessons were held? Why?
31 Why do people sometimes claim to forget what they did whilst under the influence of alcohol?
32 What did Godden & Baddeley (1975) discover when testing the recall of divers who had learned word-lists underwater?
33 Which of the above theories is most applicable to STM, and which to LTM?

Section 1: Introducing forgetting

1 *Availability* refers to whether or not material has been stored, whereas *accessibility* refers to whether or not the information can be retrieved.

2 Failures of short-term memory are most likely to be due to the information being unavailable.

Section 2: Motivated forgetting

3 Freud claims that *repression* is an unconscious process in which certain memories are made inaccessible.

4 Freud claims that memories which elicit guilt, shame or anxiety are most likely to be repressed.

5 *Psychogenic amnesia* is amnesia which does not have a physical cause.

6 The motivated forgetting theory cannot account for the sudden return of memories in people suffering from psychogenic amnesia after a period of hours or years.

7 Parkin (1993) claims that motivated forgetting may have a beneficial role in cases of post-traumatic stress disorder, where it may help sufferers to adjust.

8 Loftus (1997) claims that *false memories* are often constructed by combining actual memories with the content of suggestions from others.

Section 3: Distortion and decay theories

9 The central principle behind the *Gestalt* theory of forgetting is that memories undergo qualitative changes with time, being distorted towards a 'better', more regular and symmetrical form.

10 Wulf (1922) and James (1958) believe that studies of participants' reproductions of drawings do show distortions in the manner suggested by Gestalt theories. Baddeley (1968), however, believes that limitations in participants' drawing abilities is a more likely explanation.

11 An *engram* is a structural change in the brain which accompanies learning.

12 Decay theories claim that metabolic processes will degrade the engram over time, unless it is maintained by repetition or rehearsal.

13 According to Hebb (1949), an engram is initially delicate and liable to disruption (the *active trace*). With learning, it grows stronger and becomes permanent (the *structural trace*).

14 Procedural memories (motor skills – such as riding a bike) appear not to be lost through decay.

15 Jenkins & Dallenbach's (1924) study of recall in sleeping participants found that recall-score declined far less than in participants who were awake, suggesting that interference, *not* decay, plays the major role in forgetting.

Section 4: Interference theory

16 *Proactive interference* (or *inhibition*) and *retroactive interference* (or *inhibition*) may occur when similar material is learned within a short time-span.

17 *Paired-associate learning* involves participants learning two lists of word-pairs one after the other. The first word of each word pair is the same on both lists, but is paired with a different word in each case. Participants are then asked to recall which words were paired on either the first or second list.

18 *Retroactive inhibition* refers to interference of later learning with material learned earlier.

19 Wickens' (1972) research suggests that the major cause of proactive interference is interference with the retrieval of information from STM.

20 Interference experiments typically involve participants recalling similar lists of nonsense syllables within a short time-span. When meaningful material is used, interference effects are difficult to demonstrate. Some psychologists have argued that this shows that such explanations bear little relation to real life.

Section 5: Displacement theory

21 Displacement is most likely to occur in limited-capacity memory systems, such as STM.

22 The *serial probe task* involved presenting participants with a series of digits, then a 'probe' digit from the list to discover whether participants could recall the digit immediately following the probe.

23 Waugh & Norman (1965) found that when the number of digits following the probe was small, recall was good, but when the number of digits was large, recall was poor. This supports displacement theory.

Section 6: Retrieval-failure theory

24 Retrieval-failure theories argue that poor recall occurs because the correct retrieval cues are not being used.

25 The *tip-of-the-tongue phenomenon* is when we know that we know something, but cannot recall it.

26 Brown & McNeill (1966) discovered that participants in the 'tip-of-the-tongue' state could recall some of the features of the word (such as its first letter), despite being unable to recall the whole word.

27 Tulving & Pearlstone (1966) found that presenting participants with the *category headings* of the words which they had learned boosted recall.

28 Tulving & Thomson's (1973) *encoding specificity principle* states that recall improves if the same cues are present during recall as were present during learning.

29 Tulving (1974) uses the term *cue-dependent forgetting* to refer to state- and context-dependent forgetting.

30 Abernathy's (1940) participants recalled material best when in the same room as they had learned it. Ideally you should take exams in your teaching room.

31 Physiological states represent internal cues (e.g. alcohol acts as a cue) and memories may become inaccessible when they are absent, having been present during learning. In addition, alcohol may also impair the transfer of information from short-term to long-term memory.

32 Godden & Baddeley (1975) found that divers' recall was best under the same conditions as they had learned.

33 Displacement is most applicable to STM, with motivated forgetting, retrieval-failure, interference, distortion and decay theories applicable to LTM.

Theories of Forgetting

Availability refers to whether or not material has been stored in the first place. Mostly concerns forgetting occurring in STM.

Accessibility refers to whether or not what has been stored can be retrieved. Mostly concerns forgetting occurring in LTM.

Displacement

- Forgetting occurs due to the limited capacity of STM.
- When the system is full, oldest material is pushed out by incoming new material ('bookshelf' model).

Waugh & Norman (1965) used a *serial probe task*, presenting participants with 16 digits, then asking them to say which digit followed a digit from the list (the 'probe').
Results: the greater the number of digits following the probe, the poorer participants' recall, suggesting that later material had, indeed, displaced earlier material.

Retrieval failure

- Memories cannot be recalled because the correct retrieval cues are not being used.
- Demonstrated by the *tip-of-the-tongue phenomenon*, where we know that we know something but cannot retrieve it then and there.
- Tulving (1974) uses the term *cue-dependent forgetting* to refer to two types of forgetting.

cue-dependent forgetting

state-dependent forgetting

e.g. forgetting what one did whilst intoxicated

context-dependent forgetting

Abernathy (1940): participants recalled material best when in the same room in which they learned it.

Tulving & Pearlstone (1966): participants attempted to recall words from list of words in different categories.
Results: participants were able to recall more words if supplied with category headings. (e.g. 'animals', 'tools')

Motivated forgetting

- **Repression:** according to Freud, forgetting is a motivated process.
- **Defence mechanisms:** act to repress memories likely to cause guilt, shame or anxiety.
- **Unconscious mind:** where repressed memories reside, so they are not 'erased'.
- Freud (1901) reports on the case of a man who continually forgot the line following 'with a white sheet' in a poem. Freud claims that he was repressing a fear of death associated with seeing his dead father covered by a white sheet.

- Cases of *psychogenic amnesia* (amnesia without any physiological cause), which is linked to stressful events, may support this theory – but the theory cannot explain why these memories return when they do.
- Parkin (1993): repression may be beneficial in helping people to cope with traumatic events.
- Loftus (1997): it is difficult to investigate repressed memories, and some of the 'repressed memories' unearthed by psychiatrists may well be *false memories*.

Interference

- Forgetting is influenced more by what we do *before* or *after* learning than by the passage of time.
- Studied using *paired-associate lists* where two lists of word pairs are learned, the same words paired differently on each list (list A and list B).
- *Retroactive interference* involves later learning interfering with material learned earlier. (A ← B)
- *Proactive interference* involves earlier learning interfering with material learned later on. (A → B)

- Wickens (1972): participants became poorer at retaining information in STM on successive trials. However, if category of information was changed performance improved (release from proactive inhibition).
- This suggests that the major cause of proactive interference is interference with the retrieval of information from STM, rather than its storage.
However, Baddeley (1990) argues that such studies are not clearly related to real life and so lack ecological validity.

Distortion and decay

Gestalt theory

- Related to the Gestalt theory of perception.
- Memories undergo *qualitative changes* over time rather than being lost.
- Memories are distorted in order to become more regular, symmetrical.

- Wulf (1922) and James (1958): participants' reproductions of drawings seen earlier were changed in the direction suggested by Gestalt theory.
- Baddeley (1968): these results can be explained in terms of biases, such as the limited accuracy of participants' drawing abilities. Concluded that the theory is *sterile*.

Decay theory

- Explains why forgetting increases over time.
- Memories are stored in the brain as structural changes (*engrams*).
- Metabolic processes will tend to degrade the engram unless maintained by rehearsal ('*use it or lose it*').

Hebb (1949) identified two stages in engram formation:
1 During learning, engram is delicate and liable to disruption (the *active trace*). Equivalent to STM.
2 After learning, a stronger, permanent engram is formed (the *structural trace*), corresponding to LTM.

Jenkins & Dallenbach (1924): participants learned lists of nonsense syllables, then went to sleep and were tested for recall after either 1, 2, 4 or 8 hours.
Results: far more forgetting occurred in participants who did not go to sleep after learning words. This suggests that interference from new material, not decay, is most responsible for forgetting.

31

SOME PRACTICAL APPLICATIONS OF RESEARCH

INTO MEMORY

KEY QUESTIONS
- How accurate is eyewitness testimony?
- What factors may influence eyewitness testimony?
- How can memory be improved?
- How do 'memory experts' remember information?

Q

Section 1: Introducing eyewitness testimony
1 Which aspect of memory has cast doubts on the reliability of eyewitness testimony?
2 What sort of questions did Loftus investigate in her research into eyewitness testimony?
3 What did Loftus (1974) discover about the importance of testimony submitted by *discredited* witnesses?
4 Why, according to Brigham & Malpass (1985), are errors in identifying a suspect most likely to occur when the suspect is of a different race to the witness?
5 What other factor in identifying suspects did Wells (1993) indicate as being very important?

Section 2: The influence of leading questions
6 What is a leading question?
7 Participants in Loftus & Palmer's (1974) experiment gave widely differing estimates of how fast two cars were going, after watching a video clip of an accident. Why?
8 In a follow-up experiment, Loftus asked participants if they had seen broken glass. What did she find?
9 Do leading questions merely affect individuals' responses at the time of questioning, or do they actually distort memories for events?
10 According to Loftus & Zanni's (1975) research, which of the two questions 'Did you see *the* broken headlight?' and 'Did you see *a* broken headlight?' is most likely to elicit a positive response?
11 According to Loftus, are eyewitnesses reliable?
12 Regarding what sort of information is it easiest to mislead eyewitnesses?

Section 3: Other influences on testimony
13 What is the goal of the *cognitive interview technique* used by police in interviewing witnesses?
14 Which two steps follow on from 'reinstating the context' and 'reporting the event' in this technique?
15 What instruction, to be given by the judge to the jury, was recommended by the Devlin Committee?

Section 4: Improving memory
16 What is a *mnemonic*?
17 According to Belezza (1981), mnemonics impose meaning and structure on material. What is the other important characteristic of mnemonics?
18 What method did Snowman *et al.* (1980) use in order to boost their students' recall for concepts?
19 According to Higbee (1996), what two types of mnemonic systems are there?
20 How is the *link-word method* used to assist students in learning a foreign language?
21 How can the finding that memory is, to some extent, context-dependent (Abernathy, 1940) be used to improve memory?
22 If memory is also dependent on our internal state, what effect would you expect a state of panic to have on a student's recall abilities?
23 According to Reder & Anderson's (1980) research, why are summaries important?
24 In Thomas and Robinson's PQ4R method, what does 'PQ4R' stand for?
25 Why is it important to impose meaning on material if you wish to improve retention?
26 What should you do when material is long and complicated?
27 What is *overlearning*?
28 Of the subjects psychology, chemistry, English literature and sociology, which are most likely to cause interference if studied one after the other?

Section 5: Memory expertise
29 What two categories of 'memory experts' did Valentine & Wilding (1994) identify?
30 Name two differences between the two types of memory expert.
31 How might one criticise research into 'everyday' memory?

Section 1: Introducing eyewitness testimony

1 The reconstructive nature of memory, in particular the tendency of people to 'fill in the gaps' or modify memories so as to match existing schemas, has cast doubts on the reliability of eyewitness testimony.

2 Loftus was interested in questions such as 'Can the wording of questions cause witnesses to remember events differently?', and 'Can witnesses be misled into remembering things which did not actually occur?'

3 Loftus (1974) discovered that even *discredited* witnesses were highly influential on participants' perceptions of guilt or innocence.

4 According to Brigham & Malpass (1985), people of a given race tend to have difficulty recognising the faces of people from another race.

5 Wells (1993) suggested that the clothing worn by suspects is more important to witness identifications than facial features or height.

Section 2: The influence of leading questions

6 A leading question is one that suggests to a person the answer which should be given.

7 Participants in Loftus & Palmer's (1974) experiment gave widely differing speed estimates depending on whether the term used in the question 'How fast were the cars going when they …?' was 'hit', 'smashed', 'collided', 'bumped', or 'contacted'.

8 Loftus found that participants who had been asked questions using the term 'smashed' were far more likely to remember broken glass than those for whom the term was 'hit'.

9 The above experiment suggests that it is participants' *memories*, not merely their answers at the time, which have been affected, since in the follow-up experiment both groups of participants were asked the same question, concerning information which had not been questioned previously.

10 According to Loftus & Zanni's (1975) research, the question 'Did you see *the* broken headlight?' is most likely to elicit a positive response.

11 Loftus's (1979) answer to the question 'Are eyewitnesses reliable?' is 'sometimes' at best and 'no' at worst.

12 Eyewitnesses are most easily misled if the information concerned is peripheral to the main event.

Section 3: Other influences on testimony

13 The *cognitive interview technique* used by police in interviewing witnesses aims to improve recall for events.

14 The next two steps are 'recalling the event in a different order' and 'changing perspectives'.

15 The Devlin Committee recommended that the trial judge instruct the jury that it is not safe to convict on a single eyewitness testimony alone, unless the circumstances are exceptional or there is substantial corroborative evidence.

Section 4: Improving memory

16 A *mnemonic* is a technique for aiding recall.

17 The second important characteristic of mnemonics identified by Belezza (1981) is that they draw associations between what is to be learned and what is already in LTM.

18 Snowman *et al.*'s (1980) students used the *method of loci* technique to boost recall.

19 Higbee (1996) claims that mnemonic systems are either *visual mnemonic systems* or *verbal mnemonic techniques*.

20 The *link-word method* assists students in learning a foreign language by breaking the foreign word into similar sounding native words, then forming an image which combines those words with the word's native meaning.

21 The context-dependence (Abernathy, 1940) of memory suggests that recall will be best in the same location as learning occurred. If this is not possible, then *imagining* that location may help.

22 A state of panic, by altering a student's physical state, might make some memories inaccessible (so long as they were not in a state of panic during learning).

23 Reder & Anderson (1980) found that students do better on tests of recall having read only summaries of texts, rather than having read the whole text.

24 PQ4R stands for **P**review, **Q**uestion, **R**ead, **R**eflect, **R**ecite and **R**eview (Thomas & Robinson, 1972).

25 Craik & Watkins (1972) claim that elaborative rehearsal is far more effective than maintenance rehearsal (simply repeating words) at improving retention. The levels of processing model (Craik & Lockhart, 1972) also suggests that semantic processing should lead to better recall.

26 Long and complicated material is best dealt with by breaking it down into smaller chunks.

27 *Overlearning* is not a hazard associated with too much revision, but Ebbinghaus's (1885) finding that continuing to learn material once it could be fully recalled increased the later recall of this material.

28 Psychology and sociology are the subjects which would be most likely to interfere with recall if learned one after the other.

Section 5: Memory expertise

29 Valentine & Wilding (1994) identified *strategists* and *naturals* as being the two types of memory experts.

30 *Strategists* tend to use particular methods to store information and are better at tasks such as face-recognition and word recall, whereas *naturals* do not seem to use memory techniques and do best at tasks such as recognising snow-crystals and the temporal organisation of pictures.

31 Research into 'everyday' memory has been criticised for not employing the rigorous methodology common to laboratory experiments.

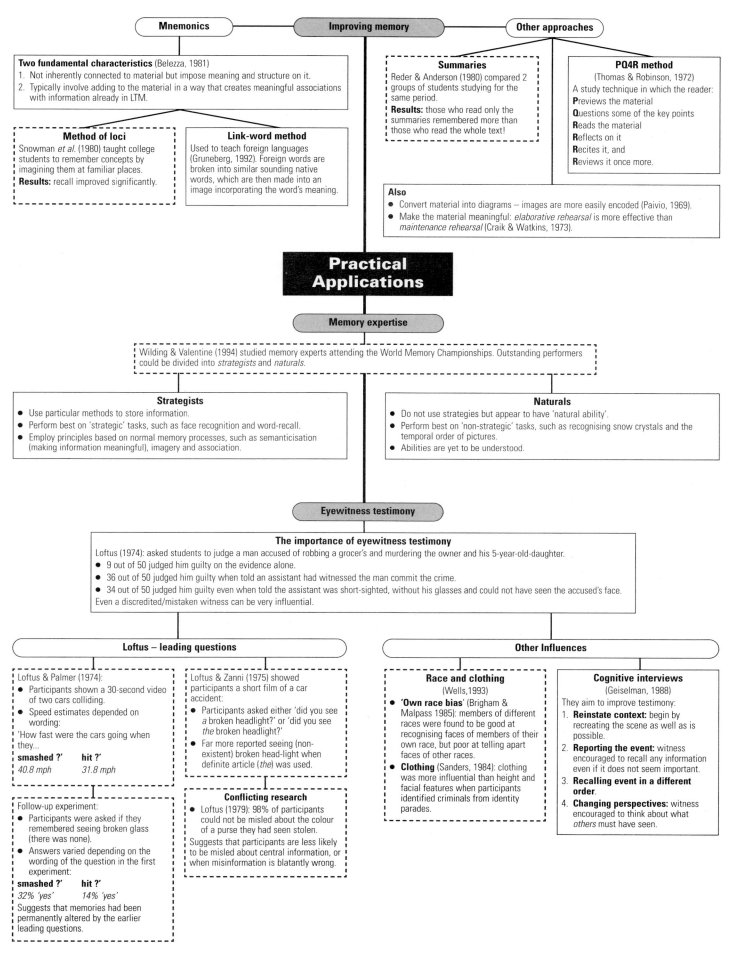

Mnemonics — **Improving memory** — **Other approaches**

Two fundamental characteristics (Belezza, 1981)
1. Not inherently connected to material but impose meaning and structure on it.
2. Typically involve adding to the material in a way that creates meaningful associations with information already in LTM.

Method of loci
Snowman *et al.* (1980) taught college students to remember concepts by imagining them at familiar places.
Results: recall improved significantly.

Link-word method
Used to teach foreign languages (Gruneberg, 1992). Foreign words are broken into similar sounding native words, which are then made into an image incorporating the word's meaning.

Summaries
Reder & Anderson (1980) compared 2 groups of students studying for the same period.
Results: those who read only the summaries remembered more than those who read the whole text!

PQ4R method
(Thomas & Robinson, 1972)
A study technique in which the reader:
Previews the material
Questions some of the key points
Reads the material
Reflects on it
Recites it, and
Reviews it once more.

Also
- Convert material into diagrams – images are more easily encoded (Paivio, 1969).
- Make the material meaningful: *elaborative rehearsal* is more effective than *maintenance rehearsal* (Craik & Watkins, 1973).

Practical Applications

Memory expertise

Wilding & Valentine (1994) studied memory experts attending the World Memory Championships. Outstanding performers could be divided into *strategists* and *naturals*.

Strategists
- Use particular methods to store information.
- Perform best on 'strategic' tasks, such as face recognition and word-recall.
- Employ principles based on normal memory processes, such as semanticisation (making information meaningful), imagery and association.

Naturals
- Do not use strategies but appear to have 'natural ability'.
- Perform best on 'non-strategic' tasks, such as recognising snow crystals and the temporal order of pictures.
- Abilities are yet to be understood.

Eyewitness testimony

The importance of eyewitness testimony
Loftus (1974): asked students to judge a man accused of robbing a grocer's and murdering the owner and his 5-year-old-daughter.
- 9 out of 50 judged him guilty on the evidence alone.
- 36 out of 50 judged him guilty when told an assistant had witnessed the man commit the crime.
- 34 out of 50 judged him guilty even when told the assistant was short-sighted, without his glasses and could not have seen the accused's face.
Even a discredited/mistaken witness can be very influential.

Loftus – leading questions

Loftus & Palmer (1974):
- Participants shown a 30-second video of two cars colliding.
- Speed estimates depended on wording:
'How fast were the cars going when they...
smashed ?'   **hit ?'**
40.8 mph   *31.8 mph*

Follow-up experiment:
- Participants were asked if they remembered seeing broken glass (there was none).
- Answers varied depending on the wording of the question in the first experiment:
smashed ?'   **hit ?'**
32% 'yes'   *14% 'yes'*
Suggests that memories had been permanently altered by the earlier leading questions.

Loftus & Zanni (1975) showed participants a short film of a car accident:
- Participants asked either 'did you see *a* broken headlight?' or 'did you see *the* broken headlight?'
- Far more reported seeing (non-existent) broken head-light when definite article (*the*) was used.

Conflicting research
- Loftus (1979): 98% of participants could not be misled about the colour of a purse they had seen stolen.
Suggests that participants are less likely to be misled about central information, or when misinformation is blatantly wrong.

Other Influences

Race and clothing
(Wells,1993)
- **'Own race bias'** (Brigham & Malpass 1985): members of different races were found to be good at recognising faces of members of their own race, but poor at telling apart faces of other races.
- **Clothing** (Sanders, 1984): clothing was more influential than height and facial features when participants identified criminals from identity parades.

Cognitive interviews
(Geiselman, 1988)
They aim to improve testimony:
1. **Reinstate context:** begin by recreating the scene as well as is possible.
2. **Reporting the event:** witness encouraged to recall any information even if it does not seem important.
3. **Recalling event in a different order**.
4. **Changing perspectives:** witness encouraged to think about what *others* must have seen.

32

LABORATORY STUDIES OF CONDITIONING AND OTHER FORMS OF LEARNING

SYLLABUS
2.4 Behaviour analysis
- theories and procedures of classical and operant conditioning

KEY QUESTIONS
- How can learning be defined?
- What processes are involved in classical conditioning?
- What processes are involved in operant conditioning?
- What other theories of learning exist?

Section 1: Introducing learning
1 Why is learning theory so important from the behavioural perspective?
2 What does it mean to say that learning is a *hypothetical construct*?
3 Complete the definition: 'Learning is the process by which relatively permanent changes occur in __ __ as a result of experience'.
4 What is the distinction between *learning* and *performance*?
5 What is the name of the theorist responsible for drawing a distinction between *operant* and *respondent* behaviour?

Section 2: Classical conditioning
6 What is the technical name for a stimulus which naturally produces a response?
7 What happens during the second stage of classical conditioning (during learning)?
8 What is a 'neutral' stimulus?
9 What is the difference between *delayed conditioning* and *trace conditioning*?
10 How effective is *backward conditioning*?
11 How does *generalisation* differ from *discrimination*?
12 What technical term is used to describe the cessation of a conditioned response after the conditioned stimulus is repeatedly presented in the absence of the unconditioned stimulus?

Section 3: Operant conditioning
13 What, according to Skinner (1938), are the important differences between *classical* and *operant conditioning*?
14 What behaviours did Thorndike (1898) observe when he placed cats in 'puzzle-boxes', rewarding them when they escaped?
15 What is Thorndike's (1898) *law of effect*?
16 What are the key features of a Skinner box?
17 What terms did Skinner introduce to replace Thorndike's 'stamping in' and 'stamping out' of a response?
18 What, according to Skinner's analysis of behaviour, is the *ABC of operant conditioning*?

19 Complete the following Skinnerian quotation: 'Behaviour is ___ and maintained by its ___'.
20 What three classes of consequence can result from a behaviour?
21 Which of these three *strengthen* behaviours?
22 What is the difference between a *primary reinforcer* and a *secondary reinforcer*?
23 Which schedule of reinforcement leads to behaviours which are the most easily extinguished?
24 Which schedule of reinforcement leads to the most resistant behaviours?
25 What type of reinforcement schedule is involved in being paid on commission?
26 What is *shaping*?
27 What applications has *shaping* had in the area of human behaviour?
28 Why, according to Skinner, is positive reinforcement a much more potent influence on behaviour than punishment?
29 What is the *law of contiguity*?
30 What, according to Seligman (1970), is *preparedness*?
31 Why, according to Mackintosh (1978, 1995), can we not reduce conditioning to the strengthening of stimulus–response connections through an automatic process called reinforcement?

Section 4: Cognitive approaches
32 In Tolman & Honzik's (1930) experiment with rats running mazes, what behaviour was especially significant?
33 How did Tolman explain this significant behaviour?
34 What is a *cognitive map*?
35 What do *social learning theorists* believe intervenes between stimulus and response?
36 What is *observational learning*?
37 What is a key factor in determining whether or not a model's behaviour is imitated?

Section 1: Introducing learning

1 Behaviourists believe that psychology is the study of behaviour, and that learning plays a central role in determining behaviour.

2 It means that learning cannot be directly observed but only *inferred* from observable behaviour.

3 'Learning is the process by which relatively permanent changes occur in *behavioural potential* as a result of experience.'

4 Learning can be seen as an organism's behavioural potential, whilst performance is the actual behaviour exhibited by an organism.

5 BF Skinner was the first psychologist to draw a distinction between operant and respondent behaviour.

Section 2: Classical conditioning

6 An *unconditioned stimulus* is a stimulus which naturally produces a response.

7 During learning, the unconditioned stimulus is paired with a conditioned stimulus until the conditioned stimulus produces the response previously produced by the unconditioned stimulus.

8 A 'neutral' stimulus is a stimulus which does not produce the conditioned response.

9 *Delayed conditioning* involves presenting the CS before and during the UCS, whilst in *trace conditioning* the CS is presented and removed before the UCS is presented.

10 *Backward conditioning* produces little, if any, learning in laboratory animals.

11 In *generalisation* the CR transfers spontaneously to stimuli similar to the original CS, whilst in *discrimination* the organism makes a *different* response to stimuli which differ from the CS.

12 *Extinction* describes the cessation of a conditioned response after the conditioned stimulus is repeatedly presented in the absence of the unconditioned stimulus.

Section 3: Operant conditioning

13 Skinner (1938) saw operant conditioning as an *active* process in which organisms *operate* on their environment, bringing about certain *consequences,* which in turn affect the *likelihood* of the behaviour being repeated.

14 Thorndike (1898) found that learning was initially *trial-and-error*; after the cats had escaped once, their escape times on successive trials decreased rapidly (from five minutes to five seconds after ten to twenty trials).

15 Thorndike's (1898) *law of effect* states that a stimulus–response connection is 'stamped in when pleasure results from the act and stamped out when it doesn't'.

16 A Skinner box is a box containing a food dispenser, a lever (or illuminated disc) and sometimes an electrified floor or light bulb.

17 Skinner replaced Thorndike's 'stamping in' and 'stamping out' of a response with the terms *strengthening* and *weakening* of a response respectively.

18 The *ABC of operant conditioning* is a representation of the relationships between *antecedents* (the stimulus conditions), *behaviours* (or operants), and *consequences* (results of operant behaviours).

19 'Behaviour is *shaped* and maintained by its *consequences*.'

20 Behaviour can result in *positive reinforcers* (rewards), *negative reinforcers* (threats) or *punishers.*

21 Both positive and negative reinforcers strengthen behaviours.

22 A *primary reinforcer* is a stimulus which is rewarding in itself (such as food, water), whereas a *secondary reinforcer* is a stimulus which acquires its reinforcing properties by being associated with a primary reinforcer.

23 *Continuous reinforcement* (reinforcing every single desired response) leads to behaviours which are very easily extinguished.

24 *Variable ratio reinforcement* schedules lead to behaviours which are highly resistant to extinction.

25 Being paid on commission involves a fixed ratio reinforcement schedule.

26 *Shaping* refers to the reinforcement of successive approximations to the desired response.

27 Shaping has been used to teach individuals with learning difficulties to use the toilet and other social skills, and in speech training with autistic children.

28 Positive reinforcement strengthens behaviours, whereas punishment can only make certain responses less likely. Nothing *new* can be taught by punishment.

29 The *law of contiguity* states that events which occur close together in time and space are likely to become associated with one another.

30 *Preparedness* is the idea that animals are biologically predisposed to learn actions that are closely related to the survival of their species (Seligman, 1970).

31 Mackintosh (1978, 1995) claims that conditioning is not an automatic response, but involves detecting and learning the *relations* between environmental events.

Section 4: Cognitive approaches

32 Tolman & Honzik (1930) found that if they reinforced a group of rats for finding their way to a goal box, having allowed these rats to wander around the maze for ten days, they reached the goal box very quickly.

33 Tolman concluded that the rats had been learning their way around the maze during the first ten days, but that this learning did not show itself until it was reinforced (i.e. learning was 'latent').

34 A *cognitive map* is a set of expectations about which part of an environment is followed by other parts.

35 *Social learning theorists* believe that *cognitive* or *mediating variables* intervene between stimulus and response.

36 *Observational learning* is learning through watching others (called *models*).

37 A model's behaviour is likely to be imitated if the *consequences* for the model are positive.

A

Studies of Conditioning

Classical/respondent conditioning

Operant conditioning

Pavlov – conditioning in dogs
- A *neutral stimulus* (which does not normally produce a response) will produce a response if associated/paired with a stimulus which *does* produce that response.
- Learning is automatic, and the learner is passive. Responses and learning are not under conscious control.

Learning: '… the process by which relatively permanent changes occur in behavioural potential as a result of experience' (Anderson, 1995a)

Thorndike – conditioning in cats
- Cats would learn to escape from 'puzzle-boxes' if rewarded with fish.
- Initially behaviour was *trial-and-error*, escape times improving when behaviour was rewarded.
- Formulated '*law of effect* (1898)': behaviours are 'stamped in when pleasure results from the act and stamped out when it doesn't'.

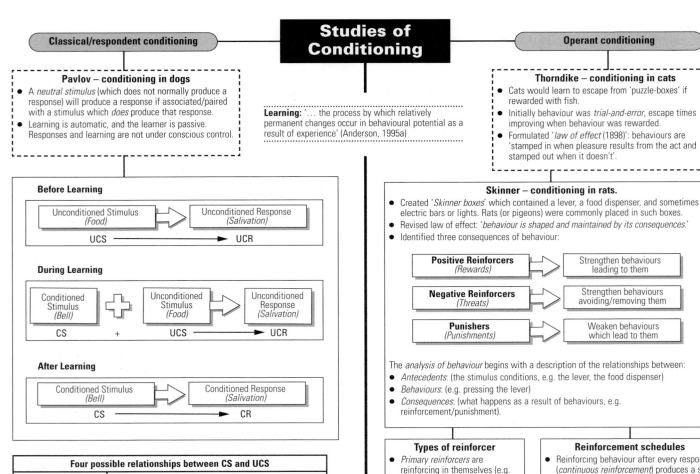

Before Learning

| Unconditioned Stimulus *(Food)* | ⟹ | Unconditioned Response *(Salivation)* |

UCS ⟶ UCR

During Learning

| Conditioned Stimulus *(Bell)* | + | Unconditioned Stimulus *(Food)* | ⟹ | Unconditioned Response *(Salivation)* |

CS + UCS ⟶ UCR

After Learning

| Conditioned Stimulus *(Bell)* | ⟹ | Conditioned Response *(Salivation)* |

CS ⟶ CR

Skinner – conditioning in rats.
- Created '*Skinner boxes*' which contained a lever, a food dispenser, and sometimes electric bars or lights. Rats (or pigeons) were commonly placed in such boxes.
- Revised law of effect: '*behaviour is shaped and maintained by its consequences.*'
- Identified three consequences of behaviour:

Positive Reinforcers *(Rewards)*	⟹	Strengthen behaviours leading to them
Negative Reinforcers *(Threats)*	⟹	Strengthen behaviours avoiding/removing them
Punishers *(Punishments)*	⟹	Weaken behaviours which lead to them

The *analysis of behaviour* begins with a description of the relationships between:
- *Antecedents*: (the stimulus conditions, e.g. the lever, the food dispenser)
- *Behaviours*: (e.g. pressing the lever)
- *Consequences*: (what happens as a result of behaviours, e.g. reinforcement/punishment).

Four possible relationships between CS and UCS

Delayed/forward	e.g. Ring bell before and during presentation of meat.
Backward	e.g. Ring bell after presentation of meat.
Simultaneous	e.g. Ring bell and present meat at the same time.
Trace	e.g. Ring bell. Stop. Present meat.

Types of reinforcer
- *Primary reinforcers* are reinforcing in themselves (e.g. food, water, sex).
- *Secondary reinforcers* have become associated with primary reinforcers (e.g. money, tokens).

Reinforcement schedules
- Reinforcing behaviour after every response (*continuous reinforcement*) produces a slow response rate and easily extinguished behaviour.
- Reinforcing behaviour after a random number of responses (*variable ratio*) produces a very high response rate and is very resistant to extinction.

Generalisation, discrimination, extinction and spontaneous recovery
- **Generalisation:** making *similar* conditioned responses to stimuli which are similar to the conditioned stimulus e.g. Pavlov found that his dogs would salivate at bells whose tones were similar to the original.
- **Discrimination:** making *dissimilar* responses to a stimulus which differs from the conditioned stimulus e.g. by presenting his dogs with meat for some tones and not for others, Pavlov taught his dogs to make fine discriminations between tones.
- **Extinction:** the *weakening* of the conditioned response in the absence of the unconditioned stimulus e.g. Pavlov found that his dogs would gradually stop salivating if he repeatedly rang bells without presenting meat.
- **Spontaneous recovery:** the *reappearance* of the conditioned response after it has stopped e.g. Pavlov found that his dogs would salivate at the sound of a bell following extinction, after a period of rest.

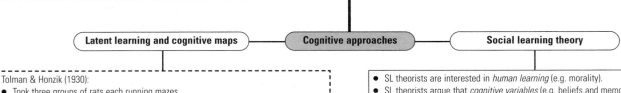

Latent learning and cognitive maps

Cognitive approaches

Social learning theory

Tolman & Honzik (1930):
- Took three groups of rats each running mazes.
- Group 1 was reinforced for finding their way to a food box (from day 1).
- Group 2 received no reinforcement (no food in food box).
- Group 3 received reinforcement after first ten days of experiment (food placed in food box on day 11).

Results: times for Group 1 to reach food box decreased steadily. Group 2 wandered aimlessly around. Group 3 wandered aimlessly until day 11 when food was presented and times to find the food *suddenly* dropped to match group 1's times.

- SL theorists are interested in *human learning* (e.g. morality).
- SL theorists argue that *cognitive variables* (e.g. beliefs and memories) intervene between stimulus and response.
- SL theorists emphasise *observational learning* which takes place spontaneously, without reinforcement.
- Imitation of another's behaviour ('*modelling*') depends partly on the consequences of the behaviour for the model.

Tolman's (1948) *place-learning theory* suggested that rats had been learning without reinforcement, although this only showed itself with reinforcement ('*latent-learning*'). Rats had not simply been conditioned, since they could navigate mazes from new starting-points – they had learned '*cognitive-maps*'.

Five major functions in observational learning (Bandura, 1974):
- **Attention:** learner must attend to important aspects of the stimulus situation.
- **Coding:** learner must form an image or semantic code in order to transfer the modelled behaviour to memory.
- **Memory permanence:** information must be retained.
- **Reproduction**: observed motor activities must be reproduced accurately and this may involve practice.
- **Motivation:** relates to the role of reinforcement (which provides us with information about what results we may achieve in the future).

DESCRIBING LANGUAGE DEVELOPMENT

KEY QUESTIONS
• How can we define language and grammar?
• What are the major components of grammar?
• What are the major stages in language development?
• What are the key features of each of these stages?

Section 1: Introducing language

1 What is *linguistics*?
2 What is *psycholinguistics*?
3 How does Brown (1965) define *language*?
4 What is the key distinction between human language and non-human 'language'?
5 Define *grammar*.

Section 2: The components of grammar

6 What do psycholinguists mean when they talk about *phones* (phonetic segments)?
7 What is the difference between a *phone* and a *phoneme* (or phonetic segments and phonological segments)?
8 What are *phonological rules*?
9 Complete the following sentence: 'Semantics is the study of the ___ of a language'.
10 What is a *morpheme*?
11 To what does the term '*syntax*' refer?
12 If, as many psychologists believe, language development follows a universal timetable irrespective of a child's culture, what does this suggest about language?

Section 3: The pre-linguistic stage

13 What form of communication do babies tend to use most in the first month of life?
14 Why are babies unable to form vowel sounds properly at six weeks old?
15 Why do babies 'coo'?
16 What are two key differences between babbling and previous forms of communication?
17 What is *phonemic contraction*?

Section 4: The one-word stage

18 At what age do children tend to produce their first word (the one-word stage)?
19 What is *jargon*?

20 What does it mean to say that the child's early word-use is very much 'context-bound'?
21 What is a *holophrase*?
22 Nelson (1973) undertook a careful analysis of children's early word use – what did she discover?
23 What conclusion was Nelson able to draw from this research?
24 Which is larger, a child's *receptive vocabulary*, or its *expressive vocabulary*?

Section 5: The two-word stage

25 Name the two sub-stages which make up the two-word sentences stage.
26 What does Brown (1965) mean when he says that between 18 and 30 months the child's speech is largely *telegraphic*?
27 Why do children at this stage employ rigid word order?
28 Which of the two, parent or child, employs *imitation with expansion*, and what does this involve?
29 What is the purpose of *motherese*?
30 What is the difference between the *pivotal rules* and *categorical rules* used by children in combining words (Brown, 1970)?
31 What is the central claim made by Cromer's (1974) *cognition hypothesis*?
32 What does it mean to say that the MLU of children increases rapidly from about 30 months?
33 What is the increase in MLU largely due to?
34 If a child who has never heard of a 'wug' tells us that two of them are two 'wugs', what can we conclude?
35 What is the term used to describe the tendency among young children to talk about 'gooses' and 'sheeps'?
36 What language task do children still have difficulty with, even at the age of five?
37 How many words would you estimate that you have in your vocabulary?

Section 1: Introducing language

1   *Linguistics* is the study of language, especially its structure, sounds and the rules governing the relation of words to sentences.

2   *Psycholinguistics* is the study of the perception, understanding and production of language.

3   Brown (1965) defines *language* as an 'arbitrary set of symbols' which make it possible for us to communicate an infinite variety of messages.

4   Human language is not limited to a finite set of utterances and allows us to create new utterances by combining units of meaning (words); this is not the case with non-human 'language'.

5   *Grammar* can be defined as the system of rules which are used to generate sentences in a given language.

Section 2: The components of grammar

6   *Phones* (or phonetic segments) refer to the basic and discrete speech sounds within a language.

7   A *phone* is a distinguishable speech sound, whilst *phonemes* are classes of such speech sounds with the same linguistic function.

8   *Phonological rules* are rules concerning which phonemes can be combined to form morphemes.

9   'Semantics is the study of the *meaning* of a language.'

10 *Morphemes* are the basic units of *meaning* within a language.

11 The term *syntax* refers to the rules used when combining words into phrases and sentences.

12 If language development does follow a universal timetable irrespective of culture, this suggests that *maturation* (the development of abilities due to a genetic 'program') plays an important role.

Section 3: The pre-linguistic stage

13 Babies' communication during the first month of life largely takes the form of crying.

14 Babies' oral cavities and nervous systems are not sufficiently mature at six weeks to allow them to form vowel sounds properly.

15 Babies' 'cooing' is associated with pleasurable states.

16 Babbling differs from previous forms of communication in that it is carried out even when the baby is alone. It also has intonational patterns and rhythms like those of adult speech.

17 'Phonemic contraction' refers to the restriction of the infant's phonemes to those used in its native language.

Section 4: The one-word stage

18 Children tend to produce their first word at about 12 months.

19 *Jargon* is the technical term for non-words produced by children during the beginning of the one-word stage.

20 The child's early word-use tends to be restricted to specific situations or contexts and it is in this sense that it is 'context-bound'.

21 A *holophrase* is a single word used to convey a complex message, such as 'Juice!' ('Please can I have some juice?').

22 Nelson (1973) discovered that the first 50 words produced by children tended to fall into six categories, with nominals and action words forming the largest groups.

23 Nelson concluded that a child's active involvement with its world determines many of its first words.

24 A child's *receptive vocabulary* (the words it understands) is much bigger than its *expressive vocabulary* (the words it can use).

Section 5: The two-word stage

25 *Stage 1 grammar* and *Stage 2 grammar* are the two substages within the two-word sentences stage.

26 *Telegraphic* is the term used by Brown (1965) to describe the near absence of purely grammatical terms (*functors*) in a child's early speech.

27 Children probably employ rigid word order in an effort to preserve a sentence's meaning.

28 Parents employ *imitation with expansion*, imitating the child's utterances whilst inserting the missing functors.

29 *Motherese* is a simplified form of language used by parents with children who have not yet mastered the full complexity of language.

30 *Pivotal rules* combine a single constant term with other terms, whilst *categorical rules* combine words in a constant category-to-category relation (Brown, 1970).

31 Cromer's (1974) *cognition hypothesis* claims that language structures can only be used correctly when permitted by our cognitive structures.

32 The mean length of utterance (MLU – the average number of words in a child's sentences) increases rapidly from about 30 months.

33 The increase in MLU is largely due to the inclusion of grammatical terms or functors, which are largely omitted in Stage 1 grammar.

34 If a child uses the term 'wugs' without ever having come across the term before, it cannot be imitating language use, so must have *internalised* the rule for forming a plural.

35 *Over-regularisation* describes the tendency among young children to talk about 'gooses' and 'sheeps'.

36 Even at the age of five, children still have difficulty with understanding *passive sentences*, such as 'the horse is kissed by the cow'.

37 Aitchison (1996) found that most 20-year-olds have vocabularies in the order of 50,000 words. This is acquired at an average of nine words per day. Your vocabulary should be in the order of 40,000 words or more (excluding psychological jargon).

Components of grammar

Phonology
(sound system)

- **Phones** are the basic speech sounds of a language (such as [p] or [d]).
- Phones may be spoken differently (e.g. by different people) without altering a word's meaning.
- **Phonemes** are functionally important *classes* of phones (e.g. [r] and [l] do the same job in Japanese, not in English).

Phonological rules regulate how we can combine phonemes (e.g. 'plort' is possible, 'xydrfq' is not).

Semantics
(meaning system)

- **Morphemes** are a language's basic units of meaning.
- Morphemes are mostly words, but also include prefixes and suffixes.
- Most morphemes are 'free', some can only be attached to others and are 'bound' (such as the plural 's').

Morphological rules: regulate how we can combine phonemes into morphemes.

Syntax
(system for relating sound to meaning)

- **Syntax** refers to the rules used in combining words into phrases and sentences (e.g. subject, verb, object).
- Language development cannot proceed without learning these rules.
- Sentences may be syntactically correct but semantically meaningless (e.g. the feather lifts the hugs with paint).

Syntactical rules: regulate how we can combine morphemes to form sentences.

Language: 'an arbitrary set of symbols which, taken together, make it possible ... to transmit and understand an infinite variety of messages' (Brown, 1965).

Language Development

Grammar: an overall description of a language, a formal device with a finite set of rules that generate the sentences in the language (Carroll, 1986).

Language development stages

Stage 1: Pre-linguistic (0–12 months)

- **Crying** dominates in the first month, with parents learning to discriminate different cries (Gustafson & Harris, 1990).
- By one month babies are able to discriminate phonemes (such as 'ba' and 'pa') despite being almost identical acoustically (Aslin *et al.*, 1983)

- **Cooing** begins at about 6 weeks and is associated with pleasurable states.
- Vowel sounds are produced but are different from those produced later, since the baby's nervous system and oral cavity are not sufficiently formed.

- **Babbling** begins between 6 and 9 months, with the baby producing combinations of consonants and vowels (e.g. 'mama', 'dada').
- Babbling is different from pre-babbling in that babies babble whilst alone, and because babbling has intonational patterns and rhythms like speech.

- **Phonemic expansion** begins shortly after babbling, with babies producing all possible phonemes.
- **Phonemic contraction** begins at 9 or 10 months, where the baby restricts its phonemes to those used in its native language.
- Mastery of phonemes is not complete until about age 7 years.

Stage 2: One-word stage (12–18 months)

- **Jargon** (non-words) are invented by children and may continue for up to 6 months.
- **Context-bound**: early words are produced only in very limited or specific situations (Barrett, 1989) (e.g. using 'duck' only to refer to toy duck whilst in bath).

- **Expressive function:** some words communicate internal states (e.g. pleasure and surprise), or
- **Directive function:** in which the behaviour of others is directed.
- **Holophrases:** a single word (e.g. 'milk') is used to convey a complex message ('Please can I have some milk') by combining gesture and tone.

Nelson (1973): identified six categories of words:

- **General nominals** (51%) – names of types of objects.
- **Specific nominals** (14%) – names for unique objects.
- **Action words** (13%) – describe/accompany actions.
- **Modifiers** (9%) – refer to properties of things.
- **Personal–social words** (8%) – relate to feelings/relationships.
- **Function words** (4%) – grammatical function words.

- Nelson (1973): it is a child's involvement with the environment which determines early word use.
- Children understand more words than they can produce.
- De-contextualisation occurs as one-word stage progresses (Barrett, 1989).

Stage 3: Two-word sentences

Stage 1 Grammar (18–30 months)

- **Telegraphic** speech (Brown, 1965): purely grammatical terms ('*functors*') are omitted from speech.
- **Rigid word order**: children use the same word order to convey the same meaning.
- Semantic relationships: children combine pairs of words according to two types of relationship rule:

Pivotal – where one word is central (e.g. *more* milk, *more* cuddles).

Categorical – where there is no constant word but constant category combinations (e.g. baby jump, daddy sit, mommy walk)

Cognition hypothesis
(Cromer, 1974)
- Language structures can only be used correctly when cognitive structures are sufficiently developed.
- Relates to Piagetian theory and ideas such as 'object permanence'.
- Children form schemata to help them understand the world.

Stage 2 Grammar (30+ months)

- **Mean length of utterance** (MLU): the average word length of a child's sentences increases rapidly, mainly due to inclusion of 'functors' (such as 'is', 'the', 'a').
- **Over-regularisation** occurs, where children apply rules too rigidly (e.g. 'gooses').
- By age four or five basic grammatical rules have been acquired, although children still have problems with passive sentences (e.g. the horse is kissed by the cow').

Berko (1958):
- Showed children a picture of a 'wug'.
- Then showed picture of two of them.
- Asked to complete the sentence 'now there are two ...'.
- Three- and four-year-olds were able to apply the rule for pluralising a word, despite never having heard the word before (so rule must have been 'internalised').

THEORIES OF LANGUAGE DEVELOPMENT

KEY QUESTIONS
- How does learning theory explain language development?
- What are the problems with this theory?
- What is Chomsky's approach to explaining language development?
- What alternatives are there to these two approaches?

Q Section 1: Learning theory

1 If the word 'mama' is initially a neutral stimulus, what unconditioned stimulus is most likely to be paired with this in order to produce a conditioned response to it?

2 Complete the following quotation: 'A child acquires verbal behaviour when relatively unplanned vocalisations, _____ _____, assume forms which produce appropriate consequences in a given verbal community' (Skinner, 1957).

3 What is the technical term used by behaviourists to describe the *reinforcement of successive approximations* to the desired behaviour?

4 What types of reinforcement might parents offer in response to a child's vocalisations?

5 When children produce *echoic responses* to their parents, what are they engaging in?

6 What did Brodbeck & Irwin (1946) discover when comparing the vocalisations of institutionalised children with those living with their natural parents?

7 According to Slobin (1975), how good are parents at teaching grammar to their children?

8 According to Brown *et al.* (1969), when mothers are responding to their children, what is it that they are responding to?

9 According to Bandura (1977), what aspect of adults' sentences do children imitate?

10 If language is established through reinforcement, as Skinner claims, what would we expect to discover, when comparing language acquisition in different cultures?

11 What is meant by saying that 'learning theory cannot explain the creativity of language'?

12 Why does the spontaneous application of grammatical rules by children pose a problem for learning theory?

Section 2: Chomsky's LAD

13 What is the central claim made by Chomsky in order to explain how children acquire language?

14 What does LAD stand for?

15 What does this mean: 'The LAD contains the TG'?

16 What are *phrase-structure rules*?

17 What is the difference between the *deep structure* and the *surface structure* of a sentence?

18 What does this mean: 'Rule (1): S ⟶ NP + VP'?

19 What is a *linguistic universal*?

20 What did Goldin-Meadow & Feldman (1977) discover when investigating congenitally deaf children?

21 According to Lenneberg (1967), how can we explain the existence of a critical period for language development?

22 Aitchison (1983) dislikes Chomsky's 'Content Cuthbert' and prefers 'Process Peggy'. What is she saying?

23 What factors do *integrative theorists* believe Chomsky has underestimated in accounting for language development?

Section 3: Alternative approaches

24 According to the *language and social interaction approach*, what is the source of language?

25 What, according to Snow (1977), is the relationship between language and an infant's social world?

26 What is *proto-conversation* (Snow, 1977)?

27 What is *visual co-orientation* (Collis & Schaffer, 1975)?

28 How does visual co-orientation help the infant to learn language?

29 What does Bruner (1975, 1978) mean by the term '*formats*'?

30 What does LASS (Bruner, 1983) stand for?

31 According to this view, what do mothers do with language in order to assist the language acquisition process?

32 What does Gauker (1990) mean when he says that language is a *cause–effect analytic device*?

33 What is *the emergence of communicative intentionality*?

34 What does Piaget (1952) believe about the growth of children's language?

Section 1: Learning theory

1 The unconditioned stimulus most likely to be paired with the word 'mama' in order to produce a conditioned response to it is the presence of the mother.

2 'A child acquires verbal behaviour when relatively unplanned vocalisations, *selectively reinforced*, assume forms which produce appropriate consequences in a given verbal community' (Skinner, 1957).

3 *Shaping* describes the *reinforcement of successive approximations* to a desired behaviour.

4 Attention, smiles, touch, and food are all reinforcements which parents commonly offer in response to a child's vocalisations.

5 *Echoic responses* are produced when children engage in imitation of their parents.

6 Brodbeck & Irwin (1946) discovered that children living with their natural parents tended to vocalise more compared with institutionalised children.

7 Very poor. Slobin (1975) points out that parents frequently reinforce incorrect grammar.

8 When mothers are responding to their children, it is the 'truth-value' or meaning of their child's utterances, not the correct grammatical form, which they respond to (Brown *et al.*, 1969).

9 According to Bandura (1977), children imitate the *general form* of adults' sentences, not the exact form.

10 If language is established through reinforcement, as Skinner claims, we would expect to discover that language acquisition proceeds differently in different cultures, depending on local reinforcement policy.

11 'Learning theory cannot explain the creativity of language' in that most of the sentences used by adults have never been used before, hence cannot have been selectively reinforced.

12 The spontaneous application of grammatical rules by children is a problem for learning theory, since the rules have never been explicitly taught and are applied in new situations for which no reinforcement can have occurred.

Section 2: Chomsky's LAD

13 Chomsky's central claim is that children are born with an innate mechanism which enables them to understand and formulate sentences in any language.

14 LAD stands for 'language acquisition device'.

15 According to Chomsky, the LAD contains transformational grammar (TG), a set of rules necessary for language comprehension.

16 *Phrase-structure rules* are the rules contained within the TG which specify what are and are not acceptable utterances in a speaker's native language.

17 The *deep structure* of a sentence is roughly that sentence's meaning, whereas the *surface structure* of a sentence is the way it is expressed in words.

18 'Rule (1): S $\longrightarrow$ NP + VP' is a phrase-structure rule, meaning that a sentence is comprised of a noun phrase and a verb phrase.

19 A *linguistic universal* is a feature common to all languages (such as nouns).

20 Goldin-Meadow & Feldman (1977) discovered that congenitally deaf children will sometimes develop gestural languages despite receiving no encouragement or training from their parents.

21 Lenneberg (1967) maintains that up until the age of puberty, the brain is relatively unspecialised and hence can still develop language-processing abilities.

22 Aitchison (1983) dislikes the Chomskian claim that TG, complete with specific rules, is innate ('Content Cuthbert') and prefers the idea that what is innate is a problem-solving mechanism capable of understanding language ('Process Peggy').

23 *Integrative theorists* believe that Chomsky has underestimated the importance of environmental input and cognitive development in language development.

Section 3: Alternative approaches

24 According to the *language and social interaction approach*, language arises from the child's pre-linguistic knowledge, especially its knowledge of social interactions.

25 Snow (1977) maintains that language is 'mapped' onto the infant's social world.

26 *Proto-conversation* (Snow, 1977) describes adults' attempts to 'involve' the infant in conversation by interpreting its grunts, gurgles, burps and giggles as primitive language.

27 *Visual co-orientation* (Collis & Schaffer, 1975) occurs when the parent and infant focus on some common object.

28 By both attending to the same thing, opportunities to interact and learn are increased.

29 Bruner's (1975, 1978) *formats* refer to rule-bound activities or routines, in which the infant has many opportunities to relate language to familiar play.

30 LASS (Bruner, 1983) stands for 'language acquisition support system'.

31 According to this view, mothers simplify linguistic input and break it down into helpful, illustrative segments.

32 Gauker's (1990) *cause–effect analytic device* is the use of language to bring about and understand changes in the speaker's environment.

33 *The emergence of communicative intentionality* refers to the infant's awareness that it is possible to bring about a desired goal by using another person as a tool.

34 Piaget (1952) believes that the growth of children's language is closely related to their cognitive skills.

A

Language Development Theories

Learning theories

Classical conditioning

- A *neutral sound* (such as 'mama') is repeatedly paired with an *unconditioned stimulus* (such as the mother).
- Words become conditioned stimuli, eliciting conditioned responses (e.g. salivating at the sound of the word 'cake').

Operant conditioning

Skinner (1957) argued that verbal behaviours are the result of *selective reinforcement*: Children imitate adult language, producing echoic responses (tacts).

↓

Adults shape the baby's sounds by reinforcing those closest to real words.

↓

Reinforcement takes the form of touch, feeding, attention.

↓

Later, correct sentences and grammar are reinforced through others' responses – incorrect grammar is ignored.

Conflicting research

- Slobin (1975): children learn grammatical rules *despite* their parents, whose use of grammar is often very poor and who frequently *reinforce incorrect grammar*.
- Brown et al. (1969): mothers do not ignore incorrect grammar but respond to what a child is *trying to say*, interpreting incomplete or primitive sentences.
- Nelson (1973): vocabulary develops more *slowly* in children whose mothers systematically correct poor pronunciation.

Other problems

- Slobin (1986): learning theory cannot explain *universal stages* in language development, since reinforcement will vary from one individual to the next.
- Chomsky (1968): learning theory cannot explain the *creativity* of language, since most of the sentences used by adults are original and therefore have never been reinforced before.
- Learning theory cannot explain how children begin using *grammatical rules*, which they have never been taught, to apply to new words.

Chomsky's LAD

Chomsky's LAD and the biological approach

- Chomsky (1957): environmental factors alone (such as reinforcement) cannot explain language development.
- Children are born with an innate **language acquisition device' (LAD).**
- LAD contains **transformational grammar** (TG) which are rules which can generate correct sentences in any language.
- TG is made up of **phrase structure rules**, which specify how to combine types of words.
- Phrase structure rules allow people to convert the **surface structure** of language (the actual words used to express something) into its **deep structure** (what it means) and back again.
- Children look for features common to all languages (**'linguistic universals'**) such as nouns, verbs, which fit into the rules.

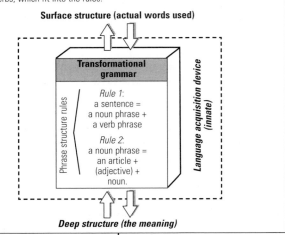

Surface structure (actual words used)

Transformational grammar

Phrase structure rules

Rule 1:
a sentence =
a noun phrase +
a verb phrase

Rule 2:
a noun phrase =
an article +
(adjective) +
noun.

Language acquisition device (innate)

Deep structure (the meaning)

Research

- Different languages do appear to have features in common and some form of TG is acquired by all people (unless brain damaged). Even those with learning difficulties acquire language, suggesting the skill is separate from learning.
- Twins raised in isolation have developed their own languages with characteristics which are common to ordinary languages (verbs, nouns, syntax) (Malmstrom & Silva, 1986).
- Aitchison (1983) agrees that children are 'wired' for language but does not believe that TG is innate, only a problem-solving mechanism.

Alternative theories

Social interaction approach
language arises from pre-linguistic knowledge

- Smith & Cowie (1991) language is used to communicate needs and intentions and as a means of entering into a community.
- Snow (1977): babies initially master a social world onto which they 'map' language.
- *Proto-language* involves adults responding to and attributing meaning to a baby's grunts, cooing and eye-contact.

Visual co-orientation
(Collis & Schaffer, 1975)
Infant and parent both focus on an object and the joint attention provides opportunities to learn.

Formats
(Bruner, 1975, 1978)
Infant and adult participate in rule-bound activity routines which provide opportunities to relate language to familiar play, and to learn the rules of social interaction.

LASS
Language acquisition support system

Bruner (1983)
Language acquisition requires more than just a model to input information into the LAD.

The parent provides the LASS:
- simplified linguistic input, breaking language down for the child, and
- 'formats' which are familiar games or routines in which the child can learn language.

Language is an extension of the interactions that the infant and caregiver have built up over the previous months.

The active child
children use a cause–effect analytic device

Gauker (1990)
During pre-linguistic stage, infants do not realise that they can achieve things by affecting others' responses ('*communicative intentionality*')
- *First order causality*: child can only understand results as the product of its own actions.
- *Second order causality*: child understands that it can achieve ends by using *others* as a tool.

Words function as a means of bringing about changes in the infant's environment, by affecting the behaviour of others.

SOME ASPECTS OF READING AND WRITING

KEY QUESTIONS
- How do we read?
- How do we recognise words?
- How can the reading process be explained?
- What theories exist to explain the writing process?

Section 1: Introducing reading

1 What does the *Stroop Effect* (Stroop, 1935) indicate about the nature of reading?
2 How can reading be defined?
3 What sort of movements does the eye make when moving across a line of print?
4 What is *phonological mediation*?
5 What is the relationship between *regressions* and the reading abilities of skilled readers?

Section 2: Word recognition and comprehension

6 What are the assumptions common to all models of word recognition?
7 What, according to Morton (1964, 1969), is a *logogen*?
8 Why, according to this model, are high-frequency words (such as 'the') recognised more easily than low-frequency words (such as 'thy')?
9 What, according to Marslen-Wilson's (1984) *cohort model*, does recognition of letters allow us to do?
10 What is the first type of recognition which takes place in Rumelhart & McClelland's (1982) *interactive-activation model*?

Section 3: Towards a theory of reading

11 Complete the sentence: 'When we read, we draw ____ to help our understanding'.
12 What is the relationship between text and knowledge, when reading?
13 In Just & Carpenter's (1980, 1992) reading model, what are the two steps which follow on from 'Get next input: move eyes'?
14 Name three things which working memory is used for in this model.
15 In what sense is reading a 'dynamic' process?
16 According to this model, what differences between individuals are most likely to account for how well language is comprehended?
17 Give two criticisms of this model.

Section 4: Learning to read

18 What was Morphett & Washburn's (1931) view concerning the mental age at which children should begin learning to read?
19 Marsh *et al.* (1981) identified four stages in learning to read. Can you name them?
20 What are *logographic skills* and *orthographic skills* (Frith, 1985)?
21 What is the difference between the *phonics* method of teaching reading and the *whole-word method*?
22 Which of these methods is more effective?

Section 5: Writing

23 According to Hayes & Flower's *information-processing model of writing* (1980, 1983), the three major processes involved in writing are: planning, _____, and reviewing. Which is the missing process?
24 What does *planning* involve?
25 What does the sub-process *generating* involve?
26 What is the difference between *organising* and *goal-setting*?
27 Name two ways in which skilled writers differ from unskilled writers in their planning of writing.
28 What cognitive component is stretched to its limits during *sentence generation*?
29 When Atwell (1981) asked skilled and unskilled writers to write with inkless pens onto carbon paper, what did he discover?
30 What is one explanation for 'writer's block'?
31 What does *reviewing* involve?
32 Two processes are involved in reviewing: reading is the first. What is the second?
33 Which type of writer – skilled or unskilled – is likely to spend longest reviewing their written material (Hayes *et al.*, 1985)?
34 What is the *rhetorical problem*?
35 Why should writers be encouraged to set goals, communicate meaning and use outlining?

Section 1: Introducing reading

1 The *Stroop Effect* (Stroop, 1935) indicates that reading is an automatic and overlearned skill to the extent that it cannot easily be 'put on hold' (Massaro, 1989).

2 Reading can be defined as 'a meaningful interpretation of written or printed verbal symbols' (Harris & Sipey, 1983).

3 The eye makes a series of stop–start jumps ('saccades') across a line of print when reading.

4 *Phonological mediation* refers to the translation of printed language into speech before meaning can be assessed.

5 *Regressions* refers to backward movements made by the eye in order to scan earlier words. Regressions occur far less frequently in skilled readers.

Section 2: Word recognition and comprehension

6 All models of word recognition assume that letter recognition is involved in recognising words, that we somehow store a representation of words known to us, and that this representation is activated in order for word recognition to occur.

7 A *logogen*, according to Morton (1964, 1969), is a representation of a word which resides in LTM.

8 High-frequency words are recognised more easily than low-frequency words, because they have a lower 'threshold of activation'.

9 According to Marslen-Wilson's (1984) *cohort model*, recognition of letters allows us to eliminate classes of words containing different letters (cohorts), so that recognition proceeds by elimination.

10 Rumelhart & McClelland's (1982) *interactive-activation model* begins with feature detection (i.e. the recognition of features of letters, such as horizontal and vertical lines).

Section 3: Towards a theory of reading

11 'When we read, we draw *inferences* to help our understanding.'

12 The relationship is mutual: text influences and modifies our existing knowledge (in the form of schemata), and our existing knowledge enables us to interpret and store the text we read.

13 The two steps which follow on from 'Get next input: move eyes' in Just & Carpenter's (1980, 1992) reading model are 'Extract physical features' and 'Assign meaning to word'.

14 Working memory is used for processing physical features, word meanings, retaining previous words, maintaining the overall gist of the material and making decisions.

15 Reading is a 'dynamic' process, because the meaning of the written word is continually influenced by context, content, prior knowledge and goals – and in turn, affects these things.

16 According to Just and Carpenter, it is WM capacity which is most likely to influence reading comprehension ability in individuals.

17 Reading comprehension difficulties do not depend solely on WM capacity, so the model's emphasis on WM reduces its overall explanatory power. In addition, the model has little to say about the eye movements which are an important part of reading.

Section 4: Learning to read

18 Morphett & Washburn's (1931) view was that children should reach a mental age of six years and six months before beginning to learn to read.

19 Marsh *et al.*'s (1981) four stages in learning to read are *glance and guess, sophisticated guessing, simple grapheme–phoneme correspondence* and *skilled reading.*

20 *Logographic skills* are the ability to recognise words as wholes (rather than building them up from letters), and *orthographic skills* involve the use of regularities in the structure of words to obtain their pronunciation (Frith, 1985).

21 The *phonics* method of teaching reading emphasises sound–symbol relationships, whilst the *whole-word method* encourages the recognition of words by sight.

22 Chall's (1967) analysis of 67 studies concluded that there was nothing to choose between them.

Section 5: Writing

23 Planning, *translating* and reviewing are the three processes.

24 *Planning* involves setting goals and organising ideas, based upon the task environment and information from LTM.

25 *Generating* involves obtaining information from LTM and the task environment which is relevant to the task.

26 *Organising* involves the selection and organisation of information into a plan, whilst *goal-setting* involves evaluating the relevance of available information.

27 Skilled writers differ from unskilled writers in the following ways: they set *goals* which focus on communicating meaning, they *generate* many ideas relating to the topic and they *organise* their communication.

28 Working memory is stretched during translation.

29 Atwell (1981) found that skilled writers were not affected, whilst unskilled writers suffered a loss of cohesion.

30 'Writer's block' can result from the need for more knowledge about a task, or adherence to 'rigid rules'.

31 *Reviewing* involves evaluating what has been written to determine how well it meets the set goals.

32 *Editing* is the second process involved in reviewing.

33 Hayes *et al.*, (1985) found that skilled writers spend longest reviewing their material.

34 The *rhetorical problem* is the writer's interpretation of the task and the achievement of the set goals.

35 *Setting goals* increases the likelihood of effective writing, enabling better reviewing of the material. *Outlining* also helps the revision process, whilst improving the quality of the writing, and writers write better when concentrating on communicating meaning, rather than the mechanics of writing.

Logogen model
(Morton, 1964, 1969)
- Each word has a representation (*logogen*) in LTM.
- A logogen has a resting *level of activity*, which is increased by hearing/seeing the word.
- When activity level reaches a certain *threshold*, the word is recognised.

Cohort model
(Marslen-Wilson, 1984)
- Words are recognised letter-by-letter from left to right.
- Each successive letter eliminates possible words (*cohorts*).
  E.g. if the word begins with 's', all non-'s' words are eliminated, and so on.

Interactive-activation model
(Rumelhart & McClelland, 1982)
Three types of recognition unit:
1. detects features of letters (e.g. curves).
2. detects the letter represented by that combination of features.
3. detects letter position, activating all words with letters in that position.

Models of word recognition

Towards a theory — **Reading** — **Learning to read**

Just & Carpenter's (1980, 1992) model:
- The main activities of reading occur in *working memory* (WM).
- Schemata affect what we take in and how we interpret it.
- Existing knowledge is modified by the new content – reading is therefore a *dynamic* process.
- **Immediacy assumption:** a word and its relationship to other words is processed as soon as it is encountered because of WM's limited capacity.

Reading readiness
- Morphett & Washburne (1931) believed reading instruction should wait until children reach a mental age of 6 years and 6 months. Others disagree.
- Marsh *et al.* (1981) identified four stages in learning to read:
  1. glance and guess
  2. sophisticated guessing
  3. simple grapheme–phoneme correspondence
  4. skilled reading.

Teaching reading
- **Phonics method:** emphasises symbol–sound relationships (such as how to pronounce 'sp' and 'br').
- **Whole-word method:** encourages the recognition of words by sight.

Chall (1967) analysed 67 studies comparing different approaches to reading and found no significant difference between them.

Reading & Writing

Reading: a meaningful interpretation of written or printed verbal symbols (Harris & Sipey, 1983)

Get next input: move eyes → Extract physical features → Assign meaning to words → Integrate with prior reading → Decide: is sentence ended? — no (loop) / yes → Assimilate meaning of sentence

Working memory

Deals with:

Physical features

Word meanings

Memory for previous words

Gist of the material

Decision making

Long-term Memory

Stores/provides

Orthography

Word meanings

Grammar

Memory for story format

LTM of content

Semantic mem.

Episodic mem.

Writing– Hayes & Flower's Model

Planning
- Involves setting goals and organising information based on the task environment and LTM.
- **Generating** occurs where relevant information from LTM is obtained.
- **Organising** involves selecting information and organising into a writing plan.
- **Goal-setting** involves evaluating the relevance of available information.

Translating
- Involves transforming the writing plan into actual phrases (sentence generation).
- **Self-questioning** occurs where writer decides how to express next sentence.
- Working memory is stretched to its limits.
- Sticking to rules too rigidly may cause *'writer's block'* – especially if the rules are inadequate (Eysenck & Keane, 1995).

Reviewing
Involves evaluating what has been written to determine how well it meets the set goals.
Parts considered unsatisfactory are improved by
- **Reading** (being sensitive to omissions, superfluous information, and errors) and
- **Editing** (re-writing, moving and changing material).

Individual differences in planning
- **Setting goals:** skilled writers produce more goals and sub-goals than unskilled writers. (Hayes & Flower, 1986).
- **Generating ideas:** Skilled writers can think of many ideas relating to what they are writing about (Raphael & Kirschner, 1985).
- **Organisation:** skilled writers plan the meaning they are going to communicate, rather than focusing on the mechanics (Geisler *et al.*, 1985).

Practical applications
Setting goals: effective writing is more likely if clear goals are established.
Outlining: outlining improves the quality of what is written and aids in reviewing it.
Generating ideas: writers should be encouraged to generate ideas.
Communicating meaning: writers should concentrate more on the meaning than the mechanics of what is to be written.
Revision: writers check writing against set goals.
Correcting and rewriting: feedback and re-submission are important in allowing writers to focus on writing correctly.

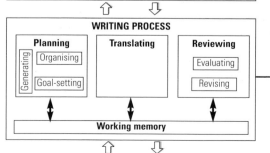

TASK ENVIRONMENT

| The rhetorical problem *Topic audience exigency* | Text produced so far |

WRITING PROCESS

Generating | Planning [Organising / Goal-setting] | Translating | Reviewing [Evaluating / Revising]

Working memory

Long-term memory
knowledge of topic, audience, plans

36

PROBLEM-SOLVING AND DECISION-MAKING

SYLLABUS
5.4 Language and thought
- models and explanations of human thought (e.g. reasoning and decision-making)

KEY QUESTIONS
- What is the nature of a problem?
- How do we go about solving problems?
- What types of errors do we make in solving problems?
- How can we explain the decision-making process?

Q Section 1: The nature of problems
1 What is the definition of a *problem*?
2 If the first two stages in problem-solving are 'representing the problem' and 'generating possible solutions', what is the third stage?
3 What is the difference between *adversary* and *non-adversary problems* (Garnham, 1988)?

Section 2: Approaches to problem-solving
4 According to the behavioural perspective, how do we go about solving problems?
5 What, according to the Gestalt approach, is *productive thinking*?
6 What name did Köhler give to the process by which his chimp, Sultan, solved the bananas-hanging-from-the-ceiling problem?
7 What is an *algorithm*?
8 What is the principal problem with using algorithms to solve problems (e.g. solving anagrams)?
9 What are *heuristics*?
10 What are the advantages of heuristic approaches to problem-solving?
11 How is a search for a solution carried out when undertaking a *means–end analysis*?

Section 3: Errors in problem-solving
12 What is *mental set*?
13 What experiment did Duncker (1945) carry out in order to demonstrate *functional fixedness*?
14 What is *confirmation bias*?

Section 4: Decision-making models and biases
15 How is *decision-making* different from *problem-solving*?
16 According to the *additive compensatory model*, how do we decide which alternative to choose?
17 What is meant by the terms *utility* and *probability* in the *utility–probability model of decision-making*?

18 What is the difference between *compensatory* and *non-compensatory models* of the decision-making process?
19 How is a *minimax strategy* applied to decision-making?
20 According to the explanation offered by the *availability heuristic model* of decision-making, why do people overestimate the chances of being a victim of violent crime (Tyler & Cook, 1984)?
21 How, according to the *representativeness heuristic*, do we judge the likelihood of something (such as the likelihood of a shy person being a librarian)?
22 In what way can this heuristic distort our judgement concerning the likelihood of events?
23 What do psychologists mean by *belief perseverance*?
24 How can *entrapment* affect our decisions?
25 What is the term used to describe our tendency to overestimate the probability that something would have happened after it has happened (the 'I-knew-it-all-along phenomenon')?
26 Why are people likely to prefer hamburgers that are 75 per cent meat to those that are 25 per cent fat?

Section 5: Computer vs. naturalistic studies
27 What name is given to the view that human cognition can be understood by comparing it with the functioning of computers?
28 What was Newell *et al.*'s (1958) *general problem solver* attempting to do?
29 When psychologists have compared experts and novices on adversarial tasks (such as chess-playing), what have they discovered about why experts make better decisions?
30 What is an *expert system*?
31 What is one criticism of such systems?
32 Why do some researchers argue that studies of decision-making should investigate *naturalistic decision-making* (NDM)?
33 What overall conclusions can we draw about human decision-making processes?

Section 1: The nature of problems

1 A *problem* is a situation in which there is a discrepancy between a present state and some goal state, with no obvious way of reducing it.

2 The third stage in problem-solving, following on from 'representing the problem' and 'generating possible solutions', is *'evaluating possible solutions'*.

3 *Adversary problems* are those in which two or more people compete for success, whereas *non-adversary problems* are those in which other people are involved only as 'problem-setters' (Garnham, 1988).

Section 2: Approaches to problem-solving

4 The behavioural perspective maintains that we go about solving problems by *trial-and-error*.

5 The Gestalt approach identifies *productive thinking* as the solution of a problem by reorganisation, or perceiving new relations among its elements.

6 According to Köhler, Sultan solved the problem by sudden *insight*.

7 An *algorithm* is a systematic exploration of every solution to a problem until the correct one is found.

8 Algorithms (e.g. as used by some chess computers) can be effective, but where the number of possible solutions is large they can be extremely time-consuming.

9 *Heuristics* are rules of thumb used in problem-solving.

10 Heuristic approaches, whilst not guaranteeing a solution, tend to reach solutions quickly.

11 A *means–end analysis* involves 'working backwards', searching for a solution by beginning with the goal and working backwards to the current state.

Section 3: Errors in problem-solving

12 *Mental set* is the tendency to continue using a previously successful strategy to solve problems, even when more efficient strategies exist.

13 Duncker (1945) investigated *functional fixedness* by providing participants with a box of drawing pins and a candle and instructing them to attach it to a wall in an upright position. They did not think to use the box as a stand which could be pinned to the wall.

14 *Confirmation bias* is a tendency to look for information which confirms our ideas and overlook contradictory information.

Section 4: Decision-making models and biases

15 *Decision-making* is a special case of *problem-solving* in which we already know the possible solutions (or choices) to a problem.

16 The *additive compensatory model* claims that we weigh up alternatives, listing features common to both and assigning weights which reflect their value. The alternative with the highest score is the most rational.

17 *Utility* refers to the value placed on potential positive or negative outcomes, whilst *probability* is the likelihood that the choice will produce the potential outcome.

18 *Compensatory models* assume that we are rational in weighing up the pros and cons of each option, whilst *non-compensatory models* assume that we do not consider all the features of alternatives, and that features do not compensate for one another.

19 A *minimax strategy* involves selecting the option with the strongest best feature, or the least weak feature.

20 According to the *availability heuristic model* of decision-making, information about violent crimes is likely to be vivid and memorable, and therefore readily available in LTM. As a consequence, we overestimate how likely it is to occur.

21 The *representativeness heuristic* allows us to judge the likelihood of something by intuitively comparing it with our preconceived ideas, which we believe represent a category.

22 The representativeness heuristic can distort our judgement by leading us to overlook important information concerning the actual frequency of objects/events in the world.

23 *Belief perseverance* refers to the tendency to cling to a belief even in the face of contrary evidence.

24 *Entrapment* refers to the reluctance to withdraw from a situation or retract a choice because of the costly investments which we have made in it.

25 The term *hindsight bias* refers to our tendency to overestimate the probability that something would have happened after it has happened.

26 People often make choices which depend to some extent on the way in which options are presented (or 'framed'), even if the choices are actually equivalent but framed differently.

Section 5: Computer vs. naturalistic studies

27 The *computer analogy* is the view that human cognition can be understood by comparing it with the functioning of computers.

28 Newell *et al.*'s (1958) *general problem solver* was an attempt to simulate the entire range of human problem-solving.

29 Psychological studies suggest that experts make better decisions, not because they are faster thinkers or cleverer than non-experts, but because they make better use of working memory.

30 An *expert system* is a computer program which applies knowledge in a specific area, enabling the computer to mimic the function of a human expert.

31 Expert systems are less flexible than their human counterparts.

32 NDM researchers argue that only by studying experienced people can we understand how decision-makers utilise both their domain knowledge and contextual information.

33 Our decision-making processes are not purely rational or unbiased, but do have the advantage over 'algorithmic' approaches of being flexible and quick.

Problem-solving

Problem: a situation in which there is a discrepancy between a present state and some goal state with no obvious way of reducing it.

Stages of problem-solving (PS)

1. *Defining / representing* the problem.
2. *Generating* possible solutions.
3. *Evaluating* possible solutions.

Types of problem

- **Adversary** – two or more competitors.
- **Non-adversary** – others involved only as problem-setters.

Problems in PS

Mental set

The tendency to continue using a previously successful strategy when more efficient strategies exist.

Luchins & Luchins (1950):
- Participants imagined using containers to solve three tasks where the goal was to obtain precise amounts of water.
- **Results:** participants continued to use strategy which was successful for Task 1 on Tasks 2 and 3, though it was not efficient (Task 2) or successful (Task 3).

Functional fixedness

A type of mental set in which we fail to see that an object may have functions other than its normal ones.

Duncker (1945):
- Gave participants a box of drawing pins and a candle.
- Told to attach upright candle to wall.
- Failed to see that empty pin box could be pinned to the wall.

Generating solutions

Algorithms

- Algorithms are systematic explorations of every possible solution until correct one is found.
- Can be very time-consuming.

Heuristics

- Heuristics are 'rules of thumb': they do not guarantee a solution but can be quick.
- They are based mainly on intuition and past experience.

Include:

Analogies: recognising that a problem is similar to another.

Means-end analysis: search for a solution begins at the goal (or end) and works backwards. Often involves breaking main goal into sub-goals (e.g. Hobbits & Orcs problem).

Perspectives on PS

Information-processing

- PS involves cognitive processes that are analysed in terms of separate stages, namely

Gestalt

- We re-structure a problem by understanding the relations between its elements.
- Approach distinguishes *reproductive* and *productive* thinking.
- Köhler's chimp *'Sultan'* solved problems with sudden 'insight'.

Behaviourist

- Problem-solving is essentially trial-and-error involving accidental success.
- Successful behaviours are reinforced and PS improves.

Decision-making

A special case of problem-solving in which we already know the possible solutions.

Models

Compensatory models

Additive compensatory model
- We start the DM process by evaluating the features of alternatives and giving each a score.
- The alternative with the highest score is the rational choice.

Utility–probability model
DM process proceeds by weighting the *desirability* of each outcome according to:
Utility: value placed on outcome.
Probability: likelihood that choice will produce potential outcome.

Non-compensatory models

Elimination by aspects
We eliminate options if they do not meet certain criteria, starting with the most important criterion.

Minimax strategy
We select the option with the strongest best feature or the least weak feature.

Conjunctive strategy
We set minimum acceptable values for each criterion, then eliminate options which do not meet these.

Computer vs. naturalistic DM

- **Computer analogy:** the assumption that human cognition can be understood by comparing it with a digital computer.
- **Expert systems:** computer programs which apply knowledge in a specific area (e.g. MYCIN which assists medical diagnoses). Whilst useful, they are much less flexible than humans.
- **Naturalistic decision-making:** researchers argue that more can be learned by studying the DM process in experienced humans who make decisions in changing environments.

Heuristics

Availability heuristic

- We base decisions on information readily available in LTM.
- We assume (often wrongly) that information is most readily available about events when they are frequent.
- Therefore, if we can easily think of information about an event, it is more likely to happen.

People tend to overestimate the probability of dying in a plane crash (Tyler & Cook, 1984) – since information about plane crashes is readily available (as compared with information about car crashes).

Representativeness heuristic

Making a decision by intuitively comparing alternatives with preconceived ideas about which characteristics belong to which categories (e.g. stereotypes).

Tversky & Kahneman (1973): gave participants a description of 'Steve' as shy, withdrawn, lover of detail.
Results: Participants were most likely to identify Steve as being a librarian when given a choice of occupations.

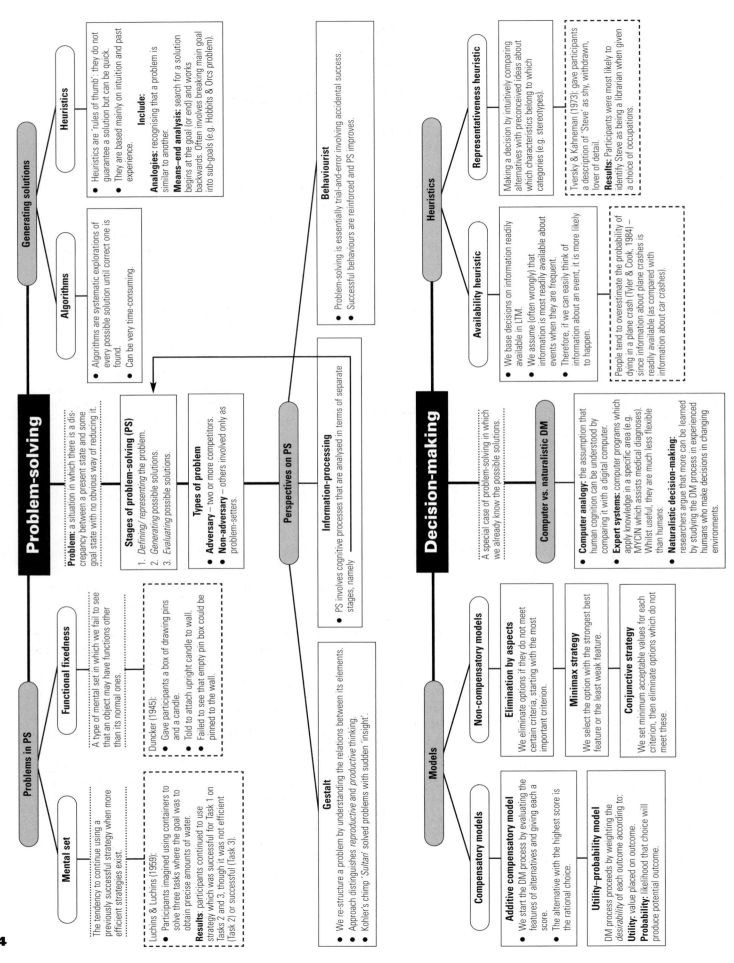

37

THE RELATIONSHIP BETWEEN LANGUAGE AND THOUGHT

SYLLABUS
5.4 Language and thought
- theories and evidence relating to the relationship between language and thought
- social and cultural variations in language in relation to thought

KEY QUESTIONS
- Are language and thought the same?
- Is thought dependent on language?
- To what extent is language dependent on thought?
- Do language and thought develop independently?

Section 1: Language and thought are the same
1 What, according to Watson's (1913) view, are thought processes?
2 Why was Watson's view called *peripheralism*?
3 What is curare and why did Smith (Smith *et al.*, 1947) inject himself with it?
4 If Watson's view were correct, what would be the consequence for people born unable to speak?

Section 2: Thought is dependent on language
5 According to *social constructionists*, what is the source of our ways of understanding the world?
6 What is meant by the expression *linguistic relativity hypothesis* (LRH)?
7 What does Whorf (1956) mean by the expression *linguistic determinism*?
8 Give three examples which support the Sapir–Whorf linguistic relativity hypothesis.
9 What is the difference between the strong and weaker versions of the LRH?
10 What did Carroll & Casagrande (1958) discover when they tested the strong version of the LRH, using Navaho-speaking and English-speaking children?
11 What did Brown & Lenneberg (1954) discover when testing the colour perceptions of Zuni Indians?
12 What did Berlin & Kay (1969) discover when investigating the use of colour terms in different cultures?
13 What are *focal colours*?
14 In Heider & Oliver's (1972) study, who were better at identifying colours which they had seen 30 seconds before – the Dani or English speakers?
15 Complete the sentence: 'Whorf's evidence was _____ rather than empirical, and he _____ the differences between Hopi and other languages' (Berry *et al.*, 1992).
16 What is a possible explanation for why Inuit Indians have many words for snow?
17 According to Hunt & Agnoli (1991), who would you expect to perform mental arithmetic more quickly – French speakers or English speakers?

Section 3: Linguistic relativity, class and race

18 When Bernstein (1961) looked at the difference between verbal intelligence scores and non-verbal intelligence scores for groups of middle-class children and groups of working-class children, what did he discover?
19 What was the name which Bernstein gave to the two types of 'codes' used by the two classes, respectively?
20 Identity four features of the 'code' which tends to be used by working-class children?
21 What is one criticism of the choice of terms 'restricted' and 'elaborated' as used to describe middle-class and working-class speech.
22 What is one major difference between Black English and White English?
23 How does Labov (1973) respond to the view that Black English is sub-standard and illogical?
24 Labov described the behaviour of a young black boy called Leon. What was Leon like?

Section 4: Language is dependent on thought
25 What was Piaget's view of the relationship between language and thought?
26 Complete the following sentence: 'As language develops it _____ onto previously acquired _____ structures, and so language is dependent on thought'.
27 What cognitive ability did children have to demonstrate in Corrigan's (1978) tests before they were capable of talking about absent objects?

Section 5: Language and thought are initially separate
28 What was the central claim made by Vygotsky (1962) with respect to the relation of language and thought?
29 What terms did Vygotsky use to describe *thinking which occurs without language* and *language which occurs without thought*?
30 According to Vygotsky, what is the difference between the *internal* and *external functions* of speech?
31 What is *egocentric speech*?

Section 1: Language and thought are the same

1 Watson (1913) believed 'thought processes' to be no more than the sensations produced by tiny movements of the speech organs too small to produce audible sounds.

2 Watson's view was called *peripheralism*, since it held that 'thinking' occurs peripherally, in the larynx, rather than in the brain.

3 Curare is a poison which produces paralysis in the skeletal muscles. Smith injected himself with it in order to discover if thought continued whilst his vocal apparatus was paralysed (Smith *et al.*, 1947).

4 If Watson were correct, people born unable to speak would also be unable to think.

Section 2: Thought is dependent on language

5 *Social constructionists* believe that we derive our ways of understanding the world from other people and our culture, rather than from objective reality.

6 The *linguistic relativity hypothesis* is the view that, since language determines *how* we think and *what* we think about, people with different languages think about the world differently.

7 Whorf's (1956) *linguistic determinism* claims that language determines our concepts. Since we can think only through the use of concepts, acquiring a language involves acquiring a world view.

8 Inuit Eskimo's have over 20 words for snow (according to Whorf), the Hanuxoo people use 92 terms for rice, the Shona people of Zimbabwe have only three words for colour and the Dani have only two.

9 The strong version of the LRH holds that language determines thought, whilst weaker versions hold that language affects perception or memory.

10 Carroll & Casagrande (1958) discovered that Navaho-only-speaking children had better shape-recognition abilities than English-speaking children (though this was not true for Navaho–English speaking children).

11 Brown & Lenneberg (1954) discovered that the Zuni Indians made more mistakes than English speakers when discriminating yellow and orange.

12 Berlin & Kay (1969) discovered that all cultures draw their basic colour terms from only 11 colours and that colour terms emerge in a sequence common to the history of all languages.

13 *Focal colours* are the basic 11 colours common to all languages.

14 Heider & Oliver (1972) found that the Dani were just as good at identifying colours which they had seen previously as English speakers.

15 'Whorf's evidence was *anecdotal* rather than empirical, and he *exaggerated* the differences between Hopi and other languages.' (Berry *et al.*, 1992)

16 Inuit Indians may have many words for snow, because snow is an important part of their environment.

17 Hunt & Agnoli (1991) argue that the French should be better at mental arithmetic, since many of their number-words contain fewer syllables than the equivalent words in English.

Section 3: Linguistic relativity, class and race

18 Bernstein (1961) found that there was no difference between verbal intelligence and non-verbal intelligence scores in groups of middle-class children, whilst groups of working-class children would often show large differences between the two measures of intelligence.

19 Bernstein claimed that middle-class children tended to use an *elaborated code*, whilst their working-class counterparts were more likely to use a *restricted code*.

20 The restricted code is grammatically crude, tends to be context-bound (i.e. assumes the listener's familiarity with the topic of discourse), rarely uses the word 'I', frequently uses uninformative emotionally reinforcing phrases ('I mean', 'you know', 'like').

21 The terms 'restricted' and 'elaborated' imply value judgements, with the latter being superior.

22 Black English tends to omit the verb 'to be' (the present tense copula).

23 Labov (1973) points out that many languages omit the verb 'to be' (such as Russian), and yet we do not consider them inferior or illogical. He argues that such a view of Black English is rooted in prejudice.

24 Leon was very different, depending on the situation. In the more formal situation, when questioned by a white or black interviewer, he was uncommunicative and silent for much of the time. With friends, he was outgoing and conversational.

Section 4: Language is dependent on thought

25 Piaget believed that language is more or less dependent on thought, or a child's level of cognitive development.

26 'As language develops it '*maps*' onto previously acquired *cognitive* structures, and so language is dependent on thought.'

27 Children had to be capable of advanced *object permanence* (knowing that objects continue to exist when they cannot be seen) before they were capable of talking about absent objects.

Section 5: Language and thought are initially separate

28 Vygotsky (1962) believed that language and thought develop independently as separate activities which interact at a certain stage of development.

29 Vygotsky used the term *pre-linguistic thought* to describe thinking which occurs without language and *pre-intellectual language* to describe language which occurs without thought.

30 The *internal function* of speech is to monitor and direct thoughts, whilst the *external function* of speech is to communicate the results of thinking to others.

31 *Egocentric speech* is talking out loud about one's plans and actions and occurs in individuals who do not adequately distinguish the internal and external functions of speech.

Peripheralism (Watson, 1913)
- 'Thought processes' are no more than the sensations produced by tiny, inaudible movements of the speech organs (thought is silent speech).
- Thinking therefore occurs 'peripherally', in the larynx.

Smith *et al.* (1947):
- Tested Watson's theory by injecting himself with *curare* – a drug causing total paralysis of the skeletal muscles.
- Despite being unable to speak, Smith was subsequently able to report on his thoughts during the paralysis.

Language & Thought

Language is dependent on thought

Thought and language are initially separate

Piaget (1950)
- As language develops, it is 'mapped' onto pre-existing cognitive structures.
- Children can be taught words, but will only be 'parroting' them if they have not yet achieved adequate cognitive growth.

e.g. Corrigan (1978): children were unable to talk about absent objects until they demonstrated an advanced level on an '*object permanence*' test (see Ch 41).

Conflicting research

Luria & Yudovich (1971):
- Studied five-year-old twin boys with only a primitive (synpraxic) level of speech, used only to accompany actions/objects.
- When they learned to use an objective language system, they were able to plan and engage in meaningful play.

Vygotsky (1962)
- Language and thought begin as separate activities (thinking mainly in images, language used as a social tool).
- At age two, *pre-linguistic thought* and *pre-intellectual language* join to form **verbal thought** and **rational speech**.
- Between ages 2 and 7, language performs two functions:
  1. **Internal function** – monitoring and directing thought
  2. **External function** – communicating results of thinking.
- Because children cannot distinguish these functions clearly, their speech is often *egocentric* (unable to think privately).

e.g. Vygotsky (1962): when 6/7-year-olds encounter a mishap in solving a problem, they often speak out loud.

Pre-linguistic thought (images, etc.)　Verbal thought and rational speech　Pre-intellectual language (crying, etc.)

Thought is dependent on language

The Sapir–Whorf linguistic relativity hypothesis:
Language determines how we think about the world and what we are able to think of.

The Whorfian hypothesis (1956)

- **Linguistic determinism** – language determines our concepts and we can only think through the use of concepts. Acquiring a language involves acquiring a 'world-view'. People who speak different languages have different world views.
- The grammar of a language may also determine an individual's thoughts and perceptions – e.g. Hopi indians do not distinguish past, present and future, and instead talk about time as it appears to the observer.

Examples
- The Hanuxoo people from the Philippines use 92 words for different types of rice.
- Eskimos have over 20 words for snow.
- The Shona people (Zimbabwe) have only three words for colour and the Dani (New Guinea) only two ('mola' for bright, warm hues, 'mili' for dark, cold hues).

Links to social class and race

Bernstein (1961):
- Working-class and middle-class children speak two different kinds of language:
  1. **Restricted code**
  2. **Elaborated code.**

Lack of an elaborated code resulted in lower scores on tests of verbal intelligence in working-class children.

Restricted code	**Elaborated code**
Grammatically crude	Grammatically complex
Context-bound	Context-independent
'I' rarely used	'I' often used
Stresses present	Stresses past and future
Doesn't allow abstract expression	Allows abstract thought expression

Black English

- Black English differs from White English (e.g. by omitting the verb 'to be': 'he gone').
- Bernstein argues that this makes Black English a restricted code, and others regard it as illogical and sub-standard.
- Labov (1973): whilst the rules of Black English differ, it is not illogical or sub-standard (other languages omit the verb 'to be') – it is prejudice which motivates such judgements.

Experimental tests of the linguistic relativity hypothesis

'Strong' version:
language determines thought

'Weak' version:
language affects perception/memory

Carrol & Casagrande (1958):
- Compared three groups on their form recognition abilities and the sequence in which they develop:
  1. Navaho-only speaking children.
  2. Navaho-American children.
  3. American children.

Results:
Navaho-only children did show superior form recognition and developed these abilities in a different sequence from Americans.
This may be because Navaho language stresses the importance of form.

Brown & Lenneberg (1954):
- Tested Zuni Indians (who have one word to describe yellow and orange) on their recognition of colours.

Results: compared with English speakers, they made more mistakes.

Conflicting research

Heider & Oliver (1972):
- Tested Dani (who have only two colour words) by showing them a colour, then later asking them to identify it from a range.

Results: Dani did not make more mistakes than English speakers in identifying the colour.

Labov (1970) illustrated **the influence of the social situation**:
- A boy called 'Leon' would say very little in a 'formal' situation when asked by white/black interviewers about a toy.
- However, when chatting with a friend and using local dialect he was a 'lively conversationalist'.

UNIT 4

Developmental Psychology

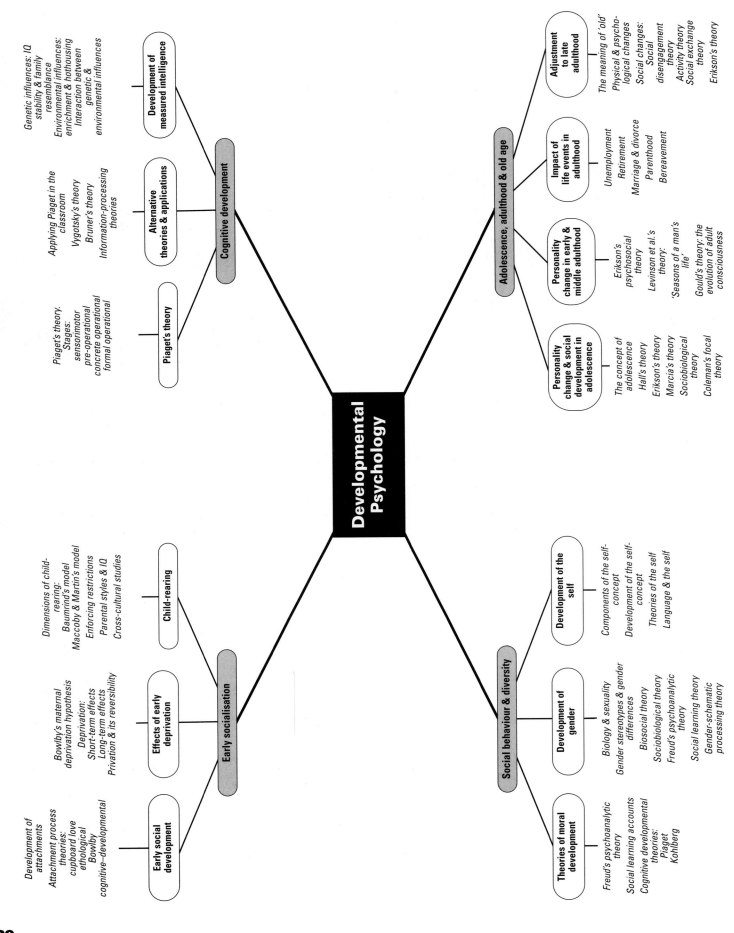

Developmental Psychology

Cognitive development

Development of measured intelligence
*Genetic influences: IQ stability & family resemblance
Environmental influences: enrichment & hothousing
Interaction between genetic & environmental influences*

Alternative theories & applications
*Applying Piaget in the classroom
Vygotsky's theory
Bruner's theory
Information-processing theories*

Piaget's theory
*Piaget's theory.
Stages:
sensorimotor
pre-operational
concrete operational
formal operational*

Adolescence, adulthood & old age

Adjustment to late adulthood
*The meaning of 'old'
Physical & psychological changes
Social changes:
Social disengagement theory
Activity theory
Social exchange theory
Erikson's theory*

Impact of life events in adulthood
*Unemployment
Retirement
Marriage & divorce
Parenthood
Bereavement*

Personality change in early & middle adulthood
*Erikson's psychosocial theory
Levinson et al.'s theory: 'Seasons of a man's life'
Gould's theory: the evolution of adult consciousness*

Personality change & social development in adolescence
*The concept of adolescence
Hall's theory
Erikson's theory
Marcia's theory
Sociobiological theory
Coleman's focal theory*

Early socialisation

Child-rearing
*Dimensions of child-rearing:
Baumrind's model
Maccoby & Martin's model
Enforcing restrictions
Parental styles & IQ
Cross-cultural studies*

Effects of early deprivation
*Bowlby's maternal deprivation hypothesis
Deprivation:
Short-term effects
Long-term effects
Privation & its reversibility*

Early social development
*Development of attachments
Attachment process theories:
cupboard love
ethological
Bowlby
cognitive–developmental*

Social behaviour & diversity

Development of the self
*Components of the self-concept
Development of the self-concept
Theories of the self
Language & the self*

Development of gender
*Biology & sexuality
Gender stereotypes & gender differences
Biosocial theory
Sociobiological theory
Freud's psychoanalytic theory
Social learning theory
Gender-schematic processing theory*

Theories of moral development
*Freud's psychoanalytic theory
Social learning accounts
Cognitive developmental theories:
Piaget
Kohlberg*

38

EARLY SOCIAL DEVELOPMENT

SYLLABUS:
6.1 Early socialisation
• theories and research relating to the process of social development in the first years of life, including the development of sociability and attachments

KEY QUESTIONS:
• What are sociability and attachments?
• What is the nature of early attachments?
• What theories exist to explain the processes of attachment-formation?

Section 1: The nature of sociability and attachment

1 Which three dimensions of *temperament* are taken to be present at birth and inherited?
2 How can *sociability* be defined?
3 How do Kagan *et al.* (1978) define *attachments*?
4 Why is our first attachment widely recognised to be crucial for healthy development?
5 Name two features of infant behaviour during the *indiscriminate attachment phase*.
6 How does the *discriminate attachment phase* differ from the *indiscriminate attachment phase*?
7 At what age do infants begin to become more independent from the caregiver?
8 What is the *Strange Situation* and what is it used for?
9 According to Ainsworth *et al.* (1978), what is the difference between *anxious–avoidant* and *anxious–resistant attachments*?
10 According to Ainsworth *et al.*, what is the crucial factor in determining the nature of a child's attachment?
11 Are attachment styles permanent characteristics?
12 What has cross-cultural research discovered regarding Ainsworth *et al.*'s attachment styles?
13 If children form secure attachments, how might this affect them later on in development?

Section 2: 'Cupboard love' theories

14 Complete the following sentence: 'According to psychoanalytic accounts, infants become attached to their caregivers because of the caregiver's ability to satisfy _____ _____.'
15 What, according to Freud, are the causes of unhealthy attachments?
16 According to the behaviourist account, what is the first step in the formation of an attachment?
17 Why does Harlow's (1959) finding that infant rhesus monkeys spend more time clinging to cloth surrogates than to wire and bottle ones cast doubt on *'cupboard love'* theories of attachment?

18 What was the consequence for the rhesus monkeys in Harlow & Suomi's (1970) experiment of being raised exclusively with cloth mothers?
19 What did Schaffer & Emerson (1964) discover (in their longitudinal study) about the target of infant attachments?

Section 3: Ethological explanations

20 Define *imprinting*.
21 Why are *precocial species* most likely to employ imprinting as an attachment mechanism?
22 What is a *critical period*?
23 Does imprinting occur in humans in the same way as it does in ducklings?

Section 4: Bowlby's theory

24 Complete the following sentence: 'Bowlby argued that because new-born infants are entirely helpless, they are _____ _____ to behave towards their mothers in ways that ensure their survival'.
25 How do infants use looking behaviour to promote the formation of a parent–child bond?
26 Why might we think that smiling behaviour is an innate behaviour?
27 Bowlby (1951) believed that there was a critical period beyond which mothering is useless – what was that period?
28 What term did Bowlby use to describe (what he believed was) the child's innate tendency to become attached to one particular individual?
29 What did Klaus & Kennell's *extended contact hypothesis* propose?
30 What did Rutter (1981) conclude about the kinds of attachment behaviour that infants display towards different attachment figures?
31 According to Bowlby, what is the value of a father to the infant?
32 What did Yogman *et al.* (1977) discover when looking at differences in the quality and quantity of mothers' and fathers' caregiving?

Section 1: The nature of sociability and attachment

1 *Sociability*, *emotionality* and *activity* are dimensions of *temperament* which are taken to be present at birth and inherited.

2 *Sociability* can be defined as seeking and being gratified by rewards from social interaction, preferring to be with others, sharing activities and being responsive to and seeking responsiveness from others.

3 Kagan *et al.* (1978) define *attachments* as an intense emotional relationship that is specific to two people, that endures over time, and in which prolonged separation from the partner is accompanied by stress and sorrow.

4 Our first attachment may well act as a *prototype* for all later attachments.

5 During the *indiscriminate attachment phase,* infants can discriminate between familiar and unfamiliar people but allow strangers to handle them without becoming distressed.

6 During the *discriminate attachment phase*, children develop specific attachments and become distressed when separated (*separation anxiety*). They may also develop a fear of strangers.

7 Infants begin to become more independent of the caregiver from about nine months onwards (though this varies from child to child).

8 The *Strange Situation* is a series of interactions between a mother, infant and a stranger, and was designed by Ainsworth *et al.* (1978) as a way of measuring the attachment styles of different infants.

9 An *anxious–avoidant attachment* is characterised by indifference towards the mother and similar behaviours towards the stranger, whilst an *anxious–resistant attachment* is characterised by an ambivalent attitude towards the mother, with distress on her departure and anger on her return.

10 *Sensitivity* to the infant's needs seems to be the crucial factor in determining the nature of a child's attachment.

11 Ainsworth *et al.* believed that attachment styles were permanent characteristics; however, Vaughn *et al.* (1980) demonstrated that attachment styles can change, depending on the circumstances.

12 Cross-cultural research reveals that different attachment styles are more or less common in different cultures.

13 According to Sroufe *et al.*'s research (1983), securely attached infants are likely to be more confident, enthusiastic and persistent in problem-solving later on, as young children.

Section 2: 'Cupboard love' theories

14 'According to psychoanalytic accounts, infants become attached to their caregivers because of the caregiver's ability to satisfy *instinctual needs*.'

15 Freud claims that either *overgratification* or *undergratification* of instinctual needs are likely to be the cause of unhealthy attachments.

16 The behaviourist account holds that the first step in attachment formation is to associate the primary caregiver with the satisfaction of physiological needs.

17 Harlow's (1959) finding suggests that *contact comfort* may be a more important factor in determining attachments than food alone.

18 The rhesus monkeys in Harlow & Suomi's (1970) experiment, having been raised exclusively with cloth mothers, were extremely aggressive as adults, rarely interacted with other monkeys and made sexually inappropriate responses.

19 Schaffer & Emerson (1964) discovered that often infants become attached most strongly to people who do not perform caregiving activities.

Section 3: Ethological explanations

20 *Imprinting* refers to the tendency of some species to form an automatic bond with whatever moving object is present during a certain critical period soon after hatching.

21 *Precocial species* are mobile from birth and therefore need a mechanism which allows them to identify caregivers and stay close to them.

22 A critical period is a restricted time period during which certain events must take place if development is to progress normally.

23 No. Humans are unlikely to attach to moving objects simply because they are present soon after birth. Human attachments are flexible and complex.

Section 4: Bowlby's theory

24 'Bowlby argued that because new-born infants are entirely helpless, they are *genetically programmed* to behave towards their mothers in ways that ensure their survival.'

25 Infants look to return a parent's gaze, inviting them to respond. Infants are distressed by lack of eye contact.

26 Smiling is probably innate since it occurs soon after birth, before the child has had an opportunity to learn, and before it has mastered control of its facial muscles.

27 Bowlby's (1951) *critical period*, beyond which mothering is useless, was two-and-a-half to three years (12 months for most children)

28 Bowlby used the term *monotropy* to describe an innate tendency to attach to a particular individual.

29 Klaus and Kennell's *extended contact hypothesis* proposed that mothers who had large amounts of contact with their new-borns were more likely to cuddle, soothe and enjoy their babies later on.

30 Rutter (1981) discovered that infants display a range of attachment behaviours towards a variety of individuals (not just the mother).

31 Bowlby claimed that the father is of no direct emotional significance to the child, only indirectly important as support for the mother.

32 Yogman *et al.* (1977) found no differences in the quality and quantity of mothers' and fathers' caregiving.

Sociability: seeking and being gratified by rewards from social interaction, preferring to be with others, sharing activities, being responsive and seeking responsiveness from others.

Early Social Development

Attachment: an intense emotional relationship that is specific to two people, that endures over time, and in which prolonged separation from the partner is accompanied by stress and sorrow (Kagan *et al.*, 1978).

Attachment phases

Age	Stage and characteristics
6 weeks–3 months	**pre-attachment phase:** infants attracted to humans in preference to inanimate objects. Nestling, gurgling and smiling are directed towards anyone.
3 months–7 months	**indiscriminate attachment phase:** infants distinguish familiar and unfamiliar faces. Infants will allow careful strangers to handle them without distress.
7 months–9 months	**discriminate attachment phase:** infants begin to develop specific attachments and display separation anxiety. Linked to emergence of object permanence. Many display a fear of strangers response.
9 months +	**multiple attachments phase:** infants become increasingly independent. Strong additional bonds formed with other caregivers and peers.

Quality of attachment

The 'Strange Situation' technique for studying attachment
(Ainsworth *et al.*, 1971, 1978)

A series of interactions in which the child's behaviour is studied:

- Mother and child enter unfamiliar room. Stranger enters. Mother leaves. Mother returns, stranger leaves. Mother leaves. Stranger returns. Mother returns. Stranger leaves.

Using the Strange Situation, Ainsworth *et al.* (1978) were able to classify children's behaviour as belonging to one of three types:

Type A (15%) **Anxious–avoidant**
Baby ignores/indifferent to mother. Both adults treated in the same way.

Type B (70%) **Securely attached**
Distressed when mother leaves. Seeks contact and is calmed when mother returns.

Type C (15%) **Anxious–resistant**
Cries more and explores less than types A or B. Very distressed when mother leaves. Anger towards her on return.

- Ainsworth *et al.* (1978): the crucial feature in determining attachment is mother's *sensitivity* – how well she interprets and responds to her baby's needs.
- Vaughn *et al.* (1980): attachment types may vary depending on the family's circumstances.
- Takahashi (1990): marked differences in %s of attachment styles cross-culturally – Type C more common in Israel and Japan.

Theories of attachment

'Cupboard love' theories

Psychoanalytic account
(Freud, 1926)

- Infants become attached to their caregivers (usually the mother) because they satisfy instinctual needs.
- Healthy attachments result from feeding practices which satisfy needs for food, security and libidinal impulses.
- Unhealthy attachments result from over- or under-gratification of these needs.

Behaviourist account
Infants become attached to those who satisfy physiological needs:
1. Caregivers become **associated** with gratification.
2. Caregivers become **conditioned reinforcers**.
3. Gratification **generalises** to a feeling of security when caregiver is present.

Conflicting research
Harlow (1959) placed infant rhesus monkeys in cages with a choice of two mothers:

wire mother – made from wire with a feeding bottle attached.

cloth mother – covered in terry cloth but with no feeding bottle.

Results: The infants spent most of their time clinging to the cloth mother and would run to it when distressed, indicating that contact comfort was more important than feeding alone.

Schaffer & Emerson (1964): a longitudinal study of infants. Roughly a third were most strongly attached to someone who *did not* perform caretaking duties (feeding, bathing, etc.)

Ethological theories

Imprinting (Lorenz, 1935)

- Some non-humans (especially precocial species) form a strong bond with the first moving object they encounter.
- The bond occurs without feeding taking place and allows the young to recognise the caregiver and stay close to it.
- A **critical period** is a restricted time-period in which certain events necessary for normal development must take place.
- Lorenz saw imprinting as being switched on and off genetically .
- Led some researchers to propose the existence of a **sensitive period** in humans.

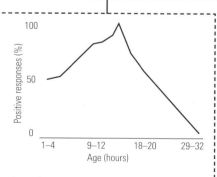

- Lorenz found that imprinting reached a peak (in ducklings) at between 12 and 17 hours after hatching .
- Imprinting was measured by following behaviour towards a model of a moving male duck.
- Lorenz saw imprinting as irreversible – supported by the finding that it affects sexual preferences later on.

Bowlby's theory

'[M]other love in infancy is as important for mental health as are vitamins and proteins for physical health' (Bowlby, 1951).

Maternal-sensitive period

- New-born infants are genetically programmed to behave in ways which ensure their survival (e.g. cuddling, eye-contact, smiling and crying).
- Also, the mother inherits a genetic blueprint for responding to the baby, producing an attachment at a critical period.
- Mothering is therefore useless if delayed for $2\frac{1}{2}$–3 years (12 months for most infants) (Bowlby, 1951).

Extended contact hypothesis
Klaus & Kennel (1976) proposed that mothers who spent more time with their new-borns would form stronger bonds with them. This led to changes in maternity ward practices.

Monotropy
Bowlby believed that children display a strong innate tendency to become attached to one particular figure (monotropy).
This attachment is qualitatively different from all others.

Conflicting research
- Rutter (1981): infants show each type of attachment behaviour towards figures other than the mother.
- Schaffer & Emerson (1964): infants form multiple attachments, in which the mother is not always the main attachment.

39

THE EFFECTS OF EARLY DEPRIVATION

SYLLABUS
6.1 **Early socialisation**
- theories and research into the effects of enrichment and deprivation on the child

KEY QUESTIONS
- What is Bowlby's maternal-deprivation hypothesis?
- What are the short-term and long-term effects of deprivation?
- What are the consequences of privation?
- Are the effects of early privation reversible?

Q

Section 1: The maternal-deprivation hypothesis

1 Bowlby based his hypothesis on two claims, one of which was that there is a 'critical period' for attachment formation. What was the other claim?

2 What, according to Bowlby, would be the consequence of breaking the mother–child bond in the first few years of life?

3 What did Goldfarb (1943) discover when investigating the development of institutionalised and fostered children?

4 Spitz (1945, 1946) and Spitz & Wolf (1946) investigated poor South American orphanages. What clinical condition resulted from the minimal attention which the children received?

5 Complete the following sentence: 'Unfortunately, Bowlby, Goldfarb, Spitz and Wolf all failed to recognise that the _____ nature of the institutional environment could be responsible for the effects they observed'.

6 What is meant by Rutter's (1981) point that Bowlby failed to distinguish *deprivation* from *privation*?

Section 2: Deprivation

7 What is the first stage in the *distress response* which a young child shows in response to short-term separation?

8 What are the important features of the final stage of distress (i.e. detachment)?

9 At what age are children likely to find separation most distressing?

10 Why?

11 Describe one way in which the distress experienced by the child following separation could be lessened.

12 Mooney and Munton (cited in Judd, 1997) investigated the effects of working mothers on children's emotional or social development. What did they find?

13 Varin (cited in Cooper, 1996a) claimed that day-care could have ill-effects. Name one characteristic consequence for the children in his study.

14 What two events are most likely to result in long-term deprivation for the child?

15 Name any four characteristics associated with *separation anxiety*.

16 What, according to Bowlby, is *school phobia*?

17 Based on Richards' (1995) research, identify any four common consequences of divorce for the child.

18 Richards' (1995) findings concerning the effects of divorce are *correlational*. How does this affect the way in which we interpret them?

19 What, according to Schaffer (1996a), is the single most damaging factor before, during and after the separation of parents?

20 What did Harlow discover about the behaviour of rhesus monkeys reared only by 'surrogate' (artificial) mothers?

Section 3: Privation

21 What would you expect an *affectionless psychopath* to be like?

22 What did Bowlby discover, when investigating the histories of 14 juvenile thieves, all of whom showed characteristics of affectionless psychopathy?

23 How might you criticise the methodology of this particular study?

24 What was the conclusion of Bowlby *et al.*'s (1956) study of children who had been separated from parents whilst in a tuberculosis sanitorium?

25 What did Quinton & Rutter (1988) attempt to determine by observing women, brought up in care, interacting with their own children?

26 What were the critical factors in reversing the early effects of intellectual privation in Skeels & Dye's (1939) study of children in American orphanages?

27 Does being kept in darkened huts for the first year of life retard the later development of Guatemalan Indian infants (Kagan & Klein, 1973)? Explain your answer.

28 In Tizard & Hodges' (1978) study of children who were adopted or returned to their natural families, which group was most likely to form close attachments?

29 What were Tizard and Hodges able to conclude?

Section 1: The maternal-deprivation hypothesis

1 The two claims on which Bowlby based his hypothesis were that infants undergo a 'critical period' for attachment formation, and that infants have a strong innate drive to form a unique attachment with a single individual (*monotropy theory*).

2 Bowlby claimed that the consequence of breaking the mother–child bond in the first few years of life would be serious and permanent damage to emotional, social and intellectual development.

3 Goldfarb (1943) discovered that the institutionalised children fell behind the fostered group on a variety of measures, ranging from IQ to tests of social maturity, from the age of three onwards.

4 Spitz (1945, 1946) and Spitz & Wolf (1946) observed high levels of *anaclitic depression*, involving symptoms such as poor appetite and morbidity.

5 'Unfortunately, Bowlby, Goldfarb, Spitz and Wolf all failed to recognise that the *unstimulating* nature of the institutional environment could be responsible for the effects they observed.'

6 Rutter (1981) pointed out that, whilst Bowlby's conclusions concerned the effects of *deprivation* (separation from the primary attachment figure), the studies on which he based his claims were actually studies of *privation* (the absence of *any* attachment).

Section 2: Deprivation

7 *Protest* is the first stage in the distress response, involving crying, kicking, screaming and struggling.

8 *Detachment* is often characterised by a superficial and uniform treatment of others, and following reunion with the mother 'rejection' of her often ensues.

9 Maccoby (1980) suggests that the period between 12 months and 18 months is associated with maximum distress.

10 Children at this age may not be able to maintain an image of the absent parent in memory, and may not be able to understand that the separation is temporary.

11 Distress may be lessened if the child has had previous positive experiences of separation (such as staying with grandparents), or if he/she has been able to form multiple attachments. Finally, the quality of substitute care is important in keeping distress to a minimum.

12 Mooney and Munton (cited in Judd, 1997) found no evidence that working mothers stunt their children's emotional or social development.

13 Varin (cited in Cooper, 1996a) found that long periods in day-care nurseries were associated with children who were more likely to behave uncooperatively and less likely to make friends.

14 Death and divorce are the events most likely to result in long-term deprivation for a child.

15 Increased aggressive behaviour, increased demands on the mother, clinging behaviour, detachment, psychosomatic reactions and fluctuations between clinging and detachment, are all characteristics associated with *separation anxiety*.

16 According to Bowlby, *school phobia* is an expression of separation anxiety, the child fearing that something dreadful will happen to its mother while it is at school.

17 Richards' (1995) research identifies lower levels of academic achievement and self-esteem, higher incidence of conduct disorders, earlier social maturity and transitions to adulthood, a tendency towards more changes of job and lower socio-economic status, a higher frequency of depression and more distant relationships with relations, as common consequences of divorce for the child.

18 Richards' (1995) findings are *correlational*: as such, they do not tell us whether the above factors are caused by divorce, or are just 'side effects' of other factors which may lead to divorce (e.g. parental discord).

19 Schaffer (1996a) claims that *inter-parental conflict* is the single most damaging factor before, during and after the separation of parents.

20 Harlow discovered that rhesus monkeys reared only by 'surrogate' mothers were disturbed in later sexual behaviour and, if female, became inadequate mothers.

Section 3: Privation

21 An *affectionless psychopath* is commonly incapable of deep feelings and consequently unable to form meaningful interpersonal relationships.

22 Bowlby discovered that seven of the 14 juvenile thieves had suffered complete or prolonged separation from their mothers, and a further two had spent nine months in hospital as two-year-olds.

23 Bowlby's study was methodologically flawed. It was a *retrospective* study and, as such, relied on fallible human memories for events.

24 Bowlby *et al.*'s (1956) study of children staying in a tuberculosis sanitorium concluded that 'part of the emotional disturbance can be attributed to factors other than separation'.

25 Quinton and Rutter aimed to determine whether children deprived of parental care in turn became depriving parents.

26 In Skeels & Dye's (1939) study of children in American orphanages, the children who suffered least from the effects of intellectual privation received more intellectual stimulation and one-to-one care from an older girl.

27 Apparently not. Kagan & Klein (1973) found that initially listless and unresponsive infants would recover completely having been allowed out of their huts after their first birthday.

28 Tizard & Hodges (1978) found that the adopted children were more likely to form close attachments than the children who were returned to their natural families.

29 Tizard and Hodges concluded that children who are initially deprived of attachments can form attachments later on, providing that adults nurture such attachments.

Early Deprivation

Bowlby's maternal-deprivation hypothesis

Based on his ideas regarding a **critical period** for attachment-formation, and his **monotropy theory** (Ch 38), Bowlby argued that the mother–infant attachment could not be broken in the first few years of life without serious and permanent damage to social, emotional and intellectual development. Based his claims on studies such as:

Goldfarb (1943):
- Fifteen children raised in institutions compared with 15 fostered children.
- Institutionalised group raised in 'social isolation' during first year.
- Institutionalised group did poorly on tests of abstract thinking, social maturity, rule-following, and at age 14 IQs averaged 72 (vs. 95 for the fostered group).

Spitz (1945, 1946):
- Studied very poor South American orphanages where children only received minimal attention.
- The children were apathetic and displayed *anaclitic depression*. After 3 months of such deprivation, complete recovery was rare.

Bowlby believed the studies showed the effects of maternal deprivation; however:
- Bowlby, Goldfarb, Spitz failed to recognise that such institutional environments were *extremely unstimulating* (not just lacking in maternal care).
- Rutter pointed out that Bowlby had failed to distinguish *deprivation* from *privation*. In fact, the results relate to *privation*.

Deprivation

Short-term effects *(associated with e.g. hospitalisation)*

The stages of distress
Protest: initial reaction takes the form of crying, screaming, clinging to mother/struggling.
Despair: child calms, may appear apathetic. Keeps anger 'locked up' and wants nothing to do with people.
Detachment: with prolonged separation, child begins to respond to others but superficially. If reunited, may 'reject' mother.

Factors influencing distress
Age: separation is most distressing between 7/8 months and 3 years (when attachments are being formed).
Gender: boys are generally more distressed than girls. Any behavioural problems are likely to be accentuated.
Separation experience: positive previous experiences of separation reduce distress.
Multiple attachments: children with multiple attachments are less likely to be distressed.

Research – day care
- Mooney & Munton (cited in Judd, 1997) reviewed 40 years research and concluded that there is no evidence that working mothers stunt their children's emotional/social development.
- Varin (cited in Cooper, 1996a): children who spend long periods in day-care are more likely to be uncooperative and less likely to have friends.

Long-term effects *(associated with e.g. death or divorce)*

Separation anxiety
Aggressive behaviour: increased together with demands on the mother.
Clinging behaviour: may not let mother out of sight – this may generalise to other relationships.
Detachment: child may appear to become self-sufficient.
Fluctuation: between clinging and detachment.
Psychosomatic reactions: e.g. bed-wetting.

Effects of divorce
(Richards, 1995)
Academic achievement: lower.
Self-esteem: lower.
Conduct: higher incidence of problems.
Social maturity: develops earlier, with transitions to adulthood (e.g leaving home, having children) occurring earlier.
Depression: higher incidence.
Relationships: more distant towards parents and kin.

Research – divorce
- Richards' research is *correlational* – Elliot & Richards (1991) found some of the above effects to be present *before* divorce.
- Schaffer (1996a): it is *inter-parental conflict* which is the most damaging factor.
- Amato (1993): conflict between parents who live together is associated with low self-esteem in children.

Privation

Effects

Affectionless psychopathy
Bowlby claimed that separation experiences in early childhood cause affectionless psychopathy – an inability to have deep feelings for others resulting in a lack of meaningful relationships.

Bowlby (1946) studied 44 juvenile thieves:
- Fourteen showed features of affectionless psychopathy (AP).
- Seven of these had experienced prolonged separation as children.
- None of a control group of juveniles showed AP.
Bowlby took this to show that AP resulted from maternal deprivation, though privation is a more likely cause.

Developmental retardation
- Dennis (1960): there is a critical period for intellectual development before age 2.
- Based claims on a study of Iranian orphanages where children adopted after age 2 seemed unable to catch up

Skeels & Dye (1939):
- Studied 25 children raised in an unstimulating orphanage.
- At age 2 those with lower IQs were transferred to a school for the mentally retarded where older girls provided one-to-one care.
Results: the average IQ of this group rose by 36 points, whilst the IQ of those remaining behind dropped by 21 points.

Reversibility

Kagan & Klein (1973):
- Studied a Guatemalan society where babies are kept in small dark huts for their first year.
- Children are not cuddled/played with and are listless and unresponsive.
- However, children leave huts after first birthday and recover, developing normally.

Tizard & Hodges (1978):
- Looked at children who were either adopted or returned to own families on leaving care.
- Children had little opportunity to form relationships whilst in institutions.
- By age 8 majority of adopted children had formed close attachments, whereas only some of those returned to their natural families had done so.

Extreme early privation
Koluchova (1972): describes the case of two Czechoslovakian boys brought up in a closet.
Boys were discovered aged 7, and by age 14 showed no psychopathological symptoms.

Characteristics (Skuse,1984)
Victims often demonstrate the following symptoms on discovery:
- motor retardation
- absent/rudimentary vocal and symbolic language
- retarded perceptuomotor skills
- poor emotional expression
- lack of attachment behaviour
- social withdrawal.
However, Skuse believes that in the absence of genetic/congenital abnormalities, the chances of recovery are still very good.

40

CHILD-REARING

KEY QUESTIONS
- What models of the child-rearing process have been proposed?
- What can cross-cultural studies tell us about the nature of child-rearing?

Section 1: Introducing child-rearing
1 What did Watson (1928) believe would be the consequence of giving children too much love?
2 Identify three pieces of advice offered by Spock (1946) in his book *Baby and Child Care*.
3 What are the two main dimensions on which parental approaches to child-rearing can be classified?
4 Identify one way in which the children of 'warm' parents have been found to differ from those of 'cold' parents.

Section 2: Models of child-rearing
5 Baumrind (1967) originally identified four dimensions of child-rearing. Name them.
6 What is the difference between *authoritarian* and *authoritative* parenting styles?
7 Baumrind (1971) found that children of authoritative parents scored highest on all four measures which comprise *instrumental competence*. Identify these four measures.
8 Complete the sentence: 'Neither the authoritarian nor permissive styles are helpful in developing children's social and emotional competence. This may be because neither style enables children to develop ____ ____'.
9 Maccoby & Martin (1983) devised a two-dimensional classification of child-rearing styles. Identify the two dimensions.
10 What, according to this model, is the difference between *indifferent–uninvolved* and *indulgent–permissive* parenting styles?
11 Baumrind (1971) identifies at least five possible reasons why the authoritative style is the most beneficial. Describe any three of them.
12 The vast majority of research into parenting styles is correlational, allowing Lewis (1981) to propose an alternative explanation for the relationship between the authoritative parenting style and social and emotional competence in children. What is this explanation?
13 What, according to Belsky (cited in Matthews, 1996b) is the cause of toddlers' temper tantrums?

14 Enforcing restrictions may be accomplished by three methods. What is involved in the *power-assertion method* of enforcing discipline?
15 What is involved in the *inductive approach* to parental discipline?
16 Identify the third technique used to enforce restrictions.
17 Which of these techniques is most effective?
18 Krebs & Blackman (1988) identify four general problems involved in the use of punishment with children – describe them.
19 Evidence suggests that *punishment* can be effective, under certain conditions. What are they?
20 What do children learn when raised in unresponsive and unstimulating environments?
21 Identify three aspects of parental styles which have been linked to higher IQ scores in children.

Section 3: Cross-cultural studies
22 Berry *et al.* (1992) have identified two main approaches to the cross-cultural study of child-rearing practices. Name them.
23 What are *ethnographic reports*?
24 Barry *et al.* (1959) argue that there are six universal dimensions of child-rearing. What are *nurturance training* and *self-reliance training*?
25 Complete the sentence: 'Barry *et al.* argued that these dimensions could all be reduced to a single dimension with pressure towards ____ at one end and pressure towards ____ at the other'.
26 Barry *et al.* also claimed that all societies differ in the manner in which boys and girls are socialised along this dimension. What is this difference?
27 According to Barry *et al.*, how does the economic mode of subsistence of a society affect the way in which children are socialised?
28 What was the overall conclusion drawn by Minturn & Lambert (1964), based on Whiting's (1963) *six cultures project*?

Section 1: Introducing child-rearing

1 Watson (1928) believed that giving children too much love would make them 'totally unable to cope with the world in which they must live'.

2 Spock (1946) advised parents to 'trust themselves', feed babies on demand and avoid physically punishing their children.

3 Approaches to child-rearing can be classified with regard to emotional responsiveness and control/demandingness.

4 The children of 'warm' parents display fewer behavioural problems and are more likely to develop values similar to those of their parents (Martin, 1975).

Section 2: Models of child-rearing

5 Baumrind (1967) identified control, demands for maturity, clarity of communication and nurturance as the four dimensions of child-rearing.

6 *Authoritarian parents* rely on strictly enforced rules, tend to be autocratic and leave little room for discussion whilst showing minimal warmth, nurturance or communication. *Authoritative parents* expect their children to meet certain standards, but encourage their children to think independently and involve them in decision-making processes.

7 *Instumental competence* comprises social responsibility, independence, achievement orientation and vitality (Baumrind, 1971).

8 'Neither the authoritarian nor permissive styles are helpful in developing children's social and emotional competence. This may be because neither style enables children to develop *internal standards*.'

9 Parent-centred–child-centred and demanding–undemanding (Maccoby & Martin, 1983).

10 *Indifferent–uninvolved* parents minimise the amount of contact which they have with their children and impose few behavioural rules. *Indulgent–permissive* parents are responsive to their children, tolerant, rarely use punishment and make few demands for mature behaviour.

11 Baumrind (1971) identifies expectations for mature behaviour, encouragement of individuality, respect for children's rights, firm enforcement of rules, two-way communication, and giving children control over their lives as possible reasons why the authoritative style is better.

12 Lewis (1981) proposes that children who are socially and emotionally well-adjusted may elicit an authoritative style from their parents.

13 Belsky (cited in Matthews, 1996b) believes that toddlers' temper tantrums are caused by their parents' 'failure to show respect for the emerging autonomy of the child'.

14 The *power-assertion method* involves coercing children into behaving in a certain way by overpowering and intimidating them.

15 The *inductive approach* to parental discipline involves trying to give children knowledge to enable them to behave appropriately in other situations (e.g. reasoning with the child).

16 The third technique is *love-withdrawal*, involving the implicit or explicit message that 'If you don't behave in this way, I won't love you any more'.

17 The inductive approach is the most effective.

18 According to Krebs & Blackman (1988), the punishing agent presents an aggressive model for the child, the negative feelings elicited by the punishment become associated with surrounding cues, punishment only teaches what not to do (not positive alternatives), and punishment may make the child insecure and erode its sense of self-esteem.

19 Punishment can be effective if it is emphatic and administered immediately (Aronfreed, 1976), if the punished child sees it as judiciously applied, and the punisher as warm and loving (Martin, 1975).

20 Children learn that nothing they do has any effect on what happens to them.

21 Parental provision of appropriate play material (Elardo *et al.*, 1975), active parental involvement with the child and the extent of home organisation and safety (Bradley & Caldwell, 1976), and emotional and verbal responsiveness (Gottfried, 1984) have all been linked with IQ.

Section 3: Cross-cultural studies

22 *Archival studies* and *field studies* are the two main approaches identified by Berry *et al.* (1992).

23 *Ethnographic reports* are reports of studies in which the investigators have become members of the societies being investigated.

24 *Nurturance training* refers to the degree to which children are trained to take responsibility for subsistence or household tasks, whilst *self-reliance training* is the degree to which children are trained to take care of themselves and to be independent of assistance from others (Barry *et al.*, 1959).

25 'Barry *et al.* argued that these dimensions could all be reduced to a single dimension with pressure towards *compliance* at one end and pressure towards *assertion* at the other.'

26 Barry *et al.* claimed that across all societies girls were more socialised for compliance and boys for assertion.

27 Barry *et al.* claimed that pastoral or agricultural societies show greater pressure towards compliance 'than hunter-and-gatherer societies'.

28 Minturn & Lambert (1964) found that there was greater variation in child-rearing practices within cultures than than between cultures.

Child Rearing

Emotional responsiveness: the first of two main dimensions, describing whether child-rearing is warm and loving, involving behaviours such as hugging and kissing or cold and rejecting.

Dimensions of child-rearing

Control/demandingness: the second of two main dimensions, describing whether child-rearing is restrictive and highly supervised, involving many rules or permissive with few rules.

Baumrind's model of child-rearing (1967, 1991)

3 styles

Permissive
- Make few demands on children.
- Reluctant to punish inappropriate behaviour.
- Little attempt at control.

May stem from indifference, preoccupation or a belief in 'freedom'.

Authoritarian
- Use strictly enforced rules.
- Make children meet their standards.
- Autocratic with little time for discussion.
- Punishment often used.
- Minimal warmth and communication.

Authoritative
- Set definite standards to be met.
- Children involved in decisions and rule-making.
- Children encouraged to think independently.
- Children's views are valued.

Results (Shaffer, 1985)

Social competencies low in both boys and girls.
Cognitive competencies low in girls, very low in boys.

Social competencies average in both boys and girls.
Cognitive competencies average in girls, low in boys.

Social competencies high in boys, very high in girls.
Cognitive competencies high in boys, very high in girls

Maccoby & Martin's model (1983)

2 dimensions

	Parent-centred	Child-centred
Demanding	AUTHORITARIAN–AUTOCRATIC	AUTHORITATIVE–RECIPROCAL
Undemanding	INDIFFERENT–UNINVOLVED	INDULGENT–PERMISSIVE

- Minimal contact with children and few/no rules.
- Children feel unloved and engage in attention-seeking behaviour.
- Children less achievement-oriented.

- Lack of rules.
- Parents are responsive and tolerant and rarely use punishment.
- Few demands for appropriate behaviours.

Authoritative styles – key elements
(Baumrind, 1971)

Expectations for mature behaviour: clear standards are set and immature behaviour is not reinforced.
Encouragement of individuality: individuality is seen as positive.
Respect for children's rights: parents recognise children's rights.
Firm enforcement of rules: commands and sanctions are used where necessary.
Two-way communication: verbal 'give-and-take' is encouraged.

Enforcing restrictions

Induction
Involves giving children knowledge enabling them to behave appropriately.
- The '*reasoning*' technique is the most widely used and involves explaining why one behaviour is better than another.
- The most effective method (Staub, 1979).

Love-withdrawal
Involves implicit or explicit use of the message '*if you don't behave in this way, I won't love you any more*'.
- Ignoring or isolating children ('time-out') or expressing disappointment in children, are commonly used techniques.

Power assertion
Involves coercing children by overpowering or intimidating them.
- Parents who use this approach often believe in the use of tangible rewards and punishment.
- Often shouting at a child is used rather than reasoning.

Parental styles and IQ
Higher IQ has been linked to:
- Emotionally and verbally responsive mothers (Gottfried, 1984).
- Active parental involvement (Bradley & Caldwell, 1976).
- Provision of appropriate play material (Elardo *et al.*, 1975).

Problems with the use of punishment
(Krebs & Blackman, 1988)
- The punishing parent presents the child with an aggressive model.
- The negative feelings elicited by the punishment may become associated with the parent, making it less likely that the child will turn to the parent in times of conflict or doubt.
- Punishing only teaches what not to do, but not the positive alternatives.
- Frequent punishment may result in an insecure child with a poor sense of autonomy and self-esteem.

Cross-cultural studies

Archival studies
based on records such as the *Human Relations Area Files* (HRAF)

Universal dimensions of child-rearing
(Barry et al., 1959) – common, in degrees, to all societies:
- **Obedience** training: obeying adults.
- **Responsibility** training: taking responsibility for household/subsistence tasks.
- **General independence** training: being free from control, domination and supervision.
- **Achievement** training: striving towards excellence in performance.
- **Self-reliance** training: taking care of oneself and being self-sufficient.
- **Nurturance** training: taking care of younger children.

- Barry *et al.* argued that these six dimensions could be reduced to two:
  1. *pressure towards compliance.*
  2. *pressure towards assertion.*
- All societies tended to socialise boys for the former and girls for the latter.
- Agricultural societies showed greater 'pressure towards compliance' than hunter-and-gatherer societies.

Field studies

Six cultures project
- Whiting (1963) studied the Ilocos (Philippines), Guisii (Kenya), Mixtecan (Mexico), Rajput (India), Taira (Japan) and Orchard Town (USA).
- Minturn & Lambert (1964) used data from this study and concluded that there was more variation *within* cultures than *between* cultures.

Overall, there is a contradiction between the results of archival studies and the results of field studies.

PIAGET'S THEORY OF COGNITIVE DEVELOPMENT

Q

Section 1: Key concepts

1 What is *genetic epistemology*?
2 Upon what research did Piaget originally base his conclusions regarding cognitive development?
3 Complete the following sentence: 'Piaget concluded that younger children's intelligence is _____ different as well as _____ different from older children's'.
4 Piaget claims that all children progress through a series of *invariant stages*. Explain what this means.
5 What is a *functional invariant*?
6 What, according to Piaget, is a *schema*?
7 What term did Piaget use to apply to the process of modifying our existing schemas to match new objects?
8 Which mental state drives the process of matching objects and schemas?

Section 2: Cognitive stages

9 According to Piaget, how many stages of cognitive development are there? What are they?
10 Name two important abilities which children master during the *sensorimotor* stage?
11 What is *object permanence*?
12 Piaget divides the sensorimotor stage into six sub-stages – how is object permanence demonstrated differently in sub-stages 3 and 4?
13 Towards the end of the sensorimotor stage *symbolic thought* emerges. What is it?
14 What is the main difference between the sensorimotor stage and the *pre-operational stage*?
15 What is *artificialism*?
16 Children display *transductive reasoning* during the pre-operational stage. What does this mean?
17 Children are unable to *decentre* at this stage. What is it that they cannot do?
18 How did Piaget & Inhelder (1956) demonstrate *egocentrism* in the pre-operational child?
19 If a child is shown equal amounts of water in identical beakers, then one of these amounts is poured into a tall, thin beaker and the child states that there is now more water in this beaker, what conclusions can we draw?
20 During the *concrete operational stage* of development, what does a child need in order to perform logical operations?
21 What can a concrete-operational child do that a pre-operational child cannot?
22 What is a *transitivity task*?
23 What is the difference between *horizontal* and *vertical décalage*?
24 What is the central difference between the child's abilities at the concrete operational and *formal operational* stages?
25 What experiment did Inhelder & Piaget (1958) conduct in order to investigate the problem-solving abilities of children at different ages?

Section 3: Evaluating Piaget

26 What did Bower & Wishart (1972) find when they turned off the lights whilst young children were reaching for an object?
27 How might misunderstandings concerning the use of the word 'more' confuse children attempting to complete a conservation task?
28 What does Gelman's (1979) finding that four-year-old children adjust their speech in order to explain things to a blind-fold listener suggest?
29 What is one criticism of Piaget & Inhelder's (1956) *'three-mountains' task*?
30 Why, according to Donaldson (1978), is the use of the pre-transformation question in conservation experiments a significant flaw?
31 What did McGarrigle & Donaldson (1974) discover by using 'Naughty Teddy'?
32 What is one methodological criticism of Piaget's work?
33 Are the stages culturally universal?
34 Based on Dasen's (1994) research, how many of your friends would you expect to have attained formal operational thought?

Section 1: Key concepts

1 *Genetic epistemology* is the term coined by Piaget to describe the study of the development of knowledge.

2 Piaget originally based his conclusions regarding cognitive development on observations of his own three children.

3 'Piaget concluded that younger children's intelligence is *qualitatively* different as well as *quantitatively* different from older children's.'

4 Piaget's *invariant stages* of cognitive development are a series of stages through which all children pass in the same sequence, without missing any stages or regressing to earlier ones.

5 A *functional invariant* is a fundamental aspect of the developmental process which remains the same throughout cognitive development.

6 A *schema*, according to Piaget, is a basic building block of intelligent behaviour – a mental structure which allows us to organise past experiences and understand future experiences.

7 Piaget used the term *accommodation* to describe to the process of modifying our existing schemas to match new objects.

8 *Equilibrium* was the term used by Piaget to describe a state of 'mental balance', which drives the process of matching objects and schemas.

Section 2: Cognitive stages

9 There are four stages of cognitive development: *sensorimotor*, *pre-operational*, *concrete operational* and *formal operational*.

10 Children master their *co-ordination* and the *concept of object permanence* during the sensorimotor stage.

11 *Object permanence* is the ability to maintain a mental representation of an object which is out of sight for a period of time. Without this, infants behave as if objects which they can no longer see have ceased to exist.

12 Object permanence is demonstrated by a child's ability to find a partially hidden object during sub-stage 3 of the sensorimotor stage, whereas they are able to find a completely hidden object during sub-stage 4.

13 *Symbolic thought* is the capacity to construct a mental representation of an object and deal with this as though it were the object.

14 The main difference between the sensorimotor stage and the *pre-operational stage* is the continued development and use of internal images, symbols and language.

15 *Artificialism* is the belief that natural features (such as the sky) have been designed and constructed by people.

16 *Transductive reasoning* is typical of the pre-operational stage and involves drawing inferences about two things based on a single shared attribute (e.g. if both cats and dogs have four legs, then cats and dogs are the same).

17 Pre-operational children are unable to *decentre*; they cannot classify things logically or systematically, since they can only focus on a single perceptual quality at a time.

18 Piaget & Inhelder (1956) demonstrated *egocentrism* by presenting children with a papier-mâché model of three mountains, placing a doll somewhere in this scene, then asking them to pick out the picture most closely resembling what the doll would see. Pre-operational children could not do this.

19 A child who cannot see that the amount of water remains the same is demonstrating an *inability to conserve liquid quantity*.

20 During the *concrete operational stage*, a child is unable to perform logical operations without the presence of real objects.

21 A concrete operational child can decentre and take another's point of view (a decline in egocentrism).

22 A *transitivity task* involves a type of inferential reasoning such as ' If Alan is taller than Bob and Charlie is taller than Alan, who is tallest?'.

23 *Horizontal décalage* refers to inconsistencies in a child's abilities *within* the same kind of operation (e.g. ability to conserve number but not weight); vertical décalage to inconsistencies *between* different abilities.

24 A concrete operational child is still concerned with manipulating things, whereas a *formal operational child* can manipulate ideas or propositions.

25 Inhelder & Piaget (1958) asked children of different ages to discover which combinations of four colourless liquids would produce a yellow liquid.

Section 3: Evaluating Piaget

26 Bower & Wishart (1972) discovered that young children would continue searching for an object for up to one-and-a-half minutes after the lights had been turned off.

27 Children may use 'more' to refer to 'larger, longer, occupying more space', whereas adults use it to mean 'containing a greater number'.

28 Gelman's (1979) finding suggests that four-year-old children are not entirely egocentric and can take into consideration another's point of view.

29 Piaget & Inhelder's (1956) 'three-mountains' task may have been an especially difficult task.

30 Donaldson (1978) points out that asking the same question before and after the transformation may imply that a new response is required.

31 McGarrigle & Donaldson (1974) used 'Naughty Teddy' to rearrange the counters in a number conservation experiment, and found that children were more likely to give the correct response than if an adult had rearranged the counters.

32 Piaget's principal technique was observation, which is not methodologically rigorous, is difficult to replicate and open to bias.

33 Although researchers accept the validity of the stages, some have suggested that there are differences in the rates of development in different cultures.

34 Dasen (1994) found that roughly one-third of adolescents and adults actually attain formal operations.

A

Functional invariants: fundamental aspects of the developmental process which stay the same and work in the same manner throughout the stages of development.

Genetic epistemology: the study of the development of knowledge. Piaget believed that cognitive development occurs through the interaction of innate capacities and environmental events.

Structure of the intellect

- **Schemas** are mental structures which organise experience.
- **Concepts** are rules which describe the properties of events and their relations to one another.
- We begin life with simple schemas (e.g. sucking and grasping).
- Through **accommodation** and **assimilation** (adaptation) the child matches its schemas and the world, achieving a state of **equilibrium** ('mental balance').

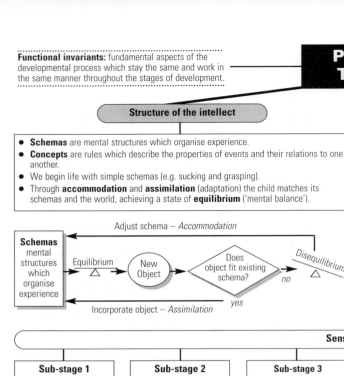

Adjust schema – *Accommodation*

Schemas mental structures which organise experience

Equilibrium △ → New Object → Does object fit existing schema? → no → *Disequilibrium* △

Incorporate object – *Assimilation* yes

Stages of cognitive development

Stage	Age	Key features
Sensorimotor	0–2 years	Developing motor skills. Object permanence develops.
Pre-operational	2–7 years	Egocentrism. Inability to decentre/conserve. Representational thought.
Concrete operational	7–11 years	Logical thinking, but requires real objects.
Formal operational	11+ years	Abstract and hypothetico-deductive thought.

Sensorimotor stage

Sub-stage 1 *0–1 month*	**Sub-stage 2** *1–4 months*	**Sub-stage 3** *4–10 months*	**Sub-stage 4** *10–12 months*	**Sub-stage 5** *12–18 months*	**Sub-stage 6** *18–24 months*
No understanding of an object (*'out of sight, out of mind'*).	Infants look briefly at where an object has disappeared.	Partially hidden object can be found. Object permanence emerges.	A completely hidden object can be found.	An object hidden under several covers can be found where last hidden.	An object placed in a container, then hidden, can be found.

→ **Object permanence increases** – children begin to search for hidden objects →

Pre-operational stage

Seriation and artificialism
Seriation: difficulty arranging objects on a particular dimension
Artificialism: the belief that natural features have been designed (e.g. the sky)

Transductive reasoning (TR) and animism
TR: faulty inferences (e.g. if cats and dogs both have four legs, then cats must be dogs)
Animism: the belief that inanimate objects are alive

Centration
Inability to focus on more than one perceptual quality at a time. (e.g. unable to sort pencils according to colour and size)

Egocentrism
Piaget & Inhelder (1956): 'three-mountain scene' – children were unable to pick out the picture corresponding to the view seen by a doll placed within the scene.

Conservation
Unable to understand that quantities remain the same despite transformations in appearance:
number – counters
volume – tall/short beakers
mass – plasticine balls

Concrete operational stage

- **Logical operations** can now be performed, but only when using actual objects (e.g. dividing a cake).
- **Decentring** is now possible, and egocentrism declines.
- **Transitivity** tasks are still difficult: e.g. 'Alan is taller than Bob, and Charlie is taller than Alan' – who is shortest?
- **Décalage** occurs, with some types of conservation mastered before others.

Formal operational stage

- Ideas/propositions can be manipulated verbally, without real objects.
- Hypothetical thought is also possible (e.g. what if people had tails?)

Systematic problem solving
(Inhelder & Piaget, 1958)
Gave participants beakers filled with a clear liquid which turned yellow when mixed in a certain combination.
- Pre-operational children simply mixed the liquids randomly,
- Concrete operational children were more systematic but failed to test all possible combinations.
- Formal operational children worked systematically, testing all alternatives.

Conflicting research

Object permanence
- Bower & Wishart (1972): even young infants would continue to search for a toy when lights had been turned off for up to 1½ minutes.

Egocentrism
- Gelman (1979): even 4-year-olds adjust their explanations to make them clearer for a blind-fold listener (i.e. 'taking their point of view').
- Critics of the 'three mountains scene' believe that it is an unusually difficult task and that simpler tasks can be performed.

Conservation
- Donaldson (1978): asking the same question before and after the transformation implies that there is a different answer (e.g. Which line contains more counters? *Now* which line contains more?).
- McGarrigle & Donaldson (1974): when 'Naughty Teddy' rearranged the counters, children were able to conserve.

Methodology and terminology
- Piaget's observations were of his own children and his general approach was unscientific.
- Some of the central concepts (e.g. schema, assimilation, accommodation and equilibrium) are vague and largely unfalsifiable.

SOME ALTERNATIVE THEORIES OF COGNITIVE DEVELOPMENT AND THEIR APPLICATION TO EDUCATION

KEY QUESTIONS
- What are the practical applications of Piaget's theory in education?
- What is Vygotsky's theory and what implications does it have for education?
- What is Bruner's theory and what implications does it have for education?
- What is the information-processing approach and what implications does it have for education?

Section 1: Applying Piaget to education

1 How can the concept of *readiness* be applied in the classroom?
2 Give an example of something which would be an appropriate part of a Piagetian curriculum.
3 What is meant by the expression *discovery learning*?
4 What is achieved by the teacher in creating disequilibrium?
5 According to Piaget, which is more important: the process of teaching or the end product?
6 What is the educational value of encouraging children to listen to others' points of view?
7 Should precisely the same curriculum be applied to each child?

Section 2: Vygotsky's theory

8 Piaget believes that cognitive development follows a course which is largely pre-determined, but for Vygotsky cognitive development arises from an entirely different source. What is this source?
9 What is meant by saying that Vygotsky saw the child 'as an apprentice'?
10 What does the term *scaffolding* mean, in Vygotsky's theory?
11 In what ways do the cognitive skills, internalised through scaffolding, remain 'social'?
12 Which strategy was most efficient in Wood *et al.*'s (1976) study of mothers helping four- and five-year-olds on a construction task?
13 What does Vygotsky mean by the *zone of proximal development*?
14 What is the value of *collaborative learning* (involving peer groups as well as teachers)?
15 Who may be able to benefit from collaborative learning, apart from children?

Section 3: Bruner's theory

16 What is Bruner's main area of disagreement with Piaget?
17 What is a *mode of representation*?

18 What type of representation is the *enactive mode*?
19 What is an *icon*?
20 At what Piagetian developmental stage does the *iconic mode* of representation emerge?
21 Complete the following sentence: 'With the emergence of the symbolic stage the child is now freed from ___ _____ _____ and begins to go beyond the information given'.
22 In Bruner & Kenney's (1966) experiment with different sizes and widths of beakers, what was the difference between a *transposition task* and a *reproduction task*?
23 At what age were 79 per cent of the children successful on the transposition task?
24 According to Bruner, what enables children to make the leap from the iconic to the symbolic mode of representation?
25 Piaget believed that cognitive development could not be significantly accelerated. What does Bruner believe?
26 What is Bruner's concept of a *spiral curriculum*?
27 Complete the following sentence: 'Educators should provide learners with means of grasping a discipline's _____, rather than just mastering factual information'.
28 How might you introduce the topic of 'volume' to a child at the sensorimotor stage of development?
29 Which theorist is child-centred and which teacher-centred – Vygotsky or Bruner?

Section 4: Information-processing theories

30 What metaphor is central to the information-processing approach to cognitive development?
31 What is a *task analysis*?
32 Name the cognitive processes that might commonly feature in a *task analysis*.
33 What is *metacognition*?
34 Complete the sentence: 'One of the teacher's main roles is to help children find strategies for reducing their _____ load' (Sutherland, 1992).

Section 1: Applying Piaget to education

1 *Readiness* (the idea that children become 'ready' to learn certain concepts at certain stages) means that the teacher must assess the child's current level of development carefully and adjust tasks as appropriate.

2 Logic (including transitive inferences), maths, science (conservation) and space (geometry) might all constitute part of a Piagetian curriculum.

3 *Discovery learning* is an expression used to convey the Piagetian view that children learn from actions, rather than from passive observation.

4 In creating disequilibrium, the teacher provides the opportunity and the motivation for children who are ready to advance to the next stage.

5 Piaget maintains that the process of teaching is more important than the end product.

6 According to Piaget, listening to others' points of view may help to break down egocentrism, as well as enabling them to learn from each other.

7 No. On a Piagetian account the curriculum should be adapted to meet the needs of individuals.

Section 2: Vygotsky's theory

8 Vygotsky maintains that cognitive development arises from a social process, involving interaction with others.

9 Vygotsky saw the child 'as an apprentice' in that she/he acquires knowledge and skills through collaboration with those who already possess them.

10 *Scaffolding* refers to the role played by parents, teachers and others, by which children acquire skills and knowledge. These people provide a 'framework' which helps to support the child during development.

11 Cognitive skills remain 'social' in two ways. First, we internalise the 'scaffolding' that others have provided in scaffolding our own learning, and secondly we develop most highly those skills which are offered by our culture.

12 Wood *et al.* (1976) found that mothers who provided specific and general interventions, according to the child's progress, were the most efficient instructors.

13 The *zone of proximal development* is the range of abilities and skills which a child is potentially capable of, but is not yet capable of alone.

14 Collaborative learning enables more advanced children to assist younger children, as well as allowing children to internalise the communicative process.

15 Foot (1994) found that collaborative learning may also be effective in adult and higher education.

Section 3: Bruner's theory

16 Bruner believes that language and interpersonal communication with experts play an important role in cognitive development, whereas Piaget does not.

17 A *mode of representation* is a form that knowledge or understanding can take.

18 The *enactive mode* involves representing the world through actions (e.g. riding a bike).

19 An icon is an 'image' of things we have experienced. By 'image' Bruner intends 'a copy', so that for example, we could say that we store an 'image' of a sound.

20 The iconic mode of representation emerges during the last six months of the sensorimotor stage.

21 'With the emergence of the symbolic stage the child is now freed from *the immediate context* and begins to go beyond the information given.'

22 A *transposition task* involved placing the beakers in an arrangement never seen before, according to a new pattern, whereas the *reproduction task* involved putting the beakers back the way they were, having been scrambled.

23 At the age of seven, 79 per cent of the children were capable of the transposition task.

24 Bruner claims that it is *language* which enables children to make the leap from the iconic to the symbolic mode of representation.

25 Bruner, unlike Piaget, believes that cognitive development can be accelerated by teachers who stimulate children.

26 A *spiral curriculum* is the idea that a subject's principles come to be understood at increasing levels of complexity.

27 'Educators should provide learners with means of grasping a discipline's *structure*, rather than just mastering factual information.'

28 Volume could be introduced to a child at the *sensorimotor* stage by allowing it to play with buckets and water.

29 Bruner is a child-centred theorist whilst Vygotsky places more emphasis on the teacher (teacher-centred).

Section 3: Information-processing theories

30 The *computer metaphor* is central to the information-processing approach to cognitive development, with human beings seen as information-processors.

31 A *task analysis* involves analysing a task's component steps in order to discover the processes necessary to solve a problem.

32 Encoding factual information, storing this information in working memory, integrating it to form a representation of the situation, encoding the question and scanning the representation for the answer are all cognitive processes that might commonly feature in a task analysis.

33 *Metacognition* is 'thinking about thinking': in this context, it is making children aware of their own learning processes.

34 'One of the teacher's main roles is to help children find strategies for reducing their *memory* load' (Sutherland, 1992).

Piaget – applications

Discovery learning: learning must be an active process of discovery where children construct knowledge for themselves.

Readiness
- The teacher should assess each child's stage of cognitive development, setting tasks which are appropriate and intrinsically motivating.

Curriculum
- Teachers guide children's discovery and should adapt the curriculum to each child's needs.
- Content might include maths (number), logic (transitive inferences) and science (conservation).

Teaching methods
- Teachers should try to create a state of *disequilibrium* to encourage children to advance to the next stage.
- Teachers should encourage children to learn from each other.
- Teaching materials should involve real objects.

Information-processing approach

- Shares the Piagetian view that there are psychological structures in people's minds which explain their behaviour.
- Uses the central metaphor of computers (e.g. inputs and outputs).
- Problem-solving failures occur because of faults in basic processes (see below).

Task analysis
To understand problem-solving, we must break it down into its component steps, e.g:
1. perceive and encode the facts,
2. store them in working memory (WM),
3. combine components in WM to form an integrated representation,
4. encode the question,
5. scan the representation to formulate an answer.

Applications
- Teachers must help children to reduce the load on WM, e.g. by encouraging them to write down the facts involved in a problem.
- **Metacognition** – making children aware of their own learning plays a vital role.
- Children should be encouraged to a) test hypotheses and b) use visual imagery to apply their answers to real-life situations.

Alternatives & Applications

Vygotsky's theory

- Opposed to Piagetian theory – saw children as acquiring knowledge and skills through graded collaboration with those who already possess them.
- Ability to think and reason for ourselves is the result of a social process (see Ch 37).
- Cognitive development involves an internalisation of problem-solving which takes place through interaction with others.

Scaffolding
- Refers to the role played by parents, teachers and others by which children acquire knowledge and skills (Wood *et al.*, 1976).
- As a task becomes more familiar to the child, those who provide support leave more for the child to do.

Research
- Wood *et al.* (1976): on a construction task with 4- and 5-year-olds, mothers used different strategies.
- The most effective were those who combined general and specific interventions according to the child's progress.

Zone of proximal development

- The ZPD is those functions which have not yet matured but are in the process of maturing (Vygotsky, 1978).
- The ZPD varies from one child to another, but with support from others the child can attain more than it would have been able to alone.

Applications
- Teachers should *scaffold* children to competence, guiding pupils in paying attention, concentrating and learning effectively.
- Rejects approaches advocating rigid control over learning in favour of extending and challenging children by controlling *activities*.
- *Collaborative learning* is important, where small peer groups enable more advanced children to help less advanced children.
- Group work allows children to internalise procedures for *communication*, enriching their intellectual capacity (Cheyne, 1995).
- For Vygotsky, there is value in direct teaching but with the child as an *active* learner.
- Shayer (cited in Sylva, 1996): applying Vygotsky's principles in designing materials for science teaching increased children's learning ability as well as scores on standardised attainment tests (SATs).

Bruner's theory

Individuals can represent the world in three ways: enactive, iconic and symbolic. These '*modes of representation*' develop one after the other and are all used by adults.

Enactive mode
- Past events are represented through motor responses (e.g. riding a bike).
- Corresponds to Piaget's sensorimotor stage.

Iconic mode
- Involves using mental copies /images of experiences (icons).
- Corresponds to the last 6 months of the sensorimotor stage and whole pre-operational stage.

Symbolic mode
- Child uses symbols to represent things.
- Language becomes more influential on thought.
- Child is freed from the immediate context.

Research
Bruner & Kenney (1966): arranged nine beakers on a 3 × 3 grid in order of width and height. Children had to perform two tasks:
1. **Reproduction task**: glasses scrambled and children had to put them back the way they had seen them (requires iconic mode)
2. **Transposition task**: children had to re-order the glasses (e.g. mirroring the arrangement) (requires symbolic mode).

Results:

Reproduction task:	60% 5-year-olds,	80% 7-year-olds successful
Transposition task:	0% 5-year-olds,	79% 7-year-olds successful.

The role of language
Bruner believes that the transition from iconic to symbolic mode is due to language, and this implies that cognitive development can be speeded up by training children in symbol use.

Applications
- Bruner believes that cognitive development can be speeded up, particularly when children are from deprived backgrounds.
- The *spiral curriculum* is the idea that a subject is re-encountered at increasing levels of complexity.
e.g. Volume can be introduced by allowing babies to play with water in buckets, at the pre-operational stage buckets of water can be used, accompanied by concepts such as 'more' and 'less'. At junior school, the word 'volume' is introduced, alongside concrete examples. At secondary school, 'volume' can be taught abstractly.
- Opposed to Piagetian notion of 'readiness' and believes that any subject can be taught in some form to a child at any stage.
- Teachers should enable learners to grasp a subject's structure, not just factual information – helps them develop their own ideas.
- Teachers should encourage learners to make links and understand the relationships within and between topics.
- Teachers should make demands on their pupils.

THE DEVELOPMENT OF MEASURED INTELLIGENCE

KEY QUESTIONS
- To what extent are IQ scores a product of genetic factors?
- To what extent do environment and upbringing influence IQ scores?
- Can an enriched environment significantly improve IQ scores?

Q

Section 1: Genetic influences on IQ scores

1 Why is it important to distinguish *measured intelligence* and *intelligence*?

2 What did Tryon (1940) discover when he bred 'maze-bright' and 'maze-dull' rats separately?

3 Why is the *stability* of IQ scores over time an important issue?

4 What is the difference between *IQ* and *DQ*?

5 What did McCall *et al.* (1973) find when they looked at IQ scores in 140 middle-class children between the ages of two-and-a-half and 17?

6 What sorts of events are most likely to cause short-term fluctuations in measured IQ?

7 What can we conclude from the low stability coefficients which we find when looking at IQ scores in individuals over time?

8 If genetic factors *do* influence IQ, why would one expect to find greater concordance between the IQ scores of brothers than between those of cousins?

9 What is the difference between *monozygotic twins* and *dizygotic twins*?

10 What is the concordance rate between monozygotic twins raised together?

11 Give two possible explanations for this finding.

12 How 'separate' were the twins raised 'separately' in Shields' (1962) and Juel-Nielsen's (1965) studies of monozygotic twins?

13 When do monozygotic twins necessarily share an environment?

14 In what way is bias introduced by the agencies responsible for placing separated twins?

15 What net effect have the problems with twin studies had on the conclusions drawn from them?

16 Why are studies of *adopted children* of relevance to the debate concerning whether or not IQ scores are a result of genetic influences?

17 What did Munsinger (1975) find when he compared correlations between adopted children and their biological parents with correlations between adopted children and their adoptive parents?

18 Identify one problem with such studies.

19 What was found by Scarr & Weinberg's (1976) 'transracial' study (black children adopted into high-income white families)?

Section 2: Environmental influences

20 According to Cooper & Zubek (1958), do genetically 'bright' rats remain brighter than genetically 'dull' rats when placed in dull environments?

21 What general difference was observed between rats raised in dull environments and those raised in stimulating environments?

22 According to Zajonc & Marcus's (1975) study, how can family size and birth order affect IQ scores?

23 Give one example of an 'environmental insult' which may affect IQ.

24 Coaching can improve IQ scores. What is it necessary to coach children in?

25 What was discovered by Skeels & Dye's (1939) study comparing children in orphanages with those raised by foster mothers?

Section 3: Environmental enrichment studies

26 What was the aim of 'Operation Headstart', begun in 1965 in the United States?

27 How long-lasting were the IQ gains resulting from this programme?

28 Give two criticisms of the 'Headstart' programme.

29 What overall conclusion can you draw about the usefulness of enrichment programmes?

30 What caution regarding the effects of enriched environments was identified by White (1971), when he provided infants with enriched visual environments?

31 Describe ways in which parents can encourage learning in their children.

32 If a certain trait is highly heritable, can we conclude that environmental factors are unlikely to influence it significantly?

Section 1: Genetic influences on IQ scores

1 *Measured intelligence* and *intelligence* may well not be the same thing. There may be different types of intelligence, aspects of which are not measured by intelligence tests, and intelligence tests may not actually measure intelligence.

2 Tryon (1940) found that the offspring of 'maze-bright' rats were also good at learning mazes and 'maze-dull' rats had offspring which were slow to learn.

3 If IQ is largely inherited, then we would expect it to be stable over time, since genetic material is stable over time. If IQ scores are not stable, then this suggests that environment may influence scores.

4 *IQ* stands for *Intelligence Quotient* and *DQ* stands for *Developmental Quotient* and is usually used with children aged two or less. DQ assesses a child's developmental rate against the average.

5 McCall *et al.* (1973) found that IQ scores fluctuated by an average of 28 points between the ages of two-and-a-half and 17, and in one case by as much as 74 points!

6 Disturbing factors (such as parental divorce) are most likely to cause short-term fluctuations in measured IQ.

7 The low stability coefficients which we find when looking at IQ scores in individuals over time suggest that, although genetic factors may play a significant role in IQ scores, a simple genetic account cannot tell the whole story.

8 Brothers share roughly 50 per cent of their genetic material, whereas cousins share only 12 per cent: if the genetic account is correct, brothers are more likely to have similar IQs.

9 *Monozygotic twins* develop from a single egg (zygote) and are therefore identical (share 100 per cent of their genes), whereas *dizygotic twins* arise from two eggs and are not identical (share 50 per cent of genes on average).

10 The concordance rate for monozygotic twins raised together is roughly 0.85 (Bouchard & McGue, 1981).

11 This may be due to the fact that they share identical genes, or that they both have similar upbringing and environments.

12 Not very separate: some of the twins went to the same school and/or played together (Farber, 1981; Horgan, 1993) and some were raised in related branches of the parents' families.

13 Monozygotic twins necessarily share the mother's womb for the first nine months of life.

14 The agencies responsible for placing separated twins often try to match the families as closely as possible, thereby increasing the similarity of their environments.

15 The problems with twin studies probably led to an *overestimation* of genetic influences.

16 By studying *adopted children* we can see whether or not their IQ scores correlate best with their natural or adoptive parents, which in turn suggests whether genetic or environmental factors are more influential.

17 Munsinger (1975) found a correlation of 0.48 between the IQ scores of adopted children and their biological parents as opposed to only 0.19 between adopted children and their adoptive parents.

18 Such studies do not take into account the similarity between the adoptive and biological parents' environments.

19 Scarr & Weinberg's (1976) 'transracial' study found that adopted children could make significant IQ gains (16 points) when adopted into families of above average intelligence, income and social class.

Section 2: Environmental influences

20 No. Genetically 'bright' rats are indistinguishable from genetically 'dull' rats when placed in dull environments (Cooper & Zubek, 1958).

21 Rats raised in stimulating environments had heavier brains than those raised in dull environments.

22 Zajonc & Marcus (1975) found that members of larger families had lower than average IQ scores, and that intelligence also declines with birth order, with the youngest children scoring lower on average.

23 'Environmental insults' include toxins, such as lead-based paint, which may be ingested by the child causing lower IQ scores (Needleman *et al.*, 1990).

24 Coaching (specific instruction and practice) in intelligence tests can improve IQ scores. This in turn casts doubt on the validity of the tests themselves.

25 Skeels & Dye (1939) found that most of the children raised by foster mothers showed significant improvements in their measured intelligence.

Section 3: Environmental enrichment studies

26 'Operation Headstart', was a compensatory programme designed to give culturally disadvantaged pre-school children enriched opportunities in early life.

27 Initial results suggested that the IQ gains were not long-lasting, disappearing within a couple of years.

28 Hunt (1969) argued that the programme was inappropriate to the children's needs. Additionally, it emphasised IQ changes as a measure of its effectiveness, rather than social competence or emotional health.

29 Enrichment programmes can be effective with children from deprived backgrounds, but are unlikely to have much of an impact on children raised in 'normal' environments (Scarr, 1984).

30 White (1971) found that the infants were advanced in some respects but delayed in others as a result of their enriched surroundings.

31 Parents can encourage learning by making learning informal; by not persisting in encouraging the child to learn when she/he is reluctant; by not being critical of the child's efforts; by giving the child their full attention sometimes; by including them in their everyday activities; talking *to* not *at* them; trying to see things from the child's perspective and directing their child towards learning opportunities.

32 No. A trait may be highly heritable but nevertheless dependent on environmental influences for its development.

Development of Measured Intelligence

Tryon (1940) divided rats into 'maze-bright' and 'maze-dull' groups. Groups bred separately in identical pens. Offspring were found to have *inherited* their parents' ability to learn mazes.

Genetic influences

IQ stability

An individual's genetic inheritance remains constant during his/her life, if IQ depends largely on genetics, IQ scores should be stable.
- Many studies have shown little fluctuation over time (e.g. Honzik *et al.*, 1973) with high *stability coefficients*.
- However, these tend to be of large groups which obscure individual differences. The stability coefficients are also *lower* than simple genetic theory suggests.
- Short-term fluctuations can be caused by disturbing life-events.

Conflicting research
McCall *et al.* (1973): in 140 middle class children, the average IQ change between 2½ and 17 years was 28 points. One child increased by 74 points!

Family resemblance studies

If genetic factors influence IQ, then the closer the genetic relationship between two people, the higher the correspondence between their IQ scores.
- **Monozygotic** (identical) twins (MZs) share 100% of their genes.
- **Dizygotic** (non-identical) twins (DZs) share on average 50% of genes.
- Bouchard & McGue (1981): the highest concordance rate for IQ scores is between MZ twins (supporting the genetic account).
- However, this result could be due to **shared environment**.

Separated twin studies
Allow us to see if concordance rates are just as high when MZs are raised apart.

Bouchard *et al.*(1990): concordance rates for MZs raised apart were lower than MZs raised together but still higher than for DZs raised together.
Suggests a strong **genetic** influence

Criticisms
- 'Separated' twins often turn out to have attended same schools, or been raised in branches of the same family.
- Twins will have had same experiences whilst in the womb.
- Agencies responsible for separating twins try to match families as closely as possible.
- Where twins have come forward to take part in the study, they may not be a representative sample.
- Different studies have used different IQ tests, making them difficult to compare.
- Burt's (1966) studies of MZ twins were partially fabricated.

Adoption studies
Allow us to see if concordance rates are closer to biological or adoptive parents.

Munsinger (1975): correlation between adoptees and biological parents was **0.48**, and only **0.19** between adoptees and adoptive parents. Suggests a strong **genetic** influence.

Criticisms
- Assessing the degree of similarity between the environments of the biological and adoptive parents is difficult.

Scarr & Weinberg (1976): studied black children adopted into white families of above average intelligence and income.
Results: Average IQ changed from 90 (before adoption) to 106 (after adoption).
Suggests a strong **environmental** component.

Environmental influences

Studies of non-humans

Cooper & Zubeck (1958): mixed groups of 'bright' rats and 'dull' rats and raised them in either dull or stimulating environments.
Results:
- Rats raised in stimulating environments had heavier brains, irrespective of whether they were 'dull' or 'bright'.
- No differences between bright rats and dull rats in either environment. Suggests a strong environmental influence.

Studies of humans

Post-natal influences

Extreme malnutrition
Stock & Smythe (1963): children suffering extreme malnutrition during infancy averaged 20 IQ points less than those with adequate diets.

Stressful circumstances
Samerof & Seifer (1989): children with no risk factors (e.g. father not living with the family) averaged 30 IQ points higher than those with 7 or 8 risk factors.

Family size
Zajonc & Markus (1975): intelligence declines with family size, and also with birth order (younger children average lower IQs).

Environmental insults
Needleman *et al.* (1990): children ingesting lead-based paint from peeling walls had lower IQs.

Enrichment studies

Milwaukee Project
- Heber & Garber (1975): worked with 40 poor, mostly black, families, (average IQ 75). Half were given job training and sent to school.
Results:
- Enriched group had an average IQ score of 126.
- However, IQ gains decreased over time.

Hothousing
White (1971): infants in enriched visual surroundings were advanced in some respects but *delayed* in others.

Howe (1995): children in hothousing regimes may miss out on experiences important for healthy development.

Operation Headstart
Begun in 1965, gave culturally disadvantaged pre-school children enriched opportunities, over 1 year period.
Results:
- Initial IQ gains disappeared within a couple of years.
- However, reviews of the long-term effects have revealed a 'sleeper effect' with lasting IQ gains re-emerging.

Encouraging learning
Howe & Griffey (1994)
- Learning should be informal.
- Parents should not encourage learning if child is reluctant.
- Children's efforts should not be criticised.
- Parents should sometimes give children full attention.
- Children should participate in parents' everyday activities.
- Talk to children, not at them.
- See things from the child's perspective.
- Guide children towards learning opportunities.

Interaction

- Both genetic and environmental factors influence measured intelligence.
- Early heritability estimates for IQ of 80% are now more likely to be 50–60%.
- Even where a trait is highly heritable, it can still be heavily influenced by environmental variables (e.g. malnourishment can stunt growth).
- Ultimately, it is impossible to separate out environmental and genetic influences entirely.

THEORIES OF MORAL DEVELOPMENT

KEY QUESTIONS
- How does Freud explain moral development?
- What do social learning theorists say about moral development?
- How does Piaget explain moral development?
- How does Kohlberg explain moral development?

Section 1: Freud's psychoanalytic theory

1 What is the role of the *ego* in Freud's model of the personality?
2 Which component of the personality is responsible for enforcing morality?
3 At what age do children acquire their sense of right and wrong?
4 What is the *Oedipus complex*?
5 What is the role of *castration anxiety* in the formation of morality?
6 Why did Freud believe that boys came to have a stronger sense of morality than girls?
7 What other influences might there be on childhood morality which are not taken into account by Freud's theory?

Section 2: Social learning approaches

8 What is the learning process central to the social learning account of moral development?
9 Name three factors that strongly influence the likelihood of a model being imitated.
10 What, according to Mischel (1973), are *self-regulatory systems and plans*?
11 In Hoffman's (1970) study, which parental technique was most likely to be associated with low levels of moral development?

Section 3: Piaget's theory

12 Complete the following sentence: 'According to Piaget (1932), morality develops gradually during childhood and adolescence with children passing through _____ different _____ of moral development'.
13 Why were the rules of marbles important to Piaget?
14 What is meant by saying that to younger children the rules of marbles were *external laws*?
15 What did children aged ten or more believe was the function of the rules of marbles?
16 Who were more likely to break the rules, older children or younger children?
17 What is the difference between *mutual respect* and *unilateral respect*?

18 When Piaget told children aged between five and ten stories about children who had broken something, what factor was most influential in determining how naughty they thought the children were?
19 What did older children feel was the most important element in determining the degree of naughtiness?
20 Why are younger children far more likely to accept collective punishment than older children?
21 What is *immanent justice*?
22 What is the difference between *heteronomous* and *autonomous morality*?
23 How much can Piaget's work tell us about practical morality?
24 What is the explanation offered by the *information-processing approach* as to why young children are more likely to concentrate on the damage done when assessing a child's naughtiness?

Section 4: Kohlberg's theory

25 Describe one similarity between Kohlberg and Piaget's views of moral development.
26 How did Kohlberg investigate moral reasoning in children aged between seven and 17?
27 Name the three *levels of moral development* proposed by Kohlberg.
28 Upon what basis are decisions made about right and wrong during the first stage of moral development?
29 According to Kohlberg, what is the highest stage of moral development attainable?
30 Which stage of moral reasoning is characteristic of adults who engage in robbery (Thornton & Reid, 1982)?
31 What problems exist with the *story-book morality technique* used by Kohlberg to assess morality?
32 According to Gilligan (1982), in what way does Kohlberg's work suffer from a *gender bias*?
33 Which of Piaget's cognitive stages corresponds to Kohlberg's *post-conventional level of morality*?

Section 1: Freud's psychoanalytic theory

1 The role of the *ego* in Freud's model is to negotiate compromises between instincts (in the form of the *id*), morality (in the form of the *superego)* and reality (often taking the form of social constraints).

2 The *superego* is responsible for enforcing morality, and is the internalisation of parental standards.

3 Freud suggests that a child acquires a sense of right and wrong at the age of about five or six.

4 The *Oedipus complex* refers to the sexual attraction of the male child to its mother and the perception of the father as a rival.

5 According to Freud, *castration anxiety*, arising from the Oedipus complex, causes the male child to identify with the feared parent (*identification with the aggressor*) and subsequently internalise (*introject*) the parent's standards, which become the superego.

6 Since girls have no fear of castration, they identify with the mother only through fear of losing her love (*anaclitic identification*) and hence do not develop such strong superegos.

7 Freud's theory does not take into account the influence of the media (especially television– understandably so) and other extra-familial influences on morality.

Section 2: Social learning approaches

8 *Observational learning*, whereby the child learns by observing another (the *model*), is central to the social learning account of the development of morality.

9 Models whose behaviour is seen as appropriate to the observer, who are seen as similar or relevant to the observer, and who behave in a consistent fashion, are most likely to be imitated.

10 Mischel (1973) uses the term *self-regulatory systems and plans* to apply to the self-imposed standards or rules which individuals use to regulate their own behaviour.

11 Hoffman (1970) found that *power-assertion* (such as physical punishment, withdrawal of privileges) was most likely to be associated with low levels of moral development.

Section 3: Piaget's theory

12 'According to Piaget (1932), morality develops gradually during childhood and adolescence with children passing through *qualitatively* different *stages* of moral development.'

13 Piaget believed that a study of children's understanding of the rules of marbles could reveal the way in which their moral reasoning develops.

14 The rules of marbles were *external laws* to younger children: they were perceived as created by others, and incapable of being changed in any way.

15 Children aged ten or more believed that the function of the rules of marbles was to prevent quarrelling and ensure fair play.

16 Older children were far less likely to break the rules than younger children, who often broke them to suit themselves.

17 *Mutual respect* involves a moral orientation towards peers, whereas *unilateral respect* is the moral attitude shown by children towards adult authority.

18 Children aged between five and ten believed that the *severity of the outcome* of the behaviour was the most important factor in assessing the naughtiness of the children who had broken something.

19 Older children understood that the child's *intentions* were the most important element in determining the degree of naughtiness.

20 Younger children are more likely to accept *collective punishment* than older children, because it is decreed by authority and accepted simply because of its source.

21 *Immanent justice* is the idea that misfortunes which befall wrong-doers are actually a form of punishment.

22 *Heteronomous morality* involves accepting and being subject to another's rules and laws, whereas *autonomous morality* involves a view of rules as the product of social agreements and co-operation.

23 Although Piaget's work was intended to increase our knowledge of practical morality, his method involved gaining answers to theoretical questions and situations, and so may not tell us very much about how people actually behave in practice.

24 The *information-processing approach* suggests that young children are unable to remember all of the details of the story, such as who did the damage.

Section 4: Kohlberg's theory

25 Both Kohlberg and Piaget believe that moral development passes through stages.

26 Kohlberg presented children with *moral dilemmas* (short stories in which they had to choose between two alternatives and justify their decision).

27 *Pre-conventional, conventional* and *post-conventional morality*.

28 During the first stage of moral development (punishment and obedience orientation), children believe that right and wrong are determined by what is punishable and what is not.

29 The highest level of moral development (*universal ethical principles orientation*) involves acting in accord with the universal principles laid down by one's conscience.

30 Thornton & Reid (1982) found adults who engage in robbery to be characterised by stage 2 reasoning ('right and wrong are determined by what brings rewards').

31 The *story-book morality technique* used by Kohlberg presents people with hypothetical moral situations. In reality, their behaviours might be very different.

32 Kohlberg's work was based solely on interviews with males. Gilligan (1982) argues that since women tend to be oriented more towards compassion and care, the gender bias causes them to be rated as conventional, rather than post-conventional in their reasoning.

33 The *formal operational stage*.

- The child begins life with only sexual and aggressive instincts (**ID**).
- The **EGO** develops to negotiate compromises between the **ID** and **REALITY** (including social constraints).
- Young boys and girls become attracted to the opposite-sex parent (**Oedipus/Electra complex**, respectively).
- Boys become anxious that the father will punish them (**castration anxiety**).
- Boys identify with the father to resolve the conflict and the internalised voice of the parent becomes the **SUPEREGO** (roughly, the conscience).
- Girls do not fear castration, only loss of the mother's love and this **anaclitic identification** leads to weaker superegos.

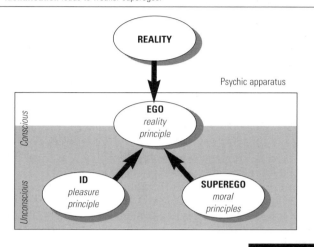

Psychic apparatus

REALITY

EGO
reality principle

Conscious

Unconscious

ID
pleasure principle

SUPEREGO
moral principles

Social learning theory

- Recognises the role of **conditioning** (reinforcement and punishment).
- **Observational learning and modelling** also play a role.
- **Cognitive factors** intervene between stimulus and response (see below).

Factors influencing likelihood of model being imitated:

- **Appropriateness:** more appropriate behaviour is more likely to be imitated. e.g. Bandura *et al.* (1961) showed that children were more likely to imitate an aggressive male than an aggressive female.
- **Relevance and similarity:** the more relevance a behaviour has, the more likely it is to be imitated, e.g. boys were more likely than girls to imitate an aggressive male (Bandura *et al.*, 1961).
- **Consistency:** children imitate behaviour which is consistent, even if that behaviour involves saying one thing and doing another (i.e. consistently being inconsistent!).

Mischel (1973):
- People develop *self-regulatory systems and plans.*
- These are internal rewards and punishments (e.g. pride and guilt) used to regulate behaviour and are *self-imposed.*
- Acquired through *observation* of parents' rewards and punishments.
- An internal image of an adult's rewarding/punishing behaviour becomes *imitative self-approval or disapproval.*

Hoffman (1970): excessive use of power-assertive techniques by parents was associated with low levels of moral development. Reasoning/explaining was associated with high levels.

Moral Development

Piaget's theory

- Children progress through *qualitatively* different stages of moral reasoning, linked to cognitive development.
- Morality of younger children is *heteronomous* (subject to another's rules) and older children *autonomous* (morality of social agreement). Change at 9/10 years, due to a reduction in egocentric thought (at 7).

Rules of marbles:
Piaget studied children's beliefs about the rules of marbles to study morality.

Moral stories:
Piaget told short stories in which children had to make moral judgements about another child.

5–9 yr-olds	**Unilateral respect**	**External responsibility**
	- Rules have always existed and been created by older children/adults/God. - Rules cannot be changed (external laws) but children broke them unashamedly.	- Could distinguish intentional/unintentional acts, but judged guilt on amount of damage done. - People should pay for their crimes (*expiatory punishment*) - Punishments accepted because of their source in authority. - *Collective punishment* seen as fair when someone doesn't 'own up'. - Naughty people who suffer misfortune are being punished (*immanent justice*).
10+ yr-olds	**Mutual respect**	**Internal responsibility**
	- Rules were invented by children and could be changed. - Rules function to ensure fair play. - Adhered rigidly to rules.	- Saw *intention* as most important in determining naughtiness. - Saw punishment as bringing home the nature of the offence and as a deterrent. - Punishing many for the misdeeds of one is immoral. - *Principle of reciprocity* – the punishment should fit the crime. - *Moral relativism* – justice is not solely tied to authority.

Conflicting research

- Nelson (1980): even 3-year-olds form moral judgements based on a person's intentions – but only if these are made explicit (they find it hard to discriminate intentions from consequences).

Kohlberg's theory

- Like Piaget, argued that children pass through stages of moral development.
- Kohlberg (1963): presented 58 males aged 7 to 17 with moral dilemmas (e.g. 'should poor Heinz steal the expensive drug to save his dying wife?') and classified the responses in three levels and six stages:

Level 1: Pre-conventional morality

Stage 1: *punishment and obedience orientation*	Right and wrong are determined by what is punishable or not. Moral behaviour is the avoidance of punishment.
Stage 2: *instrumental relativist orientation*	Right and wrong are determined by what brings rewards and what people want. Others' needs are only important because they affect us.

Level 2: Conventional morality

Stage 3: *interpersonal concordance orientation*	Moral behaviour is whatever pleases/meets with approval from others. What the majority thinks is right by definition.
Stage 4: *maintaining the social order orientation.*	Being good means maintaining the social order for its own sake and respecting authority. Laws are accepted without question.

Level 3: Post-conventional morality

Stage 5: *social contract-legalistic orientation.*	Laws are mutually agreed and can be changed by mutual agreement. Individual rights can sometimes become more important than laws.
Stage 6: *universal ethical principles orientation.*	The ultimate judge of morality is a person's own conscience guided by universal principles. Society's rules are less important than these.

Conflicting research

- Gilligan (1982): Kohlberg's stages are based on male morality and female morality is oriented more towards compassion.
- Gibbs & Schnell (1985): moral reasoning and actual behaviour do not always match – Kohlberg does not discover what people really do.
- Kohlberg (1978): later acknowledged that there may not be a separate sixth stage.

THE DEVELOPMENT OF GENDER

KEY QUESTIONS
- What biological variations may affect sexual identity?
- What psychological differences exist between the sexes?
- How do theories of gender development account for gender differences?

Section 1: Introducing gender

Q

1 What interpretation does the *feminist perspective* place on sex differences?

2 What is the view of *evolutionary psychologists* regarding sex differences?

3 What is the difference between *sex* and *gender*?

4 How do *gender roles* and *gender stereotypes* differ?

5 By what age do most children demonstrate some knowledge about their gender?

6 Name the five categories of biological sex.

7 What is the difference between a *hermaphrodite* and a *pseudohermaphrodite*?

8 Imperato-McGinley *et al.* (1979) found that of 18 DHT-deficient males who were raised as girls, all but two reverted to male gender roles at puberty. What does this suggest?

9 According to McGlone (1980), which of the two cerebral hemispheres is generally more dominant in men?

10 Which brain structure is larger in women?

Section 2: Gender stereotypes and differences

11 Identify the female characteristics and the male characteristics which Williams & Best (1994) found were associated with these gender groups.

12 How does verbal ability differ between the sexes, over the course of their development?

13 Which ability is consistently better in males during adolescence and adulthood (Maccoby & Jacklin, 1974)?

14 Complete the sentence: 'According to Eagly (1983), research has actually tended to ___ rather than ___ sex differences'.

Section 3: Theories of gender

15 What does *biosocial theory* see as central to the development of gender?

16 What did the 'baby X' experiments (Smith & Lloyd, 1978) discover?

17 What was Money & Ehrhardt's (1972) view as to whether or not it is possible to change the sex of rearing?

18 According to Money (1974), what view is supported by the case of the penectomised twin?

19 What is the central argument made by *sociobiological/evolutionary theorists*, regarding gender?

20 According to Buss (1994), what do females universally find attractive in men?

21 Outline any one criticism of the sociobiological approach.

22 According to Freud, how does the *Oedipus complex* relate to the development of gender identity?

23 To what extent do studies of children who grow up in 'atypical' families support Freud's theory?

24 According to *social learning theory*, which two processes account for the different behaviour of boys and girls?

25 What did Sears *et al.* (1957) find, when looking at parents' response to their children's aggressive behaviour?

26 According to Smith & Daglish (1977), whom do children prefer to model?

27 What feature is emphasised by the *cognitive–developmental approach* to understanding the development of gender?

28 According to this approach, what is the first stage in the development of gender identity?

29 What do children recognise during the second stage (*gender stability*)?

30 How does this stage differ from the third stage (*gender constancy* or *consistency*)?

31 What is a major problem for cognitive–developmental theory?

32 Complete the sentence: 'According to gender-schematic processing theory, then, children learn to judge themselves according to the ___ considered to be ___ to their genders'.

Section 1: Introducing gender

1 The *feminist perspective* believes that social, political, economic and cultural factors determine gender.

2 *Evolutionary psychologists* regard sex differences as 'natural', having evolved as part of the adaptation of the human species to its environment.

3 *Sex* refers to some biological fact about us (e.g. our reproductive anatomy or genetic make-up), whilst *gender* is what culture makes out of biological sex (the 'social interpretation' of sex).

4 *Gender roles* are the behaviours, attitudes, values and beliefs which a particular society considers appropriate to males and females, whilst *gender stereotypes* are widely held beliefs about psychological differences between males and females.

5 By the age of three or four, children demonstrate some knowledge about their gender.

6 The five categories of *biological sex* are: chromosomal sex, gonadal sex, hormonal sex, sex of the internal reproductive structures, and sex of the external genitals.

7 Both *hermaphrodites* and *pseudohermaphrodites* possess ambiguous external and internal reproductive structures; pseudohermaphrodites possess gonads which match their chromosomal sex (unlike true hermaphrodites).

8 Imperato-McGinley *et al.*'s (1979) finding suggests that testosterone had somehow pre-programmed masculinity into their brains.

9 McGlone (1980) claims that the *right hemisphere* is generally more dominant in men.

10 The *corpus callosum* is larger in women.

Section 2: Gender stereotypes and differences

11 Williams & Best (1994) found that terms such as 'aggressive', 'determined', and 'sharp-witted' were associated with males, whilst 'cautious', 'emotional', and 'warm' were associated with females.

12 The sexes are similar with respect to verbal ability until age 11, when females become superior, this difference increasing during adolescence and possibly beyond.

13 Spatial ability is consistently better in males during adolescence and adulthood (Maccoby & Jacklin, 1974).

14 'According to Eagly (1983), research has actually tended to *conceal* rather than *reveal* sex differences.'

Section 3: Theories of gender

15 *Biosocial theory* sees the interaction between biological and social factors as central to the development of gender.

16 The 'baby X' experiments (Smith & Lloyd, 1978) showed that adults treated babies according to the gender they believed them to be (and not their true gender).

17 Money & Ehrhardt (1972) believed that it is possible to change the sex of rearing with little psychological harm being done, provided this occurs within a 'critical' or 'sensitive' period of about two-and-a-half to three years.

18 According to Money (1974), the case of the penectomised twin supports the view that gender identity is learned.

19 The central argument made by *sociobiological/evolutionary theorists*, regarding gender, is that gender (and gender roles) has evolved gradually as part of our adaptation to the environment.

20 Buss (1994) claims that females universally find attractive in men the characteristics associated with the provision of resources.

21 The *sociobiological approach* assumes that dominance patterns are to be equated with greater aggression in males, when in fact these are more often related to status. Sociobiological approaches are difficult to test. Our hunches about which characteristics were adaptive in our evolutionary past are at best 'educated guesses'.

22 According to Freud, the *Oedipus complex* is resolved through identification with the same-sex parent, which results in the acquisition of a gender identity.

23 Studies of children who grow up in 'atypical' families do not show adverse affects in terms of their gender identity, and so do not support Freud's account.

24 According to *social learning theory*, *observational learning* and *reinforcement* play central roles in the development of gender.

25 Sears *et al.* (1957) found that parents allowed their sons to be more aggressive in their relations to other children, and intervened more frequently and quickly when girls behave aggressively.

26 According to Smith & Daglish (1977), children prefer to model the behaviour of those with whom they have most contact.

27 The *cognitive–developmental approach* emphasises the child's participation in the construction of his/her gender.

28 The first stage is *gender labelling* or *basic gender identity*.

29 During the second stage (*gender stability*), most children recognise that people retain their gender for a lifetime.

30 In the third stage (*gender constancy* or *consistency*) children realise that gender is immutable (i.e. remains constant despite transformations in appearance).

31 Cognitive–developmental theory cannot account for the appearance of gender-appropriate behaviour *before* gender constancy is achieved.

32 'According to gender-schematic processing theory, then, children learn to judge themselves according to the *traits* considered to be *relevant* to their genders.'

Gender Development

Gender differences

Aggression
Maccoby & Jacklin (1974): boys are more verbally and physically aggressive than girls, beginning as soon as play begins ($2\frac{1}{2}$ yrs).

Verbal ability
Maccoby & Jacklin (1974): sexes score similarly until age 11 when females are superior. Gap is small but increases during adolescence.

Spatial ability
Maccoby & Jacklin (1974): males' ability is consistently higher in adolescence and adulthood. However, difference is small.

Mathematical ability
Maccoby & Jacklin (1974): increases faster in boys, beginning around 12 or 13.

Biological and sexual identity

Pseudohermaphrodites
Pseudohermaphrodites possess ambiguous external and internal reproductive structures:
- Imperato-McGinley *et al.* (1979) studied 18 DHT-deficient males. Sexually, they appeared and were raised female but at puberty changed into males. All but two adopted male gender roles (suggesting masculinity is pre-programmed).
- Goldwyn (1979) cites the case of Daphne Went, who though genetically male has a female appearance and has lived happily as a woman.

Brain differences
- McGlone (1980): the right hemisphere is generally dominant in men, and the left in women.
- The *corpus callosum*, which connects the two hemispheres, is larger in women.
- Bryden & Saxby (1985): found greater activity in right hemisphere of males performing spatial tasks – both hemispheres activated in women.

However, it is unclear how and if these differences influence gender.

Sex: a biological fact about us, such as our genetic makeup or anatomy.
Sexual identity: our biological status.
Gender: what our culture makes out of the 'raw material' of biological sex.
Gender identity: our own classification of ourselves (can differ from sexual identity).

Gender/sex role: behaviours which a society considers appropriate to males or females.
Gender stereotypes: widely held beliefs about psychological differences between males and females.
Sex typing: the acquisition of a gender identity and learning the appropriate behaviours.

Biosocial theory
- Stresses the importance of the interaction between biological and social factors in producing gender and argues that they are inseparable.
- Money & Ehrhardt (1972): 'anatomy is destiny' – how an infant is labelled sexually determines how it is raised, which in turn determines gender identity and gender role.

Money & Ehrhardt (1972)
- Studied girls with adrenogenital syndrome who were raised as boys until age 3. At 3 they had surgery and were raised as girls.
- Children can change gender, provided this occurs before 3 years old.

Money (1974)
- Studied a twin who lost his penis during circumcision. He had surgery at 17 months and was raised as a girl.
- He adapted to a female role, supporting the idea that gender is learned.

Social learning theory
- Emphasises the different treatment of boys and girls by parents, who are treated in line with gender-role expectations.
- Observational learning and reinforcement of roles: children observe others and receive reinforcement for behaviours considered 'sex-appropriate' (Bandura, 1977).
- Parents tend to reinforce boys for independence and emotional control, girls for dependence and emotional expression.

Research
- Sears *et al.* (1957): parents allowed sons to be more aggressive with others than daughters.
- Bandura *et al.* (1961, 1963): boys were more likely to imitate aggressive male models than were girls.
- Maccoby & Jacklin (1974): no consistent differences in reinforcement for aggressiveness or autonomy between boys and girls.

Psychoanalytic theory
Gender identity is assumed to be flexible up until the resolution of the Oedipus complex, which is resolved via identification with the same-sex parent, leading to gender identity.

Conflicting research
- Krebs & Blackman (1988): children acquire gender-identity gradually, not in a single step.
- Golombok *et al.* (1983): parents who grow up in single-parent or lesbian families may well have 'normal' gender identity.
- Children are aware of gender roles long before the age of 5 or 6 which Freud proposed for identification.

Sociobiological theory
- Sociobiologists (evolutionary theorists) argue that gender has evolved as part of our adaptation to our environment.
- Males and females have evolved differently in line with their different contributions to domestic labour and reproduction (e.g. greater physical strength for hunting – males, milk-producing capacities – females).

Parental investment theory (Kenrick, 1994)
- Male–female partnerships arose from the needs for sexual exclusivity and protection, respectively.
- This led to different courtship displays and roles which are still evident.
- Women look for mates who can provide resources, whilst men look for mates who are capable of reproducing well.

Other theories

Cognitive–developmental theory (Kohlberg, 1969)

Three stages in the development of gender identity
- **Stage 1** *(gender labelling)*: by 3 years the child recognises that it is male or female (but unaware that this is permanent).
- **Stage 2** *(gender stability)*: by 4/5 child realises that gender is permanent – but judges gender superficially (e.g. by hair).
- **Stage 3** *(gender constancy)*: by 6/7 child realises that gender is immutable – i.e. cannot be changed (e.g. by cutting hair).

Gender-schematic processing theory (Bem, 1985)
- Children learn to judge themselves according to the traits considered relevant to their genders, depending on the label 'boy' or 'girl'.
- The self-concept becomes mixed with the gender-schemas (gender roles) of a particular culture.
- The child's self-esteem then becomes linked with how well it performs against the gender-schema.

THE DEVELOPMENT OF THE SELF

KEY QUESTIONS
- What are the components of the self?
- How does the self develop?
- What theories exist to explain the development of the self?

Section 1: The components of the self

1 What is the difference between *consciousness* and *self-consciousness*?
2 What is meant by the term *self-image*?
3 Name at least two important categories of response to the question 'Who am I?'.
4 What did Kuhn (1960) discover when he compared the responses of seven-year-olds and undergraduates to the question 'Who am I?'?
5 What is an important difference between self-image and *self-esteem*?
6 What influence was able to turn a dull and unattractive girl into an attractive and desirable girl in the space of a few days (Guthrie, 1938)?
7 What is the *ideal-self*?
8 How does self-esteem relate to the self-image and the *ideal-self*?
9 What are *self-schemata*?

Section 2: The development of the self

10 What does Piaget believe concerning the self-concept of a baby?
11 According to Maccoby (1980), in what two ways is the infant able to distinguish itself from others?
12 How do most non-human animals react to the sight of their reflections in a mirror?
13 What did Gallup (1977) discover when a mirror was placed on the cage wall of pre-adolescent chimps?
14 How did Lewis & Brooks-Gunn (1979) discover that most babies are able to recognise themselves in a mirror by the age of 18–20 months?
15 Complete the following sentence: 'Language plays an important role in consolidating the early development of self-awareness by providing _____ permitting distinctions to be made between self and non-self'.
16 Could it be that your own name has affected the type of self which you have developed? How?
17 Explain how names affected individuals from the West African Ashanti people.

18 What is meant by saying that by the age of four most children have concepts of their '*psychological selves*'?
19 What is the first category which is recognised by infants and applied to the self?
20 What is an important difference between the way in which children tend to define themselves before and after the age of seven?

Section 3: Theories of self

21 Complete the sentence: 'James (1890) was the first to make the distinction between self-as-____ ('I') and self-as-____ ('me')'.
22 What did James (1890) mean when he claimed that the self is *multifaceted*?
23 Explain what Goffman's (1959) *dramaturgical approach* to the self proposed about the self.
24 Does Cooley's (1902) *looking-glass self* theory mean that we build up a sense of self through looking in the mirror?
25 Why, according to Mead's (1934) *symbolic interactionist approach*, are language and the symbols which make up language important to developing a sense of self?
26 What is a *generalised other*?
27 By what process does a generalised other come about?
28 Complete the sentence: 'Mead does not see the self as something privately going on inside a person. Rather, the self is a cognitive process lodged in the ongoing ____ ____'.
29 In what ways can the terms 'I' and 'self' mislead us in our understanding of selves?
30 How might a culture affect an individual's experience of self?
31 How does Maori culture see experiences such as fear, anger, love and grief?
32 What is the difference between the *independent* and the *interdependent* self?
33 In conclusion, what is probably the most important influence on the development of the self?

Section 1: The components of the self

1 *Consciousness* refers to sensations such as hunger and pain shared by humans and non-humans, whereas *self-consciousness* refers to the human ability to introspect (i.e. to have a self as both thinking subject and as the object of that thought).

2 *Self-image* is how we describe ourselves (the sort of person we think we are).

3 Responses to the question 'Who am I?' are often in the form of *social roles* (such as 'student', 'friend'), *personality traits* (such as 'fun-loving') or *body image* (such as 'short').

4 Kuhn (1960) found that seven-year-olds averaged five social roles in answer to the question 'Who am I?', whilst undergraduates averaged ten social roles.

5 *Self-image* is essentially descriptive, whereas *self-esteem* is evaluative.

6 The *reaction of others*. Her male classmates decided to treat her as though she were the most desirable girl in the school, and this resulted in a change in her self-image, which in turn affected the way others treated her (Guthrie, 1938).

7 The *ideal-self* is the kind of person you would like to be.

8 Rogers (1951) claims that the relationship is simple: the greater the gap between your self-image and ideal-self, the lower your self-esteem.

9 *Self-schemata* are organised beliefs about what we are like and what we could be like.

Section 2: The development of the self

10 Piaget believes that a baby has no self-concept and cannot differentiate between 'me' and 'not me'.

11 Maccoby (1980) maintains that the infant is able to distinguish itself from others, first because only its own fingers hurt when bitten, and secondly because they are able to associate the bodily sensations with the sight of their own movements.

12 Most non-human animals react to their reflections as if they were other animals.

13 Gallup (1977) discovered that pre-adolescent chimps would react to their reflections as if they were other animals for a period of about three days, after which time they learned that they were their own reflections.

14 Lewis & Brooks-Gunn (1979) had mothers apply rouge to their babies' noses whilst pretending to wipe them, then observed whether or not the babies touched their noses more than usual when looking in a mirror.

15 'Language plays an important role in consolidating the early development of self-awareness by providing *labels* permitting distinctions to be made between self and non-self.'

16 It could well be that your name has affected your self: the *self-fulfilling prophecy* refers to the process by which stereotypes (for example, those associated with names)

influence others' expectations of an individual, which in turn affect the way that individual behaves.

17 The West African Ashanti people are named according to the day of their birth and are believed to have certain characteristics as a result. Police records show that those born on a Wednesday (the 'aggressive personality' day) are indeed more likely to commit crimes.

18 By the age of four most children believe that they have a private, thinking self that is not visible to others.

19 *Age* is the first category which is recognised by infants (recognised at between six and 12 months).

20 Children younger than seven tend to define themselves in terms of physical characteristics, whereas older children are more likely to include internal, psychological characteristics.

Section 3: Theories of self

21 'James (1890) was the first to make the distinction between self-as-*knower/subject* ('I') and self-as-*known/object* ('me').'

22 James (1890) believed that we have as many selves as we have social relationships, and in this sense the self is *multifaceted*.

23 Goffman's (1959) *dramaturgical approach* portrayed the self as largely a 'performance' designed for an 'audience'.

24 No. Cooley's (1902) *looking-glass self theory* states that we build up a sense of self through the reactions and evaluations of others.

25 According to Mead (1934), language is important for developing a sense of self, since it allows us to communicate with and understand the perspectives of others.

26 A *generalised other* is the viewpoint of people in general.

27 A 'generalised other' is built up through successive 'role-plays' of different types of people.

28 'Mead does not see the self as something privately going on inside a person. Rather, the self is a cognitive process lodged in the ongoing *social world*.'

29 The terms 'I' and 'self' may mislead us into thinking that our selves are objective things, or that they are stable and unified over time.

30 Different cultures have different 'discourses' or ways of accounting for the self. These may influence the experiences which individuals attribute to 'self'.

31 Maori culture sees experiences of fear, anger, love and grief as coming from outside the self (from unseen powers and forces), not from within the self.

32 The *independent* self, stressed in Western cultures, is the view of the self as autonomous, whilst the interdependent self, common to non-Western cultures, views the self as bound up with our social interactions.

33 *Interaction with others*, stressed by most major self-theories, is probably the most important influence on the development of the self.

Development of the Self

Language
- The structure of our language implies certain beliefs about human nature.
- Words like 'I' 'me' mislead us into thinking we are a unified entity, whilst 'self' and 'mind' do not refer to anything objective.
- Different ways of talking about selves in different cultures affect individuals' experiences of self.

Components of the self-concept

Self-image
How we would describe ourselves. Typically divides into:
- **social roles**
- **personality traits**

Also includes:
body image, which is related to gender and may change most at puberty

Kuhn (1960) asked 7-year-olds and under-graduates to give 20 answers to 'Who am I?'.
Results: The 7-year-olds gave five answers relating to social roles vs. 10 from the undergraduates.

Self-esteem
The extent to which we like or approve of ourselves.
The value attached to abilities and character-istics may vary with:
- culture
- gender
- age
- social background.

Guthrie (1938) describes an unattractive female student whose class-mates pretended she was the most desirable girl. Her self-image changed and others perceived her as more desirable.

Ideal-self
The kind of person you would like to be.
If there is a big gap between self-image and ideal-self, then self-esteem is likely to be low.

Self-schemata
We store information about aspects of ourselves, different selves and future selves in '*self-schemata*'. These are complex and inter-related perceptions of what we are like and what we *could* be like.

Theories of the self

James' & Cooley's theories
James (1890) distinguishes:
- *self-as-subject*/knower ('I')
- *self-as-known*/object ('me').
- The self is *multifaceted*; we have as many selves as social relationships.
- This is consistent with *self-presentation*, in which we create a self to suit circumstances, as a perfor-mance for an audience (Goffman, 1959).

The looking-glass self
(Cooley, 1902)
- To understand what we are like, we need to see the reactions of others who act as a 'looking glass'.
- We gradually build up a sense of self through the judgements and evaluations of others.
- Our sense of self may change, therefore, depending on who is judging us and how they judge us.

Mead's theory

Symbolic interactionism
Mead (1934)
- We exist in a symbolic as well as physical environment, because things have meanings.
- Because we interact with others and have language, we can understand others' points of view.
- We are capable of interacting with ourselves, and this gives humans their uniqueness.

The generalised other
- Through role-taking, we acquire different viewpoints (mother, father, friend, etc.)
- Over time, children learn to take the view of people in general (*the generalised other*) and see themselves from that perspective.

Development of the self-concept

Early developments
- Many psychologists (including Piaget) believe that babies have no sense of self.
- Gradually, the infant distinguishes itself from its environment.
- For Piaget, self-awareness develops as the child adapts to its environment, by exploring objects, it is also exploring its self.

Maccoby (1980): two ways in which babies can distinguish self and others:
- Their own fingers hurt when bitten but biting rattles/mothers does not produce pain.
- They associate the feelings of their own body movements with the sight of limbs and the sound of cries.

This suggests that it is the *bodily self* which is the first to develop.

Self-recognition
- Involves knowing that you are continuous in time (for photographs) or space (for mirrors).

Chimpanzees
Gallup (1977)
- Pre-adolescent chimps treated reflections as *other* chimps for 3 days, then *learned* that it was their reflection.
- When a spot was painted on their nose they looked in the mirror and touched the spot.

Lower primates are *unable* to recognise themselves.

Humans
Lewis & Brooks-Gunn (1979)
If red spots were painted on infants placed in front of a mirror:
- touching of spot did not occur before 15 months.
- 15–18 months, 25% touched it.
- 18–20 months, 75% touched it.

Self-definition
- Language provides *labels* which allow us to distinguish self and non-self ('I', 'you', etc.).
- Names are also important and may already be associated with *stereotypes*.
- Children reverse the labels 'I', 'you', when referring to others (*shifting reference*).
- Only autistic and blind children frequently fail to do this.

Self-fulfilling prophecy
Jahoda (1958)
- West african Ashanti people name children according to the day of the week on which they are born.
- Police records show that children born on a Wednesday (the day of 'natural aggression') are more likely to commit crimes than those born on Monday (the day of 'quiet, calm personalities').

It seems that people may become what their names indicate.

Psychological self
- Young children are aware that people can think and dolls can't.
- They identify the part of them that knows their name as being in the head.
- They do not believe that others can see them thinking by looking into their eyes.
- By the age of $3\frac{1}{2}$–4 they have a concept of a basic thinking self that is not visible.

Categorical self
- Age is the first category to be acquired – babies can distinguish adults and babies before 12 months of age.
- Before the age of 7 years, children tend to define themselves in physical terms (height, hair, etc.).
- Between middle childhood and adolescence, more references are made to emotions, values, competencies.

47

PERSONALITY CHANGE AND SOCIAL DEVELOPMENT IN ADOLESCENCE

KEY QUESTIONS
● What is adolescence?
● What explanations of adolescence have been proposed by Hall, Coleman, Erikson, and Marcia?

Q

Section 1: The concept of adolescence
1 What does *adolescence* mean?
2 What ages does adolescence tend to span in Western societies?
3 What is the important period which marks the beginning of adolescence?
4 Complete the sentence: 'Some researchers maintain that adolescence is difficult to define because it has been _____ _____ by Western culture and is a recent _____ of Western capitalist society'.
5 What can Plato tell us about adolescence?
6 What are the three main components of adolescence according to the classical view?

Section 2: Hall's and Erikson's theories
7 According to Hall (1904), what does each individual's psychological development 'recapitulate'?
8 What was the most revealing finding in Csikszentmihalyi & Larson's (1984) study in which students wrote a description of what they were doing and how they felt every two hours?
9 What did Rutter *et al.* (1976) discover when comparing the rates of mental disorders between ten-year-olds, 14-year-olds and adults?
10 In general, is Hall's theory well-supported by research into adolescence?
11 What view of the personality did Erikson (1963) challenge in proposing his *psychosocial stages*?
12 What does Erikson's (1963) *epigenetic principle* maintain about the pattern of social and psychological growth in an individual?
13 According to Erikson, what is the major conflict facing the individual during adolescence?
14 What are the possible positive and negative outcomes of this crisis?
15 What is meant by saying that Western societies see adolescence as a *moratorium*?
16 What is *ego identity*?
17 Name four ways in which *role confusion* may show itself during adolescence.

18 What did Simmons & Rosenberg (1975) discover when investigating self-esteem in girls?
19 Why has Erikson's research been criticised for being biased (Gilligan, 1982)?

Section 3: Marcia's and sociological theories
20 According to Marcia's four statuses of adolescent identity, what is the difference between *identity diffusion* and *identity foreclosure*?
21 Are Marcia's statuses necessarily sequential, in the way that Erikson's stages follow one after the other?
22 What did Meilman (1979) find which casts doubt on Marcia's theory?
23 What, according to sociologists, is one of the features which drives adolescent development by producing different expectations of the adolescent?
24 How does the *generation gap* relate to adolescent development?
25 Does the majority of research support the view that during adolescence there is a large amount of conflict between parents and children?
26 Name two areas in which research has shown significant disagreements between children and parents.

Section 4: Coleman's focal theory
27 What, according to Coleman & Hendry (1990), is the principal problem with other theories of adolescence?
28 What is it that *focal theory* tries to explain?
29 What did Coleman find when investigating the concerns of 800 six-, 11-, 13-, 15- and 17-year-olds?
30 What was Coleman's explanation for this important finding?
31 What prediction does focal theory make about which adolescents are most likely to experience difficulties during adolescence?
32 Overall, does the evidence support the notions of '*storm and stress*', *identity crisis* and the *generation gap* during adolescence?

Section 1: The concept of adolescence

1 *Adolescence* comes from the Latin *adolescere* meaning 'to grow into maturity' and is regarded as a prelude to and preparation for adulthood.

2 Adolescence tends to span the ages of 12–20 in Western societies, though many other cultures view this as unusually long.

3 *Puberty*, the onset of sexual maturation, marks the beginning of adolescence.

4 'Some researchers maintain that adolescence is difficult to define because it has been *artificially created* by Western culture and is a recent *invention* of Western capitalist society.'

5 Plato, writing 2000 years ago, regarded the young as being most likely to challenge the existing social order, suggesting that adolescence has been around for a long time.

6 The three main components of adolescence according to the classical view are 'storm and stress', identity crisis, and the generation gap.

Section 2: Hall's and Erikson's theories

7 According to Hall (1904), each individual's psychological development 'recapitulates' the biological and cultural evolution of the human species.

8 Csikszentmihalyi & Larson's (1984) study of students showed that they were subject to extreme mood swings and could go from extreme happiness to deep sadness (and vice versa) in the space of an hour.

9 Rutter *et al.* (1976) discovered that there was very little difference in the rates of mental disorders between the three groups, suggesting that adolescence is not quite the period of 'storm and stress' which Hall suggests.

10 No, Hall's theory is not well-supported by research. For example, Siddique & D'Arcy (1984) found that 30 per cent of adolescents reported no symptoms of psychological distress and 40 per cent reported only mild levels.

11 Erikson (1963) challenged the view that personality development stops early in life (as was suggested by Freud, among others).

12 Erikson's (1963) *epigenetic principle* holds that the pattern of social and psychological growth in an individual is genetically determined.

13 Erikson believes that adolescents face the *identity vs. role confusion conflict*, in which they must decide on an occupational role.

14 The positive (adaptive) outcome of this conflict is 'a sense of who one is', whereas the negative (maladaptive) outcome is a prolonged uncertainty about one's role in life.

15 Western societies see adolescence as a *moratorium* – an authorised delay of adulthood which frees adolescents from most responsibilities and helps them to make the transition into adulthood.

16 *Ego identity* is a firm sense of who one is and what one stands for.

17 *Role confusion* may show itself as an aimless drifting through occupations, as *negative identity* (drug taking or suicide), as fear of intimacy, or an inability to plan, work or study well.

18 Simmons & Rosenberg (1975) discovered that low self-esteem is more common in girls during early adolescence than in late childhood or late adolescence.

19 Erikson's research was largely based on white males from the middle classes and has therefore been criticised for *androcentrism* (Gilligan, 1982).

Section 3: Marcia's and sociological theories

20 *Identity diffusion* is a state in which the individual is in crisis and unable to formulate clear self-definition, goals or commitments, whereas *identity foreclosure* involves avoiding the crisis by rapidly committing oneself to a conventional goal without exploring other options.

21 No. Marcia's statuses are not necessarily sequential, and need not occur one after the other.

22 Meilman (1979) found that relatively few men achieve *identity moratorium*, an important status within Marcia's theory since he claims that it must precede *identity achievement*.

23 Sociologists see *role change* as an integral feature of adolescent development.

24 The *generation gap* represents the difference between the social norms of adults and adolescents and is significant, since sociologists claim that socialisation in adolescents is influenced more by their peer's generation than by their parent's.

25 No. In fact researchers such as Bandura & Walters (1959) and Fogelman (1976) found little disagreement between adolescents and parents.

26 Music, fashion, sexual behaviour (Noller & Callan, 1990), together with appearance and evening activities (Fogelman, 1976), are the areas likely to be most contentious.

Section 4: Coleman's focal theory

27 Coleman & Hendry (1990) point out that most other theories try to explain abnormal development through adolescence.

28 *Focal theory* tries to explain the relatively stable and stress-free transition which most adolescents manage to make into adulthood.

29 Coleman found that these concerns peaked at different ages, so that different concerns were paramount at different times.

30 Coleman believed that adolescents were able to cope with their concerns by dealing with them one at a time.

31 Focal theory predicts that adolescents forced to deal with more than one concern at a time will experience most stress.

32 No. *Storm and stress*, *identity crisis* and *generation gap* have not been found to occur in anything like the degree suggested by the classical view of adolescence.

Development in Adolescence

Adolescence: begins at puberty and regarded as a prelude and preparation for adulthood. Spans ages 12–20 in Western societies.

Puberty: onset at 10 for girls and 12 for boys. Both males and females experience a growth spurt, peaking at 12 (girls) and 14 (boys) and experience sexual changes.

Hall's theory

- Hall believed that psychological development *recapitulates* the cultural and biological evolution of the human species.
- Adolescence was seen as a time of 'storm and stress', mirroring the conflicts of the last 2000 years.

Csikszentmihalyi & Larson (1984):
- Monitored the activities and feelings of high-school students every 2 hrs.
- Moods swung from extreme happiness to deep sadness within the course of 1 hour.

Most research rejects Hall
- Bandura & Walters (1959): adolescence is no more stressful than childhood or adulthood.
- Rutter *et al.* (1976) found only small differences in the rates of mental disorders between children, adults and adolescents.

Marcia's theory

Identified four 'statuses' of adolescent identity

Identity diffusion: Individual is in crisis, unable to define self, goals or commitments.

Identity foreclosure: Avoidance of uncertainties by rapid commitment to conventional goals.

Identity moratorium: Decisions about identity postponed whilst alternative identities are explored.

Identity achievement: Individual has experienced crisis but emerged with firm goals and ideology.

- Marcia does not see the stages as sequential; however, moratorium is necessary for identity achievement.
- Research suggests that relatively few men achieve moratorium, casting doubt on the four stages.

Coleman's focal theory

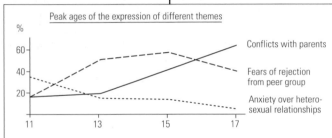

Peak ages of the expression of different themes

- Conflicts with parents
- Fears of rejection from peer group
- Anxiety over hetero-sexual relationships

Coleman & Hendry (1990): *other* theories explain individuals (who are *abnormal*) with serious problems. They propose a theory of *normal* development, which accounts for the relatively *stable* transition made by most adolescents.
- Studied 800 boys and girls: concerns about issues reached peaks (*focused*) at different ages (see above).
- Adolescents cope with change by dealing with *one issue at a time*, spreading adaptation over years.
- Those who have to deal with more than one problem at a time are most likely to experience difficulties.

Sociological theory

Role change: starting college, starting work etc. produce new expectations which speed up the socialisation process.

Conflicting demands: made by family, mass media and peers may make this a difficult time.

Generation gap: may add to these problems as adolescents are more dependent on their own generation for socialisation.

Conflicting research
- Bandura & Walters (1959): the typical American adolescent tended to *accept* most parental values quite freely and associated with other adolescents who shared such values.
- The National Children's Bureau (Fogelman, 1976): in fact both children and adults agreed on most of the issues commonly thought to be areas of disagreement. Only major disagreements were *appearance* and *evening activities*.

Erikson's theory

- **Epigenetic principle:** the entire pattern of psychological and social growth is governed by genetics.
- **Psychosocial stages:** are universal, each centring around a crisis with two possible outcomes.
- The adolescent struggles to establish a strong sense of identity (*ego identity*).

Role confusion
The failure to integrate perceptions of the self into a coherent whole, shown in:
- Fear of intimacy.
- Inability to plan for the future.
- Inability to work/study industriously.
- Negative identity (e.g drug addict/yob).

Research
- Offer *et al.* (1988): no increase in the disturbance of self-image during adolescence.
- Gilligan (1982): Erikson's sample was biased (largely middle class, white males) and is only applicable to that group.

Stage	Personal and social relationships	Crisis or conflict	Possible outcome
0–1 year	*Mother*	**Trust vs. mistrust**	Trust and faith in others or a mistrust of people.
2 yrs	*Parents*	**Autonomy vs. shame and doubt**	Self-control and mastery or self-doubt and fearfulness.
3–5 years	*Family*	**Initiative vs. guilt**	Purpose and direction or a loss of self-esteem.
6–11 years	*Neighbourhood and school*	**Industry vs. inferiority**	Social and intellectual competence or failure to thrive and develop.
Adolescence	*Peer groups, outgroups, leaders*	**Identity vs. role confusion**	A sense of 'who one is' or prolonged role uncertainty.
Early adult	*Friends, sexual partners*	**Intimacy vs. isolation**	Formation of deep relationships or failure to love others.
Middle age	*Divided labour and shared household*	**Generativity vs. stagnation**	Expansion of interests and caring for others or turning in on one's own problems.
Old age	*'Mankind', 'My kind'*	**Integrity vs. despair**	Satisfaction with the triumphs and disappointments of life or unfulfilment and a fear of death.

48

PERSONALITY CHANGE IN EARLY AND MIDDLE ADULTHOOD

SYLLABUS
6.4 Adolescence, adulthood and old age
- theories and research into personality change in adulthood, for example, those of Erikson and Levinson

KEY QUESTIONS
- How does Erikson view the changes which accompany adulthood?
- What does Levinson *et al.*'s *Seasons of a Man's Life* theory suggest?
- How does adult consciousness evolve, according to Gould?

Section 1: Erikson's theory

1 What name did Erikson give to the two crises which he believed everyone encounters in adulthood?
2 What is meant by the term *intimacy*?
3 Explain why *identity* is seen by Erikson as being a prerequisite for intimacy.
4 When would a person normally be expected to achieve intimacy?
5 What is the central task during the middle years of adulthood (40s and 50s)?
6 What is the negative consequence of failing at this task/crisis?
7 What important difference exists between the ways in which women and men achieve 'identity'?
8 According to Sanguilianio's (1978) research, what happens to a woman's identity, compared with a man's?
9 According to Sheehy (1996), to what age are many adults prolonging their 'adolescence'?
10 According to Orbach (cited in Beaumont, 1996), what is one problem with adults who refuse to grow up?

Section 2: Levinson *et al.*'s theory

11 How did Levinson *et al.* (1978) collect the data necessary to construct the *Seasons of a Man's Life* theory?
12 Complete the following sentence: 'According to Levinson *et al.*, adult development alternates between phases or periods which are _____ (or structure-_____) and _____ (or structure-_____)'.
13 What, according to Levinson *et al.*, is a person's *life structure*?
14 *Separation* is one of the key themes of the *early adult transition*. What is the difference between *internal* and *external* separation?
15 What are we trying to achieve when we work towards the *entry life structure for early adulthood*?

16 What is done during the *age-30 transition*?
17 Levinson *et al.* refer to the period between the ages of 33 and 40, as 'settling down'. What is *settling down*?
18 What does BOOM stand for and what does it involve?
19 What are *marker events* and which of Levinson *et al.*'s phases are they most likely to accompany?
20 Complete the sentence: 'It is not possible to get through middle adulthood without having at least a moderate crisis in either ____-_____ _____ or ____-____ ____'.
21 Tredre (1996) believes that *downshifting'* is often mistaken for a *mid-life crisis*. What is downshifting?

Section 3: Evaluating Levinson *et al.*

22 According to Durkin (1995), what percentage of people actually report experiencing a *crisis*?
23 Which marker events may accompany the *age-50 transition*?
24 Sheehy (1976) claims that men in their forties begin exploring another aspect of themselves – what aspect?
25 According to Levinson's (1986) *gender-splitting* account, how do women and men differ in their dreams?
26 What is the key criticism of 'stage' theories of adult development (such as Levinson *et al.*'s and Erikson's), which suggest that we progress through inevitable and universal stages?
27 What consequences might *age deviancy* have for a person?

Section 4: Gould's theory

28 What, according to Gould's theory of the *evolution of adult consciousness*, is the thrust of adult development?
29 What name does Gould give to the illusion which he believes dominates our thinking during childhood?
30 With what do we replace a sense of parental dependency?
31 How is our *sense of time* affected during our mid-30s to mid-40s?

A

Section 1: Erikson's theory

1 *Intimacy vs. isolation* and *generativity vs. stagnation* are the names which Erikson gives to the two crises which everyone encounters in early and late adulthood respectively.

2 *Intimacy* is used by Erikson to refer to the ability to form close and meaningful relationships with others without fear of losing oneself.

3 Erikson views *identity* as the reconciliation of all our various roles into a stable personality, whilst intimacy requires us to give up some of our separateness. In order to do this we must first have established a stable sense of who we are.

4 Intimacy is usually achieved in a person's 20s or 30s.

5 The central task during the middle years of adulthood is to establish life's purpose and to focus on aims and achievements, including the aim of contributing to the well-being of others.

6 If we fail in the task of achieving generativity we 'stagnate', becoming preoccupied with our own needs and desires.

7 Men generally achieve identity before intimacy, but for many women these two tasks are fused. Women come to know themselves as they are known by others.

8 Sanguilianio (1978) claims that a woman's identity is submerged into that of her partner; she seeks separate identity only in mid-life.

9 Sheehy (1996) claims that many adults are prolonging adolescence into their 30s.

10 Adults who refuse to grow up may encounter problems with their own parenting, looking to their children for emotional support (Orbach: cited in Beaumont, 1996).

Section 2: Levinson *et al.*'s theory

11 Levinson *et al.*'s (1978) data were collected by interviewing 40 men aged 35–45 from a variety of backgrounds over a period of several months.

12 'According to Levinson *et al.* adult development alternates between phases or periods which are *stable* (or structure-*building*) and *transitional* (or structure-*changing*).'

13 *Life structure* is the underlying pattern or design of a person's life at any given time.

14 *Internal separation* involves greater psychological separation from the family, whilst *external separation* involves greater physical separation (e.g moving out, financial independence).

15 The *entry life structure for early adulthood* is the first life-structure which we construct and its function is to provide a workable link between the valued self and adult society (i.e. to be the person you have become during adolescence, whilst at the same time taking on an adult role).

16 The *age-thirty transition* is a time when the first life-structure can be reviewed and its flaws and limitations worked on.

17 *Settling down* is a consolidation of the second life-structure, a time when the individual makes strong commitments to a personal, familial and occupational future.

18 BOOM stands for *becoming one's own man* and involves striving to improve our skills, contribute to and be recognised by society whilst becoming self-sufficient.

19 *Marker events* are major life-events (such as divorce, illness, death of a loved one) and are most likely to accompany middle adulthood.

20 'It is not possible to get through middle adulthood without having at least a moderate crisis in either the *mid-life transition* or the *age-50 transition*.'

21 *Downshifting* is a term used by Tredre (1996) to describe voluntarily opting out of a pressurised career in pursuit of a more fulfilling way of life.

Section 3: Evaluating Levinson *et al.*

22 According to Durkin (1995) only ten per cent of people actually report experiencing a *crisis*.

23 Divorce, re-marriage, redundancy, serious illness, the death of a loved one and children leaving home, are all marker events which may accompany the age-50 transition.

24 Sheehy (1976) claims that men in their 40s begin to explore their feminine selves (by becoming more nurturant, affiliative and intimate).

25 Levinson's (1986) *gender-splitting* account maintains that men's dreams are usually unified, focusing on career goals, whereas women's dreams are often split between career and family.

26 'Stage' theories of adult development (such as Levinson *et al.*'s and Erikson's) are often criticised for overlooking the degree of individual variability in development from one person to the next.

27 *Age deviancy* (failure to comply with the norms for one's age-group) can result in social penalties such as ridicule, pity or rejection.

Section 4: Gould's theory

28 The thrust of adult development is the realisation and acceptance of ourselves as creators of our own lives, away from the dependencies of childhood.

29 The *illusion of absolute safety* is the name given by Gould to the illusion which dominates our thinking during childhood.

30 Parental dependency must be replaced with autonomy.

31 During our mid-30s to mid-40s, we feel that time is running out and develop a sense of urgency.

Personality Change in Adulthood

Erikson's theory

The individual faces two **crises**, each corresponding to a stage of development (Ch 47):

Intimacy vs. isolation
Early adulthood (20s and 30s)
- The individual must be able to form close, meaningful relationships without fear of losing him/herself (intimacy).
- To accomplish this, we need first to have established a firm sense of identity.
- If this does not happen, then isolation can result.

Generativity vs. stagnation
Middle age (40s and 50s)
- The individual focuses on determining goals and achieving aims.
- **Generativity** means a concern for others beyond the family.
- Failure leads to **stagnation,** in which people become preoccupied with their own needs and desires.

- Men seem to achieve identity before intimacy, whereas for women the two tasks are often fused.
- Sangiuliano (1978): many women submerge their identities in partnerships and only search for separate identities in middle age.

Gould's theory

The evolution of adult consciousness
Adulthood is attained through freeing ourselves from childhood consciousness and illusions.

Gould's theory is an extension of the Freudian notion of *separation anxiety*.
- As we grow up, we have to free ourselves from **the illusion of absolute safety** which dominated childhood.
- This involves *transformations* which enable us to give up the past in order to form our own ideas.
- Parental dependency is replaced with a sense of **autonomy**.
- Our sense of *time* changes:
  - Up until 18 we are 'timeless' with infinite time before us.
  - In our 20s we are hurrying down a chosen path.
  - At the end of our 20s we must choose between options as we do not have time for them all.
  - During our mid-30s to mid-40s we feel that time is running out and become aware of our own mortality.

Levinson *et al.*'s theory

Seasons of a man's life
(Levinson *et al.*, 1978)
- Adult development comprises *eras* and *cross-era transitions*.
- Phases alternate between stable (*structure-building*) and transitional (*structure-changing*) periods.

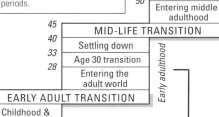

Seasons of a man's life
Levinson *et al.*(1978)
- Interviewed 40 men aged 35–45, from a variety of occupations.
- Analysed tape-recordings made over several months.
- Advanced a *life-structure theory* (the underlying pattern of a person's life at a given time), according to which adult development passes through stable and transitional phases.
- Family and work roles are seen as central to the life structure at any time.

Seasons of a woman's life:
Levinson's original work focused only on men. However, Levinson (1986) argues that a *gender-splitting* phenomenon occurs:
- Men tend to have *unified* 'dreams' which focus on career.
- Women's 'dreams' are more likely to be *split* between career and marriage.
- In addition, the transitory instability of early 30s lasts *longer* for women and the 'settling down' is much less clear cut for women, who may try to balance family and career.

Early adulthood (17–40)

Early adult transition (17–22)
Acts as a developmental 'bridge' between adolescence and adulthood.
- Incorporates the two themes of **separation**, both internal (e.g. less emotional dependence) and external (e.g. moving out) and **attachments** (forming links to the adult world).

Entering the adult world (22–28)
The first *structure-building* phase where we try to define ourselves as adults and live with our initial job, relationship and value choices.
- We try to strike a balance between *'keeping our options open'* and *'putting down roots'*.
- We try to keep the thread of our '**dreams**' alive in our choices and may look to *mentors* (more experienced others) for help.

Age-thirty transition (28–33)
We work on the problems with the first life structure.
- Most people experience an **age-30 crisis** as they realise that life is becoming more serious and less provisional.

Settling down (33–40)
A consolidating period with more commitment to choices and planning for the future. Comprises two sub-stages:
- Early settling down (33–36).
- **BOOM** (36–40): *'becoming one's own man'*: we want to contribute to society and be recognised as well as being self-sufficient.

Middle adulthood (40–60)

Mid-life transition (40–45)
A time of soul-searching where we terminate one life structure, initiate another, continuing the process of individuation started in BOOM.
- Sometimes referred to as a *mid-life crisis* where a re-assessment of life brings uncertainties and pain – though some find it fairly easy.

Entering middle adulthood (45–50)
We have resolved whether or not our commitments are worthwhile and make choices regarding a new life-structure.
- Changes may be influenced by *marker events* such as the death of a loved one, divorce, illness or change of job.

Age-50 transition (50–55)
Levinson *et al.* argue that middle adulthood cannot be reached without a crisis at either the mid-life transition or the age-50 transition.

Research
- Durkin (1995): only 10% of middle-aged people reported experiencing a crisis.
- Tredre (1996): the term 'crisis' is *misleading* in that often people are just '*downshifting*' (opting out of high-pressure lifestyles in favour of more fulfilling lives).
- Sheehy (1976): men begin to explore their more feminine side and women their more masculine side at this age.

Overall, although significant changes will occur at this age (such as death of parents, children leaving home), a crisis is not inevitable.

49

THE IMPACT OF LIFE EVENTS IN ADULTHOOD

SYLLABUS
6.4 Adolescence, adulthood and old age
• research into life events in adulthood, for example, parenting, divorce, bereavement and unemployment

KEY QUESTIONS
• How are adults affected by unemployment?
• What are the effects and phases of retirement?
• How are individuals affected by marriage, divorce and parenthood?
• What is the impact of bereavement?

Q

Section 1: Unemployment

1 What is the difference between a *normative age-graded influence* and a *non-normative influence*?
2 What is the relationship between depression and length of unemployment?
3 What is *learned helplessness* (Seligman, 1975)?
4 What explanation might account for the greater negative effect on middle-aged men of unemployment compared with young people?
5 Explain how *social support* works both to increase and reduce distress, following unemployment.
6 How would you expect the unemployment rate nationally to affect the degree of distress experienced by the unemployed?
7 Apart from depression, what two mental states are associated with unemployment?
8 Name two risks associated with unemployment (Fryer, 1992).

Section 2: Retirement

9 What is an important difference between unemployment and retirement?
10 What change are many couples likely to experience in their relationship, immediately following retirement?
11 What features are characteristic of the *honeymoon phase* of retirement?
12 What factors are most likely to contribute to *disenchantment* during this phase of retirement?
13 Which phase of the retirement process follows from the disenchantment phase?
14 What happens during the *termination phase*?
15 Complete the following sentence: 'Bromley (1988) believes that it is the _____ between employment and retirement that causes adjustment problems'.
16 Based on Bromley's (1988) research, what would be your advice to someone considering retirement?

Section 3: Marriage, divorce and parenthood

17 What percentage of adults marries at least once?
18 When Davies (1956) looked at mental disorders occurring in those engaged to be married, what did he find regarding the sorts of events which triggered the disorders, and the sorts of events which were associated with their improvement?
19 Are cohabiting couples more or less likely to get divorced than couples who have not lived together before getting married? Why?
20 How are marriage and happiness, health and longevity related?
21 Bee (1994) argues that the greatest beneficiaries of marriage are men. Why is this?
22 According to Turnbull (1995), what pattern do divorce rates take?
23 When Woollett & Fuller (cited in Cooper, 1996b) investigated how mothers who had been divorced subsequently felt about their daily activities, what did they find?
24 Describe the pattern of changes in marital satisfaction which takes place before and during parenthood.
25 What explanation do Levinson *et al.* (1978) offer for why unhappy couples might stay together?
26 What is the difference between *empty-nest distress* and *crowded-nest distress*?

Section 4: Bereavement

27 Define the terms *bereavement*, *grief*, and *mourning*.
28 Engel (1962) believes there are three phases of *griefwork*, of which *developing awareness* is the second. What are the other two?
29 Ramsay & de Groot (1977) believe that grief comprises not phases but components. Name any five.
30 Hinton (1975) identifies three *abnormal patterns of grieving*: numbness, neurotic forms of emotional distress and physical symptoms. Give two examples of behaviours from the last two patterns.
31 What is Lieberman's (1993) criticism of traditional bereavement research and its underlying assumption about bereavement?

Section 1: Unemployment

1 A *normative age-graded influence* is a biological or social change which occurs at a fairly predictable age (such as the menopause or retirement), whereas a *non-normative influence* is a change which is unpredictable and may occur at any time to different individuals (e.g. illness, unemployment).

2 Depression is strongly positively correlated with length of unemployment: the longer one has been unemployed, the more likely one is to be depressed.

3 *Learned helplessness* is a term coined by Seligman (1975) to describe a state of hopelessness and sense of being unable to affect what happens.

4 Middle-aged men may well be more adversely affected by unemployment because of the greater commitment which they have to their jobs, as compared to young people (Warr, 1987).

5 The social support associated with the relationships enjoyed at work will be lost, causing distress, which may in turn be reduced by social support from family.

6 Warr (1984) found that the perceived cause of unemployment is influential in determining the amount of distress suffered: if the unemployment rate is high, then the unemployed should experience less distress since they feel less responsible.

7 Distress, low self-esteem, anxiety, negative affect, cognitive difficulties, worry about the future, demoralisation and resignation are all associated with unemployment (Dooley & Prause, 1995).

8 An increased risk of psychological ill-health, and an increased risk to the mental health of the family, are both associated with unemployment (Fryer, 1992).

Section 2: Retirement

9 In most cases, *retirement* is anticipated whereas *unemployment* is usually sudden and unexpected.

10 Many couples will find themselves spending an increased amount of time together, following retirement.

11 The *honeymoon phase* of retirement is characterised by euphoria, partly due to a new-found freedom, and is often a busy period.

12 Unrealistic pre-retirement fantasies and inadequate preparation for retirement are both likely to contribute to disenchantment.

13 The *reorientation phase* follows from the *disenchantment phase*.

14 The *termination phase* involves illness or disability which makes self-care difficult, possibly resulting in a sick or disabled role.

15 'Bromley (1988) believes that it is the *transition* between employment and retirement that causes adjustment problems.'

16 Bromley (1988) found that those individuals most satisfied during retirement are those who discover satisfying leisure activities, with at least some of the characteristics of work. This would be good advice.

Section 3: Marriage, divorce and parenthood

17 Ninety per cent of adults marry at least once.

18 Davies (1956) found that events which hinged on the marriage date (such as booking the reception) were most likely to trigger the disorders, whilst either breaking off the engagement or getting married tended to be associated with their improvement.

19 Cohabiting couples are more likely to get divorced than couples who have not lived together before getting married, possibly because of the type of individuals, who prefers to live together (Bee, 1994).

20 Married people are happier, healthier and live longer (on average) than their unmarried counterparts.

21 Bee (1994) believes that men are less likely to provide emotional support for their spouse than are women, leading to an inequitable exchange.

22 Turnbull (1995) claims that divorce rates are highest during the first five years of relationships, then subside, peaking again at between 15 to 20 years.

23 Woollett & Fuller (cited in Cooper, 1996b) found that mothers who had been divorced experienced a sense of achievement and of 'a job well done' in their everyday activities. Apparently, this is because their divorce 'galvanises' them into taking charge of their lives.

24 Before parenthood, marital satisfaction is at its highest, dropping and remaining low with the arrival of children, then picking up when the children leave home.

25 Levinson *et al.* (1978) believed that unhappy couples might nevertheless stay together because of the satisfaction which they gain through their parenting role.

26 *Empty-nest distress* is distress resulting from the departure of dependents, whilst *crowded-nest distress* results from the non-departure of dependants who have grown up but decide not to leave home.

Section 4: Bereavement

27 *Bereavement* refers to the loss, through death, of a loved one, *grief* to the psychological and physical reactions to bereavement, and *mourning* to the observable expression of grief.

28 The other two phases of *griefwork* are *disbelief and shock* and *resolution* (Engel, 1962).

29 Ramsay & de Groot (1977) believed that shock, disorganisation, denial, depression, guilt, anxiety, aggression, resolution and reintegration, comprise the nine *components of grief.*

30 A fear of being alone, of enclosed spaces, of one's own death, and depersonalisation (*neurotic forms of emotional distress*). Fatigue, insomnia, loss of weight/appetite, headaches and palpitations (*physical symptoms*).

31 Lieberman (1993) criticises traditional bereavement research for its assumption that we need to 'recover' from bereavement and 'return to normal', rather than adapting to it.

Life Events and Adulthood

Normative age-graded influences: predictable biological and social changes (e.g. menopause or retirement).
Non-normative influences: idiosyncratic transitions (e.g. illness, divorce).

Normative history-graded influences: historical events that affect whole groups (e.g. wars, recessions).

Marriage and divorce

- Over 90% of adults marry at least once (marriage is therefore a normative age-graded influence).
- It is an important transition involving personal commitment and financial responsibilities, and can be stressful.

Marriage
- Cramer (1994): married people tend to live longer, be **happier, healthier** and less likely to suffer mental disorders.
- Bee (1994): **men tend to benefit more** from marriage since women are more likely to provide emotional support than are men.
- Rutter & Rutter (1992): women are more likely to experience **career/family conflict**.

Divorce
- Turnbull (1995): divorce rates are highest during the first **5 years** of marriage, then peak again at **15–25 years**.
- Divorce is **stressful** on parents and children, with men experiencing more stress than women.
- Woollett & Fuller (cited in Cooper, 1996b): divorced mothers experience a greater **sense of achievement** in their everyday activities.

Cohabitation
Couples who live together before marriage are more likely to divorce later on and express less satisfaction with their marriage.
- Bee (1994): this is because cohabitees are likely to be less conventional and more likely to flout social traditions.

Parenthood

- 90% of people will become parents (Bee, 1994).
- Parenthood varies in meaning and impact more than any other transition and may occur within a wide range of ages.
- Turnbull (1995): the trend towards postponing childhood has led to increasing numbers of middle-aged parents with young children.

Adaptations
- Marital satisfaction tends to be highest before children and remains low whilst children are in the home, rising again in the post-parental phase.
- Bee (1994): new parents have less time for each other (e.g. conversation, sex, affection).
- Levinson *et al*. (1978): couples who are dissatisfied with the relationships may nevertheless stay together because of the satisfaction of the parental role.

Crowded and empty nests
- Durkin (1995): most parents do not find children's departure a distressing time (*empty-nest distress*).
- Durkin (1995): empty-nest distress in women may be related to the period in which they were brought up.
- Datan *et al*. (1987): '*crowded nests*' (where grown-up children opt not to leave home) can be stressful.

Unemployment

Produces psychological and physical effects over time:
- **Depression and suicide** are more prevalent among the unemployed and relate to the length of unemployment.
- **Learned helplessness** (Seligman, 1975), where individuals see themselves as helpless and unable to change their situation.
- Loss of **self-esteem** through loss of role is common.

Sources of distress
(Argyle, 1989)
Length of unemployment: hopelessness sets in if job-hunting fails.
Commitment: committed people are most distressed.
Social support: work relationships are lost, unemployed are often stigmatised.
Activity level: keeping active lessens distress.
Perceived cause: if levels are high nationally, distress is lessened.

Effects of unemployment
(Fryer, 1992)
- Poor psychological health.
- Increased *risk* to psychological health.
- Risk to mental health of *family*.
- Effects may persist even after re-employment.
- Distress caused by *anticipation* of unemployment.
- Feelings of *powerlessness*.
- Financial pressures.

Retirement

- Unlike unemployment, retirement is expected and bearable.
- Couples may find themselves spending more time together.
- Transition to an economically unproductive role can be stressful.
- People who retire voluntarily have less difficulty adjusting.
- Retirement is a role and a process involving stages:

Six phases in retirement
(Atchley, 1982)
Pre-retirement: anxiety about lifestyle changes.
Honeymoon phase: euphoria, sense of freedom, busy.
Disenchantment phase: 'let down', depression.
Reorientation phase: more realistic expectations, new avenues explored.
Stability phase: mastery of the retirement role.
Termination phase: illness/disability role.

Research
- Bromley (1988): it is the *transition* from work to retirement which causes problems. People who are active in retirement experience fewer problems.
- Campbell (1981): retirement is an 'honourable' status, unlike unemployment and a proper reward, not a symbol of failure.

Bereavement

Three phases of 'griefwork'
Engel (1962)
Griefwork: the process of mourning through which the bereaved adjust to loss:
1. **Disbelief and shock**: refusal to accept truth (may last for days).
2. **Developing awareness**: gradual realisation of what has happened. Often accompanied by guilt, apathy, exhaustion and anger.
3. **Resolution**: The individual fully accepts what has happened and establishes a new identity.

Normal and abnormal grieving
- Parkes & Weiss (1983): prolonged, incapacitating grief is the most common variation on normal grieving.
- Hinton (1975): identifies three other abnormal patterns:
  Numbness: An exaggeration of the reaction associated with the shock of loss.
  Neurotic forms of emotional distress (e.g. fear of being alone, enclosed spaces).
  Physical symptoms (e.g fatigue, insomnia, weight loss).
- Parkes *et al*. (1969): self-neglect, suicide and cardiac disease account for increased death rates in widows and widowers.

Components of grief
Ramsay & de Groot (1977)
Shock: 'numbness' can include *depersonalisation* and *derealisation*.
Disorganisation: inability to do simple tasks.
Denial: behaving as if deceased were still alive.
Depression: 'despair' or 'desperate pining' are common following denial.
Guilt: over angry thoughts or neglect, can be real or imagined.
Anxiety: fear of losing control, going mad, the future.
Aggression: irritability and outbursts towards God, doctors, deceased, family.
Resolution: emerging acceptance of the death.
Reintegration: reorganising one's life alone.

ADJUSTMENT TO LATE ADULTHOOD

KEY QUESTIONS
● What is old age?
● What physical and psychological changes take place in old age?
● What theories have been advanced to explain social changes in old age?

Section 1: Introducing old age

1 What is the difference between a *decrement model of ageing* and a *personal-growth model of ageing*?
2 Has the proportion of older people in the British population increased or decreased in recent years?
3 Kastenbaum (1979) identified four distinct '*ages of me*' – to which of these does the expression 'You're only as old as you feel' refer?
4 What is a person's *biological age*?
5 What is one of the dangers, related to these 'ages of me', associated with *ageism*?
6 What are some of the difficulties shared by all of the sub-groups of 'the elderly'?
7 According to the *accumulated-damages theory*, why does ageing occur?

Section 2: Physical and psychological changes

8 Why do the elderly take longer to recover from stressful conditions or fractures?
9 What is the principal problem with *cross-sectional studies* of cognitive abilities, which suggest that old age is associated with a decline in these abilities?
10 What general conclusions about the relationship between ageing and cognitive abilities can be drawn from *longitudinal studies*?
11 What is the difference between *crystallised intelligence* and *fluid intelligence*?
12 Which of these two types of intelligence is most likely to decrease with age?
13 How can you explain this decline?
14 Does recall decline or improve in older adults, as compared with younger adults?
15 What percentage of people over 65 show significant deterioration of the kind associated with dementia?
16 According to Rogers *et al.*'s (1990) study of cognitive decline in the elderly, who was most likely to maintain their cognitive abilities?
17 Complete the following sentence: 'When Levy & Langer (1994) compared hearing Americans, deaf Americans and Chinese on their performance on memory tasks, they found that, amongst older participants, _____ towards _____ and memory performance were positively correlated'.
18 What explanation did Levy and Langer offer for the decline of memory abilities?

Section 3: Disengagement and activity theories

19 According to Cumming (1975), social disengagement involves two related withdrawals. What are they?
20 To what does the term *shrinkage of life space* refer?
21 According to *social disengagement theory*, what is the appropriate and successful way to age?
22 Bromley (1988) offered three main criticisms of social disengagement theory. What was his *practical* criticism of it?
23 What is meant by the criticism that social disengagement theory is less of a theory, and more of a *proto-theory*?
24 Some psychologists believe that disengagement is not the most successful way of entering old age. How did Havighurst *et al.*'s (1968) study support this view?
25 According to *activity theory*, from what does decreased social interaction in old age result?
26 What is meant by saying that it is important for older adults to maintain their role counts?
27 Complete the following sentence: 'Quite possibly, disengagement theory actually _____-estimates and activity theory _____-estimates the degree of control people have over the reconstruction of their lives'.

Section 4: Alternative approaches

28 In what way do *lifespan theorists* differ from activity or disengagement theorists in their views of adjustment to old age?
29 *Social exchange theory* sees the process of adjusting to old age as a sort of *contract* between the individual and society. What is involved in this contract?
30 According to Erikson (1963), why is it inevitable that we face a conflict between *ego-integrity* and *despair* in old age?
31 Name two characteristics of *ego-integrity*.

Section 1: Introducing old age

1 *Decrement models of ageing* see ageing as a process of decline and decay in physical and mental abilities, whilst the *personal growth model* stresses the potential advantages of late adulthood, such as an increase in leisure time.

2 The proportion of older people in the British population has increased dramatically in recent years.

3 The expression 'You're only as old as you feel' refers to a person's *subjective age*, according to Kastenbaum's (1979) '*ages of me*'.

4 A person's *biological age* refers to the state of the face and body (how old a person appears to others).

5 *Ageism* encourages us to think that people's *chronological age* is an accurate indicator of their *biological, subjective* and *functional* ages – it may well not be.

6 All of the sub-groups of 'the elderly' share to some degree the problems of reduced income, failing health and the loss of loved ones.

7 *Accumulated-damages theory* claims that ageing is a consequence of the damage resulting from the wear-and-tear of living.

Section 2: Physical and psychological changes

8 The elderly take longer to recover from stressful conditions and fractures, because their immune systems function less effectively.

9 *Cross-sectional studies* of the elderly, which initially suggested a decline in cognitive abilities, were comparing groups who had lived at different historical times and may therefore have had different experiences (the *cohort effect*).

10 *Longitudinal studies* have suggested that some people retain their intellects well into middle age and beyond, contradicting the cross-sectional studies. However, these studies did find some changes in the nature of intelligence and memory.

11 *Crystallised intelligence* results from accumulated knowledge, whilst *fluid intelligence* refers to the ability to solve novel and unusual problems.

12 *Fluid intelligence* is most likely to decrease with age.

13 This decline could be explained either through disuse of this type of intelligence, or as a result of decreased efficiency of neurological functioning as a consequence of age.

14 Generally, recall declines in older adults. However, some studies (e.g. Maylor's 1994 study of *Mastermind* contestants) have found improvements.

15 Ten per cent of people over 65 show significant deterioration of the kind associated with dementia.

16 Rogers *et al.*'s (1990) study of cognitive decline in the elderly found that those who kept mentally active were most likely to maintain their cognitive abilities.

17 'When Levy & Langer (1994) compared hearing Americans, deaf Americans and Chinese on their performance on memory tasks, they found that amongst older participants, *attitudes* towards *ageing* and memory performance were positively correlated.'

18 Levy and Langer argued that the *self-fulfilling prophecy* could account for the findings, whereby people with low expectations maintain their abilities less.

Section 3: Disengagement and activity theories

19 *Social disengagement* involves withdrawal of society from the individual and withdrawal of the individual from society (Cumming, 1975).

20 *Shrinkage of life space* refers to the fact that, as we age, we tend to interact with fewer people and occupy fewer roles.

21 According to *social disengagement theory*, the appropriate and successful way to age is to withdraw from society and to accept this withdrawal.

22 Bromley's (1988) *practical* criticism of social disengagement theory was that it encouraged segregation of and negative attitudes towards the elderly.

23 Social disengagement theory is a collection of loosely-related assumptions and arguments (a *proto-theory*) rather than a framework of ideas (a *theory*).

24 Havighurst *et al.*'s (1968) study found that the most active and 'engaged' of the elderly were the most content individuals.

25 Decreased social interaction in old age results from a withdrawal of society from the ageing individual which is not desired by the individual.

26 It is important for older adults to maintain their role counts (that is, the different roles which they have to play in society) if they are to maintain their levels of activity.

27 'Quite possibly, disengagement theory actually *under*-estimates and activity theory *over*-estimates the degree of control people have over the reconstruction of their lives.'

Section 4: Alternative approaches

28 *Lifespan theorists* see adjustment to old age as an extension of personality styles, and as continuous with other periods in an individual's life rather than discontinuous.

29 The '*contract*' proposed by *social exchange theory* involves individuals giving up their roles as economically active members of society in exchange for increased leisure time and fewer responsibilities.

30 Erikson's (1963) theory of adult development proposes the existence of a series of psychosocial stages through which we all must pass. These stages are a result of inevitable biological, psychological and social forces.

31 *Ego-integrity* is characterised by a sense of life's purpose, a sense that our lives were somehow inevitable, that all of life offers something of value and can be learned from, a deepening sympathy with our parents, and a realisation that we share birth, life and death with all others.

The meaning of 'old'

Ages of me
(Kastenbaum, 1979)

- **Chronological age:** my age in years starting from birth.
- **Biological age:** the state of my face and body – how old I look.
- **Subjective age:** the age that I feel.
- **Functional age:** (closely related to social age) – my status and lifestyle.

Ageism: beliefs about a group based solely on their chronological age. Dangerous since chronological age is not an accurate indicator of the other ages.

Theories of ageing

Genetic clock/programmed theory: ageing is built into every organism through a genetic code which tells cells when to stop working.

Accumulated damages theory: ageing is a consequence of damage resulting from the wear-and-tear of living.

Sub-groups of 'the elderly'
(Burnside et al., 1979 & Craig, 1992)

- **The young old (60–69):** a major transition – adaptations to new roles and the loss of income.
- **The middle-aged-old (70–79):** loss of friends and illness. Reduced participation and declining health.
- **The old old (80–89):** difficulty in adapting/ interacting with surroundings. Need help maintaining social and cultural contacts.
- **The very old old (90–99):** altering activities to make the most of what they have – can be joyful and serene.

Adjustment to Late Adulthood

Decrement model: sees ageing as a process of decay or decline in physical and intellectual abilities and in social relationships.

Personal growth model: stresses the advantages of 'old age' (e.g increase in leisure time, reduced responsibilities).

Psychological changes

Intelligence

Crystallised intelligence
Results from accumulated knowledge (e.g. reasoning skills, language skills). Linked to background and education and is measured by tests of general information.

Performance **increases** with age and improves until near the end of life (Horn, 1982).

Explanations
- A tendency to add to our knowledge as we grow older.
- Regular use of crystallised intelligence (Denney & Palmer, 1981).

Fluid intelligence
The ability to solve novel and unusual problems. Allows us to perceive and draw inferences about patterns of stimuli. Measured by tests using novel problems.

Performance **declines** with age, peaking between 20 and 30. Discovered using a *cross-longitudinal method* (Schaie & Hertzog, 1983).

Explanations
- May be due to reduced neurological functioning.
- Low use – few challenges to use our fluid intelligence (Cavanaugh, 1995).

Memory

Research
- **Recall tests:** older adults generally perform more poorly.
  However, older *Mastermind* contestants tended to score more highly (Maylor, 1994).
- **Recognition tests:** differences between older and younger people are slight/non-existent.
- **Everyday memory:** the elderly do have difficulty recalling events from their youth (Miller & Morris, 1993).
- **Dementia** (e.g Alzheimer's disease): 90% of people above 65 show little deterioration (Diamond, 1978).
- **Activity:** Rogers *et al.* (1990) found that those who kept mentally active were most likely to keep their cognitive abilities.

The influence of stereotypes
- Levy & Langer (1994): studied Americans, deaf-Americans and Chinese. Found that positive attitudes towards ageing and memory performance were positively correlated.
Levy & Langer believe that negative attitudes about ageing may become *self-fulfilling prophecies*, where low expectations cause a reduction in activities that help maintain memory abilities.

Social changes

Social disengagement theory

- Social disengagement: 'a systematic reduction in certain kinds of social interaction' (Bromley, 1988).
- Cumming (1975): social disengagement is the withdrawal of *society* from the individual (e.g through retirement) and the withdrawal from society of the *individual* (e.g through a more solitary life).
- Cumming: **three aspects of disengagement**:
  1. *Shrinkage of life space:* fewer interactions and roles.
  2. *Increased individuality:* governed by fewer rules/expectations.
  3. *Acceptance of change:* the individual accepts disengagement.

Bromley (1988): 1. the theory encourages negative attitudes towards and segregation of the elderly, 2. it is not a proper theory but a collection of loosely related assumptions, 3. that older people may in fact be *more likely* to seek engagement.

Psychosocial theory

Erikson (1963): the individual faces a conflict between **ego-integrity** (positive) and **despair** (negative).

Ego integrity involves:
- believing that life does have a purpose and makes sense.
- believing that all of life offers something of value.
- seeing our parents in a more sympathetic light.
- seeing that we share with all others the cycle of birth, life and death.

In contrast, despair involves a fear of death and the feeling that it is too late to undo the past.

Activity (re-engagement) theory

- Older people are essentially the same as middle-aged people with similar psychological and social needs. Decreased social interaction is the result of society withdrawing and is often not wanted.
- Optimal ageing involves staying active and maintaining interactions, especially by maintaining a high number of roles.

However, some elderly people do accept disengagement, and each individual selects styles best suited to them.

Social exchange theory

- Dyson (1980): both disengagement and activity theories fail to take into account physical and economic factors and as a result are **prescriptive** (tell us what the elderly *should* be doing)
- It is more useful to see adjusting to ageing as a **contract** between the individual and society, in which we give up our economically active roles in return for more leisure time and fewer responsibilities.

UNIT 5

Social Psychology

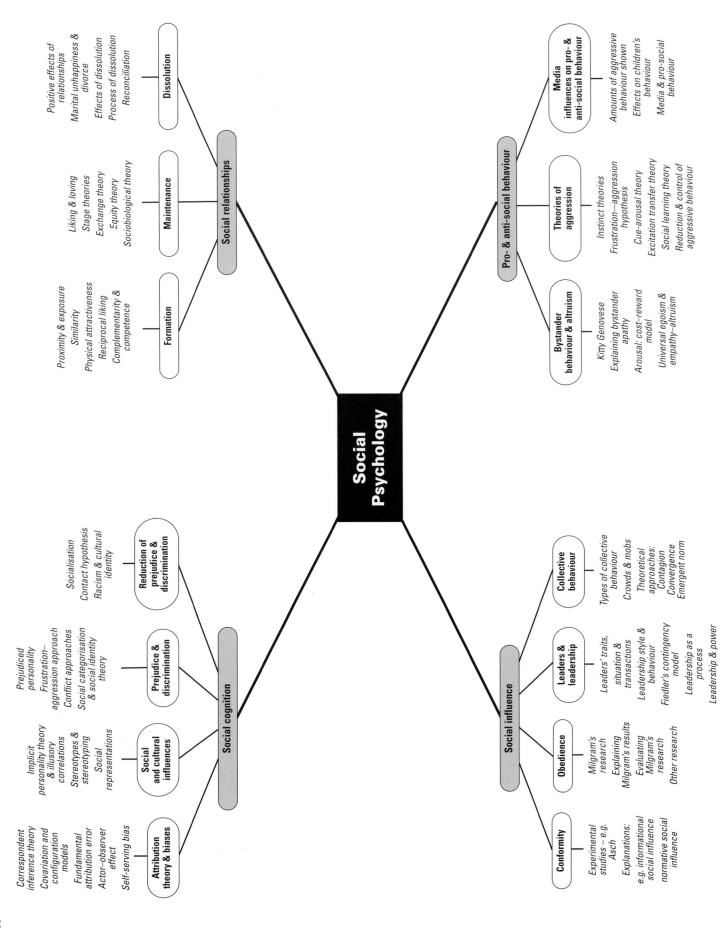

Social Psychology

Social relationships

Formation
- Proximity & exposure
- Similarity
- Physical attractiveness
- Reciprocal liking
- Complementarity & competence

Maintenance
- Liking & loving
- Stage theories
- Exchange theory
- Equity theory
- Sociobiological theory

Dissolution
- Positive effects of relationships
- Marital unhappiness & divorce
- Effects of dissolution
- Process of dissolution
- Reconciliation

Pro- & anti-social behaviour

Bystander behaviour & altruism
- Kitty Genovese
- Explaining bystander apathy
- Arousal: cost–reward model
- Universal egoism & empathy–altruism

Theories of aggression
- Instinct theories
- Frustration–aggression hypothesis
- Cue-arousal theory
- Excitation transfer theory
- Social learning theory
- Reduction & control of aggressive behaviour

Media influences on pro- & anti-social behaviour
- Amounts of aggressive behaviour shown
- Effects on children's behaviour
- Media & pro-social behaviour

Social cognition

Attribution theory & biases
- Correspondent inference theory
- Covariation and configuration models
- Fundamental attribution error
- Actor–observer effect
- Self-serving bias

Social and cultural influences
- Implicit personality theory & illusory correlations
- Stereotypes & stereotyping
- Social representations

Prejudice & discrimination
- Prejudiced personality
- Frustration–aggression approach
- Conflict approaches
- Social categorisation & social identity theory

Reduction of prejudice & discrimination
- Socialisation
- Contact hypothesis
- Racism & cultural identity

Social influence

Conformity
- Experimental studies – e.g. Asch
- Explanations: e.g. informational social influence normative social influence

Obedience
- Milgram's research
- Explaining Milgram's results
- Evaluating Milgram's research
- Other research

Leaders & leadership
- Leaders' traits, situation & transactions
- Leadership style & behaviour
- Fiedler's contingency model
- Leadership as a process
- Leadership & power

Collective behaviour
- Types of collective behaviour
- Crowds & mobs
- Theoretical approaches: Contagion Convergence Emergent norm

51

THEORIES OF ATTRIBUTION AND BIASES IN THE ATTRIBUTION PROCESS

SYLLABUS
1.1 Social cognition
- attribution theories including errors and biases in the attribution process, for example, the fundamental attribution error and the self-serving bias

KEY QUESTIONS
- What are attribution theories?
- How does the correspondent inference theory explain the attribution process?
- How does the covariation model explain the attribution process?
- What biases affect how attributions are made?

Section 1: Introducing attribution

1 What are *attribution theories* concerned with?
2 Why did Heider believe that the ordinary person was like a *naïve scientist*?
3 Why is it important that members of a culture share a *common psychology*?
4 What is a *dispositional* (or *internal*) *attribution*?
5 What is a *situational* (or *external*) *attribution*?

Section 2: Correspondent inference theory

6 What do Jones & Davis (1965) mean by the term *correspondent inference*?
7 Complete the sentence: 'Jones and Davis argue that a precondition for a correspondent inference is the attribution of _____'.
8 Once this precondition has been met, we can look for a disposition which may explain it. According to Jones and Davis, we employ an *analysis of non-common effects* for this purpose. What does this involve?
9 What influence does information regarding the *expectedness* and *social desirability* of a behaviour have on a correspondent inference?
10 Name two other factors which may influence the inference which we draw.

Section 3: Co-variation and configuration models

11 According to Kelley (1967), what is the *principle of covariation*?
12 What is the difference between *distinctiveness information* and *consensus information*?
13 If a behaviour is accompanied by *high consensus* information, is a dispositional or situational attribution more likely?
14 How do we use *consistency*, *distinctiveness* and *consensus* information, according to the *abnormal conditions focus model*?
15 What is the problem with Kelley's claim that we require three types of information in order to make an attribution?

16 What are *causal schemata*?
17 What is the difference between a behaviour which falls into the *multiple necessary causes* schema and one which falls into the *multiple sufficient causes* schema?
18 How is the *discounting principle* used?
19 Why is Kelley's model a *normative* model of the attributional process?
20 Complete the sentence: 'Our tendency to act as "cognitive _____" means that we do not analyse the interactions between personal and situational factors even if a lot of information is available'.

Section 4: Attributional biases

21 What is the *fundamental attribution error*?
22 Napolitan & Goethals (1979) had students talk with a young woman who behaved in either a cold or a warm manner. Half of the students were told that she was instructed to behave in this manner. What was the effect of this information?
23 What two explanations for the fundamental attribution error were proposed by Jones & Nisbett (1971)?
24 What did Miller (1984) discover about the attributional process in India?
25 How do the *consequences* of a person's behaviour affect the attributions made for that behaviour?
26 What is the *actor–observer effect*?
27 How does a dislike of being 'pigeon-holed' help us to explain this effect?
28 Complete the sentence '… another possible explanation suggests that actors do not perceive _____ as they act and are therefore more likely to attribute their behaviour to the situation'.
29 What experiment did Storms (1973) carry out in order to investigate the actor–observer effect?
30 What is the *self-serving bias*?
31 According to this bias, what kind of attribution are you most likely to make to explain a good exam result?
32 In which *clinical condition* is the self-serving bias reversed?

Section 1: Introducing attribution

1 *Attribution theories* are concerned with the ways in which we *explain* behaviour, in particular the general principles governing our selection and use of information to arrive at *causal explanations* for behaviour.

2 Heider believed that we are *naïve scientists* in that we try to link observable behaviours to unobservable causes.

3 Without a *common psychology*, members of a culture would find it difficult to understand and be understood by others. Social life would be impossible.

4 A *dispositional* (or *internal*) attribution is an explanation of a behaviour in terms of the enduring characteristics of the actor, such as his/her personality, motivation, or abilities.

5 A *situational* (or *external*) attribution is an explanation of behaviour by reference to external events not under the direct control of the actor, such as illness, accidents, and environmental pressures.

Section 2: Correspondent inference theory

6 A *correspondent inference* (Jones & Davis, 1965) is when we infer whether or not a person's *dispositions* correspond to their *behaviour*.

7 'Jones and Davis argue that a precondition for a correspondent inference is the attribution of *intentionality*.'

8 An *analysis of non-common effects* involves looking at the number of differences between the chosen course of action and those that are not. These can be used to explain why the individual chose a particular behaviour.

9 Behaviour which is *expected* or *socially desirable* tells us very little about a person. For example, teachers can tell very little about the characters of their students so long as they behave as students are expected to. When behaviour is unexpected or undesirable, we find it more informative.

10 *Free choice* and *prior expectations* also influence the inference we draw.

Section 3: Co-variation and configuration models

11 The *principle of covariation* states that 'an effect is attributed to one of its possible causes with which, over time, it co-varies'.

12 *Distinctiveness information* tells us whether or not the person reacts in the same way towards other similar stimuli or entities, whilst *consensus information* tells us whether or not others behave in the same way towards the same stimulus.

13 If a behaviour is accompanied by *high consensus* information a *situational attribution* is more likely.

14 We use this information to determine whether it is the actor or some aspect of the situation which is *abnormal*, attributing the cause to whatever is abnormal.

15 We frequently make attributions *without having access to all three types of information*.

16 *Causal schemata* are ready-made beliefs or preconceptions about how certain kinds of causes interact to produce certain effects.

17 Behaviour falling into the *multiple sufficient causes* schema could be caused by any number of things, whilst one which falls into the *multiple necessary causes* schema must have involved many causes.

18 The *discounting principle* is used to discount the least plausible of the explanations for a behaviour falling into the multiple sufficient causes schema.

19 Kelley's model is *normative* because it tells us how people *should* make attributions rather than how they actually do.

20 'Our tendency to act as "cognitive *misers*" means that we do not analyse the interactions between personal and situational factors even if a lot of information is available.'

Section 4: Attributional biases

21 The *fundamental attribution error* is the tendency to overestimate the importance of dispositional or personal or situational factors, and underestimate external or situational factors for other people's behaviours.

22 Nothing whatsoever. The students completely disregarded the 'situational' information in making their attributions.

23 Nisbett (1971) proposed that there is a different *focus of attention* when we see ourselves from when we judge others and that *different types of information* (such as how consistent the behaviour is) *are available* when judging our own behaviour.

24 Miller (1984) found that in India people were far more likely to give situational attributions for others' behaviour.

25 The more negative and serious the consequence of a person's behaviour, the more likely we are to blame them for it (e.g. reporters after the death of Princess Diana).

26 The *actor–observer effect* is the tendency to make different attributions for behaviour depending on whether we are performing or observing it.

27 We dislike being 'pigeon-holed', and so are less likely to explain our own behaviour in terms of trait labels (dispositional attribution).

28 '… another possible explanation suggests that actors do not perceive *themselves* as they act and are therefore more likely to attribute their behaviour to the situation.'

29 Storms (1973) showed participants a video of their behaviour from another person's perspective, and found that the direction of attributions was reversed.

30 The *self-serving bias* is the tendency to 'take credit' for positive events and 'deny responsibility' for negative events.

31 A good exam result must surely be the result of your hard work and high ability (*internal attribution*).

32 Those suffering from *clinical depression* seem to blame themselves for negative events and attribute positive events to external factors.

Attribution Theories & Bias

Attribution: an explanation of why an individual behaved in a certain way.
Attribution theory: the general principles governing our selection and use of information to arrive at causal explanations for behaviour.

Heider (1958)
The ordinary person is like a *naïve scientist*, linking behaviours to causes.
Explanations are either:
- *dispositional/internal* (e.g. ability or effort)
- *situational/external* (e.g. illness or luck).

Correspondent inference theory

Jones & Davis (1965)
- An attribution involves deciding whether or not a person's *dispositions* (e.g. kindness) correspond to their intentions (e.g. buying flowers).
- If behaviour and dispositions do not correspond, we may decide that the *situation* has caused the behaviour.
- In order to make an inference, we must first decide if the behaviour was intentional.
- If behaviour is intentional, an analysis of *non-common effects* is carried out in order to see why the person chose this option (e.g. this was the *only* available option which would have impressed a particular member of the opposite sex).
- Other important factors may then be considered:
  Free choice: if the person was pressurised, their behaviour may not reflect their dispositions.
  Expectedness/social desirability: expected/desirable behaviours tell us little about dispositions.
  Prior expectations: help us to judge whether or not a particular behaviour is in character.

Was the behaviour intentional?
1. Did they *know* what would happen?
2. Were they *capable* of doing it?

→ *no* → Not dispositional

↓ *yes*

Analysis of non-common effects.
(What are the differences between what they did and what they could have done?)

↓

Was it freely chosen? | **Was it expected/ socially desirable?** | **Was it in line with prior expectations?**

D i s p o s i t i o n s

Covariation and configuration models

Covariation model
Kelley (1967)
An attribution about the cause of a behaviour depends on the extent to which it covaries with three types of information:

e.g. Why is Pete always late for psychology?

Consensus
Extent to which others behave in the same way.

Is everyone late for psychology?
no = low consensus
yes = high consensus

Distinctiveness
Extent to which the person behaves in the same way to similar stimuli.
Is Pete also late for sociology?
no = high distinctiveness
yes = low distinctiveness

Consistency
The stability of the behaviour across time.

Is Pete always late for psychology?
no = low consistency
yes = high consistency

Research
- McArthur (1972): people do make attributions in the direction suggested by the model when given the three types of information.
- **Abnormal conditions focus model** (Hilton & Slugoski, 1986): the three types of information help tell if it is the *situation* or the actor which is *abnormal* (*e.g. if everyone else is on time, Pete is abnormal*).

Configuration model
Kelley (1972)
- In many situations we do not have all three kinds of information.
- In these '*single-event attributions*', we make attributions by slotting behaviour into '*causal schemata*' ('stereotyped' explanations).
- Causal schemata are a shorthand way of explaining events; two principal types:

Multiple sufficient causes
Any number of causes could explain the behaviour.
e.g. a pop-star advertising cola.
A *discounting principle* is used to eliminate unlikely causes.

Multiple necessary causes
Many causes are needed to produce the behaviour.
e.g. winning a marathon.

Attributional biases

The fundamental attribution error

The tendency for observers to underestimate situational influences and overestimate dispositional influences upon others' behaviour (Ross, 1977).

Napolitan & Goethals (1979)
- Students talked with a young woman who was either warm and friendly or cold and critical.
- Half were told behaviour was spontaneous, half that she was instructed to behave that way.
Results: both groups inferred that she was warm when she was friendly, and cold when unfriendly, regardless of whether they knew that she was acting as instructed.

Explanations (Jones & Nisbett, 1971)
1. *Focus of attention:* when we act, we focus on the situation; when another acts, we focus on them and not the situation.
2. *Types of information:* we have more consistency information available when judging ourselves, and know what it is we are attending to.

The actor–observer effect

The tendency to make different attributions about a behaviour depending on whether we are *performing* (*acting*) or *observing* it. If acting, we tend to make external attributions, if observing we tend to make dispositional attributions.

Storms (1973):
- Pairs of participants talked across a table and were videoed.
- When shown the video of their behaviour, they tended to make *internal* attributions, not external attributions as is typical.

Explanations
1. We do not like to be pigeon-holed, so do not explain our behaviours with trait-labels.
2. Observers assume actors always behave in the way they have seen; actors know they have behaved differently.
3. People do not *perceive* themselves, they focus on their situation. When observing, they focus on the actor, not the actor's situation.

The self-serving bias

The tendency for us to 'take the credit' (*internal attribution*) when things go right, and 'deny responsibility' (*external attribution*) when things go wrong.

- Lau & Russell (1980): American football players attributed wins to internal causes (e.g. determination) and defeats to external causes (e.g. injuries).
- Arkin et al. (1980): students regard exams in which they do well as good indicators of their abilities, and those in which they do badly as poor indicators.
- Abramson et al., (1978): depressed people reverse this pattern, attributing success to luck and failure to a lack of ability.

Explanations
Greenberg et al. (1982): the bias serves our *needs*, such as the need to maintain self-esteem. 'Taking the credit' is a *self-enhancing bias*, denying responsibility is a *self-protecting bias*.

52

SOCIAL AND CULTURAL INFLUENCES ON PERCEPTION: STEREOTYPES AND SOCIAL REPRESENTATIONS

SYLLABUS

1.1 Social cognition
- theories and research studies into the influence of social factors upon perception. These should include Cultural Identity, Social Identity Theory and Social Representations
- the origins and maintenance of social and cultural stereotypes

KEY QUESTIONS
- What is implicit personality theory?
- What are stereotypes and how can we explain them?
- What are social representations and how are they formed?

Q

Section 1: Implicit personality theory

1 What did the participants in Asch's (1946) study do when presented with a list of characteristics describing a fictitious individual?
2 What is the difference between a *central trait* and a *peripheral trait*?
3 What is the *halo effect*? Can you give an example of a term likely to induce a positive halo?
4 Bruner & Tagiuri (1954) coined the term *implicit personality theory*. What does it describe?
5 What sort of people are likely to share similar implicit personality theories?
6 What is an *illusory correlation*?

Section 2: Stereotypes

7 What is a *social stereotype*?
8 What did Katz & Braly (1933) find in their investigation of stereotyping in Princeton University students?
9 When Gagahan (1991) criticises studies of stereotyping for *social desirability responding*, what does she mean?
10 How did Razran (1950) overcome the problem of social desirability responding?
11 According to Campbell (1967), why must stereotypes contain a '*grain of truth*'?
12 Why do illusory correlations cast doubt on the 'grain of truth' hypothesis?
13 When Hamilton & Gifford (1976) read equal proportions of positive and negative statements about members of either small or large groups, what effect did they observe?
14 According to Wegner & Vallacher (1976), how do we explain 'odd' behaviour?
15 What is the *confirmation bias*?
16 Complete the following sentence: 'Tajfel sees stereotyping as a special case of categorisation which involves an exaggeration of _____ within groups and of _____ between groups'.

17 According to Brislin (1993), why should we not view stereotyping as an *abnormal cognitive process*?
18 We often assume that a stereotype is intended to apply to *all* members of a stereotyped group. What did McCauley & Stitt (1978) find when investigating stereotypes of Germans?
19 Why do we rely on stereotypes to form impressions of strangers?
20 Complete the sentence: 'Perhaps stereotypes are resistant to change because they represent ways of _____ our complex social world'.

Section 3: Social representations

21 How does Moscovici define *social representations*?
22 What is an *anchor* in social representations research?
23 What two processes are used to *objectify* an abstract concept, in order to make it concrete?
24 How has *figuration* been applied to Freud's psychodynamic model?
25 What social representation has resulted from 'split-brain' studies?
26 According to Durkin (1995), why do children make use of social representations?
27 What is the role of social representations in child-rearing practices?
28 How might social representations concerning 'intelligence' influence the way in which children are taught?
29 Why did a student protest staged by Belgian student-leaders fail, according to Di Giacomo's (1980) research?
30 According to Moscovici (1984), what features of social representations allow them to be both *durable* and *open to change*?
31 What is perhaps the major weakness with social representations theory?

Section 1: Implicit personality theory

1 The participants in Asch's (1946) study inferred further character traits from a list of characteristics describing a fictitious individual.

2 *Central traits*, such as 'warm' or 'cold', exert a *major* influence on our perceptions of others, whilst *peripheral traits*, such as 'polite' or 'blunt', exert only a *minor* influence on our overall impressions.

3 The *halo effect* involves attributing to someone a range of characteristics we associate with a particularly favourable or unfavourable characteristic. Such characteristics are usually evaluative, such as 'generous' (positive halo) or 'cruel' (negative halo).

4 *Implicit personality theory* describes the unconscious inference processes that enable us to form impressions of others based on very little evidence.

5 People from the *same culture* or *group* are the most likely to share similar implicit personality theories.

6 An *illusory correlation* is the belief that two variables (such as race and aggressiveness) are correlated, when in fact they are not.

Section 2: Stereotypes

7 A *social stereotype* is a grossly oversimplified and generalised abstraction that people share about their own or another group.

8 Katz & Braly (1933) found that Princeton University students held strong traditional stereotypes about ethnic minorities, especially derogatory stereotypes, despite having (in most cases) no personal contact with members of the stereotyped groups.

9 Gagahan (1991) is pointing out that participants in research into stereotypes may simply give the response which they believe is most *socially acceptable* or *desirable* and, as a consequence, not reveal their true attitudes.

10 Razran (1950) deceived his participants into believing that they would be rating pictures of girls according to their psychological characteristics. In fact, the same picture was given a different ethnic group name, and differences in the traits reported attributed to ethnic stereotyping.

11 Campbell (1967) claims that stereotypes originate in at least one person's experience before being communicated to others, so must contain a '*grain of truth*'.

12 In order for stereotypes to contain a grain of truth, traits must have been correctly inferred from behaviour. However, illusory correlations demonstrate that we may associate certain traits with certain behaviour *without* there being any such relationship.

13 Hamilton & Gifford (1976) found that participants rated members of the smaller group as being less desirable, despite there being no relationship between the group and this characteristic.

14 Wegner & Vallacher (1976) claim that we explain 'odd' behaviour as being due to the actor's membership in an unusual group.

15 The *confirmation bias* is the tendency for us to seek out information which confirms our existing beliefs.

16 'Tajfel sees stereotyping as a special case of categorisation which involves an exaggeration of *similarities* within groups and of *differences* between groups.'

17 Brislin (1993) argues that stereotypes are 'categories about people', and simply reflect a general need to organise, remember and retrieve potentially useful information.

18 McCauley & Stitt (1978) found that traits stereotypically assigned to Germans were *not* believed by their participants to apply to *all* Germans.

19 It might be ethically correct to form impressions based only on unique characteristics of individuals, but this *attribute-driven processing* involves more cognitive effort than *category-driven processing*, where judgements are based on group membership.

20 'Perhaps stereotypes are resistant to change because they represent ways of *simplifying* our complex social world.'

Section 3: Social representations

21 *Social representations* are the shared beliefs and explanations held by the society in which we live or the group to which we belong.

22 An *anchor* is a concept established within a pre-existing system of beliefs to which new experiences can be related.

23 *Personification* and *figuration* are used to *objectify* an abstract concept in order to make it concrete.

24 *Figuration* has led people to portray the impulsive *id* as a demon perched on one shoulder, with the moral *superego* balanced on the other.

25 Moscovici & Hewstone (1983) argue that Sperry's (1964) split-brain studies have become transformed into a social representation of a *logical left-brained* type person and an *intuitive right-brained* type person.

26 Durkin (1995) claims that children make use of social representations in order to *understand the adult world*, making 'the unfamiliar familiar' by incorporating the puzzling features of the adult world into their own collective practices.

27 Social representations help adults to know what to expect of children and what should be done with them.

28 Teachers who believe that 'intelligence' is inherited will be less inclined to stimulate under-achievers than those who believe that 'intelligence' is a product of experience.

29 Di Giacomo (1980) found that the social representation of students differed between the student-leaders and the students themselves. Leaders were more likely to associate students with solidarity.

30 Moscovici (1984) sees social representations as having a solid '*central figurative nucleus*', surrounded by '*peripheral elements*' which may change.

31 Social representations theory is *vague and 'fuzzy'*, and as a consequence *largely unfalsifiable* since it does not suggest many hypotheses which can be tested experimentally.

A

Stereotypes & Social Representation

Implicit personality theory

Bruner & Taguiri (1954)
Implicit personality theory (IPT): beliefs about which personality traits belong together. We use IPTs to 'fill in the gaps' when we have little information about people. IPTs are consistent within a culture.
Illusory correlations: may result from IPTs where we see certain variables as being related when in fact they are not.

Central and peripheral traits
Asch (1946)
- Presented participants with list of traits describing a person.
- Found that participants would infer other traits from these.
Certain words (e.g. 'warm'/'cold') had a large impact – *central* traits – whereas others (e.g. 'polite'/'blunt') did not – *peripheral* traits.
The halo effect: certain characteristics, such as 'warm' or 'cold', carry with them a positive or negative 'halo' of associations.

Stereotypes

The nature of stereotypes

Katz & Braly (1933)
- Asked Princeton University students to identify which of a list of 84 traits were most closely linked to ten ethnic groups (e.g. Negroes, Germans, Turks).
- If 75% or more agreed on a trait, this was taken to be part of the stereotype.
- Substantial agreement on stereotypes, especially derogatory ones (e.g. Negroes – lazy and ignorant).
- Most of the students had *never met* members of these groups.

Stereotyping: a form of IPT where a single item about a person (appearance or verbal label) is used to generate inferences about their character.
Individual stereotype: judgements about what a person from a given group is like.
Group stereotype: belief that all people from a given group share the same characteristics.
Social stereotypes: grossly oversimplified and generalised abstractions that people share about their own or other groups (Oakes *et al.*, 1994).

Razran (1950)
Tried to overcome the problem of *social desirability* in stereotype research.
- Asked participants to rate pictures of girls for psychological qualities.
- Same pictures given Irish-, Italian- or Jewish-sounding names.
- Participants did not know study was a study of stereotyping.
- Pictures were rated differently depending on the type of name (e.g. Jewish – rated high on 'ambition', low on 'niceness')

Explaining stereotyping

The 'grain of truth' hypothesis
Campbell (1967) believes that stereotypes arise from two sources:
- a person's experience of another person.
- communicating that experience to others.
Stereotypes therefore originate in at least one person's experience.
However, this assumes that people make logical inferences, whereas in fact *illusory correlations* may cause people to infer traits wrongly from their experiences.

Explaining illusory correlations

Hamilton & Gifford (1976):
- presented participants with both positive and negative descriptions of people from either a large or a small group.
- the small group were perceived more negatively, despite the proportion of positive descriptions being the same.

- Wegner & Vallacher (1976): illusory correlations (ICs) arise from a tendency to attribute 'odd' behaviours to membership of an unusual group.
- **The confirmation bias:** ensures that once we have made an IC we seek out information which supports it.

Stereotyping as a cognitive process

- Tajfel (1971): stereotyping is a special case of *categorisation* involving an exaggeration of differences *between* groups and similarities *within* groups.
- Brown (1986): stereotypes are 'an intrinsic, essential and primitive aspect of cognition'.
- Other psychologists see generalisations as false and illogical. However, people may not believe a stereotype applies to every member of a group (see below).

McCauley & Stitt (1978)
- asked participants to estimate the percentage of Germans who conformed to stereotypical traits.
- None of the estimates was 100%, suggesting that stereotypes only imply an average difference, when compared with other groups.

Social representations

The nature of social representations

Anchoring and objectifying
Anchors: established concepts within a pre-existing system to which new experiences can be related.
Objectifying: making abstract things concrete in a way that most people can understand. Achieved by:
1. *Personification* (linking ideas with a person's name, e.g. Freud).
2. *Figuration* (converting complex ideas into images and metaphors, e.g. 'black holes').

Social representations (SRs): the shared beliefs and expectations held by the society or group to which we belong (Moscovici, 1981).
- SRs provide the *framework* within which we can make sense of and communicate about the world.
- SRs are 'the essence of social cognition' (Moscovici, 1981).

SRs of 'split-brain' research
- Sperry (1964): the two hemispheres of the brain showed differences in functioning, and are specialised for certain tasks.
- Moscovici & Hewstone (1983): this research has been transformed into a popular belief that people are either 'logical and left-brained' or 'intuitive and right brained'.

SRs in childhood
Durkin (1995) argues that SRs apply in two ways to childhood:
1. They are used by children to make sense of the world (e.g. the rules which adults impose on them).
2. They are used by members of a society to know what expectations and beliefs to have towards children, and how to treat them as a result (e.g. whether or not intelligence is inherited).

Other research
- Di Giacomo (1980) studied a protest staged by Belgian students. Leaders' SRs saw students as 'workers' needing 'solidarity'. The students did not. The protest failed.
- Moscovici (1984): SRs are stable because they combine a stable 'nucleus' with changeable peripheral elements.

53

SOME THEORIES OF PREJUDICE AND DISCRIMINATION

SYLLABUS
1.1 Social cognition
- the origins and maintenance of prejudice and discrimination

KEY QUESTIONS
- What are prejudice and discrimination?
- Is prejudice the consequence of 'authoritarian personalities'?
- Do frustration and aggression create prejudice?
- Can social categorisation or social identity result in prejudice?

Section 1: Introducing prejudice
1 What are the three components common to all attitudes?
2 What form do these components take in prejudicial attitudes?
3 What is the difference between prejudice and discrimination?

Section 2: Personality and frustration–aggression
4 What was the aim of Adorno *et al.*'s (1950) research?
5 What did Adorno *et al.* believe about the link between upbringing and prejudice?
6 What personality inventories, aimed at measuring different aspects of personality, were devised by Adorno *et al.*?
7 Which of these inventories was found to be highly correlated with scores on all of the other inventories?
8 What name did Adorno *et al.* give to individuals who scored highly on this particular inventory?
9 Why is the problem of *acquiescent response sets* pertinent to Adorno *et al.*'s methodology?
10 What was wrong with Adorno *et al.*'s original sample?
11 What historical aspect of prejudice suggests that Adorno *et al.*'s theory is inadequate as an explanation of prejudice?
12 What did Minard (1952) discover when assessing the attitudes of white coal-miners towards their black fellow workers above ground and underground?
13 What does Dollard *et al.*'s (1939) *frustration–aggression hypothesis* state?
14 According to Dollard *et al.*, what do we do when we are prevented from being aggressive towards the source of frustration?
15 What relationship did Hovland & Sears (1940) discover between lynchings of blacks and cotton prices in America between 1880 and 1930?
16 How was Weatherley (1961) able to demonstrate *scapegoating* of Jews under laboratory conditions?

Section 3: Relative deprivation and realistic conflict

17 Complete the sentence: 'According to relative deprivation theory, the discrepancy between our ____and ____ ____ produces frustration'.
18 Why were the Los Angeles riots an example of *fraternalistic relative deprivation* rather than *egoistic relative deprivation*?
19 What is the principal source of inter-group conflict, according to *realistic conflict theory*?
20 What experiment did Sherif *et al.* (1961) carry out which supports realistic conflict theory?
21 When Tyerman & Spencer (1983) studied relations between four groups of scouts, how did their findings relate to those of Sherif *et al.*?

Section 4: Social categorisation and social identity
22 How were the boys in Tajfel *et al.*'s (1971) minimal group experiments assigned to their groups.
23 How much did these boys know about their fellow group members?
24 What did Tajfel *et al.* discover about the boys' allocation of points?
25 *Social categorisation theory* claims that people tend to divide up the world into two categories. What are these?
26 According to social categorisation theory, how is prejudice caused?
27 What is the difference between the *ingroup differentiation hypothesis* and the *illusion of outgroup homogenity*?
28 What did Wetherall (1982) discover when comparing the attitudes towards outgroups of white and Polynesian children?
29 What, according to *social identity theory*, are the two components of positive self-images?
30 What is the relationship between prejudice and maintaining a positive self-image?
31 How can social identity theory be criticised?

Section 1: Introducing prejudice

1 All attitudes have *cognitive*, *affective*, and *behavioural* components.

2 Prejudicial attitudes comprise a *cognitive component* (usually *stereotypes*), an *affective component* (usually *negative emotions* or feelings), and a *behavioural component* (*discriminatory behaviour*).

3 An unjustified negative *attitude* towards a group and its members is called *prejudice*. *Discrimination* is the *behavioural component* of this attitude.

Section 2: Personality and frustration–aggression

4 Adorno *et al.* (1950) aimed to discover whether or not a link between personality and prejudice existed, in an attempt to understand the emergence of anti-Semitism and ethnocentrism in Nazi Germany.

5 Adorno *et al.* believed that an excessively harsh disciplinary attitude might create aggression which could not be directed at parents, and so might be *displaced* onto an alternative target.

6 Adorno *et al.*'s personality inventories aimed to measure *anti-Semitism*, *ethnocentrism*, *political–economic conservatism* and *potentiality for fascism*.

7 The *potentiality for fascism scale* (*F scale*) was found to be highly correlated with scores on the other scales.

8 Adorno *et al.* called such individuals *authoritarian personalities*.

9 *Acquiescent response set* refers to a participant's tendency to agree with the remainder of a questionnaire (regardless of content) having agreed with the first few questions. Because of the wording of Adorno *et al.*'s questions, this would have resulted in *high scores* on the authoritarianism scale.

10 Adorno's original sample was *biased*, being comprised solely of white, middle-class, non-Jewish Americans.

11 Historically, prejudice has been widespread in certain cultures at certain times. It is hard to see how this could result from personality differences alone.

12 Minard (1952) discovered that 80 per cent of the white miners were friendly to their black fellow workers underground as opposed to only 20 per cent when they were above ground. This suggests that *conformity to social norms* plays a significant role in prejudicial attitudes.

13 Dollard *et al.*'s (1939) *frustration–aggression hypothesis* states that frustration always leads to aggression, and aggression is always a result of frustration.

14 Dollard *et al.* believe that if we are prevented from being aggressive towards the source of frustration, we are likely to *displace* that aggression onto a substitute or '*scapegoat*'.

15 Hovland & Sears (1940) found a *negative correlation* between lynchings of blacks and cotton prices. When the prices dropped, the number of lynchings increased.

16 Weatherley (1961) insulted students who scored either high or low on an anti-Semitism scale, then had all participants write short stories about pictures of men, some of whom had Jewish-sounding names.

Section 3: Relative deprivation and realistic conflict

17 'According to relative deprivation theory, the discrepancy between our *expectations* and *actual achievements* produces frustration.'

18 The Los Angeles riots were an example of *fraternalistic relative deprivation* because they involved a comparison between the rights of one group and those of another, not between the rights of two similar individuals (*egoistic relative deprivation*).

19 *Realistic conflict theory* maintains that the principal source of inter-group conflict is *competition for scarce resources*.

20 Sherif *et al.* (1961) generated competition between two groups of white American boys at summer camp (the 'Rattlers' and the 'Eagles'). The boys competed for rewards, and negative attitudes quickly arose.

21 Tyerman & Spencer's (1983) findings *contradicted* Sherif *et al.*'s. Their four groups of scouts maintained strong inter-group relations despite being in competition. These relationships were established before the group was divided, and suggest that competition may not always be sufficient to produce prejudice.

Section 4: Social categorisation and social identity

22 The boys in Tajfel *et al.*'s (1971) minimal group experiments were assigned *arbitrarily* (e.g. by the toss of a coin).

23 Nothing – they neither knew the identity of, nor interacted with, their fellow group members.

24 Tajfel *et al.* discovered that the boys would always allocate more points to their own groups, even when a co-operative strategy would have been to both groups' advantage.

25 People tend to divide up the world into *ingroups* ('us') and *outgroups* ('them').

26 Prejudice is caused by categorising individuals into groups, since people favour their own groups (categorisation is a *sufficient* condition for prejudice).

27 The *ingroup differentiation hypothesis* is the ingroup's tendency to see many differences amongst themselves, whilst the *illusion of outgroup homogenity* is the tendency to see members of other groups as 'all the same'.

28 Wetherall (1982) found that Polynesian children were more *generous* towards the outgroup.

29 A positive self-image is comprised of a *personal identity* and a *social identity*.

30 In order to maintain positive self-images, we need to maintain positive images of the groups to which we belong, drawing social comparisons between these and others groups. This leads to disputes between groups.

31 Support for *social identity theory* is principally from minimal group experiments, which may lack ecological validity. Additionally, research only shows a *positive* bias towards the ingroup, not *derogatory* attitudes towards the outgroup.

Prejudice & Discrimination

Prejudice: an extreme *attitude* comprising three components common to all attitudes: *cognitive* (stereotypes), *affective* (negative feelings/emotions) and *behavioural* (discrimination)

Discrimination: the *behavioural* component of prejudice, ranging from anti-locution (e.g. racist jokes) to extermination (e.g. the attempted genocide of the Jews)

Emotional sources

The prejudiced personality

The authoritarian personality (Adorno *et al.*, 1950)
- Prejudice is the result of personality development.
- Children who are harshly disciplined might displace their aggression onto alternative targets (such as minority groups), especially those who are weaker or who cannot fight back.

Adorno *et al.* (1950) devised several personality inventories to measure:
- **Anti-semitism** (*AS scale*) (negative opinions of Jews)
- **Ethnocentrism** (*E scale*) (belief in own group's superiority)
- **Political–economic conservatism** (*PEC scale*) (resistance to change)
- **Potentiality for fascism** (*F scale*) (authoritarian trends)

Results: those who scored highly on the F-scale scored highly on the other scales, and were likely to have had the childhood described above.

Problems with Adorno *et al.*'s research
- Their scales consisted of statements which would always indicate authoritarianism if agreed with. This can produce biases due to *response set*.
- The original sample was *biased* (white, middle-class, non-Jewish Americans).
- The theory cannot explain *widespread prejudice* at times in history – Minard's (1952) study of white and black coal-miners suggests that *conformity to social norms* is a more likely explanation.

Frustration–aggression hypothesis

Dollard *et al.* (1939)
- Frustration always gives rise to aggression, and aggression is always caused by frustration.
- Frustration (caused by being blocked from achieving a desirable goal) cannot always be dealt with by direct aggression and we may displace the aggression onto a 'scapegoat'.

Naturalistic studies
- Hovland & Sears (1940): the number of lynchings of blacks between 1880 and 1930 in America was negatively correlated with cotton prices. As prices decreased, lynchings increased.
- Doty *et al.* (1991) confirmed that prejudice rises significantly in times of economic and social threat.

Laboratory studies
Weatherley (1961)
had experimenters insult students who scored either low or high on measures of anti-semitism.
- Both groups had to write short stories about pictures of men, two of whom had Jewish-sounding names.
- Groups did not differ in aggression shown towards non-Jews, but high-scorers showed more aggression when writing about those with Jewish names.

Social sources

Relative deprivation theory

- Frustration is produced by the discrepancy between our *expectations* and our *actual attainments*.
- Relative deprivation occurs when attainments fall short of rising expectations.
- *Fraternalistic deprivation* occurs when individuals compare their attainments with a dissimilar group (e.g. the Los Angeles riots, based on the poor treatment of Rodney King by comparison with whites).
- *Egoistic relative deprivation* occurs when individuals make comparisons with other similar individuals.
- Vivian & Brown (1995): the most militant blacks were those with high educational status, presumably because their expectations are high and their treatment still poor.

Realistic conflict theory

Robber's Cave field experiment
(Sherif *et al.*, 1961)
- Sherif (1966) proposes that prejudice arises as a consequence of competition for scarce resources. Competition is a sufficient condition for the occurrence of hostility or conflict.
- He divided twenty-two 11- and 12-year-old white middle-class boys attending summer camp into two groups who were housed separately out of sight of each other.
- Groups created strong group identities (the 'Rattlers' and the 'Eagles').
- Competitive events were organised and the two groups came to view each other in negative ways, fighting with each other.

Cognitive sources

Social categorisation theory

- People divide themselves into *ingroups* ('us') and *outgroups* ('them').
- This categorisation is *necessary* for discrimination, and *sufficient* by itself to produce discrimination.
- Ingroups see themselves *positively* and tend to see differences among themselves (*the ingroup differentiation hypothesis*).
- Outgroups are evaluated less favourably and seen to be all alike (*the illusion of outgroup homogeneity*).

Minimal group experiments
(Tajfel *et al.*, 1971)
- 14–15-year-old Bristol schoolboys were randomly assigned to one of two groups.
- Boys were told which group they belonged to but did not meet or interact with any of the others.
- Boys worked in cubicles on tasks involving allocating points to members of both groups.
- Boys allocated more points to their own groups, even when a co-operative strategy would have earned more points overall.

Tajfel concluded that just knowing that another group exists is sufficient for discrimination to occur.

Social identity theory

Tajfel & Turner (1986)
- People strive to maintain a *positive self-image*.
- There are two components to this:
  - *personal identity* (our personal traits)
  - *social identity* (derived from group-membership)

In order to enhance self-esteem, individuals make *social comparisons* with other groups, each trying to evaluate itself more highly. This leads to *social competition*.

54

THE REDUCTION OF PREJUDICE AND DISCRIMINATION

SYLLABUS
1.1 Social cognition
• the reduction of prejudice and discrimination

KEY QUESTIONS
• How can theories of prejudice help to reduce prejudice?
• Is prejudice a product of socialisation?
• What type of contact can help to reduce prejudice?
• How does racism relate to the development of childhood identity?

Section 1: Applying theories of prejudice

1 What two factors correlate highly with high *F-scale* scores in children?
2 How could *authoritarianism* be reduced in children?
3 What suggestions for reducing prejudice can be made from the *frustration–aggression* and *relative deprivation* approaches?
4 According to the *conflict approach*, what should replace competition if we wish to reduce prejudice?
5 How could the prejudice generated by social categorisation be reduced?

Section 2: Socialisation

6 According to *social learning theory*, what is the source of negative racial attitudes?
7 What does it mean to say that 'parents should encourage self-examination in their children'?
8 Complete the sentence: 'Parents could, therefore, stress to their children the importance of remembering to attribute behaviour to people as _____ rather than as group _____'.
9 How did Elliot (1977) enable her students to experience the effects of prejudice and discrimination directly?
10 Identify two ethical concerns which might apply to Elliot's study?
11 When Weiner & Wright (1973) conducted a similar experiment to Elliot using 'green' and 'orange' groups, how were the attitudes of those who had experienced prejudice later shown to differ from those who had not?

Section 3: The contact hypothesis

12 What is *autistic hostility*?
13 What term is used to describe the phenomenon in which both groups come to see themselves in the right and the opposition in the wrong?
14 Identify four reasons why increased contact might lead to a reduction in prejudice and discrimination.

15 Why might *increased contact* not be sufficient in itself for a reduction in prejudice to occur?
16 Which two additional suggestions for the reduction of prejudice are made in Allport's (1954) *contact hypothesis*?
17 What did Deutsch & Collins (1951) find when they studied the effects of integrated housing projects?
18 How can Minard's (1952) finding that white coal miners were far more friendly towards blacks underground than they were above ground be explained?
19 How can the continued hostility that exists between black and white groups in desegregated American schools be explained?
20 If two people from different groups enjoy positive interpersonal contact, why might their positive attitudes not generalise to each others' groups?
21 How did Sherif *et al.* (1961) succeed in reducing the prejudice which they had created between two groups of boys?
22 Under what conditions might Sherif *et al.*'s approach increase antagonism between two groups?
23 What was involved in Aronson *et al.*'s (1978) *jigsaw classroom technique*?
24 How successful was Aronson *et al.*'s approach at reducing prejudicial attitudes?

Section 4: Prejudice and childhood identity

25 What is the central *disagreement* which Milner (1996, 1997) expresses with the social learning approach to explaining prejudice?
26 According to Milner, what is the *primary motivation* behind the development of prejudicial attitudes in children?
27 How does this motivation relate to the phenomenon of *misidentification*?
28 What things are likely to reduce the significance of racism during childhood as the child develops?

Section 1: Applying theories of prejudice

1 The *F-scale* scores of parents and the *level of education* correlate highly with high F scale scores in children.

2 Authoritarianism could be reduced either by *changing child-rearing practices* (specifically by allowing children to express their hostility) or by *increasing access and provision of good education*.

3 The *frustration–aggression* and *relative deprivation* approaches would suggest that providing people with ways of venting their frustration, and changing social conditions so that people's expectations and actual achievements were similar, would help reduce prejudice.

4 *Competition* should be replaced with *co-operation*, according to the *conflict approach*.

5 The prejudice generated by social categorisation could be reduced by *breaking down negative stereotypes* of outgroups, and by *making the boundaries between groups less distinct*.

Section 2: Socialisation

6 Negative racial attitudes arise from '*significant others*' (such as parents, peers or teachers) or from the *media* (especially television and films).

7 Children should be encouraged to look *more closely* at the things they do or say to determine whether or not they reflect prejudice or discrimination (e.g. 'You're alright – you're just like a white person' - type statements).

8 'Parents could, therefore, stress to their children the importance of remembering to attribute behaviour to people as *individuals* rather than as group *representatives*.'

9 Elliot artificially created prejudice and discrimination amongst some students by encouraging discrimination towards other students based on their *eye-colour*.

10 The children were only nine years old and not in a position to give *informed consent* for the experiment. In addition, some may have suffered *stress and discomfort* as a consequence of the study.

11 Weiner & Wright (1973) found that nine-year-olds who had experienced discrimination were more likely to want to go on a picnic with black children from another school than groups who did not experience discrimination (96 per cent and 62 per cent respectively).

Section 3: The contact hypothesis

12 *Autistic hostility* is the view, arising from ignorance of other groups, that others are more dissimilar from us than they actually are.

13 The *mirror-image phenomenon*.

14 Increased contact might lead to a reduction in prejudice and discrimination for the following reasons: *groups realise that they are more similar than they assumed, and this leads to liking; mere exposure to a stimulus increases the degree to which it is liked; negative stereotypes may be disconfirmed; groups come to see other groups as comprised of unique individuals and not simply 'all the same'.*

15 *Increased contact* may fail if groups are of *unequal status*. In particular the 'superior' group may rationalise the inequality.

16 Allport's (1954) contact hypothesis suggests that *equal status contact* and the *pursuit of common goals* may reduce prejudice.

17 Deutsch & Collins (1951) found that residents of integrated housing schemes were *less* prejudiced than those who did not live in integrated housing.

18 Minard's (1952) finding may well be due to the equal status of black and white miners below ground and the pressure to conform to social norms above ground.

19 The continued hostility may be due to a failure to promote equal status for minority and majority groups, and a lack of unanimous support from all authority figures involved.

20 If people are not seen as typical members of a group, then positive attitudes towards them may not be generalised to their group.

21 Sherif *et al.* (1961) engineered a problem with their shared water supply, requiring the boys to *work together* to restore the supply. Working to achieve this *superordinate goal* reduced prejudice.

22 If the joint venture *fails*, this may increase antagonism between two groups.

23 Aronson *et al.*'s (1978) *jigsaw classroom technique* involved children working in small inter-racial groups. Each child was given part of a task, but all were tested on the whole, so they had to work together to succeed.

24 The approach reduced prejudice between the students concerned, but changes in attitudes may not be long-term or generalised to whole groups.

Section 4: Prejudice and childhood identity

25 Milner (1996, 1997) believes that racial attitudes are *not* developed *passively*, by absorbing others' attitudes, but by an *active* process of *constructing an identity*.

26 Children are motivated by a need to *locate themselves* and their groups within the social world in a way which promotes positive personal and social identities.

27 Children from minority groups may choose to identify with the majority group (*misidentification*) if they are prevented from forming a positive image of their own group.

28 Other things may come to satisfy the need for a positive social identity, such as membership of clubs and teams.

A

Reduction of Prejudice

Based on theories (Ch 53)

Prejudiced personality
High 'F' scores in children are correlated with parents' scores and with education.
Solutions
- access to good education.
- change child-rearing style, e.g. allow expression of hostilities.

Frustration–aggression hypothesis and relative deprivation
Social conditions lead to frustration.
Solutions
- provide people with less anti-social ways of venting frustration.
- lower people's expectations.

Conflict approaches
Hostility arises from competition.
Solutions
- remove competition and replace it with goals requiring co-operation.

Social categorisation and social identity
Prejudice arises from group identities.
Solutions
- reduce inter-group stereotypes.
- make the boundaries between groups less distinct.

Socialisation

Social learning theory suggests that children acquire negative attitudes as a result of parents, peers, teachers and the media (e.g. seeing groups in comic or demeaning roles on TV or film).
- Ashmore & Del Boca (1976): children's racial attitudes are often closely aligned with their parents'.

Solutions
- *Discouraging others*, especially in the media, from providing negative views which children may 'model'.
- Parents could encourage *self-examination* in their children, stressing the importance of seeing people as *individuals* rather than *group representatives*. (Hogg & Vaughan, 1995).

Experience of prejudice and discrimination
Jane Elliot (1977): divided her 9-year-old pupils into **blue-eyed** and **brown-eyed** groups.
- Treated groups differently depending on eye-colour.
- Children who were treated more poorly did more poorly in homework, and became depressed and angry.
- Children 'on top' treated outgroup very badly.
- When treatment was reversed, patterns reversed.
- Children were debriefed and were later found to express more tolerance of differences and opposition to prejudice.

Weiner & Wright (1973): 9-year-olds who went through a similar exercise in discrimination were more likely to want to go on a picnic with black children than a group who did not.

Childhood identity

Milner (1996, 1997): *disagrees* with the social learning view that the development of children's racial attitudes is a *passive* process in which children simply 'absorb' implicit or explicit racism from their culture.
- Children are *actively engaged* in constructing a sense of identity.
- This identity must locate themselves and their groups in a way which establishes and sustains a *positive self-* and *social-regard*.
- Negative racial attitudes may help the child to align itself with the majority group.
- However, the minority group cannot gain in self-esteem through negative racial attitudes and *misidentification* may occur, resulting in *self-denigration*.

Black and white dolls
Clark & Clark (1947): asked black and white children aged 3–7 to choose between a black or white doll to play with.
Regardless of their own colour, children chose to play with the white dolls, describing them as prettier and nicer.
Solutions
- 'Black is beautiful' campaigns helped to eliminate the misidentification phenomenon amongst minority groups.
- The majority group are less likely to 'need' racist attitudes as they gain a positive social identity from other sources (such as supporting a winning football team).

Contact approaches

Increased contact

- People who are segregated or separated have no way of checking whether an interpretation of, or stereotype about, another group is accurate.
- **Mirror-image phenomenon:** may result where each group sees itself in the right and the other in the wrong.

Explaining the effects of contact
- **Similarity:** groups may realise that their attitudes are more similar than they assumed. Similarity leads to liking.
- **The mere expose effect:** the more familiar stimuli are, the more we like them.
- **Negative stereotypes:** increased opportunities to disconfirm these.
- **The illusion of outgroup homogeneity:** may be reduced as people are increasingly seen as individuals.

However, in the USA many whites have regular contact with blacks who play menial roles. Under these conditions, stereotypes may be *reinforced*.

Equal status contact

Contact hypothesis *(Allport, 1954)*: 'Prejudice ... may be reduced by equal status contact between minority and majority groups in the pursuit of common goals'.

Integrated housing
Deutsch & Collins (1951) compared integrated and segregated housing projects. Residents of the integrated housing showed a decrease in prejudicial attitudes towards blacks.

Coalminers
Minard (1952) studied white coalminers in the USA, and found that underground 80% were friendly towards blacks, with only 20% being friendly above ground.
This suggests that equal status below ground and social norms above ground decreased, and increased prejudice.

However, school desegregation has not *always* been followed by a reduction in prejudice (Cook, 1984). This may be due to less than wholehearted support from the authorities, or a failure to fully implement equal status.

Pursuit of common goals

The 'Robbers Cave' field experiment
(Sherif *et al.*, 1961, see Ch 53).
- Sherif created prejudice between two groups of boys at summer camp by creating competition.
- Attempts to resolve this by having them eat together, and watch movies together failed (*desegregation*).
- However, when the shared water supply was 'cut off', and groups had to work together to restore it, prejudices and negative stereotypes were greatly reduced (*superordinate goals*).

Jigsaw classroom technique
(Aronson *et al.*, 1978)
- Students are allocated to small inter-racial groups.
- Each child is given a part of the lesson to be learned, and the group is tested on the *whole* lesson.
- In order to succeed, students must co-operate.

Although Aronson's jigsaw classroom did reduce prejudice, the effects may have been short-term and may fail to generalise to other groups. In addition, if the shared enterprise *fails*, groups may blame each other.

THE FORMATION OF ADULT RELATIONSHIPS

KEY QUESTIONS
- How is the formation of relationships affected by proximity and exposure?
- How significant is similarity in relationship formation?
- How does attractiveness influence relationship formation?
- How do reciprocity, complementarity and competence influence liking?

Section 1: Affiliation
1 How do psychologists define *affiliation*?
2 Under what circumstances would you expect the need for affiliation to be greatest?
3 What did Schachter (1959) find when he led groups of female students to believe they were about to receive either painful or painless electric shocks?
4 Complete the sentence: 'According to Clore & Byrne (1974), we are attracted to people whose presence is _____ for us'.

Section 2: Proximity and exposure
5 What did Festinger *et al.* (1950) discover when investigating the patterns of relationships formed between students living in campus accommodation?
6 According to Hall (1959), what are *proxemic rules*?
7 What is meant by saying that successful relationships may require an initial establishment of '*boundary understandings*'?
8 What is Zajonc's (1968) *mere exposure effect*?

Section 3: Similarity
9 What did Newcomb (1961) discover when comparing the effects of *similarity* and *familiarity*?
10 What is the relationship between sharing of attitudes and liking?
11 Identify Rubin's (1973) five reasons why similarity is *rewarding*.
12 What explanation for the effect of similarity on liking is offered by *balance theory* (Heider, 1946; Newcomb, 1953)?
13 How does balance theory differ from Rosenbaum's (1986) *repulsion hypothesis*?

Section 4: Physical attractiveness
14 What are the differences between the ways in which attractive and unattractive people are perceived?
15 Are there any exceptions to the rule 'what is beautiful, is good', according to psychological research?

16 What did Dion (1972) find when investigating *attributions* made for the bad behaviour of *attractive* or *unattractive children*?
17 Give four examples of the different criteria that different *cultures* have for physical attractiveness.
18 What did Brehm (1992) conclude was the primary '*resource*' offered by females in her study of commercial dating services?
19 What did Langlois & Roggman (1994) discover about '*average*' faces?
20 Which features did Perrett *et al.* (1994) find were consistently rated as being attractive in their cross-cultural study?
21 What did Wells *et al.* (1995) discover were correlates of high levels of hair loss?
22 If, according to *social exchange theory*, we look to maximise our rewards in our choice of partner, why do we settle for partners who are anything less than perfectly rewarding?
23 What is a *value-match*?
24 Are we most satisfied when *matched* with the partner we most desire?
25 What did Lykken & Tellegren (1993) discover when investigating *mate selection* in 738 sets of identical twins?

Section 5: Reciprocity and competence
26 What is *reciprocal liking*?
27 Who does Aronson & Linder's (1956) *gain–loss theory* predict we should like the most?
28 How much evidence is there to support the view that '*opposites attract*'?
29 What is the general rule concerning the relationship between *competence* and *attraction*?
30 How has Duck (1995) criticised research into the formation of relationships?

Section 1: Affiliation

1 Psychologists define *affiliation* as the basic need for the company of others.

2 The need for affiliation has been found to be greatest when moving to a new neighbourhood, on termination of a close relationship, and during times of anxiety.

3 Schachter (1959) found that those expecting to receive painful electric shocks (the high anxiety condition) were twice as likely to want to wait for the experiment in a room with another participant, rather than alone.

4 'According to Clore & Byrne (1974), we are attracted to people whose presence is *rewarding* for us.'

Section 2: Proximity and exposure

5 Festinger *et al.* (1950) discovered that students were most friendly with their next-door neighbours and least friendly with those living at the end of the corridor. Those living near stairways also had more friends than those living at the end of a corridor.

6 Hall (1959) sees *proxemic rules* as rules which prescribe the physical distance that is appropriate between people in daily situations, and the kinds of situation in which closeness or distance is proper.

7 Successful relationships may require that in the initial stages partners are *invited* into each other's personal space, rather than *invading* it.

8 The *mere exposure effect* (Zajonc, 1968) refers to a general tendency of people to prefer stimuli with which they are more familiar.

Section 3: Similarity

9 Newcomb (1961) discovered that whilst *similarity* was important in determining liking, the key factor was *familiarity*, which frequently led dissimilar room-mates to like each other.

10 Individuals are strongly attracted to people who share their attitudes, and the degree of liking is proportional to the proportion of attitudes shared.

11 Rubin (1973) believes that similarity may provide the *basis for shared activities, increase our confidence and self-esteem, encourage us to believe that the person is sensitive and praiseworthy*, and make it *easier to communicate*.

12 *Balance theory* (Heider, 1946; Newcomb, 1953) proposes that *similarity* is a consequence of our need for a 'balanced' world; to have different views to those of a friend would produce an *imbalance*, which can be resolved by changing our views or rejecting our friend.

13 Rosenbaum's (1986) *repulsion hypothesis* suggests that *disagreement* is more strongly motivating than *agreement*, and that it is this discomfort which motivates us to seek out those with similar views.

Section 4: Physical attractiveness

14 *Attractive* people are perceived as sexually warm and responsive, kind, strong, outgoing, nurturant, interesting, intelligent, more likely to be sought after and popular, more likely to be employed and as happier, more socially skilled and successful.

15 Dermer & Thiel (1975) found that extremely attractive females were judged to be egoistic, vain, materialistic and less likely to be successfully married.

16 Dion (1972) found that *bad behaviour* was explained in *situational* terms for *attractive* children and *dispositional* terms for *unattractive* children.

17 *Chipped teeth, body scars, artificially elongated heads* and *bound feet* have all been regarded as attractive in certain cultures.

18 Brehm (1992) concluded that the primary '*resource*' offered by females was *physical attractiveness*.

19 Langlois & Roggman (1994) found that producing an '*average*' *face* from digitised pictures of students resulted in a face which was more attractive than 96 per cent of the individual faces.

20 *High cheek bones,* a *thinner jaw* and *large eyes* (relative to facial size) were consistently regarded as *attractive*.

21 Wells *et al.* (1995) discovered that *low self-esteem, depression, neuroticism* and *psychoticism* were all correlates of hair loss.

22 If everybody is looking to maximise their rewards, then we must strike a *compromise* and settle for somebody who is roughly as rewarding as we are.

23 A *value-match* is the most rewarding person we could realistically hope to find (in our judgement).

24 No. We are most satisfied with the partner who we feel will not reject us.

25 The *mates selected* by the identical twins were *no more similar* than those selected by random pairs of adults. In addition, less than half reported finding their co-twin's mate attractive.

Section 5: Reciprocity and competence

26 *Reciprocal liking* refers to our tendency to like those who like us.

27 According to Aronson & Linder's (1956) theory, we should like most those people who come to like us after initially disliking us.

28 Very little. Winch (1958) found some degree of *complementarity of needs* between marriage partners.

29 In general we are more attracted to *competent* than *incompetent* people.

30 Duck (1995) argues that much of the research in this area is based on analyses of interactions where the partners are students, and tends to focus on immediate judgements of attractiveness or expressions of desire to see another person again. Additionally, follow-up studies or longitudinal research are rarely carried out.

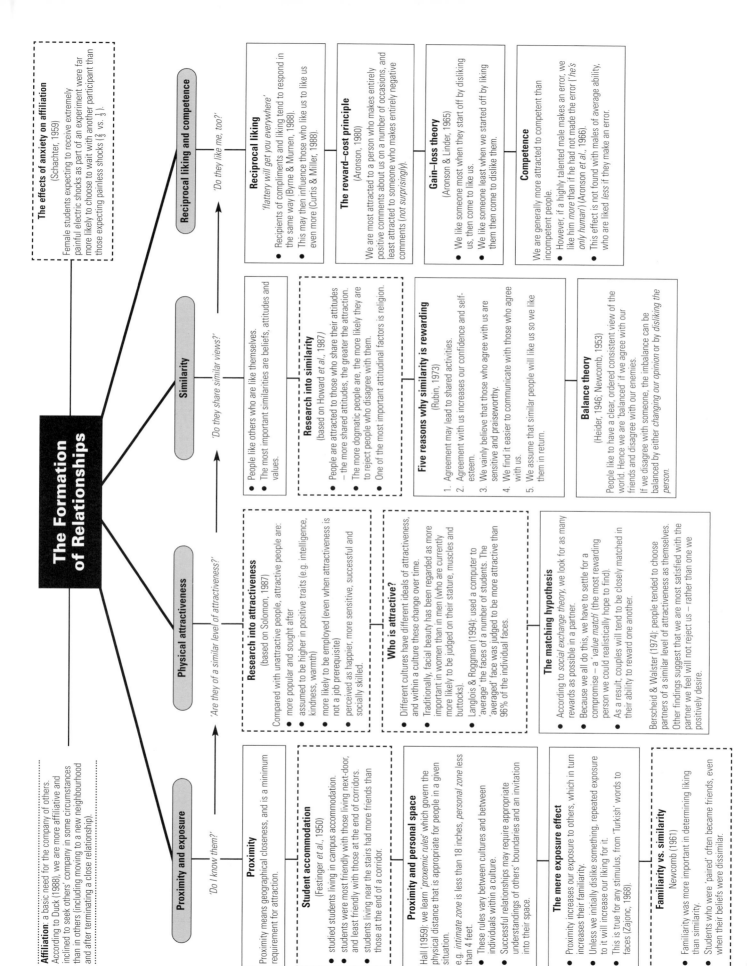

The Formation of Relationships

Affiliation

Affiliation: a basic need for the company of others. According to Duck (1988), we are more affiliative and inclined to seek others' company in some circumstances than in others (including moving to a new neighbourhood and after terminating a close relationship).

The effects of anxiety on affiliation
(Schachter, 1959)

Female students expecting to receive extremely painful electric shocks as part of an experiment were far more likely to choose to wait with another participant than those expecting painless shocks ($\frac{2}{3}$ vs. $\frac{1}{3}$).

Proximity and exposure
'Do I know them?'

Proximity

Proximity means geographical closeness, and is a minimum requirement for attraction.

Student accommodation
(Festinger et al., 1950)

- studied students living in campus accommodation.
- students were most friendly with those living next-door, and least friendly with those at the end of corridors.
- students living near the stairs had more friends than those at the end of a corridor.

Proximity and personal space

Hall (1959): we learn *proxemic rules* which govern the physical distance that is appropriate for people in a given situation.

e.g. *intimate zone* is less than 18 inches, *personal zone* less than 4 feet.

- These rules vary between cultures and between individuals within a culture.
- Successful relationships may require appropriate understandings of others' boundaries and an invitation into their space.

The mere exposure effect

- Proximity increases our exposure to others, which in turn increases their familiarity.
- Unless we initially dislike something, repeated exposure to it will increase our liking for it.
- This is true for any stimulus, from 'Turkish' words to faces (Zajonc, 1968).

Familiarity vs. similarity
Newcomb (1961)

- Familiarity was more important in determining liking than similarity.
- Students who were 'paired' often became friends, even when their beliefs were dissimilar.

Physical attractiveness
'Are they of a similar level of attractiveness?'

Research into attractiveness
(based on Solomon, 1987)

Compared with unattractive people, attractive people are:

- more popular and sought after
- assumed to be higher in positive traits (e.g. intelligence, kindness, warmth)
- more likely to be employed (even when attractiveness is not a job prerequisite)
- perceived as happier, more sensitive, successful and socially skilled.

Who is attractive?

- Different cultures have different ideals of attractiveness, and within a culture these change over time.
- Traditionally, facial beauty has been regarded as more important in women than in men (who are currently more likely to be judged on their stature, muscles and buttocks).
- Langlois & Roggman (1994): used a computer to 'average' the faces of a number of students. The 'averaged' face was judged to be more attractive than 96% of the individual faces.

The matching hypothesis

- According to *social exchange theory*, we look for as many rewards as possible in a partner.
- Because we all do this, we have to settle for a compromise – a *'value match'* (the most rewarding person we could realistically hope to find).
- As a result, couples will tend to be closely matched in their ability to reward one another.

Berscheid & Walster (1974): people tended to choose partners of a similar level of attractiveness as themselves. Other findings suggest that we are most satisfied with the partner we feel will not reject us – rather than one we positively desire.

Similarity
'Do they share similar views?'

- People like others who are like themselves.
- The most important similarities are beliefs, attitudes and values.

Research into similarity
(based on Howard et al., 1987)

- People are attracted to those who share their attitudes – the more shared attitudes, the greater the attraction.
- The more dogmatic people are, the more likely they are to reject people who disagree with them.
- One of the most important attitudinal factors is religion.

Five reasons why similarity is rewarding
(Rubin, 1973)

1. Agreement may lead to shared activities.
2. Agreement with us increases our confidence and self-esteem.
3. We vainly believe that those who agree with us are sensitive and praiseworthy.
4. We find it easier to communicate with those who agree with us.
5. We assume that similar people will like us so we like them in return.

Balance theory
(Heider, 1946; Newcomb, 1953)

People like to have a clear, ordered consistent view of the world. Hence we are 'balanced' if we agree with our friends and disagree with our enemies.

If we disagree with someone, the imbalance can be balanced by either *changing our opinion or by disliking the person.*

Reciprocal liking and competence
'Do they like me, too?'

Reciprocal liking

'flattery will get you everywhere'

- Recipients of compliments and liking tend to respond in the same way (Byrne & Murnen, 1988).
- This may then influence those who like us to like us even more (Curtis & Miller, 1988).

The reward–cost principle
(Aronson, 1980)

We are most attracted to a person who makes entirely positive comments about us on a number of occasions, and least attracted to someone who makes entirely negative comments (*not surprisingly*).

Gain–loss theory
(Aronson & Linder, 1965)

- We like someone most when they start off by disliking us, then come to like us.
- We like someone least when we started off by liking them then come to dislike them.

Competence

We are generally more attracted to competent than incompetent people.

- However, if a highly talented male makes an error, we like him *more* than if he had not made the error (*'he's only human'*) (Aronson et al., 1966).
- This effect is not found with males of average ability, who are liked *less* if they make an error.

THE MAINTENANCE OF ADULT RELATIONSHIPS

SYLLABUS

1.2 Social relationships
- explanations and research evidence relating to the maintenance of interpersonal relationships
- individual, social and cultural variations in the nature of interpersonal relationships

KEY QUESTIONS
- What is love?
- How does love differ across cultures?
- Are there stages in the development of relationships?
- Why do people stay together?

Section 1: Liking and loving

1 Define *liking*.
2 According to Rubin (1973), what are the three components of *love*?
3 What are the differences between *liking* and *loving*?
4 What three factors are correlated with couples' high scores on Rubin's '*love scale*'?
5 How does the nature of women's and men's loving differ?
6 Complete the sentence: 'For some researchers, love is a label which we learn to attach to our own state of _____ arousal'.
7 According to Berscheid & Walster (1978), what is the difference between *romantic* and *companionate love*?
8 What are the three basic components of Sternberg's (1986b, 1988) *love triangle*?

Section 2: Love across cultures

9 From which of Sternberg's (1986b, 1988) three components is *companionate* love comprised?
10 Give three reasons why it is important to study relationships across different cultures.
11 How do *individualistic cultures* differ from *collectivist cultures*?
12 What did Gupta & Singh (1992) discover when they compared Indian couples who had *married out of love* with couples who had entered into *arranged marriages*?

Section 3: Stage theories

13 Which is the first of the three filters in Kerckhoff & Davis's *filter theory* (1962), and determines the likelihood of couples meeting?
14 What do the letters SVR stand for, in Murstein's (1976, 1987) *stage theory*?
15 At which of the stages in Murstein's theory are the *external attributes* of a partner likely to be most important?
16 According to Levinger's (1980) *five-stage theory of relationships*, what is the third stage, which follows acquaintance/initial attraction, and building up the relationship?
17 What are the major criticisms levelled by Brehm (1992) against stage theories in general?

Section 4: What keeps people together?

18 In what sense is *exchange theory* an 'economic' theory of relationships?
19 What is Rubin's (1973) principal criticism of exchange theory?
20 How did research by Mills & Clark (1980) into different kinds of relationship support Rubin's criticism?
21 What is the extra component added to *reward*, *cost* and *profit* in *equity theory*?
22 According to equity theory, what is most likely to make us feel differently about a relationship?
23 Explain what is meant by the statement: 'When CL alt. exceeds the current ratio, then the relationship will be unlikely to continue'.
24 According to Argyle (1988), when are people in close relationships likely to begin thinking about rewards and costs?
25 In what way does *complementarity in resources* generally play a role in relationships?
26 What is Buss's (1988, 1989) explanation for the existence of sex differences regarding the relative importance of factors influencing their choice of partners?
27 How could the cultural and historical context in which men and women are placed offer an alternative explanation for differences in the mate selection process?
28 What type of relationship does Buss's account have difficulty explaining?
29 What factors do Hill *et al.* (1976) see as important predictors of whether or not relationships would break up?
30 According to Duck (1992), what are the characteristics of happy couples?

Section 1: Liking and loving

1 *Liking* can be defined as the *positive evaluation of another*, consisting of *respect* and *affection*.

2 According to Rubin (1973), *love* comprises *attachment, caring* and *intimacy*.

3 Rubin maintains that loving is more than an intense liking, and differs qualitatively in the ways described above.

4 Scores on the *liking scale, expectations of a permanent relationship*, and *high levels of eye-contact* are the factors which are positively correlated with couples' high scores on Rubin's 'love scale'.

5 Women are more likely to report loving same-sex friends and appear able to experience loving in a wider variety of contexts than are men, who channel loving into a single sexual relationship.

6 'For some researchers, love is a label which we learn to attach to our own state of *physiological* arousal.'

7 *Romantic love* is characterised by intense feelings of tenderness, elation, anxiety, and sexual desire, whilst *companionate love* is the affection remaining after this has subsided and is less intense, involving thoughtful appreciation of one's partner.

8 Sternberg's (1986b, 1988) *love triangle* proposed that love is comprised of *passion, intimacy* and *commitment* (or *decision*).

Section 2: Love across cultures

9 *Companionate love* lacks passion and is therefore comprised of *intimacy* and *commitment*.

10 Studying relationships across different cultures allows us to assess the degree to which theories are true universally, facilitate and understand the relationships that are increasingly occurring between people of different cultures, and comprehend differences in the rules of commerce between cultures.

11 *Individualistic cultures* place the greatest emphasis on personal achievement and self-reliance, whilst *collectivist cultures* prioritise the welfare and unity of the group.

12 Gupta & Singh (1992) discovered that couples who had *married out of love* reported diminished feelings of love after five years, whereas couples in *arranged marriages* (who were not newly-weds) reported more love.

Section 3: Stage theories

13 The first of the three filters in Kerckhoff & Davis's *filter theory* (1962) is the *sociological/demographic filter* (for example, determining the likelihood of individuals from a certain class, race, religion, meeting).

14 The letters SVR stand for *stimulus, value, role* (Murstein, 1976, 1987).

15 *External attributes* (such as physical appearance) are deemed to be most important during the *stimulus stage*.

16 The third of Levinger's (1980) five stages of relationships is the *consolidation* or *continuation stage*.

17 Brehm (1992) criticises stage theories, pointing out that there is only weak evidence for the existence of a fixed sequence of stages in interpersonal relationships, and that the expression 'phases' might better describe changes which take place at different times for different couples.

Section 4: What keeps people together?

18 *Exchange theory* is an 'economic' theory of relationships in that it proposes that our feelings for others are determined by our *profits* from them (how rewarding they are minus how costly they are).

19 Rubin (1973) points out that people are sometimes altruistic in the true sense of the word and do not consider first the rewards they might expect to receive for their actions.

20 Mills & Clark (1980) identified two types of couple, the *exchange* and *communal couples*. Only the former 'count the cost' of relationships, whilst the latter give out of concern for each other.

21 *Equity theory* proposes the extra component of *investment*.

22 Equity theory predicts that a *change in the ratio of rewards to costs* within a relationship is most likely to make us feel differently about that relationship.

23 *Comparison-level theory* proposes that we make comparisons between the ratio of rewards and costs we are currently receiving with the level we could receive elsewhere (comparison level for alternatives). If we could do better elsewhere, we will *feel dissatisfied*.

24 Argyle (1988) maintains that people begin thinking about rewards and costs in a relationship when they start to *feel dissatisfied*.

25 Generally, men seem to give higher priority to good looks in their partners, whilst women are more likely to consider men with good earning capacity.

26 Buss (1988, 1989) believes that the difference has an evolutionary basis aimed at maximising reproductive success. Hence, males choose young, healthy females, and females choose male providers who possess resources and power.

27 It could be that women choose mates with power and status because their culture denies them these things for themselves.

28 Buss's account has difficulty explaining *homosexual relationships*.

29 Hill *et al.* (1976) found that similarities of *age, intelligence, attractiveness, education* and *career plans* were important predictors of a lasting relationship, as well as *equal involvement in the relationship* and the partners describing themselves as *being 'in love'*.

30 Duck (1992) found that happy couples give more *positive and consistent non-verbal cues* than unhappy couples, *express more agreement with and approval of their partners, talk more about their relationships*, and are *more willing to compromise*.

A

Maintenance of Relationships

Liking: the positive evaluation of another, consisting of *respect* and *affection*.
Loving: qualitatively different from and more than an intense liking. Comprises *attachment* (a need for the physical presence), *caring* (a feeling of concern) and *intimacy* (the desire for close and confidential contact) towards the loved one (Rubin, 1973).

Loving

The love scale
(Rubin, 1973)

Rubin (1973) developed love scales to measure separately the degree of loving and liking:
- Couples do not always like each other to the degree that they love each other (and vice versa).
- Females report loving their female friends more than men do, and seem to experience a greater degree of intimacy.
- Men seem to channel loving into a single sexual relationship whilst women do not.

Romantic and companionate love
(Berscheid & Walster, 1978)

Romantic love: intense feelings of tenderness, elation, anxiety and sexual desire.

Companionate love: the affection that remains after romantic love subsides

The transition from romantic to companionate love is important if a relationship is to be maintained.

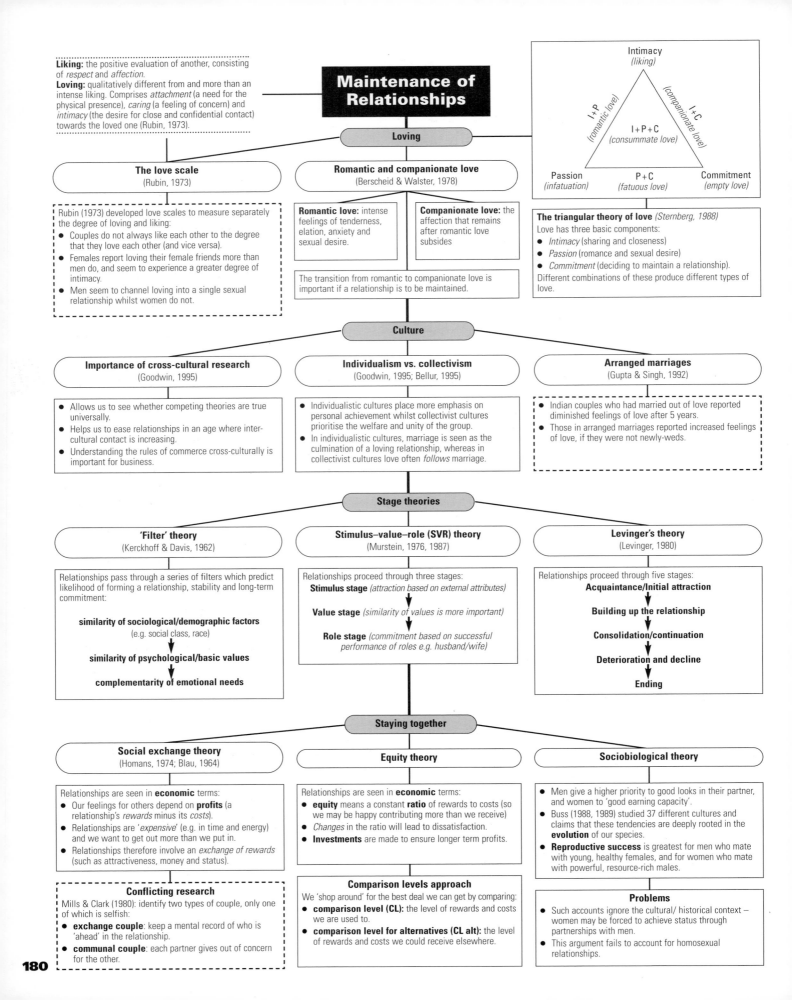

The triangular theory of love *(Sternberg, 1988)*
Love has three basic components:
- *Intimacy* (sharing and closeness)
- *Passion* (romance and sexual desire)
- *Commitment* (deciding to maintain a relationship).
Different combinations of these produce different types of love.

Culture

Importance of cross-cultural research
(Goodwin, 1995)

- Allows us to see whether competing theories are true universally.
- Helps us to ease relationships in an age where inter-cultural contact is increasing.
- Understanding the rules of commerce cross-culturally is important for business.

Individualism vs. collectivism
(Goodwin, 1995; Bellur, 1995)

- Individualistic cultures place more emphasis on personal achievement whilst collectivist cultures prioritise the welfare and unity of the group.
- In individualistic cultures, marriage is seen as the culmination of a loving relationship, whereas in collectivist cultures love often *follows* marriage.

Arranged marriages
(Gupta & Singh, 1992)

- Indian couples who had married out of love reported diminished feelings of love after 5 years.
- Those in arranged marriages reported increased feelings of love, if they were not newly-weds.

Stage theories

'Filter' theory
(Kerckhoff & Davis, 1962)

Relationships pass through a series of filters which predict likelihood of forming a relationship, stability and long-term commitment:

similarity of sociological/demographic factors
(e.g. social class, race)
↓
similarity of psychological/basic values
↓
complementarity of emotional needs

Stimulus–value–role (SVR) theory
(Murstein, 1976, 1987)

Relationships proceed through three stages:
Stimulus stage *(attraction based on external attributes)*
↓
Value stage *(similarity of values is more important)*
↓
Role stage *(commitment based on successful performance of roles e.g. husband/wife)*

Levinger's theory
(Levinger, 1980)

Relationships proceed through five stages:
Acquaintance/Initial attraction
↓
Building up the relationship
↓
Consolidation/continuation
↓
Deterioration and decline
↓
Ending

Staying together

Social exchange theory
(Homans, 1974; Blau, 1964)

Relationships are seen in **economic** terms:
- Our feelings for others depend on **profits** (a relationship's *rewards* minus its *costs*).
- Relationships are *'expensive'* (e.g. in time and energy) and we want to get out more than we put in.
- Relationships therefore involve an *exchange of rewards* (such as attractiveness, money and status).

Conflicting research
Mills & Clark (1980): identify two types of couple, only one of which is selfish:
- **exchange couple**: keep a mental record of who is 'ahead' in the relationship.
- **communal couple**: each partner gives out of concern for the other.

Equity theory

Relationships are seen in **economic** terms:
- **equity** means a constant **ratio** of rewards to costs (so we may be happy contributing more than we receive)
- *Changes* in the ratio will lead to dissatisfaction.
- **Investments** are made to ensure longer term profits.

Comparison levels approach
We 'shop around' for the best deal we can get by comparing:
- **comparison level (CL):** the level of rewards and costs we are used to.
- **comparison level for alternatives (CL alt):** the level of rewards and costs we could receive elsewhere.

Sociobiological theory

- Men give a higher priority to good looks in their partner, and women to 'good earning capacity'.
- Buss (1988, 1989) studied 37 different cultures and claims that these tendencies are deeply rooted in the **evolution** of our species.
- **Reproductive success** is greatest for men who mate with young, healthy females, and for women who mate with powerful, resource-rich males.

Problems
- Such accounts ignore the cultural/historical context – women may be forced to achieve status through partnerships with men.
- This argument fails to account for homosexual relationships.

57

THE DISSOLUTION OF ADULT RELATIONSHIPS

SYLLABUS

1.2 Social relationships
- explanations and research evidence relating to the dissolution of interpersonal relationships
- effects of interpersonal relationships, e.g. on happiness and health
- components of interpersonal relationships, for example, goals and conflicts, rules, power and roles

KEY QUESTIONS
- What are the positive effects of relationships?
- What patterns of marital unhappiness and divorce have been discovered?
- What are the effects of the dissolution of a relationship?
- How do dissolution and reconciliation occur?

Section 1: Positive effects of relationships

1 What relationship did William Farr discover in 1885 between mortality and marital status?
2 When Cramer (1994) compared single, divorced, and widowed people, what three positive effects did he find were associated with being married?
3 When Cochrane (1996) looked at mortality rates for divorced, married and single people, who were the most likely to die in any given year?
4 Identify three reasons why marriage may be beneficial.
5 What alternative explanation is offered by the *selection for marriage hypothesis*?

Section 2: Patterns of unhappiness/divorce

6 Name the factors identified by Duck (1988, 1992) as contributing to *marital unhappiness* and *divorce*.
7 According to McGhee (1996), what kind of communication strategy is a good predictor of dissatisfaction experienced by wives?
8 How do women differ from men with regard to the number and type of problems reported within relationships?
9 What two factors determine changes in marital satisfaction on Pineo's (1961) *linear model*?
10 According to Burr's (1970) *curvilinear model*, when is marital satisfaction likely to be high?
11 What alternative to Pineo's and Burr's models was proposed by Gilford & Bengston (1979)?
12 What type of attribution is an individual employing a *relationship-enhancing approach* to conflict resolution likely to make for their partner's negative behaviour?
13 What type of attribution is an individual employing a *distress-maintaining approach* to conflict resolution likely to make for their partner's negative behaviour?
14 Identify three rules which are common to most relationships, according to Argyle & Henderson (1984).

Section 3: Effects of dissolution

15 Identify the ill effects that Duck (1992) found that people in disrupted relationships are susceptible to.
16 According to Cochrane (1983, 1996), how much more likely are the *divorced* to be admitted to mental hospital in any one year than married people?
17 What important difference exists between the way men and women suffer the detrimental effects of divorce?
18 How does Fincham (1997) attempt to account for the differences between the way in which divorce affects men and women?
19 Complete the following sentence: 'Buehler & Legge (1993) found that following relationship dissolution, ___ and other reassurances to self-esteem improved the level of psychological well-being in a sample of 144 women with children'.

Section 4: Dissolution and reconciliation processes

20 Name the five stages of pre-marital romantic breakups in Lee's (1984) model.
21 Which of Lee's stages are experienced as the most dramatic and exhausting stages of the break-up?
22 What did Lee find was the effect of a particularly long transition through these stages of break-up?
23 Name the features of the first phase (*intrapsychic phase*) of Duck's (1982, 1988) model of relationship dissolution.
24 Which phase follows the *intrapsychic phase*?
25 What is the purpose of the '*grave-dressing*' *phase*, the final phase in Duck's model?
26 Rusbult (1987) has proposed an *exit–neglect–voice–loyalty model* of relationship dissolution. Which of these alternatives are *passive* or *active*, and which are *constructive* or *destructive*?
27 What is the central claim of Felmlee's (1995) *fatal-attraction model* of relationship breakdown?

Section 1: Positive effects of relationships

1 Farr discovered that married people tend to *live longer*.
2 Cramer (1994) found that married people are *happier, healthier* and have *lower rates of mental illness* than the single, widowed or divorced.
3 Cochrane (1996) found that *divorced* people were the most likely to die in any given year.
4 Marriage may protect against ill health by *boosting self-esteem,* by *providing intimacy and security, home-building, sexual satisfaction and social support.*
5 The *selection-for-marriage-hypothesis* suggests that mental health status causes marital status, and a predisposition to illness will reduce the likelihood of a person marrying.

Section 2: Patterns of unhappiness/divorce

6 Duck (1988, 1992) identifies marriages in which the partners are *younger than usual,* from *lower socioeconomic groups* and *educational levels,* from *different demographic backgrounds,* and who have experienced *parental divorce as children,* as prone to *marital unhappiness and divorce.*
7 McGhee (1996) found that *manipulative and coercive communication strategies* were good predictors of dissatisfaction experienced by wives.
8 Women report more problems, and stress basic unhappiness and incompatibility, than do men.
9 Pineo's (1961) *linear model* suggest that the *fading of the romantic 'high'* and a *reduction over time of compatibility* cause changes in marital satisfaction.
10 According to Burr's (1970) *curvilinear model,* marital satisfaction is likely to be *high* in the *earliest and later years of marriage.*
11 Gilford & Bengston (1979) propose that it is more productive to look at the pattern of positive rewards and the pattern of negative costs.
12 An individual employing a *relationship-enhancing approach* to conflict resolution is likely to make an *external attribution* for their partner's negative behaviour.
13 An individual employing a *distress-maintaining approach* to conflict resolution is likely to make an *internal attribution* for their partner's negative behaviour.
14 Argyle & Henderson (1984) identified '*respecting other people's privacy*', '*not discussing what has been said in private*' and '*being emotionally supportive*' as rules which apply to most relationships.

Section 3: Effects of dissolution

15 Duck (1992) found that people in disrupted relationships are susceptible to *coronary heart disease, alcoholism, drug dependency* and *sleep disturbances.*
16 Cochrane (1983, 1996) found that the *divorced* are *five-and-a-half times* more likely to be admitted to mental hospital in any one year than married people.
17 Men tend to suffer detrimental effects *after* divorce, whereas women tend to suffer detrimental effects *before* divorce.
18 Fincham (1997) argues that women *value* relationships more than men, and feel *greater responsibility* for making the relationship work. When it does not, this can cause depression.
19 'Buehler & Legge (1993) found that following relationship dissolution, *companionship* and other reassurance to self-esteem improved the level of psychological well-being in a sample of 144 women with children.'

Section 4: Dissolution and reconciliation processes

20 The five stages of pre-marital romantic breakups are *dissatisfaction, dissatisfaction exposed, negotiation, attempts to resolve the problem,* and *relationship terminated* (Lee, 1984).
21 Lee found that *exposure* and *negotiation* are experienced as the most dramatic and exhausting stages.
22 Lee found that a particularly long transition through these stages of break-up caused people to feel more attracted to their ex-partners and experience the greatest loneliness and fear during the break-up.
23 The intrapsychic phase is characterised by a *personal focus on the partner's behaviour,* an *assessment of the adequacy of the partner's role performance,* a *depiction and evaluation of the negative aspects of being in the relationship,* a *consideration of the costs of withdrawal,* an *assessment of the positive aspects of alternative relationships,* and *facing the 'express/repress' dilemma.*
24 The *dyadic phase* follows on from the intrapsychic phase.
25 The *'grave-dressing'* phase involves providing a credible and socially acceptable account of the relationship's life and death, helping to save face and 'justify' the original commitment.
26 *Exit* and *neglect* are *destructive,* voice and *loyalty* constructive. *Neglect* and *loyalty* are passive, exit and *voice,* active.
27 Felmlee's (1995) *fatal-attraction model* of relationship breakdown claims that the perceived characteristics of a person who initially attract someone to him/her are also the characteristics that lead to the breakdown of a relationship.

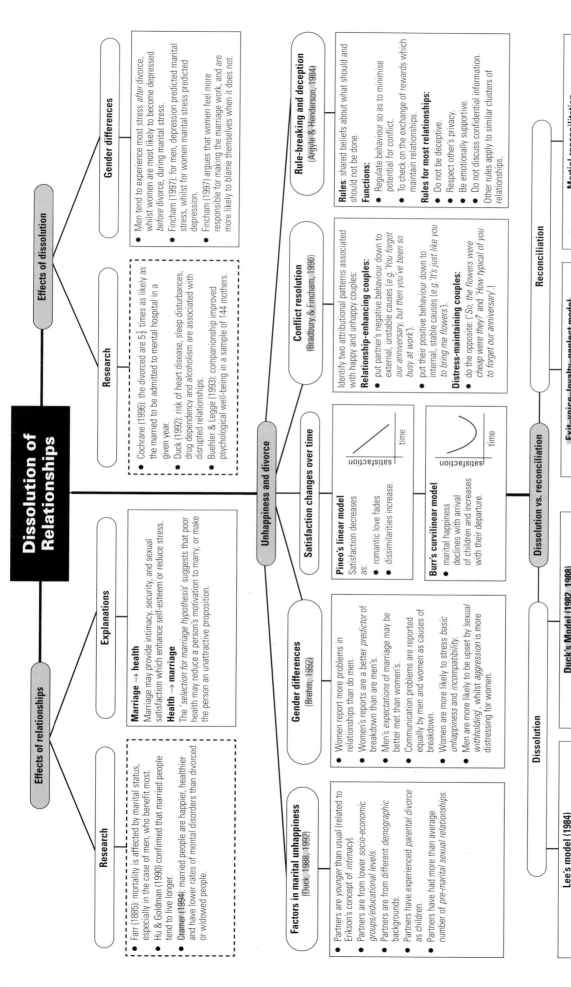

Dissolution of Relationships

Effects of relationships

Research
- Farr (1885): mortality is affected by marital status, especially in the case of men, who benefit most.
- Hu & Goldman (1990) confirmed that married people tend to live longer.
- Cramer (1994): married people are happier, healthier and have lower rates of mental disorders than divorced or widowed people.

Explanations
Marriage → health
Marriage may provide intimacy, security, and sexual satisfaction which enhance self-esteem or reduce stress.

Health → marriage
The 'selection for marriage hypothesis' suggests that poor health may reduce a person's motivation to marry, or make the person an unattractive proposition.

Effects of dissolution

Research
- Cochrane (1996): the divorced are 5½ times as likely as the married to be admitted to mental hospital in a given year.
- Duck (1992): risk of heart disease, sleep disturbances, drug dependency and alcoholism are associated with disrupted relationships.
- Buehler & Legge (1993): companionship improved psychological well-being in a sample of 144 mothers.

Gender differences
- Men tend to experience most stress *after* divorce, whilst women are most likely to become depressed *before* divorce, during marital stress.
- Fincham (1997): for men, depression predicted marital stress, whilst for women marital stress predicted depression.
- Fincham (1997) argues that women feel more responsible for making the marriage work, and are more likely to blame themselves when it does not.

Unhappiness and divorce

Factors in marital unhappiness
(Duck, 1988, 1992)
- Partners are *younger* than usual (related to Erikson's concept of *intimacy*).
- Partners are from lower *socio-economic groups/educational levels*.
- Partners are from different *demographic* backgrounds.
- Partners have experienced *parental divorce* as children.
- Partners have had more than average number of *pre-marital sexual relationships*.

Gender differences
(Brehm, 1992)
- Women report more problems in relationships than do men.
- Women's reports are a better *predictor* of breakdown than are men's.
- Men's *expectations* of marriage may be better met than women's.
- Communication problems are reported equally by men and women as causes of breakdown.
- Women are more likely to stress *basic unhappiness and incompatibility*.
- Men are more likely to be upset by *sexual withholding*, whilst *aggression* is more distressing for women.

Satisfaction changes over time

Pineo's linear model
Satisfaction decreases as:
- romantic love fades
- dissimilarities increase.

Burr's curvilinear model
- marital happiness declines with arrival of children and increases with their departure.

Conflict resolution
(Bradbury & Fincham, 1990)
Identify two attributional patterns associated with happy and unhappy couples:

Relationship-enhancing couples:
- put partner's negative behaviour down to external, unstable causes (*e.g. 'You forgot our anniversary, but then you've been so busy at work'*).
- put their positive behaviour down to internal, stable causes (*e.g. 'It's just like you to bring me flowers'*).

Distress-maintaining couples:
- do the opposite: (*'So, the flowers were cheap were they?'* and *'How typical of you to forget our anniversary'*).

Rule-breaking and deception
(Argyle & Henderson, 1984)

Rules: shared beliefs about what should and should not be done.

Functions:
- Regulate behaviour so as to minimise potential for conflict.
- To check on the exchange of rewards which maintain relationships.

Rules for most relationships:
- Do not be deceptive.
- Respect other's privacy.
- Be emotionally supportive.
- Do not discuss confidential information.

Other rules apply to similar clusters of relationships.

Dissolution vs. reconciliation

Dissolution

Lee's model (1984)
Five stages in the breakup of pre-marital romance.
1. **Dissatisfaction** (D): is discovered.
2. **Exposure** (E): dissatisfaction exposed.
3. **Negotiation** (N): about the dissatisfaction.
4. **Resolution** (R): attempts at resolution made.
5. **Termination** (T): relationship terminated.
- Of 112 pre-marital relationships surveyed, Lee found (E) and (N) to be experienced as the most dramatic.
- Where passage from (D) to (T) was prolonged, people experienced greatest loneliness and fear during breakup.

Duck's Model (1982, 1988)
Four phases in the breakup of relationships.
Intrapsychic phase: dissatisfaction is internal, focus on partner's inadequacy, assess costs of withdrawal and attractions of other relationships.
Dyadic phase: decide to confront/avoid partner, negotiate repair/withdrawal.
Social phase: problems made public, blame-placing stories constructed, 'intervention teams' (family/friends) may try to help.
Grave-dressing phase: each partner constructs an acceptable account of what went wrong to preserve their reputation.

Reconciliation

Exit–voice–loyalty–neglect model
Rusbult (1987)
4 basic responses to relationship dissatisfaction: *exit* (leaving), *neglect* (ignoring), *voice* (articulating concerns), *loyalty* (staying and accepting things.)

Martial reconciliation
Wineberg (1994)
Wineberg studied 506 white women who had attempted reconciliations. Overall, 30% were successful. The key factors linked with reconciliation were:
- Both partners were of the same religion.
- Cohabitation with a partner before marriage.
- Marriage with a partner of the same age.

Factors linked with dissolution included age at separation, duration of marriage, and education.

183

CONFORMITY

Section 1: Introducing conformity

1 How do Zimbardo & Leippe (1991) define *conformity*?
2 What is the difference between a *membership group* and a *reference group*?
3 What is the *autokinetic effect*?
4 Complete the sentence: 'By observing the convergence of participants' individual estimates when placed in a group, Sherif was able to study the development of a _____ _____ in the laboratory'.
5 Why, according to Asch (1951), did Sherif's experiments fail to demonstrate conformity?

Section 2: The Asch paradigm

6 What task did Asch devise in order to study conformity?
7 In what important way did this task differ from Sherif's task?
8 How many errors were made on Asch's task when participants were not influenced by group pressure?
9 How did Asch create *group pressure* in order to study its effects on a single participant?
10 What was the *mean conformity rate* in Asch's first studies of group pressure effects?
11 Identify five explanations given by Asch's participants in explaining their conforming behaviour.
12 When a single confederate was instructed to give the wrong answer when in a group of 16 naïve participants, what was their reaction?
13 What did Bogdonoff *et al.* (1961) discover when investigating *stress* in naïve participants in Asch-type experiments?
14 Does an increase in group size always result in an increase in conformity?
15 What is the relationship between *unanimity* and conformity?
16 How did Sistrunk & McDavid (1971) use groups of men and women to demonstrate that *task familiarity* influences conformity?
17 Do men or women conform more?

18 Identify four other factors which have been found to influence the likelihood of participants conforming to group pressure.
19 Give two criticisms of the original experimental procedure used by Asch to investigate conformity.
20 How did Crutchfield (1954) attempt to overcome criticisms of Asch's procedure?
21 According to Moscovici & Faucheux (1972), why should we see the naïve participants in Asch's studies as the *majority*?
22 What can Asch-type studies tell us about minorities, according to Moscovici and Faucheux?
23 Name three of the reasons why, according to Hogg & Vaughan (1995), *consistency* is an important factor in minority influence?

Section 3: Why do people conform?

24 What is the difference between *informational social influence* and *normative social influence*?
25 When Schachter (1951) instructed a confederate to disagree with the majority over the issue of sentencing a delinquent, how was the confederate treated?
26 What is the difference between *internalisation* and *compliance*?
27 Complete the sentence: 'The dual-process dependency model of social influence underestimates the role of _____ _____ in determining the degree of conformity'.
28 According to Abrams *et al.* (1990), when does social influence occur?

Section 4: Conformity: good or bad?

29 What valuable social purpose served by conformity is identified by Zimbardo & Leippe (1991)?
30 What assumption, implicit in much research into conformity, was made explicit by Asch (1952)?
31 Why might a conforming response sometimes be a rational response?

Section 1: Introducing conformity

1 Zimbardo & Leippe (1991) define *conformity* as 'a change in belief or behaviour in response to real or imagined group pressure when there is no direct request to comply with the group, nor any reason to justify the behaviour change'.

2 A *membership group* is a group to which one belongs, whilst a *reference group* is a group which, although one is not a member, one admires and respects.

3 The *autokinetic effect* refers to the apparent movement of a stationary point of light in an otherwise dark room.

4 'By observing the convergence of participants' individual estimates when placed in a group, Sherif was able to study the development of a *group norm* in the laboratory.'

5 Asch (1951) argued that since Sherif's task was *ambiguous*, with no right or wrong answer, one could not draw conclusions about conformity.

Section 2: The Asch paradigm

6 Asch devised a simple perceptual task involving the estimation of line lengths in order to study conformity.

7 Unlike Sherif's task, Asch's task was *unambiguous*, with responses which were clearly correct or incorrect.

8 When participants were not influenced by group pressure, very few errors were made (*0.42 per cent*).

9 Asch instructed several confederates to give unanimously wrong answers on certain critical trials. Since 'naïve participants' heard these incorrect responses before giving their own responses, they experienced pressure to conform.

10 *Thirty-two per cent* of the incorrect responses were agreed with in Asch's first studies (the *mean conformity rate*).

11 Asch's participants explained their conforming behaviour by saying that *they didn't wish to upset the experiment*, that *they doubted they could see the task material properly* or were *suffering from eye-strain*, that they *didn't wish to appear foolish/different*, or that they had been *unaware of giving incorrect answers*.

12 When a single confederate gave the wrong answer, the 16 naïve participants reacted with laughter and sarcasm.

13 Bogdonoff *et al.* (1961) discovered that naïve participants showed increases in measures of arousal associated with stress when hearing incorrect responses, and could reduce this arousal by conforming.

14 No. The relationship is not linear; a single confederate has little effect, two confederates typically produce 14 per cent conformity in Asch-type experiments, three confederates produce near-maximum conformity of 32 per cent, and subsequent increases make little difference.

15 If the *unanimity* of a group is punctured, it seems to exert far less group pressure, and conformity levels decrease.

16 Sistrunk & McDavid (1971) asked men and women to identify kitchen utensils and tools. The women were more likely to conform when identifying tools, and the men when identifying kitchen utensils.

17 Women tend to conform more than men when responses are public, but when responses are made privately this difference seems to disappear (Eagly & Steffen, 1984).

18 *Self-esteem*, *concern about social relationships*, a *need for social approval* and *attraction towards other group members* have all been found to influence the degree to which participants conform to group pressure.

19 Asch's original experimental procedure was *time consuming* to set up, and *uneconomical* in that only one naïve participant at a time could be tested.

20 Crutchfield (1954) automated Asch's procedure, placing participants in a booth with a set of lights which supposedly indicated other participants' responses. However, they were in fact controlled by the experimenter, and so no confederates were needed.

21 Moscivici & Faucheux (1972) argue that since the naïve participants are actually expressing the conventional or self-evident view, we should see them as the majority.

22 Asch-type studies can tell us how the *active minority* manages to influence the views of the majority.

23 Hogg & Vaughan (1995) see consistency as *disrupting the majority norm*, *drawing attention to the minority*, *identifying an alternative view*, *demonstrating certainty*, and *revealing the minority viewpoint as the only possible solution to a conflict*.

Section 3: Why do people conform?

24 *Informational social influence* involves making reference to others in order to determine social reality, whereas *normative social influence* is used to determine what is acceptable.

25 Schachter (1951) found that the group tried to convince the confederate to agree, and when he did not, largely ignored him.

26 *Internalisation* involves changing one's private beliefs so as to be consistent with a public belief, whilst *compliance* involves a change in behaviour which does not correspond to the individual's private beliefs.

27 'The dual-process dependency model of social influence underestimates the role of *group membership* in determining the degree of conformity.'

28 Abrams *et al.* (1990) claim that social influence occurs when we see ourselves as belonging to a group and possessing the same characteristics as others.

Section 4: Conformity: good or bad?

29 Zimbardo & Leippe (1991) believe that conformity enables us to structure our social behaviour and predict the reactions of others.

30 The assumption that independence is 'good' and conformity 'bad'.

31 If the information which we have about a situation is biased or limited, then conforming to the views or behaviour of others may be the most rational option.

Conformity

Conformity: a change in belief or behaviour in response to real or imagined group pressure (Zimbardo & Leippe, 1991).
Groups: may be those to which the individual belongs (*membership groups*) or those whom the person admires or respects (*reference groups*) but does not belong.

Group norms
Sherif (1935): had participants make estimates of the amount by which a spot of light in a dark room appeared to move (*autokinetic effect*).
Results: the private estimates made by participants converged towards an average when they were members of a group (*emergence of a group norm*).

Asch's research

Factors affecting conformity

Using the Asch paradigm, researchers have manipulated variables in order to discover their influence:

Group size
With one confederate only, conformity is low (3%). This rises to 14% with two confederates, and 32% with three. Further increases in group size have no effect.

Unanimity
When unanimity is 'punctured' (e.g. by a single non-conforming stooge), conformity decreases greatly.

Task difficulty, ambiguity and familiarity
With difficult or ambiguous tasks, conformity increases. Where the task is familiar (e.g. identifying familiar objects), conformity decreases.

Gender/individual differences
Men conform less than women when their conformity/independence will be made public. Conformity increases when naïve participants are low in self-esteem, have a strong need for social approval, or are attracted to other group members.

The Asch paradigm

Unlike Sherif's study, Asch (1951) presented participants with an *unambiguous* situation to see if they would conform to an obviously *wrong* answer.
- Asch devised a simple perceptual task involving judging which of three lines matched a comparison line in length.
- Pilot studies found an error rate of less than 0.5% when participants performed alone.
- Some participants were then selected as confederates and instructed to give incorrect answers when given a secret signal.
- A single naïve participant was placed in this group, and was last or next to last to respond.

Results: when confederates gave incorrect answers, naïve participants would give incorrect responses about one-third of the time. About three-quarters of participants conformed at least once.

Participants' explanations
- Didn't want to 'upset the experiment'.
- Didn't want to appear different/foolish.
- Weren't aware they had given incorrect responses.
- Wondered if they were suffering from eye-strain.

Bogdonoff *et al.* (1961): naïve participants experienced stress when hearing incorrect responses, but this decreased if they conformed.

Automating Asch's procedure
(Crutchfield, 1954)

Asch's experiment was time-consuming to set up and uneconomical, requiring many confederates for each naïve participant.
- Crutchfield seated participants in a cubicle with a panel of lights supposedly representing the responses of participants in other cubicles.
- In fact, the lights were controlled by the experimenter and the need for confederates was removed altogether.

Minority vs. majority influence

- Moscovici & Faucheux (1972): although naïve participants are *numerically* a minority, it is more profitable to think of them as the *majority*, since they embody the conventional view.
- We need, therefore, to understand how active minorities (in this case the confederates) were able to influence the majority.
- Moscovici (1976): the *consistency* of the minority appeared to be the most important factor.

Why is consistency important?
(Hogg & Vaughan, 1995)
- It disrupts the majority norm and produces uncertainty.
- It draws attention to the minority as an entity.
- It identifies an alternative, coherent point of view.
- It demonstrates uncertainty and commitment to that view.
- It shows that the solution to the conflict is the minority view.

Informational social influence (ISI)

Festinger's (1954) *social comparison theory* states that people have a basic need to confirm that their beliefs are correct. In ambiguous/novel situations, we look to others for 'guidance' about our social reality. The less we are able to rely on our own perceptions, the more we will be susceptible to informational influence from others.

Normative social influence (NSI)

People need to be accepted by others and create a favourable impression, so they accept the view of the majority rather than risking rejection.

Non-conformity and rejection
Schachter (1951): when a confederate was instructed to disagree with the majority over the sentencing of a fictitious delinquent ('*Johnny Rocco*'), the group initially tried to get him to conform to their views, then largely ignored and rejected him when he failed to do so.

Why do people conform?
(Deutsch & Gerard, 1955)

Internalisation and compliance

Internalisation occurs when a private belief becomes consistent with a public belief or opinion. The individual conforms 'truly', *accepting* the majority view.
Compliance occurs when people give answers which they do not really believe. Conformity may sometimes be more accurately described as 'internalisation' (as in Sherif's experiments) or 'compliance' (as is more likely in Asch's experiments).

Group belongingness

The distinction between NSI and ISI has been called the *dual process dependency model of social influence* and has been criticised for underestimating the role of group 'belongingness' in conformity.

Referential social influence
Abrams *et al.* (1990): social influence only occurs when we disagree with those with whom we *expect to agree* (e.g. when others are similar to us or belong to the same group). On this model, the degree of similarity or common group membership will influence conformity.

59

OBEDIENCE

SYLLABUS
1.3 Social influence
• research relating to obedience and independent behaviour

KEY QUESTIONS
• How do conformity and obedience differ?
• How did Milgram investigate obedience?
• What factors did Milgram find influenced the amount of obedience exhibited?
• How can we explain Milgram's findings?
• What can we learn from Milgram's research?

Section 1: Milgram's research

1 What three differences did Milgram (1992) identify between *conformity* and *obedience*?

2 What was the original purpose of Milgram's research into obedience?

3 How did Milgram obtain participants for his investigation?

4 What was the role of *Mr Wallace*?

5 What were the '*teachers*' in Milgram's experiment instructed to do?

6 In the '*voice feedback*' variation of Milgram's experiments, what did the learner do as the experiment progressed?

7 In what way did the experimenter (*Mr Williams*) deal with participants' reluctance to continue?

8 What percentage of the participants in Milgram's initial study administered the highest voltage to the 'learners'?

9 Milgram describes a number of behaviours common to the participants in the role of 'teacher'. Describe three of them.

10 How did Milgram subsequently vary the *institutional context* of his experiments?

11 What result did Milgram obtain when the teacher was in the same room as the learner or had to force the learner's hand onto a shock plate?

12 In what way did Milgram vary the *remoteness* of the authority figure in his experiments?

13 Which of Milgram's variations on his basic design produced the highest levels of obedience?

14 Complete the following sentence: 'The effects of _____ _____ are most impressive in undercutting the experimenter's authority'.

15 Which of Milgram's variations produced the lowest levels of obedience?

Section 2: Explaining Milgram's findings

16 How might the '*credibility*' of the situation provide an explanation for Milgram's findings?

17 What experiment involving caged puppies, casts doubt on the 'credibility' explanation?

18 What experiment did Hofling *et al.* (1966) carry out, suggesting that high levels of obedience are not limited to laboratory settings?

19 What is the effect of *diffusion of responsibility* on obedience levels?

20 What is the difference between an *agentic state* and an *autonomous state*?

21 What did Bickman (1974) find was the impact of visible symbols (such as uniforms) on obedience levels?

22 According to Gilbert (1981), how might the '*foot-in-the-door*' phenomenon have influenced Milgram's participants?

23 What two roles were allocated to students in Zimbardo *et al.*'s (1973) prison study simulation?

24 Why did Zimbardo *et al.* (1973) have to terminate their study after only six days, when it was planned to run for two weeks?

Section 3: Evaluating Milgram's findings

25 What did Milgram find when he replicated his experiment using *female* participants?

26 What have researchers discovered when looking at the cross-cultural replicability of Milgram's findings?

27 Give one criticism of studies which have attempted to replicate Milgram's finding cross-culturally.

28 What serious *ethical* criticism of Milgram's research was made by Baumrind (1964)?

29 How did Milgram respond to Baumrind's criticism?

30 According to Vitelli (1988), how common is some form of *deception* in social psychological studies?

31 How did Milgram attempt to minimise ethical concerns regarding the deception of participants in his experiments?

32 How did Aronson (1988) defend Milgram's use of deception?

33 Why would the view we have of ourselves lead us to reject Milgram's research?

34 When are we most likely to *rebel* against authority?

Section 1: Milgram's research

1 According to Milgram (1992), *obedience* involves an explicit instruction to act in a certain way, the presence of a higher authority who is of a different status, and a social hierarchy which sanctions the power of the authority figure (rather than a need for acceptance by one's peers).

2 Milgram wished to test the *'"Germans are different" hypothesis'*, used as an explanation for Nazi atrocities.

3 Participants were obtained by placing an advertisement in a local newspaper.

4 Mr Wallace was a confederate who always took the role of learner.

5 The *'teachers'* were instructed to teach a list of word-pairs to the learners, punishing incorrect responses with increasing levels of electric shock.

6 As the experiment progressed, the learner was heard to utter grunts, screams, protests, then fall ominously silent after refusing to answer any more questions. The learner was a confederate, suffered no shock, and all protests were played on a tape recorder.

7 The experimenter was permitted to use four verbal 'prods' (*'please continue'*, *'the experiment requires that you continue'*, *'it is absolutely essential that you continue'*, *'you have no other choice, you must go on'*) to encourage participants to continue.

8 *Sixty-two-and-a-half* per cent in the initial study (remote victim) administered the highest voltage.

9 Participants displayed *great anguish*, *verbally attacked the experimenter*, *twitched nervously*, or *broke into nervous laughter*.

10 Milgram varied the *institutional context* of his experiments by moving to a rundown office in downtown Bridgeport.

11 When the teacher was in the same room as the learner, or had to force the learner's hand onto a shock plate, the 450 volt-obedience rate dropped to 40 and 30 per cent, respectively.

12 Milgram varied the *remoteness* of the authority figure by having the experimenter leave the room, after giving the essential instructions, and give the remaining instructions by telephone.

13 Having the teacher paired with another (confederate) teacher who administered the shocks whilst the participant simply read out the word pairs, produced the highest levels of obedience.

14 'The effects of *peer rebellion* are most impressive in undercutting the experimenter's authority.'

15 When the learner demanded to be shocked, or when there were two authorities giving contradictory commands, the levels of obedience were lowest.

Section 2: Explaining Milgram's findings

16 If participants did not believe the experimental set-up in which they found themselves (for example, by guessing that the learner was not receiving electric shocks), their responses might have been affected.

17 Sheridan & King (1972) had participants administer real electric shocks to a caged puppy as part of a study of 'learning'. Seventy-five per cent of the participants administered the maximum voltage.

18 Hofling *et al.* (1966) instructed nurses by telephone to administer twice the maximum dose of a drug. Twenty-one out of 22 complied unhesitatingly.

19 *Diffusion of responsibility*, where participants pass responsibility for the consequences of their actions onto an authority figure, *increases* the obedience level.

20 Individuals in an *agentic state* see themselves as an agent of an external authority, whereas individuals in an *autonomous state* act of their own accord and assume responsibility for their actions.

21 Bickman (1974) found that people are twice as likely to pick up a paper bag or give a coin to a stranger when told to do so by someone in a guard's uniform, than when the person is in civilian clothes.

22 Gilbert (1981) says that participants may have found it difficult to extricate themselves from the experiment, having agreed to a series of gradually escalating demands (the *'foot-in-the-door'* phenomenon).

23 Students in Zimbardo *et al.*'s (1973) prison simulation study were allocated either prisoner or guard roles.

24 Zimbardo *et al.* (1973) had to terminate their study prematurely because of the *pathological reactions* of the students in the role of 'prisoners'.

Section 3: Evaluating Milgram's findings

25 Milgram obtained very similar levels of obedience with *female* participants compared with male participants.

26 Attempts to replicate Milgram's findings cross-culturally have produced a wide range of levels of obedience, ranging from 16 per cent for Australian female students (Kilham & Mann, 1974) to 92 per cent for Dutch citizens (Meeus & Raaijmakers, 1986).

27 Such studies have varied in the degree to which they accurately reproduced Milgram's experimental set-up.

28 Baumrind (1964) criticised Milgram for failing to adequately protect participants from stress and emotional conflict.

29 Milgram responded that neither of these effects was anticipated nor intended by the experimenters.

30 Vitelli (1988) claims that more than one-third of social psychological studies employ some form of deception.

31 Milgram extensively debriefed his participants, and found that 84 per cent said they were glad to have participated.

32 Aronson (1988) points out that, without deception, the results would not have reflected how people behave in real-life situations.

33 Milgram's research paints an unacceptable picture of us, as humans. It is easier to reject his research than to reject the illusion of ourselves as autonomous.

34 We are most likely to *rebel* against authority when we feel that our freedom is in danger of being lost.

Obedience

Obedience: involves an explicit instruction to behave in a certain way, a higher authority who influences behaviour, and a hierarchical structure which legitimises this authority

Stanley Milgram's studies of obedience to authority
Milgram (1963, 1964, 1974):

Milgram wished to test the idea that Nazism was the product of a German character defect (a readiness to obey authority).

- Participants (aged 20–50 years), from all walks of life, answered a newspaper advertisement for a 'study of memory' (paid $4.50).
- Participants introduced to Mr. Williams (experimenter) and Mr. Wallace (confederate), whom they believed was a harmless accountant in his 50s. Told that experiment concerned effects of punishment on learning. Drew lots – rigged so that the confederate was the learner.
- 'Teacher' looked on as learner was strapped into chair, given mild sample shock, and told both of a slight heart condition (*voice feedback variation*).
- Teacher introduced to shock generator (15–450 volts), marked '*slight, moderate, strong, very strong, intense, intense to extreme, danger: severe shock, XXX*'. Teacher is given a sample shock.
- Teacher instructed to teach word pairs to learner and told to move one switch higher on the shock generator for every incorrect response.
- Teacher heard tape-recorded grunts, screams, objections and, ominous silence after 330 volts (*voice feedback variation*).
- 4 verbal prods used by experimenter: '*Please continue*', '*The experiment requires that you continue*', '*It's absolutely essential that you continue*', '*You have no other choice – you must go on*'.
- After the experiment (when participants refused to continue or administered the maximum shock four times) full debriefing was given.

Results: Approximately 65% of participants went up to 450 volts, all to 300 *(voice feedback variation)*. Psychiatrists had predicted that less than 1% of participants would administer the highest voltage. Participants trembled, sweated, broke into nervous laughter, or verbally attacked the experimenter. Three participants suffered seizures.

Variations on Milgram's basic procedure (% going to 450 V)

A peer administers shocks (92.5%)
- The teacher is paired with another (bogus) teacher and had only to read out the word-pairs, whilst the other teacher administered the shock.
- Participants shifted responsibility onto the other teacher and obedience rose to 92.5%

Institutional context (47.5%)
- Many participants claimed that they continued administering shock because the experiment was being conducted at prestigious Yale University.
- When Milgram transferred the experiment to a rundown office in downtown Bridgeport, the 450 volt obedience rate was still 47.5%.

Proximity (40%) and touch proximity (30%)
- When learner and teacher were in the same room, the 450 volt obedience rate dropped to 40%.
- When the teacher had to force the learner's hand onto a shock plate the 450 volt obedience rate was still 30%.

Two peers rebel (10%)
- The teacher is paired with two confederate (bogus) teachers.
- The first teacher refused to continue at 150 V, the second at 210 V.
- Only 10% of participants continued on to 450 V, most stopping when one or the other teachers refused to continue.

Methodological and generalisation issues

- **Representative sample?** Milgram studied 636 participants from the New Haven area. Although participants who went to 450 V tended to be more authoritarian, people who volunteer for experiments tend to be less authoritarian on average.
- **Gender bias?** Although Milgram used mainly male participants, the 40 females in one of his experiments produced the same results as men.
- **Cross-cultural validity?** Reproducing the study in different countries produced obedience rates ranging from 16% (Australian female students) to 92% (members of the Dutch population). However, such studies often only replicated Milgram's procedure *partially*.
- **Ecological validity?** Clearly there are differences between Nazi Germany and Milgram's laboratory. Some psychologists argue that his findings do not generalise well to real-life situations. However, Hofling *et al.* (1966) (see right) showed that high levels of obedience could be obtained outside the laboratory.

Explaining Milgram's results

Credibility
Participants may not have believed the experimental set-up, and guessed that the learner was not receiving shocks.

Puppies and electric shocks (Sheridan & King, 1972)
- Participants were required to deliver *real* and increasing electric shocks to a caged puppy as part of a learning task.
- After a time, an odourless anaesthetic was released into the cage, causing the puppy to appear to 'die'.
- 75% of participants continued, and delivered the maximum shock.

Demand characteristics
Participants may simply have responded to cues in Milgram's experimental setting, making this an unusual result.

Obedience in nurses (Hofling *et al.*,1966)
- Nurses were instructed by telephone to deliver twice the maximum dosage of a drug (in fact a harmless tablet) to a patient.
- 21 out of 22 obeyed unhesitatingly.

Legitimate authority
In an organised society, individuals must give up responsibility to those of higher status in order to ensure smooth functioning. Participants may have entered this '*agentic*' state, rather than acting independently ('*autonomous*' state). Visible symbols of status (such as the lab coat) may act as prompts for this behaviour.

The Stanford prison simulation (Zimbardo *et al.*, 1973)
- Zimbardo *et al.* created a mock prison in the university basement, randomly assigning students to prisoner or guard roles.
- Prisoners wore 'smocks' and were referred to by numbers. Guards wore uniforms and sunglasses, and were referred to as 'Sir'.
- Experiment had to be stopped after six days as guards became increasingly sadistic, and prisoners suffered pathological reactions.

Ethical issues

- **Protection of participants**: Baumrind (1964) argued that Milgram had not protected participants from stress and emotional conflict. Milgram responded that the outcome (of stress) was not *anticipated*, and not therefore an *intentional outcome*.
- **Deception:** Milgram deceived his participants over the nature of the study, but Aronson (1988) points out that he could not have obtained valid results otherwise. In addition, Milgram thoroughly debriefed his participants, and 84% were glad or very glad to have participated. Moreover, 80% said they felt more experiments of this kind should be conducted.

60

SOCIAL POWER: LEADERS AND LEADERSHIP

SYLLABUS

1.3 Social influence
- theories and research into the basis of social power, including leadership and followership

KEY QUESTIONS
- What are leaders and leadership?
- Why do leaders emerge?
- What styles of leadership exist?
- How does Fiedler's model explain leader effectiveness?

Section 1: Introducing leadership
1 How does Hollander (1985) define a *leader*?
2 How can *leadership* be defined?
3 What is the difference between the *trait* and *situational approaches* to understanding leadership?

Section 2: The emergence of leaders
4 Name three of the *traits* that Stogdill (1974) found leaders were slightly more likely to have than non-leaders.
5 Give one criticism of the trait approach to understanding leadership.
6 According to Bales' (1950) *situational approach*, who is most likely to emerge as the leader in a given situation?
7 When Sherif *et al.* (1961) introduced competition between two groups of boys as part of their 'Robber's Cave' field experiment, how did this affect the groups' leaders?
8 Give one criticism of the situational approach to understanding leadership.
9 What view is advanced by those who apply *transactional theory* to the understanding of leadership?

Section 3: Leadership styles
10 Identify two differences between the behaviour of adults adopting an *autocratic style* and a *democratic style*, in Lewin *et al.*'s (1939) study of groups of ten-year-old boys.
11 Which of Lewin *et al.*'s styles produced boys who were *aggressive* towards each other?
12 Which of Lewin *et al.*'s styles influenced the boys to produce the most work?
13 Haplin & Winer (1952) identified two major categories of leader. What was involved in *initiating structure*?
14 Bales & Slater (1955) identified two categories of leader by discovering who was best liked amongst groups of students working together. Which two types of '*specialist*' emerged as the best liked?

15 What did Bales & Slater (1955) believe was the relationship between the two styles?
16 How did Stogdill (1974) view the relationship between the two styles differently?
17 What did Shaw (1981) discover when he compared autocratic and democratic leaders in terms of the resulting group dynamics and productivity?

Section 4: Fiedler's model
18 What sort of 'match' is Fiedler's (1964) *contingency model of leader effectiveness* concerned with?
19 How did Fiedler arrive at an *LPC score* for leaders?
20 How did low and high LPC scorers differ, according to Fiedler?
21 What did Fiedler intend by the expression 'the *favourableness* of the situation'?
22 Name the three situational variables that influence a situation's favourableness.
23 Why are *task-oriented leaders* the best leaders for highly favourable situations, according to Fiedler's model?
24 Why are *task-oriented leaders* also the best for highly unfavourable situations?
25 What problem is posed for Fiedler's model by the low *test–retest reliability* of LPC scores?

Section 5: Leadership – process and power
26 What is the difference between *appointed leaders* and *emergent leaders*?
27 In what ways is a leader both a *conformist* and a *deviant*?
28 What does Hollander (1958) mean by the term *idiosyncrasy credit*?
29 What important aspect of a leader's interactions with others is overlooked by approaches which focus on the leader–subordinate relationship?
30 Name the five kinds of power identified by French & Raven (1959). Name any three of them.

Section 1: Introducing leadership

1 Hollander (1985) defines a *leader* as the person who exercises the most influence in a group.

2 *Leadership* can be defined as the exercise of power over others (Hollander, 1985).

3 *Trait approaches* emphasise the characteristics of individuals which make them leaders, whilst *situational approaches* focus on identifying the conditions which influence the effectiveness of individuals appointed as leaders in a given situation.

Section 2: The emergence of leaders

4 Stogdill (1974) found that leaders were slightly more *intelligent*, *sociable*, *achievement-oriented*, *experienced*, *older* and *taller* than non-leaders.

5 The trait approach to understanding leadership is not well supported by the evidence, which suggests that leaders and followers do not show consistent personality differences. Additionally, it is clear that different traits are required of a leader, depending on the situation.

6 Bales' (1950) *situational approach* suggests that the leader is likely to be the person whose skills and competence are most useful to a group in a given situation.

7 Sherif *et al.* (1961) found that competing groups would replace their leaders with physically stronger boys.

8 The situational approach overlooks evidence suggesting that some people adopt the role of leader more readily than others, irrespective of the situation (Nydegger, 1975).

9 *Transactional theory* suggests that both the characteristics of people and the demands of the situation influence who will become a leader.

Section 3: Leadership styles

10 *Autocratic* adults told the boys what to do and with whom to work, did not explain their comments, and were aloof and impersonal. *Democratic* adults discussed options with the boys, allowed them to make their own decisions, explained their comments, and joined in with activities.

11 Both the *autocratic* and *laissez-faire styles* produced boys who were aggressive towards each other.

12 The autocratic style influenced the boys to produce the most work.

13 *Initiating structure* involves defining a group's goals, planning how those goals should be achieved, and directing the action of the group.

14 Bales & Slater (1955) identified *task specialists* and *socioemotional specialists* as being the two categories of leader that emerged in groups of students.

15 Bales & Slater (1955) believed that the styles were *inversely related*, and that no one person could display both styles simultaneously.

16 Stogdill (1974) suggested that the two styles were *independent dimensions*, and that effective leaders are those who score average on both.

17 Shaw (1981) discovered that *autocratic* leaders tended to be best at *increasing productivity*, whereas *democratic* leaders tended to produce the *happiest groups*. Shaw qualified this by pointing out that each style may be more advantageous in different situations.

Section 4: Fiedler's model

18 Fiedler's (1964) *contingency model of leader effectiveness* is most concerned with the match between a leader's qualities/style and the requirements of the group's situation.

19 Fiedler asked leaders to rate the person they found most difficult to work with on 18 bipolar scales (e.g. friendly–unfriendly); the sum of these values was their *LPC score*.

20 *Low* LPC scorers tended to be *directive*, *controlling* and *dominant* in relations with group members, whereas *high* LPC scorers were *accepting*, *permissive* and *considerate* in their relations with group members.

21 'The *favourableness* of the situation' was used by Fiedler to refer to the extent to which the situation allows the leader to exert influence.

22 Fiedler identified *quality of leader–member relations*, *task structure*, and *position-power* as the three variables which influence a situation's *favourableness*.

23 In highly favourable situations, *task-oriented leaders* do not need to waste time worrying about group morale, so an interpersonal emphasis is unnecessary.

24 In highly unfavourable situations the group may fall apart without an emphasis on production above all else.

25 The low *test–retest reliability* of LPC scores (Rice, 1978) suggests that leadership styles are not stable but can be modified.

Section 5: Leadership – process and power.

26 *Appointed leaders* are assigned by an external group to a position within a formal group structure, whereas *emergent leaders* are appointed (and can be demoted) by the members of the informal group to which the leader belongs.

27 A leader must embody a group's norms (such as its principles and goals) whilst acting as an agent of change, steering the group in new directions.

28 *Idiosyncracy credit* is the way in which a leader 'earns' the right to bring about change, by conforming closely to the group's established norms initially (Hollander, 1958).

29 Such approaches overlook the fact that leaders devote substantial time to their superiors, colleagues, and those external to the group, not simply to their immediate subordinates.

30 French & Raven (1959) identify *reward power*, *coercive power*, *legitimate power*, *expert power* and *referent power* as the five kinds of power which can be wielded.

Leaders & Leadership

Leader: the person who exercises most influence in a group.
Leadership: the exercise of power over others (Hollander, 1985).

Leadership as a process

- In order to become a leader, an individual must achieve legitimacy as a leader (**validation**). This can occur in different ways:
  Appointed leaders: assigned a leadership role and imposed on the group by an external authority (*formal group structure*).
  Emergent leaders: assigned a leadership role by the group members (*informal group structure*).
- Leadership is a complex social process involving exchanges (**transactions**) between leaders and group members.
- Leaders are both:
  conformists – because they embody the group's norms.
  deviants – because they can change prevailing norms.
- The right to make changes is often earned through initially conforming to group norms (**idiosyncracy credit**) (Hollander, 1958)

Leadership and power

Five kinds of power
(French & Raven, 1959)

Legitimate power:	the formal power associated with a role, regardless of the individual (e.g. Prime Minister)
Reward power:	power associated with the control over valued resources, such as food, money, co-operation (e.g. employers)
Coercive power:	power associated with control over feared consequences, such as demotion, loss of love (e.g. employers)
Expert power:	power associated with the possession of special knowledge (e.g. doctors, teachers)
Referent power:	power associated with personal qualities, such as charm and charisma (e.g. charismatic leaders)

Leader emergence

Trait approaches

- See leaders as extraordinary people who rise to positions of power because of certain personality traits.
- Stogdill (1974): leaders tend to be slightly more intelligent, sociable, achievement-oriented, experienced, older and taller.
- However, *overall*, leaders have not been shown to be consistently different from non-leaders in terms of their personality traits (Turner, 1991).

Transactional approaches

- Shaw (1981: applied transactional theory to both the trait and situational approaches to leader emergence. According to this theory, *both* the characteristics of people and the demands of the situation determine who will become leader.

Situational approaches

- Bales (1950) stressed the *functional demands* of the situation – the leader is the one whose skills/competencies best meet the group's needs in a particular context.
- Sherif *et al.* (1961): when competition was introduced between boys (Robbers' Cave field experiment) both groups replaced their leaders with physically stronger boys.
- However, *overall*, research shows that some people adopt positions of power more readily than others.

Leadership styles

Autocratic, democratic, laissez-faire

- Lewin *et al.* (1939) investigated the effects of three different kinds of adult behaviour on 10-year-old boys attending after-school clubs:

Leadership style	Boys' behaviour
Autocratic: told boys what to do and who to work with. Did not explain. Impersonal.	Aggressive towards each other, submissive towards leader. Stopped working if leader absent.
Democratic: discussed projects and allowed boys to choose. Joined in.	Got on well together and co-operated. Approaches to leader were task-related and worked if leader-absent.
Laissez-faire: left boys to their own devices, gave neither praise nor blame.	Aggressive towards each other, did little work when leader present or absent. Easily discouraged.

Initiating structure and showing consideration

- Halpin & Winer (1952) asked people in different groups what were the most important behaviours in a leader. Two major categories emerged:
  Initiating structure: leader should set goals, plan and direct the whole group.
  Showing consideration: demonstrating positive regard and communicating with individuals.
  These two qualities are difficult to balance and leaders may tend to demonstrate one more than the other.

Task specialists and socioemotional specialists

- Bales & Slater (1955) asked groups of students working together to identify the best-liked member.
- Found that after the second day, best-liked members were either:
  Task specialists: made suggestions, provided information, expressed opinions.
  Socioemotional specialists: helped others express themselves, cracked jokes, expressed positive feelings.
  Bales and Slater believe these styles are inversely related, but other researchers believe that the most effective leaders score average on both.

Fiedler's contingency model

The LPC scale
- A leader is asked to think of all those people who have worked for him/her.
- The most *difficult* one is then rated on 18 bipolar scales (e.g. pleasant–unpleasant).
- These scores are added to give an LPC score:
Relationship oriented leaders (*high LPC score*) are accepting and considerate.
Task-oriented leaders (*low LPC score*) tend to be directive and dominant.

Fiedler's contingency model of leader effectiveness
(Fiedler, 1964, 1981; Fiedler & Chemers, 1984)
- The model is mainly concerned with the match between a leader's style (or qualities) and the group's situation.
- Fiedler developed a scale to measure the extent to which leaders distinguished between their most and least preferred co-workers (LPC score – see left).
- Fiedler believed that leader effectiveness was contingent upon the *fit* between their *style* (as measured by the LPC scale) and the *favourableness of the situation*.
- The favourableness of the situation comprises three *variables* (see right).
- *Relationship-oriented leaders* are most effective when the favourableness of the situation is neither very high nor very low.
- *Task-oriented leaders* are most effective when the situation is either very favourable or very unfavourable (since in either case group relations are less important).

Three variables determining the favourableness of a situation:
Quality of leader–member relations: the degree of loyalty and confidence of group members.
Task structure: clarity and complexity of the task and the number of possible solutions.
Position-power: the power inherent in the leader's role.

61

COLLECTIVE BEHAVIOUR

SYLLABUS
1.3 Social influence
- explanations and research evidence into collective behaviour, including crowds and the behaviour of mobs

KEY QUESTIONS
- What types of collective behaviours are there?
- How do contagion theories explain collective behaviour?
- What is the nature of deindividuation?
- How do convergence and emergent norm theories explain collective behaviour?

Section 1: Introducing collective behaviour

1 Complete the following definition of collective behaviour, offered by Milgram & Toch (1969): 'behaviour which originates _____, is relatively _____, fairly unpredictable and planless in its course of development, and which depends upon _____ among participants'.
2 What is the difference between a *craze* and a *panic*?
3 What is the difference between *education* and *propaganda*?
4 Define a *crowd*.
5 How do *casual* and *acting crowds* differ?
6 How do Broom & Selznick (1977) define a *mob*?
7 Raper (1933) reports an example of mob behaviour involving a black man called James Irwin. What happened to James Irwin?

Section 2: Contagion theories

8 According to Le Bon (1879), what is the central question regarding the behaviour of crowds?
9 How do *suggestibility accounts* of crowd behaviour explain why individuals behave as they do?
10 What did Freud (1921) believe that crowds permitted?
11 According to Shibutani (1966), in what way are *rumours* likely to be distorted?
12 What is *social contagion* (or *interactional amplification*)?
13 How does the shooting of a black man, described by Lee & Humphrey (1943), demonstrate *impersonality*?
14 Why, according to Le Bon, does *anonymity* cause individuals to indulge in behaviour which would normally be controlled?
15 Complete the following definition of *deindividuation*, offered by Singer *et al.* (1965): 'a subjective state in which people lose their sense of _____-_____'.
16 What is Festinger *et al.*'s (1952) explanation for why deindividuation may lead to uncharacteristic behaviours?
17 How did Zimbardo (1969) demonstrate anonymity in big cities?

18 What was the effect on Zimbardo's (1969) female participants administering electric shocks when they were dressed in lab coats and hoods which hid their faces?
19 What did Diener *et al.* (1976) find in their study of 1300 'trick-or-treating' American children one Halloween night?
20 What is Diener's (1980) explanation for deindividuation?
21 What are the two types of *self-awareness*, according to Prentice-Dunn & Rogers (1982, 1983)?
22 Give any one example of a factor which may reduce each type of self-awareness, respectively.
23 What expression do Prentice-Dunn and Rogers use to describe the state which we enter as a result of *decreased self-awareness*?
24 According to Prentice-Dunn and Rogers, a deindividuated state does not, in itself, cause anti-social or aggressive behaviour. How does it relate to these behaviours?
25 Give one criticism of Zimbardo's (1969) study, in which women wearing hoods were more likely to administer high levels of electric shock.
26 According to Brown (1985), what is one of the functions of uniforms in the real world?
27 How did Gergen *et al.* (1973) show that deindividuation can sometimes cause *affiliative* behaviours?

Section 3: Convergence and emergent norm theory

28 What explanation for crowd behaviour is offered by *convergence theory*?
29 What criticisms of contagion theories are made by *emergent norm theory*?
30 What is the *'riffraff theory'* of riots?
31 In his study of thresholds of participation, which types did Brown (1954) discover were *most* and *least* easily encouraged into taking mob action?

Section 1: Introducing collective behaviour

1 'Behaviour which originates *spontaneously*, is relatively *unorganised*, fairly unpredictable and planless in its course of development, and which depends upon *inter-stimulation* among participants'.

2 A *craze* is a rush towards some satisfaction, whereas a *panic* is a rush away from some perceived threat.

3 *Education* should cultivate the ability to make discriminating judgements, whereas *propaganda* seeks to persuade people into the undiscriminating acceptance of a ready-made judgement.

4 A *crowd* is a collection of people gathered around a centre or point of common attention (Young, 1946).

5 A *casual crowd* is one whose members rarely know one another, and whose forms of behaviour are mostly unstructured (e.g. going shopping). *Acting crowds* (*mobs*) are fairly unified and single-minded in their aggressive intent.

6 Broom & Selznick (1977) define a *mob* as a crowd bent upon an aggressive act such as lynching, looting, or the destruction of property.

7 Raper (1933) reports that James Irwin was chained to a tree, had his fingers and toes cut off, was castrated, hung on a tree, set fire to, and then shot.

Section 2: Contagion theories

8 Le Bon (1879) believes that the central question regarding the behaviour of crowds is why they act in ways which are uncharacteristic of the individuals comprising them.

9 *Suggestibility accounts* propose that crowds may react readily and uncritically to authoritative commands in the absence of a leader or recognised behaviour patterns.

10 Freud (1921) believed that crowds permit the expression of behaviour usually *repressed*, such as the need (derived from our relationship to our father) to submit to a more powerful authority.

11 Shibutani (1966) points out that *rumours* are usually distorted in the direction of personal or cultural predispositions.

12 *Social contagion* is the process whereby members of a crowd stimulate and respond to one another, thereby increasing their emotional intensity and responsiveness.

13 The two men who shot the black man did not know him, but shot him because he was seen as 'the enemy', and as bad as any other member of that group.

14 *Anonymity* removes the sense of individuality from group members. Because moral responsibility is then shifted away from the individual onto the group, the individual feels free to indulge in behaviours which would normally be controlled.

15 'a subjective state in which people lose their sense of *self-consciousness*.'

16 Festinger *et al.* (1952) believe that group membership allows us to merge with that group, foregoing our individual identities, leading to a reduction of inner restraints and inhibitions.

17 Zimbardo (1969) abandoned a car in a big city location and a small town location and secretly filmed people's behaviour, recording the number of incidents of 'destructive contact'.

18 Zimbardo (1969) discovered that they delivered *twice as much shock* as females who could be easily identified.

19 Diener *et al.* (1976) found that 'trick-or-treating' American children were more likely to steal candy if their costumes prevented them from being recognised.

20 Diener (1980) argues that a person is prevented by situational factors from becoming *self-aware*. This results in a weakening of normal restraints, a lack of concern about what others will think of our behaviour, and a reduced capacity to think rationally.

21 *Public self-awareness* and *private self-awareness*.

22 *Public self-awareness* may be reduced by difficulty in recognising the individual in a crowd, by a diffusion of responsibility and by the presence of models who supply norms for behaviours. *Private self-awareness* may be reduced by drugs, arousal, physical involvement, hypnosis, and chanting.

23 Prentice-Dunn and Rogers describe this state as an '*irrational state of altered consciousness*'.

24 The deindividuated state makes us *susceptible to behavioural cues*, such as others' behaviour or the presence of weapons.

25 The hoods worn by women in Zimbardo's (1969) study resembled the hoods worn by the Ku Klux Klan, and may have led participants to believe that extreme behaviours were expected of them.

26 Brown (1985) believes that one of the functions of uniforms in the real world is to *reduce* individuality, thereby *increasing* deindividuation.

27 Gergen *et al.* (1973) left people alone in lighted or dark rooms. Towards the end of the experiment, participants in the dark (deindividuated) condition became quite intimate and physical.

Section 3: Convergence and emergent norm theory

28 *Convergence theory* claims that crowd behaviour arises from the gathering together of people who share the same needs, dislikes, impulses and purposes.

29 *Emergent norm theory* claims that contagion theory exaggerates the irrational and purposeless components of crowd behaviour, and that it cannot explain why a crowd takes one course of action rather than another.

30 The *riffraff theory* sees riots as the product of small groups of people such as criminals, drug addicts, drifters and welfare cheaters.

31 Brown (1954) claimed that the '*lawless*' needed little provocation before engaging in mob action, whereas the '*resisters*' would actively oppose mob action.

Collective Behaviour

Emergent norm theory

- **Emergent norm theory** suggests that the perceptions and grievances of a group, fed by the contagion process, lead to the emergence of a norm which justifies and limits crowd behaviour.
- Argues that contagion theories overemphasise irrational and purposeless aspects of crowd behaviour.
- Analyses of riots showed that rioters were not just 'riffraff', but comprised a cross-section of the people involved, motivated by genuine grievances. Also, burning and looting were not indiscriminate.
- **Thresholds for participation:** Brown (1954) attempted an analysis of why ordinary people become looters and rioters, identifying 'lawless', 'suggestible', 'cautious', 'yielders', 'supportive', and 'resisters' as types within the crowd who have different thresholds for physical action.

Reicher (1984): analysed riots in Bristol in 1980.
- Found that crowd directed attacks on police cars and confined its behaviour to the St Paul's district.
- The crowd behaved in what it saw as a legitimate way in response to the police presence.

Convergence theory

- Argues that crowd behaviour arises from the gathering together of people who have the same needs, impulse, dislikes and purposes.
- 'Controlled emotional contagion' may serve the useful social function of allowing people to release emotions and tensions they cannot ordinarily express (e.g. following the death of Princess Diana).
- Organised gatherings provide settings that integrate crowd behaviour into the social structure (e.g. religious services, football matches).

Contagion theories

Impersonality

Refers to the tendency to treat one member of the 'enemy' as being as bad as another.

Lee & Humphrey (1943) cite the case of two whites who decided to shoot a black stranger simply because 'other people were fighting and killing and we felt like it, too'.

Social contagion

- **Social contagion** (*interactional amplification*) is the process whereby the members of a crowd stimulate and respond to one another and thereby increase their emotional intensity and responsiveness (Horton & Hunt, 1976).
- A crowd which is so aroused needs emotional release and may act on the first suggested action which accords with its impulses.

Suggestibility

- In the absence of a leader or recognised norms for behaviour, authoritative suggestions may lead people to react readily and uncritically (Lang & Lang 1961).
- Le Bon (1879) believed that a 'racial unconscious' took over from the 'conscious personality', and Freud (1921) suggested that crowds allow repressed needs to be expressed.

The importance of rumour
(Shibutani, 1966)
- Rumours are subject to distortion typically in the direction of personal/cultural predispositions.
- Heightened suggestibility may increase the impact of rumours on collective behaviour.

Anonymity

- Le Bon (1879): the more anonymous a crowd, the greater its potential for extreme action, because anonymity removes the sense of individuality from group members.
- Moral responsibility is shifted from the individual to the group, and the normal restraints are removed.
- Festinger *et al.* (1952) proposed the concept of **deindividuation** where individuals do not single out others as individuals and do not feel that they themselves are singled out by others.
- Individuals merge with the group and, becoming anonymous, experience a reduction of inhibitions.

Deindividuation

Research
Zimbardo (1969) left cars with number plates removed and bonnets up in the Bronx area of New York and Palo Alto, California. In the more anonymous 'big city', the car was mostly stripped by clean-cut whites within one day, whereas the car in Palo Alto was left alone for seven days.
Zimbardo (1969) had female undergraduates wearing either hoods, which hid their faces, or conspicuous name tags administer electric shock to another student who pretended to be in pain. Anonymous females administered twice as much shock, irrespective of whether the student was described as 'conceited and critical' or 'honest sincere and warm'.

Diener's theory (1980)

- Argues that situational factors prevent us from becoming self-aware, and we are blocked from monitoring our own behaviour.
- Self-regulatory capacities are lost.

Prentice-Dunn & Rogers' theory (1982, 1983)

Argue that there are two types of self-awareness:
- **Public self-awareness:** concern about the impression we are giving others.
- **Private self-awareness:** the attention we pay to our thoughts and feelings.

Public self-awareness can be reduced by three factors:
- Difficulty in identifying us (e.g. in a crowd).
- Diffusion of responsibility (e.g. if others were behaving antisocially).
- Other members setting norms which can be imitated.

Private self-awareness can also be reduced:
- By drugs, chanting, physical involvement, excitement.

These two can lead to an **irrational state of altered consciousness**, in which we are susceptible to **behavioural cues** (such as weapons, others' behaviour) and can behave in aggressive and antisocial ways.

Collective behaviour: behaviour which originates spontaneously, is relatively unorganised, fairly unpredictable and planless in its course of development, and which depends on interstimulation of its participants (Milgram & Toch, 1969).

Crowd: a collection of people gathered around a centre point of common attention (Young, 1946).

Mob: a crowd bent upon an aggressive act such as lynching, looting or the destruction of property (Broom & Selznick, 1977).

Panic: a form of action in which a crowd, excited by a belief in some imminent threat, may engage in uncontrolled, and therefore dangerous, collective flight.

62

BYSTANDER BEHAVIOUR AND ALTRUISM

SYLLABUS
1.4 Pro- and anti-social behaviour
• explanations and research studies relating to altruism and bystander behaviour

KEY QUESTIONS
• How can we explain bystander apathy?
• What explanations of bystander behaviour does the arousal model offer?
• Can egoism or altruism best account for bystander behaviour?

Q

Section 1: Introducing bystander behaviour

1 How did Kitty Genovese respond when she was stabbed by her attacker?
2 How many of her neighbours in her apartment block were aware of the disturbance?
3 How many times did her attacker assault her?
4 What central question is raised by reports such as that of Kitty Genovese?

Section 2: The decision model

5 Latané & Darley (1968) proposed a 'five-step' decision model of bystander intervention. The first and last steps are *noticing the event* and *implementing the selected decision*, respectively. What are steps two, three and four?
6 What is *pluralistic ignorance*?
7 What experiment, involving the study of students completing questionnaires, did Latané & Darley (1968) carry out in order to demonstrate pluralistic ignorance?
8 Why is *social influence* one reason why groups of participants failed to respond to cries coming from an adjoining room (Latané & Rodin, 1969)?
9 What interesting result did Latané & Rodin (1969) obtain when, instead of placing *strangers* together, they placed two *friends* together, and measured their responses to a potential emergency?
10 What do Latané & Darley (1968) suggest underlies the *diffusion of responsibility* phenomenon?
11 How did Darley & Latané (1968) demonstrate diffusion of responsibility in a laboratory setting?
12 How did Darley and Latané account for the high levels of emotional arousal in participants who did not respond to a victim's plight?
13 What is the relationship between the *competence* of a bystander and his/her likelihood of intervening to help?
14 In what situations may competencies *reduce* the likelihood of bystanders intervening?

15 How did Bickman (1971) demonstrate the effect of a victim's proximity on the likelihood of a bystander intervening?
16 How can Latané and Darley's model be criticised?
17 Piliavin *et al.* carried out a number of experiments involving the collapse of a 'stooge' in a subway carriage (Piliavin *et al.*, 1969; Piliavin & Piliavin, 1972). Identify the factors which affected the likelihood of bystanders intervening.
18 What is the *reverse bystander effect* (Williams & Williams, 1983)?

Section 3: The cost–reward model

19 Piliavin *et al.*'s (1981) *cost–reward model* emphasises the interaction between two sets of factors. Give examples of factors from both sets.
20 What do Piliavin *et al.* mean by '*we-ness*'?
21 What is the role of *arousal* in the cost–reward model?
22 What name do Piliavin *et al.* give to the '*calculations*' in which bystanders weigh the benefits and costs of helping?
23 Give two examples of the *costs of helping* and two examples of *costs of not helping*.
24 In terms of the costs of helping and not helping, explain why bystanders are typically unlikely to help a 'stooge' who, clutching a bottle, collapses in a subway.
25 Give an example of both *personal costs* and *empathy costs*.
26 When is *indirect helping* most likely to occur?
27 Identify any two ways in which *cognitive reinterpretation* can be accomplished.
28 What is Piliavin *et al.*'s explanation for why *impulsive helping* occurs?

Section 4: Egoism and altruism

29 What is the difference between an *egoistic act* and an *altruistic act*?
30 What is the *paradox of altruism*?
31 What argument is advanced in the '*empathy–altruism*' hypothesis?

Section 1: Introducing bystander behaviour

1 Kitty Genovese responded by screaming 'Oh my God, he stabbed me!' and 'Please help me!'.

2 *Thirty-eight* of her neighbours were woken by her screams.

3 Her attacker assaulted her *twice*, stabbing her and returning to assault her and stab her a second time.

4 Such reports raise the question 'Why do bystanders intervene/fail to intervene?'

Section 2: The decision model

5 The second, third and fourth steps are: *interpreting the event as one requiring help*, *assuming personal responsibility*, and *selecting a way to help*.

6 *Pluralistic ignorance* refers to the lower likelihood of individuals defining a situation as dangerous if others are present.

7 Latané & Darley (1968) had smoke (actually steam) fill a room in which students were completing questionnaires. When others were present, they were far less likely to raise the alarm.

8 *Social influence* refers to the tendency of individuals to follow the reactions of others. For example, by appearing to remain calm, individuals may influence others into thinking that a situation is 'safe'.

9 Latané & Rodin (1969) found that when two *friends* were placed in an ambiguous situation, their response to a potential emergency was just as quick as when either was alone, and much quicker than when two *strangers* were together.

10 Latané & Darley (1968) suggest that a *diffusion of responsibility* occurs when individuals reason that somebody else should, and probably will, offer assistance.

11 Darley & Latané (1968) persuaded students that they were taking part in a discussion over an intercom with a number of other participants (either two or one). One of the other 'participants' (actually a tape-recording) was heard to have a seizure and response times were measured.

12 Darley and Latané believed that such participants were experiencing conflict between the fear of making fools of themselves/disrupting the experiment, and their own guilt and shame at doing nothing.

13 When bystanders have relevant *competencies* (e.g. first aid qualifications), helping is more likely.

14 If bystanders perceive others as being more competent they are less likely to help.

15 Bickman (1971) replicated Darley and Latané's 'seizure study', but led participants to believe that the other person in the discussion was either close to or distant from the victim. Participants were more likely to help when the other participant was far from the victim.

16 Latané and Darley's model does not tell us why 'no' decisions are taken at any of the five stages, and pays more attention to why people don't help, rather than why they do. Additionally, the model does not account for other factors which have been shown to affect helping (such as those identified by Piliavin *et al.*).

17 Whether or not the stooge was carrying a cane or a bottle (and smelled of alcohol), the appearance of fake blood from the victim's mouth as they collapsed, and the presence of an ugly facial birthmark all affected the likelihood of bystander intervention.

18 The *reverse bystander effect* refers to the increasing reluctance of victims to seek help as the number of potential helpers increases.

Section 3: The cost–reward model

19 The first set of factors includes *situational*, *bystander* and *victim characteristics*, whilst the second includes *cognitive* and *affective reactions*.

20 'We-ness' is used by Piliavin *et al.* (1981) to refer to the categorisation of another person as a member of one's own group.

21 The two sets of factors interact to produce *arousal*. This arousal is then attributed to some factor (such as the victim's plight), and attempts made to reduce this arousal.

22 They call it *hedonistic calculus*.

23 *Costs of helping* include *time, effort, danger, embarrassment, disruption of activities* and *psychological aversion*. *Costs of not helping* include *guilt, others' disapproval*, and the *cognitive/emotional discomfort of knowing that another is suffering*.

24 Such an individual may be perceived as dangerous or violent, and as not worthy of help. Hence the costs of not helping are low.

25 *Personal costs* include self-blame and public disapproval, whilst *empathy costs* refer to the knowledge that a victim continues to suffer.

26 *Indirect helping* is most likely to occur when both the costs of helping and the costs of not helping are high.

27 *Cognitive reinterpretation* can be accomplished by redefining the situation as one not requiring help, by denigrating the victim, or by diffusion of responsibility.

28 Piliavin *et al.* believe that *impulsive helping* occurs as a consequence of the individual being 'flooded' with arousal which focuses them toward the victim's plight, blocking out cost considerations. They suggest that the mechanism may have an evolutionary basis.

Section 4: Egoism and altruism

29 An *egoistic act* is performed solely with a view to benefit the individual acting, whilst an *altruistic act* is performed solely to benefit others.

30 The *paradox of altruism* refers to the Darwinian view that, in the long term, organisms who are altruistic are the least likely to survive.

31 The *empathy–altruism hypothesis* suggests that we feel empathic concern when others are in distress and act to reduce their distress.

A

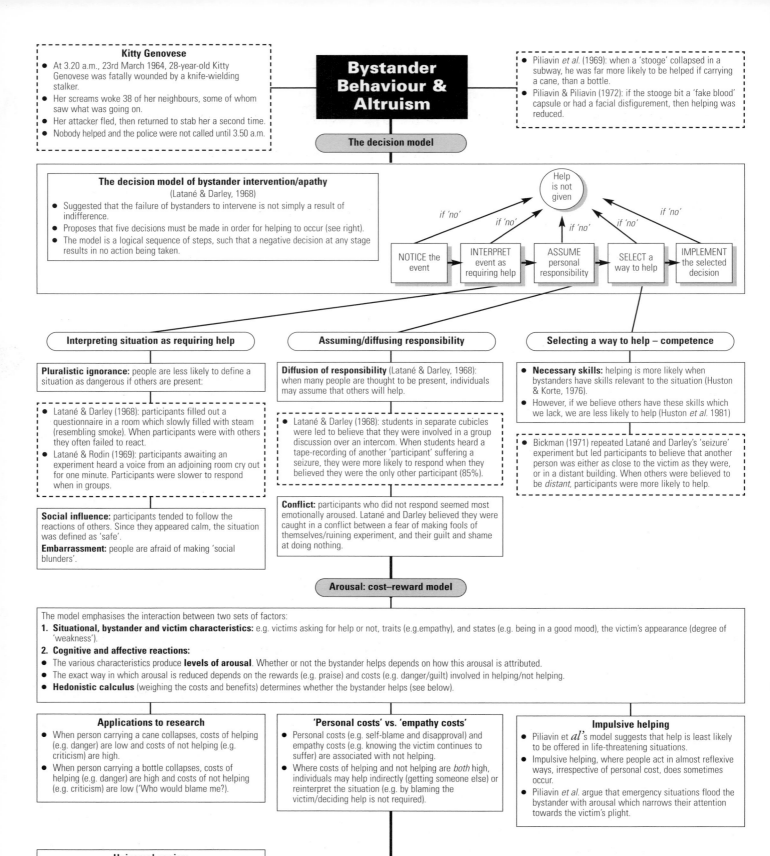

Bystander Behaviour & Altruism

Kitty Genovese

- At 3.20 a.m., 23rd March 1964, 28-year-old Kitty Genovese was fatally wounded by a knife-wielding stalker.
- Her screams woke 38 of her neighbours, some of whom saw what was going on.
- Her attacker fled, then returned to stab her a second time.
- Nobody helped and the police were not called until 3.50 a.m.

- Piliavin *et al*. (1969): when a 'stooge' collapsed in a subway, he was far more likely to be helped if carrying a cane, than a bottle.
- Piliavin & Piliavin (1972): if the stooge bit a 'fake blood' capsule or had a facial disfigurement, then helping was reduced.

The decision model

The decision model of bystander intervention/apathy
(Latané & Darley, 1968)

- Suggested that the failure of bystanders to intervene is not simply a result of indifference.
- Proposes that five decisions must be made in order for helping to occur (see right).
- The model is a logical sequence of steps, such that a negative decision at any stage results in no action being taken.

Help is not given

if 'no'   *if 'no'*   *if 'no'*   *if 'no'*   *if 'no'*

NOTICE the event → INTERPRET event as requiring help → ASSUME personal responsibility → SELECT a way to help → IMPLEMENT the selected decision

Interpreting situation as requiring help

Pluralistic ignorance: people are less likely to define a situation as dangerous if others are present:

- Latané & Darley (1968): participants filled out a questionnaire in a room which slowly filled with steam (resembling smoke). When participants were with others they often failed to react.
- Latané & Rodin (1969): participants awaiting an experiment heard a voice from an adjoining room cry out for one minute. Participants were slower to respond when in groups.

Social influence: participants tended to follow the reactions of others. Since they appeared calm, the situation was defined as 'safe'.

Embarrassment: people are afraid of making 'social blunders'.

Assuming/diffusing responsibility

Diffusion of responsibility (Latané & Darley, 1968): when many people are thought to be present, individuals may assume that others will help.

- Latané & Darley (1968): students in separate cubicles were led to believe that they were involved in a group discussion over an intercom. When students heard a tape-recording of another 'participant' suffering a seizure, they were more likely to respond when they believed they were the only other participant (85%).

Conflict: participants who did not respond seemed most emotionally aroused. Latané and Darley believed they were caught in a conflict between a fear of making fools of themselves/ruining experiment, and their guilt and shame at doing nothing.

Selecting a way to help – competence

- **Necessary skills:** helping is more likely when bystanders have skills relevant to the situation (Huston & Korte, 1976).
- However, if we believe others have these skills which we lack, we are less likely to help (Huston *et al.* 1981)

- Bickman (1971) repeated Latané and Darley's 'seizure' experiment but led participants to believe that another person was either as close to the victim as they were, or in a distant building. When others were believed to be *distant*, participants were more likely to help.

Arousal: cost–reward model

The model emphasises the interaction between two sets of factors:

1. **Situational, bystander and victim characteristics:** e.g. victims asking for help or not, traits (e.g.empathy), and states (e.g. being in a good mood), the victim's appearance (degree of 'weakness').
2. **Cognitive and affective reactions:**
- The various characteristics produce **levels of arousal**. Whether or not the bystander helps depends on how this arousal is attributed.
- The exact way in which arousal is reduced depends on the rewards (e.g. praise) and costs (e.g. danger/guilt) involved in helping/not helping.
- **Hedonistic calculus** (weighing the costs and benefits) determines whether the bystander helps (see below).

Applications to research

- When person carrying a cane collapses, costs of helping (e.g. danger) are low and costs of not helping (e.g. criticism) are high.
- When person carrying a bottle collapses, costs of helping (e.g. danger) are high and costs of not helping (e.g. criticism) are low ('Who would blame me?').

'Personal costs' vs. 'empathy costs'

- Personal costs (e.g. self-blame and disapproval) and empathy costs (e.g. knowing the victim continues to suffer) are associated with not helping.
- Where costs of helping and not helping are *both* high, individuals may help indirectly (getting someone else) or reinterpret the situation (e.g. by blaming the victim/deciding help is not required).

Impulsive helping

- Piliavin et *al*'s model suggests that help is least likely to be offered in life-threatening situations.
- Impulsive helping, where people act in almost reflexive ways, irrespective of personal cost, does sometimes occur.
- Piliavin *et al.* argue that emergency situations flood the bystander with arousal which narrows their attention towards the victim's plight.

Universal egoism

- The view that people are fundamentally selfish, and altruism is impossible (Dovidio, 1995).
- Simple Darwinian theory suggests that altruistic species should die out. However, altruism among animals *is* observed.
- The '*paradox of altruism*' can be explained if we assume that altruism is really a subtle form of *egoism* (e.g. 'investing') and this is roughly the approach taken by Piliavin *et al.*'s model.

Egoism vs. altruism

Is a bystander's response a selfish, *egoistic* act, or one performed to benefit others, with no expectation of benefit/gain (*altruistic*)?

Empathy–altruism

- The empathy–altruism hypothesis argues that sometimes we experience empathic concern for others and act to relieve their distress.
- The feelings produced by empathic concern are qualitatively different from those produced by personal distress.

63

THEORIES OF AGGRESSION AND THE REDUCTION AND CONTROL OF AGGRESSIVE BEHAVIOUR

SYLLABUS
1.4 Pro- and anti-social behaviour
- social–psychological theories of aggression, for example, social learning theory and social constructionism
- the implications of research on aggression for the reduction and control of aggressive behaviour

KEY QUESTIONS
- What theories have been advanced to explain aggressive behaviour?
- How can aggression be reduced?

Q

Section 1: Introducing aggression

1 How do Baron & Richardson (1994) define '*anti-social behaviours*'?
2 How can *aggression* be defined?
3 What is the difference between *pro-social aggression*, *anti-social aggression* and *sanctioned aggression*?

Section 2: Theories of aggression

4 According to Freud, what is *Thanatos*?
5 In Freud's *psychoanalytic approach*, what is the relationship between 'Thanatos' and aggression?
6 According to Lorenz (1966), why is aggression *instinctive* in all species?
7 What is *ritualisation*?
8 According to Lorenz, what has been the effect of '*weapons technology*' on aggression between humans?
9 What did Megargee (1966) discover about individuals who had committed brutally aggressive crimes?
10 Identify the main criticism of Freud's *instinct theory* of aggression.
11 Identify the main criticisms of Lorenz's *instinct theory* of aggression.
12 Dollard *et al.* (1939) proposed the *frustration–aggression hypothesis* in an effort to explain aggressive behaviour. What does this hypothesis state?
13 According to this account, what causes frustration?
14 What experiment, involving young children, did Barker *et al.* (1941) carry out in order to investigate the effects of frustration?
15 Complete the following sentence: 'According to Miller (1941), frustration is an instigator of aggression, but _____ factors (such as the fear of _____) may prevent actual aggression from occurring'.
16 According to Berkowitz's (1966, 1978, 1989) cue-arousal theory, what two conditions act together to produce aggression when frustration occurs?

17 In Geen & Berkowitz's experiment (1966), in which participants were insulted by a stooge and then required to administer electric shocks to the same stooge, did they administer more shock when the stooge was called 'Kirk Anderson' or 'Bob Anderson'?
18 In a similar experiment conducted by Berkowitz & LePage (1967), a stooge was subjected to higher levels of shock in the presence of certain cues. What were these cues?
19 What is the main principle behind Zillman's (1982) *excitation-transfer theory*?
20 Why did Zillman & Bryant (1974) require their participants to ride bicycles?
21 Which type of pornography is most likely to lead to a *decrease* in aggressive behaviour?
22 According to *social learning theory*, which two processes are responsible for the learning of aggressive behaviours?
23 How did Bandura (1965) use a 'Bobo doll' to demonstrate *vicarious reinforcement*?
24 How does the *social constructionist* approach suggest that we determine whether or not a behaviour is aggressive?

Section 3: Reducing/controlling aggression

25 What reasoning lies behind the *cathartic* approach to the reduction of aggressive behaviour?
26 Is *catharsis* effective, according to the research?
27 Identify one difficulty with the use of *punishment* to control aggressive behaviour.
28 What two factors, which may reduce aggressive behaviour, are suggested by the finding that exposure to aggressive models may influence aggressive behaviour?
29 How can *social skills training* help to reduce aggressive behaviour?
30 How do *cognitive interventions* help to reduce aggressive behaviours?
31 Identify five *clinical approaches* to the reduction of aggressive behaviour.

Section 1: Introducing aggression

1 Baron & Richardson (1994) define *anti-social behaviours* as those which show a lack of feeling and concern for the welfare of others.

2 *Aggression* can be defined as behaviour intended to harm or destroy another person who is motivated to avoid such treatment.

3 *Pro-social aggression* (such as the shooting of an armed robber) differs from *anti-social aggression* (such as mugging), in that it is in the interests of a society, or permitted by that society (*sanctioned aggression* – such as self-defence).

Section 2: Theories of aggression

4 *Thanatos* is a self-destructive drive directed towards death.

5 Thanatos may be directed *outwards*, towards some other thing or person, in the form of aggression.

6 Lorenz (1966) believes that aggression is adaptive, allowing animals to adapt to their environments, survive in them, and successfully reproduce.

7 *Ritualisation* is stereotyped patterns of behaviour which allow members of the same species to fight and be victorious without significant harm to either member.

8 Lorenz claims that '*weapons technology*' has enabled our intentions to override our instincts, allowing killing to take place without eye-contact or the 'safety device' of appeasement rituals.

9 Megargee (1966) found that these individuals were often *overcontrolled*, repressing their anger and allowing it to build up.

10 Freud's *instinct theory* of aggression is difficult to test empirically, since many of its essential concepts are global and inexact.

11 Lorenz's *instinct theory* of aggression cannot account for frequent instances of non-human aggression resulting in death, and fails to take into account how goals (such as mating/territory defence) may influence rituals. Lorenz's view of aggression as spontaneous rather than reactive has also been questioned.

12 The *frustration–aggression hypothesis* states that aggression always results from frustration and that frustration always leads to aggression.

13 Frustration is caused by unfulfilled desires (when an expected reinforcer is prevented from occurring).

14 Barker *et al.* (1941) showed young children attractive toys, then prevented them from playing with them. When they were eventually allowed to play with them, they threw, stomped on, and smashed the toys.

15 'According to Miller (1941), frustration is an instigator of aggression, but *situational* factors (such as the fear of *retaliation*) may prevent actual aggression from occurring.'

16 The two conditions are a *readiness to act aggressively* and the *presence of environmental cues*.

17 Participants administered more shock when the stooge was called '*Kirk* Anderson', having seen a film in which the actor *Kirk* Douglas was brutally beaten.

18 The cues were a *shotgun* and a *revolver*. The *weapons effect* refers to the tendency of weapons to stimulate violence (Berkowitz & LePage, 1967).

19 Zillman's (1982) *excitation-transfer theory* states that arousal from one source can be transferred to, and energise, some other response.

20 Zillman & Bryant (1974) had participants ride bicycles in order to raise their levels of arousal. They then investigated whether heightened arousal would affect the level of shock delivered to a stooge who had previously insulted them.

21 Donnerstein *et al.* (1987) found that '*soft*' pornography either *decreases* or has no effect on aggression, whereas 'hard core' pornography can lead to an increase in aggression.

22 *Reinforcement* and the *imitation* of aggressive models (*observational learning*) may lead to aggressive behaviour.

23 Bandura (1965) showed children videos of adults attacking a 'Bobo doll' and then being rewarded/punished/neither, and subsequently observed the children's behaviour in a similar situation.

24 The *social constructionist* approach suggests that whether behaviour is aggressive or not depends on whether it is judged to be so by the performer or an observer.

Section 3: Reducing/controlling aggression

25 The *cathartic* approach reasons that aggressive energy may 'build up', and that people can 'let off steam' through arousing but non-harmful actions (e.g. computer games).

26 No. In fact, research has suggested that cathartic activities may actually increase aggressive behaviour.

27 *Punishment* is only effective if *prompt*, *aversive* and *highly probable* following the target behaviour. Punishment *fails to teach the appropriate behaviours*, may be seen as *unjustified*, and may *provide a role model* for aggressive behaviour.

28 *Exposure to non-aggressive models*, in particular non-aggressive parents, and *non-aggressive role models* in the media, may help to counter the effects of exposure to aggressive models.

29 *Social skills training* can help to reduce aggressive behaviour by decreasing the frustration associated with an inability to cope adequately with social situations (e.g. communicating one's needs).

30 *Cognitive interventions* help to reduce aggressive behaviours by encouraging individuals to consider alternative explanations for others' behaviour (e.g. any mitigating circumstances).

31 *Desensitisation*, *active challenging*, *environmental control*, *rehearsal* and *practice* are all 'anger management' interventions.

Freud's psychoanalytic approach

- Freud proposed the existence of two drives:
  Eros – pleasure and self-preservation.
  Thanatos – self-destruction and death.
- Conflict between these two drives is resolved by Thanatos being turned *outward* as aggression.
- Cathartic activity (such as sport) may provide acceptable ways for people to express this need.

Research

- Megargee (1966): individuals committing brutally aggressive crimes were often 'overcontrolled' and repressed their anger.
- However, Freud's theories are difficult to test empirically.
- Lea (1984) cites several examples of non-human intraspecies aggression resulting in death, contradicting Lorenz's claims.

Lorenz's ethological approach

- Lorenz (1966): aggression is instinctive because it is adaptive.
- Most animals have 'built-in safety devices' which prevent them from killing their own species (e.g. **ritualisation**, where the end of combat is signalled by certain actions).
- Conflict may be avoided by **appeasement** rituals which prevent others from attacking.
- Once we became able to kill each other through weapons, appeasement rituals became ineffective and technology overrides instinct.

Instinct theories

Frustration–aggression hypothesis

- Dollard *et al.* (1939) translated Freud's work into social learning theory terms.
- Hypothesis proposes that *aggression is always a consequence of frustration* and *frustration always leads to aggression*.
- Frustration occurs when our goals are thwarted (i.e. when an expected reinforcer is prevented from occurring).
- Aggression will therefore emerge in specific situations and may be delayed, disguised, or directed towards a 'scapegoat'.

- Barker *et al.* (1941): children who were shown toys, then prevented from playing with them, were more likely to throw/smash them when allowed to play with them.
- Miller (1941): frustration is not *sufficient* for aggression, it can be expressed in ways other than aggression, and expression will depend partly on other situational factors (e.g. fear of retaliation).

Cue-arousal theory

- Berkowitz (1966, 1978, 1989): frustration does not always produce aggression. Frustration produces anger.
- Frustration is psychologically painful and psychological or physical pain can produce aggression.
- Two conditions act to produce aggression when frustration occurs:
  – **a readiness** to act aggressively
  – **environmental cues** associated with aggression/the frustrating object.

- **The weapons effect** (Berkowitz, 1968): stooges administered electric shocks to participants. Angry participants were then asked to administer shocks to the stooge. When a shotgun and revolver were placed on a nearby table, participants administered a higher level of shock than when they were absent.

Aggression

Aggression: some behaviour intended to harm or destroy another person who is motivated to avoid such treatment.

Antisocial behaviours: behaviours which show a lack of feeling and concern for the welfare of others (Baron & Richardson, 1994)

Excitation-transfer theory

- Zillman (1982): arousal from one source can be transferred to and energise some other response.
- There is a sequence in which arousal is generated then labelled, which produces a specific emotion such as anger.
- Arousal from any source (e.g. exercise, sex) can therefore produce heightened aggression (if mis-attributed).

- Zillman & Bryant (1974) aroused participants by requiring them to ride bicycles. Participants were then insulted by a stooge. Aroused participants delivered higher levels of harsh noise to stooges.

Social learning theory

- Aggressive behaviours are learned through reinforcement and imitation of aggressive models (Bandura, 1965, 1973, 1994).
- Reinforcement can take the form of praise for 'being tough,' or rewards for aggression.
- Observational learning involves observing others who serve as models for behaviour.

- **'Bobo Doll' study** *(Bandura 1965)*: children watched a video of an adult being aggressive towards an inflatable 'Bobo doll'. Children who observed the adult being rewarded for behaviour were significantly more aggressive than those who had seen the adult punished (or not rewarded) when placed in the same situation.

Clinical approaches
(Hollin & Howells, 1997)
- **Desensitisation:** using relaxation whilst imagining provoking stimuli.
- **Active challenging:** of unrealistic thoughts about other people.
- **Environmental control:** staying away from risky environments (e.g. clubs and pubs).
- **Rehearsal and practice:** of alternative ways of dealing with verbal prologue to conflict.

Reduction/control of aggression

Other approaches
(Baron & Byrne, 1994)
- **Social skills training:** reduces frustration experienced in social situations (e.g. not being able to communicate adequately).
- **Cognitive interventions:** changing the attributions which we make for others' behaviour (e.g. looking for mitigating circumstances).
- **Incompatible responses:** inducing emotional responses which are incompatible with aggression and inhibit it.

Catharsis

- Freudian and ethological approaches suggest that people can 'let off steam' through arousing but non-harmful actions.
- However, studies have suggested that attacking inanimate objects, attending sporting events, watching TV violence, may actually *increase* aggression (Baron & Byrne, 1994)

Punishment

- Punishment needs to be prompt, sufficiently strong to be aversive, and highly probable following the aggressive behaviour in order to be effective (Bower & Hillgard, 1981).
- Unfortunately, the weak link between crime and punishment in society means that most criminals are not deterred.

Exposure to non-aggressive models

- Punishment may be ineffective because those who deliver it are presenting aggressive models for behaviour.
- Children may copy aggressive behaviour from their parents and the media.
- Seeing other people behaving non-aggressively in the face of provocation may help reduce aggression (Donner-stein & Donnerstein, 1976).

64

MEDIA INFLUENCES ON PRO-SOCIAL AND ANTI-SOCIAL BEHAVIOUR

SYLLABUS
1.4 Pro- and anti-social behaviour
• media influences on pro- and anti-social behaviour

KEY QUESTIONS
- How much aggressive behaviour is shown on television?
- What are the effects of media aggression on children's behaviour?
- Can the media also have pro-social effects?
- How is media influence studied?

Q Section 1: Showing and watching aggression

1 What is the basic method used to quantify the amount of violence shown on television?

2 What was the principal finding of Gerbner's studies of violence on American television?

3 According to Cumberbatch's (1987) study of British television, what percentage of viewing time did violence occupy?

4 What was Cumberbatch's view regarding the increase in television violence in the decade up to 1987?

5 When Gunter & Harrison (1995) compared terrestrial and satellite channels for the percentage of programmes containing violent acts, what did they find?

6 According to Gunter and Harrison, in what type of programme were most of the violent acts contained?

7 What was the overall conclusion of Gunter and Harrison's study regarding the distribution of violence in television programmes?

Section 2: The effects of television on behaviour

8 What general conclusion, relevant to the study of the effects of television on children's behaviour, can be drawn from Bandura's (1965) 'Bobo doll' study?

9 How were Anderson et al. (1986) able to study the viewing habits of families?

10 Complete the following sentence: 'Anderson discovered that no-one watches the television for more than ___ per cent of the time it is on'.

11 Approximately how much time do adults spend watching television, per week?

12 At what age does the average number of hours of television watched per week peak?

13 Cumberbatch (1987) found that whilst violence in children's programmes was rare, there was one notable exception. What was it?

14 How do children differ from adults in their perception of violent acts on television?

15 How do correlational studies of television violence investigate the relationship between television violence and aggression?

16 What is the principal criticism of correlational studies of the effects of television violence on behaviour?

17 How did Liebert & Baron (1972) investigate the link between watching violent television and behaving aggressively?

18 Identify three problems associated with laboratory studies of media influences.

19 In general, what are the results of field experiments into the relationship between watching television violence and aggressive behaviour?

20 How did Williams (1986) conduct a 'natural experiment' in her study of the 'Notel' community?

21 In 1994, a study began to look at the effects of the introduction of television to the island of St Helena. The study is now in its fifth year. So far, what effects on pro-social behaviour have been found?

22 What relationship between television and arousal is proposed by Berkowitz (1993)?

23 How do the effects of television disinhibition and desensitisation differ?

24 What is probably the most direct link between watching television and the viewer's own behaviour?

25 Which type of individual is most likely to benefit from a 'cathartic' effect of watching television violence?

Section 3: Pro-social effects of the media

26 Name six pro-social effects of the media which researchers have found from laboratory studies which used specially prepared television materials.

27 What conclusion do Gunter & McAleer (1990) draw regarding the effects of televised examples of good behaviour?

28 What is involved in television literacy?

29 According to Mitchell (1983), what relation may computer games have with social interaction amongst children?

30 Identify five benefits associated with the use of computer games.

Section 1: Showing and watching aggression

1 A simple counting technique is used, with researchers defining violence objectively, then coding samples of television for incidents which match those definitions.

2 Gerbner found that although the number of programmes containing violence had not increased significantly since 1967, the number of violent episodes per show had increased.

3 Violence occupied about *one per cent* of viewing time.

4 Cumberbatch argued that whilst violence in society and concerns about violence on television had risen, this was not reflected by similar increases in violence on television.

5 Gunter & Harrison (1995) found that roughly *28 per cent* of terrestrial programmes contain violent acts, compared with *52 per cent* of programmes on satellite channels.

6 *Films* and *dramas* contained 70 per cent of the violent acts.

Section 2: The effects of television on behaviour

7 The study concluded that television violence is concentrated principally in a small number of programmes.

8 Bandura's (1965) '*Bobo doll' study* suggests that children can acquire new aggressive responses through exposure to a filmed model.

9 Anderson *et al.* (1986) installed automatic time-lapse video recording equipment in the homes of 99 families, with one camera recording people's behaviour in the room and the other focused on the television itself.

10 'Anderson discovered that no-one watches the television for more than *75 per cent* of the time it is on.'

11 Roughly *ten hours* per week (11.5 hours switched on, 7.56 hours looking at it).

12 The average number of hours of television watched per week peaks at the age of *ten*.

13 Cumberbatch (1987) found that *children's cartoons* contained relatively high amounts of violent behaviour.

14 Children differ from adults in their ratings of violence, and may not see violent acts which lack realism (such as cartoon violence) as being violent.

15 *Correlational studies* of television violence typically ask people which programmes they like most or watch most often, and then correlate this with measures of aggression, such as teacher's reports or self-reports.

16 Correlational studies can tell us whether there is a relationship between television violence and aggressive behaviour, but do not allow us to infer *causation*. It may be, for example, that naturally aggressive individuals choose to watch more violent television.

17 Liebert & Baron (1972) randomly assigned children to two groups. One group watched *The Untouchables*, which was violent, whilst the others watched a non-violent sports competition. They were then observed playing afterwards, and their aggressive acts measured.

18 Most *laboratory studies* use *small and unrepresentative samples*, under *unnatural viewing conditions*. Additionally, the *measures of viewing and aggressive behaviour are often far removed from everyday behaviour*. Overall, such studies lack *ecological validity*.

19 In general, the results show that children who watch violent television are more aggressive than those who do not (Parke *et al.*, 1977).

20 Williams (1986) studied a community where television had only recently been introduced (the 'Notel' community), comparing verbal and physical aggression with communities where there was either a single or several television channels.

21 The study of St Helena has shown that pro-social behaviours have not decreased since the introduction of television, and have actually increased slightly.

22 Berkowitz (1993) proposes that watching violence on television increases the viewer's overall level of *emotional arousal* and *excitement*.

23 *Disinhibition* is the reduction of inhibitions about behaving aggressively oneself (or coming to believe that aggression is a legitimate way of solving problems). *Desensitisation* is the reduction in emotional response to television violence (and an increased acceptance of it in real life) as a result of repeatedly viewing it.

24 *Imitation* is probably the most direct link between watching television and the viewer's own behaviour.

25 Individuals who score highly on cognitive measures of fantasy, daydreaming and imagination (Singer, 1989).

Section 3: Pro-social effects of the media

26 *Courage*, the *delay of gratification*, *adherence to rules*, *charitable behaviour*, *friendliness* and *affectionate behaviour* may all be influenced by the use of specially prepared TV material.

27 Gunter & McAleer (1990) conclude that televised examples of good behaviour can encourage children to behave in friendlier and more thoughtful ways to others.

28 *Television literacy* involves teaching children to be 'informed consumers' of television (e.g. distinguishing reality and make-believe, understanding the purpose of advertisements, and assessing stereotyping).

29 Mitchell (1983) points out that computer games may promote interaction in a beneficial way through co-operation and competition.

30 Computer games can act as *motivating devices* in the learning process, give children a *sense of confidence* in the use of IT, *equip them with computer-related skills*, can *promote social interaction*, allow the *release of aggression and stress*, *enhance cognitive skills*, *provide a sense of mastery and accomplishment*, and *reduce youth problems* (as a consequence of an addictive interest in computer games).

Media Influence on Behaviour

How much aggression is shown?

American TV – Gerbner's studies
(Gerbner, 1972; Gerbner & Gross, 1976; Gerbner et al., 1980, 1986)

- The percentage of TV shows containing violent incidents has remained the same since 1967.
- The number of violent episodes per show has gradually increased to around five violent acts per hour (prime time).
- On children's weekend shows, there were roughly 20 violent acts per hour.

UK TV – Cumberbatch's (1987) study

- 30% of programmes contained some violence (1.68 acts per hour, on average).
- Violence occupied just over 1% of viewing time.
- Death resulted from violence 26% of the time, but considerable blood and gore occurred in only 0.2% of cases.
- Perpetrators were more likely to be portrayed as 'baddies' than 'goodies'.

UK TV – Gunter & Harrison (1995)

- BBC 1 and 2, ITV, and Channel 4. 28% contained violent acts (52% for satellite channels).
- 70% of violence occurred in dramas and films, 19% in children's programmes.
- Most violent acts occurred in inner-city locations and the majority of perpetrators were young white males.
- 1% of programmes contained 19% of all violent acts.

Concluded that **violence is concentrated in a small number of programmes**.

How much do people watch?

Anderson et al. (1986):

- No one watches TV for more than 75% of the time it is on.
- Children average 12.8 hours (9.14 hours watching), adults 11.5 hours (7.56 hours watching) per week.
- Adult males look at the TV more than do adult females.
- Number of hours looking at TV increases up to age of 10 then decreases, levelling off at 17 years.

How is violence perceived?

- Cumberbatch (1987): children's cartoons contain relatively high amounts of violence.
- However, realism appears to be an important factor, since real life violence is judged as more violent than fictional violence (Gunter & McAleer, 1990).
- Although cartoons may *objectively* contain a large number of violent acts, children may *subjectively* perceive them as containing hardly any.

How does TV exert an influence?

Arousal

- Berkowitz (1993): watching violence increases a viewers' emotional arousal and excitement.
- More realistic violence is perceived by viewers as more arousing.

Disinhibition

- Refers to a reduction in the viewer's inhibitions about behaving aggressively.
- Relates to Berkowitz's 'cue-arousal' theory (see Ch 63)

Imitation

- Bandura (1965) showed that children may imitate aggressive adults (see Ch 65).
- However, cognitive factors (i.e. how violence is perceived and interpreted) will affect whether or not it is imitated.

Desensitisation

- A reduction in emotional response to TV violence and an acceptance of violence in real life.
- Increasingly violent programmes may be required to produce an emotional response (Gadow & Sprafkin, 1989).

Does viewing TV violence at an early age predict later aggression?

Comstock & Paik (1991): viewing TV violence at an early age *is* a predictor of later aggression (based on Huesmann & Eron's (1986) cross-cultural survey). However, Cumberbatch (1997) made the following criticisms:

- The Australian research showed *no* significant correlation between early TV viewing and later aggression.
- The Dutch researchers found no relationship and refused to allow their findings to be included.
- The American researchers found that when initial aggression was controlled for there was only a significant correlation in girls.
- The Polish researchers only found small effects which needed to be 'treated cautiously'.
- The Finnish researchers misunderstood their own data which in fact showed a *negative* correlation.

Media and pro-social behaviour

TV violence and catharsis

- Instinct theories suggest that watching TV violence might allow aggressive feelings to be released.
- Evidence suggests that if this effect does occur, it is restricted to individuals who score high on measures of fantasy and imagination (Singer, 1989)

Four areas of evidence for pro-social effects of TV
(Gunter & McAleer, 1990)

Laboratory studies with prepared materials: these have been shown to influence courage, delay of gratification, and promote adherence to rules, friendliness and affection.

Laboratory studies using broadcast materials specially designed for teaching (e.g. Sesame Street): children are able to identify and remember co-operative and helping behaviours emphasised.

Laboratory studies with materials from popular series: when pro-social behaviour is similar to that required of the child, programmes may influence behaviour in some circumstances.

Field studies relating pro-social viewing to pro-social behaviours: children who watch a high proportion of pro-social programmes are more likely to behave pro-socially; however, the correlations are weaker than with anti-social behaviour.

Computer games

- The long-term effects are unclear (Griffiths, 1997).
- They may promote interaction (through co-operation and competition) among children (Mitchell, 1983), have a cathartic effect (Kestenbaum & Weinstein, 1984) or provide a sense of achievement.

Methods of studying TV violence

Correlational studies

- Typically involve asking people what they watch and correlating these with reports of social behaviour by teachers, peers etc.
- Such studies are unable to infer cause and effect, and it may be that those who watch violent TV are different in some way.

Laboratory studies

- Designed to test for a causal link, and typically involve showing experimental groups of children violent programmes and observing their behaviour.
- Most use small and unrepresentative samples and unnatural viewing conditions, so it is unclear how they relate to the real world.

Field experiments

- Have greater ecological validity than laboratory experiments and typically involve assigning children to violent/non-violent viewing and measuring their behaviour.
- Poor control over extraneous variables mean that we cannot be certain what has caused differences between groups.

Natural experiments

- Researchers take advantage of naturally occurring divisions.
- Williams (1986) studied the 'Notel' community where TV was only recently introduced. Verbal and physical aggression *did* increase in the two year period following the introduction of TV.

UNIT 6

Abnormal Psychology and Atypical Development

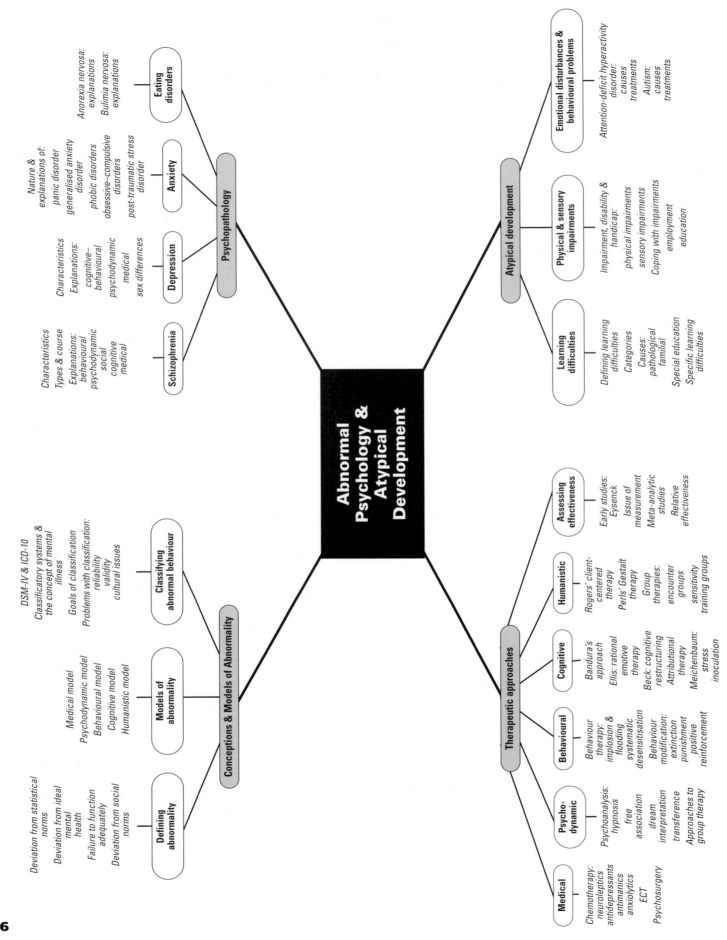

Abnormal Psychology & Atypical Development

Psychopathology

Schizophrenia
- Characteristics
- Types & course
- Explanations:
  - behavioural
  - psychodynamic
  - social
  - cognitive
  - medical

Depression
- Characteristics
- Explanations:
  - cognitive–behavioural
  - psychodynamic
  - medical
  - sex differences

Anxiety
- Nature & explanations of:
  - panic disorder
  - generalised anxiety disorder
  - phobic disorders
  - obsessive–compulsive disorders
  - post-traumatic stress disorder

Eating disorders
- Anorexia nervosa: explanations
- Bulimia nervosa: explanations

Atypical development

Learning difficulties
- Defining learning difficulties
- Categories
- Causes:
  - pathological
  - familial
- Special education
- Specific learning difficulties

Physical & sensory impairments
- Impairment, disability & handicap:
  - physical impairments
  - sensory impairments
- Coping with impairments
  - employment
  - education

Emotional disturbances & behavioural problems
- Attention-deficit hyperactivity disorder:
  - causes
  - treatments
- Autism: causes treatments

Conceptions & Models of Abnormality

Defining abnormality
- Deviation from statistical norms
- Deviation from ideal mental health
- Failure to function adequately
- Deviation from social norms

Models of abnormality
- Medical model
- Psychodynamic model
- Behavioural model
- Cognitive model
- Humanistic model

Classifying abnormal behaviour
- DSM-IV & ICD-10
- Classificatory systems & the concept of mental illness
- Goals of classification
- Problems with classification:
  - reliability
  - validity
  - cultural issues

Therapeutic approaches

Medical
- Chemotherapy:
  - neuroleptics
  - antidepressants
  - antimanics
  - anxiolytics
- ECT
- Psychosurgery

Psycho-dynamic
- Psychoanalysis:
  - hypnosis
  - free association
  - dream interpretation
  - transference
- Approaches to group therapy

Behavioural
- Behaviour therapy:
  - implosion & flooding
  - systematic desensitisation
- Behaviour modification:
  - extinction
  - punishment
  - positive reinforcement

Cognitive
- Bandura's approach
- Ellis: rational emotive therapy
- Beck: cognitive restructuring
- Attributional therapy
- Meichenbaum: stress inoculation

Humanistic
- Rogers' client-centered therapy
- Perls' Gestalt therapy
- Group therapies:
  - encounter groups
  - sensitivity training groups

Assessing effectiveness
- Early studies: Eysenck
- Issue of measurement
- Meta-analytic studies
- Relative effectiveness

65

WHAT IS ABNORMALITY?

SYLLABUS
4.2 Conceptions and models of abnormality
- alternative approaches to defining normal and abnormal behaviour, including their practical problems and ethical implications
- cultural and subcultural differences in the definition of abnormality

KEY QUESTIONS
Can we define abnormality as:
- a deviation from statistical norms?
- a deviation from ideal mental health?
- a failure to function adequately?
- a deviation from social norms?

Section 1: Deviation from statistical norms
1 What is the literal definition of *abnormality*?
2 What is the *deviation from statistical norms* definition of abnormality?
3 In what way does this definition fail to take into account the *desirability* of a behaviour or characteristic?
4 How does this definition fail to take into account the *undesirability* of a behaviour or characteristic?
5 Identify one further difficulty with the *deviation from statistical norms* definition of abnormality.

Section 2: Deviation from ideal mental health
6 How does the *deviation from ideal mental health* approach define abnormality?
7 Identify four of the 'characteristics of ideal mental health' proposed by Jahoda (1958).
8 What is the difficulty with using such characteristics to define abnormality?
9 What is an important difference between judgements of *physical health* and judgements of *mental health*?
10 What argument does Chance (1984) advance regarding the cultural variability of standards for mental health?
11 Complete the following sentence: 'Not only does the mental health definition change across cultures, it changes over ___ within a culture (it is ___-dependent)'.

Section 3: Failure to function adequately
12 What two things should every human being achieve, according to the *failure to function adequately model* of abnormality?
13 Why do Sue *et al.* (1994) use the terms '*practical*' and '*clinical*' criteria to describe the ways in which people fail to function adequately?
14 What do Miller & Morley (1986) have to say in support of the *personal distress model of abnormality*?

15 Give two reasons why this model may not be an adequate definition of abnormality.
16 Identify one other form of distress which may be used in defining abnormality.
17 Identify one difficulty with using 'others' distress' as a criterion for abnormality.
18 What does '*maladaptiveness*' mean in relation to defining abnormality?
19 What constitutes '*unexpected behaviour*', according to Davison & Neale (1994)?
20 Identify one further criterion according to which an individual could be seen as failing to function adequately.
21 What is the principal difficulty in using 'bizarreness' as a criterion for abnormality?

Section 4: Deviation from social norms
22 What is a *norm*?
23 Identify the five classes of behaviour which exist on the continuum of normative behaviour (Gross, 1995).
24 How did Gibson (1967) demonstrate that certain 'socially unacceptable' behaviours were actually statistically quite frequent?
25 What did Mead (1935) discover when studying the Mundugumor people?
26 What differences in the social norms of our own culture and that of the Trobriand Islanders did Malinowski (1929) discover?
27 Social norms clearly change across cultures. In what other way do they change?
28 How many of the characteristics which have been suggested as definitions of abnormality would you expect to be reflected in behaviours actually *classified* as being mental disorders?
29 What solution do Sue *et al.* (1994) propose to the lack of consensus on the 'best definition' of abnormality?

Section 1: Deviation from statistical norms

1 Literally, *abnormality* means deviating from the norm or average.

2 The *deviation from statistical norms* definition says that behaviours or characteristics which are statistically infrequent are abnormal.

3 Behaviours may be statistically infrequent but nevertheless *desirable* (such as creativity) and we would not want to classify such behaviours as abnormal.

4 Behaviours which are *undesirable*, and which we might wish to classify as abnormal (such as child abuse, eating disorders and depression), may in fact be statistically quite common.

5 This definition implies a 'cut-off' point for what is normal, which must be necessarily *arbitrary* (e.g. what is a 'normal' height?), and will clearly vary between cultures.

Section 2: Deviation from ideal mental health

6 By identifying the characteristics which people should possess in order to be considered 'normal', we can define abnormality as a deviation from these characteristics.

7 Amongst others, Jahoda (1958) identifies *individual choice*, *resistance to stress*, an *accurate perception of reality*, and *self-actualisation* as characteristics of ideal mental health.

8 Most of us would fall foul of at least one of these criteria, with the consequence that most of us would be considered abnormal.

9 Judgements of *physical health* make reference to the *objective physical state* of the individual and can be stated in anatomical and physical terms. Judgements of *mental health* are essentially *value judgements*.

10 Chance (1984) proposes that there must be universal standards to which we should all aspire, regardless of culture and regardless of the popularity of certain behaviours (e.g. murder can never be considered mentally healthy).

11 'Not only does the mental health definition change across cultures, it changes over *time* within a culture (it is *era-dependent*).'

Section 3: Failure to function adequately

12 According to this model, we should all achieve some *sense of personal well-being* and make some *contribution to the larger social group*.

13 Sue *et al.* (1994) use these two terms since they are often the basis on which people come to the attention of psychologists or other professionals.

14 Miller & Morley (1986) point out that people present themselves to clinics principally because their feelings or behaviours cause them distress.

15 Personal distress may sometimes be the *appropriate* response to certain circumstances, and in some cases we may wish to classify behaviours as abnormal where the individual is *not* experiencing any personal distress (such as with dissocial personality disorder).

16 The *distress to others*, caused by an individual's behaviour, may sometimes be used to determine whether or not a behaviour is abnormal.

17 Using others' distress can lead to an individual being unfairly classified as abnormal, by involving others' own judgements and values.

18 *Maladaptiveness* is when individuals are prevented from efficiently satisfying their occupational and social roles.

19 Davison & Neale (1994) claim that '*unexpected behaviour*' involves reacting to a situation or event in ways which could not be predicted or reasonably expected from what is known about human behaviour (e.g. acting in a way which is 'out of all proportion to the situation').

20 If an individual's behaviour is *bizarre* it may constitute a failure to function adequately.

21 What is 'bizarre' will vary depending on the *context* and the *justification* for the behaviour.

Section 4: Deviation from social norms

22 A *norm* is an expectation about how people should behave and think.

23 The continuum of normative behaviour includes *unacceptable*, *tolerable*, *acceptable/permissible*, *desirable*, and *required/obligatory* behaviours.

24 Gibson (1967) studied the 'confession rates' of people to prosecutable offences (such as shoplifting), and discovered relatively high rates for these behaviours.

25 Mead (1935) discovered that levels of suspicion comparable to what we would call 'paranoia' in the West were the norm, since strangers were quite likely to be hostile.

26 Malinowski (1929) discovered that Trobriand Islanders were expected to clean the bones of their dead relatives and wear them as ornaments.

27 Social norms change across *time* and are, therefore, '*era-dependent*'.

28 Any of the behaviours classified as mental disorders may reflect *one*, a *combination*, or *none* of the characteristics used to define abnormality.

29 Sue *et al.* (1994) have proposed a *multiple-perspectives* (or *multiple-definitions*) approach, according to which all points of view are considered as part of the evaluation of an individual.

Deviation from statistical norms

- The most obvious and intuitive way of defining abnormality: individuals possessing statistically infrequent characteristics or behaviours are abnormal.
- Someone who behaves in a way unlike the vast majority of people may be labelled 'abnormal'.

Problems

- **Some behaviours are statistically abnormal but desirable:** e.g. genius (Balamurali Ambati became the youngest doctor in the world at 17, Mozart performed his own concerto aged 3).
- **Some behaviours are statistically normal but undesirable:** Hasset & White (1989) point out that one in two Americans is either depressed and/or involved in child abuse.
- **How far must one deviate from the average?:** at what point does someone's height become abnormal, for example? Any chosen cut-off point will be arbitrary (Miller & Morley, 1986).

Deviation from social norms

- Norms are expectations about how people *should* behave and think. All societies have norms, but these will differ from one society to another and over time.
- Abnormality can be considered in terms of breaking society's standards or norms.

Problems

- **Most people deviate from some norms:** Gibson (1967) found high 'confession rates' amongst people for prosecutable offences from which they had escaped conviction.
- **Norms change with time:** some behaviours come to be viewed as differences in lifestyle, rather than abnormal, over time (e.g. homosexuality, which was classed as a mental disorder until 1973).
- **Norms are culture-bound:** social norms vary between cultures and any such definition of abnormality will be culture-relative.

Norms across cultures

- Mead (1935): a high degree of suspicion (which we would consider paranoia) is common among the Mundugumor people, where even male members of the same household may be hostile.
- Malinowski (1929) studied the Trobriand Islanders, where the bones of dead relatives are cleaned and worn as ornaments.

Abnormality – Definitions

Deviation from ideal mental health

- Abnormality can be defined as deviating from the characteristics and abilities which one should possess in order to be considered mentally healthy.
- This may mean possessing characteristics which should *not* be possessed (e.g. hearing voices) or *not* possessing characteristics which *should* be possessed (e.g. being able to cope with stress).
- Jahoda (1958) has suggested a number of ideals, including *individual choice, resistance to stress, accurate perception of reality, self-actualisation* (being who you want to be) as possible characteristics of mental health.

Problems

- **Most of us fail to demonstrate all these characteristics, all the time:** Maslow (1968) points out that few people achieve self-actualisation, and some of us may not always feel that we are coping with stress. As a result, most of us would be considered abnormal at some time.
- **Such ideals are value judgements, not objective judgements:** unlike physical health, which can be defined in clear physical terms (Szasz, 1960), judgements about mental health may involve cultural and personal values about what is healthy. This leaves the decision open to bias.
- **Ideals of mental health vary between cultures:** in the Sambia of New Guinea, male youths are taught that females are poison and the males engage in prescribed unlimited fellatio. On the island of Java, soccer is played with a ball that is soaked in petrol then set alight.
- **Ideals of mental health vary with time and context:** Chance (1984) claims that there are certain universal standards and that, for example, murder cannot be considered healthy even if it is popular. However, during war-time, pacifists may be considered negatively, and schizophrenic symptoms (such as hallucinations) would be seen as healthy 'visions' in a 13th-century monk (Wade & Tavris, 1993).

Failure to function adequately

- Every human being should achieve a sense of personal well-being and make some contribution to a larger social group. Abnormality is defined as a failure to function adequately in this respect.
- Such failures include the 'practical' and 'clinical' criteria below (Sue *et al.*, 1994):

Personal distress

Most people come to clinics because their feelings/behaviours cause them distress (Miller & Morley, 1986). These feelings may take forms such as anxiety, depression, and loss of appetite, and may not be obvious to other people.

Problems

- We cannot use this as a definition on its own since such feelings may be appropriate responses under some circumstances (e.g. the death of a loved one).
- Some mental disorders are not accompanied by personal distress (e.g. repeated acts of crime with dissocial personality disorder).

Others' distress

Some psychological states may not be distressing for the individual him/herself, but lead to distress in others. Being the cause of others' distress can thus constitute a failure to function adequately.

Problems

- Others can introduce their own values into a judgement (e.g. a father's distress over his son's homosexuality: Gross, 1995).

Maladaptiveness

If behaviour is maladaptive (i.e. prevents the person from efficiently satisfying social and occupational roles), then it may be classed as abnormal even if not causing distress (e.g. substance-use disorders).

Unexpected behaviour

If a person reacts in way which could not reasonably be predicted, then we may see them as functioning inadequately, for example, behaviour which is out of all proportion to the situation (such as extreme over-reactions: Davison & Neale, 1994).

Problems

- Unexpected behaviours may also involve under-reactions, which may be more difficult to identify.

Bizarreness

A person is failing to function adequately if behaviour would be considered bizarre in the circumstances (e.g. walking around a university naked).

Problems

- Under some circumstances, bizarre behaviours are not abnormal (e.g. transvestitism is common in pantomimes).

66

AN INTRODUCTION TO MODELS IN ABNORMAL PSYCHOLOGY

SYLLABUS

4.2 Conceptions and models of abnormality
- assumptions of the medical, behavioural, cognitive, humanistic and psychodynamic models of abnormal psychology including their implications for treatment and ethical implications

KEY QUESTIONS

How do the following models explain and approach the treatment of mental disorders:
- the medical model?
- the psychodynamic model?
- the behavioural model?
- the cognitive model?
- the humanistic model?

Q

Section 1: The medical model

1 Which model of abnormality was replaced by the emergence of the *medical model* in the eighteenth century?
2 What central claim regarding the nature of mental disorders is made by the medical model?
3 Upon what evidence were the early successes of the medical model based?
4 From what observation do *genetic theories* of mental disorders originate?
5 How do *biochemical theories* explain mental disorders?
6 What other term is used to describe *medical therapies*?
7 Identify two problems associated with the use of *drug therapies*.
8 Name the two other principal forms of therapy associated with the medical model.
9 Identify one criticism common to both these forms of therapy.

Section 2: The psychodynamic model

10 How did Freud explain *hysteria*, in which physical symptoms are experienced but there are no underlying physical causes?
11 Name the three interacting structures which Freud believed comprise the personality.
12 What is 'normality' according to the *psychodynamic model*?
13 According to Freud, which *psychosexual stage* of development is experienced between the ages of three and five or six?
14 What are *defence mechanisms*?
15 What did Freud call the defence mechanism in which we redirect our emotional responses from a dangerous object to a safe one?
16 What is the first aim of *psychoanalysis*?
17 What is the goal of *therapeutic regression* (Winnicott, 1958)?
18 Identify two criticisms of the methodology used by Freud in developing his psychodynamic model.
19 What is meant by the criticism that Freud's model is both *reductionist* and *deterministic*?

Section 3: The behavioural model

20 Complete the sentence: 'Whilst the medical and psychodynamic models explain disorders in terms of internal factors, the behavioural model sees disorders as _____ _____ which are learned and maintained'.
21 According to the *behavioural model*, where should we look if we wish to explain mental disorders?
22 What were Watson & Rayner (1920) able to demonstrate with Little Albert?
23 What two forms of conditioning are held to explain the origins of mental disorders?
24 Identify the three things therapies based on the behavioural model have in common.

Section 4: The cognitive model

25 What way in which individuals may learn new behaviours is identified by *social learning theorists*?
26 What is the main difference between the *cognitive model* and the *behavioural model*?
27 How does the *information-processing approach* view mental disorders?
28 Complete the sentence: 'Beck (1974) argues that disorders like depression are often 'rooted' in the ____ ways people think about themselves and the world'.
29 Identify the five types of illogical thinking which Beck (1974) identified as contributing to depression.
30 What is *cognitive restructuring*?

Section 5: The humanistic model

31 According to the *humanistic model*, what do human beings strive for?
32 According to this model, how are humans different from non-humans?
33 What is *unconditional positive regard* (Rogers, 1951)?
34 What are the aims of *humanistic therapies*?
35 How does the role of the humanistic therapist differ from the more traditional therapist role?

Section 1: The medical model

1 The *demonological model*, which saw mental disorders as resulting from supernatural forces.

2 The medical model claims that mental disorders are forms of *illness* which can be treated with medical techniques.

3 Early successes were largely based on showing that mental disorders could be linked to gross destruction of brain tissue.

4 *Genetic theories* of mental disorders originate from the observation that some mental disorders have a tendency to run in families.

5 *Biochemical theories* explain mental disorders as a result of imbalances of neurotransmitters.

6 Medical therapies are also known as *somatic therapies*.

7 Drug therapies are *rarely cures*, and usually *only treat the symptoms* of a disorder. They frequently have *unpleasant side-effects*, and have been accused of being used as a form of '*social control*'.

8 *Electroconvulsive therapy* (ECT) and *psychosurgery*.

9 Both these forms of therapy *lack a convincing scientific rationale* to explain their effects.

Section 2: The psychodynamic model

10 Freud explained *hysteria* as a result of unresolved and unconscious sexual conflicts originating in childhood.

11 The *id*, the *ego*, and the *superego*.

12 Normality is a balance between the conflicting demands of the id, ego, and superego.

13 The *phallic stage*.

14 *Defence mechanisms* are ways in which the ego prevents anxiety-arousing impulses and thoughts from reaching consciousness.

15 Freud termed this redirection of impulses *displacement*.

16 The first aim of *psychoanalysis* is to make the unconscious conscious, thereby providing people with *insight* into their problems.

17 *Therapeutic regression* enables the person to re-experience repressed feelings from childhood in a safe context, so that they can experience these feelings in a more appropriate way.

18 Freud's methods *lacked scientific rigour* (depending largely on inference rather than objective evidence) and his *samples were biased* (consisting largely of upper middle-class Viennese women aged 20–44).

19 Freud's model reduces the complexity of human behaviour to the interplay of three forces (*reductionist*), and sees people as helpless to change themselves since 'the die is cast early in life' (*deterministic*).

Section 3: The behavioural model

20 'Whilst the medical and psychodynamic models explain disorders in terms of internal factors, the behavioural model sees disorders as *maladaptive behaviours* which are learned and maintained.'

21 According to this model, we should look at the *environmental conditions* in which the behaviour is displayed.

22 Watson & Rayner (1920) were able to demonstrate that a *phobia* (in Albert's case, a phobia of white rats) could be acquired through *classical conditioning*.

23 *Operant conditioning* and *classical conditioning*.

24 Therapies based on the behavioural model *focus on maladaptive behaviours* rather than speculating as to their cause, *base the success or failure of the treatment on specific observable changes*, and believe that *the value claimed for a treatment should be related to evidence from experimental studies*.

Section 4: The cognitive model

25 *Social learning theorists* point out that certain behaviours can be acquired simply by *watching* them being performed.

26 Unlike the *behavioural model*, the *cognitive model* believes that cognitions such as thoughts, expectations and attitudes play an important role in causing mental disorders.

27 The *information-processing approach* views mental disorders as resulting from a disturbed 'input–output sequence' in the storage, manipulation and retrieval of information.

28 'Beck (1974) argues that disorders like depression are often 'rooted' in the *maladaptive* ways people think about themselves and the world.'

29 Beck (1974) identified *magnification*, *minimisation*, *selective abstraction*, *arbitrary inference* and *overgeneralisation* as examples of illogical thinking.

30 *Cognitive restructuring* involves identifying maladaptive thoughts or ways of thinking, and challenging and attempting to change them.

Section 5: The humanistic model

31 Human beings strive for *growth*, *dignity*, *self-determination* and *self-actualisation*.

32 Humans are different from non-humans in that they possess free will and a desire to achieve *self-actualisation*.

33 *Unconditional positive regard* is the assurance that we will be loved and accepted despite our shortcomings.

34 *Humanistic therapies* aim to remove blocks to self-development, put people in touch with their true selves, and promote continued growth (and self-actualisation), rather than allowing external factors to influence behaviour.

35 *Humanistic therapists* see themselves as partners in the therapeutic process (as a *facilitator*), and will consciously avoid giving advice or assuming the role of 'expert'.

A

The medical model

- Emerged in the 18th century, replacing the 'demonological' model, which saw supernatural forces as responsible for mental disorders.
- Proposed that all mental disorders are actually forms of physical illness (pathology) which could be treated with appropriate medical techniques.
- Proposed that the brain plays a central role in 'psychic functioning'. Early successes were largely based on showing that mental disorders could be linked to gross destruction of brain tissue.
- More recently, the model has looked at the role played by neurotransmitters and genetics in mental disorders.

Somatic therapies
- **Chemotherapy** (drugs) alleviate symptoms, do not offer a cure, have unpleasant side effects.
- **Electroconvulsive therapy** (electricity): effective for depression, but lacks a convincing rationale and causes some amnesia.
- **Psychosurgery** (surgery): irreversible, dangerous, and poorly understood.

Biochemical and genetic theories
- **Biochemical theories** explain mental disorders in terms of an imbalance of neurotransmitters.
- **Genetic theories** derive from the discovery that some disorders run in families, and proposes that DNA may transmit disorders.

The behavioural model

- Rejects references to internal factors and claims that mental disorders are maladaptive behaviours.
- Sees maladaptive behaviours as learned and maintained in the same way as adaptive behaviours (conditioning).
- Maintains that the best way of explaining disorders is to consider the environmental conditions in which a behaviour is displayed.
- Theorists use the case of little Albert (below) as a model for the acquisition of all abnormal fears.

Little Albert
(Watson & Rayner, 1920)
- Albert, an 11-month-old boy, was conditioned to fear a white rat by presenting the rat at the same time as striking a steel bar behind his head.
- After seven combinations, Albert not only feared the rat, but this fear had generalised to a white rabbit, cotton wool, a fur coat and the experimenter's white hair.

Behavioural therapies
- Therapies attempt to change systematically behaviour by applying learning principles.
- The success or failure of a treatment is based on specific and observable changes in behaviour.
- Therapists believe that the value of a therapy must be supported by evidence from experimental studies.

Abnormality – Models

The humanistic model

- Humanistic psychologists view people as a set of potentials who are basically good and strive for growth, dignity and self-determination.
- Humanistic psychologists view the whole personality (e.g. joy, sorrow, alienation, intimacy) as worthy of study.
- Claims that humans differ from non-humans in that they possess free will and the desire for self-actualisation.
- Sees each individual as unique, free, rational and self-determining.
- Mental disorders arise because external factors block personal growth.

Humanistic therapies:
- Aim to remove blocks to self-development, put people in touch with their true selves, and promote continued growth.
- Individuals in therapy are termed *'clients'* rather than 'patients' and are seen as partners in therapy.
  Responsibility for success is placed more with the client than the therapist (or 'facilitator').
- Therapy offers *'unconditional positive regard'* (Rogers, 1951) or 'loving us for what we are' to counter feelings that we must achieve certain standards or be a certain way in order to be accepted (resulting from 'conditional positive regard').
- Therapies focus on the 'here and now' rather than on past conflicts, and the therapist consciously avoids giving advice or assuming the role of 'expert'.
- Examples: client-centred therapy and Gestalt therapy

The cognitive model

- Accepts the behavioural account of learning but focuses on the thoughts, expectations, and attitudes (*'cognitions'*) which accompany behaviour and which may cause mental disorders.
- Social learning theorists point out that behaviours can be acquired through *observational learning* (Bandura, 1969).
- Proposes that 'mediating processes', such as thoughts, interpretations and perceptions of ourselves, are important in causing disorders (not just conditioning).
- Some approaches see individuals as *information-processors* whose input–output sequences may become disordered (e.g. by faulty storage or manipulation of information).
- Other approaches see mental disorders as resulting from faulty patterns of thinking (see below).

Cognitive therapies
(Beck & Weishaar, 1989)
Aim to teach people to:
- monitor their negative, automatic thoughts
- recognise the connection between cognition, affect and behaviour
- examine the evidence for and against distorted thoughts
- replace these with more reality-oriented interpretations
- identify and alter beliefs which pre-dispose them to distort their experiences.

Cognitive restructuring
(Beck, 1974)
Disorders such as depression often involve maladaptive ways of thinking, e.g.:
- **Magnification and minimisation:** magnifying failures and minimising successes.
- **Arbitrary inference:** arriving at a conclusion about oneself without any supporting evidence.

Therapy aims to identify and challenge such beliefs.

The psychodynamic model

- Freud argued that mental disorders were caused by psychological **conflicts** which originated in **childhood** and are **unconscious**.
- The personality is composed of **three interacting structures** (see below). When these are in balance, normality is attained, but when unconscious conflicts cannot be managed, disorders arise. Neurotic symptoms may represent compromises between these structures and reflect the stage of development at which the conflict occurred. '**Defence mechanisms**' serve to protect us from these conflicts.
- The aim of therapy is to **make the unconscious conscious** and to provide people with **insight** into their problems. Often involves **therapeutic regression** and **interpretation** (e.g. of dreams) in order to unearth **repressed** material.

Structures of the personality
ID (operates on the *pleasure principle*): present at birth, impulsive and pleasure-seeking.

EGO (operates on the *reality principle*): negotiates compromises between id and superego and helps us cope with reality.

SUPEREGO (Conscience + ego-ideal): governs moral judgements and feelings.

Psychosexual stages
Oral stage (0–1 yr): pleasure achieved through the mouth.

Anal stage (1–3 yrs): pleasure achieved through anal membranes.

Phallic stage (3–5/6 yrs): pleasure through self-manipulation of genitals.

Latency stage (5/6–12 yrs): sexual motivations recede in importance.

Genital stage (after puberty): pleasure through heterosexual relationships.

Some defence mechanisms
Repression: unacceptable thoughts/ impulses are pushed into the unconscious.

Reaction formation: the opposite of an unacceptable impulse is expressed.

Rationalisation: socially acceptable reasons are given for unacceptable motives.

Displacement: an emotional response is redirected towards a 'safe' object.

Projection: unacceptable motives/ impulses are transferred to others.

67

CLASSIFYING ABNORMAL BEHAVIOUR

SYLLABUS

4.2 Conceptions and models of abnormality
- alternative approaches to classifying normal and abnormal behaviour, including their practical problems and ethical implications. Approaches should include DSM and ICD
- cultural and subcultural differences in the definition of abnormality including biases relating to diagnosis and classification

KEY QUESTIONS
- What are DSM-IV and ICD-10?
- How do psychosis and neurosis differ?
- What issues surround the use of the term 'mental illness'?
- What are the goals of classification and difficulties in achieving these goals?
- What other issues surround classificatory systems?

Section 1: Introducing DSM-IV and ICD-10

1 Who was the first person to attempt a comprehensive classification of abnormal behaviours?
2 What is the full name of the classificatory system introduced by the World Health Organisation in 1948?
3 What are the three catagories of mental disturbance or mental disorder identified in the 1983 Mental Health Act (England and Wales)?
4 Identify any one *organic mental disorder* identified in ICD-10.
5 Into which ICD-10 category would an individual suffering from *bipolar disorder* fall?
6 Into which DSM-IV category would *multiple personality disorder* fall?
7 Into which DSM-IV category would *anorexia nervosa* fall?
8 Which of ICD-10 and DSM-IV has the larger number of *discrete categories*?

Section 2: Neurosis, psychosis and mental illness

9 In what way do *neurotics* and *psychotics* differ with regard to 'contact with reality'?
10 What is the relationship between neurosis, psychosis and the *pre-morbid personality*?
11 Do ICD-10 and DSM-IV use the terms 'neurotic' and 'psychotic'?
12 Identify the four reasons given by Gelder *et al.* (1989) for abolishing the distinction between neurosis and psychosis.
13 How does Blaney (1975) defend the decision to think of abnormal behaviour as indicative of some kind of underlying *illness*?
14 According to Szasz (1974, 1994), what political purpose is served by labels such as '*mentally ill*'?
15 What, according to Szasz, is the difference between *diseases of the brain* and *problems in living*?
16 Which term, used to describe conditions resulting in abnormal behaviour, is used by both ICD-10 and DSM-IV?

17 Why has DSM-IV removed the category *organic mental disorder* from the classificatory system?

Section 3: Goals and problems with classification

18 Identify the three common goals shared by ICD-10 and DSM-IV.
19 Briefly describe Rosenhan's (1973) first experiment which questions the *reliability* and *validity* of classification of mental disorders.
20 What did Rosenhan's follow-up experiment involve?
21 What does the term '*reliability*' refer to when used to describe a diagnosis?
22 What did Cooper *et al.* (1972) discover about the diagnoses given by American and British psychiatrists?
23 In what way were Cooper *et al.* able to reduce these differences?
24 What is *multiaxial classification*, as introduced by DSM-III (1980)?
25 Name the five '*axes*' used by the DSM system.
26 Which of DSM-IV and ICD-10 gives more prominence to the *aetiology* of disorders?
27 What does the term '*validity*' refer to when used to describe a diagnosis?
28 What did Bannister *et al.* (1964) discover when investigating the relationship between diagnosis and treatment?
29 How do critics of Rosenhan's study argue that the *pseudopatients*' behaviour after admission was not normal?
30 What percentage of the general population and what percentage of the psychiatric population are black?
31 What is an *adaptive paranoid response*?
32 According to Littlewood & Lipsedge (1989), mental illness in minorities is an intelligible response to what?
33 Why does Littlewood (1992) criticise DSM-IV for being *ethnocentric*?

Q

Section 1: Introducing DSM-IV and ICD-10

1 Kraepelin (1913) was the first to attempt a comprehensive classification of abnormal behaviours.

2 The full name is the *International Standard Classification of Diseases, Injuries and Causes of Death*.

3 The 1983 Mental Health Act identifies *mental illness, personality disorder* and *mental impairment* as the three categories of mental disturbance.

4 Dementia in Alzheimer's disease, personality and behavioural disorders due to brain disease, damage and dysfunction (e.g. BSE) are all examples of organic mental disorders (ICD-10).

5 *Bipolar disorder* falls into the category '*mood (affective) disorders*'.

6 *Multiple personality disorder* falls into the category '*dissociative disorders*' in DSM-IV.

7 *Anorexia nervosa* falls into the DSM-IV category, '*eating disorders*'.

8 *DSM-IV* has the larger number of *discrete categories* and *ICD-10* a smaller number of more *general categories*.

Section 2: Neurosis, psychosis and mental illness

9 *Neurotics* maintain contact with reality, whereas *psychotics* lose contact (e.g. hallucinations and delusions).

10 Neurotic disturbances are related to the individual's personality prior to the disorder (the *pre-morbid personality*), whereas psychotic disorders are not.

11 ICD-10 uses the term neurotic and DSM-IV the term psychotic.

12 Gelder *et al.* (1989) believe that disorders included under these categories actually have little in common; these categories are less informative than more specific classifications (e.g. schizophrenia); the criteria used to distinguish neurosis and psychosis all have exceptions; the groupings are based on supposed common origins (related to the psychodynamic model) rather than observable commonalities.

13 Blaney (1975) argues that the term 'ill' is more *humane* than alternatives, since a person so described is seen as a 'victim' and not blameworthy.

14 Szasz (1974, 1994) believes that labels such as '*mentally ill*' may serve the political purpose of excluding those who have upset the social order.

15 Szasz argues that the term *diseases of the brain* should be applied to mental disorders resulting from a known organic cause, and *problems in living* to describe 'functional disorders' (i.e. those for which there is no known physical basis).

16 *Mental disorder* is the term used by both ICD-10 and DSM-IV.

17 The category *organic mental disorder* has been removed from DSM-IV because it implies that other disorders in the manual do not have an organic component.

Section 3: Goals and problems with classification

18 ICD-10 and DSM-IV share the goals of providing a common shorthand language (L), understanding the origins (O) of mental disorders, and identifying appropriate treatment (T) plans (LOT).

19 Rosenhan (1973) instructed eight psychiatrically normal people to present themselves to psychiatrists, complaining of hearing voices. Each was able to gain admission to psychiatric hospitals and most were diagnosed as schizophrenic.

20 In Rosenhan's follow-up experiment, he warned members of a teaching hospital that *pseudopatients* would be trying to gain admittance and to try to identify them. There were no pseudopatients; nevertheless, roughly one-quarter of (presumably) genuinely disturbed individuals was suspected of being pseudopatients by at least one member of staff.

21 *Reliability* refers to the consistency of a diagnosis across repeated measurements.

22 Cooper *et al.*(1972) found that American psychiatrists were far more likely to diagnose schizophrenia whereas manic depression was more likely to be diagnosed by British psychiatrists.

23 Cooper *et al.* were able to reduce these differences by establishing specific criteria and training clinicians in these.

24 *Multiaxial classification* involves assessing patients on five different axes which represent different areas of functioning. This gives a broader and more in-depth picture.

25 The five 'axes' are *clinical syndromes* and other conditions that may be a focus of clinical attention, *personality disorders*, *general medical conditions*, *psychosocial and environmental problems*, and *global assessment of functioning*.

26 ICD-10 gives more prominence to the *aetiology* (*cause*) of disorders within its various categories.

27 *Validity* refers to the extent to which a diagnosis reflects an actual disorder (i.e. how accurate it is).

28 Bannister *et al.* (1964) discovered no clear-cut relationship between diagnosis and treatment.

29 Critics argue that a normal person would say 'I'm not crazy, I just pretended to be. Now I want to be released'.

30 Black people make up *five per cent* of the general population and *25 per cent* of the psychiatric population.

31 *Adaptive paranoid response* describes a mental disorder brought about by a hostile environment.

32 Littlewood & Lipsedge (1989) see mental illness in minorities as an intelligible response to *disadvantage and racism*.

33 Littlewood (1992) believes that Axis V (global assessment of functioning) of DSM-IV's multiaxial classification makes ethnocentric assumptions regarding family life, occupation and education.

ICD-10 (*International Standard Classification of Diseases, Injuries and Causes of Death*)

Major categories
- **Organic, including symptomatic, mental disorders:** e.g. Alzheimer's disease.
- **Mental and behavioural disorders due to psychoactive substance use:** e.g. alcoholism.
- **Schizophrenia, schizotypal and delusional disorders:** e.g. paranoid schizophrenia.
- **Mood (affective) disorders:** e.g. bipolar affective disorder.
- **Neurotic, stress-related and somatoform disorders:** e.g. phobias.
- **Behavioural syndromes associated with physiological disturbances and physical factors:** e.g. anorexia nervosa.
- **Disorders of adult personality and behaviour:** e.g. specific personality disorders.
- **Mental retardation:** e.g. profound mental retardation.
- **Disorders of psychological development:** e.g autism.
- **Behavioural and emotional disorders with onset usually occurring in childhood and adolescence:** e.g. hyperkinetic disorder.

Comparing DSM-IV and ICD-10
- DSM and ICD overlap extensively and, for many categories, are virtually identical.
- DSM-IV uses a larger number of discrete categories, whereas ICD-10 uses a smaller number of more specific categories.
- The single category 'neurotic, stress-related and somatoform disorders' in ICD-10 accounts for 4 categories in DSM-IV (anxiety disorders, somatoform disorders, dissociative disorders and adjustment disorders).
- DSM-IV has a single category for 'disorders first diagnosed in infancy, childhood and adolescence' which corresponds to 3 categories in ICD-10.

ICD-10 & DSM-IV

DSM-IV (*Diagnostic and Statistical Manual of Mental Disorders*)

Major categories
- **Delirium, dementia, amnestic and other cognitive disorders:** e.g. Alzheimer's disease.
- **Substance-related disorders:** e.g alcoholism.
- **Schizophrenic and other psychotic disorders:** e.g. paranoid schizophrenia.
- **Mood disorders:** e.g bipolar disorder.
- **Anxiety disorders:** e.g. phobias.
- **Somatoform disorders:** e.g. hypochondriasis.
- **Dissociative disorders:** e.g. multiple personality disorder.
- **Adjustment disorders:** e.g. adjustment disorder with disturbance of conduct.
- **Disorders first diagnosed in infancy, childhood or adolescence:** e.g. retardation.
- **Personality disorders:** e.g. borderline personality disorder.
- **Sexual and gender identity disorders:** e.g. paraphilias.
- **Impulse control disorders not elsewhere classified:** e.g. kleptomania.
- **Factitious disorders:** e.g. factitious disorder
- **Sleep disorders:** e.g. narcolepsy.
- **Eating disorders:** e.g. anorexia nervosa.
- **Mental disorders due to a general medical condition not elsewhere classified:** e.g. catatonic disorder due to medical condition.
- **Other conditions that may be a focus of clinical attention:** e.g. sexual abuse.

Abnormality – Classification

Psychosis & neurosis

The concept of mental illness

Distinctions between neurosis and psychosis
Personality: only a part of the personality is affected in neurosis.
Reality: the neurotic maintains contact with reality, whereas the psychotic does not.
Insight: the neurotic recognises that a problem exists.
'Normal' behaviour: neurotic behaviours are exaggerations of normal behaviour.
Pre-morbid personality: neurotic disorders are related to the individual's personality prior to the disorder.
- Present classificatory systems have dropped the distinction, although ICD-10 still uses the term 'neurotic', and DSM-IV, 'psychotic'.
- The categories are too broad and unspecific to be of much use, and the distinction stems from the psychodynamic model, not current observations of disorders (Gelder *et al.*, 1989).

Neither DSM-IV nor ICD-10 uses the term 'mental illness', although much of the vocabulary is medical (e.g. symptoms, diagnosis, cure).
Blaney (1975): the label 'ill' is more humane than 'mad' since it removes any sense of blame.
Szasz (1974, 1994):
- There is no such thing as mental illness, only illnesses ('diseases of the brain') or 'problems in living' (where an organic cause is not known: *The Myth of Mental Illness*).
- There is no known organic basis for the majority of 'mental illnesses'.
- Such labels are used to stigmatise and exclude those who have upset the social order, and psychiatry is largely 'social policing'.
DSM-IV has removed the category 'organic mental disorders' because it implies that the other disorders do not have an organic component.

The goals of classification

3 goals common to ICD-10 and DSM-IV: language, origins, treatment (LOT)
Providing a common shorthand language: i.e. a common set of terms with agreed-on meanings, enabling effective communication.
Understanding the origins of disorders: grouping people with similar behavioural symptoms into categories can help to identify common causes.
Treatment plans: accurate diagnosis is necessary to match a disorder to a treatment to ensure maximum benefit for the individual.

Problems with reliability
- Reliability refers to the consistency of a diagnosis across repeated measurements.
- Cooper *et al.* (1972): the same video of a patient was more likely to lead to a diagnosis of schizophrenia in America and manic depression in Britain.
- Agreement can be increased using standardised interview schedules.
- DSM-III (1980) introduced a multi-axial system of classification according to which patients are assessed on 5 different axes: clinical syndrome, personality disorders, general medical conditions, psychosocial and environmental problems, global assessment of functioning.

Rosenhan (1973):
- Instructed 8 psychiatrically normal people to complain of hearing voices. All 8 *'pseudopatients'* were admitted to hospital, most with a diagnosis of schizophrenia. Once admitted, patients acted normally, although it took between 7 and 52 days for staff to be convinced they were well enough to be discharged (with a diagnosis of 'schizophrenia in remission').
- In a second study, Rosenhan warned institutions to be on the look out for 'pseudopatients'. Roughly 1/4 of genuine individuals admitted were thought to be 'faking' by at least one member of staff. However, there were **no** pseudopatients.

Problems with validity
- Validity refers to an estimation of a particular measure's accuracy (whether the diagnosis reflects the actual disorder).
- Since there is no objective test for most disorders, validity is difficult to assess.
- Bannister *et al.* (1964) found no clear-cut relationship between diagnosis and treatment. This suggests diagnoses may lack validity.
- Defenders of psychiatric diagnosis point out that medical diagnoses are often incorrect (e.g. 34% of 'causes of death' disagree with later post-mortems).

- 5% of the British population are black, but 25% of hospitalised psychiatric patients are black.
- Black patients are more likely to see a junior, rather than senior doctor (Littlewood & Lipsedge, 1989).
- Of those Afro-Caribbeans diagnosed as schizophrenic, only 15% show the classic diagnostic indicators.

Transcultural psychiatry
Until recently, Western diagnostic categories were seen as applicable to all cultures. Increasingly, this assumption is being questioned.

- Littlewood & Lipsedge (1989): the delusion of persecution displayed by ethnic minorities is actually an intelligible response to disadvantage and racism.
- Littlewood (1992): DSM-IV is **ethnocentric**, especially the assessment of the global level of functioning (Axis V).

68

SCHIZOPHRENIA

SYLLABUS
4.3 Psychopathology
- alternative explanations of psychological disorders, including the possible contributions of genetic/neurological and social/psychological factors; disorders described and explained should include schizophrenia

KEY QUESTIONS
- What are the characteristics of schizophrenia?
- How many types of schizophrenia are there?
- What phases are there in schizophrenia's development?
- How do genetic/neurological and social/psychological factors contribute to schizophrenia?

Q

Section 1: The nature of schizophrenia
1 Bleuler coined the term *schizophrenia* in 1911. To what does it refer?
2 In what way are *first rank symptoms* more significant than other symptoms?
3 What is *thought broadcasting*?
4 Define the term *hallucination*.
5 What form of hallucination is the most common in schizophrenics?
6 Define the term *delusion*.
7 What is a *delusion of reference*?
8 How can *thought process disorders* such as the loosening of associations, be explained?
9 What is '*word salad*'?
10 Name the three types of *disturbance of affect*.
11 What is the difference between *catatonia* and *stereotypy*?

Section 2: Types and phases of schizophrenia
12 Name the five types of schizophrenia.
13 Which type of schizophrenic shows the highest level of functioning and the least impairment in ability to carry out daily functions?
14 Which type of schizophrenia tends to appear during late adolescence, have a slow, gradual onset, and be characterised by aimlessness, a decline in academic/occupational performance and a withdrawal from reality?
15 Name the three '*phases*' which occur in the course of schizophrenia.
16 What percentage of schizophrenics regain the capacity to function normally?
17 Why do some psychologists argue that the concept of schizophrenia is 'almost hopelessly in tatters' (Carson, 1989; Sarbin, 1992)?

Section 3: Explaining schizophrenia
18 What is Ullman & Krasner's (1969) *behavioural* explanation for schizophrenia?
19 What is the principal problem with this explanation?

20 Complete the sentence: 'Freud believed that schizophrenia results from _____ to an infantile stage of development'.
21 Identify one criticism of the *psychodynamic* explanation of schizophrenia.
22 According to Bateson *et al.* (1956), what is a *double-bind communication*?
23 According to Fromm-Reichman (1948), what is a '*schizophrenogenic mother*'?
24 Donne *et al.* (1985) found that the recurrence of schizophrenic symptoms in sufferers could be reduced by changes in their parents' behaviours. Identify these changes.
25 According to the *cognitive model*, which 'mechanism' is impaired in schizophrenics?
26 What is the likelihood of an individual developing schizophrenia if they have one schizophrenic parent?
27 What does Gottesman & Shields' (1972) discovery of a *concordance rate* of 42 per cent for schizophrenia in MZ (monozygotic) twins suggest?
28 What did Gottesman (1991) find when comparing concordance rates for MZ twins raised together with rates for MZ twins separated at birth?
29 What explanation for schizophrenia is offered by the *inborn-error of metabolism hypothesis*?
30 Which type of receptor sites were found to be far more prevalent in the brains of schizophrenics than non-schizophrenics?
31 How does the *diathesis–stress model* explain the cause of schizophrenia?
32 When Chua & McKenna (1995) reviewed the literature concerning structural abnormalities in the brains of schizophrenics, what did they discover was the most well-established difference?
33 Why is the finding that more schizophrenics are born in late winter and early spring significant?

Section 1: The nature of schizophrenia

1 '*Schizophrenia*' originally referred to a splitting of the mind's various functions so that the personality loses its unity.

2 *First rank symptoms* are significant in that (in Britain) the presence of one or more of these is likely to lead to a diagnosis of schizophrenia.

3 *Thought broadcasting* is a thought disturbance in which people believe their thoughts are being broadcast or otherwise made known to others.

4 The term *hallucination* refers to perceptions of stimuli that are not actually present.

5 *Auditory hallucinations* (hearing voices) are the most common from of hallucination in schizophrenics.

6 A *delusion* is a false belief which persists even in the presence of disconfirming evidence.

7 A *delusion of reference* is the belief that objects, events and so on have a (typically negative) personal significance.

8 *Thought process disorders* can be explained in terms of a failure to maintain an attentional focus, as a consequence of an impairment of selective attention.

9 '*Word salad*' refers to the complete incoherence of some schizophrenic speech resulting from an extreme loosening of associations.

10 *Disturbances of affect* include *blunting, flattened affect*, and *inappropriate affect*.

11 *Catatonia* involves assuming a posture which is maintained for hours or days, whilst *stereotypy* refers to a pattern of purposeless, repetitive movements such as rocking back and forth.

Section 2: Types and phases of schizophrenia

12 The five types of schizophrenia are *hebephrenic, simple, catatonic, paranoid*, and *undifferentiated*.

13 *Paranoid schizophrenics* show the highest level of functioning and the least impairment in their ability to carry out daily functions.

14 *Simple schizophrenia*.

15 The course of schizophrenia usually occurs in the following phases: *prodomal phase, active phase*, and *residual phase*.

16 Approximately 25 per cent of schizophrenics regain the capacity to function normally.

17 With the exception of paranoid schizophrenia, other forms of schizophrenia are difficult to distinguish in practice, and may in fact be different disorders rather than types of one disorder. Hence, it is argued, diagnoses of schizophrenia lack *validity*.

Section 3: Explaining schizophrenia

18 Ullman & Krasner (1969) argue that people show schizophrenic behaviour when it is more likely than normal behaviour to be reinforced.

19 The explanation cannot account for the acquisition of schizophrenic behaviours when there has been no opportunity to learn them.

20 'Freud believed that schizophrenia results from *regression* to an infantile stage of development.'

21 Schizophrenic behaviour does not resemble infantile behaviour, and the psychodynamic model has poor predictive power.

22 A *double-bind communication* is one in which a child is placed in a 'no-win' situation by its parents, for example by their giving contradictory verbal and non-verbal messages.

23 A '*schizophrenogenic mother*' (Fromm-Reichman, 1948) is a mother who produces schizophrenic children because she is domineering, cold, rejecting and guilt-producing.

24 Donne *et al.* (1985) found that a *reduction in parents' hostility, criticism* and *intrusiveness* could reduce the recurrence of schizophrenic symptoms.

25 The *selective attention mechanism* is impaired in schizophrenics, according to the *cognitive model*.

26 An individual with one schizophrenic parent has a *one in five chance* of developing schizophrenia themselves.

27 Gottesman & Shields' (1972) discovery suggests that genetics play an important role in the likelihood of schizophrenia. However, other factors, such as environmental influences, also play an important role.

28 Gottesman (1991) found that the concordance rates for MZ twins raised together were the *same* as rates for MZ twins separated at birth.

29 The *inborn-error of metabolism hypothesis* suggests that some people inherit a metabolic error which causes the body to break down naturally occurring chemicals into toxic ones which cause schizophrenia.

30 Dopamine receptor sites are far more likely to be found in the brains of schizophrenics than in non-schizophrenics.

31 The *diathesis–stress model* argues that we inherit a genetic pre-disposition towards schizophrenia (a *diathesis*) which may be triggered by environmental *stress* (such as exams, leaving home, job loss).

32 Chua & McKenna (1995) argue that the only well-established structural abnormality in schizophrenia is *lateral ventricular enlargement* (and that even this is modest and overlaps with the non-schizophrenic population).

33 The finding that more schizophrenics are born in late winter and early spring (Torrey *et al.*, 1977) supports the theory that schizophrenia may result from a *viral infection* affecting children during the second trimester of pregnancy, when crucial brain interconnections are formed.

Characteristics

first rank symptoms

Passivity experiences & thought disturbances

Thought insertion: belief that thoughts are being inserted into the mind from outside.
Thought withdrawal: belief that thoughts are being removed from the mind.
Thought broadcasting: belief that thoughts are being 'broadcast' to others.

Hallucinations

Hallucination: the perception of stimuli not actually present.
Auditory hallucinations: (most common) typically involve voices offering a running commentary, commands, or insults.
Somatosensory hallucinations: changes in how the body feels.
Depersonalisation: the person feels separated from the body.

Primary delusions

Delusion: a false belief which persists even in the presence of disconfirming evidence.
Delusion of grandeur: belief that person is or was very important.
Delusion of persecution: belief that others are conspiring against the person.
Delusion of reference: belief that events (e.g. the news) have personal relevance.

other symptoms

Thought process disorder

Schizophrenics are unable to maintain an attentional focus, resulting in:
- loose associations
- word salad
- clang associations
- neologisms

Disturbances of affect

Emotional disturbances include:
- **Blunting:** lack of emotional sensitivity or response.
- **Flattened affect:** general absence of emotional expression.
- **Inappropriate affect:** displaying incongruous emotions.

Psychomotor disorders

May take the form of:
Catatonia: a (unusual) posture is maintained for hours/days.
Stereotypy: purposeless, repetitive movements

Lack of volition

The tendency to withdraw from interactions with others. More disturbed individuals may be oblivious to the presence of others.

Types of schizophrenia

Schizophrenia

The course of schizophrenia

- **Hebephrenic:** ('silly mind') predominantly active symptoms, e.g. disorganised behaviour and speech, delusions, hallucinations, flattened/inappropriate affect.
- **Simple:** slow onset, withdrawal from reality, deterioration of academic/occupational performance.
- **Catatonic:** impairment of motor activity often with catatonia.
- **Paranoid:** delusions and hallucinations (usually of persecution). Otherwise relatively unaffected.
- **Undifferentiated:** 'catch-all' category for people not clearly falling into one type.

Prodromal phase
Usually occurs in early adolescence or early adulthood. The individual becomes more withdrawn, eccentric, emotionally flat, unkempt, with reduced productivity.

Active phase
Major characteristics of schizophrenia appear. Varies in duration from months to a lifetime.

Residual phase
Lessening of the major characteristics and more-or-less return to the prodomal phase.

Explanations

Behavioural

- Ullman & Krasner (1969): schizophrenia results from reinforcement of bizarre behaviour or the absence of reinforcement for appropriate behaviours.
- However, without an opportunity to observe such behaviours, the model cannot explain how they are acquired.

Psychodynamic

- **Regression** to an earlier stage of functioning occurs when the ego is overwhelmed by the id or superego. The individual returns to the oral stage when self and world are no longer distinguished. Fantasies and reality are confused.
- However, schizophrenic behaviour is not similar to infantile behaviour.

Social/family relationships

- Bateson *et al.* (1956): parents predispose children to schizophrenia by communicating in ways which leave them in 'no-win' situations ('double binds').
- **Schizophrenogenic mothers** (Fromm-Reichman, 1948) may generate schizophrenic children by being cold, domineering, rejecting and guilt-producing.

Cognitive

- Sees schizophrenia as resulting from disturbances of thought and perception.
- Maher (1968): bizarre language use is a result of faulty information processing.
- Catatonia may result from a breakdown of selective attention, resulting in the senses being overloaded.

Medical

Genetic

Schizophrenia tends to run in families: the likelihood of developing it is 1 in 100, but this rises to 1 in 5 with one schizophrenic parent, and 1 in 2 with two schizophrenic parents.

- Gottesman & Shields (1972) looked at concordance rates for MZ (identical) and DZ twins. The concordance rate was 42% for MZ twins (but not 100%), suggesting that both genetics and environment play a role.
- Gottesman (1991): the concordance rate for MZ twins reared together and apart is the same.
- Attempts to identify the gene responsible have not yet been successful.

Biochemical

- **Inborn-error of metabolism hypothesis:** a tendency to break down naturally-occurring chemicals into toxic ones (resembling hallucinogens) is inherited.
- **Excess dopamine utilisation:** schizophrenics possess an abnormally large number of dopamine-receptor sites. Drugs which block the functioning of these sites reduce schizophrenic symptoms (Kimble, 1988).
- **Diathesis–stress model:** genes may cause a biological vulnerability (*diathesis*) which puts a person at risk from environmental *stressors* (like exams, leaving home, losing a job).

Neurodevelopmental

- **Brain damage:** resulting from disease, difficult birth, (resulting in lack of oxygen) may be related to schizophrenia.
- **Structural abnormalities:** Chua & McKenna (1995) identify lateral ventricular enlargement as the most well-established structural abnormality, although even this is slight and overlaps with the normal population.
- **Viral theories:** significantly more people who develop schizophrenia are born in late winter and early spring (Torrey *et al.*, 1977). This may relate to infection with the influenza virus during the stage when crucial inter-connections in the brain are being formed.

69

DEPRESSION

SYLLABUS
4.3 Psychopathology
• alternative explanations of psychological disorders, including the possible contributions of genetic/neurological and social/psychological factors; disorders described and explained should include depression

KEY QUESTIONS
• What are the characteristics of depression?
• What sex differences are there in depression?
• How do genetic/neurological and social/psychological factors contribute to depression?

Section 1: Characteristics of depression

1 What name is given to the disorder characterised by alternating phases of *mania* and *depression*?
2 Why does Seligman (1973) refer to depression as the 'common cold' of psychological problems?
3 Identify any three of the characteristics which need to accompany persistent low mood in order for a diagnosis of depression to be made.
4 What percentage of adults in Britain will experience serious depression at some time?
5 What is the difference between *endogenous* and *exogenous depression*?
6 Which of the mood disorders is equally prevalent in men and women?

Section 2: Explanations of depression

7 What was Ferster's (1965) *behavioural explanation* for depression?
8 According to Lewisohn's (1974) expansion of Ferster's theory, what important role do friends and relatives play in depression?
9 Why, according to Lewisohn's account, are people lacking in *social skills* most at risk from depression?
10 How did Seligman & Maier (1967) demonstrate *learned helplessness*?
11 According to Abramson *et al.* (1978), what types of *attribution* do depressed people make for failure and success?
12 According to Beck (1974), depression may result from a *cognitive triad*. What is a cognitive triad?
13 According to Freud's psychodynamic model, to what is depression a response?
14 What is the relationship between depression and childhood, according to Freud?
15 What is Freud's explanation for feelings of guilt, unworthiness or despair, which may accompany depression?
16 What explanation do psychodynamic theorists propose for *bipolar disorder*?

17 Complete the following sentence: 'There is little evidence for a direct connection between early ___ and the risk of ____ in adult life (Crook & Eliot, 1980)'.
18 How much more likely is an individual to suffer from a mood disorder if they have a first degree relative with a mood disorder, than if they do not?
19 What conclusion can be drawn from the fact that *concordance rates* for bipolar disorder and major depression differ significantly?
20 What difficulty in investigating the *genetic* contribution to depression is overcome by *adoption studies*?
21 What did Wender *et al.* (1986) discover when investigating adopted children who developed mood disorders as adults?
22 What might the link be between a gene called SERT and depression?
23 Name the two neurotransmitters which are thought to be involved in affective disorders.
24 How does the urine of depressives differ from that of manics?
25 According to Kety's *permissive-amine theory of mood disorder*, what is the relationship between the two key neurotransmitters?
26 What reason do we have for suspecting that drugs which alleviate depression (such as *Prozac*) do not do so simply by increasing levels of key neurotransmitters?
27 According to Wehr & Rosenthal (1989), what is the cause of *winter depression*?
30 What other naturally occurring phenomenon has been identified by some researchers as a possible contributor to depression?

Section 3: Sex differences in depression

31 Identify three potential sources of *hormonal changes* in women which may contribute to depression.
32 Complete the sentence: 'Girls are very much more likely to be victims of ____ as children than are boys'.

Section 1: Characteristics of depression

1 *Bipolar disorder.*

2 Because depression is the *most common* psychological problem people face.

3 The characteristics are: *poor appetite* and *weight loss* or *increased appetite and weight gain, difficulty in sleeping or sleeping longer than usual, loss of energy or extreme tiredness, observable slowing down or agitation, loss of interest/pleasure in previously enjoyable activities, feelings of self-reproach or excessive guilt, diminished ability to concentrate,* and *recurrent thoughts of death and/or suicide.*

4 *Five per cent* of British adults will experience serious depression at some time.

5 *Endogenous depression* describes depression which 'comes from within' (*biological disturbances*), whilst *exogenous depression* 'comes from outside' (*stressful life experiences*).

6 *Bipolar disorder* is equally prevalent in men and women.

Section 2: Explanations of depression

7 Ferster (1965) believed that depression results from a *reduction in reinforcement.*

8 Lewisohn (1974) argues that friends and relatives may *reinforce* the depressed behaviour by giving the individual their concern and attention.

9 People lacking in *social skills* are least likely to receive positive reinforcement from those around them (e.g. laughter at their witty comments), and are therefore most at risk from depression.

10 Seligman & Maier (1967) subjected dogs to unavoidable electric shocks, then later placed them in a situation in which they could avoid the shocks. They made no attempt to avoid them.

11 Abramson *et al.* (1978) believe that depressed people attribute *failure* to *internal, stable* and *global factors,* and *success* to *luck.*

12 A *cognitive triad* (Beck, 1974) consists of three interlocking *negative beliefs* concerning the *self,* the *world* and the *future.*

13 Freud's *psychodynamic model* claims that depression is a response to loss which may be either actual (e.g. the loss of a friend) or symbolic (e.g. the loss of a job).

14 According to Freud, the greater the experience of loss during childhood, the greater the susceptibility to, and depth of, depression.

15 Freud believed that such feelings represent the individual's hostility (towards parents) which is *repressed* and *directed inwards,* towards the self.

16 Psychodynamic theorists propose that *bipolar disorder* results from the alternating domination of the personality by the superego and the ego.

17 'There is little evidence for a direct connection between early *loss* and the risk of *depression* in adult life (Crook & Eliot, 1980).'

18 An individual who has a first degree relative with a mood disorder is *ten times* more likely to suffer from a mood disorder than one who has not.

19 The difference in *concordance rates* suggests that the genetic factors involved in the disorders are different.

20 *Adoption studies* overcome the problem that children who share the same genes often share similar environments, so that is it difficult to determine their respective contributions.

21 Wender *et al.* (1986) discovered that such children were far more likely to have biological parents with a mood disorder, or who suffered from alcoholism or committed suicide, than children who did not suffer from a mood disorder.

22 Ogilvie *et al.* (1996) discovered that cells use SERT in the production of *serotonin transporter proteins,* and that the SERT gene is shortened in depressives. Serotonin is strongly linked to mood disorders.

23 *Serotonin* and *noradrenaline.*

24 The urine of *depressives* contains *low* levels of compounds produced when noradrenaline and serotonin are broken down, whereas the urine of *manics* contains *high* levels of these compounds.

25 Kety's *permissive-amine theory of mood disorder* suggests that one of the neurotransmitters (*serotonin*) acts to regulate the level of the other (*noradrenaline*).

26 Drugs which alleviate depression alter levels of neurotransmitters for only a short period (immediately after they are taken), and their anti-depressant effects do not occur during this period.

27 Wehr & Rosenthal (1989) claim that *winter depression* is caused by the desynchronisation of melatonin production as a result of decreasing light exposure.

28 *Geomagnetic phenomena* (e.g. the aurora borealis which is a source of geomagnetic changes) may be linked with depression.

Section 3: Sex differences in depression

29 The *menstrual cycle, childbirth,* the *menopause, oral contraceptives, brain chemistry* and *diet* are all sources of hormonal changes in women, and may contribute to depression.

30 'Girls are very much more likely to be victims of *abuse* as children than are boys.'

Depression

| **Depression** | Gender differences

Clinical depression

Persistent low mood for at least 2 weeks plus at least 5 of the following:
- poor appetite or weight loss, or increased appetite or weight gain.
- difficulty in sleeping (insomnia) or sleeping longer than usual (hypersomnia).
- loss of energy or tiredness to the point of being unable to make the simplest everyday decisions
- an observable slowing down or agitation (e.g. hand wringing).
- a markedly diminished loss of interest or pleasure in activities that were once enjoyed.
- feelings of self-reproach or excessive or inappropriate guilt over real or imagined misdeeds.
- complaints/evidence of diminished ability to think or concentrate.
- recurrent thoughts of death, suicide, suicidal thoughts without a specific plan, or a suicide attempt or a specific plan for committing suicide.

- **Unipolar depression** (depression without mania): can occur at any age. In the USA, 15% of adults experience serious depression at some time, and is far more prevalent in women.
- Psychiatrists distinguish *endogenous* ('coming from within'/biochemical) depression from *exogenous* ('coming from the outside'/stressful experience) depression.
- **Bipolar disorder** (alternating depression and mania, or mania on its own): is equally prevalent in men and women and generally appears in the early 20s.

Women are 2–3 times more likely than men to be diagnosed as clinically depressed (Williams & Hargreaves, 1995).

Biological explanations
- Hormonal fluctuations may play a role in depression, and are associated with the menstrual cycle, childbirth, the menopause, oral contraceptives, brain chemistry and diet. However, a specific causal mechanism has not yet been identified.
- Diksic *et al.* (cited in Highfield, 1997d): men's brain stems manufacture serotonin at a rate 52% higher than do women's. One possibility is that dieting during teens may alter brain biochemistry.

Non-biological explanations
Cochrane (1995) has summarised non-biological explanations:
- Girls are far more likely than boys to be sexually abused, and victims of abuse are 2 times more likely than non-victims to suffer depression.
- The difference is greatest between the ages 20–50, when most women experience marriage, child-bearing, motherhood and the empty-nest syndrome.
- An acceptance of the traditional female role may contribute to learned helplessness, in which the woman sees herself as having little control over her life.
- Depression may be a coping strategy in response to the social and political circumstances in which women find themselves.

Explanations

The behavioural model

Lewisohn (1974):
- certain events (e.g. death of a loved one) reduce positive reinforcement. Less activity leads to concern and attention which reinforces the depression.
- socially unskilled individuals are more at risk since they are less able to elicit positive reinforcement from others.

| Few potentially reinforcing events related to personal characteristics |
| Little availability of reinforcement in the environment |
| Little operant activity by the individual |

→ Low rate of positive reinforcement / Social reinforcement for depression (concern etc.) → **Depression**

The psychodynamic model
- Freud argued that actual losses (e.g. death of a loved one) and symbolic losses (e.g. loss of job) lead us to re-experience feelings of loss and dependence from our childhood.
- Repressed hostility towards one's parents is experienced as anger during loss. This anger is turned inwards and becomes guilt and despair and may lead to suicide.
- Bipolar disorder is seen as alternating dominance of the superego (depressive phase) and the ego (manic phase).

- However, there is little evidence that experience of loss in early life leads to an increased risk of depression, or that depressed people interpret the death of a loved one as desertion/rejection.

The cognitive–behavioural model

Learned helplessness
Seligman & Maier (1967): restrained dogs so that they could not avoid electric shock. Dogs became passively resigned to receiving shocks and made no attempt to escape when the opportunity arose.
- Argued that dogs' behaviours (including lethargy and loss of appetite) were similar to those of depressed humans.

Attributional style
Abramson *et al.* (1978): people who attribute failure to internal, stable and global causes ('It's my fault, it's always going to be like this, whatever I do'), and success to luck, are more likely to become depressed.

Beck's cognitive triad model
- Beck (1974): believes that certain childhood experiences lead to a cognitive triad of three interlocking negative beliefs concerning *self*, *world* and *future*.
- These lead people to magnify bad and minimise good experiences (see Chapter 66).

The medical model

Genetic influences
- Weissman (1987): people with first-degree relatives with a mood disorder are 10 times more likely to develop a mood disorder than people without affected relatives.
- Concordance rates are different for bipolar and unipolar depression, suggesting that different genetic factors are involved.

Serotonin transporter proteins
Ogilvie *et al.* (1996) found that cells use a gene called SERT to manufacture serotonin transporter proteins. Serotonin is strongly linked to depression. In a significant number of people with depression, this gene is shorter than normal.

Biochemical influences
- Schildkraut (1965): **noradrenaline** causes depression and mania in low and high amounts, respectively. Later research suggested that **serotonin** plays a similar role.
- Kety (1975): since serotonin can be low during mania, serotonin regulates noradrenaline levels and low levels permit noradrenaline to fluctuate.
- However, drugs that alleviate depression (e.g. Prozac) affect serotonin/noradrenaline levels immediately after taking them, but take weeks to work, suggesting that they affect the sensitivity of neurons utilising serotonin/noradrenaline.

External factors & biochemistry
Lower levels of noradrenaline and serotonin may be the *result* of, rather than the *cause* of, depression, e.g.:
- **Seasonal affective disorder** (SAD) such as summer depression and winter depression. Summer depression is associated with deficient serotonin levels, whilst winter depression is caused by the desynchronisation of melatonin production as a result of decreasing natural light exposure (Wehr & Rosenthal, 1989).
- Kay (1994): **geomagnetic storms** affect melatonin production and may partly account for both summer and winter depression.

70

ANXIETY DISORDERS

SYLLABUS

4.3 Psychopathology
- alternative explanations of psychological disorders, including the possible contribution of genetic/ neurological and social/psychological factors; disorders described and explained should include anxiety disorders (e.g. phobias and post-traumatic stress disorder)

KEY QUESTIONS
- What are the characteristics of panic disorder, generalised anxiety disorder, phobic disorders, obsessive–compulsive disorder, and post-traumatic disorder?
- How do genetic/neurological and social/psychological factors contribute to these anxiety disorders?

Q **Section 1: Panic disorder (PD) and generalised anxiety disorder (GAD)**

1 Define *anxiety*.
2 What are the physiological reactions accompanying *panic attacks* similar to?
3 At what time of day do anxiety attacks occur?
4 What is *anticipatory anxiety*?
5 In what ways is *generalised anxiety disorder* different from *panic disorder*?
6 Clark (1993) proposes that abnormalities in thinking are the core disturbance in panic. What form do these abnormal cognitions take?
7 Outline two explanations proposed by the *psychodynamic model* for the origins of anxiety disorder.
8 What percentage of first degree relatives of sufferers of panic disorder have the disorder themselves?
9 According to Eysenck (1967), what exactly is inherited in panic disorder and generalised anxiety disorder?
10 What is *autonomic lability*?
11 Papp *et al.* (1993) argue that panic disorder is caused by a dysfunction of receptors in the brain. In what way do these receptors cause panic attacks?

Section 2: Phobic disorders

12 What is a *phobia*?
13 What is a *social phobia*?
14 In what ways does a *specific phobia* differ from a social phobia?
15 What is the third category of phobia identified by DSM-IV?
16 What was Freud's (1909) explanation for Little Hans' phobia of horses?
17 What alternative explanation for Hans' phobia is offered by the *behavioural model*?
18 How does Mowrer's (1947) *two-process* (or *two-factor*) *theory* explain the way in which phobias are maintained and are resistant to extinction?

19 What aspect of phobias is difficult for the behavioural model to explain?
20 What explanation did Rosenhan & Seligman (1984) propose to explain the finding that certain classes of stimuli (such as snakes) can more easily be made a conditioned stimulus than others (such as flowers)?

Section 3: Obsessive–compulsive disorder (OCD)

21 How do an *obsession* and a *compulsion* differ?
22 Identify the four most common characteristics of obsessive thought.
23 According to Tallis (1994), why might the finding that first degree relatives of sufferers of OCD often have some sort of anxiety disorder themselves not necessarily suggest a strong genetic component to the disorder?
24 What difference in brain activity do OCD sufferers show compared with non-OCD sufferers?
25 How does the *psychodynamic model* explain obsessive thoughts?
26 How does the *anxiety-reduction hypothesis* account for OCD's maintenance?
27 How can Skinner's (1948a) *superstition hypothesis* account for the behaviour of soccer players who insist on putting on the left sock before the right sock?

Section 4: Post-traumatic stress disorder (PTSD)

28 What is *post-traumatic stress disorder*?
29 Identify three of the symptoms of PTSD shown by Vietnam war veterans.
30 What did Hunt (1997) find when studying PTSD in people in their sixties and seventies who had been disturbed by their experiences during World War II?
31 How do explanations of PTSD differ from explanations of other disorders?
32 Why isn't classical conditioning the only mechanism involved in PTSD?
33 Identify three factors which may influence the likelihood that individuals experiencing trauma will develop PTSD.

Section 1: Panic disorder (PD) and generalised anxiety disorder (GAD)

1 *Anxiety* is a general feeling of dread and apprehensiveness, typically accompanied by various physiological reactions (including increased heart rate, rapid and shallow breathing, sweating, muscle tension, and dryness of the mouth).

2 The physiological reactions accompanying *panic attacks* (PD) are similar to those occurring during a *heart attack*.

3 Attacks are more common during wakefulness, but can occur at any time, even during sleep.

4 *Anticipatory anxiety* is a worry about when the next attack will occur, and the avoidance of situations in which it has occurred.

5 *Generalised anxiety disorder* (*GAD*) involves similar sensations to those in *panic disorder,* but these are more persistent and less intense.

6 Clark (1993) proposes that the core abnormal cognition is the interpretation of increased physiological activity in catastrophic ways (e.g. 'I'm having a heart attack').

7 The *psychodynamic model* sees GAD as the result of unacceptable unconscious conflicts blocked by the ego which break through (as a panic attack) when defences are weakened. Alternatively, PD may result from separation anxiety which re-occurs later in life.

8 Around *40 per cent* of first degree relatives of sufferers of panic disorder have the disorder themselves (Balon *et al.*, 1989).

9 Eysenck (1967) believes that what is inherited is a *highly reactive autonomic nervous system* (ANS).

10 *Autonomic lability* refers to the ease with which some people are aroused by environmental stimuli.

11 Papp *et al.* (1993) argue that a dysfunction of receptors which monitor levels of oxygen in the blood causes sufferers to fear that they are suffocating and to hyperventilate.

Section 2: Phobic disorders

12 A *phobia* is a strong, persistent, and irrational fear of, and desire to avoid, particular objects, activities or situations.

13 A *social phobia* is an intense and excessive fear of being in a situation in which one may be scrutinised by others, and a fear of acting in an embarrassing or humiliating way.

14 *Specific phobias* are fears of specific objects or situations, whilst social phobias apply to classes of social situation.

15 *Agoraphobia*.

16 Freud (1909) believed that Hans' unconscious fear of his father (as a result of the Oedipus complex) was displaced onto horses, which symbolised his father.

17 The *behavioural model* argues that the phobia was developed by conditioning, after Hans had witnessed a terrible accident involving a horse pulling a cart.

18 Mowrer's (1947) *two-process theory* suggests that phobias which have been acquired through classical conditioning are maintained by negative reinforcement, since avoiding the phobic stimulus leads to a reduction in anxiety. This reinforcement makes the phobia resistant to extinction.

19 The behavioural model cannot explain the failure of many phobics to report any traumatic experiences.

20 Rosenhan & Seligman (1984) proposed that we are *genetically prepared* to fear things which were sources of danger in our evolutionary past.

Section 3: Obsessive–compulsive disorder (OCD)

21 An *obsession* is a recurrent thought or image (often senseless or repugnant) that does not feel voluntarily controlled. A *compulsion* is a irresistible desire to engage in repetitive behaviours.

22 *Impaired control over mental processes, concern over losing motor control over behaviours, contamination,* and *checking rituals.*

23 Tallis (1994) points out that in over half the cases of OCD, family members become actively involved in the rituals, suggesting that learning may play a role.

24 OCD sufferers show increased metabolic activity in the left frontal lobe.

25 The psychodynamic model maintains that obsessive thoughts are defence mechanisms that serve to displace more threatening thoughts.

26 The *anxiety-reduction hypothesis* proposes that thoughts or behaviours which lead to a reduction in anxiety are more likely to be repeated, since the reduction in anxiety is a form of reinforcement.

27 Skinner's (1948a) *superstition hypothesis* holds that behaviours which have, coincidentally, been associated with success (positive reinforcement) will be repeated and maintained by the anxiety which is aroused when they are not repeated.

Section 4: Post-traumatic stress disorder (PTSD)

28 *Post-traumatic stress disorder* is a response to an extreme psychological or physical trauma outside the range of normal human experience.

29 Amongst others, they include *tiredness, apathy, depression, social withdrawal, nightmares, hyperalertness* and *flashbacks.*

30 Hunt (1997) found that traumatic memories of experiences during World War II seemed to be coming back to disturb them, after they had retired.

31 Explanations of PTSD recognise that the disorder can be explained largely in environmental terms.

32 Since not everybody who experiences a potentially traumatising event develops PTSD, classical conditioning cannot be the only mechanism involved in the disorder.

33 *Individual differences in the way in which people perceive events,* the *recovery environment* (such as support groups), and the *difference between what was expected and what was actually encountered* may all influence the likelihood that individuals experiencing trauma will develop PTSD.

Panic disorder
- Panic attacks come 'out of the blue', and can occur during sleep.
- Sufferers often believe they are having a heart attack.
- Attacks can last from minutes to hours.
- Attacks may be followed by anticipatory anxiety (fear of having an attack) which may develop into agoraphobia.

Generalised anxiety disorder
- Characterised by persistent high levels of anxiety and worry.
- The sensations associated with PD are also present, though more persistent and less intense.
- May cause people to become tired, irritable and socially inept.

explanations

Psychodynamic
- GAD is the result of unconscious conflicts blocked by the ego. We repress these impulses but defences sometimes weaken, leading to a panic attack.
- PD may represent unresolved separation anxiety.

Cognitive
- Clark (1993): increased physiological activity is interpreted in catastrophic ways (e.g as a heart attack).
- This abnormal cognition leads to even more physiological activity which confirms the catastrophic belief.

Genetics and biochemistry
- 40% of 1st degree relatives of PD suffer from the disorder (Balon *et al.*, 1989). Eysenck (1967) claims that a predisposition is inherited in the form of a highly reactive ANS.
- Papp *et al.* (1993): PD is caused by a dysfunction in receptors that monitor oxygen levels in the blood.

Phobic disorders

- **Agoraphobia:** a fear of open spaces typically involving a fear of being unable to escape/be helped. Accounts for 10–50% of all phobias and mostly affects women.
- **Social phobia:** intense and excessive fear of being scrutinised by others and embarrassing or humiliating oneself.
- **Specific phobia:** an extreme fear of a specific object (e.g. spiders) or situation (e.g. enclosed spaces).
Phobias are the most common type of anxiety disorder and usually develop in childhood.

explanations

Psychodynamic
- Phobias are the surface expression of deeper conflicts.
- Freud (1909) described **'Little Hans'** – a 5-yr-old with a phobia of horses. Horses symbolised Hans's father, whom Hans saw as a rival for his mother's affection (Oedipus complex).

Behavioural
- Phobias may be acquired by classical conditioning (see 'Little Albert': Ch 66).
- The **two-process theory** (Mowrer, 1947) claims that phobias are acquired by classical conditioning then maintained by operant conditioning (avoiding the stimulus is reinforced by reduced anxiety).

Biological and genetic
- Rosenhan & Seligman (1984): we are genetically prepared to fear certain stimuli (e.g. spiders).
- Slater & Shields (1969): found a 41% concordance rate among MZ twins, but only a 4% rate between DZ twins.

Anxiety: a general feeling of dread typically accompanied by physiological reactions including increased heart rate, rapid and shallow breathing, sweating, muscle tension and dryness of the mouth.

Anxiety Disorders

Obsessive–compulsive disorder

- **Obsessions:** recurrent thoughts or images (often senseless or repugnant) which cannot be controlled.
- **Compulsions:** irresistible urges to engage in repetitive behaviours aimed at preventing some undesirable event.
Often compulsions arise from obsessions (e.g. a hand-washing compulsion from a fear of contamination).
In Britain, roughly 1½ million people suffer from the disorder. It is slightly more common in women than in men.

explanations

Psychodynamic
- Obsessions are **defence mechanisms** which occupy the mind so as to displace more disturbing thoughts.
- However, it is hard to see what thoughts of killing a loved one (which are common to sufferers of OCD) could displace.

Behavioural
- OCD is a way of reducing anxiety. If a behaviour or thought reduces anxiety, then it becomes reinforced and therefore more likely to occur.
- **Superstition hypothesis** (Skinner, 1948a): chance associations between behaviours and reinforcers leads the individual to repeat those behaviours.

Biological and genetic
- People with OCD show increased activity in the left frontal lobe. Drugs which reduce this activity reduce symptoms of OCD.
- Comings & Comings (1987): first degree relatives of OCD sufferers often have the disorder.

Post-traumatic stress disorder

- Occurs in response to an extreme psychological or physical trauma outside the range of normal human experience (Thompson, 1997).
- May result from involvement in a disaster, physical threats to self/family, and witnessing another's death.
- May occur immediately after the event or months later.
- Symptoms include tiredness, apathy, depression, social withdrawal, nightmares, flashbacks, hyperalertness.

Children and PTSD
- Yule (1993): child survivors of recent disasters show symptoms of PTSD, including distressing memories of the event, avoidance of reminders, disturbed sleep and poor concentration.

explanations

- Unlike other disorders, PTSD can be explained in environmental terms.
- Classical conditioning is involved (Kolb, 1987): sufferers often show reactions to stimuli present at the time of the trauma.
However, not everyone who suffers a traumatic event experiences PTSD.

- Green (1994): PTSD develops in about 25% of those who experience potentially traumatic events (12% for accidents, 80% for rape).
- Paton (1992): differences between what workers *expected* to find and what they *actually* found were a source of stress for relief workers at the Lockerbie disaster.

- **Individual differences** in how people perceive events, as well as the **predictability** of events, seem to influence the degree of stress experienced.
- The **recovery environment** (such as support groups) may also play an influential role.
- The effects of drugs on victims of PTSD suggest that disturbed opioid function may play a role (van der Kolk *et al.*, 1989), and the *locus coeruleus* (the brain's 'alarm centre') may also be involved.

EATING DISORDERS

KEY QUESTIONS
- What are the characteristics of anorexia nervosa and bulimia nervosa?
- How do genetic/neurological and social/psychological factors contribute to these eating disorders?

Section 1: Characteristics of anorexia nervosa

1 How long have the characteristics of what is now called *anorexia nervosa* been known about?
2 By what ratio do female anorectics outnumber male anorectics?
3 At what age is onset of the disorder most common?
4 What is the principal characteristic of anorexia nervosa?
5 Complete the sentence: 'For a diagnosis of anorexia nervosa to be considered, the individual must weigh less than __ per cent of normal or expected weight for height, age and sex'.
6 Identify two physical problems which frequently accompany anorexia nervosa.
7 In what percentage of cases is anorexia nervosa fatal?
8 What is the literal meaning of anorexia nervosa?
9 What is the difference between the *restricting sub-type* and *binge eating/purging sub-type* of the disorder, as identified by DSM-IV?
10 Why do anorectics fail to recognise their bodies' thinness?

Section 2: Explaining anorexia nervosa

11 Which area of the brain plays an important role in the regulation of eating?
12 How does the action of *noradrenaline* on this area affect the behaviour of non-humans?
13 What is the relationship between the neurotransmitter *serotonin* and appetite?
14 What is the principal problem in drawing conclusions from studies of changes in neurotransmitter levels?
15 Park *et al.* (1995) suggest that changes in the levels of corticotrophin-releasing hormones might trigger anorexia. What did they suggest might bring about such changes in hormonal levels?
16 What is the *concordance rate* for anorexia nervosa in MZ twins brought up in the same environment?
17 According to the *psychodynamic model*, why might an overdependence on parents lead to anorexia?

18 A further psychodynamic explanation proposes that anorexia represents an attempt to avoid a particular issue. What is that issue?
19 According to Bemis (1978), why is there a link between being a 'good girl', doing well in school, and anorexia nervosa?
20 Identify two criticisms of psychodynamic accounts of anorexia nervosa.
21 Crisp (1967) believes that anorexia nervosa can be seen as a specific *phobia*. What is it a phobia of?
22 What research suggests that Western societal norms may be influential in causing anorexia nervosa?

Section 3: Characteristics of bulimia nervosa

23 What behaviours are characteristic of *bulimia nervosa*?
24 What percentage of bulimics are men?
25 What percentage of the population may be affected by bulimia?
26 Identify two reasons why many cases of bulimia go unnoticed by friends and family.
27 Name any three physiological effects associated with purging.

Section 4: Explaining bulimia nervosa

28 What is the relation between *plasma endorphins* and bulimia nervosa?
29 Explain how Ruderman's (1986) *disinhibition hypothesis* accounts for bulimia nervosa.
30 Identify the reasons given by Garner (1992) for believing that it is misleading to see anorexia nervosa and bulimia nervosa as psychologically dissimilar.
31 Complete the sentence: 'According to Waller (1993) ____, ____ is related to eating disorders, particularly those involving bulimic features'.
32 According to Cooper (1995), in what two ways may *depression* relate to eating disorders?
33 What general conclusions can be drawn regarding the causes of eating disorders?

Section 1: Characteristics of anorexia nervosa

1 The characteristics of what is now known as *anorexia nervosa* been known about for several hundred years (Hartley, 1997).

2 Female anorectics outnumber male anorectics by 15:1.

3 Onset is most common in adolescence, peaking at between 14 and 16 years of age.

4 The principal characteristic of anorexia nervosa is a prolonged refusal to eat adequate amounts of food, resulting in deliberate weight loss.

5 'For a diagnosis of anorexia nervosa to be considered, the individual must weigh less than *85* per cent of normal or expected weight for height, age and sex.'

6 These include a *decline in general health, low blood pressure, low body temperature, constipation* and *dehydration*.

7 Between *5–15 per cent* of anorexia cases are fatal (Hsu, 1990).

8 'Anorexia nervosa' literally means '*nervous loss of appetite*'.

9 The *restricting sub-type* of anorectics loses weight through constant fasting and physical activity, whilst the *binge eating/purging sub-type* alternates between fasting and bingeing.

10 Due to a distorted body image, the individual does not recognise the body's thinness.

Section 2: Explaining anorexia nervosa

11 The *hypothalamus* plays an important role in the regulation of eating.

12 *Noradrenaline* acts on the hypothalamus to cause non-humans to begin eating, with a preference for carbohydrates.

13 *Serotonin* induces satiation and suppresses appetite.

14 Conclusions from studies of changes in neurotransmitter levels do not tell us whether these changes are causes of the disorder, effects of it, or merely correlates.

15 Park *et al.* (1995) suggested that *viral-* or *immune-induced alterations* in central homeostasis might bring about such changes.

16 Askevold & Heiberg (1979) report a *concordance rate* for MZs of 50 per cent, whilst Holland *et al.* (1984) found a concordance rate of 55 per cent for MZ twins.

17 The *psychodynamic model* suggests that girls who are over-dependent on parents may fear becoming sexually mature and independent, becoming anorectic in an effort to remain pre-pubescent and avoid adult responsibilities.

18 A further psychodynamic explanation proposes that it is *adult sexuality*, particularly *pregnancy*, which is feared.

19 Bemis (1978) argues that females who are habitually co-operative and well-behaved may feel controlled by others, and attempt to assert their individuality by assuming control over their bodies.

20 Some psychodynamic accounts seem to apply only to females, and they have difficulty explaining the occurrence of the disorder in adulthood.

21 Crisp (1967) believes that anorexia nervosa is a phobia of *gaining weight*.

22 Research which shows that in at least some non-Western societies the incidence of anorexia nervosa is much lower, suggests that cultural and social norms may influence its prevalence.

Section 3: Characteristics of bulimia nervosa

23 *Bulimia nervosa* is characterised by periodic episodes of 'binge' eating, followed by 'purging' of the digestive tract using laxatives, self-induced vomiting or diuretics.

24 Only *five per cent* of bulimics are men.

25 Bulimia may affect as much as *five per cent* of the population.

26 Bulimics are often secretive in their behaviours, and appear to eat normally in public. Also, there is not a constant weight loss as there is in anorexia nervosa.

27 Purging may lead to '*puffy*' facial appearance, a *deterioration in tooth enamel, calluses on the back of the hand, digestive tract damage, dehydration*, and *nutritional imbalances*.

Section 4: Explaining bulimia nervosa

28 *Plasma endorphins* are elevated in people with bulimia nervosa (and in those who self-mutilate: Parkin & Eagles, 1993), although it is not clear if this is a cause, effect, or correlate of the disorder.

29 Ruderman's (1986) *disinhibition hypothesis* proposes that 'restricted' eaters who have 'all-or-nothing' rules regarding dieting may feel that they have over-eaten, and, having broken their diet, feel disinhibited about consuming more food. Alcohol may also lead to disinhibition.

30 Garner (1992) points out that anorectics and bulimics share many psychological traits (such as perfectionism) and the goal of maintaining a sub-optimal weight, and that individuals may move between the two disorders.

31 'According to Waller (1993), *sexual abuse* is related to eating disorders, particularly those involving bulimic features.'

32 Cooper (1995) suggests that *depression* may contribute to the initiation, or the maintenance of an eating disorder.

33 No single theory emerges as a definitive account of the origins of eating disorders. It seems likely that disorders do not have single discrete causes, but result from a combination of factors.

Anorexia nervosa

Facts

- Anorexia nervosa literally means 'nervous loss of appetite', but anorectics are often both hungry and pre-occupied with thoughts of food.
- The characteristics of the disorder have been known about for several hundred years (Hartley, 1997).
- Female anorectics outnumber males by 15:1.
- Onset is usually in adolescence, with the 14–16 period being most common (Hsu, 1990).
- Estimates of the disorder's incidence range from 1 in 100 to 4 in 100 (Sahakian, 1987).

Characteristics

- Characterised by a prolonged refusal to eat adequate amounts of food, resulting in deliberate weight loss (85% of normal weight for anorexia diagnosis).
- Physical consequences include cessation of menstruation, low blood pressure and body temperature, constipation and dehydration.
- **Restricting types** lose weight through fasting and physical activity.
  Binge eating/purging types use laxatives and vomiting, alternating between fasting and binge eating.
- **Distorted body image** causes the individual not to recognise her/his body's thinness.

explanations

Biological explanations

- A dysfunction of the *hypothalamus* (which plays an important role in regulating eating).
- Changes in neurotransmitter levels (*noradrenaline* can trigger eating in non-humans, whilst *serotonin* suppresses appetite).
- Park *et al.* (1995) have suggested that viral- or immune-induced alterations (e.g. glandular fever-like illnesses) could trigger restrictive anorexia.
- Lask (cited in Kennedy, 1997) believes a deficient blood flow to the *anterior temporal lobes*, which interpret vision, may explain why anorectics see themselves as fat.

Genetic explanations

- First and second degree relatives of anorectics are significantly more likely to develop the disorder (Strober & Katz, 1987).
- Holland *et al.* (1984): found concordance rates of 55% for MZ twins and 7% for DZ twins. However, twins were raised together and the genetic component is likely to be small.

Psychodynamic explanations

- The disorder represents an unconscious effort to remain pre-pubescent (anorexia may cause menstruation to cease and retard puberty). Sexual maturity is feared because the girl is over-dependent on parents.
- Alternatively, the disorder prevents the girl from having to address the issue of her sexuality (especially pregnancy), allowing her to take on a 'boy-like' appearance.
- Finally, the disorder may reflect an attempt by anorectics to assert their own independence and individuality by assuming control over their bodies. Many anorectics are 'good girls' who are cooperative and well-behaved, and this may lead them to feel that they are being controlled by others (Bemis, 1978).
- However, some of the above can only be applied to females, and cannot explain anorexia in adults.

Behavioural explanations

- Anorexia is a 'weight phobia' (Crisp, 1967) resulting from social norms, values and roles.
- The cultural idealisation of the slender female in the West may be one cause of a fear of being fat (Petkova, 1997).
- Wooley & Wooley (1983): cultural standards of thinness are related to the increase in the incidence of eating disorders.
- Lee *et al.*, (1992): much lower incidences of anorexia in other cultures support this explanation.
- Hill (cited in Uhlig, 1996a): classmates, mothers and toys (such as Sindy dolls) are more influential than fashion magazines, shaping young girls' perceptions of desirability.

Conflicting research

- Touyz *et al.* (1988): describe the case of an anorectic who was blind from birth. This is difficult for the behavioural model to explain.

Eating Disorders

Bulimia nervosa

Facts

- The word 'bulimia' comes from the Greek *bous* meaning 'ox' and *limos* meaning hunger.
- Fewer than 5% of cases are men (Cooper, 1995).
- Bulimia nervosa is more common than anorexia nervosa and may affect up to 5% of the population.
- The disorder usually begins in adolescence/early adulthood.
- The frequency with which binges occur ranges from 2–3 times a week to 30 times a week.
- Associations between self-mutilative behaviour and bulimia have been found (Parry-Jones & Parry-Jones, 1993).

Characteristics

- Characterised by periodic episodes of compulsive 'binge' eating which are terminated either by abdominal pain or (in the purging type) the expulsion of food using diuretics, laxatives or self-induced vomiting.
- Like anorectics, bulimics are unduly concerned with their body shape and weight and they fluctuate between weight gain and loss.
- Guilty feelings resulting from the behaviour mean that it is often carried out in secret and the disorder may go unnoticed.
- Physiological effects of purging include puffy facial appearance, deterioration in tooth enamel, calluses on the back of the hand, digestive tract damage, dehydration and nutritional imbalances.

explanations

Biological explanations

- Abnormal neurotransmitter levels may be involved (e.g. serotonin levels are increased by carbohydrate bingeing).
- Hormones and endorphins may be involved – elevated levels of plasma endorphins have been found in bulimics and those who self-mutilate (Parkin & Eagles, 1993).
- However, it is not clear whether these changes are a cause, consequence or correlate of the disorder.

Genetic explanations

- The genetic evidence is much weaker than with anorexia.
- Kendler *et al.* (1991): concordance rate of only 23% for MZs and 9% for DZs.

Sexual abuse

- Waller (1993): sexual abuse is related to eating disorders, particularly bulimia, with borderline personality disorder linking the abuse to the eating disorder.
- Piran *et al.* (1985): sufferers of eating disorders often had a history of affective disorders (particularly depression), suggesting that vulnerability to eating disorders is increased by depression.
- Cochrane (1995) points to sexual abuse as an explanation of depression (Ch 69).

Other explanations

- Garner (1986): it is misleading to regard bulimia and anorexia as being psychologically dissimilar. Anorectics and bulimics share the same goal of maintaining a sub-optimal body weight and may move between the two disorders.

The disinhibition hypothesis

- Ruderman (1986): distinguishes between restrained eaters (who constantly diet) and unrestrained eaters.
- Restrained eaters may believe they have over-eaten and since they have broken their diet feel disinhibited and consume more food. Alcohol is also a 'disinhibiting factor'.
- This is later followed by purging in an attempt to reduce this weight gain.
- This 'all-or-nothing' rigidity makes people susceptible to binge eating.

THERAPIES BASED ON THE MEDICAL MODEL

SYLLABUS

4.4 Therapeutic approaches
- alternative types of treatment therapies for psychological disorders, including assessment of their appropriateness and effectiveness. These should include somatic approaches
- ethical issues involved in therapy and intervention (e.g. informed consent, confidentiality and the choice of goals)

KEY QUESTIONS
- How is chemotherapy used to treat mental disorders?
- How is ECT used to treat mental disorders?
- How is psychosurgery used to treat mental disorders?
- What ethical and other issues are involved in the use of these therapies?

Q

Section 1: Chemotherapies

1 Identify one reason why the *neuroleptics* were seen as a great advance in the treatment of seriously disturbed individuals.
2 What are other names for the neuroleptics?
3 Identify three disorders which neuroleptics are commonly used to treat.
4 Identify the three inter-related but discriminable ways in which neuroleptics function.
5 What are *akathisia* and *tardive dyskinesia*, commonly reported by users of neuroleptics?
6 Are the *positive* or *negative* symptoms of schizophrenia least likely to be affected by typical neuroleptics?
7 Identify two criticisms relating to the use of neuroleptic drugs.
8 To what class of drug do the *antidepressants* belong?
9 Name any two disorders, not including depression, for which antidepressants are commonly prescribed.
10 Name any one member of the *tetracyclic* group of antidepressants.
11 Why are *monoamine oxidase inhibitors* (*MAOIs*) so called?
12 The tetracyclics are also known as *SSRIs*. What do the letters SSRI stand for?
13 Identify two side-effects common to both MOAIs and tricyclics.
14 Identify one drawback in using antidepressants with patients considering *suicide*.
15 What effect do *lithium salts* have on *bipolar disorder*?
16 What is the mode of action of *lithium carbonate*?
17 Identify two side-effects associated with lithium salts.
18 To what class of drug do the *anxiolytics* belong?
19 What disorders are the anxiolytics used for?
20 For which type of anxiety disorder are the anxiolytics of little use?
21 Complete the sentence: 'The general effect of anxiolytics is to depress ____ activity, which causes a decrease in activity of the ___ branch of the ___'.
22 Identify two side-effects associated with the use of anxiolytics.

23 What is *rebound anxiety*?
24 Identify two dangers associated with the use of anxiolytics.

Section 2: Electroconvulsive therapy (ECT)

25 What did von Meduna advocate, based on his observation that schizophrenia and epilepsy were *biologically incompatible*?
26 Which therapeutic technique was pioneered by Cerletti and Bini?
27 What is the purpose of giving ECT patients an *atropine sulphate* injection, 45–60 minutes before the treatment?
28 Which two other types of drug are administered to patients before treatment?
29 What current flowing at what voltage is passed across the electrodes, and for what period of time?
30 Name three disorders for which ECT is primarily used today.
31 Why is it unlikely that the effects of ECT are due to the memory disruption caused by the treatment?
32 Why is it unlikely that the effects of ECT can be attributed to patients denying their symptoms to avoid the 'punishment' of therapy?
33 What is the most plausible account of ECT's effectiveness?
34 What did Breggin (1979) discover when investigating the effects of ECT in non-humans?

Section 3: Psychosurgery

35 To what does the term *psychosurgery* refer?
36 What was the rationale behind Moniz and Lima's procedure in which the neural connections between the pre-frontal areas and the hypothalamus and thalamus were severed?
37 What was involved in the original '*apple corer*' *technique*?
38 What is the principal criticism of the theoretical rationale behind Moniz's operation?
39 What is involved in a *capsulotomy*?

Section 1: Chemotherapies

1   *Neuroleptics* were seen as a great advance since they lessened the need for the physical restraint of seriously disturbed individuals.

2   Neuroleptics are also called *antipsychotics* and *major tranquillisers*.

3   Neuroleptics are commonly used to treat *schizophrenia, mania* and *amphetamine abuse*.

4   Neuroleptics function by *blocking dopamine receptors* in the brain, by *inhibiting the functioning of the hypothalamus*, and by *preventing arousal signals from reaching higher brain regions*.

5   *Akathisia* is restlessness, whilst *tardive dyskinesia* is an irreversible movement disorder resembling Parkinson's disease.

6   *Negative symptoms* (such as apathy and withdrawal) are least likely to respond to typical neuroleptics.

7   Neuroleptic drugs are *not cures* but only treat the symptoms of pychosis. In addition, they *do not treat social incapacity or assist the patient in adjusting to life outside a therapeutic setting*.

8   Antidepressants are classed as *stimulants*.

9   Antidepressants are commonly prescribed for *anxiety, agoraphobia, obsessive–compulsive disorder* and *eating disorders*.

10   *Prozac* (fluoxetine) is a *tetracyclic* antidepressant.

11   *Monoamine oxidase inhibitors* (MAOIs) are so called because they inhibit the uptake of the enzyme which deactivates the monoamine neurotransmitters noradrenaline and serotonin.

12   *SSRI* stands for *selective serotonin re-uptake inhibitors*.

13   MOAIs and tricyclics are both associated with *cardiac arrhythmias* and *heart block, dry mouth, blurred vision* and *urinary retention*.

14   Antidepressants do not work immediately and may take weeks to begin working. For patients considering suicide this may be too long.

15   *Lithium salts* flatten out cycles of manic behaviour.

16   *Lithium carbonate* functions by increasing the re-uptake of noradrenaline and serotonin.

17   Lithium salts are associated with *depressed reactions, hand tremors, dry mouth, weight gain, impaired memory* and *kidney poisoning*. In high concentrations they may cause *nausea, diarrhoea* and *death*.

18   *Anxiolytics* are classed as *depressants*.

19   Anxiolytics are used to treat *anxiety and tension* in people whose disturbances are not severe enough to warrant hospitalisation.

20   Anxiolytics are of little use in treating panic disorder.

21   '(The) general effect (of anxiolytics) is to depress *CNS* activity, which causes a decrease in activity of the *sympathetic* branch of the *ANS*.'

22   Anxiolytics are associated with *drowsiness, lethargy, tolerance, dependence, withdrawal* and *toxicity*.

23   *Rebound anxiety* refers to anxiety which is even more intense than the original anxiety, and occurs when the drug is stopped.

24   Overdose of anxiolytics can lead to *death*, especially when taken with alcohol. They may also lead to addiction.

Section 2: Electroconvulsive therapy (ECT)

25   Von Meduna advocated inducing major epileptic fits in psychotics in order to 'cure' their schizophrenia.

26   Cerletti and Bini (Bini, 1938) were the first to advocate passing an electric current across the temples to induce an epileptic fit.

27   An *atropine sulphate* injection is given in order to prevent the heart's normal rhythm from being disturbed, and to inhibit the secretion of mucus and saliva.

28   A *muscle relaxant* and an *anaesthetic* are administered before treatment.

29   A current of 200 milliamps, flowing at 110 volts, for a period of 0.5–4 seconds.

30   ECT is primarily used to treat *severe depression, bipolar disorder* and *certain obsessive–compulsive* disorders.

31   *Unilateral* ECT minimises memory disruption, but is nevertheless effective at reducing depression.

32   *Sub-convulsive shocks* have been applied to patients, and although these are likely to be just as unpleasant and threatening as convulsive shocks, they do not seem to be as beneficial.

33   The most plausible account of ECT's effectiveness suggests that it produces biochemical changes in the brain, particularly in levels of *serotonin* and *noradrenaline*, which are greater than those produced by drugs.

34   Breggin (1979) discovered that ECT caused brain damage to non-humans, immediately following its administration.

Section 3: Psychosurgery

35   The term *psychosurgery* refers to surgical procedures that are performed on the brain to treat mental disorders, where the intention is to alter purposely psychological functioning.

36   Moniz and Lima's procedure aimed to disconnect thought (mediated by the cortex) from emotion (mediated by the lower brain centres).

37   The original '*apple corer*' technique involved drilling a hole in the skull on either side of the head, then inserting a blunt instrument which was rotated in a vertical arc.

38   The theoretical rationale behind Moniz's operation was *vague and misguided*, with researchers not entirely clear why beneficial effects should occur.

39   A *capsulotomy* involves cutting two tiny holes in the forehead, which allow radioactive electrodes to be inserted into the frontal lobe, to destroy tissue by means of beta rays.

A

Psychosurgery

Facts
- Refers to surgical procedures which are performed on the brain with the intention of altering psychological function.
- Moniz and Lima pioneered the *leucotomy* or *prefrontal lobotomy*. The procedure involved severing the connections between the prefrontal areas ('rational area') and the hypothalamus and thalamus ('emotional areas').
- Original 'apple corer' technique involved inserting a blunt instrument into either side of the head and rotating it. A 70% 'cure' rate was claimed by Moniz and Lima after one year.
- Freeman & Watts (1942) popularised the prefrontal lobotomy, and Freeman developed the *transorbital lobotomy* involving the insertion of a probe into frontal area via the eye socket.

Reasons for abandoning psychosurgery
- **Psychotherapeutic drugs:** introduced in the late 1950s.
- **Lack of scientific basis:** David (1994) has suggested that, even today, knowledge of the frontal lobes is psychiatry's 'pseudoscience'.
- **Consistency and irreversibility:** psychosurgery is irreversible and its effectiveness varies between individuals.
- **Side-effects:** apathy, seizures, intellectual impairments, memory loss, hyperactivity, impaired learning ability, and death are possible.
- **Lack of evaluation:** the consequences of many forms of psychosurgery are poorly researched.
- **Consent:** psychosurgery was routinely used with people who could not give their consent to the operation.

Modern techniques
- Over 20 operations a year are still conducted in Britain (Snaith, 1994).
- Modern labotomies involve the insertion of radioactive rods into the frontal lobes, or the use of a heated electrode.
- Techniques are used with depressives and obsessive–compulsives, and reduce the risk of suicide in depressives from 15% to 1% (Verkaik, 1995).

Electroconvulsive therapy

Facts
- Involves passing an electric current across the brain in order to induce an epileptic fit.
- von Meduna claimed that schizophrenia and epilepsy were *'biologically incompatible'*, and used Cardiazol to induce epileptic fits.
- Cerletti and Bini (Bini, 1938) advocated the use of electric currents to induce epileptic fits.
- Typically, a number of treatments are administered over several weeks. Around 20,000 people per year undergo ECT in Britain.
- Originally used to treat schizophrenia, now mostly used to treat depression, bipolar disorder and obsessive–compulsive disorder.
- ECT has a negative public image and has been criticised on ethical grounds and even outlawed in Berkeley, California.
- Heather (1976): the treatment is unscientific, and Breggin (1979) cites studies of non-humans which suggest that ECT may cause brain damage.

Procedure
- An atropine sulphate injection is given to prevent disturbance of the heart's rhythm, followed by a short-acting anaesthetic and a muscle relaxant.
- In unilateral ECT, a current of around 200 milliamps at 110 volts is passed across the temples for between 0.5 and 4 seconds. In unilateral ECT, only one hemisphere (the non-dominant hemisphere) is affected.

Explaining ECT's effectiveness
- Benton (1981): whilst ECT is clearly effective in some cases, little is known about how it works.
- It is possible that a person denies their symptoms to avoid the 'punishment' that ECT is perceived as being. However, 'sub-convulsive shocks' are equally unpleasant but do not reduce depression equally.
- ECT may produce biochemical changes greater than those produced by drugs. It is difficult to establish which of the physical changes occurring during ECT is responsible. Lilienfeld (1995) suggests that *serotonin* and *noradrenaline* are most likely to be affected.

Somatic Therapies

Chemotherapy

	Neuroleptics	Antidepressants and antimanics	Anxiolytics
Facts	<ul><li>Also known as **antipsychotics/major tranquillisers.**</li><li>Introduced in the 1950s following the discovery that they calmed psychotics without impairing consciousness.</li><li>Seen as a great advance since they lessened the need for physical restraints.</li><li>Antipsychotics do not cure schizophrenia but reduce its prominent symptoms.</li></ul>	<ul><li>Antidepressants are classified as **stimulants** and were introduced in the late 1950s. Prozac is popular today.</li><li>Used to treat depression, anxiety, agoraphobia, obsessive–compulsive disorders.</li><li>None of the antidepressants exerts immediate effects (most take two weeks).</li><li>Lithium salts flatten out cycles of manic behaviour.</li></ul>	<ul><li>Classified as **depressants** and known as **anti-anxiety drugs** or **minor tranquillisers**.</li><li>Used to reduce anxiety and tension.</li><li>Anxiolytics are effective in reducing the symptoms of GAD, but less effective for panic attacks.</li><li>Overdose can lead to death, especially if mixed with alcohol, and they are addictive.</li></ul>
Examples	<ul><li>Largely derive from phenothiazines and include Thorazine, Largactil.</li><li>Recently a dibezazepine (Clozaril) has been used and has fewer side-effects.</li></ul>	<ul><li>MAOI (monoamine oxidase inhibitors) include Nardil. The tetracyclic group (selective serotonin reuptake inhibitors – SSRIs) include Prozac.</li><li>Lithium salts include Camoclit and Litarex.</li></ul>	<ul><li>The propaneidol group includes Miltown.</li><li>The benzodiazepine group includes Librium and Valium.</li></ul>
Mode of action	<ul><li>Most neuroleptics block D2 dopamine receptors in the brain.</li><li>Also inhibit the hypothalamus, which secretes dopamine.</li><li>Prevent arousal signals from reaching higher brain regions.</li></ul>	<ul><li>MAOIs block the uptake of an enzyme which deactivates noradrenaline and serotonin. Tetracyclics deactivate the enzyme which removes serotonin.</li><li>Antimanics increase the re-uptake of noradrenaline and serotonin.</li></ul>	<ul><li>CNS activity is depressed, causing a decrease in the activity of the sympathetic branch of the ANS.</li><li>This produces decreased heart and respiration rate, reducing feelings of nervousness and tension.</li></ul>
Side-effects	<ul><li>**Neuroleptic malignant syndrome:** delirium, coma and death.</li><li>**Extrapyramidal symptoms:** restlessness, abnormal body movements and tardive dyskinesia (irreversible shaking resembling Parkinson's disease).</li></ul>	<ul><li>MAOIs can cause death if combined with certain foods (e.g. cheese and yeast extracts), whilst tetracylics may impair sexual functioning and heighten aggression.</li><li>Antimanics may cause tremors, dry mouth, weight gain, impaired memory.</li></ul>	<ul><li>Include drowsiness, lethargy, tolerance, dependence, withdrawal and toxicity.</li><li>*Rebound anxiety*, which is even more intense than the original anxiety, can occur when use is stopped.</li></ul>

THERAPIES BASED ON THE PSYCHODYNAMIC MODEL

KEY QUESTIONS
- What techniques are used in psychoanalysis?
- How do psychoanalytically oriented psychotherapists differ from traditional psychoanalysts?
- What are the psychodynamic approaches to group therapy?
- What ethical and other issues concern therapies based on the psychodynamic model?

Section 1: Psychoanalytic techniques

1 According to Freud's *psychodynamic model*, how does the ego defend itself from demands of the id or superego with which it is to weak to cope?
2 According to Freud, why is a change in behaviour not enough to bring about a permanent cure?
3 Why did Freud view a person's present problems as not belonging to the *psychoanalyst's* domain?
4 What is the purpose of *psychoanalysis*?
5 What is *insight*?
6 What is the rationale behind providing an analysand with insight?
7 Why did Freud abandon *hypnosis*?
8 Complete the sentence: 'Unconscious impulses are expressed in dreams as a form of ___ ___'.
9 What is the difference between *manifest* and *latent content*?
10 Why are *parapraxes* important to a psychoanalyst?
11 What name is given to the technique in which an analysand is encouraged to say whatever comes to mind?
12 Why is it important that analysts should not reveal personal information about themselves, nor express emotion or evaluation of an analysand?
13 Give two examples of ways in which *resistance* may be demonstrated?
14 What does resistance demonstrate to a psychoanalyst?
15 What is *confrontation*?
16 What is the role of *transference* in the psychoanalytic process?
17 What is *countertransference*?
18 In what way do modern commentators (such as Thomas, 1990) differ from Freud in their opinion of countertransference?
19 What is meant by Freud's claim that *working through* is necessary since troubles are usually *over-determined*?

Section 2: Psychoanalytical orientations

Q

20 Identify two ways in which *focal psychotherapies* differ from *classical psychoanalysis*.
21 What is the principal way in which *ego analysts* disagree with Freud's psychodynamic model?
22 What criticism of brief therapies was advanced by Roth and Fonagy (1996)?

Section 3: Psychodynamic group therapies

23 From what need did Moreno (1946) believe that most human problems arise?
24 What occurs during *psychodrama*?
25 What name is given to the individual who is dramatising his/her conflicts in psychodrama?
26 How does *doubling* in psychodrama differ from *mirroring*?
27 Identify three of the reasons Moreno gives for psychodrama's usefulness.
28 According to Berne (1964), personality is comprised of three ego states. Name these three states.
29 What is a *complementary interaction*?
30 What type of interaction is most likely to lead to problems?
31 What name is given to the analysis of games involving enacting different ego states and observing the effects of these on others?
32 What is the goal of this type of analysis?

Section 4: Psychodynamic model – issues

33 What is probably the major problem with Freud's work?
34 What is the principal problem with evidence derived from *case studies*?
35 What is an *intellectual insight*?
36 Explain what is meant by saying that the 'escape clause' of intellectual insight makes the argument for insight's importance completely circular.

Section 1: Psychoanalytic techniques

1 The ego defends itself by repressing the demands into the unconscious.

2 In order to bring about a permanent cure, the problems giving rise to the behaviours must also be changed.

3 Present problems will already have received attention in the form of sympathy and advice from family and friends.

4 The purpose of *psychoanalysis* is to uncover the unconscious conflicts responsible for a person's mental disorder.

5 *Insight* is a conscious awareness of repressed conflicts.

6 The rationale is that once a person understands the reason for a behaviour, the ego can deal more effectively with it and resolve the conflict.

7 Freud abandoned *hypnosis* on discovering that some analysands denied the accuracy of reports made under hypnosis, whilst others revealed information which was too painful or premature.

8 'Unconscious impulses are expressed in dreams as a form of *wish fulfillment*.'

9 *Manifest content* refers to the symbolic form of a dream, whereas *latent content* refers to its hidden meaning.

10 *Parapraxes* (faulty actions or 'Freudian slips') may reveal unconscious thoughts and desires.

11 *Free association*.

12 It is important that the analyst remain anonymous since such an interaction ensures that the analysand does not form a close, personal relationship with the analyst, but views him/her as an ambiguous stimulus.

13 *Resistance* may be demonstrated in behaviours such as *disrupting sessions*, *changing the subject*, *joking*, *arriving late for sessions*, or *missing sessions altogether*.

14 Resistance demonstrates that the analyst is getting close to the source of the problem, and that the unconscious is struggling to avoid 'giving up its secrets'.

15 *Confrontation* involves the analyst telling the analysand exactly what is being revealed in free association.

16 *Transference* occurs when the unconscious conflict has been unearthed and displaced onto the analyst, who now becomes the object of the analysand's emotional responses. The conflict can then be 'lived out'.

17 *Countertransference* is when the analyst transfers his/her own feelings onto the analysand.

18 Modern commentators (such as Thomas, 1990) often see countertransference as an unavoidable outcome of the psychoanalytic process.

19 Freud maintains that troubles seldom stem from a single source (i.e. are *over-determined*), and all aspects of the conflict and their implications must be dealt with before the conflict can be resolved (*working through*).

Section 2: Psychoanalytical orientations

20 *Focal psychotherapies* are usually briefer, involve face-to-face interaction, and pay more attention to the analysand's current life and relationships than does *classical psychoanalysis*.

21 *Ego analysts* believe that Freud over-emphasised the influence of sexual and aggressive impulses, and underestimated the ego's importance.

22 Roth and Fonagy (1996) argue that there is a high 'relapse rate' in all types of brief therapies when those who have undergone treatment are not followed up for long periods of time.

Section 3: Psychodynamic group therapies

23 Moreno (1946) believed that most human problems arise from the need to maintain social roles which may conflict with each other and a person's essential self.

24 *Psychodrama* involves participants and other group members acing out their emotional conflicts.

25 The *protagonist*.

26 *Doubling* involves the group leader or therapist also acting out the protagonist's role, whilst *mirroring* involves other group members minimising or exaggerating the protagonist's behaviour in order to provide feedback.

27 Moreno believes psychodrama is useful because it *helps to prevent destructive and irrational acting out in everyday life*, *enables feelings which cannot be adequately described to be expressed*, and *encourages individuals to reveal the deepest roots of their problems*.

28 *Adult*, *parent* and *child*.

29 A *complementary interaction* occurs when aspects of individuals' personalities are matched in interaction.

30 *Crossed interaction*.

31 *Transactional analysis*.

32 Transactional analysis aims to help people understand their behaviour and change it in a way which will give them greater control over their lives.

Section 4: Psychodynamic model – issues

33 Probably the major problem with Freud's work is that it is difficult to study scientifically, as many of the key concepts are vague or difficult to measure.

34 Evidence derived from *case studies* may well be biased.

35 *Intellectual insight* occurs when an analysand accepts an insight into a behaviour, but does not change that behaviour.

36 The argument for insight's importance is completely circular, since if the analysand improves, this improvement is attributed to insight, and if they do not improve then it is argued that only 'intellectual', rather than real insight, occurred.

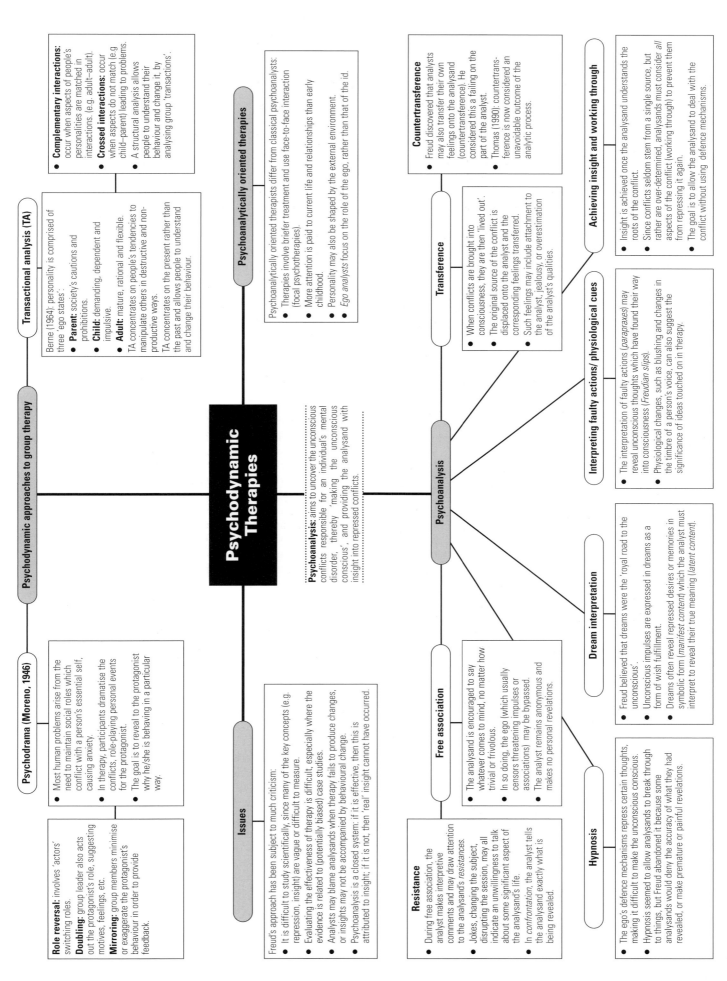

Psychodynamic Therapies

Psychoanalysis: aims to uncover the unconscious conflicts responsible for an individual's mental disorder, thereby 'making the unconscious conscious', and providing the analysand with insight into repressed conflicts.

Psychodynamic approaches to group therapy

Psychodrama (Moreno, 1946)

- Most human problems arise from the need to maintain social roles which conflict with a person's essential self, causing anxiety.
- In therapy, participants dramatise the conflicts, role-playing personal events for the protagonist.
- The goal is to reveal to the protagonist why he/she is behaving in a particular way.

Role reversal: involves 'actors' switching roles.

Doubling: group leader also acts out the protagonist's role, suggesting motives, feelings, etc.

Mirroring: group members minimise or exaggerate the protagonist's behaviour in order to provide feedback.

Transactional analysis (TA)

Berne (1964): personality is comprised of three 'ego states':

- **Parent:** society's cautions and prohibitions.
- **Child:** demanding, dependent and impulsive.
- **Adult:** mature, rational and flexible.

TA concentrates on people's tendencies to manipulate others in destructive and non-productive ways.

TA concentrates on the present rather than the past and allows people to understand and change their behaviour.

- **Complementary interactions:** occur when aspects of people's personalities are matched in interactions. (e.g. adult–adult).
- **Crossed interactions:** occur when aspects do not match (e.g child–parent) leading to problems.
- A structural analysis allows people to understand their behaviour and change it, by analysing group 'transactions'.

Psychoanalytically oriented therapies

Psychoanalytically oriented therapists differ from classical psychoanalysts:

- Therapies involve briefer treatment and use face-to-face interaction (focal psychotherapies).
- More attention is paid to current life and relationships than early childhood.
- Personality may also be shaped by the external environment.
- *Ego analysts* focus on the role of the ego, rather than that of the id.

Issues

Freud's approach has been subject to much criticism:

- It is difficult to study scientifically, since many of the key concepts (e.g. repression, insight) are vague or difficult to measure.
- Evaluating the effectiveness of therapy is difficult, especially where the evidence is related to (potentially biased) case studies.
- Analysts may blame analysands when therapy fails to produce changes, or insights may not be accompanied by behavioural change.
- Psychoanalysis is a closed system: if it is effective, then this is attributed to insight; if it is not, then 'real' insight cannot have occurred.

Psychoanalysis

Transference

- When conflicts are brought into consciousness, they are then 'lived out'.
- The original source of the conflict is displaced onto the analyst and the corresponding feelings transferred.
- Such feelings may include attachment to the analyst, jealousy, or overestimation of the analyst's qualities.

Countertransference

- Freud discovered that analysts may also transfer their own feelings onto the analysand (countertransference). He considered this a failing on the part of the analyst.
- Thomas (1990): countertransference is now considered an unavoidable outcome of the analytic process.

Achieving insight and working through

- Insight is achieved once the analysand understands the roots of the conflict.
- Since conflicts seldom stem from a single source, but rather are over-determined, analysands must consider *all* aspects of the conflict (working through) to prevent them from repressing it again.
- The goal is to allow the analysand to deal with the conflict without using defence mechanisms.

Interpreting faulty actions/ physiological cues

- The interpretation of faulty actions (*parapraxes*) may reveal unconscious thoughts which have found their way into consciousness (*Freudian slips*).
- Physiological changes, such as blushing and changes in the timbre of a person's voice, can also suggest the significance of ideas touched on in therapy.

Dream interpretation

- Freud believed that dreams were the 'royal road to the unconscious'.
- Unconscious impulses are expressed in dreams as a form of wish fulfillment.
- Dreams often reveal repressed desires or memories in symbolic form (*manifest content*) which the analyst must interpret to reveal their true meaning (*latent content*).

Free association

- The analysand is encouraged to say whatever comes to mind, no matter how trivial or frivolous.
- In so doing, the ego (which usually censors threatening impulses or associations) may be bypassed.
- The analyst remains anonymous and makes no personal revelations.

Resistance

- During free association, the analyst makes interpretive comments and may draw attention to the analysand's *resistances*.
- Jokes, changing the subject, disrupting the session, may all indicate an unwillingness to talk about some significant aspect of the analysand's life.
- In *confrontation*, the analyst tells the analysand exactly what is being revealed.

Hypnosis

- The ego's defence mechanisms repress certain thoughts, making it difficult to make the unconscious conscious.
- Hypnosis seemed to allow analysands to break through to things, but Freud abandoned it because some analysands would deny the accuracy of what they had revealed, or make premature or painful revelations.

THERAPIES BASED ON THE BEHAVIOURAL MODEL

KEY QUESTIONS
- What do therapies based on classical conditioning involve?
- What do therapies based on operant conditioning involve?
- What ethical and other issues concern these therapies?

Q

Section 1: Behaviour therapy

1 What did Watson & Rayner (1920) demonstrate in their experiments with 'Little Albert'?
2 What is the principle common to both *implosion therapy* and *flooding*?
3 Outline the procedures in implosion therapy.
4 What is *stimulus augmentation*?
5 How does flooding differ from implosion therapy?
6 Wolpe (1973) describes the case of an adolescent girl with a fear of cars. How was this fear overcome?
7 Identify one difficulty with the use of flooding as a form of therapy.
8 What is learned during *systematic desensitisation* (SD) that is not learned during either implosion therapy or flooding?
9 How was Jones (1924) able to eliminate fear responses in children?
10 What is an *anxiety hierarchy*?
11 What are the next two steps during SD which follow the construction of an anxiety hierarchy?
12 What does the *principle of reciprocal inhibition* maintain, as applied to phobias?
13 What source of variation between individuals poses a problem for SD?
14 What is meant by saying that *in vivo* desensitisation is always the most effective form of desensitisation?
15 Which of flooding, implosion therapy, and SD is the most effective?
16 What is the objective of *aversion therapy*?
17 In what way is aversion therapy applied in the treatment of *alcohol abuse*?
18 Identify one other behaviour which aversion therapy has been used to treat.
19 Identify one highly controversial (and non-fictitious) use of aversion therapy.
20 Complete the sentence: 'In some cases, ___ factors will 'swamp' the conditioning process, and this is one reason why aversion therapy is not always effective'.

21 In what way does aversion therapy also involve *operant conditioning*?
22 How does *covert sensitisation* differ from aversion therapy?

Section 2: Behaviour modification

23 During any form of therapy based on *operant conditioning*, the first step is to identify the maladaptive behaviour. What is the next step?
24 What is the rationale behind therapies based on *extinction*?
25 Identify one problem which a therapist faces in attempting to implement therapies based on extinction.
26 How were Cowart & Whaley (1971) able to eliminate self-mutilating behaviour in an emotionally disturbed infant?
27 Identify two reasons why therapies based on *punishment* are not as effective as those based on positive reinforcement.
28 What name is given to therapies in which successive approximations to desired behaviours are rewarded?
29 How does Ayllon & Azrin's (1968) *token-economy system* work?
30 Ayllon & Azrin's (1968) therapies were effective in eliciting and maintaining desired behaviours. What further effect did they have on staff and patients?
31 Identify two problems associated with the use of token economies.

Section 3: Behavioural therapies – issues

32 Complete the sentence: 'Although critics accept that therapies based on the behavioural model can alter behaviour, they argue that such therapies fail to identify a disorder's ___ ___'.
33 What is *symptom substitution*?
34 Identify one further practical problem associated with the use of behaviour therapies.
35 Outline one ethical issue of behavioural approaches to therapy.

Section 1: Behaviour therapy

1 Watson & Rayner (1920) showed that a fear response to a neutral stimulus could be conditioned, by pairing the neutral stimulus with an unpleasant one.

2 Both *implosion therapy* and *flooding* work on the principle that a stimulus which evokes a fear response will lose this power if it is repeatedly presented without the unpleasant experience.

3 Implosion therapy involves the therapist repeatedly exposing the person to vivid mental images of the feared situation whilst in the safe therapeutic setting.

4 *Stimulus augmentation* is when verbal descriptions of the feared stimulus are used by the therapist to supplement the person's imagery.

5 Flooding differs in that the individual is forced to *confront the feared object or event*, rather than simply imagining it.

6 The girl's fear of cars was overcome by forcing her into the back of one and driving her around for four hours.

7 For some people, such therapies lead to increased anxiety or are too traumatic.

8 *Systematic desensitisation* teaches the adaptive and desirable response, whereas implosion therapy and flooding only extinguish the undesirable behaviour.

9 Jones (1924) was able to eliminate fear responses in children by gradually introducing the feared object, whilst at the same time giving them candy.

10 An *anxiety hierarchy* is a series of scenes or events rated from lowest to highest in terms of the anxiety they elicit.

11 Following the construction of an anxiety hierarchy, SD involves *relaxation training*, then *relaxing whilst imagining scenes from the hierarchy*.

12 The principle maintains that it is impossible to experience anxiety and relaxation at the same time.

13 Individuals differ in their abilities to conjure up vivid *mental images*.

14 *In vivo* desensitisation involves *live* encounters with the feared object or situation, and is more effective than other desensitisation techniques.

15 Flooding.

16 *Aversion therapy* aims to extinguish the pleasant feelings associated with socially undesirable behaviours.

17 *Alcohol* is paired with vomiting by giving people a drug which induces vomiting when combined with it, or inducing vomiting immediately after alcohol is taken.

18 Aversion therapy has also been used to treat *cigarette smoking*, *overeating* and *children's self-injurious behaviour*.

19 Aversion therapy has also been used to 'treat' *homosexuality*.

20 'In some cases, *cognitive* factors will "swamp" the conditioning process, and this is one reason why aversion therapy is not always effective.'

21 Aversion therapy also involves *operant conditioning* in that once the classically conditioned fear has been learned, the person is inclined to avoid contact with the stimulus in the future (operant response).

22 *Covert sensitisation* differs from aversion therapy in that people are trained to punish themselves using their imaginations (rather than aversive stimuli).

Section 2: Behaviour modification

23 Once the maladaptive behaviour has been identified, the next step is to *identify the reinforcers that maintain such behaviour*.

24 Therapies based on *extinction* maintain that operant conditioning can be used to eliminate abnormal behaviour by removing reinforcers which maintain such behaviour.

25 In order to be effective, the therapist must be able to identify and eliminate the reinforcer(s) which maintain the behaviour, and this is not always easy.

26 Cowart & Whaley (1971) were able to eliminate self-mutilating behaviour by delivering electric shocks to the infant via his leg, every time he showed the maladaptive behaviour.

27 Behaviours learned through *punishment* may *overgeneralise* to behaviours related to the punished behaviour, and punishment tends only to produce a *temporary suppression* of undesirable behaviours.

28 *Behaviour shaping.*

29 Ayllon & Azrin's (1968) *token-economy system* works by rewarding disturbed individuals with tokens for desirable behaviours. These tokens can then be exchanged for 'privileges'.

30 Token economies improved staff and patient *morale*, with patients less apathetic and irresponsible, and staff more enthusiastic about their patients and therapy.

31 Patients who are re-introduced to the community may not be successfully 'weaned off' the token, and token economies may lead to 'token learning' where patients only perform a behaviour if rewarded for it.

Section 3: Behavioural therapies – issues

32 'Although critics accept that therapies based on the behavioural model can alter behaviour, they argue that such therapies fail to identify a disorder's *underlying causes*.'

33 *Symptom substitution* occurs when removing one symptom simply results in another occurring in some other form.

34 Behaviour therapies may condition behaviours which, since they are learnt in a therapeutic setting, do not generalise well to other conditions.

35 Behavioural approaches to therapy have been criticised on a number of ethical grounds, in particular, techniques involving punishment have been seen as authoritarian, dehumanising and akin to 'brainwashing'. Others argue that behaviour therapies manipulate people and deprive them of their freedom.

A

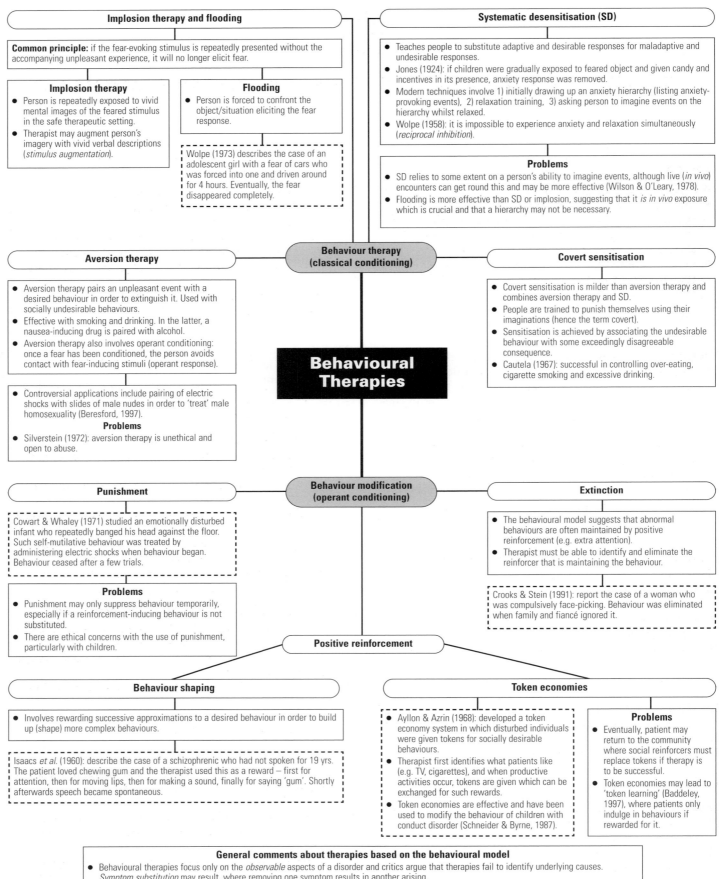

Behavioural Therapies

Behaviour therapy (classical conditioning)

Implosion therapy and flooding

Common principle: if the fear-evoking stimulus is repeatedly presented without the accompanying unpleasant experience, it will no longer elicit fear.

Implosion therapy
- Person is repeatedly exposed to vivid mental images of the feared stimulus in the safe therapeutic setting.
- Therapist may augment person's imagery with vivid verbal descriptions (*stimulus augmentation*).

Flooding
- Person is forced to confront the object/situation eliciting the fear response.

Wolpe (1973) describes the case of an adolescent girl with a fear of cars who was forced into one and driven around for 4 hours. Eventually, the fear disappeared completely.

Systematic desensitisation (SD)
- Teaches people to substitute adaptive and desirable responses for maladaptive and undesirable responses.
- Jones (1924): if children were gradually exposed to feared object and given candy and incentives in its presence, anxiety response was removed.
- Modern techniques involve 1) initially drawing up an anxiety hierarchy (listing anxiety-provoking events), 2) relaxation training, 3) asking person to imagine events on the hierarchy whilst relaxed.
- Wolpe (1958): it is impossible to experience anxiety and relaxation simultaneously (*reciprocal inhibition*).

Problems
- SD relies to some extent on a person's ability to imagine events, although live (*in vivo*) encounters can get round this and may be more effective (Wilson & O'Leary, 1978).
- Flooding is more effective than SD or implosion, suggesting that it *is in vivo* exposure which is crucial and that a hierarchy may not be necessary.

Aversion therapy
- Aversion therapy pairs an unpleasant event with a desired behaviour in order to extinguish it. Used with socially undesirable behaviours.
- Effective with smoking and drinking. In the latter, a nausea-inducing drug is paired with alcohol.
- Aversion therapy also involves operant conditioning: once a fear has been conditioned, the person avoids contact with fear-inducing stimuli (operant response).

- Controversial applications include pairing of electric shocks with slides of male nudes in order to 'treat' male homosexuality (Beresford, 1997).

Problems
- Silverstein (1972): aversion therapy is unethical and open to abuse.

Covert sensitisation
- Covert sensitisation is milder than aversion therapy and combines aversion therapy and SD.
- People are trained to punish themselves using their imaginations (hence the term covert).
- Sensitisation is achieved by associating the undesirable behaviour with some exceedingly disagreeable consequence.
- Cautela (1967): successful in controlling over-eating, cigarette smoking and excessive drinking.

Behaviour modification (operant conditioning)

Punishment

Cowart & Whaley (1971) studied an emotionally disturbed infant who repeatedly banged his head against the floor. Such self-mutilative behaviour was treated by administering electric shocks when behaviour began. Behaviour ceased after a few trials.

Problems
- Punishment may only suppress behaviour temporarily, especially if a reinforcement-inducing behaviour is not substituted.
- There are ethical concerns with the use of punishment, particularly with children.

Extinction
- The behavioural model suggests that abnormal behaviours are often maintained by positive reinforcement (e.g. extra attention).
- Therapist must be able to identify and eliminate the reinforcer that is maintaining the behaviour.

Crooks & Stein (1991): report the case of a woman who was compulsively face-picking. Behaviour was eliminated when family and fiancé ignored it.

Positive reinforcement

Behaviour shaping
- Involves rewarding successive approximations to a desired behaviour in order to build up (shape) more complex behaviours.

Isaacs *et al.* (1960): describe the case of a schizophrenic who had not spoken for 19 yrs. The patient loved chewing gum and the therapist used this as a reward – first for attention, then for moving lips, then for making a sound, finally for saying 'gum'. Shortly afterwards speech became spontaneous.

Token economies
- Ayllon & Azrin (1968): developed a token economy system in which disturbed individuals were given tokens for socially desirable behaviours.
- Therapist first identifies what patients like (e.g. TV, cigarettes), and when productive activities occur, tokens are given which can be exchanged for such rewards.
- Token economies are effective and have been used to modify the behaviour of children with conduct disorder (Schneider & Byrne, 1987).

Problems
- Eventually, patient may return to the community where social reinforcers must replace tokens if therapy is to be successful.
- Token economies may lead to 'token learning' (Baddeley, 1997), where patients only indulge in behaviours if rewarded for it.

General comments about therapies based on the behavioural model
- Behavioural therapies focus only on the *observable* aspects of a disorder and critics argue that therapies fail to identify underlying causes. *Symptom substitution* may result, where removing one symptom results in another arising.
- Behaviours which are learned under one set of conditions (e.g. therapeutic setting) may not *generalise* to another (e.g. real life). Therapists try to counter this by working in environments which are representative of real life.
- Behaviour therapies have been criticised for being unethical. Punishment techniques are authoritarian, and other therapies may manipulate people and deprive them of their freedom. Therapists respond that patients give consent, and are encouraged to control their own behaviours.

THERAPIES BASED ON THE COGNITIVE MODEL

SYLLABUS
4.4 Therapeutic approaches
- alternative types of treatment therapies for psychological disorders, including assessment of their appropriateness and effectiveness. These should include cognitive–behavioural therapies
- ethical issues involved in therapy and intervention (e.g. informed consent, confidentiality and the choice of goals)

KEY QUESTIONS
- What is Bandura's approach to therapy?
- What is Ellis's approach to therapy?
- What is Beck's approach to therapy?
- What are attributional approaches to therapy?
- What is Meichenbaum's approach to therapy?
- What other applications of the cognitive model are there?
- What ethical and other issues concern therapies based on the cognitive model?

Section 1: Bandura's approaches

1. How do both *SD* and *covert sensitisation* incorporate *cognitive processes* into their methodology?
2. What name do *social learning theorists* give to learning in which humans learn from others without direct experience?
3. Under what conditions is our restraint against performing an action likely to be lowered (*response disinhibition*)?
4. What is involved in *participant modelling*?
5. How is participant modelling applied in the area of *assertiveness training*?
6. Complete the sentence: 'Bandura (1977) believes that one reason for modelling's effectiveness is the development of ___-___.'

Section 2: Ellis: rational–emotive therapy

7. What is the aim of *rational–emotive therapy (RET)*?
8. In Ellis's *A-B-C model* what do the letters A, B and C stand for?
9. Identify two of the common maladaptive cognitions suggested by Ellis.
10. What does it mean to say that the therapist is an 'exposing and nonsense-annihilating scientist'?
11. Why do rational–emotive therapists not offer people warmth, love and support?
12. What was Ellis's (1984) view concerning the consequence of fidelity to interpersonal commitments (e.g. marriage)?
13. In what sense is RET *argumentative*?
14. Name one characteristic of individuals for whom RET is effective.
15. For which types of disorders is RET ineffective?

Section 3: Beck: cognitive restructuring therapy

16. What does Beck's *cognitive restructuring therapy* have in common with Ellis's RET?
17. What type of disorder is Beck's therapy specifically designed to treat?

18. What is the *cognitive triad* from which depressed people suffer?
19. Give four examples of faulty thinking identified by Beck.
20. For which other disorder has Beck's therapy also been found to be effective?

Section 4: Attributional therapy

21. What do *attributional therapists* believe are sometimes the cause of depression?
22. What does it mean to say that in depressed people the *self-serving bias* is reversed?
23. How do attributional therapists train people to overcome depression?
24. Identify one outcome, apart from a reduction in depression, which may arise from attributional therapy.
25. Identify one advantage which attributional therapy has over many other forms of therapy.

Section 5: Meichenbaum: stress inoculation

26. What is Meichenbaum's (1976, 1985) explanation for why people sometimes find situations stressful?
27. What is involved in the first stage of *stress-inoculation therapy* (*cognitive preparation*)?
28. What is involved in the final stage of stress-inoculation therapy?
29. Give three examples of reinforcing self-statements suggested by Meichenbaum (1976).

Section 6: Other applications

30. For which type of anxiety disorder are cognitive therapies particularly helpful?
31. What is *hypervigilance*?
32. What did James & Blackburn (1995) discover about the effectiveness of cognitively based therapies in treating *obsessive–compulsive disorders*?
33. Identify one medical condition on which cognitively based therapies have been found to have a significant impact.

Section 1: Bandura's approaches

1 Both *SD* and *covert sensitisation* involve the use of visual imagery, which is a *cognitive process*.

2 *Observational learning.*

3 *Response disinhibition* is likely to occur when we observe a positive outcome for a behaviour.

4 *Participant modelling* involves an individual observing the therapist's behaviour and then imitating it.

5 In *assertiveness training*, people with difficulty asserting themselves in interpersonal situations are required to perform in the presence of a group who provide feedback on the adequacy of the performance. The therapist may then model the appropriate behaviour, and the individual is required to imitate the therapist.

6 'Bandura (1977) believes that one reason for modelling's effectiveness is the development of *self-efficacy*.'

Section 2: Ellis: rational–emotive therapy

7 *Rational–emotive therapy* aims to help people find flaws in their thinking, and to replace these maladaptive cognitions with more rational ones.

8 The letters A, B and C stand for a *significant activating event* (A), a person's *belief system* (B), and the highly charged emotional *consequence* (C).

9 Ellis identifies people's belief that they are *worthless unless they are perfectly competent at everything they try*, and that they *must be approved of and loved by everyone they meet*.

10 The therapist is responsible for exposing irrational beliefs and substituting more rational alternatives in a scientific fashion, by reference to observations.

11 Rational–emotive therapists believe that offering people warmth, love and support may reinforce their need for love (which is often at the core of their circumstances), and create a dependence on therapy or the therapist.

12 Ellis (1984) believed that fidelity to interpersonal commitments, such as marriage, leads to harmful consequences.

13 RET is *argumentative* in that the therapist attacks those beliefs which he/she believes are illogical or foolish.

14 RET tends to be effective with people who are *self-demanding and feel guilty*, or that they are *not living up to their own standards of perfection*.

15 RET is ineffective for people with *severe thought disorders* (such as *schizophrenia*).

Section 3: Beck: cognitive restructuring therapy

16 Beck's *cognitive restructuring therapy* and Ellis' RET both assume that disorders stem primarily from *irrational beliefs*.

17 Beck's therapy is specifically designed to treat people suffering from *depression*.

18 Depressed people suffer from the *cognitive triad* of *negative beliefs about themselves*, their *futures*, and their *experiences*.

19 Beck identifies *magnification* and *minimisation*, *selective abstraction*, *arbitrary inference* and *overgeneralisation* as types of faulty thinking.

20 Beck's therapy has also been found to be effective with *eating disorders*.

Section 4: Attributional therapy

21 *Attributional therapists* believe that unrealistic or faulty attributions concerning their own behaviour are sometimes the cause of people's depression.

22 Depressed people tend to attribute *failures* to *internal causes* and *success* to *external causes* (the opposite attributional pattern to the self-serving bias).

23 Attributional therapists train people to overcome depression by perceiving success as resulting from internal factors, and at least some failures from external factors beyond their control.

24 Attributional therapy can result in *increased self-esteem*, *greater confidence*, and *better performance*.

25 Attributional therapy can result in beneficial changes after only a *small number of therapy sessions*.

Section 5: Meichenbaum: stress inoculation

26 Meichenbaum believes that people sometimes find situations stressful because they think about them in 'catastrophising' ways.

27 The first stage of *stress-inoculation therapy* involves the therapist and person exploring the way that stressful situations are thought about.

28 The final stage of stress-inoculation therapy (*application* and *follow-through*) involves the therapist guiding the person through progressively more threatening situations that have been rehearsed in actual stress-producing situations.

29 Meichenbaum (1976) proposed reinforcing self-statements such as '*it worked, you did it*', '*wait until you tell your therapist about this*', '*it wasn't as bad as you expected*', '*you made more out of the fear than it was worth*', '*you did it!*', '*it's getting better each time you use the procedures*'.

Section 6: Other applications

30 Cognitive therapies are particularly helpful in the treatment of *panic disorder*.

31 *Hypervigilance* involves people repeatedly scanning their bodies for signs of danger.

32 James & Blackburn (1995) discovered that of the few well-controlled studies examining the effectiveness of cognitively based therapies, there was little evidence to suggest that improvement occurred.

33 Cognitively based therapies have been found to have a significant impact of *chronic fatigue syndrome*.

Cognitive Therapies

Bandura

Modelling

Observational learning: according to Bandura (1969) and other social learning theorists, humans can learn simply by observing the behaviour of another. If we see a positive outcome for a behaviour, we are more likely to perform it (**response disinhibition**); if we see a negative outcome, we are less likely to perform it (**response inhibition**).

Modelling: maladaptive behaviours can be eliminated by exposing sufferers to models who demonstrate the appropriate actions. Participant modelling involves the individual observing, then imitating, the therapist.
Used effectively with a variety of phobias.

Assertiveness training
- Individuals demonstrate problem behaviours in front of a group who provide feedback.
- Therapist then models appropriate behaviour.
- Individual then tries again, alternating between modelling and behavioural rehearsal.
- Used in social skills training.

Self-efficacy
Bandura (1977): one reason for modelling's effectiveness is it increases a person's evaluation of the degree to which he/she can cope with difficult situations (self-efficacy), by encouraging them to perform behaviours which were previously impossible.

Ellis

Rational–emotive therapy (RET)
- The aim of RET is to help people find flaws in their thinking and alter these maladaptive cognitions by creating a dispute belief system (D), which does not lead to severe emotional consequences (see below).
- Ellis proposes that two common cognitions are:
  1) *I am worthless unless I am perfectly competent.*
  2) *Everyone must approve of me and love me.*
- Therapy involves substituting more realistic thoughts in place of the maladaptive and self-defeating ones (the therapist is 'an exposing and nonsense annihilating scientist').
- People are seen as having the capacity for rational understanding and the resources for personal growth.

The A-B-C model
- Ellis (1991): significant activating events (A) are often followed by highly charged emotional consequences (C) because of a person's belief system (B).
- As a result, inappropriate emotional responses (e.g. depression, guilt) can only be abolished if there is a change in beliefs or perceptions.

Effectiveness
- Fancher (1995): it is false to think that therapists are capable of identifying 'faulty thinking'.
- Effective in producing behaviour change amongst the self-demanding or perfectionists (Brandsma *et al.*, 1978).
- Ineffective with severe thought disorders (Ellis, 1993).

Beck

Cognitive restructuring therapy (Beck, 1967)
- Assumes that disorders stem primarily from irrational beliefs.
- Specifically designed to treat depressed people.
- Depressed people suffer from a *'cognitive triad'* of negative beliefs about themselves, their future and their experiences (Beck *et al.*, 1979 – see Ch 66).
- Therapy aims to identify implicit and self-defeating assumptions, substituting more adaptive ones.
- The approach is gentler and less confrontational than RET, disproving the person's negative self-image (Williams, 1992).
- Most effective in the treatment of depression (Andrews, 1991), but has also been used in treating eating disorders.

Meichenbaum

Stress inoculation therapy (Meichenbaum, 1976, 1985)
- Assumes that people sometimes find situations stressful because they think about them in catastrophic ways.
- Therapy consists of three stages:
  1) Cognitive preparation: therapist and person explore the way stressful situations are thought about (e.g. 'I can't cope').
  2) Skill acquisition: negative self-statements are replaced with positive ones which are then practised.
  3) Application and follow-through: therapist guides the person through progressively more threatening situations that have been rehearsed.
- Meichenbaum *et al.* (1982): 'the power of positive thinking' approach is particularly effective in relation to anxiety and pain.

Attribution therapy
- Attributions are beliefs about the causes of our own/other people's behaviour.
- Attributional therapists hold that in some cases depressed people make faulty attributions which are responsible for their distress.
- Depressed people do not show the *self-serving bias*, instead attributing their failures to internal causes and successes to external causes, resulting in low self-esteem.
- Therapists train sufferers to perceive success as resulting from internal factors, and at least some failures from external factors beyond their control.
- Beneficial changes can occur after only a small number of therapy sessions (Brockner & Guare, 1983).

Other applications
- Cognitively-based therapies can be particularly effective in treating panic disorder. Clark (1993) argues that the core disturbance is an abnormal interpretation of physiological changes as signs of impending mental or physical catastrophe, leading to hypervigilance of their physical condition.
- Clark *et al.* (1994) and Shear *et al.* (1994): cognitive therapies are highly effective at changing cognitions and behaviours in 90% of those treated.
- However, James & Blackburn (1995) found that cognitively-based therapies were not effective in treating obsessive–compulsive disorder.

THERAPIES BASED ON THE HUMANISTIC MODEL

Q ## Section 1: Rogers' client- (or person-) centred therapy

1 Why was Rogers' therapy once also called *non-directive therapy*?
2 What, according to Rogers (1986), is the central premise of *person-centred therapy*?
3 According to Rogers, there are three major elements necessary for the right 'therapeutic atmosphere'. What is *genuineness*, the first of these?
4 Why is genuineness the most important of the three elements?
5 What is *unconditional positive regard*?
6 Identify and describe the third element necessary for the correct therapeutic atmosphere.
7 How often are Rogerian sessions typically held?
8 What is *active listening*?
9 What is *reflection*, and which of the three elements does it relate most closely to?
10 What is meant by saying that the therapist's *passive reflection* is gradually replaced by *active interpretation*?
11 Complete the sentence: 'The therapy helps ___-___ by providing an encouraging atmosphere in which clients can explore various choices and paths'.
12 How did Rogers ensure that his therapeutic techniques could be evaluated?
13 Identify one conclusion which can be drawn from Traux's (1966) finding that only those clients who showed progress were regularly followed by positive comments by Rogers?
14 In what way might giving people unconditional positive regard be harmful?
15 For what type of disorders is Rogerian therapy not appropriate?
16 Identify one further criticism of the Rogerian approach to therapy.

Section 2: Perls' Gestalt therapy

17 What is the principal difference between Rogerian therapy and *Perls' Gestalt therapy*?
18 What assumption regarding mental disorders is shared by Perls and Freud?
19 What did Perls believe about the significance of *dreams*?
20 Why did Perls apply the term *Gestalt* to his therapy?
21 According to Perls' approach, what is the essential difference between psychologically healthy people and those suffering from mental disorders?
22 Complete the sentence: 'Gestalt therapy's primary focus is on moment-to-moment ___-___'.
23 To what does Kempler (1973) liken the client–therapist relationship?
24 What happens during an *empty-chair exercise*?
25 What occurs during the technique called *dialogue*?
26 What does *speaking in the first person* help people to do?
27 Why do Gestalt therapists argue that Gestalt therapy cannot be evaluated in the same way as other therapies?

Section 3: Humanistic group therapies

28 What, according to Graham (1986), is the role of *encounter groups*?
29 What are participants in such groups encouraged to do?
30 What is the nature of the *therapeutic atmosphere* which the facilitator aims to create?
31 What was the original aim of *sensitivity training groups (T-groups)*?
32 What is the principal difference between T-groups and encounter groups?
33 Some critics have claimed that T-groups may have detrimental effects. What are these effects?
34 Identify the three characteristics which are most likely to be possessed by leaders who have '*casualties*' among their groups.
35 Identify one other destructive characteristic sometimes present in T-groups.

Section 1: Rogers' client- (or person-) centred therapy

1 The therapy was also called *non-directive therapy* because Rogers refused to tell people what to do or think.

2 Rogers (1986) claims that the central premise of person-centred therapy is that the individual is capable of change and self-direction, but only in a climate of facilitative psychological attitudes.

3 *Genuineness* refers to real human relationships in which therapists honestly express their feelings.

4 Genuineness is the most important of these elements because a meaningful relationship demands that *empathy* and *positive regard* are honest and real.

5 *Unconditional positive regard* means respecting clients as important human beings, and accepting them for what they are without reservation.

6 The third element is *empathy*. It is the process of perceiving the world from the client's perspective and understanding what they are feeling.

7 Rogerian sessions are typically held once a week.

8 *Active listening* involves the therapist attempting to grasp both the content of what the client says and the feeling behind it.

9 *Reflection* involves summarising the client's message and feeding this back. It relates most closely to *empathy*.

10 As therapy progresses, the therapist goes beyond summarising the overt messages in what the client has said and responds to what he/she senses, beginning to confront the client more.

11 'The therapy helps *decision-making* by providing an encouraging atmosphere in which clients can explore various choices and paths.'

12 Rogers *recorded* his sessions so that his techniques could be evaluated.

13 Traux's (1966) findings suggest that *social reinforcement* is a powerful influence on behaviour, and that Rogerian therapy was not non-directive.

14 Unconditional positive regard may result in clients leaving therapy with the unrealistic expectation that everything they do will meet with society's approval.

15 Rogerian therapy is not appropriate for *psychoses*, such as *schizophrenia*.

16 The Rogerian approach may be wrong in viewing human beings as basically 'good' (in line with the humanistic model), and has been criticised for treating people in the same way, regardless of their disorder.

Section 2: Perls' Gestalt therapy

17 Unlike Rogerian therapy, *Perls' Gestalt therapy* is highly directive, with the therapist leading the client through planned experiences.

18 Both Perls and Freud agree that mental disorders result from *unconscious mental conflicts*.

19 Perls saw *dreams* as disowned parts of the personality.

20 Perls used the term *Gestalt* (meaning 'organised whole'), since therapy was intended to enable the person to become 'whole' and resume normal growth.

21 Psychologically healthy people are *aware of themselves*, whereas mental disorders involve a *blockage of awareness*.

22 'Gestalt therapy's primary focus is on moment-to-moment *self-awareness*.'

23 Kempler (1973) likens the client–therapist relationship to that between *apprentice* and *master*.

24 During an '*empty-chair exercise*', the client moves back and forth between two chairs to play opposing roles in a conflict.

25 During *dialogue*, the client undertakes verbal confrontations between his/her opposing wishes and desires.

26 *Speaking in the first person* helps people to recognise and take responsibility for their own actions.

27 Gestalt therapists argue that the therapy is so individualised that it cannot be evaluated in the same way as other therapies.

Section 3: Humanistic group therapies

28 Graham (1986) claims that *encounter groups* enable people to break through their own barriers in order to react freely and openly with others.

29 Participants in such groups are encouraged to act out their emotions through bodily contact and 'games'.

30 The facilitator aims to create an atmosphere of *mutual trust* in which participants feel free to express themselves.

31 *Sensitivity training groups* (*T-groups*) were originally aimed at helping group leaders improve the functioning of groups by democratic methods.

32 T-groups differ from encounter groups in that they were originally limited to 'subtler' emotional expressions.

33 Some critics have claimed that T-groups may precipitate or even cause psychological disturbances.

34 Leaders who have 'casualties' among their groups are more likely to be *aggressive*, *highly charismatic* and *authoritarian*.

35 The pressure to have some *ecstatic* (or '*peak*') *experience*, which is viewed as necessary for continuing mental health, may also be a destructive influence.

A

Genuineness

- Also called authenticity or congruence – refers to therapeutic relationships where therapists honestly express their feelings and thoughts towards the client (e.g. boredom).
- Rogers (1980): clients can detect a fake concern on the part of the therapist and this will impede their personal growth.

Unconditional positive regard

- Respecting clients as important human beings and accepting them for what they are without reservation.
- Therapists must convince clients that they actually like and respect them and that this does not depend on what the client says or does.

Empathy

- The process of understanding the world from the client's perspective. The client must be convinced that he/she is understood by the therapist. Otherwise, the client may feel that they are accepted or respected, but not as they really are.

Encouraging personal growth

Techniques   **Rogers' client-centred therapy**   **Application and evaluation**

- The therapy was also called **non-directive therapy** as Rogers refused to tell people what to do or think, instead clarifying feelings by paraphrasing what they have said (**reflection**) and repeatedly asking them what they feel and think.
- Sessions are typically held once a week, with client and therapist facing each other.
- **Active listening** by the therapist involves grasping both the content and the feeling behind what the client is saying.
- This is gradually replaced by **active interpretation**, where the therapist responds to what is sensed to be the client's true feelings and may confront the client with inconsistencies.
- The focus is on present, not past, feelings.
- By accepting themselves, clients 'get it together' and experience **congruence**.

- Used in human relations training with professionals such as nurses, crisis workers and counsellors.
- Aids decision-making by providing an encouraging atmosphere in which to explore options.

Truax (1966): analysed therapy sessions (which Rogers recorded with clients' permission). Only those clients who showed progress were regularly followed by positive comments by Rogers, suggesting that social reinforcement is a powerful influence.

Criticisms

- People are treated in the same way, regardless of their disorder.
- Unconditional positive regard may *harm* people by leaving them with unrealistically high expectations of approval.
- Ineffective for psychoses, and the assumption that people are basically 'good' may be wrong in certain cases (e.g. with antisocial personality disorder).

Humanistic Approaches

Encounter groups   **Group therapy – humanistic**   **Sensitivity training groups**

Originally developed by Rogers to enable people to react more openly and freely with one another.

- Participants are encouraged to act out their emotions through bodily contact and structured 'games'.
- The leader (facilitator) attempts to create an atmosphere of mutual trust in which group members feel free to express their feelings.
- Rogers (1973): this reduces defensiveness and promotes self-actualisation ('being who you want to be').

Introduced in the late 1940s, with the intention of helping group leaders to improve the functioning of groups by democratic methods.

- Such 'T-groups' encourage expressions of emotion which are subtler than those expressed in encounter groups.
- Some claimed that such groups can precipitate psychological disturbances, especially where leaders are charismatic, authoritarian and aggressive.
- Particularly destructive is the pressure to have some ecstatic experience required for continued mental health.

Assumptions   **Perls' Gestalt therapy**   **Techniques**

Like Rogers, Perls believed that therapy should help people to integrate conflicting aspects of their personalities.

- Gestalt therapy differs in that it is highly **directive** and the therapist leads the client through **planned experiences**.
- Saw dreams as 'disowned parts of the personality' and emphasised the 'here and now'.
- Mental disorders occur as a result of a **blockage of awareness,** resulting in limited control over behaviours.
- When therapy is complete, disowned fragments are integrated and the person becomes an '**organised whole**' (Gestalt) and can resume normal growth, fully aware of themselves (**organismic self-regulation**).
- Primary focus is on developing moment-to-moment **self-awareness**, with the therapist directing the client.

Effectiveness

- Proponents argue that the growth of this therapy is an indicator of its effectiveness.
- Rimm & Masters (1979): there have been few controlled studies to validate Gestalt therapy.
- Therapists argue that because the therapy is so individualised, it cannot be evaluated in the same way as other therapies.
- Simkin & Yontef (1984): techniques like amplification can be effective.

Role play: a person may act out different roles in an important conflict, moving between roles (*empty chair exercise*). This helps the client to complete 'unfinished business'.

Amplification: client is asked to exaggerate a behaviour or feeling so as to become more aware of it.

Dialogue: the client undertakes verbal confrontations between conflicting wishes and ideas (e.g. 'don't take chances' and 'take risks in order to progress').

Speaking in the first person: people are encouraged to recognise and take responsibility for their own actions, restating comments (e.g. 'some people might disagree') in the first person (e.g. 'I disagree')

ASSESSING THE EFFECTIVENESS OF THERAPIES

SYLLABUS
4.4 Therapeutic approaches
• alternative types of treatment therapies for psychological disorders, including assessment of their appropriateness and effectiveness

KEY QUESTIONS
• What did early attempts at assessing the effectiveness of therapies suggest?
• How can the effectiveness of therapies be measured?
• What do meta-analytic studies suggest?
• What problems are there in attempting to compare the effectiveness of different types of therapies?

Section 1: Effectiveness – early studies

1 Why had the effectiveness of *psychotherapeutic* approaches not been seriously questioned prior to Eysenck's (1952) study?
2 According to Eysenck, what percentage of cases treated with psychoanalysis could be considered 'cured' or 'improved'?
3 What is *spontaneous remission*?
4 What percentage of the control group in Eysenck's study underwent spontaneous remission?
5 Complete the sentence: 'Eysenck claimed that there appeared to be an ___ correlation between recovery and psychotherapy'.
6 What additional *ethical issue* did Eysenck raise?
7 Some researchers questioned the way in which Eysenck had classified 'failures'. What criticism did they make?

Section 2: Issues of measurement

8 What criterion of success would those who support the *behavioural model* be likely to apply?
9 How would *psychoanalysts* disagree with this criterion?
10 Identify one difficulty with involving family and friends of the person who has received therapy in assessing effectiveness.
11 Why is a person's therapist unlikely to be used to assess the effectiveness of a therapy?
12 What did Sloane *et al.* (1975) find concerning the relative effectiveness of psychotherapy and no treatment at all?
13 Identify three ethical concerns which arise from studies such as Sloane *et al.*'s.
14 What are *recidivism rates*?
15 What is Luborsky *et al.*'s claim about the *dose–effect relationship*?

Section 3: Meta-analytic studies

16 What is a *meta-analytic study*?
17 Complete the sentence: 'On the basis of their meta-analytic study, Smith *et al.* (1980) concluded that the average person who receives therapy is better off at the end of it than __ per cent of persons who do not.'
18 What criticism did Smith *et al.*'s study attract, concerning the nature of their sample?
19 What overall conclusion can be reached concerning the issue of psychotherapy's effectiveness?

Section 4: Comparing relative effectiveness

20 Identify the five therapies which May (1975) attempted to compare in his study of their relative effectiveness?
21 Which two therapies did May conclude were the most effective?
22 What further conclusion was May able to reach, based on the relative effectiveness of these two therapies?
23 Why is it difficult to compare the 'improvements' made during different forms of therapy?
24 What did Russell (1981) discover when comparing the effectiveness of experienced and novice therapists?
25 What is *technical eclecticism*?
26 What did Strupp & Hadley (1979) find when they asked warm, empathetic university professors to 'treat' students experiencing depression and anxiety?
27 What is the *placebo effect*?
28 What type of *somatic therapy* is most effective for severe thought disorders (e.g *schizophrenia*)?
29 What type of therapy is likely to be most effective with *agoraphobia*?
30 Name two types of disorder for which *spontaneous remission* rates are relatively high.
31 What is the *YAVIS effect*?

Section 1: Effectiveness – early studies

1　Prior to Eysenck's (1952) study, the value and effectiveness of *psychotherapies* was not questioned (at least by therapists), since many people seeking treatment improved and reported themselves satisfied with the therapies.

2　Eysenck claimed that *44 per cent* of such cases could be considered 'cured' or 'improved'.

3　*Spontaneous remission* refers to the improvement of a psychological problem without any professional treatment.

4　*Sixty-six per cent* of the control group underwent spontaneous remission.

5　'Eysenck claimed that there appeared to be an *inverse* (or *negative*) correlation between recovery and psychotherapy.'

6　Eysenck claimed that it was *unethical* for therapists to charge people for their services, when research suggested that they were paying for nothing.

7　Eysenck had classified those who dropped out of therapy as failures, and it is not necessarily the case that someone who leaves therapy is not cured.

Section 2: Issues of measurement

8　Those who support the *behavioural model* would be likely to identify *behaviour change* as an appropriate criterion of success.

9　*Psychoanalysts* would argue that for therapy to be effective, unconscious conflicts must be resolved.

10　The family and friends of the person who has received therapy may actually be the *cause* of a person's problems.

11　A person's therapist is unlikely to be used to assess effectiveness since they have a stake in believing that their therapies are effective, and are likely to be biased.

12　Sloane *et al.* found that 80 per cent of those who had received psychotherapy had improved, compared with only 48 per cent of those assigned to a waiting list.

13　It may be unethical to *assign people to waiting lists* (e.g. if they are depressed and suicidal), *assign them to therapies other than that which they have specifically requested*, and *to deceive them as to which therapy they are receiving in order to reduce expectation effects*.

14　*Recidivism rates* are statistics which show whether or not individuals are readmitted for therapy, or seek additional therapy after an initial course of therapy has ended.

15　Luborsky *et al.* (1975) claim that the more psychotherapy sessions that take place, the better the outcome (the *dose–effect relationship*).

Section 3: Meta-analytic studies

16　A *meta-analytic study* is one in which researchers combine the results of all the studies conducted in a given area to produce an 'averaged' result.

17　'On the basis of his meta-analytic study, Smith *et al.* (1980) concluded that the average person who receives therapy is better off at the end of it than *80* per cent of persons who do not.'

18　Most of the participants in Smith *et al.*'s study were students, who do not form a *representative sample* of the population as a whole.

19　Overall, it is fair to say that the issue of psychotherapy's effectiveness has yet to be resolved.

Section 4: Comparing relative effectiveness

20　May (1975) compared the effectiveness of *psychoanalytic-type therapy*, *phenothiazine drugs*, a *combination of psychotherapy* and *drugs*, *ECT*, and *milieu therapy*.

21　May concluded that *drugs alone* and *psychotherapy plus drugs* were the most effective.

22　May concluded that, since drugs and drugs plus psychotherapy were equally effective, psychotherapy had little or no tangible effects.

23　Is it difficult to compare 'improvements' made during therapy since different therapies define 'improvement' in different ways.

24　Russell (1981) discovered that experienced therapists were generally more effective than novice therapists.

25　*Technical eclecticism* refers to therapy in which techniques are borrowed from different therapies to tailor treatment to individual patients.

26　Strupp & Hadley (1979) found that warm, empathic university professors were as effective as professional therapists in producing change in students experiencing depression and anxiety.

27　The *placebo effect* is the expectation that a treatment will be effective to bring about an actual improvement.

28　*Drugs* are the most effective treatment for severe thought disorders (e.g schizophrenia).

29　*Behaviour therapy*.

30　*Spontaneous remission* rates are relatively high for *GAD* and *depression*.

31　The *YAVIS effect* refers to the increased effectiveness of certain types of therapy (e.g. psychoanalysis) with people who are **Y**oung, **A**ttractive, **V**erbal, **I**ntelligent and **S**uccessful.

Assessing Effectiveness

Early studies of effectiveness

Eysenck (1952)
Looked at studies conducted between 1920 and 1951, comparing psychoanalysis, eclectic therapies (a variety of approaches is used) and a control group (who received no therapy).

Results:

Psychoanalysis	-	44% improved
Eclectic	-	64% improved
No therapy	-	66% improved.

Concluded that **no treatment is at least as effective or more effective than treatment**, and suggested that it was unethical for therapists to charge for treatment (Eysenck, 1992).

Disputing Eysenck
- Eysenck's figures were re-analysed, so as not to include as 'failures' those who dropped out of therapy, taking the success rate for psychoanalysis to 66% (Oatley, 1984).
- Bergin (1983): success rate for psychoanalysis rose to 83% if 'improvement' was measured differently.
- Malan *et al.* (1975): even untreated individuals had had one assessment interview, which may have motivated self-induced change.

Meta-analytic studies

Smith *et al.* (1980)
Attempted to overcome the possibility that certain types of measurement may favour certain therapies by looking at **all** types of measurement. Looked at 475 studies using a total of 1776 outcome measures.

Results
Concluded that the average person who receives therapy is better off than 80% of persons who do not.

Disputing Smith *et al.*
- Over half the people receiving treatment in the 475 studies were students (hardly representative).
- Shapiro & Shapiro (1982): some of the problems being treated were not that serious (e.g. smoking).
- Prioleau *et al.* (1983): only 32 of the studies were free from methodological flaws, and the effectiveness of psychoanalysis was yet to be demonstrated.
- Andrews (1993): dynamic psychotherapy is no better than routine clinical care.

The issue of measurement

Criterion of success
- Therapists differ as to what they regard as an appropriate measurement: behaviour therapists stress changes in observable behaviour, psychoanalysts the resolution of unconscious conflicts.
- Even if behaviour change were the appropriate criterion, the therapist who judges whether a behaviour change has taken place may be biased.
- The subjective reports of the person undergoing therapy may also be unreliable.
- Family and friends cannot necessarily be relied upon as they may be the cause of a person's problems.

Sloane *et al.* (1975) attempted to circumvent such problems by using the reports of therapists not involved in treatment:
- 90 people suffering from anxiety/personality disorders were matched for age, sex, severity of disorder.
- Assigned randomly to psychotherapy, behaviour therapy, or a waiting list.

Results
- After 4 months, independent clinicians judged 80% of the two therapy groups as either having improved or recovered.
- 48% of the control group had improved/recovered.

Ethical issues
- There are ethical concerns over whether suicidal participants, assigned to a 'control group', should be denied therapy.
- Similarly, it seems unethical to assign participants to one therapy when they have requested a different therapy.
- Ideally, participants should not know which therapy they were receiving (to reduce expectation effects). However, this would be difficult and possibly unethical.

Comparing effectiveness

May (1975) assigned schizophrenics not previously hospitalised to one of 5 groups (psychoanalytic-type therapy, antipsychotic drugs, psychotherapy and drugs, ECT, milieu therapy). Criteria of success were assessments by nurses and clinicians, release rates, and duration of hospitalisation.

Results
Drugs alone, and psychotherapy plus drugs were the most effective. May concluded that psychotherapy had little or no effects.
However, others have argued that no one therapy is better than another (Smith *et al.*, 1980), or that factors other than the type of therapy influence effectiveness.

The therapist's influence
- Therapists using the same therapy are not equally effective (Wolpe, 1985).
- Experienced therapists are generally more effective than novices (Russell, 1981).
- One reason may be increased *technical eclecticism* (borrowing techniques from different therapies as required).
- Truax & Carkhuff (1964): therapists who genuinely care, are empathic, and offer trust, are most effective.
- Luborsky (1984): the therapeutic alliance (working together in a warm relationship) is the most important factor, suggesting that a 'placebo effect' is responsible for improvements (i.e. people improve because they expect to).

The disorder's influence
- Some types of therapy are more effective for certain disorders (e.g. drugs for schizophrenia).
- Behaviour therapies are better for treating agoraphobia, and some of these therapies (e.g. flooding) are better than others.
- Smith *et al.* (1980): psychodynamic therapies more effective with anxiety disorders than with schizophrenia.
- Bergin & Lambert (1978): people suffering from depression or GAD are more likely to undergo spontaneous remission than those suffering phobias or obsessive–compulsive disorder.

The person's influence
- Garfield (1980): psychodynamic therapies are most effective with well-educated, articulate, motivated and confident people with non-severe depression, anxiety disorders or inter-personal problems.
- Individuals differ and so does the nature of each therapeutic session, making it difficult to assess what exactly is most influential.
- Therapies which lack cultural sensitivity and do not take into account differing norms and educational standards will be of little use in treating members of other cultures (Baron, 1989).

LEARNING DIFFICULTIES

Section 1: Definitions and classification

1 How do both ICD-10 and DSM-IV define an individual as *mentally retarded*?

2 What term is used to apply to individuals with IQ scores of less than 20 or 25?

3 Describe the criterion used by the American Association of Mental Retardation to classify mental retardation.

4 Why did Burt (1921) originally advocate a 'cut-off' point, corresponding to an IQ score of 70, in classifying mental retardation?

5 What recommendation was made by the Warnock report concerning the emphasis which should be applied in dealing with learning difficulties?

6 Describe the characteristics of children with *mild learning difficulties*.

7 At what point in their development are children with *severe learning difficulties* most likely to be integrated into the mainstream curriculum?

8 What is the difference between the *delay* and *difference models* of cognitive abilities in people with learning difficulties?

Section 2: The causes of learning difficulties

9 According to Frude (1998), if an individual inherits a low IQ, which of the two categories of causes, '*pathological*' or '*familial*', of causes, would this fall into?

10 What is the nature of the genetic abnormality responsible for the vast majority of *Down's syndrome* cases?

11 Why has the incidence of Down's syndrome decreased significantly in recent years?

12 Why do some sufferers of Down's syndrome have speech difficulties?

13 How successful are sufferers of Down's syndrome in academic pursuits?

14 Why is *fragile X syndrome* more common in males than females?

15 How does *phenylketonuria* (PKU), which can cause learning difficulties, occur?

16 Identify two pre-natal *teratogens*.

17 How much *alcohol* use is 'safe' during pregnancy, according to *behavioural teratologists*?

18 Identify three *peri-natal influences* on subsequent learning difficulties.

19 Complete the sentence: 'In the majority of children with mild and moderate learning difficulties, however, there are no known ___ problems'.

20 In what way can learning difficulties be explained on statistical grounds alone?

21 What, according to Rutter & Madge (1976), is the *cycle of disadvantage*?

Section 3: Special education

22 Who is responsible for issuing a *statement of special educational needs*?

23 Identify three types of individual likely to be involved in the decision to issue such a statement.

24 Bloom (1984) found that one-to-one teaching was highly effective with children with special needs. Identify one problem with this approach to special education.

25 What argument in favour of special education is proposed by its proponents?

26 How do opponents disagree with this argument?

Section 4: Specific learning difficulties

27 Complete the sentence: 'People with dyslexia have ___ general cognitive abilities'.

28 Approximately what percentage of the world's population are dyslexic?

29 What ability is affected by *phonological dyslexia*?

30 What is *CoPS*?

31 On what basis is the claim made that dyslexia may have an underlying physical basis?

32 Why, according to Fletcher *et al.* (1994), is a sub-skill deficit in phonological awareness unlikely to be the cause of dyslexia?

33 What is the *multisensory approach*?

34 Why, according to Booth & Goodey, (1996) is dyslexia the 'cuckoo in the nest' of special educational needs?

Section 1: Definitions and classification

1 Both ICD-10 and DSM-IV define an individual as *mentally retarded* if his/her IQ score is *less than 70*.
2 Individuals with IQ scores of less than 20 or 25 are described as *profoundly retarded*.
3 The American Association of Mental Retardation classifies retardation based on the *intensity of needed support* (the amount of support a person needs to function in the environment).
4 Burt (1921) originally advocated this 'cut-off' on the grounds that it best suited the amount of *available accommodation*.
5 The Warnock report recommended that children's learning *needs* be emphasised.
6 Children with *mild learning difficulties* have some difficulties with normal school work, but can cope with the normal curriculum.
7 Children with *severe learning difficulties* are most likely to be integrated into the mainstream curriculum during early schooling, when the curriculum is more child-centred and developmental.
8 The *delay model* of cognitive abilities suggests that children with learning difficulties develop in the same way as other children, only more slowly, whilst the *difference model* suggests that there is a qualitative difference in the way the two develop.

Section 2: The causes of learning difficulties

9 If an individual inherits a low IQ, this falls into the '*familial*' causes category.
10 *Down's syndrome* is usually the result of an extra chromosome (chromosome 21).
11 The availability of *diagnostic tests* which can detect Down's syndrome early on in pregnancy has led to an increased number of terminations in such cases.
12 Sufferers of Down's syndrome may have speech difficulties as a result of a relatively small mouth and relatively large tongue.
13 Academic progress is generally slower, but ability levels vary, with at least some sufferers of Down's syndrome experiencing a high degree of success.
14 *Fragile X syndrome* is caused by a defect of the X chromosome. Since males only have one copy of this chromosome (females have two), they are particularly vulnerable to the disorder.
15 *Phenylketonuria* (*PKU*) causes a deficiency in enzyme production, leading to a build-up of a toxin (*phenylalanine*) in the brain.
16 *Infections* (e.g. rubella), *toxic chemicals* (such as cocaine and alcohol), *radiation* and *pollutants* are all pre-natal teratogens.
17 *Behavioural teratologists* do not agree on a 'safe' level of maternal alcohol drinking during pregnancy.
18 *Birth trauma*, *prematurity* and *asphyxiation* are *peri-natal* influences on subsequent learning difficulties.

19 'In the majority of children with mild and moderate learning difficulties, however, there are no known *pathological* problems.'
20 Assuming that variations in intelligence are a result of genetic variations, some individuals will lie at the lower end of this range and be classed as having learning difficulties.
21 The *cycle of disadvantage* describes the manner in which parents with low abilities provide unstimulating environments for their children, who in turn raise their own children similarly.

Section 3: Special education

22 A local educational authority is responsible for issuing a *statement of special educational needs*.
23 *Parents*, the *class teacher*, the *school's special educational needs co-ordinator*, the *local education authority* and *external agents* (e.g educational psychologists) are all likely to be involved.
24 One-to-one teaching is economically unsustainable.
25 Proponents of special education argue that children who have evidently failed in mainstream schools need help in different and separate schools.
26 Opponents argue that such schooling does not necessarily result in better learning outcomes, and isolates children socially by separating them from their local peer groups.

Section 4: Specific learning difficulties

27 'People with dyslexia have *normal* general cognitive abilities.'
28 Around *ten per cent* of the world's population are dyslexic.
29 *Phonological dyslexia* affects letter–sound conversion, so that individuals cannot convert written words to their sounds directly.
30 *CoPS* (*cognitive profiling system*) is an interactive CD-ROM, consisting of ten skills tests (presented as games) designed to identify a child's cognitive weaknesses.
31 The discovery that developmental and acquired dyslexia (resulting from brain injury) share characteristics, suggests that dyslexia may have an underlying physical basis.
32 Fletcher *et al.* (1994) found that difficulties with underlying phonological awareness characterise children with all types of reading failure, whether they are just behind or specifically delayed.
33 The *multisensory approach* to teaching children with dyslexia argues that such children require teaching which integrates visual, auditory and physical work.
34 Booth & Goodey (1996) point out that dyslexia accounts for over 40 per cent of cases coming before the SEN appeals tribunal, and that it has a distorting effect on a school's special needs budget, at the expense of children who have 'genuine' disabilities.

A

Learning difficulties

Definitions

- In both DSM-IV and ICD-10, an individual is designated mentally retarded if his/her IQ is less than 70.
- The American Association of Mental Retardation (AAMR) bases classification on the intensity of needed support (not IQ).
- Today the terms 'learning difficulties' and 'special needs' are used in preference to 'mental retardation'.

The use of an IQ score of 70 has been criticised on the ground that the original advocate, Burt (1921), calculated this level based on the amount of *accommodation* available, not the individual's *needs*.

Categorising

The Warnock report (Special Educational Needs, 1978) recommended that children's learning needs be emphasised, introducing 'mild' 'moderate' and 'severe' learning difficulties to replace categories such as 'educationally sub-normal'.

Mild
(IQ 50–55 – 70)
Some difficulties with school work, but can cope with normal curriculum given appropriate support.

Moderate
(IQ 35–40 – 50–55)
Limited progress in literacy and numeracy, despite support. Additional help required achieved by 'statementing'.

Severe
(IQ 20–25 – 35–40)
Communication and academic attainment very limited. May attend special schools.

- The term 'profound learning difficulties' is used to apply to children with an IQ below 20–25.
- Some children may also be identified as having a 'specific learning difficulty' (often called dyslexia).

Special education

- Special education is the most widespread form of intervention for those with learning difficulties (Frude, 1998).
- The largest category of special needs is mild learning difficulties, embracing those failing in the classroom.
- One-to-one teaching can be highly effective (Bloom, 1984) but economically unsustainable.
- Some statemented children are educated separately in special schools: class sizes are smaller, teachers have specialist qualifications and curriculum is matched to children's needs. Cost is roughly 3 times that of 'mainstream' education (Audit Commission, 1992).

Statementing
- *Identifying children with special needs:* class teachers, the school's special educational needs coordinator, external agents (e.g. educational psychologists) and the local education authority (LEA) will all be involved.
- The LEA issues a *statement of special educational needs*, and provides appropriate support/school placement. Parents are involved at all stages and the statement is reviewed regularly.

Segregated education – issues
- Proponents argue that children who have failed in ordinary schools need help in different and separate schools (Hall, 1996).
- Opponents argue that such schooling does not necessarily result in better learning outcomes and isolates children socially.
- Some parents prefer mainstreaming (educating a child with learning difficulties in a normal school), but such children may not have their special educational needs met (Frude, 1998).

Specific learning difficulties

- People with specific learning difficulties (or dyslexia) have normal general cognitive abilities and no visual/auditory impairments.
- About 10% of the world's population are dyslexic (75% are boys).

Phonological dyslexia: individual cannot convert written words to sounds directly.
Surface dyslexia: individual cannot recognise a word by sight (only by sounding it out).
Deep dyslexia: individual is unable to pronounce aloud non-words and will sometimes substitute words with similar meaning.

Diagnosis
- Usually made by an educational psychologist.
- Young dyslexics have trouble remembering two or more instructions, catching a ball, and are often clumsy and inattentive (Fawcett & Nicholsson, 1994).
- The CoPS interactive CD-ROM consists of 10 skills tests presented as games, and allows diagnosis of children as young as 5 years.

Causes
- In *acquired dyslexia* (following brain injury), damage is to the left posterior hemisphere.
- In *developmental dyslexia*, there is atypical asymmetry of the planum temporale (associated with phonological coding.)
- Children with a dyslexic parent are 17 times more likely to be dyslexic, suggesting a genetic basis.
- Some argue that dyslexia results from specific sub-skill deficits (such as phoneme processing).

Dealing with dyslexia: Presland (1991) argues that dyslexics do not require special remedial techniques, whilst others (e.g. Hornaby & Miles, 1980) argue for a multisensory approach.
Political issues: some argue that dyslexia is a convenient label for poor academic performance, and that resources should go to children with other special needs.

Causes

Pathological causes

Genetic abnormalities
- **Down's syndrome** is caused by an extra chromosome 21. Characterised by slow progress in physical and mental skills.
- The likelihood of a woman giving birth to a Down's syndrome child increases with age. Amniocentesis has led to a greater number of terminations in such cases.
- Lewis (1987): stimulating environments can affect the cognitive development of children with Down's syndrome, suggesting that genetic factors set a limit on cognitive development, whilst environmental factors determine progress towards that limit.
- **Fragile X syndrome** is characterised by hyperactivity, learning, and memory difficulties.
- The syndrome is caused by a defect of the X chromosome, in which a gene sequence expands, 'looping out' and shutting it off.
- **Phenylketonuria** (PKU) is a rare genetic disorder causing a build-up of phenylalanine which is toxic to the brain. Without early treatment, severe retardation may result.

Non-genetic biological factors
Environmental factors (*teratogens*), commonly occurring pre-natally can cause learning difficulties.
Pre-natal influences include infections (e.g. rubella), toxins (e.g. alcohol, cocaine), radiation, and pollutants.
Foetal alcohol syndrome (FAS) may result from excessive alcohol use during pregnancy and may lead to mild or moderate retardation.
Peri-natal influences include birth trauma, prematurity and asphyxiation.
Post-natal influences include exposure to toxins (e.g. pesticides), malnutrition, tumours and infections (e.g. meningitis), and brain damage due to child abuse.

Familial causes
- In the majority of children with mild and moderate learning difficulties there are no known pathological problems.
- This may be largely due to the normal distribution of intelligence.
- Relatives of people with mild learning difficulties also tend to have low IQs, suggesting a genetic basis.
- Such families are also often characterised by emotional/cognitive deprivation, poverty, lack of education and poor nutrition, which may combine with genetic factors (Bee, 1997).
- Rutter & Madge (1976) used the term *'cycle of disadvantage'* to describe the effects of the poor environments provided by low ability parents.

79

PHYSICAL AND SENSORY IMPAIRMENTS

SYLLABUS
4.1 Atypical development
- research into the psychological effects of physical and sensory impairments, including the problems of coping with such impairments

KEY QUESTIONS
- What do the terms 'impairment', 'disability' and 'handicap' mean?
- What are the nature and effects of physical impairments?
- What are the nature and effects of sensory impairments?
- How do sufferers cope with their impairments?

Section 1: Impairment, disability, handicap

1 Identify any two types of individual classed as having mobility problems.
2 According to the World Health Organisation, what is the distinction between *disability* and *handicap*?
3 What is an *impairment*?
4 Identify two impairments which are not normally identified as a disabilities.

Section 2: Physical impairments

5 Identify three *chronic illnesses*.
6 Identify four psychological effects associated with chronic illnesses.
7 What is the role of *psychological decision theory* in the lives of those affected by chronic illness?
8 How do *problem-focused approaches* differ from *social approaches*?
9 To what does the term *cerebral palsy* refer?
10 How does *hemiplegia* differ from *quadriplegia*?
11 Complete the sentence: 'However, in some individuals with cerebral palsy normal ___ processes are masked by physical difficulties in communication'.
12 What incorrect conclusion may teachers sometimes reach, based on the failure of students with cerebral palsy to produce work equivalent to that of their able-bodied peers?

Section 3: Sensory impairments

13 In what way does *conductive* deafness differ from *perceptive* deafness?
14 Identify four common causes of conductive deafness.
15 What is the most obvious sign of serious hearing loss in a newborn child?
16 What is the most widely used method for assessing hearing impairments in infancy?
17 Why is this method not always reliable?
18 Identify two differences between the early language development of hearing-impaired babies and that of normal babies.

19 What did Harris (1991) discover when looking at sign language acquisition of hearing-impaired children born to hearing-impaired parents?

20 Approximately what percentage of children suffer temporary conductive hearing loss?
21 Identify two methods of communication which may be taught in residential schools for the hearing-impaired.
22 Identify one advantage and one disadvantage of teaching hearing-impaired children in mainstream schools.
23 Complete the sentence: 'The Makaton language programme (Walker, 1996) is a sign language consisting of a special selection of ___ words, structured in ___ of increasing complexity'.
24 What are *Blissymbols*?
25 What argument is proposed by *oralists*, concerning effective communication in the hearing-impaired?
26 Identify four causes of visual impairment.
27 What is *Braille*?
28 What types of words commonly have their meanings reversed by children with visual impairments?

Section 4: Coping with impairments

29 What does the law say regarding discrimination in employment towards a person disabled by virtue of physical or mental impairment?
30 Under what conditions can less favourable treatment be justified?
31 Identify one factor which is sometimes used by employers to legitimise discrimination.
32 Why, apart from the legal issues, is discrimination *not* in an employer's interests?
33 Why might people with impairments be limited in their choices when applying to universities?
34 What two things, according to a survey by the charity SCOPE, did many people with impairments report concerning their treatment at school?

Section 1: Impairment, disability, handicap

1 People who use wheelchairs some/all of the time, people with visual impairments, and people with partial sight/blindness all have mobility problems.

2 The World Health Organisation identifies a *disability* as the effects of an impairment on everyday activities, whilst a *handicap* is the effects of an impairment on social and occupational roles.

3 An *impairment* is an objective pathology or psychological difficulty.

4 *Short-sightedness* and *colour blindness* are not normally identified as disabilities.

Section 2: Physical impairments

5 *Chronic illnesses* include *cystic fibrosis, diabetes* and *congenital heart disease.*

6 *Increased behavioural problems, greater difficulties in coping and adjustment, adverse effects on family members and family functioning,* and a *higher incidence of emotional disturbances,* are all psychological effects associated with chronic illnesses.

7 *Psychological decision theory* aims to help affected individuals and their families to reach illness-related decisions in a systematic and beneficial way.

8 *Problem-focused approaches* prepare children to cope better with painful or stressful medical procedures or an illness's symptoms, whilst *social approaches* are aimed at the family or community of an affected child and include administrative interventions (e.g in areas such as education and delivery of care).

9 *Cerebral palsy* refers to various neurological defects resulting from brain damage either before birth or early in life.

10 *Hemiplegia* involves movement difficulties on one side of the body, whilst in *quadriplegia* all four limbs are affected.

11 'However, in some individuals with cerebral palsy normal *cognitive* processes are masked by physical difficulties in communication.'

12 Teachers may sometimes incorrectly conclude that students with cerebral palsy also have *learning difficulties.*

Section 3: Sensory impairments

13 *Conductive* deafness differs from *perceptive* deafness in that the former results from sound waves not being conducted efficiently through the external and middle ears to the inner ear, whilst the latter results from damage to the inner ear, auditory nerve or brain.

14 Conductive deafness is commonly caused by *wax, foreign bodies, blocking of the Eustachian tube* or *inflammation of the middle ear.*

15 The most obvious sign is congenital absence or abnormality of the external ear.

16 The *distraction test.*

17 Children are sometimes able to pick up visual 'cues' from those administering the test and give the impression that they have heard a sound.

18 Hearing-impaired babies stop babbling at around nine months, and acquire words at a slower rate than normal babies.

19 Harris (1991) discovered that such children acquired language at a similar, if not faster, rate than oral language is normally acquired.

20 Around *20 per cent* of children suffer temporary conductive hearing loss.

21 *Sign language, speech, lip-reading* and *finger-spelling* may all be taught in residential schools for the hearing-impaired.

22 Mainstream schools offer social and emotional advantages for hearing-impaired children, but hearing may be difficult in a large class with poor acoustics, and teachers are unlikely to have been specially trained.

23 'The Makaton language programme (Walker, 1996) is a sign language consisting of a special selection of *essential* words, structured in *stages* of increasing complexity.'

24 *Blissymbols* are picture symbols which are translatable into any language.

25 Oralists believe that effective communication may best be accomplished by teaching hearing-impaired children lip-reading and spoken language, and by providing them with hearing aids.

26 Visual impairment may be caused by *infection, trauma, congenital cataracts, pituitary gland tumours* and *occipital lobe* or *optic fibre* damage.

27 *Braille* is a writing system using patterns of raised dots to represent letters, words, numbers or musical notes, which can be read by touch.

28 *Personal pronouns* ('you' and 'I') commonly have their meanings reversed by children with visual impairments.

Section 4: Coping with impairments

29 It is against the law to treat such individuals less favourably than someone else, solely on the basis of their disability, unless there is a good reason.

30 Less favourable treatment can be justified when it is relevant to an individual's circumstances and there is a 'substantial' reason.

31 Employers may use the *unsuitability of a post*, the *unsuitability of premises*, or *difficult access/journey to work* to legitimise discrimination.

32 Discrimination is *not* in an employer's interests, since workers with disabilities stay in the same job longer and are less likely to take sick leave or sustain industrial injuries.

33 Choices may be limited to the few universities which are accessible or have appropriate facilities.

34 Many people with impairments believe that teachers had underestimated them, and reported that they had been bullied at school because of their impairments.

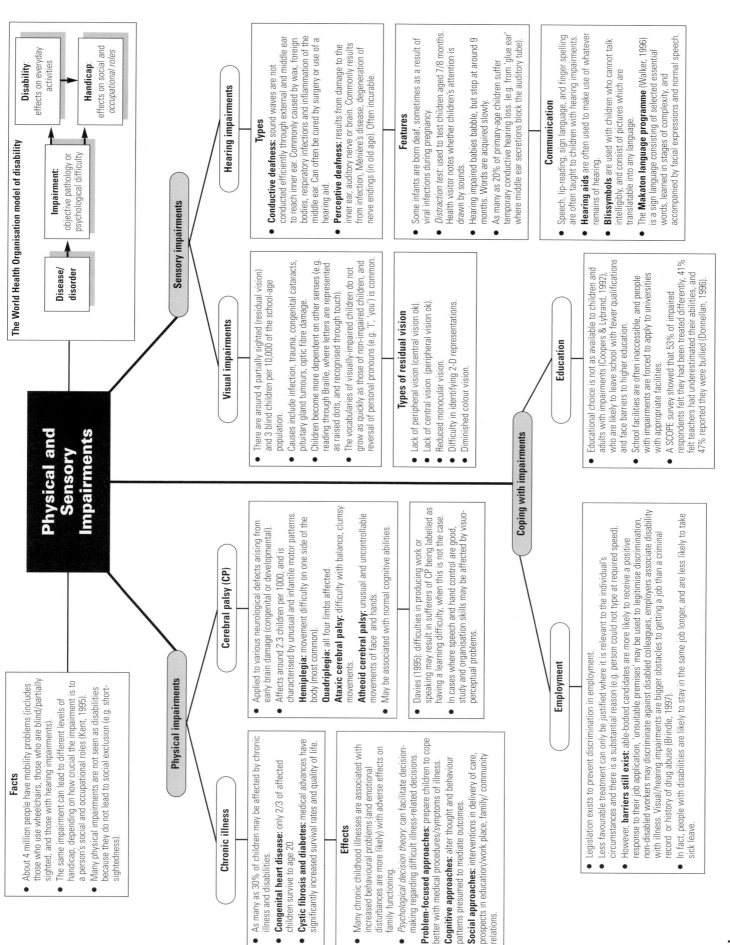

Physical and Sensory Impairments

The World Health Organisation model of disability

Disease/disorder → **Impairment:** objective pathology or psychological difficulty → **Disability:** effects on everyday activities → **Handicap:** effects on social and *occupational roles*

Facts
- About 4 million people have mobility problems (includes those who use wheelchairs, those who are blind/partially sighted, and those with hearing impairments).
- The same impairment can lead to different levels of handicap, depending on how crucial the impairment is to a person's social and occupational roles (Kent, 1995).
- Many physical impairments are not seen as disabilities because they do not lead to social exclusion (e.g. short-sightedness).

Sensory impairments

Hearing impairments

Types
- **Conductive deafness:** sound waves are not conducted efficiently from external and middle ear to reach inner ear. Commonly caused by wax, foreign bodies, respiratory infections and inflammation of the middle ear. Can often be cured by surgery or use of a hearing aid.
- **Perceptive deafness:** results from damage to the inner ear, auditory nerve or brain. Commonly results from infection, Ménière's disease, degeneration of nerve endings (in old age). Often incurable.

Features
- Some infants are born deaf, sometimes as a result of viral infections during pregnancy.
- *Distraction test:* used to test children aged 7/8 months. Health visitor notes whether children's attention is drawn by sounds.
- Hearing impaired babies babble, but stop at around 9 months. Words are acquired slowly.
- As many as 20% of primary-age children suffer temporary conductive hearing loss. (e.g. from 'glue ear' where middle ear secretions block the auditory tube).

Communication
- Speech, lip-reading, sign language, and finger spelling are often taught to children with hearing impairments.
- **Hearing aids** are often used to make use of whatever remains of hearing.
- **Blissymbols** are used with children who cannot talk intelligibly, and consist of pictures which are translatable into any language.
- The **Makaton language programme** (Walker, 1996) is a sign language consisting of selected essential words, learned in stages of complexity, and accompanied by facial expressions and normal speech.

Visual impairments
- There are around 4 partially sighted (residual vision) and 3 blind children per 10,000 of the school-age population.
- Causes include infection, trauma, congenital cataracts, pituitary gland tumours, optic fibre damage.
- Children become more dependent on other senses (e.g. reading through Braille, where letters are represented as raised dots, and recognised through touch).
- The vocabularies of visually-impaired children do not grow as quickly as those of non-impaired children, and reversal of personal pronouns (e.g. 'I', 'you') is common.

Types of residual vision
- Lack of peripheral vision (central vision ok).
- Lack of central vision (peripheral vision ok).
- Reduced monocular vision.
- Difficulty in identifying 2-D representations.
- Diminished colour vision.

Physical impairments

Chronic illness
- As many as 30% of children may be affected by chronic illness and disabilities.
- **Congenital heart disease:** only 2/3 of affected children survive to age 20.
- **Cystic fibrosis and diabetes:** medical advances have significantly increased survival rates and quality of life.

Effects
- Many chronic childhood illnesses are associated with increased behavioural problems (and emotional disturbances are more likely) with adverse effects on family functioning.
- *Psychological decision theory:* can facilitate decision-making regarding difficult illness-related decisions.
- **Problem-focused approaches:** prepare children to cope better with medical procedures/symptoms of illness.
- **Cognitive approaches:** alter thought and behaviour patterns presumed to mediate outcomes.
- **Social approaches:** interventions in delivery of care, prospects in education/work place, family/ community relations.

Cerebral palsy (CP)
- Applied to various neurological defects arising from early brain damage (congenital or developmental).
- Affects around 2.3 children per 1000, and is characterised by unusual and infantile motor patterns.
- **Hemiplegia:** movement difficulty on one side of the body (most common).
- **Quadriplegia:** all four limbs affected.
- **Ataxic cerebral palsy:** difficulty with balance, clumsy movements.
- **Atheoid cerebral palsy:** unusual and uncontrollable movements of face and hands.
- May be associated with normal cognitive abilities.
- Davies (1995): difficulties in producing work or speaking may result in sufferers of CP being labelled as having a learning difficulty, when this is not the case.
- In cases where speech and hand control are good, study and organisation skills may be affected by visuo-perceptual problems.

Coping with impairments

Education
- Educational choice is not as available to children and adults with impairments (Coopers & Lybrand, 1992), who are likely to leave school with fewer qualifications and face barriers to higher education.
- School facilities are often inaccessible, and people with impairments are forced to apply to universities with appropriate facilities.
- A SCOPE survey showed that 53% of impaired respondents felt they had been treated differently, 41% felt teachers had underestimated their abilities, and 47% reported they were bullied (Donnellan, 1996).

Employment
- Legislation exists to prevent discrimination in employment.
- Less favourable treatment can only be justified where it is relevant to the individual's circumstances and there is a substantial reason (e.g. person could not type at required speed).
- However, **barriers still exist:** able-bodied candidates are more likely to receive a positive response to their job application, 'unsuitable premises' may be used to legitimise discrimination, non-disabled workers may discriminate against disabled colleagues, employers associate disability with illness. Visual/hearing impairments are bigger obstacles to getting a job than a criminal record or history of drug abuse (Brindle, 1997).
- In fact, people with disabilities are likely to stay in the same job longer, and are less likely to take sick leave.

251

80

EMOTIONAL DISTURBANCES AND BEHAVIOURAL

PROBLEMS IN CHILDHOOD AND ADOLESCENCE

KEY QUESTIONS
- What is attention-deficit/hyperactivity disorder (ADHD)?
- How is ADHD caused and how can it be treated?
- What is autism?
- How is autism caused and how can it be treated?

Q
Section 1: Attention-deficit/hyperactivity disorder

1 Identify two examples of *attentional* problems.
2 Identify two examples of *hyperactivity* problems.
3 What type of children are often referred to as *hyperactive*, even though they may not meet the diagnostic criteria for this disorder?
4 What is the difference between '*pervasive*' ADHD and '*true*' ADHD?
5 According to some experts, to whom is the diagnosis of ADHD too readily applied?
6 According to Prentice (1996), approximately what percentage of the school-age population may be affected by ADHD?
7 How do ADHD children respond to structured situations?

Section 2: Causes and treatments

8 What did Morrison (1980) discover when looking at the parents of children with ADHD?
9 Which theoretical perspective on the causes of ADHD was proposed by Feingold (1975)?
10 Outline the research which led Harley *et al.* (1978) to conclude that Feingold's claims were 'seriously overstated'.
11 Identify one reason for believing that genetic factors are implicated in ADHD.
12 Identify three factors which may lead to the sorts of neurological impairment that might result in ADHD.
13 What did Zametkin (1990) discover when using PET to examine *glucose metabolism* in hyperactive and normal adults?
14 Which class of drugs has been particularly effective in treating ADHD?
15 Complete the sentence: 'According to one explanation, the brains of ADHD-children lack ___ and their behaviours are an attempt to seek more ___'.
16 Identify two difficulties with the drugs used to treat ADHD.
17 In what way is the use of drug therapies with children open to abuse?

18 Identify three other forms of treatment used with children suffering from ADHD.
19 What does it mean to say that ADHD may best be explained in interactionist terms?

Section 3: Autism

20 Literally, what does *autism* mean?
21 During what period of life can autism be acquired?
22 Complete the sentence: 'Some researchers argue that autism and childhood ___ are earlier and later manifestations of the same childhood psychosis'.
23 Identify three symptoms of the 'social and interpersonal isolation' demonstrated by autistics.
24 What term is used to describe the *ritualistic behaviours* engaged in by many autistic children?
25 Apart from the social world, what else are autistic children frequently insensitive to?
26 How common is autistic disorder?

Section 4: Causes and treatments

27 What factors did Kanner (1943) believe could exacerbate (inborn) autism?
28 How did Bettelheim (1967) expand upon Kanner's theory?
29 Identify four reasons for thinking that explanations which attribute autism to parental behaviours are invalid.
30 What does the term *mindreading* refer to?
31 According to Baron-Cohen *et al.* (1985), what is *mind-blindness*?
32 Identify the four modules which Baron-Cohen (1995) proposes are involved in mindreading.
33 According to Kalat (1984), which naturally occurring chemical is over-produced in autistic children?
34 What observation has led to treatments for autism involving low carbohydrate diets?
35 Which therapeutic approach has been used to eliminate autistic self-mutilative behaviour?
36 What is *symptom substitution*?
37 What is involved in *structural therapy*?

Section 1: Attention-deficit/hyperactivity disorder

1 *Attentional* problems include being *easily distracted, failing to follow instructions or respond to commands, difficulty in completing tasks* and *paying little attention to detail.*

2 *Hyperactivity* problems include *excessive or exaggerated motor activity* (e.g. fidgeting, aimless running), *impulsiveness* and a *lack of self-control.*

3 Children with *short attention spans.*

4 'Pervasive' ADHD is displayed in different situations, whereas 'true' ADHD is displayed in all situations.

5 Some experts claim that the diagnosis is too readily applied to children whom teachers and parents find difficult to control.

6 Prentice (1996) claims that as many as *five per cent* of the school-age population may be affected by ADHD.

7 ADHD children are extremely disruptive in structured situations.

Section 2: Causes and treatments

8 Morrison (1980) discovered that many of the parents of children with ADHD have clinical diagnoses of *personality disorder* or *hysteria.*

9 Feingold (1975) proposed that ADHD is caused by *dietary factors*, such as food additives.

10 Harley *et al.* (1978) placed 36 school-age boys on experimental and control diets, and found that although 30 per cent were rated as less hyperactive when on the experimental diet, there were no differences in other measures (e.g. concentration and intelligence).

11 The *concordance rate* is higher for MZs (identical twins) than for DZs (non-identical twins).

12 *Lead poisoning, foetal alcohol syndrome* and *chromosomal abnormalities* may all lead to neurological impairments.

13 Zametkin (1990) discovered that hyperactive adults showed slower *glucose metabolism* in the brain structures associated with attention and the inhibition of inappropriate responses.

14 *Stimulants* (particularly *amphetamines*) have been particularly effective in treating ADHD.

15 'According to one explanation, the brains of ADHD-children lack *arousal* and their behaviours are an attempt to seek more *stimulation.*'

16 Stimulant medication is only effective in around 70 per cent of cases, and only appears to treat the symptoms rather than the cause.

17 Drugs may be administered to all 'problem children' (even those whose problems stem from family conflict, for example) as a way of 'keeping the peace'.

18 *Behaviour modification* (particularly *token economies*), *relaxation training*, and *cognitive–behavioural therapy* are all used to treat ADHD.

19 ADHD may be the result of an *interaction* between biological predispositions and environmental triggers.

Section 3: Autism

20 Literally, *autism* means 'selfism'.

21 Autism can be acquired at any time during the first three years of life.

22 'Some researchers argue that autism and childhood *schizophrenia* are earlier and later manifestations of the same childhood psychosis.'

23 Autistics largely *ignore other people*, show *little attachment* (even to their parents), and *retreat into a 'private world'.*

24 *Stereotyped behaviours.*

25 Autistic children are frequently insensitive to *pain.*

26 About one child per 5000 is autistic.

Section 4: Causes and treatments

27 Kanner (1943) believed that cold, detached and unresponsive parents could exacerbate autism.

28 Bettelheim (1967) proposed that autism is the result of parental failure to provide stimulation in the first nine months of life.

29 First, autistic children's parents are not significantly different from those of children with other disorders. Second, brothers and sisters of autistic children are typically not autistic. Third, children who are seriously neglected do not usually show the characteristics of autism. Fourth, even if parents are *unresponsive*, it is not clear whether this is a cause, correlate or consequence of autism.

30 *Mindreading* is used to refer to our attempts to make sense of the social world around us (e.g. by interpreting it in terms of people's mental states).

31 *Mindblindness* is the inability to perceive mental states in oneself and others.

32 The four modules are the *intentionality detector* (*ID*), *eye-direction detector* (*EDD*), *shared-attention mechanism* (*SAM*), and the *theory of mind mechanism* (*ToMM*).

33 Kalat (1984) claims that *endorphins* are over-produced in autistic children.

34 The observation that certain allergies produce behaviours similar to those seen in autism.

35 A *behavioural approach* (particularly *behaviour modification*) has been used to eliminate autistic self-mutilative behaviour.

36 *Symptom substitution* is when one maladaptive behaviour is replaced with another.

37 *Structural therapy* involves structuring a child's environment to provide it with spontaneous physical and verbal stimulation in the form of play and games.

Facts

- ADHD stands for **attention deficit/hyperactivity disorder.**
- Both DSM-IV and ICD-10 identify 2 broad types, one characterised by attentional problems, and the other by hyperactivity, although both may occur together.
- **Attentional problems include** being easily distracted, failing to follow instructions or respond to commands, difficulty in completing tasks/paying attention to detail.
- **Hyperactivity problems include** excessive/exaggerated motor activity, impulsiveness and a lack of self-control.
- Prentice (1996): around 5% of the school-age population may be affected, and it is far more prevalent in boys.
- ADHD children are extremely disruptive in classroom situations and show poor social and emotional adjustment, possibly resulting in fights, tantrums, and poor self-image later in life.

Classificatory issues

- Whether attentional problems and hyperactivity are the same or different disorders is unclear.
- Children with 'short attention spans' are often referred to as 'hyperactive', although they may not meet the diagnostic criteria for this disorder, and are simply 'overactive'.
- 'Pervasive' ADHD is evident in only some situations, whilst 'true' ADHD is displayed in all situations.
- Some experts maintain that the diagnosis is applied too readily to children whom parents/teachers find difficult to control, or used as a label to 'pathologise' children who are boisterous.

ADHD

Causes

Family variables: many parents of children with ADHD have clinical diagnoses of personality disorder or hysteria (Morrison, 1980). However, such factors may be the cause of, or caused by, ADHD.

Dietary factors: Feingold (1975) argued that food additives (e.g artificial colour/flavours) caused disruptiveness and hyperactivity. However, some researchers (e.g Harley *et al.*, 1978) found few differences between groups of boys on experimental and control diets.

Genetic and biological factors: some parents of hyperactive children have had long histories of hyperactivity (Dendy, 1995), although neurological impairments might also result from lead poisoning and foetal alcohol syndrome. The reticular activating system, involved in attention, also shows a higher glucose metabolism in those with ADHD (Zametkin, 1990).

Treatments

Stimulant drugs (e.g. amphetamines) result in a marked reduction of activity by increasing the ability to pay attention and concentrate.

The brains of children with ADHD may be 'underaroused', and their activity an attempt to seek optimum levels of arousal. However, such drugs do not cure ADHD, have adverse side-effects, and are a 'social handicap' They are effective in only about 70% of cases.

Behaviour modification (e.g token economies) has been used successfully with ADHD.

Cognitive–behavioural therapy teaches children to stop and think before they undertake behaviours.

Parent training involves supervising medication and developing good parenting strategies (e.g. breaking long assignments into small tasks).

Emotional Disturbances and Behavioural Problems in Childhood and Adolescence

Facts

- Literally, autism means 'selfism' and was coined by Kanner (1943) to describe 11 children who were unresponsive to social stimuli, engaged in self-destructive behaviour, and became upset when objects they had arranged were moved or changed.
- The disorder can be acquired at any time during the first 3 years of life, and some researchers have argued that autism and childhood schizophrenia are manifestations of the same psychosis.
- Autistic disorder affects about 1 in 5 000 children and is more frequent in boys.
- Autism affects children from all ethnic backgrounds.
- Prognosis is generally poor, but children who have developed some meaningful speech by age 5 are most likely to benefit from treatment.

Characteristics

- **Social and interpersonal isolation:** autistics largely ignore others.
- **Stereotyped behaviours:** e.g. rocking back and forth.
- **Disturbances of movement:** e.g. hyperactivity/inactivity.
- **Resistance to changes in routine:** insisting on sameness.
- **Abnormal responses to sensory stimuli:** ignoring sounds, being startled by mild sounds.
- **Insensitivity to pain:** e.g. cuts, burns, extreme hot or cold.
- **Inappropriate emotional expression:** e.g. sudden bouts of fear.
- **Poor speech development:** some autistics never develop speech (mutism). Where speech is developed, it is not used for social interaction.
- **Specific limited intellectual problems:** performance on intellectual tasks is generally poor, although some children may show extraordinary abilities in some areas.

Autism

Causes

Parental failure: Bettelheim (1967) argued that failure to provide stimulation during first 9 months would lead the child to withdraw into a private world. However, autistic parents do not differ significantly from others. Brothers and sisters of autistics are typically normal, and seriously neglected children do not show autistic characteristics.

Cognitive deficiencies: Baron-Cohen *et al.* (1985) suggested that a deficiency in the ability to understand others' mental states ('*mindreading*') might account for autism, and autistic children might suffer from '*mindblindness*'.

Proposed the existence of 4 modules involved in 'mindreading':

- intentionality detector (ID)
- eye-direction detector (EDD)
- shared attention mechanism (SAM)
- theory of mind mechanism (ToMM).

Genetic factors: Folstein & Rutter (1977) found a higher concordance rate for MZs than DZs.

Endorphin production: Kalat (1984) found that autistic children suffer from the over-production of endorphins, resulting in lowered pain thresholds. When autistics are given drugs to block endorphin production, they become more responsive to their social environment.

Treatment

Biologically-based treatments: neuroleptics and serotonin-reducing drugs have been used, but results have been disappointing and use is associated with side-effects. Low carbohydrate diets have been used, based on the observation that certain allergies result in self-mutilative behaviours similar to those seen in autistics.

Behavioural approaches use positive reinforcement or extinction to eliminate self-mutilative behaviour. However, these approaches will only provide children with enough adaptive behaviours to cope more efficiently in the world.

> Lovaas (1977): electric shocks were extremely effective at reducing self-mutilative behaviour.

Cognitive approaches involve structural therapy, aiming to increase the amount of stimulation children receive, in order to make them more aware of their environment and relate to it more.

UNIT 7

Perspectives

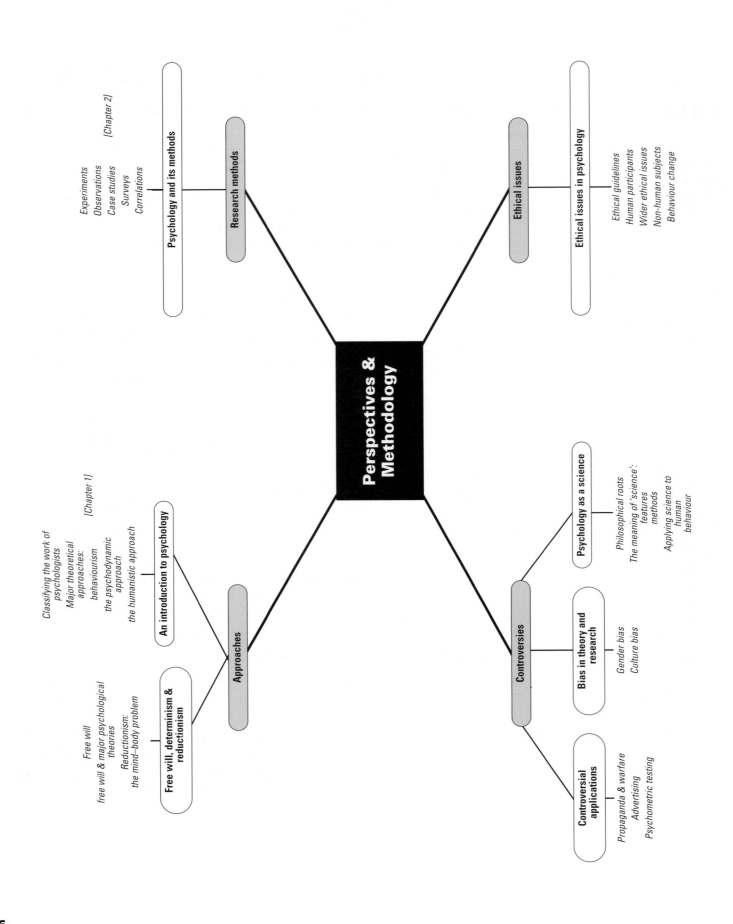

Perspectives & Methodology

Research methods

Psychology and its methods

Experiments
Observations
Case studies
Surveys
Correlations

[Chapter 2]

Ethical issues

Ethical issues in psychology

Ethical guidelines
Human participants
Wider ethical issues
Non-human subjects
Behaviour change

Approaches

An introduction to psychology

Classifying the work of psychologists
Major theoretical approaches:
behaviourism
the psychodynamic approach
the humanistic approach

[Chapter 1]

Free will, determinism & reductionism

Free will
free will & major psychological theories
Reductionism:
the mind–body problem

Controversies

Psychology as a science

Philosophical roots
The meaning of 'science':
features
methods
Applying science to human behaviour

Bias in theory and research

Gender bias
Culture bias

Controversial applications

Propaganda & warfare
Advertising
Psychometric testing

256

81

THE NATURE OF THE PERSON IN PSYCHOLOGY: FREE WILL AND DETERMINISM, AND REDUCTIONISM

KEY QUESTIONS
- What is free will?
- How do the major psychological theories view the issue of free will?
- What is reductionism?
- What is the mind–body problem?

Section 1: What is free will?
1 What name is given to the condition characterised by uncontrollable verbal and behavioural tics?
2 What human 'ability' is described by the term *free will*?
3 Complete the sentence: 'Determinism implies that behaviour occurs in a regular manner which is (in principle), totally ___'.
4 What was demonstrated by Penfield's (1947) experiments, in which he stimulated the cortex of patients in order to produce movements of their limbs?
5 What is *psychological reactance*?
6 What are the two levels of functioning, besides deliberate control, which Norman & Shallice (1986) suggest we are capable of?
7 Identify two further ways in which free will can be defined (besides 'deliberate control' and 'behaving voluntarily').
8 According to Koestler (1967), what are the two enemies of free will?
9 In general terms, what is the relation between mental disorders and free will?
10 Identify three important roles which a psychiatrist may play in advising a court of law.
11 What are the implications of determinism for morality (is it possible to derive an 'ought' from an 'is')?

Section 2: Free will and psychological theories
12 According to James's *soft determinism*, what type of cause is required for our behaviours to be free?
13 What further distinction did James draw?
14 According to Freud, what is *psychic determinism*?
15 Which psychoanalytic technique most clearly demonstrates this principle?
16 What is *overdetermination*?

17 What does Skinner eliminate all reference to in his *radical behaviourism*?
18 According to Skinner, what determines what we do?
19 What is the principal argument in Skinner's (1971) book *Beyond Freedom and Dignity*?
20 With what does Skinner equate the terms 'good' and 'bad' in order to remove morality from human behaviour?
21 What is the *behaviour therapist's dilemma*?
22 Complete the sentence: 'For Rogers, therapy and life are about ___ human beings struggling to become more ___'.
23 According to Rogers, what are the two elements which determine whether or not impulses are translated into behaviour?

Section 3: Reductionism
24 According to *reductionism*, what can psychological explanations be replaced by?
25 Outline one way in which the *mind–body relationship* poses a problem.
26 What is the difference between *dualism* and *monism*?
27 What did Descartes believe regarding the relationship between mind and body?
28 What is the difference between an *epiphenomenologist* and a *psychophysical parallelist*?
29 What name is given to those reductionists who attempt to replace psychological accounts with neuro-physiological ones?
30 What argument does Penrose (1990) put forward, regarding the way in which individual neurons and their synaptic connections work?
31 Complete the sentence: 'Consciousness, intelligence, and memory are properties of the brain as a ___ which ___ from interactions between the units that compose it'.
32 According to Rose (1992), how is it possible to be a materialist without being a reductionist?

Section 1: What is free will?

1 *Tourette's disorder* is characterised by uncontrollable verbal and behavioural tics.

2 *Free will* describes the ability of people to choose their own courses of action.

3 'Determinism implies that behaviour occurs in a regular manner which is (in principle) totally *predictable*.'

4 Penfield's (1947) experiments demonstrated that the subjective experience which we have of voluntarily moving our limbs is not the same as that when the appropriate brain region is stimulated (implying that the former cannot be simply reduced to the latter).

5 *Psychological reactance* describes the attempt to regain or reassert our freedom when we feel that it is threatened.

6 Norman & Shallice (1986) identify *fully automatic processing* and *partially automatic processing* in addition to deliberate control.

7 Free will can also be defined as 'having a choice' and 'not being coerced or constrained'.

8 Koestler (1967) identifies habit and strong emotions as the two enemies of free will.

9 In general terms, mental disorders can be seen as the partial or complete breakdown of the control people normally have over their thoughts, emotions and behaviours.

10 Psychiatrists may advise the court about fitness to plead, mental state at the time of the offence, and diminished responsibility.

11 If determinism were true, then we could not be held responsible for our actions, and it would be impossible to say that behaviours were 'right' or 'wrong'.

Section 2: Free will and psychological theories

12 According to James's *soft determinism*, a behaviour is free if it has as its immediate cause processing by a system such as *conscious mental life*.

13 James also distinguished between the scientific and non-scientific worlds.

14 *Psychic determinism* refers to the idea that all behaviours (even apparently 'accidental' ones) have their causes in the unconscious mind.

15 *Free association* clearly demonstrates this principle.

16 *Overdetermination* refers to the idea that much of our behaviour has multiple causes, both conscious and unconscious.

17 Skinner eliminates all reference to mental or private states in his *radical behaviourism*.

18 Skinner claims that the environment, in the form of punishments, rewards and threats, determines what we do.

19 In *Beyond Freedom and Dignity*, Skinner (1971) argues that the notion of 'autonomous man' is both false and has many harmful consequences.

20 Skinner equates the terms 'good' and 'bad' with 'beneficial to others' and 'harmful to others' respectively.

21 The *behaviour therapist's dilemma* refers to the conflict between ethical and legal constraints on therapeutic practice, which obliges therapists to recognise the autonomy of the individual, and behaviour therapy, which does not.

22 'For Rogers, therapy and life are about *free* human beings struggling to become more *free*.'

23 According to Rogers, social conditioning and voluntary choice determine whether or not impulses are translated into behaviour.

Section 3: Reductionism

24 According to *reductionism*, psychological explanations will be replaced by explanations in terms of brain functioning, or even in terms of physics and chemistry.

25 It is difficult to see how the physical (body) and the non-physical (mind) could be related, since they do not share any properties. In addition, it is unclear how something non-physical could influence something physical.

26 *Dualism* proposes that there are two types of substance, mind and body, whilst *monism* proposes that there is only one (mind or body).

27 Descartes believed that the mind can influence the brain (or body), but not vice versa.

28 An *epiphenomenologist* sees the mind as a kind of by-product of the brain, whilst a *psychophysical parallelist* sees that there is no interaction between mind and brain at all (the two are synchronised).

29 *Eliminative materialists*.

30 Penrose (1990) argues that there is a built-in indeterminacy in the way that individual neurons and their synaptic connections work.

31 'Consciousness, intelligence, and memory are properties of the brain as a *system* which *emerge* from interactions between the units that compose it.'

32 According to Rose (1992), it is possible to have distinct and legitimate languages (*levels of description*) which are not reducible to one another.

Defining free will and determinism
- Free will: intuition tells us that people have the ability to choose their own courses of action and determine their own behaviours.
- Determinism: the idea that everything is the effect of some cause and that all behaviour is (in principle) totally predictable.

Free will & determinism

Psychology and free will
- For much of its history, psychology has operated as if there were no difference between physical phenomena and thought or behaviour.
- Between 1913 and 1956, Skinner's behaviourist model argued that behaviour is determined by punishment or reward.

Meanings

Having a choice
The individual could have behaved differently, given the same situation, i.e. their behaviour is not entirely determined by the circumstances.

Not being coerced or constrained
The individual was not forced (e.g. by being threatened with a gun) to do something. Related to 'soft determinism' (see below).

Voluntary
- The individual's behaviour is not automatic/reflex (e.g. the blink reflex).
- Penfield (1947): electrical stimulation of patients' brains could cause them to move limbs. However, they did not experience this in the same way as they would a voluntary movement, showing that the two cannot be the same.
- In addition, people often respond to the feeling that their freedom is threatened by attempting to regain it (*psychological reactance*).

Deliberate control
- Norman & Shallice (1986): there is a limit to the amount of information we can attend to at one time. Processing is either *fully automatic* (e.g. reading), *partially automatic* (e.g. driving) or governed by *deliberate control*. Free will corresponds to the last of these.
- Koestler (1967): freedom has two enemies:
  1. *habit* ('men can become like machines').
  2. *strong* (especially negative) *emotions* ('I couldn't help it').

Mental disorders
- In general terms, mental disorders can be seen as the partial or complete breakdown of the control people normally have over their thoughts, emotions and behaviours.
- e.g. compulsive behaviours, obsessional thoughts, panic attacks, thought insertion (a symptom of schizophrenia).

Free will and abnormality

Forensic psychiatry
- Psychiatrists can play important roles in
  1) advising the Court about fitness to plead,
  2) mental state at the time of the offence,
  3) diminished responsibility.
- If a plea of diminished responsibility is accepted, there is no trial and a sentence of manslaughter is passed.

James and soft determinism
- James distinguished between the scientific and non-scientific worlds, allowing both types of explanation.
- James distinguished soft and hard determinism:

soft determinism: if our conscious mental life is the immediate cause of our actions, then they are free.

hard determinism: if our behaviour is caused by anything at all, then our actions cannot be free.

Free will in major psychological theories

Rogers, freedom and the fully functioning person
Rogers' humanistic, phenomenological approach emphasises the extent to which we create our own world, struggling to become more free:
- Social conditioning may influence the individual, but what we do still depends on voluntary choice.
- Through such choices we aim to grow and become fully-functional ('*self-actualised*').

Freud and psychic determinism
For Freud, *psychic determinism* implied that there are no 'accidents' in the mind and that unconscious causes can determine behaviour:
- *Free association* is used to study the way in which unconscious conflicts or desires cause neurotic behaviour.
- One of the aims of psychoanalysis is to 'free' the patient's ego from such causes.
- Much of our behaviour has multiple causes, both conscious and unconscious (*overdetermination*).

Skinner and the illusion of free will
- Skinner argued that the 'illusion of free will' is only preserved because we are unaware of the forces, punishments and threats in our environment which teach us to act as we do:
- Skinner's *radical behaviourism* rejects all reference to mental events, and free will as 'explanatory fictions'.
- Skinner's claims conflict with the notion of moral responsibility, a conflict which Skinner solves by equating 'good' with 'what is rewarded' and 'bad' with 'what is punished'.
- The *behaviour therapist's dilemma*: the tension between believing that human beings are not free and ethical guidelines (such as informed consent and the right to withdraw) which imply that they are.

Free Will, Determinism & Reductionism

Reductionism: the idea that psychological explanations can be replaced by explanations in terms of brain functioning or even in terms of physics and chemistry' (Garnham, 1991).

Reductionism

Materialism and reductionism
Although most materialists (who believe that only matter exists) are also reductionists, it is possible to be a materialist and argue that since 'minds' and 'brains' are different levels of description, that one cannot be reduced to the other.

Dualism: both mind and matter exist

The mind–body problem

Monism: only mind or matter exists

Descartes   Interactionism   Epipheno-menology   Parallelism

- Although we normally assume that we have both a conscious 'mind' and a physical 'brain', it is difficult to see how two such substances could be related or influence one another.
- Whilst *eliminative materialists* argue that the mind can be reduced to a description of neurons, others argue that abilities such as consciousness are properties of the system as a whole and cannot be described in terms of individual neurons.

Mentalism   *or*   Materialism
(idealism)

Mind–brain identity theory   *Eliminative materialism*

CONTROVERSIAL APPLICATIONS

Section 1: Psychology, propaganda and warfare

1 According to Richards (1996b), in what way does war present psychology with a dilemma?

2 Which theory arose from research into the problems
pilots experience when taking off and landing?

3 What were Milgram's obedience studies intended to test?

4 What do the letters PTSD stand for?

5 What did Eysenck identify while he was treating Second
World War soldiers at the Mill Hill hospital in London?

6 Which military task was crucial to the development of
American psychology between 1917 and 1918?

7 In what way did the carnage of the First World War affect
Freud's psychoanalytic theory?

8 Identify the effects of war on the Bosnian children studied by Udwin (1995).

9 According to Milgram & Milgram (1976), which Israeli
children suffered the most anxiety in response to the Yom
Kippur War of 1973?

10 Complete the sentence: 'Propaganda is the communication of a point of view with the ___ goal of having the
recipient of the appeal come to '___' accept this position
as if it were his or her own (Pratkanis & Aronson, 1991)'.

11 According to Brown (1963), how is propaganda intended
to affect in-group and out-group attitudes?

12 How is repetition used for the purposes of propaganda?

13 How is selection used for propaganda purposes?

14 Identify other specific techniques used in propaganda.

15 Why are drink-driving campaigns not normally seen as
propaganda?

Section 2: Advertising

16 According to Scott's (1909) textbook, what is the most
fundamental principle of advertising?

17 In what way did Jim Vicary first demonstrate the power
of *subliminal advertising*?

18 In what way have department stores made use of barely
audible subliminal messages?

19 Why is it important that subliminal stimuli should affect
general reactions?

20 Why are subliminal sounds less likely to be effective than
visual messages?

21 What general conclusion was reached by Zimbardo &
Leippe (1991) regarding claims about the power of subliminals?

22 Complete the sentence: 'Subliminals are an unethical
technique of persuasion since they ___ people of an
opportunity to ___ it'.

Section 3: Psychometric testing

23 What does *psychometric* mean?

24 What is *reification*?

25 There are two major issues which need to be addressed
regarding psychometric tests in general. What are they?

26 Name the three types of personality test identified by
Kline (1995).

27 Identify the main advantages of personality questionnaires as compared to other types of personality test.

28 In which area has the use of personality testing been
increasing steadily over the past 20 years?

29 Identify one use of personality testing which is particularly controversial and explain why it is controversial.

30 What arguments have been put forward in favour of the
use of such tests?

31 Complete the sentence: 'Intelligence tests are a kind of
___ test, designed to measure underlying constructs, and
contrasted with ___ tests (such as spelling tests)'.

32 What is a *norm-referenced assessment*?

33 Identify one argument in favour of the use of IQ assessment with children.

34 According to Bee (1994), what is the most serious objection to the use of IQ tests?

35 What may be the effect of life stress on a child's IQ
score?

36 What is meant by saying that traditional tests focus on
school intelligence?

Section 1: Psychology, propaganda and warfare

1 Richards (1996b) points out that whilst the majority of psychologists see war as an evil pathology, they will also feel bound to support the war efforts of their host society.

2 Gibson's (1950) *theory of (direct) perception.*

3 Milgram intended to test the idea that Hitler could not have carried out his plans without the characteristic obedience of the German population.

4 *Post-traumatic stress disorder.*

5 Eysenck identified the traits of *introversion–extroversion* and *neuroticism–stability.*

6 *Intelligence testing of new recruits* was crucial to the development of American psychology.

7 Freud's experiences of the mass killings of the First World War led him to propose the existence of a *death instinct* (*Thanatos*).

8 The Bosnian children studied by Udwin (1995) suffered high levels of anxiety, sleeping and concentration problems, depression, withdrawal and behavioural difficulties.

9 Milgram & Milgram (1976) found that children who had the lowest levels of peacetime anxiety suffered the most anxiety in response to the Yom Kippur War.

10 'Propaganda is the communication of a point of view with the *ulterior* goal of having the recipient of the appeal come to '*voluntarily*' accept this position as if it were his or her own.'

11 Propaganda is intended to build up strong in-group attitudes and enhance feelings of hatred for the enemy as a dangerous out-group.

12 If a statement is repeated often enough, it will eventually come to be accepted by the audience.

13 Selection involves choosing certain (supportive) facts from a mass of complex information for propaganda purposes, and sometimes censoring others.

14 Propaganda also involves the use of *stereotypes*, the *substitution of names*, *assertion*, *pinpointing the enemy* and *appeals to authority.*

15 Drink-driving campaigns are aimed at benefiting the audience and encouraging independence of judgement and individuality.

Section 2: Advertising

16 *Association* is the most fundamental principle of advertising, according to Scott (1909).

17 Jim Vicary arranged for messages such as 'Hungry? Eat Popcorn' and 'Drink Coca-Cola' to be flashed quickly onto a cinema screen during a film.

18 Department stores have mixed barely audible messages (e.g. 'I am honest. I will not steal.') with their piped music, in order to reduce shoplifting.

19 If subliminal stimuli do not affect general reactions, then reactions to the stimulus (such as text) may not change reactions to associated stimuli (such as the product named).

20 Subliminal sounds are more likely to go totally unrecognised than are subliminal images.

21 Zimbardo & Leippe (1991) concluded that the claims made for subliminals have not been borne out by scientific research.

22 'Subliminals are an unethical technique of persuasion since they *deprive* people of an opportunity to *resist* it'.

Section 3: Psychometric testing

23 *Psychometric* means 'mental measurement'.

24 *Reification* refers to the error of assuming that if a measure for something exists, then the thing supposedly measured must also exist.

25 The two major issues are: 'Is the test a good test?' and 'What is the test being used for?/How will it affect the person's future?'.

26 Kline (1995) identifies *personality questionnaires and inventories*, *projective tests*, and *objective tests.*

27 Personality questionnaires are quick and easy to use, can be given to many people at the same time, can be standardised and can be computerised.

28 Personality testing has been increasing steadily in the area of *occupational assessment.*

29 The use of personality testing for promotion and redundancy is controversial since the individual is already working for the organisation, which should be able to assess him/her without the use of tests.

30 Such tests may be fairer than more informal (interview) procedures, provide standardised, numerical information allowing comparisons, produce explicit and specific indicators of temperament, and have good scientific foundations.

31 'Intelligence tests are a kind of *ability* test, designed to measure underlying constructs, and contrasted with *aptitude* tests (such as spelling tests).'

32 A *norm-referenced assessment* is one in which the individual's score is compared with the typical score for members of the individual's age group.

33 IQ assessment has prevented some children from being segregated into special schools or classes.

34 Bee (1994) claims that the most serious objection is that such tests are biased, especially against minority groups.

35 Life stress may cause a child's IQ score to fluctuate.

36 Traditional tests focus on the specific range of skills needed for school success and ignore other abilities, such as creativity and social intelligence.

Controversial applications

Psychology may influence the individual
- **passively**: where knowledge of a theory or research alone is influential (e.g. Freud's psychoanalytic theory) or
- **actively**: by deliberately changing attitudes and behaviours (e.g. in advertising).

Social influence
- 'Controversial' may mean 'ethically dubious' where knowledge is applied in order to influence 'the general public' in ways which they are unaware of and which may not be in their best interests.
- Similar considerations may also apply to psychotherapy and psychiatry.

Propaganda & warfare

- Richards (1996b): war presents psychologists with a dilemma, since they often feel bound to support their host society, whilst simultaneously viewing war as an evil pathology.
- The army IQ tests (1917—18) were crucial in professionalising American psychology.
- Freud (1920, 1923) identified the psychological roots of war in *Thanatos*, the death instinct.

Theory and research stimulated by war
- Gibson (1950) based his *theory of (direct) perception* on studies of the problems faced by pilots.
- *Intelligence tests* were first introduced in America for army recruiting during the First World War.
- *Milgram's obedience studies* were intended to test the view that Nazism was a product of certain German character traits.

The effects of war on children
- Milgram & Milgram (1976): Israeli children who enjoyed the lowest levels of peacetime anxiety suffered the greatest increases in anxiety following the Yom Kippur War (1973).
- Udwin (1995) found high levels of anxiety, sleep and concentration problems, depression and withdrawal in Bosnian children.

Propaganda
Involves a deliberate attempt to manipulate, often by concealed means, the minds of others for ulterior ends (Brown, 1963).

The aims of propaganda
- to direct hatred against the enemy and undermine the enemy's morale
- to convince the home public of the rightness of cause and maintain fighting spirit
- to develop the support and friendship of neutrals
- to promote a picture of the enemy which justifies the entry into conflict
- to build in-group attitudes and strengthen negative attitudes towards the out-group.

Techniques used
- **Stereotypes:** promoting a negative caricature.
- **Substitution of names:** e.g. 'Huns/Krauts' for Germans.
- **Selection:** choosing only certain facts to publicise.
- **Repetition:** repeating a statement until it is accepted.
- **Assertion:** using bald statements instead of argument to support a cause.
- **Pinpointing the enemy:** identifying a 'scapegoat'.
- **Appeal to authority:** e.g. to a religious figure.

Education vs. propaganda
- Although some education campaigns (e.g. safe sex) seem similar to propaganda, they are aimed at benefiting the audience, encouraging independence and individuality.
- However, textbooks which ignore the contributions made by minorities, or distort their histories, can be seen as propaganda.

Psychometric testing

- Trying to quantify psychological phenomena has always been difficult: a measurement may change what is being measured, phenomena are often unobservable and may only exist hypothetically.
- Two major issues emerge:
  1) Is the test a good test (i.e. is it reliable, valid, standardised and does it have discriminatory power)?
  2) What is it being used for (e.g. in order to influence the person's educational/occupational future)?

Personality measurement
- The use of personality tests in occupational assessment has been increasing over the past 20 years.
- However, with issues such as promotion and redundancy many employees feel that their employer should be able to assess their capabilities via the normal appraisal system and that such tests are insensitive and intrusive.

Arguments for
- Tests are fairer than many informal procedures.
- Tests provide numerical information, allowing easy comparisons.
- Good tests produce explicit and specific indications rather than vague comments (e.g. 'high-flyer').
- Good tests have a sound scientific basis.

Arguments against
- Personality measurement may assess between 15–30 different 'traits'. Which combinations are best for a given job is not clear.
- A person's performance in a job will be influenced by the situation and the people he/she works with, and relatively little is known about these interactions.

Intelligence measurement
- The Weschler Intelligence Scale for Children (WISC) is a commonly used way of assessing ability (rather than attainment) and includes tests of verbal and non-verbal abilities.
- Proponents argue that IQ tests can prevent some children from being segregated into special schools and that they can be used to identify children with special learning needs.

Arguments against the use of intelligence tests
- Bee (1994): they are biased, especially against minority groups.
- Bee (1994): all IQ tests measure achievement to some degree, when they are really intended only to measure competence.
- Individual children's IQ scores can and do fluctuate, especially in response to life stress.
- Traditional tests fail to measure a whole range of cognitive and social skills likely to be useful for getting on in the world (e.g. creativity, social intelligence) and instead focus on 'school intelligence'.
- Children with low IQs but good social skills may be inappropriately excluded from the classroom.
- Knowing an IQ score may result in a *self-fulfilling prophecy* with children receiving differential treatment, depending on this score.

Advertising

- Scott (1909, cited in Brown, 1963) wrote the first textbook published in Britain on advertising, identifying *association* as the most fundamental principle.

The effectiveness of subliminal messages
In order to be effective, subliminal messages must:
- **be able to influence judgements** when superimposed onto consciously attended-to material. Greenwald *et al.* (1989) found that they can have an impact under such conditions.
- **affect general reactions** (e.g. buying popcorn rather than just liking the word 'popcorn' more). Bargh & Pietromonaco (1982) subliminally presented stimuli can affect evaluations of related stimuli.
- **be strong and persistent enough to affect mental processes** that lead to subsequent behaviour (little evidence).

Subliminal advertising
- Originated with Jim Vicary, an American market researcher. He arranged for messages such as *'Hungry? Eat Popcorn'* to be flashed onto the screen too quickly for them to be consciously perceived. Sales of popcorn rose by 50%.
- Subliminal messages were legally outlawed (before it was established whether or not they really worked).
- Despite this, they made a comeback in the 1970s:
  - *The Exorcist* (1974) flashes a death mask onto the screen to increase the 'horror',
  - Department stores in America began mixing barely audible whispers (e.g. 'I am honest, I will not steal') with their music, reporting decreases in shoplifting as a result.

Ethical acceptability
- The British Institute of Practitioners in Advertising banned all of its 243 affiliated agencies from using it in 1963, arguing that subliminal advertising interfered with 'The free choice of the public to accept or reject …'.
- Any technique used to influence others (excluding physical methods) can be considered unethical if:
  a) it relies on deception
  b) prohibits exposure to opposing messages
  c) unfairly prevents efforts to resist it.
Since we are not aware of subliminal advertising, it is unethical with regard to c).

PSYCHOLOGY AS A SCIENCE

SYLLABUS
7.2 Controversies in psychology
• arguments for and against psychology as a science

KEY QUESTIONS
• What are the philosophical roots of science and psychology?
• What does 'science' mean?
• Are scientific methods appropriate for the study of human behaviour?

Section 1: Philosophical roots

1 What does the expression *philosophical dualism* mean?
2 Complete the sentence '___ became the ideal of science, and was extended to the study of human behaviour by Comte in the mid-1800s, calling it ___'.
3 What do *empiricists* believe about knowledge?
4 Why is 1879 widely accepted as the 'birthdate' of psychology?
5 According to Wundt, what were the two components of conscious experience?
6 What name is given to Wundt's attempts to analyse conscious experience?
7 What is the famous definition of psychology provided in James's *The Principles of Psychology*?
8 Which approach, which emphasises behaviour's purpose and utility, did James inspire?
9 For what reason did Watson (1913) reject introspective reports?
10 According to Watson, what should the subject matter of psychology be?
11 What did Watson see as the two *goals* of psychology?
12 Which approach emerged during the *cognitive revolution*?
13 What analogy is central to this approach?
14 What does *scientism* maintain, regarding the study of human behaviour?

Section 2: The meaning of 'science'

15 Identify the four major characteristics which must be possessed for a discipline to be a science.
16 What is a *theory*?
17 According to common belief, what is the starting point for scientific discovery?
18 What alternative view of this 'starting point' has been proposed?
19 Name the two phases which Kuhn (1962) identifies in the history of a science.
20 Complete Deese's (1972) equation: '___' = data + ___.

21 According to Popper's (1972) version, what is the starting point for the *scientific method*?
22 According to Kuhn (1962), under what condition can a field of study be legitimately called a science?
23 According to Kuhn, what name is given to the stage of development in which psychology remains?
24 What argument does Valentine (1982) give in support of the view that psychology is 'normal science'?
25 One view argues that psychology is not yet a normal science, since it does not have a paradigm. What are the two other views relating to this issue?
26 Complete the sentence: 'According to Richardson (1991), science is a very ___ business'.
27 What suggestion does Richardson (1991) make to increase the 'objectivity' of science?
28 Why, according to Kuhn, does 'scientific truth' have little to do with objectivity?

Section 3: Human behaviour and scientific method

29 What is the problem of *experimenter bias*?
30 In what way did Rosenthal & Fode (1963) and Rosenthal & Lawson (1961) illustrate the problem of *experimenter bias*?
31 What are *demand characteristics*?
32 In what way does experimental psychology adopt a *nomothetic approach*?
33 Why does psychology suffer from '*the problem of representativeness*'?
34 Why is *artificiality* in laboratory settings a source of problems?
35 What social factor makes the laboratory such an unnatural setting?
36 For what reason may psychological experiments lack *internal validity*?
37 Which types of variable pose a special problem for psychologists?

Section 1: Philosophical roots

1 *Philosophical dualism* is the distinction between mind and matter (as two 'types' of substance).
2 '*Objectivity* became the ideal of science, and was extended to the study of human behaviour by Comte in the mid-1800s, calling it *positivism*.'
3 *Empiricists* believe that the only source of true knowledge is sensory experience.
4 In 1879 Wundt established the first 'laboratory' of experimental psychology at Leipzig.
5 According to Wundt, conscious experience is composed of *sensations* and *feelings*.
6 Wundt's attempts at analysis were called *structuralism*.
7 James defines psychology as 'the science of mental life'.
8 James inspired *functionalism*.
9 Watson (1913) rejected introspective reports, since they are impossible to verify accurately (as they are subjective experiences).
10 According to Watson, the only valid subject matter of psychology is *behaviour* (both human and non-human).
11 Watson saw the two goals of psychology as the *prediction* and *control* of behaviour.
12 The *information-processing approach* emerged during the cognitive revolution.
13 Central to this approach is the *computer analogy*.
14 *Scientism* maintains that human behaviour can and should be studied using the methods of natural science (such as the laboratory experiment).

Section 2: The meaning of 'science'

15 In order for a discipline to be a *science*, it must possess a *definable subject matter*, demonstrate *theory construction*, generate *testable hypotheses*, and use *empirical methods* of investigation.
16 A *theory* is a complex set of inter-related statements which attempts to explain observed phenomena.
17 According to common belief, the starting point for scientific discovery is simple, unbiased observation.
18 An alternative view of this 'starting point' argues that there is no such thing as 'unbiased' observation, and that our observation is always selective, interpretative, pre-structured and directed.
19 Kuhn (1962) claims that the history of a science demonstrates long peaceful periods called 'normal science', and 'scientific revolutions'.
20 '*Fact*' = data + *theory* (Deese, 1972)
21 Popper (1972) claims that the starting point for the scientific method is a problem (usually a refutation of an existing theory or prediction).
22 According to Kuhn (1962), a field of study can only be called a science if the majority of its workers subscribe to a common, global perspective or *paradigm*.

23 Psychology remains in a state/stage of *pre-science*, according to Kuhn.
24 Valentine (1982) argues that behaviourism comes as close as anything could to a paradigm.
25 The two other views maintain that psychology has had a number of paradigms and corresponding revolutions, and that psychology has, simultaneously, a number of paradigms.
26 'According to Richardson (1991), science is a very *social* business.'
27 Richardson (1991) suggests that researchers must universally agree conventions for reporting observations and findings, so that others can replicate them.
28 According to Kuhn, 'scientific truth' has more to do with the popularity and acceptance of a particular framework within the scientific community.

Section 3: Human behaviour and scientific method

29 The problem of *experimenter bias* refers to the way in which the particular characteristics of the researcher may, inadvertently, influence the participant(s).
30 Rosenthal & Fode (1963) and Rosenthal & Lawson (1961) found that researchers who were deceived into thinking they were using 'maze-bright' rats in their experiments found faster rates of learning in these rats than did those deceived into thinking their rats were 'maze-dull'.
31 *Demand characteristics* are those cues in an experimental situation which convey the experimental hypothesis to participants ('giving the game away').
32 Experimental psychology adopts a *nomothetic approach* in that it attempts to establish *general laws of behaviour*, by generalising from limited samples of participants to 'people in general'.
33 Psychology suffers from *the problem of representativeness* in that the participants in traditional experiments have not been representative of 'people in general' (e.g. they have largely been psychology undergraduates).
34 *Artificiality* is a source of problems since we cannot be sure whether the behaviour of people in a laboratory is an accurate indicator of how they are likely to behave outside it.
35 The fact that the experimenter has all the 'power' and is responsible for structuring the situation makes the laboratory an especially unnatural setting.
36 Psychological experiments may lack *internal validity*, since it is difficult to know when all *extraneous variables* have been controlled.
37 *Participant variables* pose a special problem for psychologists.

James's contribution
- James published *The Principles of Psychology* in 1890, in which he discusses instinct, brain function, consciousness, the self, attention, memory, perception, free will and emotion.
- James inspired *functionalism* – an approach which emphasises the utility and purpose of behaviour.

Watson's contribution
- Watson rejected introspectionism, arguing that psychology must be the *science of behaviour* and confine itself to *measurable* and *observable* events.
- The *goals* of psychology should be the *prediction* and *control* of behaviour.
- Watson believed that the *conditioned reflex* could become the foundation of psychology.
- Behaviour was seen as shaped by the environment and analysable into *stimulus–response* units.

The cognitive revolution
- The *information-processing approach* compared human cognition to the functioning of a digital computer (the *computer analogy*).
- It became acceptable again to study 'the mind' and psychologists began to explore the possibility of modelling human intelligence on computers.

Philosophical roots
- Descartes was the first to distinguish between mind and matter (*philosophical dualism*).
- *Objectivity* became the ideal of science and Comte's *positivism* extended this approach to the study of human behaviour.
- Descartes also advocated *mechanism* and *reductionism* (the world can be reduced to physical interactions).
- *Empiricism* is the idea that the only source of knowledge about the world is sensory experience.

Wundt's contribution
- Wundt founded the first psychological laboratory, at Leipzig in 1879.
- He attempted to analyse conscious mental states into their component *sensations* and *feelings* by the use of *introspection*.
- This approach is known as *structuralism*.

Mainstream psychology
- Central assumptions and practices have remained the same (referred to as mainstream psychology).
- *Scientism*: the borrowing of methods and vocabulary from the natural sciences (e.g. studying phenomena in the laboratory) in a value-free way (with no investigator bias).

Psychology as a Science

What is a 'science'?

The major features of science
- **A definable subject matter:** in psychology, this changed from human thought to behaviour to cognitive processes.
- **Theory construction:** e.g. Watson's attempt to account for human behaviour in terms of classical conditioning.
- **Hypothesis testing:** making and testing specific predictions deduced from the theory.
- **The use of empirical methods:** used to collect data relevant to the theory.

The scientific method
- **Theory** (an explanation) → *deduction* / *support* → **Hypothesis** (a testable statement)
- *data*
- **Empirical methods** e.g. experiment, observation, survey
- Subject matter e.g. human behaviour

Common beliefs	Alternative views
Scientific discovery begins with unbiased observations.	Observations are always biased and influenced by our preconceptions.
From the resulting data/sense data generalised statements of fact will emerge.	Fact = Data + Theory. Facts do not exist objectively, all data is partly interpreted.
The essential feature of scientific activity is the use of empirical methods.	Data alone cannot make a science, since without theory data are meaningless.
Science discovers the objective truth about the world.	Scientific theories reflect the prevailing values and assumptions.
Science involves the steady accumulation of knowledge.	Sciences involves a series of peaceful periods and 'scientific revolutions'(Kuhn, 1962).

Can psychology be a science if psychologists cannot agree what psychology is?
- Kuhn (1962): a field of study is only a science if the majority of its workers subscribe to a common perspective or *paradigm*.
- Kuhn argues that there are three stages in the development of a science (and that psychology is still a pre-science):
1) **Pre-science:** no paradigm has evolved and there are several schools of thought (Kline, 1988, sees psychology as having several paradigms).
2) **Normal science:** a paradigm has emerged providing a framework for interpreting results. Workers explore the limits of the theory.
   Valentine (1982): behaviourism 'with its clearly defined subject matter, methodology and assumptions' is as close to a paradigm as you can get.
3) **Revolution:** the old paradigm has to be abandoned and replaced by a new one because of the weight of conflicting evidence.
   Palermo (1971) and LeFrancois (1983): psychology has already undergone several paradigm shifts (see above).

The problem of objectivity
- Kuhn stresses the role of agreement and consensus among scientists, so the 'truth' of a theory may have more to do with its acceptability.
- Richardson (1991): argues for the importance of universally agreed conventions on reporting and measurement in order to ensure a theory's 'truth value'.

Human behaviour & scientific methods

The problem of representativeness
- The *nomothetic* ('law like') approach to psychology involves generalising from experimental samples to 'people in general'.
- However, the participants in American psychology experiments are typically undergraduates who may not be representative of 'people in general', thus introducing *ethnocentrism*.

The problem of artificiality
- Heather (1976): we cannot be sure that the way people behave in the laboratory is an accurate indicator of how they will behave outside it.
- Particularly unnatural is the way in which one 'participant' (the experimenter) has all the power and structures the situation.

The psychology experiment as a social situation
Experimenters and participants influence each other:
1. **experimenter bias:** the experimenter's expectations may cause participants to behave differently.
   - Rosenthal & Fode (1963) found that experimenters who had been informed that their rats were 'maze-bright' obtained better learning than did those with the 'maze-dull' group, despite the fact that the rats were actually randomly allocated!
2. **demand characteristics:** any cues in the experimental situation which convey the expected outcome may be detected by the participant, who may then decide to play the role of 'good' or 'bad' participant.

Internal vs. external validity
- Whilst an experiment may be *ecologically valid* (*external validity*), it will lack *internal validity* if all relevant extraneous variables have not been controlled.
- Participants vary and we cannot assume that they all perceive the IV in the same way.
- In attempting to increase the control, we also increase the situation's artificiality.

BIAS IN PSYCHOLOGICAL THEORY AND RESEARCH

Q

Section 1: Gender bias
1 Identify two common themes within *feminism*.
2 What is the role of *individualism* within psychology in relation to gender bias?
3 Complete the sentence: 'Most psychological research is conducted on ___ samples'.
4 Identify one way in which women's behaviour is often viewed when it differs from men's.
5 What do psychological explanations of women's behaviour tend to emphasise?
6 What is *heterosexism*?
7 Complete the sentence: 'Psychology's claims to be a science are based on its methods and the belief that it is a ___-___ discipline'.
8 Identify the two major problems identified by Nicholson (1995) which are associated with adherence to the 'objective' investigation of behaviour.
9 What is meant by the claim that 'scientific psychology has reified concepts such as personality and intelligence'?
10 What was the practical consequence of gender bias for many women living in the state of Virginia between 1924 and 1972?
11 In what way did psychology influence the 1924 Immigration Restriction Act in the USA?
12 What is *androcentrism*?
13 According to Caplan (1991), what does *masochistic disorder* (proposed as an addition to DSM-III-R) represent in relation to women?
14 According to Tavris (1993), what type of causal attributions are often made for men's and women's socially unacceptable behaviours, respectively?
15 According to Tavris, what view is central to the 'mismeasure of woman'?
16 In what way may gender bias show itself in the formulation of research questions?

17 What problem is raised by the failure of many studies to report the sex and race of participants, researchers and any confederates?
18 In what way may gender bias enter into the conclusion formulation of studies?
19 Name one developmental theory which has been identified as sexist.

Section 2: Culture bias
20 According to Smith & Bond (1993), what does *cross-cultural psychology* study?
21 What is *ethnocentrism*?
22 According to Moghaddam (1987), which individuals comprise the core of psychology's 'First World'?
23 Complete the sentence: 'An implicit equation is made between "human being" and "human being from ___ ___" (the Anglocentric bias)'.
24 What is the independent variable for cross-cultural psychologists?
25 How does Herskovits (1955) define *culture*?
26 Which terms are used to describe the two aspects of culture?
27 What does *cultural complexity* refer to?
28 What label is used to describe cultures in which identity is largely defined by personal choices and achievements?
29 What do *tight cultures* expect?
30 What is meant by an *etic approach* to the study of a culture?
31 What is an *imposed etic*?
32 According to Brislin (1993), why may etics cause difficulties with regard to the concept of intelligence?
33 What is the problem of *equivalence*, as identified by Brislin?
34 Complete the sentence: 'Cross-cultural research allows investigators to highlight ___ ___'.
35 Identify some other advantages of cross-cultural research.

Section 1: Gender bias

1 Two common themes within *feminism* are the valuation of women as worthy of study in their own right, and recognition of the need for social change on behalf of women.

2 *Individualism* obscures the social and structural operation of male power by concentrating its analysis on people as individuals.

3 'Most psychological research is conducted on *male* samples.'

4 Women's behaviour is often viewed as pathological, abnormal or deficient in some way when it differs from men's.

5 Explanations of women's behaviours tend to emphasise *biological causes.*

6 *Heterosexism* is taking heterosexuality to be the norm, so that homosexuality is seen as abnormal.

7 'Psychology's claims to be a science are based on its methods and the belief that it is a *value-free* discipline.'

8 Nicholson (1995) points out that the experimental environment takes the 'subject's behaviour,' as distinct from the 'subject' herself, as the unit of study (becoming deliberately blind to the behaviour's *meaning*), and occurs in a very specific context which typically disadvantages women.

9 Scientific psychology has treated abstract concepts (such as personality and intelligence) as if they were 'things' or entities.

10 More than 7500 women were forcibly sterilised, using mental age (as measured by the Stanford–Binet intelligence test) as a criterion.

11 The army alpha and beta tests of intelligence, which suggested that certain cultures were of 'inferior intelligence', influenced the 1924 Immigration Restriction Act.

12 *Androcentrism* refers to male-centredness, the tendency to take maleness as a standard or norm against which to compare women.

13 Caplan (1991) claims that masochistic disorder represents a way of calling psychopathological the behaviour of women who conform to social norms for a 'feminine woman'.

14 Tavris (1993) claims that such behaviours are likely to be attributed to men's upbringings and to women's psyches or hormones.

15 According to Tavris, the view that men are the norm and women the opposite, lesser or deficient beings, is central to the 'mismeasure of woman'.

16 It is often assumed that topics relating to white males are more important and 'basic' than those relating to females and/or ethnic minorities.

17 This failure may lead researchers to overlook the significance of interactions between variables, such as sex and race.

18 In the formulation of conclusions, results based on one sex only are often applied to both.

19 Both Erikson's (1950) theory of lifespan development and Kohlberg's (1969) theory of moral development have been criticised for sexism.

Section 2: Culture bias

20 *Cross-cultural psychology* studies variability in behaviour among the various societies and cultural groups around the world (Smith & Bond, 1993).

21 *Ethnocentrism* is the tendency to use our own ethnic or cultural group's norms and values to define what is 'natural' and 'correct' for everyone else.

22 Moghaddam (1987) points out that historically white, middle-class males living in the USA have comprised the core of psychology's 'First World'.

23 'An implicit equation is made between "human being" and "human being from *Western culture*" (the Anglocentric bias).'

24 For cross-cultural psychologists, the independent variable is culture.

25 Herskovits (1955) defines *culture* as the 'human-made part of the environment'.

26 Culture can be broken down into *objective aspects* and *subjective aspects.*

27 *Cultural complexity* refers to how much attention people within a culture pay to time.

28 *Individualistic* cultures.

29 *Tight cultures* expect their members to behave according to clearly defined norms.

30 An *etic approach* to the study of a culture looks at a behaviour from *outside* that cultural system.

31 An *imposed etic* refers to the imposition of concepts or research tools by a 'visiting' psychologist on an 'alien' culture, for which these are assumed to be valid.

32 Brislin (1993) points out that definitions of what constitutes a 'problem' (a common element of intelligence tests) vary between cultures.

33 The problem of *equivalence* refers to the difficulty in knowing that we are studying the same process across different cultures.

34 'Cross-cultural research allows investigators to highlight *implicit assumptions*.'

35 Cross-cultural research also allows investigators to separate a behaviour from its context, extend the range of variables available to study, separate the influence of variables which are frequently confounded within a particular culture, and test theories to discover whether they are relevant outside a particular cultural context.

A

The feminist critique of science

- Some feminists argue that scientific enquiry itself is biased.
- Nicholson (1995) identifies 2 major problems with the 'objective' investigation of behaviour:
1) The experimental situation takes the 'subject's behaviour' as distinct from the 'subject' herself as the unit of study. Because of this it blinds itself to the behaviour's *meaning* and the personal, social and political contexts in which it occurs.
2) Experimental psychology takes place in a context which disadvantages women. Women are stripped of their social roles and expected to respond to the needs of a (usually) male experimenter.

Gender bias

- *Feminist psychology* argues that women are worthy of study in their own right and that there is a need for social change on behalf of women.
- Feminist psychology challenges the way in which psychology excludes women or assimilates them to male norms.
- By focusing on the individual, psychology neglects the social context and the mechanisms of oppression.

Major feminist criticisms

- Much research is conducted on all-male samples, then generalised to women.
- Where women's behaviour differs from men's, it is often judged to be abnormal or deficient.
- Explanations tend to emphasise biological causes, ignoring social causes and giving the impression that psychological differences are inevitable.

Practical consequences of gender bias

Intelligence testing and sterilisation

- Prince & Hartnett (1993): psychologists have *reified* concepts such as personality and intelligence (treating them as if they really exist), and this has led to assaults on women. Between 1924 and 1972, more than 7500 women in the State of Virginia were forcibly sterilised, based on a measure of intelligence (using the Stanford–Binet intelligence test).

Complicity

- Gilligan (1982): psychologists have a responsibility to make their values explicit regarding social and political issues, and failure to do so may result in them (unwittingly) contributing to prejudice, discrimination or oppression.

The masculinist bias (androcentrism) – a closer look

The male norm as standard

2 examples (Tavris, 1993):
- In 1985: the mental disorder *'masochistic personality'* was proposed as an addition to DSM-III-R. It was to include symptoms such as putting others first and seeking failure at home and at work. Caplan (1991) argues that this would have labelled as pathological the behaviour of many women who conform to social norms (the 'good wife syndrome').
- When men behave in socially unacceptable ways, causes are looked for in their upbringing (*external attribution*), whereas women's problems are seen as a result of their psyches or hormones (*internal attribution*).

The 'mismeasure of woman'

Tavris (1993): man is viewed as the norm and woman as opposite and deficient by comparison (e.g. research which aims to discover why women aren't 'as something' as men).

Example:
- Wilson (1994): the reason why 95% of bank managers, company directors and professors in Britain are men is that men are more competitive and dominant (because of their hormones).
- Wilson also claims that men are more productive than women and that those women who do reach top positions probably have 'masculinised' brains.

Sexism in research

The APA's *Guidelines for Avoiding Sexism in Psychological Research* (Denmark *et al.* 1988) identify gender bias at all stages of research:
1. **Question formulation:** it is assumed that topics relating to white males are more important than others.
2. **Research methods and design:** often the sex and race of the researchers, participants and any confederates are not specified.
3. **Data analysis and interpretation:** where sex differences are found, these are often reported in misleading ways.
4. **Conclusion formulation:** results based on one sex are then applied to both.

Sexism in theory

Gilligan (1982): psychology describes the world from a male perspective and confuses this with truth:
- Erikson (1950): describes a series of 8 universal stages of lifespan development (based on a study of males only). Despite recognising that there are sex differences, his epigenetic chart remains the same.
- Kohlberg (1969): claimed that his six stages of moral development are universal, despite the fact that his sample comprised 84 boys. His theory also suggests that females rarely develop beyond stage 3 (so are relatively morally deficient).

Bias in Psychology

What is culture?

Culture: the human-made part of the environment (Herskovits, 1955).
Includes:
objective aspects (e.g. tools, roads)
subjective aspects (e.g. norms, roles)
- Humans make and are made by culture in an interactive way (Moghaddam *et al.*, 1993).
- Research often fails to identify the sub-cultural groups (e.g. Welsh) represented within a sample of a national culture (e.g. British). This can lead researchers to overlook important sub-cultural differences and also implies that national cultures are unitary, harmonious systems.

Culture

How do cultures differ?

Triandis (1990) identifies 3 cultural syndromes (patterns of beliefs and behaviour which can be used to contrast different cultures):
1. **Cultural complexity:** how much attention people pay to time (related to the number and diversity of roles which members of a culture play).
2. **Individualism–collectivism:** whether the person's identity is defined by personal choices and achievements (individualism) or by characteristics of the group to which the person is attached (collectivism).
3. **Tightness:** tight cultures define norms clearly and do not tolerate much deviation from these.

Ethnocentrism

Ethnocentrism: the human tendency to use our own ethnic or cultural group's norms and values to define what is 'natural' and 'correct' for everyone.
- Moghaddam (1987): historically, psychology has been dominated by white, middle-class male Americans (psychology's 'First World') who applied Anglocentric theory and research to people in general.
- *Cross-cultural psychology* helps to correct ethnocentrism by treating culture as the independent variable and identifying differences and similarities between cultures.

The emic–etic distinction

Pike (1954) used the distinction to refer to different approaches to the study of behaviour:
- **Etic:** looking at a behaviour from outside a particular cultural system. 'Etics' refers to culturally general concepts.
- **Emic:** looking at a behaviour from the inside. 'Emics' are culturally specific concepts.
- **Imposed etics:** occur when 'visiting' psychologists bring an emic valid for the 'home' culture, which they then assume to be valid in the 'alien' culture. This often leads to the imposition of cultural biases onto the phenomena being studied (e.g. 'intelligence').

Advantages of cross-cultural research

- **Highlighting implicit assumptions:** allowing researchers to examine the influence of their own beliefs and assumptions.
- **Separating behaviour from context:** allowing researchers to appreciate the impact of situational factors on behaviour.
- **Extending the range of variables:** expanding the range of variables which can be explored.
- **Separating variables:** allowing researchers to identify variables which are often confounded within a particular culture.
- **Testing theories:** discovering whether Western theories are relevant outside their own cultural contexts.

ETHICAL ISSUES IN PSYCHOLOGY

KEY QUESTIONS
- What are the ethical issues surrounding human participants?
- What are the wider ethical concerns?
- What are the ethical issues surrounding non-human participants
- Which ethical concerns relate to psychologists as practitioners?

Section 1: Introducing ethics

1 Complete the sentence: 'Just as Orne (1962) regards the psychological experiment as a ___ situation, so every psychological investigation is an ___ situation'.

2 What are the two major *professional bodies* responsible for publishing ethical guidelines?

3 Identify one reason why ethical guidelines must be continually updated.

Section 2: Human participants

4 Complete the sentence: 'The essential principle is that the investigation should be considered from the ___ of all ___'.

5 Explain what is required for *informed consent* to be given.

6 What accusation did Baumrind (1964) level against Milgram?

7 In what ways did Zimbardo *et al.* (1973) follow the current *Ethical Principles* (BPS, 1993)?

8 In what way did Milgram contravene the principle of the *right to withdraw* (Coolican, 1990)?

9 Where participants are deceived, what procedure should be carried out at the earliest opportunity?

10 Which types of deception are the most serious?

11 What did Milgram (1974) point to as the central moral justification for his use of deception?

12 How great a risk of harm to participants is acceptable in psychological investigations?

13 Identify one purely pragmatic argument for guaranteeing confidentiality to participants.

Section 3: Wider ethical issues

14 Complete the sentence: 'Whilst individual participants may be protected from overt harm, the ___ ___ to which they belong may be harmed as a consequence of the research findings'.

15 Identify one area of research in which the above concern has not been considered sufficiently.

16 What is the nature of the *double obligation dilemma* which psychologists face?

17 What type of 'socially beneficial' studies were carried out by Latané & Darley (1968)?

Section 4: Non-human subjects

18 What are the two fundamental questions regarding the use of non-humans in psychological research?

19 According to Dawkins (1980), how can we discover if apparently healthy animals are actually suffering?

20 According to Gray (1987), what are the two main justifications for non-human experimentation?

21 According to Gray (1987), why is food deprivation not a source of suffering?

22 What is a *cost–benefit analysis* in relation to non-human experimentation?

23 Identify areas of medical advance in which non-human experimentation has played a vital role.

24 What do opponents of non-human experimentation argue, regarding medical advances?

25 Complete the sentence: 'Gray (1991) argues that not only is it ___ wrong to give preference to the interests of one's own species, one has a ___ to do so'.

26 Identify one major problem with this argument.

Section 5: Psychologists as practitioners

27 Identify the two beliefs which Fairburn & Fairburn (1987) believe may cause psychologists to overlook professional ethics.

28 In what important way do psychotherapists regard their work as different from behaviour modification?

29 In what way does Wachtel (1977) criticise the institutional use of the *token economy*.

30 What does Masson (1988) believe regarding the needs of individuals seeking therapy?

Section 1: Introducing ethics

1 'Just as Orne (1962) regards the psychological experiment as a *social* situation, so every psychological investigation is an *ethical* situation.'

2 The *British Psychological Society* (BPS) and the *American Psychological Association* (APA).

3 They must be updated to take into account the changing political and social contexts.

Section 2: Human participants

4 'The essential principle is that the investigation should be considered from the *standpoint* of all *participants*.'

5 Participants need to be informed of the objective of the study and any other aspects which might reasonably be expected to influence their willingness to participate.

6 Baumrind (1964) accused Milgram of failing to protect his participants from stress and emotional conflict.

7 Zimbardo *et al.* (1973) terminated their study because of the prisoners' distress, obtained informed consent and consulted the legal council of Stanford University.

8 Milgram urged participants to continue when they wished to stop, using harsh verbal prods and prompts.

9 Where participants are deceived, a full *debriefing* should be carried out at the earliest opportunity.

10 Deceptions which affect the participants' self-image (especially self-esteem) are the most serious.

11 The central moral justification was that the participants had judged the experiment to be acceptable.

12 The risk of harm should be no greater than in ordinary life.

13 If participants' confidentiality is not guaranteed, it is unlikely that members of the public would volunteer for psychological experiments.

Section 3: Wider ethical issues

14 'Whilst individual participants may be protected from overt harm, the *social groups* to which they belong may be harmed as a consequence of the research findings.'

15 Research into the intellectual inferiority of races (or genders) fails to acknowledge the harm that may be caused by such research.

16 The *double obligation dilemma* refers to the ethical obligation which psychologists have towards individual participants and society at large.

17 Latané & Darley (1968) investigated the nature of *bystander intervention*.

Section 4: Non-human subjects

18 The two fundamental questions are 'How do we know non-humans suffer?' and 'What goals can ever justify subjecting them to pain and suffering?'.

19 According to Dawkins (1980), careful observation and experimentation with a species enables us to discover the signs of suffering.

20 The main justifications are the *pursuit of scientific knowledge* and the *advancement of medicine* (Gray, 1987).

21 Rats are maintained at 85 per cent of their 'free-feeding' body weight, and are actually healthier than if allowed to eat freely (Gray, 1987).

22 A *cost–benefit analysis* involves considering non-human pain, distress and death versus acquisition of new knowledge and the development of new medical therapies for humans.

23 The causes and vaccines for infectious diseases, the development of antibacterial and antibiotic drugs, open-heart surgery, organ transplantation, kidney failure, diabetes, malignant hypertension and gastric ulcers.

24 Opponents argue that medical advances have been delayed because of misleading results from non-human experiments.

25 'Gray (1991) argues that not only is it *not* wrong to give preference to the interests of one's own species, one has a *duty* to do so.'

26 Many medical advances are possible only after scientific understanding has been developed. In the early stages of this process, suffering is imposed on non-humans with little immediate benefit to humans.

Section 5: Psychologists as practitioners

27 The two beliefs that psychology is a value-free science and that therapists should be value-neutral (or 'non-directive') may detract from an explicit consideration of professional ethics.

28 *Psychotherapists* regard their work as fostering the autonomous development of the patient, whereas *behaviour modification* removes control from the patient.

29 Wachtel (1977) believes that the *token economy* is open to abuse in institutional settings and renders the patient powerless.

30 Masson (1988) believes that individuals seeking therapy need protection from the therapist's constant temptation to abuse, misuse, profit from and bully the client.

The Code of Conduct for Psychologists (British Psychological Society, 1985) identifies the responsibilities and obligations common to both the scientist and practitioner roles.

The psychological investigation is also a *social situation* (Orne, 1962) and therefore an *ethical situation*. Ethical guidelines are difficult to apply in a hard and fast way and must take into account the social and political context.

Human participants

The introduction to *The Ethical Principles for Conducting Research with Human Participants* (BPS, 1990, 1993) states 'The essential principle is that the investigation should be considered from the standpoint of all participants;...'.

Consent, informed consent and the right to withdraw
- The *Ethical Principles* state that participants should be informed of the objectives of the research and any aspects which might be expected to influence their willingness to participate.
- In addition, researchers should not pressurise participants to take part in or remain in the investigation.

Coolican (1990): Milgram (1963, 1965 – see Ch 59) violated this latter principle (by the use of harsh verbal 'prods').

Deception
- The *Ethical Principles* state that intentional deception of participants should be avoided where possible.
- Where there are no alternatives to deception, participants should be debriefed at the earliest possible opportunity.
- Social psychological research often makes use of 'stooges' and care must be taken with regard to participants' self-esteem.

- Milgram's study has been criticised for its use of deception. However, Aronson (1988) defended its use, pointing out that realistic results could not have been obtained otherwise.
- Psychologists must consider whether or not a means can be sufficiently justified by an end.
- In defence of his experiments, Milgram pointed out (1974) that all participants were debriefed and most were glad to have participated.

Protection of participants
- The *Ethical Principles* state that investigators have a responsibility to protect participants from physical and mental harm.
- Debriefing, confidentiality and the right to withdraw are all means of ensuring that this happens.

- Baumrind (1964) criticised Milgram for exposing participants to stress and emotional conflict.
- Milgram (1974): stress was neither an anticipated nor intended outcome and 'momentary excitement' is not harm.

Debriefing
The *Ethical Principles* state that investigators should provide the participants with any information necessary to complete their understanding of the research.

Milgram carried out thorough debriefings and one year later participants were assessed by an independent psychiatrist for signs of psychological harm.

Confidentiality
- The *Ethical Principles* state that information obtained about a participant is confidential unless otherwise agreed in advance.
- Only in situations where there are direct dangers to a human life might an investigator contravene this rule.

Non-human subjects

The *Guidelines for the Use of Animals in Research* (BPS Scientific Affairs Board, 1985) identifies four general obligations:
1. avoid or minimise discomfort to living animals
2. discuss any future research with colleagues and the HO inspector
3. seek advice as to whether the end justifies the use of animals
4. consider alternatives to the use of animals.
These raise two fundamental questions:

(a) How do we know that non-humans suffer?
1. Disease and injury are major causes of suffering. Brady's (1958) 'executive monkey' experiments are unacceptable today.
2. Mental suffering due to confinement may show in bizarre behaviours.
3. Careful study of a species can increase our knowledge of their requirements (Dawkins, 1980).
However, Bateson (1992) points out that the boundaries between organisms which can and cannot experience pain are 'fuzzy'.

(b) How can we justify experiments with non-humans?
Gray (1987): the main justifications are the *pursuit of scientific knowledge* and the *advancement of medicine*.

However, in some cases the scientific justification is clear but the immediate medical justification much less so.

Olds & Milner (1954) implanted electrodes in the brains of non-humans to study self-stimulation. Although such experiments had practical applications (e.g. pain relief), they were not conducted with this objective in mind.

Safeguards for non-human subjects
- Gray (1987): food deprivation in rats is not a source of suffering, as rats are maintained at 85% of their free-feeding weight. The level of electric shock is controlled by Home Office (HO) inspectors and does not cause extreme pain.
- Procedures causing pain and distress/surgical procedures are illegal unless the experimenter holds a HO licence.
- Experimenters are required to undertake a *cost–benefit analysis* before any non-human experiment can proceed.

The medical justification argument
- **Supporters** of such experiments argue that there are no basic physiological differences between laboratory animals and humans, and that vaccines and surgical techniques could not be developed without them.
- **Opponents** argue that tests on different species produce different results and that the stress of confinement may affect the outcome unpredictably. Some important medical advances have been delayed because of misleading results from such experiments.

Speciesism: Gray (1991) argues that discriminating against another species is justified since one has a duty to give preference to one's own species, where we have to choose between human and non-human suffering.
- However, many medical advances are only possible with the advancement of scientific knowledge, during which stage non-humans may be sacrificed with no saving of human life.

Psychologists as practitioners

Psychology as value-free science
The scientist–practitioner model of helping sees clinical psychology as being guided by the general scientific method. However, at the point where psychological knowledge is applied, the psychologist is responsible for the choice of technique and its application.

Therapists as value-neutral
- **Therapist influence:** therapist neutrality is a myth. Therapists influence their clients in subtle but powerful ways. Whether these influences are in the client's interests and whether they are aware of them are important questions.
- **Freedom and behavioural control:** therapies based on operant conditioning (e.g. token economies) may place the patient in a powerless position relative to the institution enforcing the therapy.
- **The abuse of patients:** Masson (1988) believes patients need protection from therapists who have emotional power over the patient and can cause emotional, sexual and financial abuse.

Wider ethical issues

Protecting the individual vs. harming the group: whilst individual participants may be protected from harm, groups may not be protected from the wider implications of damaging research (e.g. Herrnstein's, 1971, research into the 'intellectual inferiority' of African Americans). Such research may be used to justify unacceptable attitudes or prejudices.

Protecting the individual vs. benefiting society: focusing on the protection of individual participants may occasionally discourage psychologists from carrying out socially meaningful and beneficial research, e.g. Milgram's experiments may have been unethical but furthered our understanding of obedience (and in 1965 was awarded the prize for outstanding psychological research by the APA).

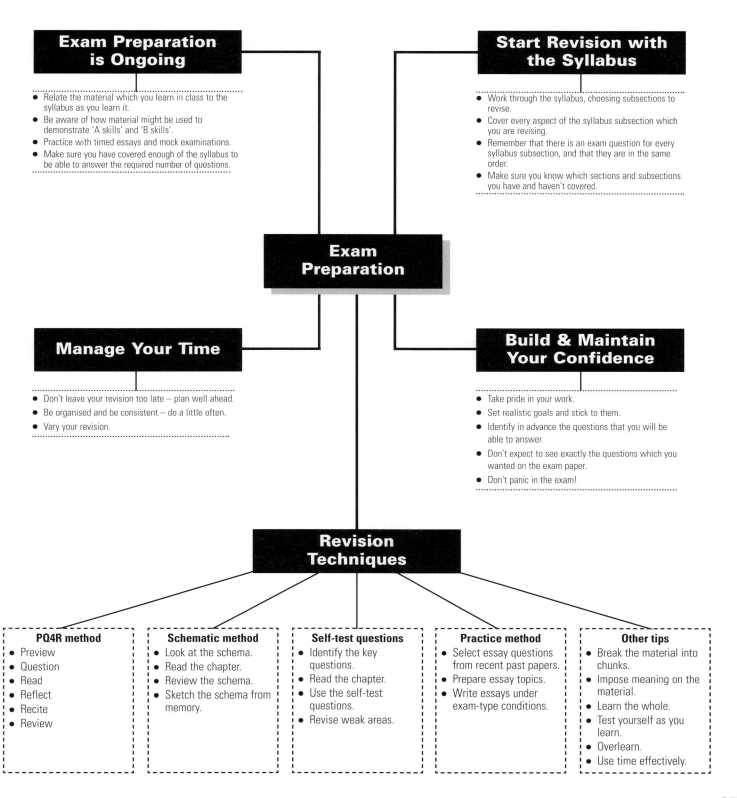

A

EXAM PREPARATION

Exam Preparation is Ongoing

- Relate the material which you learn in class to the syllabus as you learn it.
- Be aware of how material might be used to demonstrate 'A skills' and 'B skills'.
- Practice with timed essays and mock examinations.
- Make sure you have covered enough of the syllabus to be able to answer the required number of questions.

Start Revision with the Syllabus

- Work through the syllabus, choosing subsections to revise.
- Cover every aspect of the syllabus subsection which you are revising.
- Remember that there is an exam question for every syllabus subsection, and that they are in the same order.
- Make sure you know which sections and subsections you have and haven't covered.

Exam Preparation

Manage Your Time

- Don't leave your revision too late – plan well ahead.
- Be organised and be consistent – do a little often.
- Vary your revision.

Build & Maintain Your Confidence

- Take pride in your work.
- Set realistic goals and stick to them.
- Identify in advance the questions that you will be able to answer.
- Don't expect to see exactly the questions which you wanted on the exam paper.
- Don't panic in the exam!

Revision Techniques

PQ4R method
- Preview
- Question
- Read
- Reflect
- Recite
- Review

Schematic method
- Look at the schema.
- Read the chapter.
- Review the schema.
- Sketch the schema from memory.

Self-test questions
- Identify the key questions.
- Read the chapter.
- Use the self-test questions.
- Revise weak areas.

Practice method
- Select essay questions from recent past papers.
- Prepare essay topics.
- Write essays under exam-type conditions.

Other tips
- Break the material into chunks.
- Impose meaning on the material.
- Learn the whole.
- Test yourself as you learn.
- Overlearn.
- Use time effectively.

One of the fundamental errors made by many A level students is to assume that revision and exam success can be achieved by 'knowing the facts'. Many students who think they 'know the facts' do badly, because they do not know *how* to use the information they know, *where* to use it, how to manage their *time*, and how to *comment* on what they know. Consequently, many students find themselves unable to relate what they know to the question, or comment on or evaluate information. Knowing information is, therefore, only a part of successful exam preparation. In this chapter, we will look at how best to prepare for a psychology exam and address some of the above issues.

A1 Exam preparation is ongoing

You must **relate material to the syllabus as you learn**, so that at any time you are able to answer questions such as 'Which areas of the syllabus have I covered'? It is an excellent idea to bring a copy of the syllabus to every lesson. By doing this, you ensure that you know how the material relates to specific sections and subsections, and are familiar with the precise wording of the syllabus, which is often used by examiners in setting A level questions.

In every examined essay, half of the available marks are awarded for 'A skills' (knowledge) and half for 'B skills' (commentary). As you learn, you should **be aware of how the material can be used to demonstrate both A and B skills**.

Time management should develop as you learn – **timed essays and practice examinations** can be very useful in developing these skills.

Make sure you have covered enough of the syllabus to be able to answer the required number of questions in the exam. Most schools and colleges teach two or three subsections from each of the syllabus sections (e.g. perception and attention from the Cognitive psychology section). It is very unwise for you to study only one subsection from each syllabus section, since if the question is worded in such a way as to make it difficult for you to answer, you may be unable to answer the required number of questions.

A2 Revision must start with the syllabus

The best way to approach revision is to **work through the syllabus**, choosing syllabus areas to revise and 'ticking off' those areas as you cover them.

Make sure you **cover every aspect of the syllabus subsection** which you are revising. If you do not study *every* aspect of the subsections which you have chosen to cover, it is possible that you will be unable to answer *any* of the questions on the paper.

View the syllabus as a list of possible questions which may be asked. Increasingly, AEB examiners will set examination questions using wording drawn from the syllabus. This is helpful, in that it allows you to know precisely what material they are looking for in your answer, but only if you are familiar with the syllabus.

Remember that **there is an examination question for every subsection of the syllabus** (e.g. there will always be one question on 'perceptual processes', one question on 'attention and performance limitations', one question on 'memory' and one question on 'language and thought' in the Cognitive psychology section of the examination paper).

The exam questions are in the same order on the paper as the topic material in the syllabus subsections (so it is possible to work out in advance of the examination the numbers of the questions you should be able to answer).

Exam questions very rarely 'span' the bullet points on syllabus subsections so that if, for example, there are four bullet points under the heading '5.1 Perceptual processes', then there are four basic 'types' of question corresponding to four areas of material relating to perceptual processes.

It is important to know which questions you cannot answer. Exam questions relate to fairly specific areas of material on the syllabus, and if you have not covered this material your chances of answering an exam question successfully are greatly reduced.

A3 *Manage your time*

Many students underestimate how long it will take them to revise, and overestimate the amount of time which will be available for revision. **If you leave your revision too late it can be very demoralising**, as you realise that you do not have time to revise adequately.

Plan well ahead. Most students will cover between 17 and 25 of the bullet points on the syllabus. If you were to cover two of these per week (e.g. 'perceptual processes' and 'attention and performance limitations'), you might expect to revise for between 9 and 13 weeks. If you can only cover one bullet point per week, revision will take considerably longer.

Managing time involves organisation and consistency. It is important to set a realistic timetable in which you know *what* you are going to revise and *when* you are going to revise it. Like physical exercise, it is far more beneficial to do a little, regularly, than attempt a lot in one go. Work steadily through the syllabus.

Remember that **it is difficult to organise your time in a space which is cluttered with stuff and continual interruptions**. In the exam you will have a pen, a desk, some paper and three hours of silence. Your revision environment should not be too dissimilar.

Vary your revision, incorporating techniques such as studying with friends, timed essays, self-tests, 'sketches' from memory of syllabus areas, together with time in which you revise both your own notes and the contents of the textbook (see specific revision strategies below).

A4 *Build and maintain your confidence*

See your revision as developing strengths and competencies, not as a chore. If you take pride in your work, studying can become an important source of self-esteem, and others may respect you for it and look to you for advice and assistance.

Don't set unachievable goals ('I'm going to revise solidly all weekend'), but do stick to the goals which you set yourself (e.g. revising for 45 minutes, then taking a break for 15 minutes).

Reward yourself and remind yourself of the areas which you have covered, and how much you have achieved.

It may help to **identify in advance the questions which you will be able to answer** on the exam paper, once you have covered a bullet point thoroughly.

Don't expect to see precisely the question which you wanted to see on the paper. If a question looks unfamiliar or confusing, remember to slow down and remind yourself that although the question may be different, the material needed to answer it stays the same, and that you know this material. Do not simply revise from essays that have earned a high mark; 'prepared answers' will rarely be appropriate to the exam question. If someone asks you a question, you often have to think before you reply, and this is equally true of questions on a psychology examination paper. You are being asked to use material to answer a question, not just show that you know it. You can tackle *any* question by applying what you know thoughtfully.

Don't panic! It's easier said than done, but it is worth remembering that memory can be affected by your physical and mental state, and that flooding your system with adrenaline may temporarily leave you feeling that you can't remember anything at all! Plenty of practice examinations, timed essays, a good familiarity with the exam setting and procedures, and confidence in your own abilities will all prevent you from panicking. If you find yourself panicking, think about something pleasant, or think back to a psychology lesson which you enjoyed.

A5 *Revision techniques*

'THE PQ4R' METHOD
(Thomas & Robinson, 1972)

According to this approach, revising is best accomplished by carrying out the following steps:

> **P**review – the reader previews the material to familiarise him/herself with the topics and issues covered in a particular chapter.
>
> **Q**uestion – the reader prepares questions which focus on key concepts and issues.
>
> **R**ead – bearing the key questions in mind, the reader reads the material.
>
> **R**eflect – the reader takes time to reflect on the meaning of the information, and its relation to what is already known.
>
> **R**ecitation – the reader then recites what has been read, using the questions as reminders.
>
> **R**eview – finally, the material is reviewed in the reader's mind, using questions to structure the task.

THE SCHEMATIC METHOD

The *schemas* contained in this Guide can be used to provide a 'road map' of a specific chapter before the chapter is covered, and can then be used to revise that chapter, for example, by using highlighter pens to highlight specific points, and then attempting to reproduce the information in structural form on a sheet of A3 paper.

An excellent way to prepare is to produce an essay plan/schema for example essays, drawn from each of the bullet points covered under a subsection. This is not as time-consuming as writing the essays themselves, but allows you to revise the factual content and practice structuring this content at the same time.

SELF-TEST QUESTIONS

Tests of recall (such as *self-test questions*) are a good way of determining how much information has been remembered and can be retrieved in an exam situation.

Teachers may use self-test questions, and then require students to mark each others' papers, or students may test themselves. When the answers are checked, new information can be learned and students can develop the ability to view their answers from an examiner's perspective, and judge the quality of what they have written more objectively.

THE PRACTICE METHOD

Skills in performing specific tasks, such as essay-writing under time constraints, are most likely to be best developed by practising the same skills. Students who prepare material by writing 'key notes' onto small cards may not develop skills which generalise perfectly to essay-writing.

Practice at timed essays under conditions similar to those in the examination setting can help students to develop skills such as time management, essay planning, and essay writing, as well as providing familiarity with the exam situation.

THE 'BLUE PETER' MODEL

One approach sometimes adopted by students is to write and memorise 'prepared answers' which they then reproduce in the exam ('Here's one I did earlier'). Typically, if a student covers twenty syllabus 'bullet points', then they might write twenty essays, one for each topic.

Although this technique is good at developing essay skills, and encourages students to learn and structure the material, it can lead to failing to answer the question asked, instead simply giving a set response. Since only material which is relevant to the question can be credited, this may in turn lead to them failing the exam, so **it is not a recommended approach**. However, if a student can intelligently adapt a prepared essay in a way which makes it relevant to the examination question, then prepared essays can occasionally be useful.

OTHER APPROACHES
(adapted from Crooks & Stein, 1991, cited in Gross & McIlveen 1998)

- **Reduce the material to a manageable amount:** even if you could remember every single point in a textbook, not every one will be important. Revise efficiently, by focusing on the key points that you would need to make (and have time to make) in a forty minute essay on the topic.

- **Impose meaning on the material:** material which is related in some way to other material, or to your own experiences, is more easily remembered, so try to relate the material to real life and understand the way in which material is structured (the schemas below are designed to help with this).

- **Learn the whole:** memory tends to be better if related material is revised as a whole, rather than in small parts.

- **Test yourself during learning:** it is quite possible to read material, then be unable to remember what you have just read! Test yourself as you go – if the material has not been learned, revise the material again. If this doesn't work, it may be time for a break!

- **Engage in overlearning:** continuing to learn material, after you have reached 100 per cent accuracy on recalling it, can improve the retention of that material in the longer term.

- **Use study breaks and rewards:** you can only function at maximum efficiency for a certain period of time before your concentration starts to wane. Taking a break every so often allows you to return refreshed.

- **Space study sessions:** two three-hour or three two-hour study sessions usually result in better retention than a single six-hour session.

- **Avoid interference:** revising similar topics (such as sociology and psychology) within a relatively short time period, can cause the memories to interfere. Plan your study sessions so that similar subjects are revised on different days.

- **Use time effectively:** try to develop a study schedule which incorporates revision time and leisure time. Once you have planned your schedule, stick to it!

ESSAY WRITING GUIDE

Skills	Process	Notes
	Read the Question	• Identify how many studies/theories you are required to discuss. • Check if question asks specifically for 'research studies'. • Does the question say 'including' or 'for example'?
Making the material relevant to the question.		
	Decide which Syllabus Area it Refers to	• There is one question per syllabus subsection. • Questions are in the same order as the syllabus subsections. • Questions often use the syllabus wording.
Balancing the A & B skills (knowledge & commentary) equally.	**Identify A & B Skill Areas using Injunctions**	• Half your marks are for 'A' skills, half for 'B' skills. • Injunctions inform you where 'A' and 'B' skills are required. • 'B' skills are commentary, not just criticism!
	Sketch a Quick Essay Plan	• Don't waste too much time drawing complex plans. • Don't cross essay plans out – they earn marks if the essay is incomplete.
Managing your time carefully.	**Write an Introduction Defining Key Terms or Key Studies**	• Define key terms in the question. • Outline central issues/debates. • Describe an introductory study. • Do not waste time saying what you are going to do.
Leaving out personal opinion and waffle.	**Set out Research/Theory Relevant to the Question**	• *Any* research/theory which informs the answer is credited. • Summarise clearly - don't spend too much time on one memorable study. • Names are more helpful than dates.
	Comment on the Research/Theory as Required	• Learn to distinguish between commentary and waffle. • Use the injunctions to tell you precisely where to comment on material - don't include commentary if not required.
Using link sentences to make sense of the material.	**Relate each Paragraph back to the Question**	• Use link sentences to make material relate to the question. • Write a sentence at the end of each paragraph relating it back to the question. • Make comments informative.

It is not difficult to describe a good A level Psychology essay. The examiner is simply looking for a considered and informed answer to the question which has been set. However, for most students, learning to write such an essay takes both hard work and practice, which involve the acquisition of new skills and a good awareness of the way in which essays are graded. This final point is very important: without knowing how your essays will be assessed by an examiner, you cannot know what is required of you in them. Many students assume that essay writing is simply a matter of putting what they *know* on paper, and fail to appreciate that this will only earn them, at best, half marks. In this chapter, we will be taking a close look at what an examiner is looking for in a psychology essay.

B1 Read the question

Students are often criticised for not answering the question. This is often due to a failure to read and understand it.

Every question requires you to do two things: demonstrate **knowledge** of a given area and demonstrate an ability to **comment** on this area. These two skills (A and B skills – discussed below) are allocated the same proportion of marks in every essay question, with half of the marks available for each skill. One way to approach an essay question, therefore, is to ask yourself 'How do I demonstrate both A and B skills here?'.

The precise wording of essay questions is very important: if, for example, you are asked to *describe two theories* and you only describe one, you will incur a 'partial performance' penalty, which means that full A skill marks cannot be obtained. Describing more than two theories will result in the examiner only crediting the best two.

The terms 'including' and 'for example' have very different meanings. If a question uses the term 'including', you *must* discuss whatever is included, whereas if the question says 'for example' you are *not required* to discuss the example(s) unless you wish to.

Where the question uses the term 'research studies' you *must* discuss empirical studies alone. Any other usage of the term 'research' (e.g. 'research into') permits you to discuss both empirical studies *and* theory.

Read the question more than once. Under pressure, students do misread questions!

Read *all* the questions on the paper: this will help you to separate those questions which you can answer from those which you can't, *before* you begin answering them.

B2 Decide which syllabus area the question refers to

It is very important that you get this right. In theory, it is easy: since **questions on each subsection on the paper follow the same order as they do on the syllabus**, you can work out in advance which questions correspond to which bullet point (e.g. 'perceptual processes' will always be the first question on the Cognitive section).

Just to make things easier, **the examiner tries to use the same wording in the exam questions as are in the syllabus**.

Finally, **there is always one question per syllabus subsection**, so there will always be a question corresponding to the subsections (e.g. memory) which you have learned.

Despite this, many students fail to produce material relevant to the question. Most commonly, this is because they do not know their syllabus and instead rely on words which they recognise (such as 'cognitive' or 'language'). This often fails, since these words may be used in questions which apply to entirely different areas of the syllabus (e.g. 'Discuss theories and research findings into the process of language acquisition' (Cognitive psychology) as opposed to 'Critically consider attempts to teach human language to non-human animals' (Comparative psychology)). Once again, you cannot succeed if you do not know your syllabus.

B3 Identify where A and B skills are to be demonstrated, using the injunctions

The AEB chooses from a limited list of terms ('*injunctions*'), each of which determines where the A and B skills are to be assessed within an essay question. **You must be familiar with the injunctions** to the extent that you are able to identify whether they call for A skills, B skills, or a combination of both.

In any essay, half of the marks are allocated for demonstrating skill A and the other half for skill B. In practice, more than one injunction is often used to achieve this distribution of marks. Consider the following question:

(a) Describe *one constructivist* theory of perception
(*6 marks*)

(b) Critically consider one other theory of perception
(*18 marks*)

Where are the A skill and B skill marks to be found? 'Describe' is a skill A term, so this accounts for six of the marks. Since 'critically consider' is a Skill A and B term, the other six of the A skill marks must be found here, together with the twelve B skill marks.

In this example, therefore, part **b** of the question would obviously require twice as much skill B material as skill A material.

The situation can be represented as a table:

Part **a**	A skills (6 marks) Description of one constructivist theory of perception	
Part **b**	A skills (6 marks) Demonstration of knowledge and understanding of one other theory	B skills (12 marks) Awareness of strengths and weaknesses of this theory

Many students make the mistake of assuming that B skills are equivalent to *criticism*, and that in order to demonstrate B skills they must come up with criticisms of the theories or research which they mention. In fact **B skills are commentary**, which includes both positive and negative evaluative points (e.g. the strengths and weaknesses of a theory), as well as comparisons and informative comment.

Exercise 1

Look at the following terms and try to sort them into skill A terms, skill B terms, and skill A and B terms:

analyse/critically analyse   critically consider   consider
explain   distinguish between   assess/critically assess
criticise   justify   examine
evaluate/critically evaluate   describe   discuss
define   compare/contrast   state

Now check your answers against the table at the bottom of the page. How did you do?

Exercise 2

Draw up tables to represent the balance of A and B skills for the following essays:

1 Discuss one theory of cognitive development.
2 Discuss any two methods used to study perceptual development.
3 Describe and evaluate two theories of interpersonal relationships.

Often, commentary will take the form of an explanation of a theory or piece of research which you have just introduced. For example, having just explained Piaget & Inhelder's (1956) 'three mountains scene', in a developmental psychology essay you might continue: 'This research demonstrates what Piaget called "egocentrism", which is the inability of the child to take another's point of view. However, other researchers dispute Piaget's conclusion, arguing that the task is particularly difficult and that on simpler tasks children *can* demonstrate an ability to take another's perspective'. All of the above constitutes commentary on the research.

Sometimes, **B skills can be greatly improved by the use of link sentences, or link structures**. These are pre-set ways of presenting or linking material, which enhance the style and quality of the essay. In the example above, the linking structure is 'This demonstrates that … . However, …'.

Overleaf is a list of link sentences and structures which you could try to introduce into your work.

Exercise 1 – answers

Skill A	Skill B	Skill A and Skill B
consider	analyse/critically analyse	compare/contrast
define	assess/critically assess	critically consider
describe	criticise	distinguish between
examine	evaluate/critically evaluate	discuss
explain	justify	
outline/state		

Link sentences and link structures
This suggests that …
This demonstrates that …
According to …
However, …
Clearly, …
Psychologists have investigated …
Research conducted into … has shown that …
Psychologists investigating … have found that …
Whilst some studies have supported … other researchers have found that …
… believes that …, whilst … believes that …
In an attempt to resolve the issue …
Despite this, other researchers …
There are, however, a number of weaknesses with …
Unfortunately, … cannot account for …
By contrast … believes that …

Many industrious and intelligent students make the error of writing essays which are condensed accounts of the facts relating to a given topic. Although it is important to be able to do this, such essays frequently score highly for their A skills content but achieve low marks for their demonstration of B skills. Often, this is largely because they have *failed to explain* what research means or demonstrates.

As a rule of thumb, you should **explain any technical term, and state the conclusion which can be drawn from any piece of research which you cite**. Link sentences can be used to encourage the 'framing' of research, and to enable students to produce essays which flow better, sound more professional, and score more highly on B skills.

Exercise 3

Example essay: Stage 1

In the following exercise you can see how an essay which has high factual content can be improved to score more highly on B skills. Read the essay below and try to identify material which can be cut without affecting the marks which the essay will gain. Focus on whether or not material is informative or adds to the reader's understanding of the topic, and on whether or not material is relevant to the essay question.

Discuss the view that perceptual abilities are largely innate. (24 marks)

This question forms a part of the wider 'nature–nurture' debate in psychology. In answering this question I will first say what the terms 'nature' and 'nurture' refer to, then I will discuss research findings relevant to the question. Psychologists on the 'nurture' side of the debate are called 'empirists' and argue that

abilities develop largely as a consequence of learning and may be influenced by our experiences, whilst 'nativists' believe that abilities are largely innate and develop as a result of inherited genetic factors which pre-determine their development in a process called 'maturation'. I will now answer the question using psychological research which is relevant to the question, making reference to the question as I go.

The 'nature–nurture' debate as it applies to perception is a difficult one to answer. Psychologists have investigated perceptual abilities in a number of different ways in an attempt to resolve the issue including studies of human infants, human cataract patients, studies of sensory restriction in non-humans, perceptual readjustment studies and cross-cultural studies. In this essay I will discuss some of this research which is relevant to the question (and which I have time for!).

First of all I am going to discuss infants, who are extremely relevant to the study of perception. Bornstein (1976) used a technique called 'habituation' to investigate colour perception in infants. Using this technique Bornstein discovered that most babies possess largely normal colour vision at the age of two months. Infants also show the pupillary reflex and blink response at birth. This relates to the question of whether or not perception is inborn.

Fantz (1961) looked at pattern recognition and the perception of facedness in infants. In order to discover whether infants could discriminate pattern and form Fantz used the preferential looking technique. This is a technique which is used by psychologists to investigate perception. By presenting one- to 15-week-old infants with discs on which were painted colours, a bull's-eye, a patch of printed matter and a face, Fantz discovered a preference for more complex figures over simple ones, with infants spending most time looking at the human face. This was a very interesting finding as it showed us that children do have perceptual abilities fairly early on. Fantz presented infants with a normal face and a 'scrambled' face in which all the normal features were present but not placed in a normal arrangement on the disc. Fantz found that infants spent significantly longer looking at the normal face. Overall, I think that these studies tell us a great deal about perception and the way in which perception is either inborn or innate.

Gibson & Walk (1960) constructed an apparatus in which infants were placed on a sheet of plexiglass below which was a checkerboard pattern. Personally I think this was cruel and I don't know how the mothers of these children agreed to let them do it. On the 'shallow' side the pattern was immediately below the glass, whilst on the 'deep' side the pattern was placed at a distance of about four feet, giving the impression of a drop. I have drawn a detailed diagram of the apparatus used (see attached sheet). The researchers placed the infant on the shallow side of the visual cliff apparatus, and observed their behaviour when called by their mother from across the deep side. Gibson and Walk found that most babies aged between 6 and fourteen months would not crawl onto the deep side. I don't think this is very surprising, myself – I don't expect that adults would want to crawl onto the deep side! Some people said that the babies used by the researchers were too old. Campos *et al.* (1970) devised a method of assessing babies younger than six months. In their experiment babies were placed on either the shallow or deep sides of the cliff whilst their heart rates were monitored. Campos *et al.* found that heart rates would increase or decrease significantly. This showed that the babies were probably really scared by the experience.

'Sensory restriction' studies can be carried out on non-humans. Riesen (1947) raised chimpanzees in total darkness for the first sixteen months of life. As a result they failed to show a blink response and only noticed objects when they were accidentally bumped into. I think that these studies are unethical and should be banned since they cause harm to their participants. Weiskrantz (1956) argued that the visual deficiencies shown by Riesen's chimps were a consequence of degeneration of the retina in the absence of stimulation by light. Which demonstrated that Riesen's experiments were cruel and that they didn't prove anything.

Riesen (1965) conducted a second experiment in which he raised three chimps, Debi, Kova, and Lad. Lad was reared under normal conditions, Debi in total darkness and Kova was exposed to one-and-a-half hours of light per day whilst wearing opaque goggles. These goggles were worn by Kova for one and a half hours every day. Riesen found that though Kova's retina had developed normally, her receptive fields had failed to develop normally. This shows that wearing goggles can cause some blindness.

Some other psychologists have also investigated non-human perception. Blakemore and Cooper raised kittens in cylindrical chambers which had either vertical or horizontal stripes painted on the inside. The kittens were kept in the drums whether or not they wanted to be in the drums. The kittens wore collars to prevent them from seeing their own bodies and so were only exposed to lines of a particular orientation. When tested the kitten who had only been exposed to horizontal lines made no response to a rod which moved vertically, and kittens in vertical-only environments were equally 'behaviourally blind' to a rod moving in a horizontal direction. This means that kittens could not see things that they had not experienced in their lives. Studies of their visual cortex revealed that the kittens did not possess cells which were sensitive to lines of orientations which they had not experienced.

In conclusion, I think that such studies are really unnecessary. 'Is the value of this research worth the cost of life?' is the question we should ask. As for studies of infants they show that infants can perceive things from birth, although I feel that should have been obvious, really.

Example essay: Stage 2

In the essay below, irrelevant or unhelpful comments have been removed, leaving the factual material. It is interesting to note just how little factual material is required for a full answer to an essay question which you could reasonably be expected to produce in an exam. Read through the essay and try to decide where

and how commentary can be introduced in order to increase the B skills content of the essay.

Discuss the view that perceptual abilities are largely innate. *(24 marks)*

This question forms a part of the wider 'nature–nurture' debate in psychology. Psychologists on the 'nurture' side of the debate are called 'empirists' and argue that abilities develop largely as a consequence of learning and may be influenced by our experiences, whilst 'nativists' believe that abilities are largely innate and develop as a result of inherited genetic factors which pre-determine their development in a process called 'maturation'.

Psychologists have investigated perceptual abilities in a number of different ways in an attempt to resolve the issue including studies of human infants, human cataract patients, studies of sensory restriction in non-humans, perceptual readjustment studies and cross-cultural studies.

Bornstein (1976) used a technique called 'habituation' to investigate colour perception in infants. Using this technique Bornstein discovered that most babies possess largely normal colour vision at the age of two months. Infants also show the pupillary reflex and blink response at birth.

Fantz (1961) looked at pattern recognition and the perception of facedness in infants. In order to discover whether infants could discriminate pattern and form Fantz used the preferential looking technique. By presenting one- to 15-week-old infants with discs on which were painted colours, a bull's-eye, a patch of printed matter and a face, Fantz discovered a preference for more complex figures over simple ones, with infants spending most time looking at the human face. Fantz presented infants with a normal face and a 'scrambled' face in which all the normal features were present but not placed in a normal arrangement on the disc. Fantz found that infants spent significantly longer looking at the normal face.

Gibson & Walk (1960) constructed an apparatus in which infants were placed on a sheet of plexiglass below which was a checkerboard pattern. On the 'shallow' side the pattern was immediately below the glass, whilst on the 'deep' side the pattern was placed at a distance of about four feet, giving the impression of a drop. The researchers placed the infant on the shallow side of the visual cliff apparatus, and observed their behaviour when called by their mothers from across the deep side. Gibson and Walk found that most babies aged between 6 and fourteen months would not crawl onto the deep side. Campos *et al.* (1970) devised a method of assessing babies younger than six months. In their experiment babies were placed on either the shallow or deep sides of the cliff whilst their heart rates were monitored. Campos *et al.* found that heart rates would increase or decrease significantly.

'Sensory restriction' studies can be carried out on non-humans. Riesen (1947) raised chimpanzees in total darkness for the first sixteen months of life. As a result they failed to show a blink response and only noticed objects when they were accidentally bumped into. Weiskrantz (1956) argued that the visual deficiencies shown by Riesen's chimps were a consequence of degeneration of the retina in the absence of stimulation by light.

Riesen (1965) conducted a second experiment in which he raised three chimps, Debi, Kova, and Lad. Lad was reared under normal conditions, Debi in total darkness and Kova was exposed to one-and-a-half hours of light per day whilst wearing opaque goggles. Riesen found that though Kova's retina had developed normally, her receptive fields had failed to develop normally.

Blakemore and Cooper raised kittens in cylindrical chambers which had either vertical or horizontal stripes painted on the inside. The kittens wore collars to prevent them from seeing their own bodies and so were only exposed to lines of a particular orientation. When tested the kitten who had only been exposed to horizontal lines made no response to a rod which moved vertically, and kittens in vertical-only environments were equally 'behaviourally blind' to a rod moving in a horizontal direction. Studies of their visual cortex revealed that the kittens did not possess cells which were sensitive to lines of orientations which they had not experienced.

Example essay: Stage 3

Here, commentary and link sentences have been added to the essay above in order to improve the B skills score, as well as assisting with the flow and style. The additional commentary is indicated by the use of italics.

Discuss the view that perceptual abilities are largely innate. (24 marks)

Psychologists have long been interested in the question whether perceptual abilities are predominantly inborn or whether they are a product of learning. This question forms a part of the wider 'nature–nurture' debate in psychology. Psychologists on the 'nurture' side of the debate are called 'empirists' and argue that abilities develop largely as a consequence of learning and may be influenced by our experiences, whilst 'nativists' believe that abilities are largely innate and develop as a result of inherited genetic factors which pre-determine their development in a process called 'maturation'.

Psychologists have investigated perceptual abilities in a number of different ways in an attempt to resolve the issue, including studies of human infants, human cataract patients, studies of sensory restriction in non-humans, perceptual readjustment studies and cross-cultural studies. *In this essay I will consider research from studies of human infants, and studies of sensory restriction in non-humans.*

Studying the perceptual abilities of newborn infants would seem to be the most direct way of assessing which perceptual abilities are inborn, since it is unlikely that abilities present at birth can have been learned. However, the study of infant perception poses some problems for researchers; in particular infants cannot tell us what they perceive. To get round this problem, researchers have developed a range of techniques which allow us to infer what infants can and cannot perceive.

Bornstein (1976) used a technique called 'habituation' to investigate colour perception in infants. *The technique is based on the finding that infants attend less to stimuli which they recognise (to which they have become habituated). Novel stimuli presented after familiar stimuli will tend to re-excite attention.* Using this technique Bornstein discovered that most babies possess largely normal colour vision at the age of two months. Infants also show the pupillary reflex and blink response at birth. *This suggests that infants can perceive brightness and movement to some extent, and that such abilities are likely to be inborn.*

More complex perceptual abilities have also been investigated. Fantz (1961) looked at pattern recognition and the perception of facedness in infants. In order to discover whether infants could discriminate pattern and form Fantz used the preferential looking technique. *This involves presenting infants with two or more different stimuli. If the infant spends significantly longer looking at one stimulus rather than another we can conclude both that they can tell the stimuli apart, and that they prefer one over the other.* By presenting one- to 15-week-old infants with discs on which were painted colours, a bull's-eye, a patch of printed matter and a face, Fantz discovered a preference for more complex figures over simple ones, with infants spending most time looking at the human face, *suggesting that a preference for complexity is inborn.*

Whether a preference for faces is innate, or whether infants prefer looking at faces because they are complex, is unclear. In an attempt to resolve the issue Fantz presented infants with a normal face and a 'scrambled' face in which all the normal features were present but not placed in a normal arrangement on the disc. Fantz found that infants spent significantly longer looking at the normal face. *This suggests that a preference for faces is inborn. However, the difference in looking times was small and other researchers have failed to replicate Fantz's findings.*

Another area of neonate studies has focused on the question 'Can infants perceive depth?'. In an ingenious experiment, Gibson & Walk (1960) constructed an apparatus in which infants were placed on a sheet of plexiglass below which was a checkerboard pattern. On the 'shallow' side the pattern was immediately below the glass, whilst on the 'deep' side the pattern was placed at a distance of about four feet, giving the impression of a drop. The researchers placed the infant on the shallow side of the visual cliff apparatus, and observed their behaviour when called by their mothers from across the deep side. *The researchers reasoned that if the infant was reluctant to crawl onto the deep side, then it can be inferred that they were able to perceive the drop.* Gibson and Walk found that most babies aged between 6 and fourteen months would not crawl onto the deep side. *This suggests that depth perception is innate. However, since infants needed to be at an age where they could crawl, it is possible that they may have learned to perceive depth by this age.* Campos *et al.* (1970) devised a method of assessing babies younger than six months. In their experiment babies were placed on either the shallow or deep sides of the cliff whilst their heart rates were monitored. Campos *et al.* found that heart rates would increase or decrease significantly *suggesting that babies were able to detect the change, and could therefore perceive depth from birth.*

Overall studies of neonates suggest that many perceptual abilities, such as the detection of brightness, pattern, depth and colour, are innate, although they may not mature fully until some time after birth.

One difficulty with studies of neonates is that it is not possible for ethical reasons to discover the extent to which the environment may influence the development of perceptual abilities by restricting their opportunities for perceptual learning to take place. 'Sensory restriction' studies can be carried out on non-humans. *Researchers typically deprive newborn animals of normal sensory stimulation and record the effect which this has on perception.*

Riesen (1947) raised chimpanzees in total darkness for the first sixteen months of life. As a result they failed to show a blink response and only noticed objects when they were accidentally bumped into. *This would seem to contradict the findings of infant studies which suggest that such abilities are innate. By way of explanation,* Weiskrantz (1956) argued that the visual deficiencies shown by Riesen's chimps were a consequence of degeneration of the retina in the absence of stimulation by light. *Because of this, abilities which may have been present at birth might have been lost due to retinal damage.*

In response to this observation, Riesen (1965) conducted a second experiment in which he raised three chimps, Debi, Kova, and Lad. Lad was reared under normal conditions, Debi in total darkness and Kova was exposed to one-and-a-half-hours of light per day whilst wearing opaque goggles. *The purpose of the opaque goggles was to allow light stimulation to maintain the retina, whilst preventing Kova from being exposed to patterned light.* Reisen found that though Kova's retina had developed normally, her receptive fields had failed to develop normally.

Riesen's studies show that some light is necessary for the development of the visual system and that patterned light is necessary for more complex visual abilities to develop.

Other researchers have attempted to investigate the impact of more specific aspects of the environment on perceptual development. Blakemore and Cooper raised kittens in cylindrical chambers which had either vertical or horizontal stripes painted on the inside. The kittens wore collars to prevent them from seeing their own bodies and so were only exposed to lines of a particular orientation. When tested, the kitten who had been exposed to only horizontal lines made no response to a rod which moved vertically, and kittens in vertical-only environments were equally 'behaviourally blind' to a rod moving in a horizontal direction. Studies of their visual cortices revealed that the kittens did not possess cells which were sensitive to lines of orientations which they had not experienced.

Although this research suggests that the environment can play an important role in the development of more complex perceptual abilities, it may be that these abilities were present at birth but deteriorated in the absence of appropriate stimulation. It is also important to note that we cannot necessarily assume that the findings of studies of non-humans can be generalised to human abilities, even when the systems are biologically similar.

In conclusion it is clear that many simple perceptual abilities mature in accordance with an innate programme. During maturation specific environmental factors may be required for perceptual development to proceed normally. The evidence regarding more complex perceptual abilities, such as recognising human faces, is less clear and such abilities may be more heavily dependent on learning.

B4 Sketch a quick essay plan

Essay plans are very useful: they encourage you to stop and **think about the structure of the essay before you begin writing** (rather than making it up as you go along), and to **put the key facts which you can remember down on paper for easy reference** (rather than hoping that you will remember them as you go along). They also allow you to concentrate on writing the essay, having taken care of the structure and the information.

In the event that the essay is unfinished or incomplete, essay plans will be marked by the examiner, so **don't cross them out!**

However, it is also true that detailed essay plans can waste time which would be better spent in writing the essay: *essay plans should be an overview of the main points and take no more than five minutes to sketch.*

Essay plans can be sequential or schematic depending on which you prefer. Sequential plans list the points that you aim to cover in the order in which you aim to cover them. Schematic plans present the points in diagrammatic form, showing how they relate to one another. Examples of both types of plans for a sample essay title are given overleaf:

Discuss top-down and bottom up approaches to understanding perceptual processing. *(24 marks)*

Sequential plan

Intro

Define sensation and perception.
Explain top-down and bottom-up.

Body

Introduce Gregory's theory 'perception as interpretation'.
Support from illusions and constancies.
Give example – Müller Lyer.
Identify problems (What is a hypothesis?, how is it formed?, how does theory relate to real life?).
Introduce Gibson's theory 'perception is direct'.
Explain optic array and three components: texture gradient, optic flow patterns, affordances.
Supporting research – swaying room.
Identify problems (difficulty (Marr), can't explain illusions, affordances).

Conclusion

Alternatives – transactionalists, Neisser (perceptual cycle).

Schematic Plan

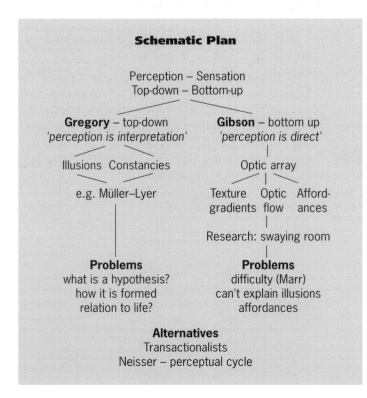

Exercise 4

- Select six essay titles from different areas of the syllabus from *recent* past papers.
- Draw up essay plans for each from memory.
- Identify information which is missing from these plans.
- Go back to your notes and revise this information.
- Re-write the essay plans.

As pointed out earlier, drawing up essay plans is a very good way to assist revision. The plans can help you to think about how the material can be used in an essay, how it is structured and how much you need to know.

B5 Write an introduction

An introduction need not be very long but is usually necessary. **The primary role of an introduction is to link the question to your response** (your essay). Typically, an introduction will 'set the scene', such as with a single sentence like ' … is one of the most enduring questions which psychologists have faced'.

An introduction can often be used to **define or introduce the key terms of the question**, such as 'bottom-up', 'obedience', 'memory', and to provide a brief overview of the subject area, e.g. 'Explanations of schizophrenia have focused on the genetic, biological and environmental factors which may contribute to the disorder'.

An introduction may also include a brief account of a key study relating to the area (perhaps the first research to be done in the area), or which illustrates the general importance of the question.

An introduction will often conclude with **a single sentence summary of what you intend to say in your essay** ('**In the following essay** I will …'). It is not necessary to say in advance precisely what you are going to do, since this will be clear from what you write.

B6 Set out research studies and/or theories relevant to the question

Examiners will credit any theory or research study which informs the question. However, they will be interested in *psychological* research, and are less likely to credit news reports (with a few notable exceptions, such as the case of Kitty Genovese). They are also highly unlikely to give you many marks for anecdotes (personal accounts of events).

It is a grave mistake not to answer the question. If material is not relevant to the question, it will gain no marks. For this reason, it is very important not simply to read the question but to answer it as well.

Students who memorise pre-prepared answers in the hope that their favourite questions will come up are not likely to succeed using this method. It is important to **be sure of what the question is asking before you begin to answer it**. When you know what the question is asking for, you must stop and think about which of the items of material that you know are relevant. This cannot be done in advance, and is one of the objectives of drawing up essay plans.

Be aware of the syllabus. In most cases, the only material which will be relevant to an exam question will come from the corresponding syllabus subsection. Only sometimes can material from one syllabus subsection be used effectively in answer to a question on another section (exceptions include questions on major theoretical orientations in psychology). **You must be able to identify the syllabus subsection to which a question 'points', and know which material is covered in that subsection.**

Stay 'on task'. Make sure that you do not drift off into related areas, such as a discussion of ethical considerations and research in similar sounding areas (for example, an essay on animal language should not end up including Skinner's theory of language development in humans).

It is very important to develop the ability to **summarise research studies and theories clearly and concisely**. A good summary of a study should include key points such as who the participants were, what the experimental conditions were, what was manipulated and what the results were. Lengthy and lurid descriptions which include a lot of extraneous detail earn very few marks and are time-consuming. Summaries which simply include the conclusions of research, without saying how the researchers arrived at these conclusions are also inadequate. A good study to practice on is Milgram's study of obedience. Try summarising the key points in a single paragraph.

Students often worry about whether or not they have to memorise *names of researchers* and *publication dates of research*. The AEB examiner requires that research studies be *recognisable*, so often a clear description of research is adequate, although the name of the researcher lends clarity to the essay. A date is rarely very important, although a general idea of when research studies were carried out can be useful (e.g. Milgram's studies of obedience were carried out *after* the second world war).

B7 Comment on the research studies and/or theories as required

Remember that half of your marks come from commentary (B skills), and that commentary can take a variety of forms.

The precise extent to which you are required to comment on theories will be determined by the injunctions used in the question. Students often make the mistake of wasting time *evaluating* studies or theories, despite the fact that the question only requires them to *describe* the research or theories. **Avoid the temptation to put down what you know, just because you know it!**

Whilst commentary is credited, waffle is not! Although the difference is not always obvious, waffle is generally uninformative, whilst commentary informs the answer. Commentary could therefore be an explanation or clarification of a previous point, but should not be a repetition of that point.

B8 Relate each paragraph back to the question

Although not strictly required, relating what you have said back to the question at the end of each paragraph can be a useful strategy, both because it draws the examiner's attention to the point that you have made and its relation to the question, and because it forces you to systematically relate what you say back to the question.

Even if you are only stopping to *check* at the end of each paragraph that what you have said relates to the question, this is a useful exercise: it will help you to address the question, rather than simply slipping into a recitation of whatever material you know.

B9 *Make the most of your time*

Learning how to manage your time, and concentrating for extended periods of time, are skills which you will master with practice. Timed essays are an important part of your preparation.

If you finish writing your essays before time, take a short break, relax, then review your work. Students invariably make errors when writing essays under pressure, and it may be possible to spot some of these and make corrections.

Writing an essay for the first time

All these comments make essay-writing seem more daunting than it really is. Many of these points are obvious, and the remainder you will probably learn to do automatically.

However, if you are writing an essay for the first time just remember that an essay should **summarise the psychological research and theory which relates to the question and say what it means**. If you do this, you cannot go far wrong.

If it helps, look at the way in which textbooks are written. They will be far more comprehensive than your essay, but they can give you a good idea of the 'style' to use (for example 'I think ...' is never used).

COURSEWORK GUIDE

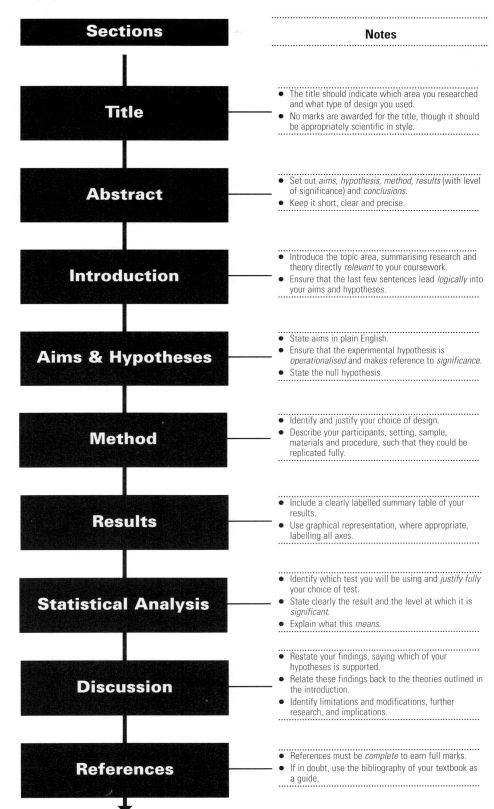

Guidelines (AEB)

Sections

Notes

Title

- The title should indicate which area you researched and what type of design you used.
- No marks are awarded for the title, though it should be appropriately scientific in style.

Pieces of coursework must be drawn from different syllabus sections.

Abstract

- Set out *aims, hypothesis, method, results* (with level of significance) and *conclusions*.
- Keep it short, clear and precise.

Coursework must comprise 1 experimental and 1 non-experimental design.

Introduction

- Introduce the topic area, summarising research and theory directly *relevant* to your coursework.
- Ensure that the last few sentences lead *logically* into your aims and hypotheses.

Marks are awarded for style and grammar.

Aims & Hypotheses

- State aims in plain English.
- Ensure that the experimental hypothesis is *operationalised* and makes reference to *significance*.
- State the null hypothesis.

Students may not work in groups larger than 3.

Method

- Identify and justify your choice of design.
- Describe your participants, setting, sample, materials and procedure, such that they could be replicated fully.

Pooled class data cannot be used.

Results

- Include a clearly labelled summary table of your results.
- Use graphical representation, where appropriate, labelling all axes.

Work within the 2000 word limit.

Statistical Analysis

- Identify which test you will be using and *justify fully* your choice of test.
- State clearly the result and the level at which it is *significant*.
- Explain what this *means*.

Title each subsection of your work clearly.

Discussion

- Restate your findings, saying which of your hypotheses is supported.
- Relate these findings back to the theories outlined in the introduction.
- Identify limitations and modifications, further research, and implications.

Have a copy of the marking scheme beside you as you write.

References

- References must be *complete* to earn full marks.
- If in doubt, use the bibliography of your textbook as a guide.

Many students find coursework a bewildering and difficult part of their course. In fact, it is not difficult to write a good piece of coursework given that you **know the criteria against which your coursework will be assessed**. The most common mistake which students make is to fail to familiarise themselves with the precise *format* required by their examination board, with the consequence that they produce elaborate and original pieces of coursework which *cannot* be awarded many marks, because they fail to meet many of the marking criteria. A good piece of coursework can *only* be written by a student fully acquainted with the marking scheme. Below is a guide to writing your coursework, together with some suggestions for coursework designs and a sample piece in outline.

C1 *Choosing your design*

There are two important questions to raise when choosing a coursework design. Firstly, **'Will the results be easy to collect, quantify and analyse?'**: it may seem 'back-to-front' to consider your statistical test before you have obtained your results, but if you collect results which are difficult to analyse or quantify you may lose marks both for your analysis and your design decisions. Results should be in an '*operationalised*' form (for example 'scores', or 'number of participants', or 'seconds', rather than 'attitude' or 'feelings').

Secondly, **'Does the investigation relate closely to an area on the syllabus?'**. Students are required (by the AEB) to choose investigations which relate to the syllabus, but it is also wise to choose an area with full and straightforward literature support, so that you do not have to struggle to complete the introduction and discussion.

Try to keep things simple. It is usually a good idea to concentrate on a single variable, or measure. With more than one variable, you are likely to require more than one experimental hypothesis and corresponding increases in the complexity of the statistics and discussion.

Consider the BPS's *Ethical Guidelines* (1993). The BPS guidelines are summarised in your textbook, but the following are likely to be particularly relevant:

- **Avoid deceiving your participants** where possible.

- Always obtain **informed consent** (designs involving children should be avoided for this reason).
- Inform participants in advance of their **right to withdraw**,
- Inform participants in advance that their results will be **confidential**, and maintain this confidentiality.
- **Debrief** participants fully, and thank them for their participation.
- Undisclosed observations are unacceptable, except in situations where participants might reasonably expect to be observed.
- **Under no condition expose participants to conditions which might cause distress or pain** (for this reason avoid designs involving non-human animals).

Bear in mind that these considerations apply whatever the experimental design (for example, a 'survey' still requires informed consent).

Remember that the AEB requires that one design is **experimental**, and the other **non-experimental**. **Surveys, correlations** and **observations** are all non-experimental designs.

Be aware of the limitations on group size, and on the use of pooled class data (the AEB allows groups of up to three students, and disallows the use of pooled class data).

Follow the advice of your teacher regarding your choice of design. Although you will lose some marks if your teacher has supported you, coursework produced with teacher support tends to score more highly on many of the other areas (bear in mind that your teacher will also probably be responsible for assessing your work!).

Ensure that procedures are standardised, and that methodological problems (such as participant variables, practice effects, and other extraneous variables) are anticipated, and the design adjusted to minimise their effects.

Don't worry if your results do not support your experimental hypothesis. Students are often disappointed if the experimental hypothesis is not supported. However, this makes no difference whatsoever to the marks awarded.

If you are working as part of a group, bear in mind that although both the design and results may be a 'joint effort', the 'write-ups' should not be (plagiarism can result in disqualification).

Below are some suggestions for coursework designs:

Suggested coursework outlines

SYLLABUS AREA 1.1
Attribution
Design: survey

Literature: attribution theory and biases

Procedure: students investigate the different attributions given by fellow students for failures/successes of their own/rival football teams

Results: nominal, in the form of external/internal attributions for failures/successes

Prejudice
Design: experimental (independent subjects)

Literature: origins, maintenance and reduction of prejudice

Procedure: students present two groups of fellow students with the same description of an individual, in which only the name has been changed (male/female, Western/non-Western), asking participants to assess their suitability for interview

Results: nominal, in the form of 'suitable/unsuitable' judgements

Design: experimental (independent)

Literature: origins, maintenance and reduction of prejudice

Procedure: students leave copies of 'bogus' UCAS forms, together with instructions to return to reception if lost. Application materials are identical except for the name (male/female, Western/non-Western)

Results: nominal, in the form of how many of each type have been returned

SYLLABUS AREA 1.2
Relationships
Design: correlational

Literature: theories of relationships; the matching hypothesis

Procedure: students ask fellow students if they wish to join a pilot 'dating service'. Assured that information will be kept confidential, asked to complete a questionnaire concerning their traits and their desired partner's traits (all scored on a ten point scale). Scores can be correlated

Results: ordinal in the form of ratings for own/partner's attractiveness

SYLLABUS AREA 3.4
Motivation, emotion and stress
Design: natural experiment

Literature: theories of emotion and motivation

Procedure: fellow students either waiting for an important exam (anxiety condition) or a bus (low anxiety conditions) are asked to rate a photograph of a member of the opposite sex of 'near average' attractiveness for attractiveness. Aroused participants should rate the photograph more highly

Results: interval/ordinal in the form of attractiveness scores

SYLLABUS AREA 5.1
Perceptual processes
Design: experiment (independent)

Literature: theories of perception, perceptual set

Procedure: participants are asked to identify an ambiguous figure, having first been exposed to stimuli which create an expectation. (e.g. showing a rabbit/duck figure after either a series of rabbits or ducks)

Results: nominal, in the form of what was identified

SYLLABUS AREA 5.3

Memory

Design: experimental (related)

Literature: theories of memory

Procedure: participants are instructed to use either imagery or rehearsal to remember a list of concrete word pairs. The first word of each word pair is presented, participants recall scores for the second word of each pair recorded in each condition

Results: interval, in the form of recall scores

SYLLABUS AREA 6.2

Cognitive development

Design: survey

Literature: Piagetian theory and theories of cognitive development

Procedure: tests of formal operational thinking are administered to participants aged 16+. Results are compared with Piaget's predictions

Results: nominal, in the form of correct/incorrect, or interval in the form of number of correct responses

C2 Title

The title does not actually merit any marks by itself, but marks are allocated for the overall style of the coursework, so the title should be appropriately scientific.

A title should be suggestive of **the area you have investigated and the method which you have used**, such as '*An experiment into the effectiveness of different memory techniques*', or '*A survey into gender stereotypes*'.

C3 Abstract

An abstract is a **clear and concise summary of your investigation**, which allows the reader to understand what you did and what you discovered. The moderator will be checking for clarity and conciseness and ensuring that you have clearly stated your **aims, hypothesis, method, results and conclusions**. Below is a possible template for an abstract:

Abstract

The aim of this [experiment/survey/observation] was to investigate the relationship between [two variables]. The experimental hypothesis was that [experimental hypothesis – see below].

A [repeated measures/independent measures/matched pairs, experimental design]/ [survey/observational/correlation method] was used. Participants were selected using a [quota/opportunity] sample. Results obtained were in the form of … [scores /ratings …/ seconds …] and [were/were not] significant at the $p < $ [0.05/0.01/0.001] level of significance. It was concluded that [conclusion].

C4 Introduction

An introduction is not dissimilar to an essay. It should **introduce the key terms relevant to the topic, outline the general theoretical background, then describe any research studies directly relevant to the study**. It is not assessed according to A and B skills, but according to the *relevance* of the material to the investigation. Beware of being 'unselective' in your choice of material – you may lose a mark. **And remember the word limit!**

In order to gain the remaining marks which are awarded for the introduction, **you must write a logical lead in to your aims and hypothesis**. If you have outlined the relevant theories correctly, this should simply mean adding a couple of link sentences onto the end of the introduction, along the lines of 'If X's theory is correct it would be anticipated that …, whilst if Y is correct … . In this investigation it is intended to discover which of these outcomes is more likely, by …'.

C5 Aims and hypotheses

The aims and hypotheses need to be **clear and testable** in order to earn full marks.

The aim is a **plain statement of what you intend to demonstrate**, for example 'This study aims to discover which of the memory techniques, rehearsal or imagery, is more effective in remembering word pairs', or 'The aim of this experiment is to find out whether or not participants' perceptions of an ambiguous figure will be influenced by the context of presentation'.

The experimental hypothesis is a **precise and testable statement**, and must be more exact than the aims. As a rule of thumb, the hypothesis usually makes reference to **significance**, and to **operationalised** terms (terms stated in a manner which is measurable, e.g. participants' 'recall scores' rather than participants' 'memories'). There is no set way to write a hypothesis, but below is a template which works for most designs:

Hypothesis Template:

There will be a significant [difference/correlation] between the [scores, ratings, responses] of participants [condition1] and the [scores, ratings, responses] of participants [condition2].

e.g. There will be a significant difference between participants' scores in the divided attention condition and participants' scores in the control condition.

Where appropriate, you should state the direction of the difference/correlation and justify the direction.

e.g. There will be a significant positive correlation between [X] and [Y]. The hypothesis is [uni-/bi-directional] because …

When you have written your hypothesis, judge for yourself whether or not it is unambiguous and testable.

The **null hypothesis should also be stated**. This is the same in any design and states simply that 'There will be no significant [difference/correlation] between …, and any [difference/correlation] there is reflects the operation of chance factors'.

C6 *Method*

The central task in your reporting of the method is to **ensure that all aspects of the investigation are reported clearly and in sufficient detail for full replication to be possible**.

You should **state the design which you used and defend it** (e.g. a repeated measures experimental design was used because it reduces the effects of participant variables).

You should **describe the participants used** (without identifying them individually), **and the sampling method used to obtain them**, e.g. 'A total of twenty male students between the ages of 17 and 18 were used, selected on an opportunity basis, since this was the best sampling method given the available time and money'.

You should identify the experimenter(s), location, time, and any other relevant conditions under which the investigation was conducted.

In the case of an experimental investigation, you should **say which were the independent and dependent variables** and any confounding or extraneous variables, together with the level of measurement (i.e. whether the data is nominal, ordinal or interval). You should also **identify any experimental or control conditions**, and any measures which you have taken to reduce practice or order effects.

Your materials should be listed, and it would be a good idea to **include (in your appendix) one copy of any stimulus materials used**.

You should **state the procedure which was followed and include copies of any standardised instructions**, e.g. 'Students who appeared to be on their own were approached on an opportunity basis by the experimenter and asked if they wished to participate in an experiment into memory. If the participant replied that s/he would, s/he was read the standardised instructions (see Appendix)'.

C7 *Presentation of results*

Results should be presented clearly. This almost always means that you must **draw up a clearly labelled table**, using appropriate descriptive statistics.

Graphical representations (such as bar charts or line graphs) may then follow, if appropriate. Many students are now adept at producing such representations using spreadsheet software. Unfortunately, this has led to a tendency to prize aesthetic merits over genuine informativeness (e.g. students occasionally produce pie-charts which show that half of the participants are male, and half female). **Do not produce graphical representations simply because they can be produced.** A graphical representation of data should make the pattern of results clearer than does the summary table; **one well-chosen graphical representation is usually sufficient** to do this.

C8 *Statistical analysis*

In order to earn full marks for your use of inferential statistics, you must **state the statistical test which you intend to use, then justify it fully, making reference to your data**. The criteria for use of a statistical test can usually be found in textbooks which detail the methods used in psychological research.

The mathematical calculations can be presented in an appendix. Statistical tests can be performed by computer: no marks are lost so long as calculations are correct.

In the results section of your coursework, you must **state the observed value for your test of statistical significance** (i.e. the value produced by the statistical test) **and the critical value which it must exceed (or, in the case of some statistical tests, be smaller than) in order for the outcome to be significant. State which level of significance you are using, and how many degrees of freedom (or, in the case of some statistical tests, the 'N' value) are involved.** For example, if using the t-test of significance you might state 'the value of t for our results is 7.844, which exceeds the critical value of 3.84 ($p < 0.05$ with 20 degrees of freedom)'.

Say whether or not the outcome is significant, whether this allows you to reject or accept the null hypothesis and accept or reject the experimental hypothesis.

Finally, **say what your result means**, e.g. 'This means that participants recalled significantly more word pairs using the imagery rather than the rehearsal technique'.

C9 Discussion

A discussion must **begin with a restatement of the outcome**, e.g. 'The results showed that participants recalled significantly more word pairs using the imagery rather than rehearsal technique ($p<0.05$)'.

Relate the outcome to the hypotheses (again), explaining which of the hypotheses has been accepted and rejected.

Relate the findings back to the research and/or theory which was outlined in the introduction. Explain which research and/or theory is supported and which not supported.

You can **broaden your discussion** to include criticisms of the research and/or theory outlined in the introduction or other areas of research or theory which relate to your findings.

Following this, **you must examine actual or potential limitations of your research design and suggest modifications which might remedy these**. Many students make only token attempts to do this, resulting in a loss of valuable marks. Try to identify *at least three actual or plausibly potential* problems with your design and *three plausible modifications* which might be made.

Identify implications of your findings and ideas for further research. Again, many students rush this part, unaware that as many marks are earned here as for other parts of the discussion. Do not confuse implications with suggestions for further research. **Try to include at least three of each.**

C10 References

Marks are awarded for full, appropriate references. You will not gain full marks if you have referred to any research or theory in the text which cannot be found in the references, or if your references are not appropriate.

If you are in doubt as to how to produce references in the appropriate format, you may look in the back of any textbook. These contain references to all publications cited in the main text.

C11 Appendices

Appendices should be included in your list of contents, and contain any **further information required for a full understanding of your study**. They are not intended to be a repository for any odd bits of paper, or illegible scribblings produced *en route* to the finished product. Neither should appendices contain, for example, every single questionnaire returned by participants (although they should contain one sample copy).

C12 Style and quality of language

The AEB awards marks for your report style and the quality of the language used.

Full marks for style are awarded for reports which are **concise, logically organised into sections and written in an 'appropriately scientific style'**. Guidelines on style can be found in the chapter on essay writing in this book; otherwise any textbook will give you a good idea as to what a scientific style is.

Full marks for quality of language are awarded for reports in which **ideas are expressed accurately, a broad range of specialist terms are used precisely, with only minor errors in spelling, punctuation or grammar**. The use of a spell-check facility (available on most word-processors) can help here.

C13 Submitting your coursework

Before you submit your coursework, use a copy of the examination board's marking criteria to check that, as far as possible, you have fulfilled the requirements.

Some examination boards permit students to revise a marked piece of coursework, then resubmit it before it receives a final grade. You will need to check with your teacher whether or not this is the case. If it is the case, then it is a good idea to submit your coursework well in advance of the examination board's deadline.

The AEB will award a grade X (no grade) for students who do not submit *any* coursework. However, it is clearly to your advantage to submit the required amount of coursework.

If you are re-sitting your A level examination, it might be possible to resubmit previously submitted pieces of coursework. Check with your teacher.

C14 Sample coursework outline

Below is a sample coursework outline that was submitted by a student. It has been written in 'note form' and is therefore not intended as a guide to appropriate report style. It identifies the report headings which you would be advised to use, together with the type of material and structure which *might* typically comprise a piece of coursework (although it is by no means perfect!).

Under no conditions should this sample be copied and submitted as a report (since this is likely to result in disqualification). However, bear in mind when deciding on a design that *it is permissible* for a design to be based on that of a previously published work. Have a copy of the marking scheme beside you as you write.

REHEARSAL AND IMAGERY
SAMPLE COURSEWORK OUTLINE

Title
An experimental investigation into the effectiveness of imagery and rehearsal as techniques of remembering word pairs.

Abstract
The aim of this investigation was to discover whether imagery or rehearsal is the more effective technique of remembering, as tested by recall of word pairs. Atkinson & Shiffrin (1971) suggest that repeating words to oneself (*rehearsal*) is the most effective technique, whilst Paivio (1984), proposes that forming a mental image of the words to be recalled (*imagery*) is better.

A repeated measures experimental design was used to gain the responses, in the form of rehearsal and imagery scores for each participant. There were two experimental conditions, participants remembering word pairs using either imagery or rehearsal. A total of 7 participants were used, all of whom were psychology students. Participants were selected on an opportunity basis.

The results were analysed using the repeated measure t-test, and there was a significant difference ($p<0.05$) between the number of word pairs recalled in each condition. This suggests that imagery is indeed the superior technique of remembering.

Introduction
Definition of memory: 'the retention of learning and experience' (keep this brief).

Components: *registration, storage and retrieval.* In order to remember something we have to be able to store and retrieve it (keep this brief).

Theories of memory
- Theory 1: Multi-store model/dual-memory theory (Atkinson & Shiffrin, 1971) attempts to explain memory in terms of the transfer of information from short-term memory (STM) to long-term memory (LTM). The key process in doing so is *rehearsal.* Dual-memory theory suggests that rehearsal is the principal technique of remembering. But this model cannot explain memory for faces, or for things which we have not rehearsed.
- Theory 2: Paivio's dual-code hypothesis – Paivio (1986) says that we can store concrete nouns (but not abstract nouns) in both a verbal form and an imaginal form (images). Forming an image to go along with a word causes it to be stored in both forms, so we remember it better. Paivio (1984) would predict imagery to be the superior technique.

Logical lead into experiment: according to Atkinson & Shiffrin (1971), we might expect rehearsal scores to be higher, but Paivio (1986) believes the opposite … in this experiment we hope to discover which of these two theories is best supported.

Aims
The aim of this experiment is to discover which technique (imagery or rehearsal) is the more effective method of remembering word pairs.

Experimental hypothesis
There will be a significant difference between the recall scores of participants in the imagery and rehearsal conditions. Imagery scores will be higher. This is a uni-directional hypothesis because the direction the outcome will take has been stated.

Null hypothesis
There will be no difference between recall scores of participants in the imagery and rehearsal conditions. Any difference reflects the operation of chance factors.

Method
Design: repeated measures experimental design.

Justification: an experiment offers good control of extraneous variables, allowing us to manipulate an independent variable and draw inferences about cause and effect. Repeated measures are used, since by using the same participants twice we can reduce the number of participant variables and consequently need fewer participants.

Sample: selected on an opportunity basis, obviously biased but the best possible with the available time and money.

Participants: psychology students at school on a Monday morning. Aged 16–19.

Controlled variables: location, distractions kept to a minimum, quiet conditions, good lighting, time for each technique to be used. Procedure standardised (copy in appendix). The 'recency effect' eliminated by getting participants to count backwards for 30 seconds at the end.

Extraneous variables: the presence of other students may have affected performance. Difficult to control absolutely which technique was used. Word pairs were read out, not presented on a tachistoscope/computer, meaning that at least some acoustic processing was necessary, even when forming an image. Age was not representative. Sex was not representative.

Independent and dependent variables: memory technique used, versus recall score for each technique.

Materials

    Stop-watch
    Copy of standardised procedure
    Pencils
    Paper
    List of word pairs (copy in appendix)

Procedure

The experimenter asked a group of students, selected on an opportunity basis, whether they wished to participate in an experiment into memory.

Once consent had been obtained and participants had been informed of their right to withdraw, the experimenter explained that the experiment was into the effectiveness of recall techniques on word pairs and that participants would be required either to form a mental image of the word interacting in some way or rehearse the pair silently to oneself.

The experimenter explained that s/he would read the word pair to be remembered, followed by the technique to be used, after which participants would be allowed ten seconds to remember the words.

Finally, the experimenter explained that at the end of the experiment, on the instruction 'count', participants would be required to count backwards from 100 until the experimenter said 'stop'. At the end of this procedure, the experimenter read out the first of each word pair, and participants were required to write down the correct second word.

The experimenter asked if the participants had any questions, then began the experiment.

(copy of standardised procedure in appendix)

Results

1 Summary table showing participants' scores for each condition, with average score for each condition.
2 Bar chart showing difference in average performance.

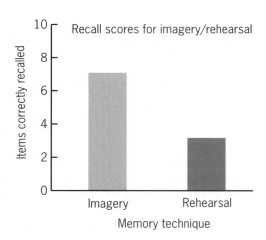

Statistical analysis: repeated measures t-test (workings in appendix). Justified because participants' scores were in the form of interval data, because participants were identical in each condition (so the design and test are *related*).

The value of t is calculated as 7.84, which exceeds the critical value of t (t = 3.84) at the p<0.05 level, with 20 degrees of freedom. This means that participants recalled significantly more word pairs using the imagery technique (average = 7.1) as compared with the rehearsal (average = 3.2) technique.

Discussion

Restate the results.

Relate this back to the experimental and null hypotheses, which are supported or rejected.

Supports Paivio's dual-coding approach (1986) and rejects Atkinson & Shiffrin's (1971) dual-memory theory.

Clearly there are flaws in dual-memory theory. We remember faces, smells, sensations – and often our memory for distinctive events doesn't seem to require rehearsal.

In addition, rehearsal is sometimes ineffective, so Craik & Watkins (1973) distinguish *rote rehearsal* (which just keeps information in STM) and *elaborative rehearsal*, where the information is linked with other things, given more associations (which transfers information into long-term memory).

Craik & Lockhart's (1972) *levels-of-processing model* suggests that images are remembered better, not because of better memory for images, but because in forming an image we increase the number of associations the words have (a form of semantic processing). Could this have happened in this investigation?

Although the findings from this experiment support Paivio's theory, the dual-coding approach is not without its critics, who point out that storing images would require an impossible amount of memory space and that we would still need a system to 'decode' these images even if we could store them.

Summary

Perhaps it is not that images are stored better but just that the *way* in which images are stored is better.

Limitations of the design and modifications

The presence of other students may have affected performance; ideally, students should be tested individually under controlled conditions. However, this would be more time-consuming and expensive.

It was difficult to control absolutely which technique was used. This variable cannot be controlled, although PET scans *might* be able to ascertain which areas of the brain are active during a task.

Word pairs were read out, meaning that at least some acoustic processing was necessary, even when forming an image. Presentation of stimulus words on a tachistoscope/computer might be better.

The age and sex of participants was not representative of the population at large. A quota sample drawing people from each gender and age range might be preferable.

Further study

A comparison of males' and females' imagery and rehearsal scores could be carried out, based on suggestions by some researchers that males possess better visuo-spatial skills and females better verbal ability.

The experiment could be repeated using a recognition rather than recall test, in an attempt to discover whether the different techniques affected the *availability* of information or simply its *accessibility*.

Lists could be learned until they could be correctly recalled twice, using either imagery or rehearsal. Recall scores could then be tested one month later, to see if there was any difference in the 'durability' of the memory traces created by the two techniques.

Implications

We can remember information (like shopping lists or stories) better if we convert it to images (e.g. the 'method of loci' where items to be remembered are mentally 'placed' at locations along a familiar route).

This suggests that diagrams are valuable aides to memory, and should be used in teaching.

In advertising, 'an image is worth a thousand words'. The conclusion suggests that images will be better remembered than 'voice-overs', or text.

References

ATKINSON, R.C. & SHIFFRIN, R.M. (1971) The control of short-term memory. *Scientific American*, 224, 82–90.

PAVIO, A. (1986) *Mental Representations: A dual-coding approach*. Oxford: Oxford University Press.

CRAIK, F. & LOCKHART, R. (1972) Levels of processing. *Journal of Verbal Learning & Verbal Behaviour*, 12, 599–607.

CRAIK, F.I.M. & WATKINS M.J. (1973) The role of rehearsal in short-term memory. *Journal of Verbal Learning & Verbal Behaviour*, 12, 599–607.

Appendix

Copy of stimulus materials (word pairs)

Copy of standardised procedure

t-test workings